The
Basics

The Basics:
A really useful cookbook

ANTHONY TELFORD

ALLEN&UNWIN

First published in 2009

Allen & Unwin
83 Alexander Street
Crows Nest NSW 2065
Australia
Phone: (61 2) 8425 0100
Fax: (61 2) 9906 2218
Email: info@allenandunwin.com
Web: www.allenandunwin.com

National Library of Australia
Cataloguing-in-Publication entry:

Telford, Anthony, 1970-

The basics : a really useful cookbook / Anthony Telford.

978 1 74175 214 4 (pbk.)

Includes index.

Cookery.

641.5

Cover and text design by Phil Campbell
Cover photograph by Greg Elms
Indexes by Puddingburn
Printed in Australia by Ligare Book Printer, Sydney
10 9 8 7 6 5 4 3 2 1

To *Sapphire Ocean*,
my seventh child and newest cook in the family

and

In loving memory of my mother,
Jeanette Caroline Telford (1942–1984)

Acknowledgements

XXXXXXXXXXXXXXXXXXXXXXXXXXXXXXXXXXXXXXXXXXXXXXXXXXXXXXXXXXXXX

Every great project requires the commitment of a significant few. I thank those committed to this book immensely. To the Allen & Unwin team led by the sage Sue Hines, including editor Siobhán Cantrill, copy-editor Susin Chow, publishing assistant Andrea Rejante, cover and book designer Phil Campbell and cover photographer Greg Elms. For inspiration I thank the doyens of Australian cookbook writing: Margaret Fulton, Joan Campbell, Stephanie Alexander and Maggie Beer. To Vassy Kritharelis, the as-yet-undiscovered talent of domestic cookery, thank you for the recipes, recipe testing and editing. Thank you to my dearest friends who have also inspired me and encouraged me past the deadline: Vee Waterston, Vassy, Anne-Marie and Kylie, Nicola Archer, Adam Cohen, Ren Marley, Rish and Lynds, Sue Shepherd, Alistair McLeod and David Carruthers. Most importantly, I am eternally grateful to my family. To my beloved Victoria for your support and the often unrewarded work of a mother—know that it will come back to you sevenfold. And to my children whom I live for: Jesse, Harley, Ty, Alannah, Indiana, Chile and Sapphire—I love you.

Introduction

'A cook must be born a cook, he cannot be made.' This is a quote from the chef Louis E. Ude, a quote I used in the introduction to my first book *The Kitchen Hand: A Miscellany of Kitchen Wisdom*. I recklessly questioned the nature of his statement only to realise after deciding to write this book that he was not simply being philosophical but he was indeed correct. I will come to why this statement is relevant to this book shortly, but firstly let me explain how I realised its validity.

I grew up as one of three boys to a well-respected agricultural scientist. A rural life dominated my first 16 years. Through my parents I was privileged to witness the law of the land: the realisation that Mother Nature is the boss, that the 'hunter-gatherer' gene has not been extinguished from modern man.

As long as I could remember, my backyard had been an edible kitchen. What I find interesting—the point which adds credibility to Udes' remark—is that my two brothers were exposed to the very same environment. Yet my younger brother Paul is a barrister and enjoys the very last stage of an ingredients journey with little interest as to how the dish was created—fortunately he married an Italian lady who is innately in tune with food, thanks to her heritage and her mamma. My older brother Cam, who is a captain in the army—the last bastion of mass-produced gruel—was more interested in the workings of things electrical than the simple pleasures that home-grown produce can provide. So why was I constantly drawn to the kitchen? To my brothers I say: it wasn't to get out of digging post holes, straining fences or any other fundamental back-breaking chore. Nevertheless, the interest I had in food came from deep within, a trait not shared by blood.

My parents were a formidable 'paddock-to-plate' duo. My father's deft hand at growing food was only matched by my mother's creativity in cooking or preserving it. How devastating it was when at the age of 14 my mother died. I had not only lost my mother, but one half of this inspirational team. It was soon after this life-changing experience that I looked to cooking as my life's path.

This book is a long-awaited tilt at acknowledging the influence of not only my parents but also friends, contemporaries, my family (including my brothers) and the world's cooks, past and present.

The Basics: A Really Useful Cookbook was, from the outset, intended to be both of those things: basic and useful. What you will find is a wealth of recipes from times past that are as relevant today. These are recipes I grew up with and you can set about cooking with confidence. More importantly, it is the hints and tips that accompany each recipe that set this apart from all other cookbooks.

Keeping in mind the opening statement, I recognise that not everyone thinks of cooking in the same way. That in fact, no matter the upbringing, an individual seems almost predestined to be who they become. And so, for those not born to be a cook, this book will, I hope, assist in making life in the kitchen just that bit more enjoyable.

I have endeavoured to minimise mistakes and discrepancies in this book, but should they appear, I take full responsibility.

Enjoy.

Anthony

Contents

xxxxxxxxxxxxxxxxxxxxxxxxxxxxxxxxxxxxxxxxxxxxxxxxxxxxxxxxxxxxxxxxxxxxxxxxxxxx

INTRODUCTION   IX

THE USEFUL RECIPES

1. BREAKFAST   1

Bircher muesli   2
Boiled eggs   4
French toast   5
Fruit salad   6
Hash brown potato   8
Omelette   10
Scrambled eggs   12
Slow-roasted tomatoes   14
Super fluffy pancakes   16

2. DIPS AND ACCOMPANIMENTS   19

Baba ghanouj   20
Caramelised onions   21
Chilli jam   22
Guacamole   24
Hummus   25
Mint jelly   26
Onion jam   28
Pesto   30
Pistou   32
Quince paste   33
Salsa verde   34
Tapenade   36
Tomato chutney   38
Tomato relish   40
Tomato jam   42
Tzatziki   43

3. SOUPS   45

Cauliflower soup   46
Chicken and sweet corn soup   48

Chicken soup with matzoh balls   50
Crab chowder   51
French onion soup   52
Gazpacho   54
Minestrone   56
Miso soup   58
Mushroom soup   59
Pea and ham soup   60
Potato and leek soup   61
Pumpkin soup   62
Seafood gumbo   64
Tomato soup   66
Vegetable and barley soup   68

4. SEAFOOD   71

Cooking whole fish   72
Crab cakes   74
Fish fillets, pan-fried   76
Fish pie   77
Garlic prawns   78
Prawn cocktail   80
Salmon patties   81
Salt and pepper squid   82
Seafood crepes   84
Tuna bake   86

5. POULTRY   89

Apricot chicken   90
Chicken Kiev   92
Chicken liver parfait   94
Crispy skin chicken breast   96
Peking duck   98
Roast chicken   100
Roast duck with cherry sauce   102
Roast turkey buffet   104

6. MEAT   **107**

Baked ham   108
Barbecue-style spare ribs   110
Beef casserole   112
Beef stroganoff   114
Bolognaise sauce   116
Braised beef brisket   118
Braised lamb shanks   120
Chilli con carne   122
Corned beef   124
Cottage pie   126
Lasagne   128
Meat loaf   130
Moussaka   132
Osso buco   134
Rissoles   136
Roast beef   138
Roast lamb   140
Roast pork and crackling   142
San choy bao   144
Sausages and mash with pepper sauce   146
Steak and kidney pie   148
Thai beef salad   150
Veal schnitzel   152

7. VEGETABLES   **155**

Baked potato in cream   156
Bubble-and-squeak   158
Corn on the cob   160
Pickled vegetables   162
Potato mash   164
Ratatouille   166
Roasted vegetables   168
Vegetable and noodle stir-fry   170
Vegetarian lasagne   172
Zucchini slice   174

8. SALADS   **177**

Caesar salad   178
Chef's salad   180
Coleslaw   182
Fattoush   184
Greek salad   186
Green salad   188
Niçoise salad   190

Panzanella   192
Pasta salad   194
Potato salad   196
Rice salad   198
Tabbouleh   200

9. GRAINS AND PULSES   **203**

Couscous with preserved lemon and saffron   204
Fried rice   206
Lentil burgers   208
Macaroni cheese   210
Firm polenta   212
Soft polenta   213
Risotto   214
Spaghetti carbonara (traditional, no cream recipe)   216
Spaghetti carbonara (westernised creamy version)   217
Spring rolls   218

10. DRESSINGS, SAUCES AND BUTTERS   **221**

Savoury Sauces   **222**
Aïoli   222
Caesar dressing   224
Cocktail sauce   226
Garlic butter   227
Ginger soy   228
Hollandaise   229
Mayonnaise   230
Mee goring sauce   232
Napoli sauce   233
Pad Thai sauce   234
Red wine sauce   235
Plum sauce   236
Satay sauce   238
Shallot dressing   240
Sweet and sour sauce   241
Teriyaki sauce   242
Thai chilli sauce   243
White sauce   244
Vinaigrette   246
Yoghurt dressing   247
Sweet Sauces   **248**
Apple sauce   248
Butterscotch sauce   250
Caramel sauce   252

Chocolate sauce 254
Raspberry sauce 256

11. DESSERTS **259**

Apple and rhubarb crumble 260
Apple pie 262
Apple strudel 264
Baked cheesecake 266
Baked quince 268
Baked ricotta cheesecake 270
Banana split 272
Brandy snaps 274
Bread and butter pudding 276
Bread and butter pudding with soy 277
Chocolate mousse 278
Chocolate self-saucing pudding 280
Christmas pudding 282
Crepes 284
Junket 286
Lemon delicious 288
Lemon meringue pie 290
Lemon tart 292
Pannacotta 294
Pavlova 296
Peach Melba 298
Pecan pie 300
Pumpkin pie 302
Queen of puddings 304
Raspberry fool 306
Stewed rhubarb 307
Rice pudding 308
Sticky date pudding 310
Summer pudding 312
Syrup pudding 314
Tiramisu 316
Trifle 318
Yoghurt and lemon mousse 320
Zabaglione 322

12. CAKES, BISCUITS AND PASTRIES **325**

Almond bread 326
Anzac biscuits 328
Baklava 330
Bacon and egg pie 332
Banana bread 334
Banana cake 336

Basic biscuits 338
Biscotti 340
Carrot cake 342
Cheese twists 344
Chocolate brownies 346
Chocolate crackles 347
Chocolate fudge 1 348
Chocolate fudge 2 349
Coconut ice 1 350
Coconut ice 2 350
Cupcakes 352
Devil's food cake 354
Flourless chocolate cake 356
Flourless orange cake 358
Friands 360
Fruit cake 362
Fruit mince pies 364
Gingerbread people 366
Hedgehog 368
Honeycomb 369
Hot cross buns 370
Hummingbird cake 372
Lumberjack cake 373
Macaroons 374
Marshmallows 376
Melting moments 378
Meringues 380
Muffins 381
Nanaimo bars 382
Peanut brittle 384
Pecan biscuits 385
Pikelets 386
Praline 387
Quiche Lorraine 388
Raspberry cheesecake 390
Sausage rolls 392
Scones 394
Spanakopita 396
Sponge cake 398
Swiss roll 400
Tea cake 402
Toffee 403
Vanilla slice 404

13. TOPPINGS **407**

Basic icing 408
Cream cheese frosting 409

Devil's chocolate frosting 410
Custard 411
Italian meringue 412
Lemon curd 414
Pastry cream 415
Marmalade 416
Strawberry jam 418

14. DRINKS 421

Banana smoothie 422
Eggnog 423
Hot chocolate 424
Lemon and ginger tea 425
Lemonade 426
Punch 427

15. BASIC RECIPES 429

Apple, prune and spice stuffing 430
Beer batter 432
Blini 434
Chicken stock 436
Clarified butter 438
Club sandwich 440
Crème fraîche 442
Croutons 443
Curry powder 444
Dashi stock 446
Fish stock 447
Fondue 448
Frittata 450
Garlic bread 452
Garlic confit 453
Lavosh 454
Nachos 456
Pasta dough 458
Sweet pastry 460
Sweet shortcrust pastry 461
Shortcrust pastry 462
Quick puff pastry 463
Choux pastry 464
Pizza dough 466
Preserved lemons 468
Sugar syrup 470
Vanilla sugar 471
Vegetable stock 472

THE REALLY USEFUL INFORMATION

Avocados 476
Beans 476
Cheese 479
Chillies 480
Chocolate 480
Corn 484
Cream 484
Eggs 486
Fats 490
Fish 491
Flour 493
Herbs 497
Lemons 500
Meat 500
Mushrooms 505
Oil 505
Onions 507
Pasta 508
Pastry 509
Potatoes 510
Poultry 511
Quinces 515
Rice 515
Salt 519
Sauces 521
Seafood 523
Spices 527
Sugar 532
Tomatoes 536
Food allergies, intolerances and food
   additives 537
Basic pantry essentials 545
Essential kitchen equipment 546
Cooking techniques 549
Basic preserving 558
Conversion charts 561

THE INDEXES

RECIPE INDEX 575

GENERAL INDEX 579

----
xxxxxxxx The Useful Recipes xxxxxxxx

```
----------------------------------------
xxxxxxxxxxxx 1. Breakfast xxxxxxxxxxxxx
----------------------------------------
```

BIRCHER MUESLI

Serves 2

xxxxxxxxxxxxxxxxxxxxxxxxxxxxxxxxxxxxxxxxxxxxxxxxxxxxxxxxxxxxxxxxxxxxxxxxxxxxxxxxxxxxxxxx

1 cup rolled oats
½ cup fresh orange juice
½ cup natural yoghurt
¼ cup currants or sultanas
¼ cup chopped dried apricots
pinch of ground nutmeg
large pinch of ground cinnamon
1 Granny Smith apple, grated, to serve
2 tablespoons natural yoghurt, extra
1 cup seasonal fresh berries, to serve

Method:

1. Combine the oats, juice, yoghurt, currants or sultanas, chopped apricots, nutmeg and cinnamon in a large bowl and stir well. Chill overnight.

2. To serve, stir in the grated apple, put into serving bowls and garnish with the extra yoghurt and the berries.

HINTS AND TIPS:

----

* You will need—large bowl, vegetable peeler, grater, cup, liquid and spoon measures and a large spoon.

* When in season, passionfruit is a wonderful addition to bircher muesli, so try adding the pulp of 4 passionfruit to this recipe. If you cannot wait for the season to begin, use a small can of passionfruit pulp, readily available at the supermarket.

* There are many varied recipes for bircher muesli and it should be remembered that this recipe—like all recipes in this book—is just a guide and so the addition of a favourite ingredient or removal of any ingredients that are not so liked is easy and encouraged.

* For gluten intolerance, the use of 'oat' style cereals can be substituted. One in particular is made from rice-meal; however, like most foods that are a gluten substitute, the end result will certainly have a different texture, one which coeliacs are quite used to.

* For a dairy-free option, simply replace the yoghurt with the same quantity of orange juice, or any other fruit juice, like apple, pineapple, mango, apricot or peach.

* Fruit yoghurts can be substituted for natural yoghurt, the only difference being that the end result will be just a bit sweeter.

* Any dried fruit can be substituted for the ones mentioned in the recipe, as long as the overall quantity for this recipe doesn't exceed ½ cup.

* Other spices that could be used in this recipe include mixed spice or allspice to replace the cinnamon and nutmeg. If no spices are on hand, simply omit from the recipe altogether.

* As much as bircher muesli is intended for breakfast, it makes for a great after-school snack for very hungry children.

* Once made, store the muesli in an airtight container in the refrigerator for 2 days. Even though it may last up to 5 days, it does begin to break down too much by day 3 and is considered a fresh product once the orange juice is added.

* Mixing in freshly grated apple adds a refreshing crunch to the bircher muesli. Topping with yoghurt and berries is just one example of how to serve this dish. Serving a dollop of bircher muesli with cold milk is simple and still delicious. Chopped fresh banana or melons can replace the fresh berries.

BOILED EGGS

xxxxxxxxxxxxxxxxxxxxxxxxxxxxxxxxxxxxxxxxxxxxxxxxxxxxxxxxxxxxxxxxxxxxxxxxxxxxxxxxxxx

hens' eggs, room
   temperature
water

Method:

1. There are many written methods for boiling an egg—see **Hints and tips** for why this one is the best.

2. Gently place room temperature eggs into a saucepan and cover with cold water by at least 5 cm.

3. Bring the water to the boil, then turn down to a barely recognisable simmer for 8–10 minutes for hard-boiled eggs. For the best results, the water should not be boiling. See **Hints and tips** for soft-boiled eggs.

4. Remove from the water with a slotted spoon and drop into cold or iced water to stop the cooking. Boiled eggs in the shell will keep in the fridge for 7 days.

HINTS AND TIPS:

----

* You will need—saucepan and slotted spoon.

* As tempted as you are to drop eggs from the fridge into boiling water, stop now and read on. The main reason eggs crack when boiled is due to temperature difference. A cold egg cooked in hot water will most probably crack, and no amount of salt or vinegar in the water will prevent this. All salt and vinegar can hope to achieve is to quickly set the egg white that flows from a cracked egg. The other reason is that eggs cooked in a rapid boil are knocked about, causing the egg to crack.

* The only reason why eggs are hard to peel once boiled is because they are very fresh. The fresher the egg, the harder it is to peel. The best eggs for boiling and then peeling are those that are about 2 weeks old. Keep the really fresh ones for poaching, frying or scrambling and for making cakes.

* For **really soft eggs**—both yolk and white—use the method mentioned, but remove the eggs after 2–3 minutes instead of 10 minutes. These are also known as 'coddled eggs'.

* For **soft yolks** and set whites, cook for 5 minutes. For a medium cooked yolk, cook for 6–7 minutes.

* All these times are approximations and much depends on the size of the egg, temperature of the egg and even the temperature of the water added in the beginning.

FRENCH TOAST

Serves 4

xxxxxxxxxxxxxxxxxxxxxxxxxxxxxxxxxxxxxxxxxxxxxxxxxxxxxxxxxxxxxxxxxxxxxxxxxxxxxxxxxxx

4 eggs
250 ml milk
1 teaspoon ground cinnamon
2 tablespoons caster sugar
1 teaspoon vanilla essence
150 g butter
4 slices of sourdough
   bread or thickly sliced
   white bread (French
   bread stick and Turkish
   bread will also work)

Method:

1. Place the eggs, milk, cinnamon, sugar and vanilla essence in a bowl and whisk.

2. Heat a frying pan or the flat plate of a barbecue (on lowest setting) and melt the butter. Soak each slice of bread in the egg mixture until wet through.

3. Place the soaked bread in the pan or on the flat plate and cook until golden brown. Turn and cook the other side. It is important to cook on a low–medium setting so the egg mixture cooks and sets, rather than cooking on a higher heat which will burn the outside and leave the inside soggy.

4. Once cooked, transfer to a plate and serve with your choice of toppings—bacon, maple syrup, **honeycomb butter**, fresh berries, ice-cream or lemon and sugar— or simply eat it on its own.

HINTS AND TIPS:

★ You will need—cutting board, bread knife, weight, spoon and liquid measures, sauté pan or frying pan.

★ French toast, like pancakes, is great for a special weekend breakfast. French toast is certainly much easier to prepare than pancakes and is a great place to start for beginner cooks.

★ This dish is also known as 'eggy bread' in the UK; and in France, it is known as 'pain perdu'.

★ Cooking French toast in butter adds to the richness of the dish.

★ Adding milk to the eggs is optional. Using just eggs mixed with the spices and sugar will give a richer and more eggy flavour.

★ You could take 2 pieces of bread and sandwich sliced bananas or grated apple between them, then dip the sandwich in the egg mixture before frying.

★ For a child's birthday party, use star- or people-shaped cutters to cut shapes from the bread before cooking.

★ Try serving French toast as a dessert instead of a breakfast dish.

★ French toast is often served as a sweet dish but can work as a savoury alternative. Try replacing the cinnamon, vanilla and sugar with 1 cup grated parmesan cheese and salt and pepper to taste. Dip the bread in the egg mixture before cooking.

FRUIT SALAD

Serves 4

XXXXXXXXXXXXXXXXXXXXXXXXXXXXXXXXXXXXXXXXXXXXXXXXXXXXXXXXXXXXXXXXXXXXXXXXXXXXXXXXXXXXXXX

¼ rockmelon (cantaloupe), peeled and seeds removed
¼ pineapple, peeled and cored
1 apple, peeled and cored
2 bananas, peeled
1 cup green grapes, washed
2 passionfruit
natural yoghurt, to serve

Method:

1. Cut the rockmelon, pineapple, apple and banana into roughly 2-cm pieces.

2. Mix all the fruit in a bowl then serve with fresh, natural yoghurt.

3. Store the fruit salad (without the yoghurt) in an airtight container for up to 2 days.

HINTS AND TIPS:

* You will need—cutting board, cook's knife, peeler, paring knife, cup measure, bowl and storage container.

* This is the most basic fruit salad recipe and can therefore be adapted to any fruit, but please consider the following tips.

* When cutting fruit, it is recommended that all fruit is cut the same size, but not necessarily the same shape. This means fruit can be cut into large pieces, about 5 cm, or into small pieces, 1 cm or less—but don't be tempted to mix the two sizes as it will look odd, and the smaller pieces can become damaged and mushy from the size and weight of the larger pieces.

* Never be tempted to add many fruits to a fruit salad to make it impressive. Sometimes a combination of 3 well-matched fruits is better than having a mixture of 10.

* Fruit salad is best eaten on the day or, at the very latest, the next day. Some fruits will certainly last longer; however, once mixed, some soft fruits will rapidly break down.

* Bananas, being a very soft fruit, should only be added just before serving. Once mixed and then stored, banana in a fruit salad will begin to soften quickly and become brown and mushy, making a great fruit salad look unappetising the next day.

* Think about matching hard fruits (as in the recipe) or soft fruits (as in the examples below).

* **Melon fruit salad**—a mix of equal parts watermelon, rockmelon and honeydew.

* **Mixed berry and mango salad**—once in season, make the most of fresh berries and counter their tartness by adding a mango cut into small pieces.

* **Pineapple, papaya and mint salad**—mix ½ pineapple, 1 pink papaya (peeled and black seeds removed) and ¼ cup shredded mint.

* **Citrus fruit salad**— 4 oranges, 6 mandarins, 2 pink grapefruit and 1 lime (mint would go well with this salad).

* **Banana, strawberry and passionfruit salad**— 3 bananas, 300 g strawberries and 3 passionfruit (the passionfruit will prevent the banana from browning).

* **Strawberry, grape and mango salad**—500 g strawberries (hulled and quartered), 500 g green grapes (washed) and 3 mangoes (cut into 2-cm pieces).

* **Tropical fruit salad**— make use of any tropical fruits like papaya, lychee, mango, longan, dragon fruit, pineapple, star apples, carambola (star fruit), chocolate pudding fruit, mangosteen and bananas.

HASH BROWN POTATO

Serves 4

XXXXXXXXXXXXXXXXXXXXXXXXXXXXXXXXXXXXXXXXXXXXXXXXXXXXXXXXXXXXXXXXXXXXXXXXXXXXXXXXXXXXXXXXXXXXXXX

500 g (about 2 large) potatoes
2 tablespoons vegetable or canola oil
2 tablespoons butter
salt and pepper, to taste

Method:

1. Scrub the potatoes—they do not need to be peeled—then coarsely grate. Squeeze the grated potato slightly to remove some of its water (this makes for a crispier end result).

2. Heat a 30-cm frying pan, preferably nonstick, over medium–high heat. Add the oil and butter.

3. When hot, add the potatoes and push down with a spatula to spread evenly in the bottom of the pan. Sprinkle the top with salt and pepper. Cook until the bottom is browned and crispy, about 10 minutes. Do not try to flip until it is browned, or the potatoes might stick.

4. Flip the hash brown, cut into sections if necessary, and cook another 10 minutes, or until browned and crispy on the other side.

5. Serve immediately, or cool and simply reheat in the microwave or preferably in a hot oven (210°C) for 5 minutes.

HINTS AND TIPS:

* You will need—grater, bowl, weight and spoon measures, nonstick frying pan and spatula.

* There are many different styles of hash browns. This recipe is about as easy and as fast as they come—and is, in fact, that of a Swiss potato dish called 'Potato rosti'. Other recipes suggest boiling and mixing the potato with all kinds of ingredients—they're not wrong. So the term 'hash brown' becomes quite loose, especially when made with sweet potato or even carrots.

* A standard supermarket potato is all that is required, this usually means a Sebago, Coliban or Nadine.

* To avoid discolouration of the grated potato, work quickly and squeeze the moisture out as soon as possible. If making a large batch, keep the grated potato in water until ready to assemble, then be sure to thoroughly squeeze out all the water before cooking.

* If using a nonstick pan, the use of oil and butter can be eliminated to reduce fats in the diet.

* For a variation, after squeezing excess moisture from the grated potato, try adding 1 egg yolk, 1 onion (finely chopped) and ¼ teaspoon hot (or mild) paprika. Instead of paprika, ½ teaspoon of finely chopped herbs like rosemary or sage marry well with potato.

* Or add the kernels from a cob of corn to the recipe with 1 tablespoon chopped parsley, ½ red capsicum (chopped) and 1 fresh red chilli (chopped). Then top this with Guacamole and bacon.

* Once cooked, top regular hash browns with crispy bacon then grated cheese and finish in a hot oven for 5 minutes.

* Remember, if using a nonstick pan, use a plastic spatula not a knife to flip the hash brown and cut it.

* Here's an easy way to flip the whole hash brown: slide the hash brown out of the pan and onto a plate. Invert the pan over the plate and the hash brown and turn the whole thing over together. The browned part is now on top.

* A large disk of hash brown can be used as a pizza base for those with wheat and gluten intolerance—simply top with all your favourite pizza goodies.

* When cooking individual hash browns, do not overcrowd the pan at the risk of the hash browns sticking together as they cook and tearing apart as they are turned.

* Individual hash browns can be used as a base for eggs Benedict, instead of an English muffin; in which case it becomes quite a different dish, especially if ham is replaced with smoked salmon— yum! This is especially good for those with wheat and gluten intolerance.

* For a cocktail party or dinner party, cook small hash browns then top with smoked salmon and crème fraîche, or trout dip and chives, or sour cream and salmon roe, or simply mayonnaise and capers.

OMELETTE

Serves 1

XXXXXXXXXXXXXXXXXXXXXXXXXXXXXXXXXXXXXXXXXXXXXXXXXXXXXXXXXXXXXXXXXXXXXXXXXXXXXXXXXXXXXXXXX

3 large eggs
2 tablespoons warm water
large pinch of salt flakes
pinch of ground white pepper
2 tablespoons butter
1 teaspoon olive oil

Method:

1. Combine the egg, water, salt and pepper in a bowl
and whisk until well combined. The water evaporates as
the omelette cooks making it light and fluffy.

2. Place a nonstick frying pan over medium—high heat,
add the butter and olive oil and heat until the butter
begins to bubble without browning.

3. Add the egg mixture to the pan. As the egg begins
to set, use a rubber or plastic spatula to move the
egg from the outer part of the pan to the middle, to
allow the uncooked egg to fill any exposed parts of the
pan.

4. When half-cooked and still runny on top, add any
flavours you like (some ideas are listed opposite) and
continue to cook until set or better still cook the
top of the omelette under the grill section of the
oven. This will only take 1—2 minutes.

5. Remove from the heat and shake the pan to loosen
the omelette from the base of the pan. Shake the
omelette to one side, tilting so that the top third
can be folded over, and then turn onto a plate.

HINTS AND TIPS:

* You will need—cutting board, cook's knife, bowl, spoon measures, whisk, spatula, shallow frying or sauté pan or crepe pan.

* This recipe is a classic French-style omelette which means it is folded as it is served. Another version is the Spanish omelette which is not folded, but served flat from the pan. Fans of the Spanish omelette have been known to cook their omelette in a shallow terracotta baking dish, eating it straight from the dish.

* A simple mixture of chopped fresh herbs can be added to the egg mixture. A quantity no more than 1 tablespoon of chopped herbs like parsley, thyme, sage, oregano, mint, chervil or tarragon can be used in any combination.

* **Bacon, spinach and goat's cheese omelette**—1 rasher of bacon (chopped and fried), 1 cup spinach (chopped and wilted by cooking it in the pan after the bacon), and ¼ cup goat's cheese (crumbled). Loosely mix all ingredients in a bowl, ready to place in the middle of the half-cooked omelette. The goat's cheese can be replaced with fetta, ricotta, brie or grated cheddar.

* **Mushroom, tomato and spinach omelette**—1 cup sliced Swiss brown mushrooms (cooked in 2 tablespoons olive oil), 1 ripe tomato (peeled, de-seeded and chopped), and 1 cup spinach (chopped and wilted by cooking it in the pan after the mushrooms). Loosely mix all the ingredients in a bowl, ready to place in the middle of the half-cooked omelette. Fresh tomato can be replaced with ¼ cup semi- or sun-dried tomatoes. Spinach can be replaced with rocket. Mushrooms can be replaced with grilled artichoke hearts.

* Try other fillings like some of the combinations mentioned in the hints and tips list for **frittata**.

* An omelette is considered a benchmark for any good chef, a sign of solid training and of a good understanding of the basics. In some kitchens, fail the omelette test and you fail to get the job. Domestic cooks need not place so much pressure on themselves, just remember practice makes perfect.

SCRAMBLED EGGS

Serves 2

XXXXXXXXXXXXXXXXXXXXXXXXXXXXXXXXXXXXXXXXXXXXXXXXXXXXXXXXXXXXXXXXXXXXXXXXXXXXXXXXXXXXXXXXXX

4–6 eggs (depending on size)
2 tablespoons thick cream (35 per cent fat)
salt and freshly ground pepper, to taste
75 g butter
chopped chives, to garnish

Method:

1. In a bowl, crack the eggs, add the cream and season with salt and pepper.

2. Whisk lightly with a fork—the whites and yolks don't have to be completely mixed and the mixture should contain some air; over-whisking the mixture expels the air and makes for heavier scrambled eggs.

3. Melt the butter in a heavy-based nonstick pan over medium heat. When the butter begins to bubble, add the egg mixture and reduce heat to low. As it begins to cook and thicken, fold the thicker bits towards the centre of the pan—uncooked egg will moat around the cooked egg. Repeat this process until the eggs are close to ready but still a little runny, then remove from the heat and move the mixture once or twice more as the heat of the pan will complete the cooking.

4. Serve immediately—scrambled eggs become tough and dry if you attempt to keep them warm. Garnish with the chives or other fresh green herbs.

HINTS AND TIPS:

* You will need—bowl, whisk or fork, weight measure, silicon spatula and nonstick pan.

* For great tasting eggs, try to source eggs from a farmers market or at the very least use free range eggs.

* The degree to which people like their eggs cooked—whether scrambled, poached, fried or boiled—can vary greatly. However, the two most common are runny and hard. This is very true when making scrambled eggs, so as much as this recipe calls for the eggs to be just set, some may feel it necessary to cook them to within an inch of dust; this is completely up to the individual. Expect that in restaurants eggs should always be 'just' cooked, and it is up to the customer to express 'firm' or 'well done' when ordering.

* If cooking scrambled eggs for more than 2, then unfortunately it becomes a lengthy process. Too many serves in one pan, although achievable, will create havoc with overcrowding, possibly causing much spillage. Also, it would mean the eggs are exposed to heat for a longer period, meaning that while some parts of the eggs are not cooked, other parts are beginning to overcook, become rubbery and then watery.

* Cooking scrambled eggs on a high heat can be done; however, there is the risk of browning parts of the eggs and leaving unsightly spots throughout the mixture. Also, eggs are a delicate protein that do not respond well to high heat.

* Adding cream—as this recipe suggests—results in very smooth, creamy and decadent scrambled eggs. Replacing the cream with milk or low fat milk can be done, but be very careful not to overcook the eggs as it will toughen the mixture and leave you with a heavily weeping mass of tough egg curds and watery milky whey as the proteins in milk also overcook and coagulate.

* For lactose intolerance, use 2 tablespoons of water instead of cream or milk—again, so long as the mixure is only just cooked, this version of scrambled eggs can still be quite amazing. Water added to scrambled egg mixture can create fluffy eggs as the water begins to steam the beaten eggs.

* Surprising as this may seem, serving scrambled eggs for an entrée at a dinner party can be quite a hit. A regular serve of scrambled eggs (2 eggs per person) plus some smoked salmon and a small green salad is a very acceptable way to begin a meal.

* For an extra special treat, just as the eggs are nearly ready, add 1 tablespoon mascarpone cheese or crème fraîche or 2 tablespoons goat's cheese. Stir once or twice and serve.

* This recipe for scrambled eggs can be slightly undercooked and then poured onto 2 tortillas. Top each one with ¼ avocado and a slice of good ham then roll like a burrito, place on a tray and top with a small handful of grated tasty cheese. Bake in a hot oven (210°C) for 5 minutes. Breakfast Burrito! Tabasco sauce or a fresh salsa made of 1 fresh tomato (chopped), ½ red onion (chopped), 2 tablespoons chopped coriander, salt and pepper, and 1 tablespoon extra virgin olive oil will finish this breakfast or brunch meal.

SLOW-ROASTED TOMATOES

Serves 4–8

XXXXXXXXXXXXXXXXXXXXXXXXXXXXXXXXXXXXXXXXXXXXXXXXXXXXXXXXXXXXXXXXXXXXXXXXXXXXXXXXXXXXXXXXXX

8 Roma or vine-ripened tomatoes
3 tablespoons olive oil
2 tablespoons salt flakes
1 tablespoon freshly ground black pepper

Method:

1. Preheat the oven to 110°C.

2. Slice the tomatoes in half and place, cut side up, on a baking tray lined with baking paper.

3. Brush or drizzle with the olive oil. Sprinkle with the salt and pepper.

4. Roast in the oven for 3 hours.

5. Remove from the oven, cool and keep refrigerated, covered, for up to 5 days.

HINTS AND TIPS:

* You will need—cutting board, cook's knife, spoon measure, baking tray and baking paper.

* These tomatoes freeze well for up to 2 months.

* Try adding 2 thinly sliced garlic cloves, placed on the tomatoes, before roasting.

* The marriage of basil and tomato is perfect, so try adding 6 basil leaves. You can also use other herbs like oregano, parsley, mint or thyme. Chop the herbs finely and sprinkle over the tomatoes before roasting.

* Finely chop 4 shallots or 1 small brown onion and sprinkle over tomatoes before roasting. Shallots are favoured over onions as they tend to be less pungent, but they are a bit more fiddly to peel and chop.

* Roasted tomatoes are fantastic with breakfast, in a salad, chopped into a frittata, served with roasted or grilled meats, or on a mezze or antipasto platter.

* Once cooked, drizzle tomatoes with balsamic vinegar and scatter with goat's cheese; serve with a simple salad or as a side dish.

* To use with pasta—peel skins from the roasted tomatoes and place in a food processor, then blitz to make a simple yet full-flavoured passata (fine tomato sauce). Homemade tomato sauce is an indispensable ingredient in any kitchen, especially for beginner cooks looking for an easy meal.

* For good storage of the roasted tomato sauce—place the hot puree in sterilised jars and seal with a lid. The heat from the sauce will create a vacuum while cooling.

* For a juicier sauce, try cooking the tomatoes at a higher temperature for a shorter time. Preheat the oven to 170°C and roast for 1½ hours until softened. These tomatoes are less intense but still very tasty; try grilling or pan frying when reheating, or simply puree to use as pasta sauce.

SUPER FLUFFY PANCAKES

Serves 7 children and 2 adults

xxxxxxxxxxxxxxxxxxxxxxxxxxxxxxxxxxxxxxxxxxxxxxxxxxxxxxxxxxxxxxxxxxxxxxxxxxxxxxxxxxxx

750 ml milk or buttermilk
8 eggs, separated
few drops of vanilla essence (optional)
600 g self-raising flour
100 g caster sugar
about 125 g unsalted butter, for cooking

Method:

1. In one bowl, mix the milk or buttermilk and egg yolks, whisking until the egg yolks are combined. At this point the vanilla essence can be added, if using.

2. Place the egg whites in a second, large bowl, ready for whisking.

3. In a third large bowl, sift the flour and sugar, making a well in the centre. Pour the milk mixture into the centre of the flour/sugar mixture and begin combining with a wooden spoon, slowly drawing in the flour to form a thick batter. Do not worry if the mixture is excessively lumpy. By not whisking the milk mixture into the flour, you ensure that the flour is not overworked thereby tightening the batter—also, the lumps NEVER appear in the final pancakes.

4. Whisk the egg whites until soft peaks form then fold into the batter.

5. Cover and allow to rest in the fridge for 1 hour— although I'm unbelievably impatient and usually cook them straightaway.

6. Cooking them requires the use of a large frying pan (or barbecue flat plate if you're a large family) set on low—medium heat. Add a good knob of the butter and melt. Spoon in the pancake mixture according to your preferred size. When bubbles begin to appear evenly on the surface, turn over. The second side will only require 1—2 minutes to cook.

HINTS AND TIPS:

---

* You will need—3 bowls, whisk or electric beaters, large spoon, egg flip or spatula, frying pan, butter knife, weight and liquid measures.

* This super fluffy pancake recipe takes a little extra time and uses 3 bowls. Do not shy away, as the results are sensational.

* The mixture can be halved as it makes a very large batch (enough for my 7 children and us parents). Any leftover batter will last until the next day; after that, however, the egg whites will begin to lose their bubbles and the mixture will become grey and lifeless.

* Toppings can range from the usual suspects—maple syrup, lemon and sugar, grilled banana or fresh berries—to the more exotic, **poached rhubarb**, blueberries in vanilla syrup, confit pineapple or **honeycomb butter**—all of which love ice-cream!

* Leftover mixture can also be cooked into smaller pancakes, refrigerated and used in school lunch boxes the next day.

* Whisking the egg whites is entirely optional. The egg whites certainly do make a difference, giving the pancakes a ´light as air´ texture. But time and washing up permitting, simply beat the whole eggs into the milk and stir the wet mixture into the dry mixture. Remember to not overwork the batter.

* Cooking the pancakes in butter gives the edges of the pancakes a crisp, frilly side which is a delight to eat and a great contrast to the soft, fluffy centre.

----

xxxxx **2. Dips and Accompaniments** xxxxx

BABA GHANOUJ

Makes 4 cups

XXXXXXXXXXXXXXXXXXXXXXXXXXXXXXXXXXXXXXXXXXXXXXXXXXXXXXXXXXXXXXXXXXXXXXXXXXXXXXXXXX

2 medium eggplants
1 garlic clove, crushed
juice of 1 lemon
100 g tahini
300 g natural yoghurt
¼ teaspoon allspice
salt flakes and freshly
    ground pepper, to taste

Method:

1. Prick the eggplants all over with a fork.

2. Place each over a naked gas flame, set to medium. Cook for 5–7 minutes, turning constantly until blistered and blackened. Alternatively, this can be done on the barbecue grill but will take much longer.

3. Eggplants are cooked when very soft to press. Place in a bowl and cover with plastic wrap.

4. When cool enough to handle, drain excess liquid and gently remove skin with a small knife. Allow the skin to come away from the flesh without force (any flesh coming off with the skin will have a bitter flavour).

5. In a bowl, mash the eggplant pulp with a fork or place in a food processor and mash using the pulse button. Drain well, discarding any juice from the eggplant.

6. Combine the remaining ingredients in a bowl, add the eggplant and mix well.

HINTS AND TIPS:

* You will need—cutting board, knife, fork, weight and spoon measures, 2 bowls, spoon and food processor (optional).

* Pricking the eggplant all over allows the heat to reach the centre and it will cook more evenly.

* Cooking the eggplant over a naked flame imparts a very smoky flavour to the dip. This flavour can be too strong for some palates. The eggplants can be pricked and then roasted in the oven at 220°C until completely soft, then continue as per the method given.

* Baba ghanouj as a dip should be drizzled with excellent extra virgin olive oil and a few grinds of fresh pepper.

* Baba ghanouj is fantastic served with meats instead of a sauce. It's especially good with grilled pork and lamb cutlets.

* As a spread on rolls and flat bread with **roasted vegetables**, cold roast meats and salads, baba ghanouj is a healthy alternative to butter or margarine.

* This recipe should yield enough dip for 10 people when served on its own with crusty bread and vegetable batons.

* Refrigerated, baba ghanouj will last up to 7 days. Before serving, bring to room temperature to enhance the flavours.

CARAMELISED ONIONS

Makes about 1 cup

xxxxxxxxxxxxxxxxxxxxxxxxxxxxxxxxxxxxxxxxxxxxxxxxxxxxxxxxxxxxxxxxxxxxxxxxxxxxxxxxxxxxxxxxxxxxxxxxx

100 ml olive oil
3 red or brown onions,
    peeled and sliced

Method:

1. Heat the oil in a heavy-based saucepan over medium heat.

2. Add the onion and cook until beginning to wilt. Reduce the heat to low and continue to cook for a further 20 minutes, stirring frequently to avoid the onions sticking to the base of the pan.

3. Once golden in colour, remove from the pan and cool. Store in a sealed container or jar in the refrigerator. Caramelised onions will last 5–7 days covered and refrigerated.

HINTS AND TIPS:

* You will need—cutting board, cook's knife, paring knife, liquid measure, roasting tray, saucepan and wooden spoon.

* Keep onions in the fridge—this is the best way to avoid crying when cutting the onion. The cold of the fridge subdues the substance known as 'allicin' which is produced when the onion is cut into.

* Don't confuse caramelised onions with onion jam. Caramelised onion refers to the browning or 'caramelisation' of the sugars that are naturally present in onions. **Onion jam**, you will notice, is made with sugar.

* Even though red or brown onions are called for in this recipe, purple onions, white onions, pickling onions and even shallots will make good alternatives.

* Adding fresh herbs is a nice option. To the above recipe, try adding in the beginning 1 sprig rosemary or 2 sprigs thyme. Or add 1 bay leaf and 5 black peppercorns.

* Caramelised onions have a wide variety of uses. For breakfast, they make a great addition to any fry-up. Even spread on toast with a few pieces of grilled bacon or avocado for a simple breakfast idea. Try also adding to an **omelette**.

* For lunch, use the onions in a roll or sandwich—or as an accompaniment to an antipasto plate with goat's cheese, olives, **roasted garlic** and toasted flat bread. Mix some caramelised onion in a quiche or frittata.

* At dinner, any time a roast or grilled meats are to be served, use caramelised onions as an alternative to mustard and sauce. They also marry brilliantly with **roasted vegetables**, grilled vegetable salad, or leftover vegetables that have been made into bubble-and-squeak for breakfast the next day. Mix into pasta dishes just before serving or spread over a pizza base. Probably the most famous way of serving caramelised onions is with gravy, grilled sausages and mashed potato; and they are great to serve with **sausages and mash with pepper sauce**.

CHILLI JAM

Makes about 4 cups

xxxxxxxxxxxxxxxxxxxxxxxxxxxxxxxxxxxxxxxxxxxxxxxxxxxxxxxxxxxxxxxxxxxxxxxxxxxxxxxxxxxxxxxxxxxx

4 red capsicums
6 tomatoes
100 ml olive oil
2 garlic cloves, minced
8 long red chillies, sliced in half lengthways, seeds
    removed and chopped
100 ml malt vinegar
300 g brown sugar
2 teaspoons salt

Method:

1. Place capsicums on a roasting tray lined with baking paper and bake at 250°C, turning every 5 minutes until the capsicums are blackened on all sides. Remove from the oven and place in a bowl to cool before peeling.

2. Peel the tomatoes while the capsicums are roasting. Bring a saucepan of water to the boil. With a small kitchen knife or paring knife, remove the tomato stem area. Score the opposite end of the tomato with a criss-cross pattern. Cook the tomatoes in the boiling water for 20 seconds. Remove, cool slightly and peel off the skins. Slice the tomatoes in half (between the top and bottom) then, using a teaspoon, remove the seeds. Chop roughly and set aside.

3. Peel the capsicums and discard any seeds and stem. Chop into small pieces.

4. Heat a heavy-based saucepan over medium heat and add the olive oil.

5. Add the garlic and chilli and fry gently for 1 minute.

6. Add the chopped capsicum and tomato and cook for 5 minutes.

Method cont.

7. Add the vinegar, sugar and salt, cook on medium heat for 15 minutes, then reduce the heat slightly and cook until the jam has thickened.

8. Pour into a sterilised jar (if storing), cool, cover and refrigerate. If using immediately and often, store in a jar or plastic container with a lid and keep refrigerated.

HINTS AND TIPS:

---

* You will need—cutting board, cook's knife, paring knife or small kitchen knife, roasting tray, baking paper, heavy-based saucepan, weight, spoon and liquid measures and a wooden spoon.

* Peeling the capsicum and tomato may seem like a lot of work, and it is a step that could be skipped; however, it is important as both capsicum and tomato skin do not break down when cooked and stay stringy and chewy in the jam if not removed.

* To skip roasting, peeling and de-seeding the capsicum, simply buy 300 g roasted capsicum from a good delicatessen and roughly chop before adding to the recipe.

* 6 large whole tomatoes will yield about 600 g peeled and de-seeded tomato.

* It may seem strange that there is lots of capsicum and tomato in a dish called chilli jam. Fortunately, capsicum, tomato and chilli are all from the 'nightshade' family of plants with the first 2 ingredients adding body to the jam. Chilli on its own, as a jam, would be too strong and would require too much mucking around to get enough even for a small jar.

* The chilli heat in this recipe is very mild, therefore if you require some real chilli kick in your jam, add 4–8 bird's eye chillies to the recipe, preparing them the same way as the long red chillies but being extra careful in handling the smaller hot chillies. After handling small hot chillies and even after washing your hands, there will be chilli residue on your hands for an hour or more—so be careful. Try washing your hands with straight lemon juice—it will help.

GUACAMOLE

Makes about 2 cups

xxxxxxxxxxxxxxxxxxxxxxxxxxxxxxxxxxxxxxxxxxxxxxxxxxxxxxxxxxxxxxxxxxxxxxxxxxxxxxxxxxxxxxxxxxx

2 ripe avocados
½ cup lemon juice
salt

Method:

1. Carefully cut each avocado down to the seed using a sharp knife. Turn the avocado around the blade of the knife to cut it in half lengthways. Twist the halves in opposite directions, lifting as you twist to reveal two halves, one with the seed still attached. To remove the seed, give it a short, sharp chop with the knife; this will bury the blade a few millimetres into the seed's woody surface. Twist the knife and the seed is free.

2. Scoop the flesh from the skin using a spoon. Place in a bowl and mash with a fork, keeping it quite chunky.

3. Add the lemon juice and salt to taste.

HINTS AND TIPS:

* You will need—cutting board, sharp cook's knife, bowl, cup measure, spoon and fork.

* This is the most basic and original recipe for guacamole. Adding other ingredients is a matter of taste. Following is a more recognised recipe which can have all or just some of the mentioned ingredients mixed into the basic recipe: 2 fresh tomatoes (finely chopped), ½ onion (finely chopped), 1 bird's eye chilli (finely chopped) and 2 tablespoons finely chopped fresh coriander.

* Use basic guacamole instead of butter or margarine on salad sandwiches.

* Use with **nachos** as an alternative to sour cream.

* Serve as part of an antipasto platter.

* To refrigerate, cover with a film of plastic wrap to prevent browning—it will keep for about a week.

* If you want the guacamole to be of a thicker consistency, add ¼–½ cup of fresh breadcrumbs.

* For a smoother consistency, blend in a food processor.

* Lime juice can be substituted for lemon juice.

* You can stir through cottage cheese or sour cream for a variation.

HUMMUS

Makes about 600 g

XXXXXXXXXXXXXXXXXXXXXXXXXXXXXXXXXXXXXXXXXXXXXXXXXXXXXXXXXXXXXXXXXXXXXXXXXXXXXXXXXXXXXXXXXX

250 g dried chickpeas
1 litre cold water
6 tablespoons tahini
4 garlic cloves, crushed
juice of 4 lemons
salt

Method:

1. Place the chickpeas in a large container and cover with the water. Soak overnight.

2. Drain the chickpeas, place in a large pot, and add enough fresh cold water to cover by 10 cm. Simmer until tender, about 1 hour.

3. Remove from the heat and drain, keeping some of the cooking water.

4. Process the chickpeas, tahini, garlic and lemon juice in a food processor, adding just enough of the cooking liquid to bring the mixture to a creamy consistency. Season with salt to taste.

HINTS AND TIPS:

★ You will need—cutting board, cook's knife, large pot, weight and spoon measures, food processor, plastic spatula and bowl.

★ When simmering the chickpeas, to prevent foam forming on the water's surface, add 1 tablespoon vegetable oil to the water before it comes to the boil.

★ The older the chickpeas the longer the cooking time.

★ Once cooked, the chickpeas can be placed in cold water so the loose skins float to the top.

★ When soaking and cooking dried chickpeas, it is worth remembering they double in weight and size.

★ Canned chickpeas can be used as a substitute for the dried variety; be careful when seasoning because the canned varieties are already salted.

★ Do not salt the water when cooking, this will toughen the chickpeas.

★ Use hummus as a dip or as a spread in rolls, flat breads and sandwiches.

★ When serving as a dip, drizzle with extra virgin olive oil and sprinkle with a few pinches of paprika.

★ As an alternative to extra virgin olive oil, drizzle with olive oil infused with basil or chilli.

★ Try adding 2 teaspoons ground cumin to the hummus.

★ Hummus can be served warm as is traditional in the east of Turkey. In fact hummus is the Arab word for chickpea.

★ Dried chickpeas can be soaked and cooked a couple of days in advance and kept in the fridge.

★ Cooked chickpeas can be frozen.

★ Changing the water once it has reached the boil reduces intestinal gas because the indigestible sugars which cause the gas dilute in the water.

★ Store dried chickpeas in an airtight container for no more than 1 year.

MINT JELLY

Makes about 1 litre

XXXXXXXXXXXXXXXXXXXXXXXXXXXXXXXXXXXXXXXXXXXXXXXXXXXXXXXXXXXXXXXXXXXXXXXXXXXXXXXXXXXXXXXXXXXXXX

1 kg Granny Smith apples
500 ml water
½ bunch mint, washed and chopped with the stalks
1 cup cider vinegar
white sugar

Method:

1. Roughly chop the apples; leave the skin on and do not core.

2. Place the apples, water and mint in a saucepan over medium heat and cook gently until the apples are soft and pulpy, about 20 minutes.

3. Add the vinegar, remove the pan from the heat and mash the apples with a potato masher.

4. Set up a pot with a colander or large strainer lined with muslin cloth sitting on top. Pour the apple mixture into the cloth-lined strainer and leave to drain overnight—do not squeeze the mixture unless a cloudy jelly doesn't worry you.

5. Measure the strained juice and pour into a saucepan then add an equal quantity of sugar. Place the pan over medium heat, stirring to dissolve the sugar. Bring to the boil and use a spoon to remove any scum forming on the surface. Simmer for 15 minutes or until the temperature reaches 103–105°C on a sugar thermometer.

6. Pour into 4 x 300-ml hot sterilised jars, and allow to cool before sealing. The jelly will continue to set over a few days. Keeps in a cool dry place for 1 year. Once opened, refrigerate.

HINTS AND TIPS:

* You will need—cutting board, cook's knife, saucepan, cup, weight and liquid measures, potato masher, wooden spoon, colander, muslin cloth, 4 x 300-ml preserving jars and lids and sugar thermometer.

* It's important to understand that homemade mint jelly does not look like the commercially prepared stuff. Homemade is more of a golden amber colour, not bright green. Bright green can be achieved by adding a few drops of green food colouring and 1 teaspoon dried mint to give that 'real' mint effect to the jelly.

* There is never any need to peel or core fruit such as apples when making a jelly, this adds to the flavour and helps to make the jelly set. See **Basic preserving**.

* Although the sugar and vinegar preserve the jelly, the biggest risk is mould. Keeping the jelly at room temperature for 1 year can be done, but if this makes you nervous, then store it in the refrigerator. Once opened, all preserves must be refrigerated.

* Several things may have an effect on the jelly not setting. **1.** Not enough pectin in the fruit—tart apples, like Granny Smiths, are required due to the higher amount of pectin than sweet eating apples. **2.** The amount of sugar—sugar helps the jelly set, therefore the ratio of sugar to liquid must be right. **3.** Evaporation— simmering the liquid at the end needs to be done long enough so the required amount of water evaporates, leaving the right proportion of sugar to liquid; this is why a sugar thermometer is used.

* Sometimes a jelly will not have set when everything seems to have gone right; to try to remedy this, bring back to the boil and add some cream of tartar or lemon juice.

* A clear jelly can only be achieved by the undisturbed straining of the fruit puree. Force it through and the jelly will be cloudy.

* A very firm jelly may 'weep', sometimes seen in homemade jams and jellies given out by relatives. This weeping is a result of too much acid being added to the mixture.

ONION JAM

Makes about 2 cups

XXXXXXXXXXXXXXXXXXXXXXXXXXXXXXXXXXXXXXXXXXXXXXXXXXXXXXXXXXXXXXXXXXXXXXXXXXXXXXXXXXXXXXXXXXXXXXXXXXX

200 g white sugar
50 ml water
2 large onions, finely diced
100 ml port
salt

Method:

1. Place the sugar in a pan and add just enough water to soften. Bring to the boil then allow to simmer until it is quite dark in colour—this is the caramel.

2. Add the onion immediately, followed by the port (being careful not to have it splatter on you), then stir to combine the ingredients. At this stage, the caramel may form clumps; do not panic as these will dissolve.

3. Season with the salt.

4. Reduce the heat slightly and simmer until the onion is thoroughly cooked and takes on a dark brown colour. Have water by the pan as the jam tends to lose all of its liquid before it is ready, so add a little more to keep it moist.

5. Once thick and fragrant, remove from the heat. Onion jam can be served warm or chilled and will store, covered, in the refrigerator for 4–6 weeks.

HINTS AND TIPS:

* You will need—cutting board, cook's knife, weight and liquid measures, saucepan and wooden spoon.

* Onion jam is great with chicken or duck liver pâté and any meat terrines as well as with roast beef or lamb.

* Onion jam is fantastic served with very ripe brie or camembert. For a more basic taste, whip some room temperature cream cheese until soft, spoon into a bowl then dollop with onion jam and serve with plain biscuits. Crusty bread served with blue cheese and onion jam is a great way to finish off a dinner party.

* Substitute the port for balsamic vinegar for a different yet stunning onion jam.

* Serve onion jam in burgers, as an accompaniment for a hot breakfast or simply with grilled meats.

* As a delicious snack, serve onion jam alongside Persian fetta (which is creamier and less salty than regular fetta cheese), **roasted** or **garlic confit** and crusty bread.

* Use red or brown onions in this recipe.

* Many recipes will ask that the onions are cooked in butter until naturally caramelised (see **caramelised onions**) then the remaining ingredients are added. That method is fine as well but I prefer a 'jam' or 'preserve' made without dairy products just in case somebody is allergic to dairy.

PESTO

Makes about 8 cups

xxxxxxxxxxxxxxxxxxxxxxxxxxxxxxxxxxxxxxxxxxxxxxxxxxxxxxxxxxxxxxxxxxxxxxxxxxxxxxxxxxxxxx

4 cups well packed basil leaves
6 garlic cloves, peeled and sliced
1 cup pine nuts or walnuts (or a combination of the
    two)
1½ cups extra virgin olive oil
salt and pepper
1 cup freshly grated parmesan or pecorino cheese (or a
    combination of the two)

Method:

1. Place the basil leaves and garlic in a food
processor or blender and process until the basil is
finely chopped.

2. Add the nuts and process until the nuts are also
finely chopped.

3. With the motor running, add the oil in a slow,
steady stream. After the oil is incorporated, turn off
the machine and add the salt and pepper to taste. Add
the cheese and process until combined.

4. If not using immediately, store in an airtight
container with a thin coating of olive oil on top to
keep the pesto from going dark. Pesto covered with oil
will keep well in the refrigerator for 2 weeks.

HINTS AND TIPS:

* You will need—cutting board, cook's knife, cup measure and food processor or blender.

* 4 cups of basil leaves will require about 2 large bunches of basil. If this seems too much, simply halve the recipe.

* Using just pecorino cheese and increasing the quantity of garlic to 8 cloves will make a more intense, sharply flavoured pesto.

* Toasting the pine nuts will also add flavour. To do this, place the pine nuts on a baking tray and roast in the oven at 200°C, tossing every 3–4 minutes until evenly brown. This is a job that requires the cook to stay in the kitchen as the pine nuts will burn easily.

* The amount of olive oil can be adjusted depending on the desired final consistency (thicker or thinner). Try adding or removing ½ cup olive oil.

* Mix 1 tablespoon pesto through 4 tablespoons softened butter and keep in the fridge. It can be sliced and placed on top of hot meats just before serving.

* Cut a chicken breast in half, spread with pesto and a generous slice of camembert cheese and a thin slice of prosciutto, secure with a toothpick and bake in a moderate oven for 20 minutes until the chicken starts to turn golden.

* Use pesto as a sandwich spread.

* Pesto can be frozen for up to 6 months. The easiest way to control portions is by freezing in ice cube trays, and once frozen, transferring to a clip lock bag.

* Serve as part of an antipasto platter.

* Add a generous dollop to **minestrone**.

* Toast good quality bread in a moderate oven, spread with the pesto and serve as crostini.

* Add pesto to roasted asparagus, stir through gnocchi, risotto, scrambled eggs or omelettes, or mix through a potato salad.

* For the advanced cook, add more parmesan and less oil, and use as a filling for homemade tortellini or ravioli.

* Use on a pizza base instead of tomato sauce.

* Chopped basil browns quickly so add a layer of oil to the top of the jar to prevent it from discolouring, and the pesto will keep longer because air is kept out.

PISTOU

Makes about 1 cup

XXXXXXXXXXXXXXXXXXXXXXXXXXXXXXXXXXXXXXXXXXXXXXXXXXXXXXXXXXXXXXXXXXXXXXXXXXXXXXXXXXXXXXXXX

4 garlic cloves, peeled
2 cups loosely packed
   fresh basil leaves
   (1 bunch)
½ cup extra virgin olive
   oil
about ¼ teaspoon salt
   flakes

Method:

1. Puree the ingredients in a small food processor until a smooth paste is formed. (Or, pound the garlic and salt in a mortar and pestle, then start adding the basil, pounding until pasty, and blend in the olive oil.)

2. Serve immediately or, like **pesto**, cover with a thin layer of olive oil and refrigerate for up to 5 days. It will freeze successfully if done in small amounts.

HINTS AND TIPS:

* You will need—cutting board, cook's knife, cup measure and food processor or mortar and pestle.

* Pistou is the French version of Italy's pesto. Therefore they are very similar in quantities and usage. The main difference is the French pistou does not have the nuts and parmesan cheese included in the pesto.

* Pistou is associated with the French provincial soup similar to minestrone. The pistou is served on the side or added to the individual bowl.

* This is the most traditional and basic pistou recipe; a common variation has the addition of ½ cup grated parmesan cheese stirred in at the end.

* Like many traditional recipes, there are many variations based on the area where the raw ingredients are sourced. Therefore it should come as no surprise that some recipes for pistou contain parmesan, nuts, tomato or even ham—any of which would be considered correct depending on which provincial cook you spoke to.

* See **pesto** for more tips on how to use pistou.

QUINCE PASTE

Makes about 3 kg

xxxxxxxxxxxxxxxxxxxxxxxxxxxxxxxxxxxxxxxxxxxxxxxxxxxxxxxxxxxxxxxxxxxxxxxxxxxxxxxxxxxxxxxxxxxx

3 kg quinces
white sugar
150 ml lemon juice,
    strained
3 cinnamon sticks

Method:

1. Choose quince which are yellow with a slight green tinge to them. This indicates that the quince is still a little under-ripe which in turn means the pectin levels are higher. Wash any 'down' from the surface of the quinces and chop roughly—at this point there is no need to peel or core the fruit. Place the chopped quinces in a saucepan with 750 ml water. Bring to the boil, reduce heat and simmer until soft.

2. Drain off the excess water and pass the softened fruit through a sieve. Weigh the quince puree then place in a deep, heavy-based pot with an equal weight of sugar. Add the lemon juice and cinnamon sticks.

3. Use a long-handled wooden spoon to stir over low heat, then increase the heat and boil until the mixture turns pink and begins to thicken. As it thickens, it is important to stir constantly so the paste doesn't catch on the base of the pot and burn.

4. Once thick, pour the paste into sterilised jars or containers. Leave to cool before covering. If properly sealed in sterilised containers, quince paste will last at least 1 year in a cool, dry area. Once opened, keep refrigerated.

HINTS AND TIPS:

----

* You will need—cutting board, cook's knife, weight and liquid measures, a long-handled wooden spoon, lemon juicer and a large heavy-based pot.

* A native fruit of Persia, quince are said to be the fruit of love. But it's their alchemy-like cooking act that inspires many cooks. The raw quince has flesh as pale as a ghost and is so hard it verges on being inedible yet it is nothing short of a culinary miracle that it transforms into a soft, ruby-red, beautifully perfumed food.

* Quince paste is a delicious accompaniment to any cheese plate, especially suited to blue cheese and ripe brie.

* Quince paste can be served with roast pork or roast turkey. Or make a sauce by heating 4 tablespoons quince paste, 4 tablespoons water, 4 tablespoons port and the zest of 1 orange, season with a small amount of salt, strain and serve on the side.

SALSA VERDE

Makes about 2½ cups

xxxxxxxxxxxxxxxxxxxxxxxxxxxxxxxxxxxxxxxxxxxxxxxxxxxxxxxxxxxxxxxxxxxxxxxxxxxxxxxxxxxxxxxxxxxx

1½ tablespoons salted capers
1 cup flat-leaf or curly parsley leaves
1 cup mint leaves
1 cup basil leaves
3 garlic cloves, minced
6 anchovy fillets
1 cup olive oil
lemon juice
salt and pepper

Method:

1. Wash the capers and soak in fresh water for an hour. Drain and squeeze dry in a tea towel.

2. In a food processor, blend the capers, herbs, garlic and anchovies until combined. Alternatively, you can use a mortar and pestle and pound the ingredients into a paste.

3. With the machine still running, gradually add the olive oil.

4. When a thick paste forms, turn the machine off and stir in the lemon juice.

5. Season to taste, transfer to a jar or bowl and cover with a layer of oil to seal; keep, covered, for up to 7 days.

HINTS AND TIPS:

★ You will need—cutting board, bowls, sieve, cup measure, food processor or mortar and pestle and plastic spatula.

★ Salsa verde directly translates as 'green sauce'.

★ For a different version of this sauce, omit the capers and anchovy fillets and add 1 tablespoon Dijon mustard.

★ To make a 'sweet and sour' green sauce known as 'Salsa verde agrodolce', add to the basic recipe 4 tablespoons lemon juice or red wine vinegar, 2 tablespoons caster sugar and 2 slices white bread with the crusts removed.

★ The herbs used in salsa verde can vary according to what you have fresh at hand. Parsley is recommended in all combinations with the addition of 2 other fresh green herbs, such as mint, basil, sorrel, marjoram, sage, tarragon, thyme, watercress, chervil or coriander to name a few.

★ Salsa verde is served with fish, seafood, chicken, grilled and boiled meats, and chargrilled or **roasted vegetables**.

★ Salted capers can be substituted with pickled capers—which are more common in the supermarket. However, salted capers are a far better product compared to the more readily available, spongy, pickled variety.

★ It is recommended to cover the salsa with oil for longer storage. Without the oil, the salsa will need to be used within 2—3 days, after which the salsa will begin to oxidise and lose flavour and pungency. The salsa can also be frozen in ice cube trays; once frozen, place the cubes into a clip lock bag.

★ Drizzle some salsa verde in **minestrone**.

★ Serve with pasta as you would pesto pasta.

TAPENADE

Makes about 3 cups

XXXXXXXXXXXXXXXXXXXXXXXXXXXXXXXXXXXXXXXXXXXXXXXXXXXXXXXXXXXXXXXXXXXXXXXXXXXXXXXXXXXXXXXXXXX

500 g kalamata olives, pitted (see **Hints and tips**)
100 g capers, rinsed
100 g anchovy fillets
200 ml olive oil

Method:

1. Place all the ingredients in a food processor and blend until smooth. Or chop and then pound in a mortar and pestle, leaving the oil until last.

2. Store, covered with a thin layer of oil, in a sealed container in the refrigerator for up to 5 days.

HINTS AND TIPS:

★ You will need—food processor or mortar and pestle, weight and liquid measures, plastic spatula, cook's knife (optional) and jar for storage.

★ Pitting olives is as simple as squashing the olives either with your fingers and removing the pit or by placing the olive on a cutting board and squashing it with the base of a glass or bottle, then removing the pit.

★ Tapenade can be made using large green olives. Any style of olive can be used, just make sure that olives kept in a brine are soaked for 30 minutes in cold water before using to remove the salty flavour. However, don't buy pitted olives, especially the Spanish variety; they will not lend enough flavour and you will be disappointed.

★ The capers should be rinsed under cold water and squeezed dry in the hand to get rid of the briny taste.

★ The addition of 2 teaspoons seeded mustard to the above recipe after blending is recommended.

★ 2 tablespoons balsamic vinegar can be added for extra kick in the tapenade.

★ To sweeten and add body to the mixture, add 1 cup chopped dried figs.

★ Try adding chopped leaves from a sprig of thyme to the blended mixture.

★ Mince or chop 1 garlic clove and add before blending the mixture.

★ In some recipes, the addition of 100 ml dark rum or brandy can replace 100 ml olive oil.

★ A little goes a long way. Smear a thin layer of tapenade on a piece of bread, taste and adjust the amount according to personal taste.

★ Tapenade is often served as an accompaniment or appetiser with chargrilled flat bread or sourdough bread.

★ As a stir-through pasta sauce, try adding an extra clove of minced garlic and a cup of Italian tomato sauce (sugo casa) then stir into the cooked pasta before topping with torn flat-leaf parsley leaves.

★ For an easy pasta sauce add tapenade and tinned tuna in olive oil to hot pasta. Sprinkle with some fresh oregano and finish with some crumbled fetta cheese.

★ Smear some tapenade mixed with equal parts ricotta under the skin of a roast chicken before baking in the oven.

★ Spread tapenade on round croutons or bruschetta then top with your favourite ingredients to serve as a light lunch or dinner starter.

★ Tapenade can be used on a pizza base rather than tomato sauce.

★ Serve tapenade as part of an antipasto plate.

★ Press out small rounds of puff pastry with a 5-cm pastry cutter, brush with tapenade, top with a slice of potato, sprinkle with dried rosemary and flaked salt and bake for 15 minutes at 180°C.

★ Add chilli to taste or juice of ½ lemon. You can also add ¼ cup roasted mushrooms or ¼ cup sundried tomatoes (finely chopped).

★ Substitute black olives for green olives and replace the anchovies with ¼ cup ground almonds.

★ Substitute the anchovies with 50 g tinned tuna.

TOMATO CHUTNEY

Makes about 1½–2 litres

xxxxxxxxxxxxxxxxxxxxxxxxxxxxxxxxxxxxxxxxxxxxxxxxxxxxxxxxxxxxxxxxxxxxxxxxxxxxxxxxxxxxxxxxxxxxxxxxxxx

1 kg ripe tomatoes, peeled (see **tomato jam**)
500 g brown onions, peeled and cut into 1-cm dice
1 tablespoon salt
250 g sultanas or raisins, chopped
250 ml white vinegar
300 g brown sugar
2 bay leaves
1 teaspoon **curry powder**
½ teaspoon ground coriander
½ teaspoon ground turmeric
½ teaspoon freshly ground black pepper
¼ teaspoon ground cloves

Method:

1. Dice the tomatoes and place in a glass or plastic bowl with the onion. Sprinkle with salt, cover and refrigerate overnight. The following day pour off excess liquid.

2. Place the tomato and onion mixture in a pot and bring to the boil.

3. Add the sultanas or raisins, vinegar, sugar and bay leaves, and simmer until the sugar dissolves.

4. In a small pan or wok, toast the curry powder and spices for 30 seconds. Remove the pan from the heat, and add some liquid from the tomato mixture to form a paste. Then add the spice paste to the chutney.

5. Simmer for 1½–2 hours or until the mixture resembles a soft jam consistency. Remember to stir occasionally to prevent it from burning.

6. Pour into hot sterilised jars and seal with a lid. Cool before storing in the pantry. Keep refrigerated

HINTS AND TIPS:

after opening.

★ You will need—knife, cutting board, bowls, weight, liquid and spoon measures, heavy-based saucepan, frying pan, wooden spoon, a strong heatproof bowl or ladle and preserving jars with lids.

★ Try adding 500 g peeled and diced Granny Smith apples to this recipe.

★ Toasting the spices brings out their fragrance; however, it is an optional step in this recipe. Do keep in mind that it is a 30-second job and adds greatly to the end result.

★ Peeling the tomatoes may not seem all that important, especially given the time it takes. But it really is essential as tomato skins do not break down once cooked and remain as chewy strips not dissimilar to rubber bands. Keep in mind that tomato chutney will last for months on end and so the extra time taken to peel the tomatoes is certainly more than made up for in preservation time.

★ Like **tomato relish**, chutney is best stored for 4–6 weeks (preferably several months) before using to allow the vinegar to mellow and the flavours to marry.

★ Tomato chutney, with its great preserving power, is always good to have on hand for barbecues and roasts. It's also great with homemade pies, or spread on rolls or sandwiches.

★ For a **green tomato chutney**, substitute the red, ripe tomatoes for green (unripe) tomatoes and add 250 g peeled and diced Granny Smith apples. Cook as per the method given.

★ Consider the tomatoes used when making a chutney. Depending on the variety and the natural sweetness of the tomato, the amount of sugar used can vary. Green tomatoes will need more sugar than sweet red tomatoes. Even red tomatoes differ in natural sugars. Do not expect your first batch to be your best; the more you make and refine the recipe, the better it will become.

★ As always, any homemade preserve stored in a nice bottle and labelled with a funky name makes for a great gift all year round.

TOMATO RELISH

Makes about 2 litres

XXXXXXXXXXXXXXXXXXXXXXXXXXXXXXXXXXXXXXXXXXXXXXXXXXXXXXXXXXXXXXXXXXXXXXXXXXXXXXXXXXXXXXXXXXXXXXX

1 kg ripe tomatoes
500 g (about 4 medium) onions, diced
1 tablespoon salt
300 g brown sugar
1–2 cups malt vinegar
1 tablespoon dry mustard powder
1 bay leaf
1 teaspoon mixed spice
½ teaspoon ground cinnamon
¼ teaspoon cayenne pepper
¼ teaspoon ground cumin

Method:

1. Peel the tomatoes (see **Hints and tips**) and roughly
chop. Place the tomatoes and onion in a bowl, sprinkle
with the salt and refrigerate overnight. This draws
out the liquid and intensifies the flavour.

2. The following day, pour off the excess liquid and
put the mixture in a heavy-based saucepan. Add the
sugar and enough vinegar to only just cover.

3. Bring the relish to the boil, reduce heat and
simmer for 1 hour.

4. While the tomatoes are simmering, dry fry the
spices over medium heat in a frying pan or wok,
stirring constantly to avoid burning. This will take
about 30 seconds. Remove the pan from the heat and
add a few tablespoons of the tomato cooking liquid
and mix to form a paste. Add this spice paste to the
tomato relish and simmer, stirring often because as it
thickens it will tend to stick and burn, for another
30 minutes or until the mixture thickens.

5. Ladle into hot, sterilised jars with plastic lids.
Relish needs to be stored for 3 months or more to
allow the flavours to mature. Eating this relish within
weeks is fine but the flavour is overpowered by vinegar.

HINTS AND TIPS:

* You will need—knife, cutting board, bowl, weight, spoon and cup measures, heavy-based saucepan, wooden spoon, ladle and preserving jars and lids.

* There is surprisingly very little difference between a relish and a chutney. A relish can be made with similar ingredients used in a chutney, although in different quantities. A relish is generally cooked for less time, which helps retain the texture of the ingredients, whereas chutney is cooked for longer and the texture is therefore thicker and more even.

* To peel a tomato—score the skin very lightly with the point of a sharp knife. Then blanch in boiling water for 10–15 seconds, no more— the longer the tomato cooks, the more flesh will be ripped off when you peel the tomato. Don't drop the tomatoes in iced water after blanching, as this will dilute their flavour.

* Relishes make great gifts and friends are always impressed when you give them something you have made yourself.

* This relish will keep in sterilised jars for up to 12 months. Once opened, keep in the fridge and use within 4 weeks.

* Serve this relish as part of an antipasto platter; it goes really well with hard cheeses.

* Substitute red tomatoes for green; they are difficult to find but if you are fortunate enough to have your own vegetable patch, it is a great way to utilise the tomatoes that do not ripen at the end of the season.

* Serve with **nachos** instead of sour cream for a lighter alternative.

* Because relish is a condiment, it really can be served with anything either hot or cold; use in sandwiches or with **rissoles**, **sausage rolls**, savoury scones, roast meat or cold meats.

* Use as a pizza base or in tacos.

* Over time, the relish will darken a bit which is fine as the flavour will intensify.

TOMATO JAM

Makes about 1¼ litres

xxxxxxxxxxxxxxxxxxxxxxxxxxxxxxxxxxxxxxxxxxxxxxxxxxxxxxxxxxxxxxxxxxxxxxxxxxxxxxxx

1 kg ripe tomatoes, peeled
   (see **Hints and tips**)
1 kg white sugar
juice of 1 lemon

Method:

1. Cut the tomatoes in half, thinly slice and place in a heavy-based saucepan.

2. Gently bring the tomatoes to the boil.

3. Add the sugar and lemon juice and stir until dissolved.

4. Continue to boil, stirring occasionally, until the jam reaches setting point.

5. Pour into hot, sterilised jars or if using immediately into a container to cool, before refrigeration.

HINTS AND TIPS:

* You will need—knife, cutting board, bowl, weight measure, juicer, heavy-based saucepan, heatproof jug or ladle and preserving jars and lids.

* To peel a tomato—score the skin very lightly with the point of a sharp knife. Then blanch in boiling water for 10–15 seconds, no more— the longer the tomato cooks, the more flesh will be ripped off when you peel the tomato. Don't drop the tomatoes in iced water after blanching, as this will dilute their flavour.

* **Green tomato jam**—2 kg green tomatoes (1 kg after cleaning), 900 g caster sugar, and juice and zest of 2 small lemons. Rinse tomatoes in cold water and dry with a tea towel. Cut into wedges and remove the seeds, juice and remove the white centre parts. Dice the tomatoes (about 2 cm) and place in a bowl with the sugar and lemon juice. Cover with plastic wrap and stand overnight. The next day, pour the tomato mixture into a heavy-based saucepan. Bring to the boil, reduce heat to low and cook for 10 minutes, stirring occasionally. Pour back into the bowl, cover with plastic wrap and again refrigerate overnight. On the third day, bring the mixture to the boil, skim if necessary, and continue cooking on low heat for 10 minutes, stirring occasionally. Check to see if the jam is thick enough and cook a few minutes more if needed. Put the jam into sterilised jars immediately and seal, or for small batches, just refrigerate.

TZATZIKI

Makes about 600 g

XXXXXXXXXXXXXXXXXXXXXXXXXXXXXXXXXXXXXXXXXXXXXXXXXXXXXXXXXXXXXXXXXXXXXXXXXXXXXXXXXXXX

500 g natural yoghurt
    (see **Hints and tips**)
1 continental cucumber,
    seeds removed and
    grated
2 garlic cloves, crushed
juice of ½ lemon
1 teaspoon shredded mint
salt

Method:

1. Place the yoghurt in a bowl and beat with a whisk to thicken slightly.

2. Add the remaining ingredients and mix well.

3. Serve with a drizzle of extra virgin olive oil or store in a container, refrigerated. It will keep for 1–2 days but will then become watery.

HINTS AND TIPS:

* You will need—2 bowls, cutting board, knife, juicer, grater, spoon measure and spoon.

* The yoghurt needs to be as thick as possible. Use a sheep's milk yoghurt or strain 750 g natural yoghurt overnight (in the fridge) through a clean muslin cloth set in a strainer over a bowl to catch the liquid. Discard the cloudy liquid. The strained yoghurt is known as 'labna'. 750 g strained yoghurt will produce about 500 g thick yoghurt after 12 hours. Strain the yoghurt for 24–36 hours and it would be too thick for tzatziki and is best used as labna cheese.

* If making tzatziki in advance and to reduce the water content, place the grated or sliced cucumber in a bowl and sprinkle with 1 tablespoon salt, allow to

stand for 30 minutes, rinse under cold water and squeeze gently to remove excess water.

* Tzatziki can be given more tang by adding the extra juice of ½ lemon, or mellow the flavour by mixing 2 tablespoons mayonnaise to the basic recipe.

* Pepper is deliberately missing from the recipe as it is not usually added. However, if you are a fan, add some to taste.

* Small amounts of leftover tzatziki can be used as a marinade for lamb cutlets, chops or roasting joint, or chicken thigh and breast fillets. Leave overnight and grill, barbecue or roast the next day.

* Serve with **roasted vegetables**, **lentil** or chickpea **burgers** or as an accompaniment to steamed beans.

* To serve as a dip, try hollowing out the inside of a round 'cob' loaf and fill the centre with the tzatziki. Toast the inside of the loaf in the oven to make chunky croutons that can be dipped into the tzatziki. Then break off parts of the crusty outer loaf and dip that in as well.

* Replace the mint with basil. On occasions, especially if serving with fish, replace the mint with fresh dill.

* Leftover **roast lamb** can be sliced and heated in a pan or on the barbecue to resemble 'gyros'. Dollop tzatziki on the lamb and roll in flat bread with lettuce and tomato.

* Although tzatziki has a special affinity with barbecued or grilled lamb, try it with lamb burgers and grilled chicken breast.

----
xxxxxxxxxxxxxx 3. Soups xxxxxxxxxxxxxx

CAULIFLOWER SOUP

Makes about 1 litre or 4 serves

XXXXXXXXXXXXXXXXXXXXXXXXXXXXXXXXXXXXXXXXXXXXXXXXXXXXXXXXXXXXXXXXXXXXXXXXXXXXXXXXXXXXXXXXXX

1 medium cauliflower
500 ml water
250 ml milk (optional)
salt

Method:

1. Remove leaves from the cauliflower. Cut into small pieces, including the entire stem as that is where most of the flavour is.

2. Place in a saucepan with the water and milk. Milk is optional—especially if lactose intolerant—and should be replaced with more water. Bring to the boil and simmer for 30 minutes or until the cauliflower is soft.

3. Remove from the heat and let stand for 10 minutes before blending. It is best to do this with a hand-held blender or benchtop blender and not a food processor which produces a less refined result.

4. Place back on the stove, bring back to the boil and season with salt to taste.

5. Serve as is or with a drizzle of extra virgin olive oil.

HINTS AND TIPS:

* You will need—cutting board, cook's knife, liquid measure, saucepan and hand-held or benchtop blender.

* When using cauliflower for this soup, find one that is free from blemishes and is firm to touch.

* The amount of liquid used is a guide and should only just cover the cauliflower. Too much liquid and the soup will be too thin; it is best to have a very thick soup that can have more liquid added after it is pureed.

* The reason it is recommended the soup stand before blending is that it is extremely hot and can cause a nasty burn if rushing the blending stage. A well-trained cook may get away with it; however, I've seen some bad burns from hot soups.

* It is important to re-boil the soup, especially if refrigerating leftovers or making the day before. This is because the air bubbles created when blending will hold bacteria when the soup is cooling and in some cases can make the soup 'sour' overnight.

* The use of onion and garlic in this soup is entirely unnecessary. The notion that all soups start with the gentle sautéing of these two ingredients is ridiculous. It may add a flavour profile that is too powerful for the main ingredient.

* For a smooth, velvety texture, bring the pureed soup back to the boil, remove from the heat and stir in 1 tablespoon butter or double cream.

* Peel and chop 2 large potatoes and add to the soup with the cauliflower. The potatoes will thicken the soup. Be sure to test the potatoes to check that they are thoroughly cooked to the point of breaking up in the soup.

CHICKEN AND SWEET CORN SOUP

Serves 6–8

xxxxxxxxxxxxxxxxxxxxxxxxxxxxxxxxxxxxxxxxxxxxxxxxxxxxxxxxxxxxxxxxxxxxxxxxxxxxxxxxxxxxxxxxxxx

250 g chicken breast, finely chopped
1 teaspoon minced ginger
100 ml shaoxing rice wine
1½ litres chicken stock (see **Hints and tips**)
1 x 400 g tin creamed corn or 400 g fresh corn kernels,
    blanched in boiling water and blended
1 teaspoon salt flakes
3 tablespoons cornflour mixed with 1 tablespoon cold
    water
3 egg whites, lightly beaten
1 teaspoon sesame oil
finely chopped spring onion, to garnish

Method:

1. Mix the chicken, ginger and rice wine in a bowl and set aside.

2. In a pot, bring the chicken stock, corn and salt to the boil, then reduce heat to a simmer. Add the chicken mixture and stir well.

3. Mix the cornflour with just enough cold water to make a smooth paste. Stir the cornflour paste into the simmering soup, bring back to the boil and remove from the heat.

4. Stir in the egg whites then add the sesame oil.

5. Serve in bowls with a sprinkle of spring onion.

HINTS AND TIPS:

* You will need—cutting board, cook's knife, weight, spoon and liquid measures, 2 bowls, whisk and serving ladle.

* This basic Chinese soup which is so very popular with the Western diner is very simple to make. But the true secret of a great chicken and sweet corn soup is the quality of the ingredients, especially the chicken stock. It is worth the effort to make **chicken stock** to truly appreciate this timeless classic.

* The time-poor cook will not have the 3–4 hours it takes to make a stock so I suggest using stock cubes until ready to take it to the next level.

* Fresh stock should be used within 3 days or freeze in handy 1- or 2-litre containers—old milk containers, thoroughly washed and drained, make excellent freezer containers for stock.

* Vegetable stock can be substituted for chicken stock. If making a vegetarian version, omit the chicken breast and stir in 250 g silken tofu at the very end.

* A dry sherry can be substituted for Chinese cooking wine.

* Finely chopped chilli with the seeds removed can be added to the cooking process.

* Canned sweet corn can be used instead of creamed corn but will still need to be drained and processed to a smooth consistency.

* Leftover soup can be frozen.

* Leftover egg yolks can be used to make a **mayonnaise**. Keep the yolks in a bowl covered with plastic film to prevent a skin from forming on the yolks. 1–2 days is ideal.

CHICKEN SOUP WITH MATZOH BALLS

Serves 4–6

xxxxxxxxxxxxxxxxxxxxxxxxxxxxxxxxxxxxxxxxxxxxxxxxxxxxxxxxxxxxxxxxxxxxxxxxxxxxxxxxxxxxxxxxxx

Matzoh balls

100 ml vegetable oil
2 medium onions, finely
   diced
½ bunch chives, chopped
6 eggs, lightly beaten
300 g matzoh meal
salt and pepper
1 litre **chicken stock**

Method:

1. Heat the oil in a pan and sauté the onions until lightly golden. Remove from the heat.

2. In a bowl, mix the chives, eggs, matzoh meal and the sautéed onion. Season with salt and pepper, and mix well. Taste the mixture to ensure it is well seasoned.

3. Refrigerate for 1–2 hours.

4. Divide the mixture into four and roll each into a thin sausage shape and cut into 35–40 even pieces— this will save time ripping at the mixture, guessing the same size balls.

5. Roll each cut piece into a ball and place on a tray.

6. Bring a pot of salted water to the boil and cook the balls for 30 minutes.

7. Remove the cooked balls and set aside ready for use.

8. Remember to reheat before using in the chicken soup.

9. Reheat the chicken stock, add the matzoh balls (4 per serve) and serve.

HINTS AND TIPS:

★ You will need—cutting board, knife, large stock or soup pot, fine sieve, some muslin cloth (optional), sauté pan, wooden spoon, tray, saucepan, and weight and liquid measures.

★ Leftover soup can be used as a stock for many other soups. Or freeze in containers for another day.

★ Traditionally, a chicken soup was made as above but using a whole chicken and then the meat from the bird was added back into the soup. The problem with this is the meat has relinquished all of its nutrients into the stock and is too dry.

★ Some cooks like to finish the soup with green peas and diced carrot.

★ If you want to add some chicken meat to the strained soup, use some chicken breast fillets, thinly sliced and poached for several minutes in the simmering soup.

★ A common catchcry throughout this book is that there are as many recipes as there are cooks. And so ... for all the Jewish cooks who cross this recipe—my apologies.

CRAB CHOWDER

Serves 4

XXXXXXXXXXXXXXXXXXXXXXXXXXXXXXXXXXXXXXXXXXXXXXXXXXXXXXXXXXXXXXXXXXXXXXXXXXXXXXXXX

100 g butter
½ brown onion, finely chopped
2 celery sticks, finely chopped
1 cup water
3 medium potatoes, peeled and diced
2 cups milk
300 g cooked crab meat
¼ teaspoon Tabasco sauce
¼ teaspoon ground pepper
salt

Method:

1. Melt the butter in a heavy-based pot or saucepan over medium heat. When the butter is bubbling, add the onion and celery and cook without colouring for 5 minutes.

2. Add the water and potatoes and bring to the boil. Reduce the heat and simmer for 10 minutes.

3. Add the milk, bring back to the boil, reduce the heat to low and simmer until the potatoes are tender (ready to eat).

4. Stir in the crab meat, Tabasco, pepper and salt to taste.

HINTS AND TIPS:

* You will need—cutting board, cook's knife, cup, weight, liquid and spoon measures, wooden spoon and heavy-based pot or saucepan.

* This is a very basic version of chowder. There are many additions and alternative ingredients for this soup while still being classed as chowder.

* Although chowder has its debated origins in Bordeaux, France, and Cornwall in the southwest of England, it owes its popularity to the Americas. Even in America it is argued which style of chowder is the best as there are 3 styles; the creamy version (above), a clear, broth style, and a tomato-based chowder. One thing, however, is common in all and that is the addition of seafood.

* The quality of seafood is paramount to the success of this dish. Crab meat is readily available at most fish shops. Always pick over the crab meat as often it has bits of shell in it.

* The best option is to cook and pick over the crab yourself, as this guarantees freshness.

* Do not be tempted to use tinned crab meat—the flavour is distinct and can affect the chowder.

* Clam chowder or seafood chowder are two alternatives to the recipe provided. Simply substitute the crab meat with the same weight of any other seafood combination. Be sure to sauté raw seafood before stirring into the chowder at the last minute.

FRENCH ONION SOUP

Serves 6

xxxxxxxxxxxxxxxxxxxxxxxxxxxxxxxxxxxxxxxxxxxxxxxxxxxxxxxxxxxxxxxxxxxxxxxxxxxxxxxxxxxxxxxxxx

100 g butter
3 large brown onions, thinly sliced
250 ml red wine
1 litre brown beef stock, **vegetable stock**, **chicken
    stock** or water
salt and pepper
1 tablespoon fresh thyme leaves, finely chopped
6 slices French stick or small sourdough
1 cup grated gruyère cheese

Method:

1. In a heavy-based pot or casserole dish, melt the
butter until it begins to foam and starts to brown
slightly. Quickly add the onions, reduce the heat to
medium and cook the onions for 15–20 minutes or until
the onions take on a light caramel colour.

2. Add the wine and reduce by half.

3. Add the stock or water, bring to the boil and
simmer for 10 minutes.

4. Remove from the heat, season with salt and pepper
to taste, and sprinkle in the thyme.

5. Heat the grill and toast the bread slices on both
sides, top one side of each slice with cheese and
place back under the grill to melt.

6. Place a cheese crouton in each bowl and ladle the
soup over the top, or ladle the soup in first then top
with a crouton.

HINTS AND TIPS:

* You will need—cutting board, cook's knife, cup, liquid, weight and spoon measures, baking tray, heavy-based pot or casserole dish and wooden spoon.

* Use brown onions and not red onions in this soup, as red onions can make the soup go slightly cloudy unless really well cooked and finished with a splash of balsamic or red wine vinegar.

* Always be careful with the quantity of salt you add at the end. Remember that instant stocks can be quite salty.

* The soup can be made well in advance and the cheesy bread grilled just before serving.

GAZPACHO

Serves 4–6

xxxxxxxxxxxxxxxxxxxxxxxxxxxxxxxxxxxxxxxxxxxxxxxxxxxxxxxxxxxxxxxxxxxxxxxxxxxxxxxxxxxxxxxxxxxx

6 large ripe tomatoes, peeled, seeded and chopped
1 long red chilli, seeds removed and minced
4 garlic cloves, minced
1 continental cucumber, peeled, seeded and diced
1 red capsicum, seeded and diced
1 red onion, peeled and finely diced
1 litre **vegetable stock** or **chicken stock**
2 tablespoons lemon juice
2 tablespoons sherry vinegar
2 tablespoons chopped fresh basil
2 tablespoons chopped fresh flat-leaf parsley
salt flakes and freshly ground black pepper
125 ml best-quality extra virgin olive oil

Method:

1. Combine all of the vegetables in a large bowl.

2. Add the stock, lemon juice and vinegar and stir very briefly.

3. Stir in the fresh herbs and season with salt and pepper to taste.

4. Chill the soup for at least 1 hour before serving.

5. Remove from the refrigerator, stir, let rest for 15 minutes and then pour the olive oil over the soup and serve.

HINTS AND TIPS:

* You will need—cutting board, cook's knife, paring knife, vegetable peeler, juicer and liquid and spoon measures.

* This full-bodied version of contemporary gazpacho is best at the peak of harvest, when all of the vegetables are perfectly ripe. On a hot day, there is nothing more refreshing.

* Alternatively, combine all the ingredients in a food processor and pulse until smooth but still with chunks in it.

* It is important to cut the vegetables to the same size. This is not only for the aesthetics of the dish but when eating, even pieces of each vegetable can be consumed in equal amounts in one mouthful.

* **Ajo blanco**—is the white gazpacho and although served chilled has little else in common with the more commonly known tomato-based soup. To make ajo blanco, you need—250 g blanched almonds, 750 ml iced water, 5 slices stale white bread (with crusts removed) soaked in water, 5 garlic cloves, 3 tablespoons extra virgin olive oil, 4 tablespoons sherry vinegar, 1 teaspoon salt flakes and ground white pepper. In a food processor, blitz the almonds. Add 1 cup iced water, then squeeze the bread of excess water and add to the almonds with the garlic. With the machine running, add more water, the olive oil and the vinegar. Check the seasoning then chill in the refrigerator. Serve topped with fresh muscatel grapes.

MINESTRONE

Serves 8

xxxxxxxxxxxxxxxxxxxxxxxxxxxxxxxxxxxxxxxxxxxxxxxxxxxxxxxxxxxxxxxxxxxxxxxxxxxxxxxxxxxxxxxxxxxxxxxxxx

3 litres **chicken stock**, **vegetable stock** or water
500 g fresh borlotti beans, shelled to yield 250 g
   (see note below) or 1 x 440 g can borlotti beans
250 g tomatoes, peeled and seeded
200 g carrots, peeled and cubed
1 celery stick, trimmed, coarsely chopped
1 large potato, peeled and diced
150 g rice (arborio if possible)
200 g white cabbage or cavolo nero (black cabbage),
   shredded
200 g green beans, cut into pieces, or fresh green peas
200 g small zucchini, washed, cut in half and
   thinly sliced
2 large ripe tomatoes, peeled, seeded and
   coarsely chopped
1 tablespoon chopped fresh flat-leaf parsley
salt flakes
chopped fresh basil or **pesto**, to serve
freshly grated parmesan cheese, to serve
extra virgin olive oil, for drizzling
freshly ground black pepper, to serve

Method:

1. Bring the stock to the boil. Add the borlotti beans
and simmer for 15 minutes—if using canned beans,
drain and rinse under cold water and add with the hard
vegetables.

2. Puree the tomatoes in a blender. Add to the stock
along with the carrots, celery, potato and rice, and
simmer for 15 minutes. With 5 minutes of cooking time
to go, add the cabbage, green beans or peas, zucchini
and chopped tomato. When completely cooked, check the
seasoning. It should be a thick soup; however, if it
is too thick, add more stock or water.

3. Serve in individual bowls with chopped basil or
pesto. Pass around the parmesan, extra virgin olive
oil, and pepper.

HINTS AND TIPS:

* You will need—cutting board, cook's knife, vegetable peeler, strainer, grater, blender, pot or large saucepan, wooden spoon, weight, liquid and spoon measures.

* Minestrone is a rustic country soup that should be served hot in winter and autumn, and cool or even chilled in summer. It may take time to prepare, but the results are worth it—recruit somebody to help you prepare the vegetables. There really is no set recipe for minestrone which makes the recipe just a guide. Although it's usually made from vegetables in season, beans, stock and pasta or rice, the actual quantities do not have to be exact. This really is the best opportunity to cook a meal without a recipe and as long as the soup is packed with vegetables and has a thick consistency, minestrone can be very simple.

* If chicken stock is unavailable then simply use water, just be sure to season the soup properly at the end. As this recipe asks for chicken stock—and as romantic as it may be to use homemade stock which will take several hours—stock cubes, powder or even pre-made packet stock will be fine. Be aware, however, that these 'quick' options can tend to be quite salty, so be careful before adding extra salt as the soup may need only a little, if any at all.

* 150 g dried white beans may be substituted for the borlotti. Soak overnight and cook until tender. Add to the broth with the vegetables.

* Fresh tomatoes for the puree can easily be replaced with a small can of crushed tomatoes. The tomatoes added at the end of the cooking are still best to be kept fresh and chunky.

* Rice can be replaced with a pasta, like small shells or macaroni.

* Other ingredients can go into the soup like cauliflower, parsnip, turnip, swede or celeriac. Bacon rinds can be added in the beginning to add a smoky flavour to the soup.

* One option is to start the soup by frying 1 finely chopped onion and 2 crushed garlic cloves in 3 tablespoons olive oil before adding the chicken stock. Or pre-boil 2 Italian sausages for 15 minutes, cool and slice into rounds then brown in the olive oil before adding the onion and garlic; continue as per the recipe.

* Serve with fresh Italian bread, no butter.

* Rather than serving in individual bowls, place the pot in the middle of the table and as everyone sits at the table, ask how much they would like. This allows people to have only what they feel like as well as the option of asking for seconds. Have all the accompaniments around the pot of soup. Bread, parmesan, extra virgin olive oil and **pesto** are perfect to add to minestrone.

MISO SOUP

Serves 4

xxxxxxxxxxxxxxxxxxxxxxxxxxxxxxxxxxxxxxxxxxxxxxxxxxxxxxxxxxxxxxxxxxxxxxxxxxxxxxxxxxxx

1 litre dashi stock

75 g Inaka miso

200 g silken bean curd
(tofu)

1 tablespoon finely sliced
spring onions, green
part only

Method:

1. Bring the dashi stock to the boil, then reduce the heat to a simmer.

2. Add the miso paste, stirring to dissolve.

3. Gently cut the tofu into 1-cm cubes and place in 4 serving bowls.

4. Ladle the miso soup over the top of the tofu and sprinkle each with some sliced spring onion.

HINTS AND TIPS:

★ You will need—cutting board, cook's knife, liquid, weight and spoon measures and pot or saucepan.

★ This is probably the easiest soup in the book due to everything being readily available at Japanese and other Asian grocers.

★ Although simply finished here with spring onions, alternative garnishes include toasted sesame seeds, toasted nori flakes or chives. Try also asparagus spears, bean sprouts, snow peas, fresh sliced shiitake mushrooms or fine julienne of carrot.

★ Do not boil miso soup as it can change the flavour slightly. Bring to the boil and turn down immediately.

★ Miso soup is high in valuable nutrients and is considered a great 'pick me up'.

★ Dashi is fundamental in Japanese cuisine as a soup stock and flavour base in many dishes. Generally made with dried fish (sardines or bonito) and kombu (a seaweed available fresh, dried, frozen and pickled), dashi can also be vegetarian, made with mushrooms. Instant dashi is a powder that simply needs boiling water added. Although quick and easy, it is frowned upon by purists. If you have a recipe for homemade dashi, have a go: there are after all only 2 or 3 ingredients involved and one of them is water—how hard can it be?

MUSHROOM SOUP

Serves 4

xxxxxxxxxxxxxxxxxxxxxxxxxxxxxxxxxxxxxxxxxxxxxxxxxxxxxxxxxxxxxxxxxxxxxxxxxxxxxxxxxxxxx

750 g mushrooms, torn into
   pieces
100 ml olive oil
1 brown onion, finely
   chopped
2 garlic cloves, crushed
750 ml chicken stock or
   vegetable stock
150 ml thickened cream
½ cup fresh flat-leaf
   parsley leaves,
   shredded
salt and freshly ground
   black pepper

Method:

1. Chop 100 g of the mushrooms and set aside to garnish.

2. Heat the oil in a large saucepan over medium heat. Add the onion and garlic and cook, stirring often, for 3–4 minutes or until soft but without colour.

3. Add the torn mushrooms and cook, stirring occasionally, for 10 minutes or until mushrooms are tender.

4. Add the stock and bring to the boil. Reduce the heat to medium-low and simmer, uncovered for 10 minutes, stirring occasionally.

5. Remove from the heat, and using a hand-held blender or benchtop blender, process soup to a smooth even consistency.

6. Return to the saucepan and stir in the cream and parsley. Place back on a medium-low heat, and reheat, without boiling, until hot. Season with salt and pepper, ladle into bowls and serve garnished with reserved mushrooms.

HINTS AND TIPS:

★ You will need—cutting board, cook's knife, liquid, weight and cup measures, wooden spoon, heavy-based pot, hand-held blender or benchtop blender.

★ The raw, chopped mushrooms added at the end will heighten the mushroom flavour in the soup.

★ The reason it is recommended the soup stand before blending is that it is extremely hot and can cause a nasty burn if rushing the blending stage. A well-trained cook may get away with it; however, I've seen some bad burns from hot soups.

★ For dairy intolerance, simply omit the cream.

PEA AND HAM SOUP

Serves 4–6

XXXXXXXXXXXXXXXXXXXXXXXXXXXXXXXXXXXXXXXXXXXXXXXXXXXXXXXXXXXXXXXXXXXXXXXXXXXXXXXXXXXX

250 g dried green split
  peas (see **Hints and
  tips**)
1 litre **chicken stock** or
  water
1 smoked ham hock (about
  500 g)
1 small brown onion,
  peeled and finely diced
1 carrot, peeled and diced
1 celery stick, diced
2 garlic cloves, crushed
2 sprigs thyme
2 sprigs oregano
2 sprigs mint
salt

Method:

1. Place the split peas in a pot with the chicken stock and ham hock.

2. Bring to the boil, reduce heat to low and simmer gently for 1 hour. Keep the liquid level the same by topping up with stock or water as needed.

3. Add the onion, carrot, celery, garlic and herbs and continue to simmer for 30 minutes.

4. Check to make sure the vegetables are tender and the split peas are mushy, if not add more liquid and continue to cook. Remove the ham hock and herbs. Season with salt to taste and serve.

HINTS AND TIPS:

* You will need—cutting board, cook's knife, vegetable peeler, liquid and weight measures, large pot and wooden spoon.

* To cut the cooking time in half, soak the split peas overnight in 1 litre of cold water.

* To gain extra flavour from the vegetables, sauté in 100 ml olive oil over medium heat in a separate pan for 5 minutes before adding to the soup, allowing 20 minutes to cook until tender.

* The flavour of the soup will develop if left to sit in the fridge for 2 days before being reheated and consumed with crusty bread.

* Use the chopped meat from the ham hock to go back into the soup or add to an entirely different dish. Combine with leftover roasted vegetables in a fry-up like **bubble-and-squeak** or make homemade baked beans and add the hock meat before being baked.

* Too often this soup is made way too thick. Use water or stock to thin the soup if it is getting too thick.

* As painful as it may appear, it is important to sort through the peas as small stones and debris can be found among them. Once sorted, rinse under cold water to remove any dust from manufacturing, soak in plenty of cold water and drain well.

* Omit the ham hock entirely to produce a delicious split pea soup.

POTATO AND LEEK SOUP

Serves 4–6

xxxxxxxxxxxxxxxxxxxxxxxxxxxxxxxxxxxxxxxxxxxxxxxxxxxxxxxxxxxxxxxxxxxxxxxxxxxxxxxxxxxx

3 leeks, white part only
100 ml olive oil
1 brown onion, finely diced
2 garlic cloves, sliced
   finely
6 large potatoes, peeled
   and chopped into 2-cm
   pieces
boiling water or **vegetable
   stock**
salt
150 ml cream (optional)

Method:

1. Slice the leeks in half lengthways and run under cold water to remove any dirt; drain and finely slice.

2. Heat the oil in a large pot over medium heat. Add the leeks, onion and garlic and sauté until softened but without colouring, about 10 minutes. Then add the potatoes.

3. Add enough boiling water or stock to cover the vegetables by 3 cm and simmer for about 15 minutes.

4. Remove from the heat and let stand for 10 minutes before blending. Use a hand-held or benchtop blender and then strain the soup back into the pot. It is important but not entirely necessary to strain the soup as leeks can be quite stringy.

5. Return to medium heat, bring just to the boil, and season with salt and cream, if desired, before serving.

HINTS AND TIPS:

★ You will need—cutting board, cook's knife, liquid measures, large pot, wooden spoon and hand-held blender (preferable for safety) or benchtop blender.

★ The reason it is recommended for the soup to stand before blending is that it is extremely hot and can cause a nasty burn if rushing the blending stage.

★ Use boiling water from the kettle—adding boiling water or stock will quicken the time it takes for the soup to come back to the boil.

★ If I wanted a more dominant flavour from the leeks—enough to call the soup a 'leek and potato'—I would double the quantity of leek and halve the potato quantity.

★ To make a **vichyssoise** (chilled potato and leek soup) puree the soup and place in the refrigerator to cool completely. Check the seasoning and make sure it is very tasty before stirring in the cream.

PUMPKIN SOUP

Serves 6–8

xxxxxxxxxxxxxxxxxxxxxxxxxxxxxxxxxxxxxxxxxxxxxxxxxxxxxxxxxxxxxxxxxxxxxxxxxxxxxxxxxxxxxxxxxxxxxxxxx

1 kg butternut pumpkin
100 ml olive oil
1 medium brown onion, thinly sliced
1.5 litres water
200 ml cream (optional)
salt

Method:

1. Peel the pumpkin using a vegetable peeler, not a knife. Cut in half lengthways and remove the seeds with a spoon. Cut into quarters lengthways and then slice thinly in the opposite direction.

2. Heat the olive oil in a pot large enough to hold all the ingredients. Cook the onions over medium–low heat without colouring.

3. Add the pumpkin and cook for a further 5 minutes, then increase the heat to high, add the water and bring to the boil. Reduce the heat and simmer for 30–40 minutes or until the pumpkin is completely soft.

4. Remove from the heat and stand for 10 minutes before blending using a hand-held or benchtop blender.

5. After blending, return to the heat, add the cream, if using, and salt to taste. Bring back to a simmer before serving.

HINTS AND TIPS:

* You will need—cutting board, cook's knife, vegetable peeler, weight and liquid measures, wooden spoon, heavy-based pot and hand-held or benchtop blender.

* When peeling pumpkin, to avoid the sticky orange film that builds up on your hand, rub a small amount of oil onto the hand that holds the pumpkin. You may need to re-apply on occasion.

* Butternut pumpkin is ideal for this soup, but other great varietals include Japola (Jap), Kent, or any dark-fleshed pumpkin.

* The dollop of cream at the end gives a smooth, velvety texture. Try adding a dollop of coriander pesto or **salsa verde**. Or sprinkle with grated parmesan or some **croutons**.

* Try roasting the pumpkin either in pieces or whole. Roasting vegetables caramelises their natural sugars which in turn enhances the flavour of the vegetable, making the soup just that bit richer and fuller flavoured.

* Adding spices to pumpkin soup is recommended to create another dimension. For example, use 1 tablespoon red curry paste and 200 ml coconut cream in the basic recipe.

* Substitute sweet potato for the pumpkin in this recipe.

* Pumpkin in the US and UK refers to a type of sweet pumpkin reserved for making pumpkin pie or jack-o'-lanterns (these have a large seed cavity and pale orange flesh). Pumpkin in Australia and New Zealand refers to all hard-skinned squash including the likes of butternut, Japola, golden nugget and Queensland blue. These and several other cultivars are all known as 'winter squash' in the US or 'squash' in the UK.

SEAFOOD GUMBO

Serves 6

xxxxxxxxxxxxxxxxxxxxxxxxxxxxxxxxxxxxxxxxxxxxxxxxxxxxxxxxxxxxxxxxxxxxxxxxxxxxxxxxxxxxxxxxxxxxxx

100 g plain flour
100 ml olive oil
1 litre **fish stock**, strained
4 garlic cloves, finely chopped
1 onion, peeled and finely chopped
2 celery sticks, finely chopped
1 red capsicum, de-seeded and finely chopped
500 g okra
800 g can tomatoes, drained and chopped
4 tablespoons tomato paste
2 bay leaves
1 teaspoon dried oregano
2 teaspoons dried thyme leaves
1 teaspoon cayenne pepper
2 tablespoons Worcestershire sauce
12 green prawns, peeled and de-veined
18 black mussels
1 kg white fish fillets
1 teaspoon Tabasco sauce
salt and pepper
3 cups **cooked rice**
6 blue swimmer crab claws, cooked
fresh basil leaves
fresh thyme leaves

Method:

1. Mix the flour and oil in a large saucepan. Stir constantly over medium heat until the flour turns 'chocolate' brown, about 15 minutes.

2. Stir in the stock and cook for 5–6 minutes, stirring constantly until thickened.

3. Stir in the garlic, onion, celery, capsicum and okra and cook over low heat for 5–6 minutes. Stir in the tomatoes, tomato paste, herbs, cayenne pepper and Worcestershire sauce. Bring to the boil, reduce heat and simmer for 40 minutes.

Method cont.

4. Stir in the prawns, mussels and fish, and poach for 3–4 minutes until cooked. Season with Tabasco sauce and salt and pepper.

5. Spoon ½ cup rice into each bowl and ladle over the soup. Decorate with crab claws, basil and thyme.

HINTS AND TIPS:

* You will need—cutting board, cook's knife, paring knife, wooden spoon, cup, weight, liquid and spoon measures, heavy-based pot.

* It is very important to get the flour and oil mixture (a roux) to be chocolate brown before proceeding. This adds the unique flavour that a gumbo should have.

* Finishing this soup with file powder or okra is entirely optional and any cook who suggests that it isn't a gumbo without these ingredients must not be aware of how many hundreds of versions of this soup there really are—I'm almost embarrassed by providing just one.

* Apart from the dark roux, the other point that is very important is the use of a good fish stock in this recipe. Water, although passable, will not deliver the goods.

TOMATO SOUP

Serves 4

XXXXXXXXXXXXXXXXXXXXXXXXXXXXXXXXXXXXXXXXXXXXXXXXXXXXXXXXXXXXXXXXXXXXXXXXXXXXXXXXXXXXXXXXXXXX

2 kg ripe tomatoes (see **Hints and tips**)
100 ml olive oil
1 small onion, finely diced
2 garlic cloves, minced
1 bay leaf
1 tablespoon sugar
200 ml water
300 ml thickened cream (optional)
salt and pepper

Method:

1. Slice the tomatoes in half exposing a cross-section of the tomato—it is then easier to remove the seeds with a teaspoon. Dice the flesh roughly. Do not worry that the tomatoes are not peeled as the soup needs to be strained.

2. Heat the olive oil in a pot large enough to hold all the ingredients. Cook the onions and garlic over medium–low heat, without colouring, for 5 minutes.

3. Add the chopped tomatoes, bay leaf, sugar and water, bring to the boil then reduce the heat to low and simmer until reduced by half.

4. Remove from the heat and pass through a sieve using a ladle to push the pulp through. Only the skin of the tomatoes should remain in the sieve. Do not be tempted to blend this soup as the skin will break up and make the soup grainy and slightly bitter.

5. Return the strained soup to low heat and simmer for a few minutes, adding cream, if using, and salt and pepper to taste. Serve.

HINTS AND TIPS:

----

* You will need—cutting board, cook's knife, liquid, weight and spoon measures, large heavy-based pot, and wooden spoon.

* It is very important that only ripe tomatoes are used—preferably vine-ripened or hydroponic—to get the best flavoured tomato soup.

* Adding the cream is optional. The resulting soup without cream may be slightly sour in which case add 1 teaspoon sugar. Top the soup with **pesto** or **croutons**.

* If fresh tomatoes are not around and you have an urge to make tomato soup, then use canned tomatoes. Try and find a good organic brand which should indicate good flavour.

* Use leftover roasted tomatoes to make a small serve of soup or roast the tomatoes for the soup.

VEGETABLE AND BARLEY SOUP

Serves 12–16

xxxxxxxxxxxxxxxxxxxxxxxxxxxxxxxxxxxxxxxxxxxxxxxxxxxxxxxxxxxxxxxxxxxxxxxxxxxxxxxxxxx

300 g pearl barley
100 ml olive oil
1 onion, finely diced
1 leek, white part only,
    sliced in half, washed
    and chopped
2 garlic cloves, minced
8 pale inner celery
    sticks, chopped
1 fennel bulb, cut into
    1-cm dice
2 carrots, scrubbed and
    cut into 1-cm dice
1 cup celery leaves,
    also from the centre,
    shredded
1 teaspoon dried basil
2½ litres **vegetable** stock
    or water
1 bay leaf
2 medium potatoes,
    scrubbed and cut into
    1-cm dice
800 g can diced tomatoes
salt
100 g spinach leaves,
    shredded

Method:

1. Soak the pearl barley in hot water for 45 minutes, drain and rinse.

2. Heat the oil in a large pot, fry the onion, leek and garlic without colouring for 5 minutes over medium heat.

3. Add the celery, fennel and carrot and cook for a further 5 minutes. Then add the celery leaves and basil, cook for 1 minute.

4. Add the stock or water and bring to the boil. Add the barley and bay leaf, reduce the heat to low and simmer for 30 minutes. Add the potatoes and tomatoes, simmer for 15–20 minutes, making sure the potatoes are soft and the barley is cooked. Add more stock or water if necessary. Just before serving, season with salt and stir in the spinach.

HINTS AND TIPS:

★ You will need—cutting board, cook's knife, paring knife, vegetable peeler, bowls and cup, liquid, weight and spoon measures.

★ For **vegetable soup**—omit the barley and add extra vegetables. To the basic recipe, add 2 large potatoes (peeled and diced chunky), 300 g pumpkin (peeled and diced chunky), 2 zucchini (diced), 150 g cabbage (diced), 100 g green beans (tailed and sliced into 2-cm lengths), 75 g spinach leaves (chopped). Add the potato and pumpkin when the stock is added. Add the zucchini, cabbage and green beans with 5 minutes remaining. Stir in the spinach just before serving.

★ There is not too much difference between this soup and a **minestrone**. If anything I would tend to simplify the vegetables in this soup, keeping to mostly root vegetables and perhaps a bit of chopped parsley at the end.

★ This great winter warmer will freeze well but is best made and consumed on the day.

★ Grate some parmesan or pecorino cheese and sprinkle over the top when serving.

★ Pearl barley is more refined (polished) than hulled barley. It is less chewy and cooks faster than hulled barley, but because it has been polished further, it is less nutritious, which could be said for all grains that become more and more refined.

★ I prefer to keep my grains in the refrigerator unless I know I'm going to use them within a month. Although the shelf life of barley and other grains is long—12 months in an airtight container, in a cool, dry area—the fact is that it takes one larvae and it's finished. Also, weather permitting, the constant change can have an effect and the natural oils will become rancid sooner than you expect.

★ Pearl barley doesn't really need soaking; I do it so it really breaks open in the soup. Hulled barley needs to be soaked for several hours before cooking and needs at least an hour to cook through.

xxxxxxxxxxxxx **4. Seafood** xxxxxxxxxxxxx

COOKING WHOLE FISH

Serves 2

XXXXXXXXXXXXXXXXXXXXXXXXXXXXXXXXXXXXXXXXXXXXXXXXXXXXXXXXXXXXXXXXXXXXXXXXXXXXXXXXXXXXXXXXXX

1 whole fish, about 1.5 kg cleaned weight
100 ml olive oil
2 sprigs fresh rosemary
6 sprigs fresh lemon thyme
½ lemon, in wedges
2 garlic cloves, finely sliced
½ bird's eye chilli, seeds removed and finely sliced
100 ml white wine
½ punnet grape tomatoes
125 ml water
12 black mussels, de-bearded and shells scrubbed
¼ cup torn fresh flat-leaf parsley leaves

Method:

1. Preheat the oven to 180°C.

2. First, ensure all the scales have been removed from the fish. Wipe dry inside and out with paper towel. Rub with a little of the oil and fill the cavity with the herbs and lemon wedges, then seal shut with several tooth picks.

3. Score the skin with a sharp knife making 4–5 incisions along the thickest part of the fish (not the tail end)—this allows the heat to penetrate the skin and the fish to cook more evenly.

4. Heat 1 tablespoon olive oil in a sauté or frying pan over low–medium heat, and fry the garlic and chilli without colouring. Add the fish and white wine.

5. Cook for a further minute, add the tomatoes, water and mussels. Place in the oven for approximately 15–20 minutes.

6. Remove from the oven and carefully lift the fish on to a serving platter, add the parsley to the pan, stir well and pour the sauce over the fish.

HINTS AND TIPS:

* You will need—cutting board, cook's knife, large sauté pan or frying pan, spatula, wooden spoon and cup and liquid measures.

* This is just one recipe for cooking whole fish—it can be grilled, steamed, baked or poached—but the recipe is a good basic start.

* Ingredients can be added or left out of the recipe, depending on taste. The mussels in this recipe are optional; however, they not only add an additional protein source, but will also create great flavour in the sauce itself.

* It is a growing trend in good restaurants to use a meat probe (thermometer) when cooking fish and other meats to ensure that the item is cooked perfectly every time. Even though many years of experience will tell you when it is ready, a meat probe is still favoured when dealing with the ever-increasing expense of fish and other meats and the desire to not waste it by overcooking. For most fish, an internal temperature of 45–55°C is ideal.

* The most important tip to consider with this recipe is the freshness and quality of the fish. See **Fish** in **Really Useful Information**.

* A very common practice for cooking whole fish is wrapping it in foil with a bunch of aromatic herbs and vegetables. The fish is either baked in the oven or cooked on a barbecue grill plate.

CRAB CAKES

Makes 6 crab cakes

xxxxxxxxxxxxxxxxxxxxxxxxxxxxxxxxxxxxxxxxxxxxxxxxxxxxxxxxxxxxxxxxxxxxxxxxxxxxxxxxxxxxxxxxx

500 g fresh or frozen crab meat
2 tablespoons olive oil
½ small onion, chopped
2 large eggs
1½ teaspoons Worcestershire sauce
1 teaspoon salt flakes
1 teaspoon hot paprika
½ teaspoon freshly ground black pepper
1 spring onion, sliced
2 slices firm white sandwich bread, crusts removed,
    torn into small pieces
1 cup fresh bread crumbs
60 g butter

Method:

1. Pick over the crab meat to remove any bits of shell and cartilage, being careful not to break up the lumps of crab.

2. Heat 1 tablespoon of the oil in a pan over medium heat and cook the onion without colouring for 5 minutes. Remove the pan from the heat and cool.

3. Whisk together the eggs, Worcestershire sauce, salt, paprika, pepper and cooled onion.

4. Gently mix in the crab meat, spring onion and torn bread. At this stage the mixture will be quite wet.

5. Press the mixture into 6 even-sized crab cakes, each one 2 cm thick. Line a tray or dinner plate with plastic wrap and sprinkle with half of the bread crumbs. Set the crab cakes in one layer on the top of the crumbs and sprinkle with the remaining bread crumbs. Cover the crab cakes loosely with more plastic wrap and chill for 1 hour. This is important to help set and hold the crab cakes together when cooking.

Method cont.

6. Melt the butter and the remaining olive oil in a large nonstick pan over medium–high heat until the butter begins to foam. Cook the crab cakes until golden brown, about 3 minutes on each side.

HINTS AND TIPS:

* You will need—cutting board, cook's knife, bowl, cup, spoon and weight measures, wooden spoon and sauté pan.

* Crab cakes are an American favourite. They can be as simple as fresh crab meat, bread crumbs, eggs and seasoning to something a bit more complex. They can be grilled, baked, pan-fried or deep-fried.

* Make the crab cakes smaller and serve as an appetiser or finger food at your next party. Make them well ahead of time and pan-fry once the guests arrive.

* Serve crab cakes with **aïoli** or **tartare sauce** as well as a simple green salad.

* To reduce the fat content, spray the crab cakes with oil and pan-fry instead of cooking in butter and oil as mentioned.

* Crab meat is readily available at most fish shops. Always pick over the crab meat as often it has bits of shell in it.

* The best option is to cook and pick over the crab yourself to guarantee freshness.

FISH FILLETS, PAN-FRIED
Serves 4

XXXXXXXXXXXXXXXXXXXXXXXXXXXXXXXXXXXXXXXXXXXXXXXXXXXXXXXXXXXXXXXXXXXXXXXXXXXXXXXXXXXXXXXXXXXXX

4 x 200g white fish fillets,
   skin left on
1 tablespoon olive oil
salt

Method:

1. Use a sharp knife and lightly score the skin on each fish fillet at 1-cm intervals.

2. Rub fish with olive oil and season with salt.

3. Place the fish fillets, skin side down, in a medium—hot nonstick pan and cook without moving for 3 minutes. See Hints and tips for cooking times especially if the fish is quite thick.

4. When the skin is crisp and lightly browned, turn fillets over, reduce heat to low and cook for a further 3–4 minutes. (The fish is cooked when any juices run clear; if the juices are cloudy, it is still slightly undercooked; and if the juices solidify and turn hard white, the fish is overcooked.)

HINTS AND TIPS:

* You will need—cutting board, cook's knife, spoon measure, sauté pan and spatula.

* The time taken to cook fish depends on the thickness of the fish fillet. From the head end where most of the bones will be, fish fillets will be quite thick and on a low temperature the fish will take 7–10 minutes to cook through. From the tail end where there are no bones, the fillet is half the thickness and may only take 5 minutes to cook through.

* The protein in fish is very delicate, similar to that of egg whites. Egg whites are best cooked over a gentle heat. Fish is the same. I tend to cook the skin side over high heat to impart colour and texture to the skin, I then turn the heat down to the lowest setting and cook it gently and slowly for as long as it takes for the proteins in the fish to just set.

* Fish need only be seasoned with a light sprinkling of salt. If you are a fan of pepper, wait until it is served and then grind some fresh pepper over the top. Black specks of pepper on the soft white flesh of the fish fillet are unappealing and pepper tends to burn in a pan and become bitter. Try white pepper instead.

* To avoid excess smoke in the kitchen or on a barbecue, rub the fish with oil rather than adding the oil to the pan or hot plate. This minimal amount of oil is less likely to send a plume of smoke through the house.

* Do not be scared to slightly undercook fish. If you have ever eaten sushi or sashimi—Japanese staples using raw fish—then the notion of fish a bit underdone should set your mind at ease. Undercooked fish will not make you sick unless the fish was old before it was cooked.

FISH PIE

Serves 4

XXXXXXXXXXXXXXXXXXXXXXXXXXXXXXXXXXXXXXXXXXXXXXXXXXXXXXXXXXXXXXXXXXXXXXXXXXXXXXXXXXXXX

2 tablespoons olive oil
800 g sliced onions
400 ml **fish stock**
200 ml cream
salt and pepper
800 g white fish fillets
1 tablespoon truffle oil
   (optional)
2 spring onions, sliced
1 packet frozen puff
   pastry, defrosted
2 egg yolks, lightly
   beaten, for glazing

Method:

1. Preheat oven to 200°C.

2. **For the sauce**—Heat the oil in a pan over low heat and add the sliced onions. Cover and sweat gently until very soft and translucent, even a little bit of colour is fine. Add the fish stock and reduce by half. Add the cream and reduce by half or until a thick consistency is reached. Remove from the heat and puree.

3. In the bottom of each pie dish, place some of the sauce and about 200 g fish, some of the spring onions then another layer of the sauce. Repeat in each dish.

4. Cover the dish with the puff pastry, brush with egg yolk, set in the fridge for 1 minute and re-coat with egg yolk.

5. Bake for 25–30 minutes on the middle shelf of the oven until the pastry is golden and puffed.

HINTS AND TIPS:

* You will need—cutting board, cook's knife, weight, spoon and liquid measures, saucepan, 4 x 12-cm diameter, 5-cm deep pie dishes and pastry brush.

* This is a beautiful pie recipe and is in stark contrast to the easy-to-make **tuna bake**.

* To make this really special, use the **quick puff pastry**—although more effort is required, the results are well worth it.

* If you are concerned about bones when buying fish for this dish, request pieces of fish from the tail end as a guarantee of no bones. Or you could ask your supplier to take the bones out and dice the fish for you—at a possible extra charge.

* Instead of the puff pastry lid, try topping the pie with mashed or crushed potato. Cut some butter into small dice and sprinkle over the mash topping before baking—same temperature and time. Or you could sprinkle grated cheese over the mash topping.

* From fish pie to seafood pie—use the combination of seafood mentioned in the recipe for **seafood crepes**.

* Any number of vegetables can be added to this pie, the most common being peas. Adding vegetables is not necessary and if serving with a good salad, there is no need to worry about a lack of greens with this dish.

GARLIC PRAWNS

Serves 2

XXXXXXXXXXXXXXXXXXXXXXXXXXXXXXXXXXXXXXXXXXXXXXXXXXXXXXXXXXXXXXXXXXXXXXXXXXXXXXXXXXX

10 large green tiger prawns, peeled
1 tablespoon olive oil
1 tablespoon butter
2 tablespoons crushed garlic
200 ml thickened cream
1 tablespoon chopped fresh flat-leaf parsley

Method:

1. Remove the vein from the back of the prawn by slicing with a knife and scraping out the dark waste tract running the length of the prawn. You can also remove the head of the prawn if you like—if you do, refer to Hints and tips.

2. Heat the olive oil and butter in a sauté pan. When the butter begins to foam, add the prawns and cook for 1 minute either side. Remove from the pan and set aside.

3. Add the garlic to the pan and sauté without colouring for 30 seconds then add the cream. Simmer, and reduce the cream by one-third. Return the prawns to the sauce for 2 minutes, remove from the heat, stir in the parsley and serve.

HINTS AND TIPS:

* You will need—cutting board, cook's knife, paring knife, spoon and liquid measures, sauté pan, tongs and wooden spoon.

* When talking prawns, 'green' refers to them being raw, not their colour. Green prawns can be purchased whole or already peeled and any shop selling seafood knows this term.

* It is worth investing in steel soap (a piece of stainless steel in the shape of a soap 'bar'); it never wears down and it removes the smell of seafood, garlic and onion from your hands without stripping them.

* If you do remove the prawn heads, you can add them to a fish stock, or freeze them for when you get around to making the stock. This can be made with 1 onion (roughly chopped), 1 carrot (roughly chopped), 1 celery stick (roughly chopped), 1 kg fish heads or bones, 1 cup dry white wine, 12 peppercorns, 1 bay leaf and enough water to cover in a large pot. Bring to the boil then reduce to a simmer for 1 hour. Strain and either use straightaway or freeze in various-sized containers so you don't have to defrost the lot and waste any.

* Fresh green prawns should be consumed the day they are purchased or defrosted; after 24 hours although still edible, they tend to oxidise and blacken.

* Fresh green prawns are best but the frozen variety can be used. The frozen prawns are sold as green prawn 'cutlets' and should not be mistaken for a crumbed prawn cutlet. The frozen variety is good in that the prawns are snap-frozen while on the fishing trawlers out at sea, guaranteeing an almost perfect fresh/frozen product.

* You can use either basil or coriander instead of parsley.

* Chopped chilli can be added with the seeds removed.

* This recipe can be served as a pasta sauce with long pasta like fettuccine or linguine.

* Alternatively, serve with steamed rice or simply with crusty bread and a crisp white wine.

* You can omit the cream and add 1 cup white wine for a lighter version, but allow several minutes simmering for the wine to reduce. Or use a light cream instead of the heavy cream suggested.

PRAWN COCKTAIL

Serves 6

XXXXXXXXXXXXXXXXXXXXXXXXXXXXXXXXXXXXXXXXXXXXXXXXXXXXXXXXXXXXXXXXXXXXXXXXXXXXXXXXXXXXXXXXXXX

1 iceberg lettuce, very
    finely shredded
24–36 fresh cooked prawns,
    peeled with tail intact
2 lemons, sliced into
    wedges

Cocktail sauce
250 ml **mayonnaise**
60 ml Worcestershire sauce
60 ml brandy
120 ml tomato sauce
1 tablespoon grated
    horseradish
salt and pepper
60 ml pouring cream,
    lightly whipped

Method:

1. For the cocktail sauce—Mix all ingredients except cream. When combined, fold in the whipped cream. Refrigerate, covered, until needed.

2. To assemble—There are several ways to put this dish together. The old way uses prawn cocktail glasses probably available at a 'trash and treasure' market on any given Sunday. The new way is to form a small mound of shredded lettuce in the centre of a plate, prop the prawns against the lettuce and drizzle with cocktail sauce, serving each with a lemon wedge.

HINTS AND TIPS:

* You will need—cutting board, cook's knife, paring knife, bowls, liquid and spoon measures and the equipment needed to make mayonnaise.

* The prawn cocktail was a dinner party hit in the 70s and early 80s, and made a tasteful comeback in some restaurants in the late 90s. It still appears now and then, and if done well will be one dish that will never quite go away.

* Depending on the size of the prawns, 4–6 per person for an entree is enough. If this is to be more of a substantial dish, then use as many as would fit in the dish.

* Always check prawns for freshness, and ask when they were cooked and if frozen, how long they have been frozen for. Waterlogged or tired, old prawns will make this dish horrid.

* At a dinner party, wrap half a lemon in muslin or cheesecloth and tie neatly. This will prevent seeds from getting into the salad.

* Shred a small handful of flat-leaf parsley and mix into the lettuce to give the iceberg lettuce some lift.

* Make bite-sized prawn cocktails as finger food by using the inner leaves of cos lettuce as an edible cup—shred some of the outer leaves, chop up the prawns and drizzle with the sauce and serve in the smaller inner leaves.

SALMON PATTIES

Serves 4

xxxxxxxxxxxxxxxxxxxxxxxxxxxxxxxxxxxxxxxxxxxxxxxxxxxxxxxxxxxxxxxxxxxxxxxxxxxxxxxxxxxxxxxx

3 cups mashed potato, room
   temperature

415 g can pink salmon,
   drained

2 spring onions, finely
   chopped

1 tablespoon chopped fresh
   flat-leaf parsley

2 eggs, lightly beaten

1 teaspoon salt

freshly ground black
   pepper

½ cup bread crumbs or
   plain flour

2 tablespoons olive oil

Method:

1. In a bowl, mix the mashed potato, salmon, spring onions, parsley, eggs, salt and pepper until thoroughly combined.

2. Shape into patties using a ½ cup measure—this will ensure the patties are all the same shape and size. Place on a tray lined with plastic wrap and rest in the fridge for at least 1 hour to allow the mixture to set before cooking.

3. When ready to cook, dip each patty in bread crumbs or flour.

4. Heat the oil in a frying pan over medium heat, add the salmon patties and cook until golden brown, flip and repeat on the other side.

HINTS AND TIPS:

----

* You will need—cutting board, cook's knife, 2 bowls, frying pan, cup and spoon measures.

* This recipe yields about 12 small patties.

* Serve salmon patties with a **simple green salad** and **mayonnaise**.

* To make **salmon croquettes**—roll the mixture into small log shapes, dip in plain flour, then dip in beaten egg and roll in dried bread crumbs. Set on a tray until all are done. Leave in the fridge for 1 hour or

so before deep-frying. If you're not comfortable with deep-frying, then shallow-fry in plenty of butter. Great as finger food served with a **tartare sauce** or a simple **mayonnaise**.

* Try adding ½ cup corn kernels and ½ cup frozen peas to the mixture.

* Use leftover roasted vegetables from the previous night's roast instead of the mashed potato. It will add an extra richness to the patties and is an alternative to making **bubble-and-squeak**.

* As a healthy option, place the patties on a baking tray lined with baking paper and

bake in the oven at 220°C for 10–15 minutes or until hot. This way you avoid the excess oil or butter and make the most of the omega 3 from the salmon.

* As a cocktail food, halve the size of the patties, fry as per recipe and top each with a dollop of sour cream and a sprig of dill.

SALT AND PEPPER SQUID

Serves 6

xxxxxxxxxxxxxxxxxxxxxxxxxxxxxxxxxxxxxxxxxxxxxxxxxxxxxxxxxxxxxxxxxxxxxxxxxxxxxxxxxxxxxxxxxxxx

1 kg squid tubes, halved lengthways
250 g rice flour
200 g cornflour
3 tablespoons salt flakes
4 tablespoons ground white pepper
2 teaspoons caster sugar
4 egg whites, lightly beaten
vegetable oil, for deep-frying (approx. 2 litres)
lemon or lime wedges, for serving

Method:

1. Open out the squid tubes, wash and pat dry. Place on a cutting board with the inside facing upwards. Score a fine diamond pattern on the squid, being careful not to cut all the way through. Cut into pieces about 5 cm x 3 cm. Alternatively, keep the tubes whole and slice into rings or cut open as above and slice into strips.

2. Combine the rice flour, cornflour, salt, pepper and sugar in a bowl. Fill a deep-fryer or large saucepan one-third full of oil and heat to 180°C (350°F), or until a small cube of white bread dropped into the oil turns golden brown in 15 seconds.

3. Dip the squid into the egg white and then into the flour mixture, shaking off any excess. Cook batches of the squid for 1–2 minutes, or until the flesh turns white and curls. Drain on paper towels. Serve with lemon wedges.

HINTS AND TIPS:

★ You will need—cutting board, cook's knife, 2 bowls, weight and spoon measures, and a deep-fryer or large, heavy-based pot or wok for deep-frying.

★ Squid and calamari are in fact two different creatures but are as close as cousins. In this recipe 'either or' should be your motto. Try also using the very tasty cuttlefish, a stumpier version of the aforementioned. Never use frozen squid tubes, especially large ones; they are watery and tough and you'd do better with a bag of rubber bands.

★ Other pepper can be used in this recipe; replace the white pepper with 2 tablespoons black pepper (crushed and ground) and 2 tablespoons Sichuan pepper. It is recommended that the salt and peppers are dry-toasted in a pan for several minutes, cooled on a tray and then pound in a mortar and pestle or a spice/coffee grinder to enhance their fragrance.

★ To check the temperature of the oil—other than dropping a piece of bread into it—use a sugar thermometer.

★ To dispose of used deep-frying oil, there are several steps that need to be followed. **1.** Allow the oil to cool completely, preferably until the next day. **2.** Make sure you keep the container and lid in which the oil came or have an alternative container (like a used milk container with screw-cap lid). **3.** If the oil can be used again, it will need to be strained. This can be done through a paper towel-lined sieve, which is placed on a funnel directly over the storage container. **4.** If the oil is being kept, keep it in the fridge until it is needed again. This keeps it out of the light and the coldness will keep the oil from turning rancid too soon. **5.** If the oil is to be thrown out, pour the cold oil straight into the bottle, fasten the lid and place in the bin. **6.** Or, if you deep-fry often, speak to your local council as they may have a collection depot nearby where you can drop off used cooking oil which they then on-sell to companies that make truck fuel or soap—true.

★ Other flours can be used instead of the rice and cornflour mentioned in this recipe. If there is only plain flour in the pantry and the recipe must go ahead, then use plain flour. Self-raising flour will also work. In fact, any type of flour can be used with only minimal difference to the final outcome.

★ Other seafood can also be adapted to this recipe. Try thinly sliced white-fleshed fish, or whole scallops. Some fish may not work quite as well and these include most oily fish like salmon, tuna, marlin and swordfish.

★ Serve these tasty seafood morsels with a dipping sauce. **Tartare sauce**, **thousand island dressing**, sweet chilli, soy sauce or shoyu are all recommended. Accompaniments like lemon, lime, fresh chilli and coriander can also be served on the side.

SEAFOOD CREPES

Serves 6

xxxxxxxxxxxxxxxxxxxxxxxxxxxxxxxxxxxxxxxxxxxxxxxxxxxxxxxxxxxxxxxxxxxxxxxxxxxxxxxxxxxxxxxxx

100 g butter
1 tablespoon olive oil
500 g white fish fillets, diced
12 green prawns, peeled, de-veined and sliced
12 local mussels, cooked and removed from shell
250 g crab meat, cooked
½ teaspoon crushed garlic
100 ml white wine
1 tablespoon chopped fresh dill
salt and pepper
1 recipe quantity **mornay sauce**
12 **savoury crepes**

Method:

1. Heat the butter and oil in a pan. As the butter begins to foam, add the fish and prawns. When almost cooked, add the mussels and crab meat. Sauté for another 2 minutes on high heat.

2. Add the garlic, sauté quickly without colouring and then pour in the wine, sprinkle in the dill and season. Remove from the heat and drain juices into a bowl.

3. Mix the seafood with the mornay sauce, adding some of the seafood juices if too thick.

4. Spoon into crepes and roll, folding in the ends as each crepe is being rolled. Place on a tray lined with baking paper, and bake in a hot oven (220°C) for 3 minutes.

HINTS AND TIPS:

* You will need—cutting board, cook's knife, large pot, wooden spoon, weight, spoon and liquid measures, baking tray, baking paper and equipment needed for making crepes and mornay sauce.

* There are 3 recipes required for this dish so take your time and use the experience for a special occasion.

* The crepes can be made well in advance and kept frozen until the day they are needed.

* The mornay sauce is best made and kept warm ready for the seafood. The warm sauce and the hot seafood will be easier to mix together, providing an evenly dispersed seafood filling.

* The crepes can be filled and refrigerated the day before they are to be baked. Do not freeze as the mornay sauce will become watery.

* Dill can be substituted with fennel tops. If either of these herbs cannot be found, then parsley, chervil, tarragon, chives or lemon thyme could be used.

* Crab meat is available already picked from seafood shops. I recommend picking over the meat as the pre-picked stuff will almost certainly have some shell in it.

* You will notice the cooking time of the seafood is minimal. Adhere to the quick cooking time to avoid overcooking the seafood when baked in the crepes.

* Leftover seafood filling can be used to make a **seafood pie**. Use pre-made puff pastry from the freezer section of the supermarket. Place the filling in individual ceramic dishes, top with a disc of puff pastry, brush with beaten egg and bake at 180°C for 20 minutes or until the pastry is flaky and golden brown.

TUNA BAKE

Serves 6

XXXXXXXXXXXXXXXXXXXXXXXXXXXXXXXXXXXXXXXXXXXXXXXXXXXXXXXXXXXXXXXXXXXXXXXXXXXXXXXXXXXXXXXXXXXXX

800 ml **mornay sauce**
2 tablespoons olive oil
1 medium onion, finely diced
2 celery sticks, diced
1 red capsicum, diced
1 cob corn, kernels removed
310 g can creamed corn
425 g can tuna in spring water, drained and crumbled
3 cups cooked pasta or rice
¼ cup chopped fresh flat-leaf parsley
salt and pepper
200 g fresh bread crumbs
grated zest of 1 lemon
½ cup grated parmesan

Method:

1. Place the mornay sauce in a bowl and set aside.

2. Heat a nonstick pan over medium heat, add the oil, onion and celery and cook without colouring for 3 minutes. Add the capsicum and corn and cook for a further 2 minutes. Remove from the heat and cool.

3. Add the creamed corn to the mornay sauce, and mix with a wooden spoon. Then add the tuna, cooked pasta or rice, parsley, salt and pepper to taste and the cooled onion mixture, stir until well combined and place in a deep baking dish.

4. In a separate bowl, mix the bread crumbs, lemon zest and parmesan and mix until well combined. Sprinkle over the tuna mixture and bake at 180°C for 30 minutes.

HINTS AND TIPS:

* You will need—cutting board, cook's knife, weight, liquid, spoon and cup measures, saucepan, bowls, baking dish and wooden spoon.

* The simplest version of tuna bake is to omit all the vegetables and just mix tuna, cooked pasta or rice and the mornay sauce, place in a baking dish, top the lot with grated cheese and bake for 20 minutes—for teenagers and those who can't be bothered, it can be that easy, if somewhat boring, so maybe try adding frozen peas and drained canned corn for colour.

* Easier again is to not make the cheese sauce, just mix the tuna, cooked pasta, 500 g sour cream and 250 g grated cheese together and bake.

* An alternative topping is to cut the crust off a bread stick or ciabatta and roughly chop into pieces, sprinkle over the top and bake.

* Try mashing 1 kg potatoes mixed with butter and cream and spreading over the filling before baking.

* If you don't like tuna, then try crispy fried bacon; use 8 rashers, chopped and fried, for this recipe. If you don't eat meat, omit it altogether. But without tuna it simply becomes a pasta bake of any sort.

* Use short pasta for this recipe—like orecchiette, shell, macaroni or fusilli.

* Try adding leftover roasted vegetables, chopped and stirred into the mixture before baking.

----
xxxxxxxxxxxxx **5. Poultry** xxxxxxxxxxxxx

APRICOT CHICKEN

Serves 4

xxxxxxxxxxxxxxxxxxxxxxxxxxxxxxxxxxxxxxxxxxxxxxxxxxxxxxxxxxxxxxxxxxxxxxxxxxxxxxxxxxxxxxxxxxxxxxxxxxx

8 chicken thigh fillets
salt and pepper
2 tablespoons vegetable oil or olive oil
40 g packet French onion soup
425 g can apricot nectar

Method:

1. Trim the thigh fillets of any excess fat then season with salt and pepper. Over medium heat, fry the chicken in the oil for 3 minutes on each side or until golden brown.

2. Mix the packet soup and the apricot nectar in a bowl; pour over the chicken when browned on both sides. If the pan has a lid, cover and reduce the heat to low and cook gently for 15 minutes. If there is no lid, cover with foil and bake in the oven at 180°C for 15 minutes.

3. Serve immediately with salad, rice or vegetables.

HINTS AND TIPS:

* You will need—cutting board, cook's knife, bowl, sauté or frying pan, tongs and wooden spoon.

* It is recommended to use chicken thigh fillets for this dish as they stay moist and tender with the extra cooking time. With chicken breast, there is always the possibility of overcooking the meat and making it dry and chewy.

* The above recipe is as basic as it could get. To make this dish more exciting while still keeping the name, try replacing the apricot nectar with 200 g apricot chutney, 8 dried apricots (quartered) and 250 ml chicken stock. Replace the packet onion soup by frying 2 garlic cloves (chopped) and 1 small onion (diced) in 2 tablespoons olive oil. The sauce can be thickened by dusting the chicken pieces in plain flour before browning.

* For gluten-intolerance, follow the previous tip, then, instead of dusting in plain flour before browning, use a gluten-free flour (see p. 494).

* Sometimes apricot chicken is cooked with canned apricots as well as the apricot nectar; this is, of course, a personal choice and if so desired add a can of apricot halves to the mixture.

* Whole chicken pieces on the bone can be used, like chicken drumsticks. If this were to happen, extend the cooking time by 15 minutes and keep an eye on the sauce as it may dry out with the extra cooking time. Keep it saucy by adding ¼ cup water or chicken stock every 10–15 minutes.

* For extra kick, add 1 bird's eye chilli (sliced thinly) to the sauce before it goes onto the chicken.

* For extra flavour, once the chicken has been browned, add 100 ml white wine to the pan, reduce by half, and then add the sauce mixture.

* Alternatives to apricots in this recipe include dry or canned peaches or mangoes, and peach or mango nectar.

* If microwaving this dish (or any chicken dish) and the skin is still intact, the skin will need to be pierced with a skewer in several spots to allow the steam to escape to avoid the chicken 'popping' and splattering in the microwave oven.

* Serve with mashed potato, steamed rice or couscous.

CHICKEN KIEV

Serves 4

XXXXXXXXXXXXXXXXXXXXXXXXXXXXXXXXXXXXXXXXXXXXXXXXXXXXXXXXXXXXXXXXXXXXXXXXXXXXXXXXXXXXXXXXXXXXXXX

Butter filling
185 g butter, softened
salt and pepper
2 tablespoons chopped fresh flat-leaf parsley
1 tablespoon chopped fresh chives
¼ teaspoon grated lemon zest

4 chicken breast fillets
3 eggs
¼ cup milk or water
½ teaspoon salt
¼ teaspoon freshly ground black pepper
½ cup flour
1 cup dried bread crumbs
vegetable oil, for deep-frying (about 1 litre)

Method:

1. For the butter filling—combine the butter with all
the ingredients, mix well. Divide the mixture into 4
and shape into 4 rolls. Refrigerate until very firm.

2. Place each chicken breast between a sheet of baking
paper and pound, using a meat mallet or rolling pin,
to about 1.5 cm thick; be careful not to 'break' the
chicken—if it does tear, fold part of the chicken
over the torn area. Wrap and refrigerate until
seasoned butter is cold and hard.

3. When the butter is firm, place 1 piece on each
chicken breast, fold in edges of chicken and roll to
encase butter completely.

4. In a small bowl, beat eggs with milk or water. In a
shallow dish, mix together the salt, pepper and flour.
Place the bread crumbs in a separate shallow dish.
Dip the chicken rolls in the seasoned flour, then the
egg mixture, then the crumbs. Repeat by dipping in the
egg mixture again then the bread crumbs. Place in a
shallow dish, cover and refrigerate for 1 hour.

Method cont.

5. Heat the oil in a large pot over medium–high heat.
When the oil is hot, deep-fry the chicken rolls
for about 3 minutes, then roll over and continue
to fry for another 3 minutes or until golden and
cooked through. Do not have the oil too hot or the
breadcrumbs will brown too quickly before the chicken
is cooked through.

6. Drain on paper towels, serve with lemon wedges.

HINTS AND TIPS:

★ You will need—cutting
board, cook's knife, weight,
spoon, cup and liquid
measures, several bowls, a
frying pan and spatula.

★ How easy would it be to
buy those nasty excuses for
Kiev from the freezer section
of the supermarket? But the
satisfaction for a young or
inexperienced cook to make
their own is very gratifying,
and there's much personal
satisfaction whenever they
triumph over a dish—whether
it's chicken Kiev or another
recipe.

★ One of the main dangers
of this dish is burning the
breadcrumbs on the outside
before the inside is cooked.
Therefore, it is worth paying
a great deal of attention to
this stage of the cooking to
ensure a successful result.

★ The uncooked Kievs could
be frozen for another day. In
which case, defrost overnight
in the refrigerator, then re-
roll in bread crumbs before
cooking to help guarantee a
crunchy outside.

CHICKEN LIVER PARFAIT

Serves 8–10 as an entree

xxxxxxxxxxxxxxxxxxxxxxxxxxxxxxxxxxxxxxxxxxxxxxxxxxxxxxxxxxxxxxxxxxxxxxxxxxxxxxxxxxxxxxxxxxx

50 g butter
olive oil
1 small onion, finely diced
2 sprigs fresh thyme
1 garlic clove
1 bay leaf
1 pinch of freshly grated nutmeg
2 teaspoons salt
pinch of pepper
200 ml vermouth
60 ml brandy
60 ml port
500 g chicken livers, cleaned and drained
4 eggs
150 g butter, melted and cooled

Method:

1. Preheat oven to 100°C.

2. Heat the butter and a splash of oil over medium heat. Add the onion, thyme, garlic, bay leaf, nutmeg, salt and pepper and sauté until the onion is transparent.

3. Add the alcohol and cook until reduced by half. Remove from the heat and cool completely.

4. Pour the onion mixture into a food processor, blitz and add the chicken livers and eggs and finish with the melted and cooled butter.

5. Pass the mixture through a very fine sieve. Pour into a ceramic terrine mould or loaf tin, place the tin in a roasting pan, add hot water to reach halfway up the sides of the mould and bake for approximately 1.5 hours or until the parfait is set like firm jelly through to the centre.

6. Remove from the oven and cool on a cake rack. Refrigerate overnight before slicing.

HINTS AND TIPS:

* You will need—cutting board, cook's knife, weight and liquid measures, saucepan, wooden spoon, plastic spatula, fine sieve, food processor or blender, loaf tin or terrine mould and roasting dish.

* Chicken livers are available from butchers and most supermarkets. If you can get them, free range is best. If replacing with duck livers, you may need to inform your butcher in advance or they may be more readily available at good delicatessens.

* To prepare chicken livers, first rinse and drain. Then using a small sharp knife, set about peeling off any membrane and cutting off any excess fat attached to the livers. Much of the membrane missed in cleaning will be caught when straining through a fine sieve before cooking.

* The most important thing to remember about making a liver parfait is that it only needs to just set. It is very similar to a baked custard in that it should still wobble in the centre as it will continue to cook as it cools. If overcooked, it will be very noticeable when set cold as it will be slightly crumbly and grainy in texture.

* The parfait can be cooked at a higher temperature for a shorter period—150°C for 45 minutes–1 hour. The only real risk here is that the outside of the parfait will be just a bit more overcooked compared to the centre.

* Cooking the parfait in individual ceramic ramekins (moulds) will also reduce the cooking time—150°C for about 30 minutes.

* Covered, the parfait will keep for 3–4 days in the fridge.

* For storage before use, melt 150 g butter and pour over the cold parfait before placing back in the fridge.

* Some recipes call for the addition of green peppercorns (in brine). For the given recipe, use 1 tablespoon green peppercorns, washed and dried and stirred through the mixture before pouring into the terrine mould (or loaf pan).

CRISPY SKIN CHICKEN BREAST

Serves 4

XXXXXXXXXXXXXXXXXXXXXXXXXXXXXXXXXXXXXXXXXXXXXXXXXXXXXXXXXXXXXXXXXXXXXXXXXXXXXXXXXXXXXXXXXXX

4 chicken breast fillets, skin on
salt and pepper
2 tablespoons olive oil

Method:

1. Preheat the oven to 200°C.

2. Season the skin of the chicken breasts with salt
and pepper.

3. Heat the oil in a pan over medium–high heat. Add
the chicken breasts, skin side down. Cook until skin
is well browned. Do not turn over, but place in the
oven for 7–10 minutes depending on how big the chicken
breasts are.

4. Serve immediately with vegetables or **couscous** with
preserved lemon and **saffron**.

HINTS AND TIPS:

* You will need—sauté pan or frying pan with an ovenproof handle and baking tray.

* The reason for not turning the chicken in the pan and browning the other side is so it doesn't break or rupture the surface of the flesh and allow moisture to escape. As soon as it comes out of the oven, turn the chicken over so the skin stays crispy.

* The chicken is done when it is firm to the touch. It is okay to slice the breast in half to check for doneness. If the chicken is still a bit undercooked when sliced, place back in the pan or on the tray and return to the oven for an extra 2 minutes.

* For rosemary skewers— using a bamboo or metal skewer, pierce each breast through the middle, lengthways. Then skewer each breast with a long rosemary sprig through the hole left by the bamboo or metal skewer. Cook as per the instructions.

* Try making a herb butter using 2 tablespoons chopped fresh herbs and 1 garlic clove (finely chopped) mixed into 4 tablespoons butter. Place under the skin of the chicken breast and cook as suggested. As the butter melts and the skin becomes crisp, baste the breast with the melted butter.

* For a simple sauce for this dish—remove the breast from the pan and set aside. Place the pan back on the heat. Add ½ cup white wine or water to the pan to lift any cooked-on chicken juices (i.e. deglaze the pan). Reduce slightly then add some salt and pepper to taste. Remove from the heat and add 2 tablespoons butter and stir until melted—do not re-boil or the sauce will separate. Serve the chicken and drizzle with the sauce. Try adding a cup of mushrooms to the pan as the chicken is cooking then continue to make the sauce mentioned with the mushrooms in it. Also, the butter can be replaced with ½ cup cream, keep it on the heat and reduce by half before serving.

* Cook an extra chicken breast at the same time and keep refrigerated for lunch the following day. Use in a salad or chop and mix with homemade **mayonnaise**.

* Often, recipes will ask for chicken breast skin off—this is, of course, for health reasons which I fully endorse, but is entirely unnecessary. The skin provides protection for the soft, tender meat, while at the same time basting the breast with its own fat adds flavour. Therefore, my suggestion for the health conscious is to cook it with the skin on and remove the skin once cooked, then pat the breast meat dry using paper towel to remove excess fat and oil.

PEKING DUCK

Serves 2–4

XXXXXXXXXXXXXXXXXXXXXXXXXXXXXXXXXXXXXXXXXXXXXXXXXXXXXXXXXXXXXXXXXXXXXXXXXXXXXXXXXXXXXXXXXXXXXXXXXX

200 g plain flour
230 ml hot water
sesame oil
1 red roasted duck (purchased from a Chinese barbecue
   shop)
plum sauce or hoisin sauce
1 bunch spring onions, white and light green parts sliced
   on an angle
1 continental cucumber, seeds removed and cut into batons

Method:

1. To make the Mandarin pancakes, mix the flour, hot
water and 2 tablespoons sesame oil in a bowl to form a
smooth dough. Knead to stretch the gluten. Allow to rest
for 30 minutes before rolling.

2. Roll out the dough to form a long thin log and cut
into pieces. Roll out one ball at a time and brush with
some sesame oil on one side. Roll out the next, again
brushing with oil, then sandwich the two oiled sides
together; continue until all the dough has been used.

3. In a sauté pan or on the barbecue hotplate, cook the
double pancakes for 2 minutes on each side. Remove and
separate, folding each pancake in half, then half again;
then steam for 10 minutes to ensure they are chewy and
fully cooked. Alternatively, cook each pancake on the
hotplate on low–medium heat for 2–3 minutes each side;
however, they will be a bit drier and tougher. Last
resort is to buy pre-made pancakes (which are never as
good).

4. Remove the skin from the duck and slice. Traditionally
it is the skin and a very small amount of the meat which
is served in the pancakes as a first course.

5. To assemble, lay out some of the cooked and slightly
warm pancakes, smear with some plum sauce or hoisin
sauce, add some of the duck meat, duck skin, cucumber
batons and spring onion slices, then roll and serve.

HINTS AND TIPS:

* You will need—cutting board, cook's knife, bowl, rolling pin, sauté or frying pan, steamer (optional) and liquid, weight and spoon measures.

* Peking duck makes an excellent starter or entree at a dinner party. Although some work is required in making the pancakes, it more than makes up for not having to make the Peking duck itself. It would be too stressful (even for professional cooks) to attempt the duck at home, which is why some things are best left for restaurants.

* A quick way to make Peking duck at home is to buy everything pre-done from a good Chinese restaurant or barbecue shop and simply put it together at home. This is a great way for a beginner cook to get the idea of what Peking duck is. From there they can advance to making the pancakes and then on to a 3-course Peking meal.

* Traditionally, Peking duck is a 3-course mini banquet. First, the duck is presented and carved at the table with the crispy skin and a small amount of the meat used in the pancakes. The remaining duck is taken back to the kitchen where the highly skilled chefs prepare the remaining 2 courses from the one duck. The pancakes are followed by a soup course then a stir-fry course. Some chefs pride themselves on making as many dishes as possible from the one bird.

* At a cocktail party, Peking duck will always be a hit and never out of fashion.

* Leftover pancakes can be frozen. Wrap flat in plastic wrap and place in a clip lock bag. Defrost in the refrigerator overnight.

* Hoisin sauce is a thick, reddish-brown sauce made from brown bean sauce, garlic, mild chilli, salt, spices and additives (check labels). Brands can vary in taste and texture, some being particularly sweet and red, while better brands are more rounded in flavour, less sweet and browner. Hoisin is used extensively in Chinese cooking, in sauces, sauce mixes, marinades (pork and chicken) and for glazing. Translated, 'hoi sin' means 'sea freshness', although it neither contains nor is used with seafood. Also known as 'Chinese barbecue sauce' (nothing like the Western version of barbecue sauce), it is found in Asian grocers and supermarkets.

ROAST CHICKEN

Serves 4

xxxxxxxxxxxxxxxxxxxxxxxxxxxxxxxxxxxxxxxxxxxxxxxxxxxxxxxxxxxxxxxxxxxxxxxxxxxxxxxxxxxxxxxxxxx

1 x 1.8 kg chicken
salt
olive oil

Method:

1. Rinse the chicken in cold water washing inside and out, and remove any deposits of fat in the cavity. Pat dry with paper towel—this step is very important.

2. Sprinkle the skin with salt, cover with plastic wrap and set aside for 30 minutes. See Hints and tips.

3. Remove the plastic wrap, pat dry again, rub with olive oil and lightly season with salt a second time.

4. Place in a preheated 180°C oven for 1 hour. The chicken is ready when the juices in the leg joint run clear; if the juices are still a bit pink, roast for another 10 minutes.

5. Remove from the oven and rest for 15 minutes before carving.

HINTS AND TIPS:

* You will need—roasting dish, paper towel, carving knife and tongs.

* This is the most basic recipe for a roast chicken I could come up with. Once this basic method is mastered, many ingredients can be added to enhance the roast, such as other spices or dry herbs to the outside and stuffing to the inside.

* The idea of rinsing and patting dry the chicken is to remove any blood and to increase the crispness of the skin. Salting the skin and resting the chicken also increases the crispy skin by drawing out moisture.

* Stuffing the cavity with cut lemon, herbs and flavours like garlic and ginger can add to the flavour, but in my experience it is almost undetectable for an everyday roast. I would suggest filling the cavity with a basic stuffing to add value to the meal.

* Trussing a chicken is a more advanced technique and one worth looking into if roast chicken is something you think you may do often. The idea is that it holds the wings and legs close to the body of the chicken, which in turn helps the bird keep moist as well as making it a good-looking roast. It is a method that needs to be shown to understand and if you are keen, might I suggest going to your local butcher and have them show you how it is done.

* Should the chicken be browning too soon, lower the temperature or cover with foil to finish off. Perhaps the thermometer in your oven is broken.

* Try roasting the chicken slightly elevated from the base of the roasting pan. Use a trivet or small cake rack covered with a piece of baking paper. This will allow the heat to circulate around the roast, evenly browning all over.

* While resting, gather the juices at the base of the pan and pour them over the chicken. Or pour the juices into a small saucepan, add 1 cup **chicken stock** or white wine or water. Bring to the boil, season with salt and pepper and thicken with 1 teaspoon cornflour mixed with 1 teaspoon cold water. Stir into the sauce as it boils.

* To make a simple stuffing—place 6–8 slices fresh bread (crust removed and diced) in a bowl with 1 cup milk. Stand for 20 minutes for the bread to absorb the milk. Mix with salt and pepper and any flavours—herbs and spice—that you have handy. Any combination of crispy fried bacon, sautéed onion and garlic, or dried fruits can be mixed into the soft bread mixture.

ROAST DUCK WITH CHERRY SAUCE

Serves 6

XXXXXXXXXXXXXXXXXXXXXXXXXXXXXXXXXXXXXXXXXXXXXXXXXXXXXXXXXXXXXXXXXXXXXXXXXXXXXXXXXXXXXX

3 x size 15 (1.5 kg) ducks, rinsed, necks and
    wing tips removed
2 brown onions, skin on and roughly chopped
2 carrots, washed and roughly chopped
2 celery sticks, washed and roughly chopped
zest of 1 orange
1 teaspoon butter
250 ml white wine (chardonnay)
250 ml reduced brown duck stock (optional, see Hints
    and tips)
500 g fresh cherries, pitted, crushed and chopped
    roughly
sea salt and freshly ground black pepper
2 tablespoons cornflour mixed with 1 tablespoon
    cold water

Method:

1. There are two ways to begin this dish. One is to
place the ducks on the chopped vegetables, season with
salt and pepper and roast in the oven at 180°C for 1½
hours. My method is to place the ducks in a pot with
the necks and wing tips, cover with water and bring to
the boil, then simmer for 30 minutes (this removes fat
and impurities, and is the beginning of a duck stock).
Then I transfer the duck to the tray of vegetables and
brown in the oven at 200°C for 45 minutes. Choose the
method that best suits you—either way I tend to do
this job the day before I serve the final dish.

2. Sauté the orange zest in the butter, add the wine
and reduce by half. Add the stock and reduce by one-
quarter.

3. Add the cherries with any juices, season with salt
and pepper and thicken with the cornflour paste.

Method cont.

4. If the duck is pre-roasted, then it gives you the chance to remove most of the bones. To do this, cut the ducks in half lengthways, remove the breast bones and thigh bones, leaving only the wing bones and the drumstick bones intact. (These excess bones then go into the stock.)

5. Reheat the duck in the oven at 200°C for 10 minutes. Slice and serve coated with the sauce. Serve with asparagus and baked potato in cream.

HINTS AND TIPS:

★ You will need—cutting board, cook's knife, weight, spoon and liquid measures, large stock pot, saucepan and large roasting tray.

★ For the stock—the best way to make use of the water the ducks have simmered in is to continue to simmer it while roasting the ducks. When the ducks have cooked, remove them from the tray of vegetables and continue to roast the vegetables until brown all over, then add these to the stock to add colour. When the ducks have cooled, remove the bones as mentioned in the method, add the bones to the stock, continue to simmer for 2—3 hours, then strain the stock. Place the strained stock back on the heat and simmer until reduced to 1 litre. It is important that from the beginning, any fat and impurities that float to the top are removed with a ladle; this is done to avoid making the stock cloudy and soapy tasting.

★ For **duck in orange sauce**—use the same method but replace the cherries in the sauce with the juice of 6 oranges and the zest of 3 oranges. The wine and duck stock stay the same, as does thickening with cornflour.

★ When thickening with cornflour, remember to add small amounts at a time, bringing the sauce back to the boil between each addition until the right consistency is reached.

ROAST TURKEY BUFFET

Serves 8

XXXXXXXXXXXXXXXXXXXXXXXXXXXXXXXXXXXXXXXXXXXXXXXXXXXXXXXXXXXXXXXXXXXXXXXXXXXXXXXXXXXXXXXXXXXXXXX

1 turkey buffet (approximately 3.5 kg)
olive oil
salt and pepper
500 g rindless bacon rashers

Method:

1. Preheat the oven to 180°C.

2. Use paper towel to pat the turkey breast dry inside
and out. Rub with olive oil and season with salt and
pepper. Place on a roasting tray and lay the bacon
rashers over the breast, then roast in the oven for
45 minutes.

3. Remove the bacon, baste the turkey with pan juices
and cook for a further 45 minutes, basting at least
3 more times.

4. Allow 30 minutes cooking time per kilogram,
therefore a 3.5-kg buffet will take approximately
1¾ hours. Always test with a skewer, making sure the
juices run clear after inserting and removing the
skewer.

5. When cooked, remove, cover with foil and rest for
15–30 minutes (depending on size) before carving.
Resting time ensures the juices settle throughout the
meat, leaving the entire breast moist and tender.

HINTS AND TIPS:

* You will need—cutting board, cook's knife, weight measure and roasting tray.

* The turkey buffet is the first choice of chefs as it can provide large quantities of moist, white turkey meat and little wastage. Although turkey drumsticks may appear to be succulent, they are tougher and chewier than their chicken equivalents.

* Depending on numbers, about 400 g raw weight per person should do. This means for 8 people you will be looking at a buffet breast around 3–3.5 kg.

* If serving at Christmas, allow for the fact that several other meats are usually served at the Christmas table and that leftover turkey meat is a prized item over the following few days.

* 50 g butter for basting may be substituted for olive oil.

* If there are not enough cooking juices to baste, sprinkle with hot water.

* Remove the turkey from the fridge to allow ample time for it to reach room temperature before cooking.

* Never cook a partially thawed bird; the bird may appear cooked through, but if the internal flesh has not reached 75°C, dangerous micro-organisms may have survived.

* When roasting meats, a wise investment is a digital meat thermometer (probe) which is inserted into the thickest part of the meat and away from any fat or bones (which have a higher temperature reading while cooking) as it goes into the oven and stays there the entire time the meat is roasted.

* Cook fresh poultry within 2 or 3 days of purchasing.

* If ample cooking juices remain once the turkey has been cooked, use to baste roast vegetables for added flavour.

* Leftover turkey is ideal for sandwiches and salads the next day. Try the **chef's salad**.

----

xxxxxxxxxxxxxxx 6. Meat xxxxxxxxxxxxxxx

BAKED HAM

Serves 6—8

xxxxxxxxxxxxxxxxxxxxxxxxxxxxxxxxxxxxxxxxxxxxxxxxxxxxxxxxxxxxxxxxxxxxxxxxxxxxxxxxxxxxxxxxxxxxx

1.5 kg cooked leg ham
whole cloves
125 ml fruit juice (orange, pineapple or apple)
3 tablespoons Dijon mustard
3 tablespoons brown sugar
1 tablespoon balsamic vinegar
125 ml white wine

Method:

1. Preheat the oven to 180°C.

2. Carefully slice the skin from the ham, score the surface fat with a diamond pattern and place in a deep baking dish. Press a clove in the centre of each diamond.

3. To make the glaze—in a bowl, mix the juice, mustard, brown sugar and vinegar. Brush the glaze over the prepared ham.

4. Pour the white wine into the baking dish to prevent the ham from sticking (or use baking paper if wine is not available). Bake the ham, basting occasionally, for approximately 30 minutes or until glossy and deep golden.

HINTS AND TIPS:

* You will need—bowl, spoon and liquid measures and deep baking dish.

* Remember the ham has to fit in both the fridge and the oven; so depending on the size, this may mean removing a shelf in the fridge and 1 or 2 shelves from the oven.

* Leftover baked ham is great in sandwiches, **frittata**, **omelette** or salads.

* Try the recipe for **chef's salad** for leftover Christmas ham and turkey.

* Ham freezes well, in which case cut into large pieces and freeze. Remove and defrost overnight before slicing thinly for sandwiches. Ham will last about 2 months in the freezer before it begins to break down slightly.

* Try adding 2 minced garlic cloves to the glaze and use maple syrup or honey instead of brown sugar.

* For extra flavour, pour the glaze over the ham and marinate in the fridge for 24 hours, turning every 6 hours, then bake and baste.

* If you own a meat thermometer, cook the ham to 65°C (internal), keeping the thermometer clear of any bone in the meat.

* Or allow 20 minutes cooking time for every 1 kg of meat.

* Other alcohol can replace the fruit juice and wine; for an adult-themed ham, use beer or bourbon as a substitute. I've even eaten a 'bourbon and coke' baked ham, the coke replacing the fruit juice and the bourbon replacing the wine—and it was wicked.

* Carving a ham on the bone may seem a daunting task if you are unfamiliar with the way the bone bends its way through the plump layer of meat. To make life easier, an 'Easy Carve' ham has been produced which looks identical to the full bone ham—it even has its knuckle bone left in for you to hang on to as you carve easily into the balloon of meat attached.

BARBECUE-STYLE SPARE RIBS

Serves 4

xxxxxxxxxxxxxxxxxxxxxxxxxxxxxxxxxxxxxxxxxxxxxxxxxxxxxxxxxxxxxxxxxxxxxxxxxxxxxxxxxxxxxxx

1 teaspoon Cajun spice
1 teaspoon dried oregano
1 teaspoon ground cumin
2 tablespoons barbecue sauce
1 rack baby back ribs of pork (see Hints and tips)
1 tablespoon olive oil
1 medium onion, chopped
150 ml white vinegar
250 ml tomato sauce
250 ml **chicken stock**
2 tablespoons Worcestershire sauce
1 teaspoon salt
1 teaspoon cayenne pepper

Method:

1. In a bowl, mix the Cajun spice, oregano, ground cumin and barbecue sauce together, rub into the ribs and leave to marinate for 2 hours. Make the sauce while the ribs are marinating.

2. For the sauce—heat the oil in a saucepan over medium heat and sauté the onion until softened. Add remaining ingredients; stir well. Bring to the boil, reduce heat and simmer, uncovered, for 1 hour, stirring occasionally. Remove from the heat and cool.

3. In a bamboo, metal or electric steamer, place the racks of ribs and steam for 45–60 minutes. Remove the ribs from the steamer and cool.

4. Preheat the oven to 180°C.

5. Cover the ribs with the sauce and roast in the oven for 20–25 minutes, constantly basting. Or grill on the barbecue grill or hotplate on the lowest setting and to the side, to avoid burning them. The meat is done when a skewer goes through the meat like it's soft butter.

HINTS AND TIPS:

----

* You will need—cutting board, cook's knife, bowl, spoon and liquid measures, wooden spoon, saucepan, steamer, and roasting tray.

* Although this recipe is intended for 4, it may only serve 2 depending on the size of the ribs.

* There are two styles of rib used—the 'spare ribs' are generally meatier and are cut from the stomach area, whereas the 'back ribs' or 'baby back ribs' are cut from the area closer to the spine and are also more curved in appearance. Both styles are ideal for this recipe.

* Ribs and other tough cuts of meat on the bone have a lot of strong tissue that holds the muscle together and binds it to the bone. They have a lot of flavour, but this connective tissue is only softened by long, gentle cooking. This can be accomplished in several ways. One way is to cook on indirect heat on the barbecue for hours and hours on end, the indirect heat being the area of the barbecue that is off but has enough heat in it from the area of the barbecue that is on. The other way is used in the method provided which takes a lot less time, and which may offend the traditionalists, especially because you don't need to use a barbecue for this recipe, hence the word 'style'.

* Although the method asks that the ribs are steamed, they can also be parboiled (simmered) for the same amount of time. To do this, parboil until the meat is tender and just about falling off the bone. Cooking much beyond that will tend to dry out and reduce the flavour in the meat.

* Available in some supermarkets and butchers is 'liquid smoke'—add ½ teaspoon to the marinating rub for an authentic 'barbecue' flavour without even touching the hotplate.

* Remember to sauce only for the last 30 minutes once the meat is cooked and tender or it will burn.

BEEF CASSEROLE

Serves 4

XXXXXXXXXXXXXXXXXXXXXXXXXXXXXXXXXXXXXXXXXXXXXXXXXXXXXXXXXXXXXXXXXXXXXXXXXXXXXXXXXXXXXXXXXXXXXXXXX

3 tablespoons olive oil
1 onion, diced
3 garlic cloves, crushed
1 teaspoon chopped rosemary
1 kg chuck or blade steak, trimmed and cut into cubes
300 ml red wine
400 ml beef stock
100 g tomato paste
4 tablespoons cornflour
2 tablespoons cold water
2 potatoes, peeled and cut into 5-cm dice
2 carrots, peeled and chopped
2 celery sticks, trimmed and coarsely chopped
150 g button mushrooms, halved
salt and pepper
¼ bunch coarsely chopped flat-leaf parsley

Method:

1. Preheat the oven to 160°C.

2. Heat 1 tablespoon oil in a large heavy-based
saucepan on medium–low heat. Sauté the onion, garlic
and rosemary for 3–4 minutes or until softened.
Transfer to a large casserole dish.

3. Cook the beef in 2 batches until browned, using
1 tablespoon oil for each batch. Add the browned beef
to the onions.

4. Keep the saucepan on the heat and add the wine,
stock and paste. Bring to the boil stirring well to
lift the cooked-on meat juices. Mix the cornflour and
cold water to a paste and add to the boiling sauce.
Simmer for 3 minutes.

5. Add the potatoes, carrots and celery to the
casserole dish. Pour the hot sauce over the casserole
and bake, covered, for 1 hour.

Method cont.

6. Mix through the mushrooms, season with salt and pepper to taste and continue to bake, this time uncovered, for a further 45–60 minutes or until the beef is very tender. Remove from the oven and stir through the parsley.

HINTS AND TIPS:
----

* You will need—cutting board, cook's knife, large heavy-based saucepan, casserole dish, liquid, weight and spoon measures, vegetable peeler and wooden spoon.

* There are only 3 things to serve with this great winter warmer—creamy mashed potato, crisp steamed green beans and crusty bread. A good glass of red wine and great company is also highly recommended.

* This recipe is rich in red wine which may be too strong for some, in which case reduce the wine by half and replace with extra beef stock. This dish is still very successful with no wine at all, just substitute for beef stock.

* This dish will last in the fridge for 5 days. It also freezes well for up to 3 months.

* Use leftovers to make a chunky beef pie.

BEEF STROGANOFF

Serves 4

XXXXXXXXXXXXXXXXXXXXXXXXXXXXXXXXXXXXXXXXXXXXXXXXXXXXXXXXXXXXXXXXXXXXXXXXXXXXXXXXXXXXXXXXX

600 g beef fillet or rump
2 tablespoons olive oil
3 tablespoons butter
1 medium onion, finely chopped
150 ml white wine
150 ml fresh cream
salt and pepper
200 g sour cream
1 tablespoon chopped fresh flat-leaf parsley

Method:

1. Cut the beef into strips 1 cm x 5 cm, trimming off any fat or gristle.

2. Place 1 tablespoon oil and 1 tablespoon butter in a frying pan over high heat, and when the butter begins to foam, add half the beef and cook rapidly for the beef to brown but still be underdone. Place the beef in a colander or strainer to drain. Repeat this process.

3. Place the pan back on the heat and add the remaining butter to the pan, add the onion and cook gently until softened.

4. Add the wine and reduce to one-third, then add the cream and reduce by half. Add the beef, stir and season with salt and pepper. Bring to the boil and remove from the heat. Stir in the sour cream.

5. Place in a serving dish and sprinkle with the parsley.

HINTS AND TIPS:

★ You will need—cutting board, cook's knife, tongs, wooden spoon, colander or strainer and spoon, weight and liquid measures.

★ The history of many dishes is often surrounded by conflicting theories as to their origins—and beef stroganoff is no different. What is known is that it is a Russian dish made in the late 19th century and definitely named after a famous person by the name of Stroganoff. The year it was made is argued about as is the person—either the diplomat Count Paul Stroganoff or Count Pavel Stroganoff, a celebrity of that era.

★ It is recommended to cook the beef in 2 or even 3 batches to keep the heat high in the pan so the beef actually fries and colours and does not become grey and stew in its own juices. Draining the beef only serves to stop the beef stewing in the residual heat in a pool of its own juices. These juices can be kept and used to thin the sauce at the end of cooking should it get too thick.

★ This is a very fast cooking dish which is why lean, tender cuts of meat are used.

★ Often mushrooms are added to this dish, although not traditionally. If wanting to add mushrooms, use 200 g button mushrooms cut into quarters. After browning the beef, fry the mushrooms using an extra tablespoon of butter, until cooked through, then drain in the colander with the beef. Then continue with the recipe as stated.

★ Beef stroganoff is great served with fettuccine tossed in butter or with plain rice.

★ Try adding 2 tablespoons roughly chopped gherkins, sprinkled over the top before serving.

BOLOGNAISE SAUCE

Makes about 2 litres

xxxxxxxxxxxxxxxxxxxxxxxxxxxxxxxxxxxxxxxxxxxxxxxxxxxxxxxxxxxxxxxxxxxxxxxxxxxxxxxxxxxxxxxxxx

3 tablespoons olive oil

1 large onion, finely chopped

4 garlic cloves, crushed

1 carrot, peeled and finely chopped or grated

1 celery stick, finely chopped or grated

1 bay leaf

200 g bacon, diced

1 kg beef or pork mince or a combination of the two

2 x 400 g cans diced tomatoes

2 tablespoons tomato paste

salt and pepper

Method:

1. In a large pot or casserole dish, heat the oil over medium heat. Add the onion, garlic, carrot and celery, and cook until softened and aromatic. Add the bay leaf and bacon, and cook for a further 3 minutes.

2. Turn up the heat, add the mince and stir with a wooden spoon for 5 minutes to break up the mince and give it a bit of colour. It doesn't need to be browned all over.

3. Add the tomatoes and tomato paste, bring to the boil, then reduce the heat to low and cook gently for 2–3 hours, stirring occasionally and adding water or stock should the sauce become too thick. Season well with salt and pepper.

4. Serve immediately, or cool and refrigerate for 1 week or freeze for up to 3 months.

HINTS AND TIPS:

* You will need—cutting board, cook's knife, weight and spoon measures, several bowls for the chopped ingredients, large pot or casserole dish and wooden spoon.

* There are as many versions of bolognaise sauce as there are Italian mammas cooking it, and so this is just one more.

* The addition of celery and carrot is probably the first point of contention—to add or not to add. These two ingredients certainly do contribute to the overall flavour, but more importantly add a natural sweetness to counterbalance any tartness of the tomatoes.

* Grating the carrot and celery will help it 'disappear' in the sauce and look as if it was never added.

* The meat used in a bolognaise sauce is of great importance. Lean beef, although sounding healthy, will dry out after the required cooking time as it lacks any connective tissue and fat to keep the meat moist and unctuous. Adding a 50/50 ratio of beef mince and pork mince will help.

Veal mince is also highly recommended.

* Making your own mince is easy if you own a food processor. Simply buy about 1.2 kg beef, like chuck, skirt or blade. Remove any large pieces of fat and sinew, cut into 5-cm dice then, in small batches, begin to process. If adding pork to the dish, purchase pork belly—skin off—then dice like the beef. The pork belly will be quite fatty, but do not attempt to separate the fat from the meat on the pork belly as the fat will add great flavour and moistness to the bolognaise.

* Bacon is optional as well. Sometimes it is good to keep some bacon rinds in the freezer and add 6 rinds to the recipe to impart some flavour—it's cheaper too.

* Fresh tomatoes can easily replace the tinned variety— allow 1 kg fresh tomatoes which need to be peeled and sliced in half before scraping out the seeds with a teaspoon, then roughly chopped before adding. See **slow-roasted tomatoes** for a wicked tomato sauce.

* ½ cup fresh basil leaves can be shredded and added at the very end of the cooking.

* Always make more bolognaise than you think you need. Leftovers are great over the coming days as the flavour develops and becomes richer with time.

BRAISED BEEF BRISKET

Serves 6–8

xxxxxxxxxxxxxxxxxxxxxxxxxxxxxxxxxxxxxxxxxxxxxxxxxxxxxxxxxxxxxxxxxxxxxxxxxxxxxxxxxxxxxxxxxxxxx

2.5 kg beef brisket
salt and pepper
2 tablespoons olive oil
4 carrots, roughly chopped
3 celery sticks, roughly chopped
2 onions, roughly chopped
2 bay leaves
10 peppercorns
375 ml red wine
600 ml beef stock

Method:

1. Preheat the oven to 140°C.

2. Cut the beef brisket in half lengthways and season with salt and pepper. Heat a braising pot or flameproof casserole dish on high, add the oil and seal the meat until browned all over.

3. Remove the meat then add the vegetables and cook over medium heat until lightly coloured. Place the meat on the bed of vegetables, add the spices, wine and stock.

4. Take a piece of foil and place directly on the meat (do not tuck over the rim of the braising pot). Or if the pot has a lid, simply put the lid on.

5. Braise in the oven for 3–4 hours. The meat is perfectly cooked when a skewer inserted meets no resistance. When cooked, remove from the pot and set aside. Reserve some of the cooking liquor for serving. The meat should be tender enough to pull strips from it instead of having to slice it.

HINTS AND TIPS:

* You will need—cutting board, cook's knife, wooden spoon, tongs, liquid and spoon measures and braising pot or casserole dish or deep roasting pan.

* If during the colder months of the year you plan on cooking several braised dishes, then it may be worthwhile to invest in a heavy (cast iron) cooking pot with a lid.

* Importantly, the meat is not sealed (browned) to lock in its juices, but rather to add colour as well as flavour—through the addition of salt and pepper as well as the caramelising of the meat. Also the browning of the meat and vegetables adds greater depth of colour and flavour to the resulting sauce.

* Drain the liquid from the vegetables after the meat has been removed, reserving the liquid for further use. Place the vegetables (removing the bay leaves and peppercorns) in a food processor with a small amount of the juices and puree to produce a thick and tasty sauce to go with the meat. Remember to season with salt and pepper.

* Another sauce idea is to strain the liquid into a saucepan (discarding the vegetables and spices) over medium heat and reduce by one-third. Then add 2 anchovy fillets and 1 tablespoon Dijon mustard. Surprisingly, the anchovies dissolve into the sauce without leaving a distinct anchovy flavour, but rather adding a different form of saltiness to the sauce.

* This dish is ideally matched to a sauce called **salsa verde**.

* As an accompaniment for dinner, serve with creamy mashed potato and steamed baby vegetables.

* Alternative cuts of beef for this dish are skirt or blade. Lamb and veal shank, pork and lamb necks, and osso buco and beef shoulder are other cuts of meat ideally suited to braising. It then becomes a matter of taste as to what liquid, vegetables, herbs and spices match the cut of meat.

* Braising works with tough cuts of meat because collagen, a key connective tissue, converts to gelatine when cooked for long periods in a slow oven. Collagen is prominent in muscles the animal uses most often. For example, the shoulder in beef is used in walking and standing, and is quite tough; while the tenderloin (eye fillet) is used hardly at all and is very tender. Braising doesn't work well with tender cuts of meat because they have little collagen, and the long cooking times contracts and tightens the muscle fibres too much—an effect exactly like wringing out a wet towel—leaving the meat dry and stringy.

BRAISED LAMB SHANKS

Serves 4

XXXXXXXXXXXXXXXXXXXXXXXXXXXXXXXXXXXXXXXXXXXXXXXXXXXXXXXXXXXXXXXXXXXXXXXXXXXXXXXXXXXXXXX

4 lamb shanks, frenched
salt and pepper
2 tablespoons plain flour
2 tablespoons olive oil
1 medium onion, finely chopped
2 garlic cloves, crushed
125 ml white wine
400 g can diced tomatoes
500 ml **chicken stock**
sprig of rosemary

Method:

1. Preheat the oven to 160°C.

2. Season the shanks with salt and pepper, and lightly dust with flour, shaking off the excess.

3. Heat the oil in a large flameproof casserole dish on high. Cook the shanks until evenly browned all over, remove from the dish and set aside.

4. Add the onion to the same dish and sauté on medium heat for 5 minutes or until softened. Add the garlic and cook for 1 minute.

5. Add the wine then return the shanks to the pan with the tomatoes, stock and rosemary.

6. Cover with the lid or with foil and bake for 2 hours or until the meat is very tender. Season to taste.

HINTS AND TIPS:

----

* You will need—cutting
board, knife, flameproof
casserole dish with lid and
liquid and spoon measures.

* 'Frenched' is a term that
describes the way meat on the
bone is trimmed. All butchers
know what it means and how
to do it, so simply ask for
'frenched lamb shanks' when
ordering. The reason it is
done is for presentation—the
meat on the bone shrinks
slightly, exposing more of
the bone which in turn makes
the meat stand out more. It
is not vital that it is done
and cooking lamb or veal
shanks without trimming will
still work with this recipe.

* Use a frying pan and
transfer to a casserole or
baking dish if you do not
have a flameproof casserole
dish.

* Try adding 1 carrot
(peeled and diced) and 1
celery stick (diced) with the
onion.

* Soak 300 g chickpeas
overnight, drain and add to
the shanks with the tomatoes,
stock and rosemary.

CHILLI CON CARNE

Serves 8

XXXXXXXXXXXXXXXXXXXXXXXXXXXXXXXXXXXXXXXXXXXXXXXXXXXXXXXXXXXXXXXXXXXXXXXXXXXXXXXXXXXXXXXXXXXX

3 tablespoons olive oil
2 small onions, chopped
3 garlic cloves, crushed
1 green capsicum, chopped
1 kg beef mince
300 ml red wine
2 x 400 g cans diced tomatoes
3 tablespoons tomato paste
2 tablespoons ground chilli
1 teaspoon ground cumin
1 teaspoon ground coriander
1 cinnamon stick
1 tablespoon Worcestershire sauce
1 beef stock cube
salt and freshly ground black pepper
2 x 400 g can red kidney beans, drained and rinsed
fresh coriander leaves
2 limes, quartered

Method:

1. Heat the oil in a large, heavy-based saucepan and fry the onion and garlic until softened. Increase the heat, add the capsicum and beef, and cook quickly, stirring constantly with a wooden spoon, until the meat is well browned.

2. Add the wine, tomatoes, tomato paste, chilli, cumin, coriander, cinnamon, Worcestershire sauce and stock cube. Season well with salt and pepper. Bring to a simmer, cover with a lid and cook over gentle heat for at least 1 hour, stirring occasionally, until the mixture is rich and thickened.

3. Add the kidney beans and cook for a further 10 minutes, uncovered, before removing from the heat. Garnish with coriander leaves and lime wedges. Serve with steamed rice, steamed or boiled chat potatoes or crusty bread, as well as guacamole, sour cream and a green salad.

HINTS AND TIPS:

---

* You will need—cutting board, cook's knife, paring knife, large saucepan, wooden spoon and spoon and liquid measures.

* Chilli con carne is also known simply as chilli, especially in Texas.

* Like most slow-cooked dishes, chilli con carne is much tastier a day or two after it's cooked. Simply leave to cool, stick in the fridge and gently heat before serving.

* I always recommend making more than is needed as the leftovers can be frozen in individual portions in clip lock sandwich bags.

* Chilli con carne (chilli with meat) does not traditionally have beans in the recipe as beans are considered a cheap filler. However, for a perfectly acceptable vegetarian version of this dish substitute the minced beef with its weight in cooked (or canned) red kidney beans.

* Cooking the mince until it begins to brown—although not entirely necessary—does stop the 'meat' smell from developing after the dish is cooked.

* Use diced stewing beef like chuck to give the dish a chunky texture. Cook for longer (2½ hours), adding a cup of water to allow for evaporation.

* You may like to finish this dish with 1 tablespoon lime juice and 1 tablespoon brown sugar.

CORNED BEEF

Serves 8

xxxxxxxxxxxxxxxxxxxxxxxxxxxxxxxxxxxxxxxxxxxxxxxxxxxxxxxxxxxxxxxxxxxxxxxxxxxxxxxxxxxxxxxxx

2 kg corned beef girello or silverside
2 large carrots, peeled and cut into rounds
1 large onion, quartered
2 bay leaves
6 whole cloves
6 peppercorns
wine vinegar (100 ml for every 1 litre of water)

Method:

1. Tie the beef neatly with string to hold it together and place into a deep pot with the remaining ingredients. Cover with cold water and bring very slowly to the boil. Simmer gently for 2 hours and 40 minutes. Check if the meat is ready by inserting a skewer into the beef—the skewer should meet little resistance when inserted and removed.

2. When the meat is cooked, remove from the liquid, place onto a large serving platter and cover with foil to keep warm. Reserve some of the cooking liquor to use as a sauce (see Hints and tips).

HINTS AND TIPS:

* You will need—cutting board, cook's knife, large pot and cooking twine.

* Cooking or kitchen twine or string is available from all supermarkets but I prefer to buy only what I need from the local butcher. Butchers usually carry commercial strength twine made from either cotton, polyester or rayon.

* The reason for tying the meat is to stop it from curling and shrinking too much. Ask your butcher to do this job for you. Once tied, the beef will retain its shape, although it will have lost moisture and be smaller in size.

* Depending on the size of the meat, allow a simmering time of 40 minutes for every 500 g meat.

* Leave the skin on the onion when cutting into quarters as the skin will add a nice amber colour to the stock.

* The wine vinegar in this recipe can be substituted with cider vinegar, white vinegar or malt vinegar.

* Small Dutch carrots and peeled pickling onions can be added to the simmering stock in the last 20 minutes of cooking. Serve with the meat.

* Reserve 250 ml of the cooking liquor, strain, and mix with 1 tablespoon chopped flat-leaf parsley to make a very easy sauce. Serve with mustard on the side.

* Cook 250 g Savoy cabbage (sliced) in 2 tablespoons butter. Add 1 tablespoon chopped flat-leaf parsley. Cook the cabbage until just wilted. Do not be tempted to cook it in the stock with the beef—this is an outdated method that produces overcooked, mushy cabbage with no flavour.

* Serve with **white sauce, caramelised onions, parsley** and **crushed white vegetables** or **mashed potato**.

* Girello is an Italian word for the 'eye of silverside' or 'eye of round', meaning a more tender cut running through the centre of a normally tougher cut of meat. The recommendation of girello is because of its cylindrical shape which, when tied, delivers perfect discs of tender corned beef.

* Leftover corned beef is great in sandwiches the next day. It is also great as **Corned beef hash**—mix 200 g corned beef (diced) with 150 g cooked potato (diced), and season with salt and pepper. Heat 100 g butter in a sauté pan, add the hash mixture and flatten to form a pancake. Cook on one side until brown and crispy, use an egg flip to turn, then brown the other side. Serve with a squeeze of lemon.

COTTAGE PIE

Serves 6

XXXXXXXXXXXXXXXXXXXXXXXXXXXXXXXXXXXXXXXXXXXXXXXXXXXXXXXXXXXXXXXXXXXXXXXXXXXXXXXXXXXXXXXXX

1 kg potatoes, peeled and quartered
2 tablespoons butter
200 ml milk
salt
1 tablespoon olive oil
1 brown onion, diced
2 garlic cloves, crushed
1 carrot, grated
2 celery sticks, diced
1 x 400 g can diced tomatoes
1 kg beef mince
1 bay leaf
250 ml beef stock
2 tablespoons Worcestershire sauce
2 tablespoons chopped fresh flat-leaf parsley
1 tablespoon tomato paste
salt and pepper

Method:

1. Preheat the oven to 200°C.

2. For the mashed potato topping—cover the potatoes
with cold water, cover the saucepan with a lid and
bring to the boil. Reduce heat to low and simmer until
soft. Drain and mash with the butter, milk and salt to
taste.

3. Place the oil in a frying pan over medium heat.
Add the onion and fry for 2 minutes before adding the
garlic. Cook until the onion is soft. Add the carrot
and celery, cook until soft.

4. Add the tomatoes and cook for 10 minutes to enhance
the tomato flavour.

5. Add the beef and cook through, ensuring you break
up the mince by pressing and stirring with a wooden
spoon—the mixture should resemble large bread crumbs.

6. Add the bay leaf, stock and Worcestershire sauce, and reduce until most of the moisture is absorbed.

7. Add the parsley and tomato paste to thicken and add colour to the mixture, cook for a further 3 minutes. Add salt and pepper to taste.

8. Pour into a deep baking dish and top with the mashed potato, using a fork to fluff and spread evenly.

9. Bake in the oven for 20 minutes, allowing the potato mash to crisp and brown slightly.

HINTS AND TIPS:
----

* You will need—cutting board, cook's knife, vegetable peeler, spoon, liquid and cup measures, bowls, saucepan with a lid, frying pan, wooden spoon, potato masher and deep baking dish.

* Sprinkle 1 cup grated tasty cheese or 1 teaspoon nutmeg over the potato mash before baking the pie.

* This pie made with beef mince is known as a 'cottage pie', while it is said that a true 'shepherd's pie' is made with lamb mince. A mix of half beef mince and half lamb mince can be used—basically, it doesn't really matter as

long as it's cheap to make and filling on a cold winter's night.

* 1 cup of peas, corn or button mushrooms can be added during step 5.

* Add chilli with the parsley to suit individual tastes or even a large pinch of curry. You do not really taste the curry but it gives the meat a lift.

* If you do not want to use mince, use leftover roast meat; this will usually make a smaller dish but it eliminates any waste from the roast.

* You can substitute the cup of beef stock with 1 cup gravy for a thicker, richer taste.

* This pie can remain in the fridge for up to 1 week before it is baked.

* For a 'fancier' pie, eliminate the can of tomatoes from the above recipe, make the mince mixture then, in the baking dish, layer the mince, sliced fresh tomato and a layer of corn, and repeat. Top with the mashed potato and bake.

LASAGNE

Serves 6

XXXXXXXXXXXXXXXXXXXXXXXXXXXXXXXXXXXXXXXXXXXXXXXXXXXXXXXXXXXXXXXXXXXXXXXXXXXXXXXXXXXXXXXXX

1 tablespoon butter
1 litre **bolognaise sauce**
500 g fresh lasagne sheets
1.2 litres **béchamel sauce**
1 cup grated parmesan cheese

Method:

1. Preheat the oven to 180°C.

2. Grease a large rectangular baking dish and spoon some bolognaise sauce into the base of the dish. Cover with a layer of lasagne sheets. Top the pasta with a layer of meat sauce (making sure that the pasta is completely covered), then drizzle some béchamel sauce over the meat sauce and sprinkle over a light dusting of cheese.

3. Repeat layering the pasta sheets, sauces and cheese in this manner until all have been used, ending with a topping of béchamel sauce and cheese.

4. Bake the lasagne covered with foil for 30 minutes, unwrap and return to the oven for 15 minutes or until golden brown. Remove from the oven and rest for 10 minutes to firm before serving.

HINTS AND TIPS:

* You will need—large baking dish (approximately 20 cm x 30 cm) as well as the equipment mentioned in the recipes for bolognaise and béchamel sauce.

* Instant or dried lasagne sheets work just as well with the cooking times staying the same.

* Drizzle the béchamel sauce on each layer—don't try to 'spread' the béchamel as this will only mix it into the meat sauce, creating a mess.

* The bolognaise sauce needs to be made first as it takes a while to cook. The béchamel (white) sauce is made last and kept warm to make drizzling easier. If the béchamel sauce goes cold, it will also go firm and lumpy, making it much harder to use.

* A mixture of cheese can be used, try mozzarella and cheddar with the parmesan.

* Bocconcini—a type of fresh mozzarella cheese available at supermarkets and delicatessens—can be broken into small pieces and sprinkled between the layers. You will need 250 g for this recipe.

* Using a mornay sauce instead of a béchamel sauce is fine.

* Instead of beef mince in the bolognaise sauce, try using 500 g pork mince and 500 g veal mince; although only slightly more expensive, the meat in the sauce will be moister and more tender.

* Making 2 trays of lasagne is a good idea, which at the time appears like a lot of work. Bake one for your dinner, wrap the other one in plastic wrap and freeze for dinner another day; this way only one set of dishes is created to produce 2 meals.

* For a vegetarian alternative, see **vegetable lasagne**.

* For people with coeliac disease or gluten intolerance, use gluten-free lasagne or rice sheets available in health food shops and supermarkets. The flavour and texture will differ slightly and yet will be suitable because of the flavour of the sauces.

MEAT LOAF

Serves 4–6

XXXXXXXXXXXXXXXXXXXXXXXXXXXXXXXXXXXXXXXXXXXXXXXXXXXXXXXXXXXXXXXXXXXXXXXXXXXXXXXXXXXXXXXXXXXXX

250 g beef mince
250 g pork mince
250 g veal mince
1 medium carrot, peeled and grated
8 button mushrooms, sliced
4 rindless bacon rashers, diced
1 medium brown onion, peeled and grated
2 tablespoons Worcestershire sauce
½ cup tomato puree (passata)
1 egg
2 tablespoons chopped fresh flat-leaf parsley
salt and pepper

Method:

1. Preheat the oven to 180°C. Line a deep loaf tin
with baking paper.

2. Mix all the ingredients in a large mixing bowl.

3. Tightly pack the mixture into the loaf tin. This
will make slicing easier.

4. Place in the oven for 1 hour or until browned
on top.

HINTS AND TIPS:

* You will need—cutting board, cook's knife, vegetable peeler, vegetable grater, spoon, weight and cup measures, large bowl, deep loaf tin and baking paper.

* This recipe can be created with almost anything you happen to have on hand in the fridge and the minces can be increased or varied depending on taste. You could even use chicken or sausage mince.

* Mixing with your hands helps you gauge the consistency of the mixture. If it is too wet, add 1 cup dried bread crumbs.

* If the loaf becomes too dry while baking, pour 1–2 tablespoons boiling water or stock over the top.

* Chilled meat loaf can be served as part of an antipasto platter.

* Instead of using bacon in the mixture, place slices of streaky bacon over the baking paper and allow it to overhang the edge of the tin. Fill with the mixture and fold the overhanging bacon over the top of the meat loaf. This will help keep the meat loaf moist.

* To add depth of flavour, cook the carrot, mushrooms, bacon and onion in 1 tablespoon butter then add to the mixture.

* Leftover meat loaf can be used in sandwiches.

* Any leftover mixture can be made into burger patties and frozen, or freeze and make sausage rolls at a later date.

* Pack into muffin trays for individual serves and bake for 20 minutes.

* 1 cup grated tasty cheese can be sprinkled on top about 10 minutes before removing from the oven. Do not do this if you have layered bacon on top.

* Boil 4 eggs, peel and place into the meat loaf. Do this by filling the loaf tin one-third full with mince, lay the eggs lengthways in the centre of the loaf tin then top with the remaining mince before baking.

* This recipe can be made in advance and frozen unbaked.

MOUSSAKA

Serves 6

xxxxxxxxxxxxxxxxxxxxxxxxxxxxxxxxxxxxxxxxxxxxxxxxxxxxxxxxxxxxxxxxxxxxxxxxxxxxxxxxxxxxxxxxxxxx

2 medium eggplants
2 tablespoons cooking salt
5 tablespoons cooking oil
1 medium onion, peeled and finely diced
2 garlic cloves, minced
500 g lamb mince
3 tablespoons tomato paste
1 teaspoon dried oregano
1 cinnamon stick
250 ml beef stock
salt and pepper
300 g potatoes, peeled and cooked
50 g grated kefalograviera cheese

Sauce
30 g butter
30 g plain flour
375 ml milk
50 g grated tasty cheese

Method:

1. Slice the eggplant, spread on a plate and sprinkle
with the cooking salt. Leave for 30 minutes. Rinse and
pat dry with paper towel.

2. Fry the eggplant in a little oil until brown on
both sides. Set aside.

3. Heat the remaining oil and cook the onion and
garlic until softened. Add the mince and cook until
browned.

4. Stir in the tomato paste, oregano, cinnamon, stock
and seasonings. Bring to the boil, cover and simmer
for 30 minutes.

5. Slice the cooked potatoes. When the meat has
cooked, remove the cinnamon stick.

Method cont.

6. Line the base of a large baking dish with half the eggplant and pour over half the meat mixture. Top with the rest of the eggplant, then add the remaining meat and finally add a layer of sliced potatoes.

7. For the sauce—melt the butter, stir in the flour and cook over medium heat until the mix turns a sandy colour. Remove from the heat and add all the milk at once. Return to the heat and, using a whisk, stir the sauce until it comes back to the boil then continue to boil for 2 minutes. Remove from the heat and stir in the tasty cheese.

8. Pour the sauce over the moussaka, sprinkle with the kefalograviera cheese and bake in a preheated 180°C oven for 30 minutes or until golden brown.

HINTS AND TIPS:
----

* You will need—cutting board, cook's knife, 2 bowls, 2 saucepans, sauté or frying pan, wooden spoon, whisk, grater, spoon, liquid and weight measures, large baking or lasagne dish.

* Like many traditional dishes steeped in history, there will always be debate over which is the true recipe. Well, there are many true recipes of traditional dishes as every region of every country has its own interpretation of a national dish—and moussaka is no different.

* This recipe includes cinnamon, which some regional cooks of Greece would disagree with, while others swear by it. I add it because I love the subtle aroma it gives the meat sauce, and it also masks the meaty smell perfectly.

* Kefalograviera is a style of hard cheese used for saganaki (fried cheese). It is ideal to use in this dish. Available from all good delicatessens, it can be substituted for regular tasty cheese or parmesan.

OSSO BUCO

Serves 6

XXXXXXXXXXXXXXXXXXXXXXXXXXXXXXXXXXXXXXXXXXXXXXXXXXXXXXXXXXXXXXXXXXXXXXXXXXXXXXXXXXXXXXXX

6 pieces osso buco (veal shank cut into slices
   3–4 cm thick)
salt and pepper
4 tablespoons butter
2 tablespoons olive oil
2 medium carrots, finely diced
1 medium onion, finely diced
1 celery stick, finely diced
2 garlic cloves, crushed
1 tablespoon fresh thyme leaves
250 ml white wine
2 tablespoons tomato paste
400 g can diced tomatoes
500 ml **chicken stock** or beef stock
zest of 1 orange

Method:

1. Preheat the oven to 160°C.

2. Season the osso buco pieces with salt and pepper.

3. Heat 2 tablespoons butter and the olive oil in a
heavy-based flameproof casserole dish and sauté the
veal on both sides until golden brown. Remove the veal
from the dish and place on a tray.

4. Add 2 tablespoons butter to the casserole dish,
then add the onion, carrot, celery, garlic, and thyme,
and cook for 10 minutes. If necessary, add a little
more butter.

5. Pour the wine into the dish, bring to the boil
and simmer for a few minutes. Add the tomato paste,
tomatoes and stock, bring to the boil, then add the
osso buco.

6. Top with the orange zest, cover tightly with a lid
and cook for 2 hours.

HINTS AND TIPS:

* You will need—heavy-based flameproof casserole dish or roasting pan, wooden spoon, tongs and liquid and spoon measures.

* Osso buco literally means 'bone with a hole'.

* If the osso buco is already cut, then try and find 6 large pieces; alternatively, look for 12 smaller, thinner cuts of osso buco. As the hind legs are bigger than the front legs, the size of the shins and consequently the size of the slices cut from the hind legs will yield greater amounts of meat and tend to be more tender.

* When cooked properly, osso buco will not need a knife as the meat falls off the bone and can be broken into pieces with a fork.

* Traditionally osso buco is served with teaspoons to scoop out the marrow.

* This very same recipe lends itself well to whole veal shanks or lamb shanks, or even other tougher cuts of meat from brisket and blade to forequarter chops. The smaller the piece of meat, the less time it may take in the oven; therefore check for doneness after 1½ hours.

* With 15 minutes of cooking time left, remove the dish from the oven and add 1 cup of your favourite olives, then place back in the oven, uncovered. When about to serve, instead of the gremolata, sprinkle some baby capers over the dish for added zing.

* Saving bacon rinds in the freezer is handy—add 6 rinds to the osso buco in the beginning. Also add 300 g pickling onions (peeled and kept whole) to the dish with 45 minutes to go.

* Serve with simple **risotto Milanese** or **mashed potatoes**. If avoiding starches, serve with grilled field mushrooms and wilted baby spinach with lemon wedges on the side, or simply serve with some good crusty bread and a leafy green salad.

* **Gremolata** (gremolada) is a traditional accompaniment to osso buco but some may find the flavour too sharp for the rich flavour of the dish. It is sprinkled on top of the osso buco before serving. Mix thoroughly—½ cup curly parsley (finely chopped), zest of 1 lemon (chopped), and 1 garlic clove (finely chopped).

* The orange zest can be substituted with lemon zest.

* Osso buco can also be cooked on the stovetop in a saucepan. Follow steps 1 to 5 of the recipe then cover with a lid and cook over low heat for 2 hours or until the meat falls off the bone. Check occasionally to see if more stock is required.

RISSOLES

Serves 4

XXXXXXXXXXXXXXXXXXXXXXXXXXXXXXXXXXXXXXXXXXXXXXXXXXXXXXXXXXXXXXXXXXXXXXXXXXXXXXXXXXXXXXXXXXX

1 tablespoon olive oil
1 small brown onion, finely diced
2 garlic cloves, crushed
750 g lamb mince
½ cup bread crumbs
1 tablespoon chopped fresh flat-leaf parsley
1 egg
salt and pepper
½ cup plain flour
½ cup vegetable oil, for frying

Method:

1. Place the olive oil, onion, garlic, mince, bread crumbs, parsley, egg and salt and pepper in a large mixing bowl and mix thoroughly.

2. With wet hands—this prevents the mince from sticking to your hands—grab a handful of mince and shape into a large patty.

3. Coat with the flour and repeat with the remaining mince.

4. Shallow-fry on low–medium heat until golden brown, about 3–4 minutes, depending on thickness.

5. Turn and cook for 2–3 minutes on other side.

HINTS AND TIPS:

★ You will need—cutting board, cook's knife, cup and spoon measures, bowl, frying pan and tongs.

★ Using a nonstick frying pan means less oil is needed for frying the rissoles.

★ Onion is often better grated for burgers, rissoles and meatballs, as it 'melts' into the meat and eliminates an overpowering onion taste.

★ Add the finely grated zest of 1 lemon to the mince.

★ For best results, it is highly recommended that the rissoles be placed in the refrigerator for 1 hour before cooking to allow the proteins to set firm and hold once cooked.

★ The rissoles can be cooked on the barbecue, or in the oven, or grilled until golden brown.

★ Rissoles can be made in advance and frozen. It is best to lay them flat on plastic wrap, then freeze solid before placing in an airtight container with sheets of baking paper between each one. This makes it easy to separate if only needing to defrost a couple at a time.

★ Make smaller rissoles for an antipasto platter and serve with tomato relish or sweet chilli sauce.

★ Any mince can be used— beef, pork, chicken, or a mixture of beef and lamb or chicken and pork. You could also use sausage mince mixed in equal quantities with any of the other minces.

★ To keep the rissoles moist, add ½ cup ricotta cheese or 1 grated Granny Smith apple or 1 cup grated zucchini. It is best to use regular rather than lean mince because that will also help to keep the rissoles moist.

★ Crush 1 cup pine nuts and add to the mixture.

★ Add ¼ cup parmesan cheese to the plain flour.

ROAST BEEF

Serves 8

XXXXXXXXXXXXXXXXXXXXXXXXXXXXXXXXXXXXXXXXXXXXXXXXXXXXXXXXXXXXXXXXXXXXXXXXXXXXXXXXXXXXXXXXXXXXX

1 x 2.5 kg beef roast (sirloin, wing-rib, blade,
    rump, scotch or eye fillet)
½ cup olive oil
sea salt
freshly ground black pepper
1 cup water

Method:

1. Preheat the oven to 180°C.

2. Heat a heavy-based roasting pan or a large
ovenproof frying pan. Rub the beef with the oil and
salt. Place the beef in the pan and brown on all
sides, then sprinkle with the pepper. Remove the pan
from the heat. Place the roast on a trivet or rack
that fits in or over the roasting pan, add the water to
the pan and place in the oven.

3. Bake for 2½ hours. Depending on how well you want
the roast cooked, use a meat thermometer—45°C for
rare, 55°C for medium and 65°C for well done—or use
the old 'time by weight' method of 30 minutes for
every 500 g.

4. Once cooked, remove from the oven, move the roast
to a warm area and rest for 20 minutes.

HINTS AND TIPS:

★ You will need—roasting pan or large ovenproof frying pan, metal trivet or small wire rack and cup measure.

★ There are several methods for roasting beef. Roasting it on a trivet so it is elevated from the base of the pan is one way—the water in the base produces a bit of steam in the oven to help keep the meat moist as well as being the beginning of a gravy. Raising the meat from the base of the pan ensures it won't burn underneath.

★ Cooking the roast on a bed of vegetables also prevents its base from burning, and adds minimal flavour to the roast as well as the gravy. Roughly chop 1 carrot, 1 large brown onion and 2 celery sticks, place in the roasting pan and place the beef on top.

★ I recommend leaving the roast at room temperature, covered, for about 2–3 hours (depending on size) prior to cooking. This ensures that the meat is more evenly cooked instead of too well done on the outside and too rare in the centre.

★ Slow-roasting the beef can be done to minimise moisture loss, at a temperature of 120°C or less, for 6–8 hours—the beef will not shrink as much and will stay juicy throughout. The joint of meat needs to be seared on the outside as the lack of heat in the oven will fail to brown it.

★ Roasting on a high heat can also be done but is not recommended by professional cooks and food scientists as they know all too well what happens to the delicate proteins in meat when exposed to the vicious dry heat of an oven. Roasting meat at 200°C or above forces the meat to contract, squeezing out valuable juices and ultimately leaving the meat with a small, juicy centre and a much larger, dry outer area.

★ Searing the beef before it is roasted is more for flavour than for keeping in the juices. Oil and salt rubbed into the meat also add flavour. The pepper is only added after it is seared as pepper tends to burn easily.

★ Resting the beef after roasting is important to allow the meat fibres to relax and for the blood (juices) to distribute evenly throughout the whole joint. Which explains why if ever you've cut into a roast (or even a steak) immediately after it comes from the oven, it almost gushes blood and juice all over the cutting board. This will not happen if the meat is well rested.

★ For a **simple gravy**—keep adding water to the pan as it evaporates in the oven, this will be a good start. Once cooked, place the pan back on the heat and add 2 cups beef or chicken stock, and reduce slightly. Season with salt and pepper, and thicken with 1 tablespoon cornflour mixed with 2 teaspoons cold water whisked into the gravy. Bring to the boil and pour into a jug.

★ For **Yorkshire pudding**—add 1–2 tablespoons olive oil or beef dripping to each cup of a muffin tray and place in a preheated 220°C oven. Make a batter by mixing 150 g plain flour with 240 ml milk and 3 eggs. Place 2 tablespoons of batter into each hot oiled cup and bake for 10–15 minutes or until puffed and golden. Do not open the oven door until ready as the puddings may not rise. Leftover puddings freeze well and can be reheated for another day.

ROAST LAMB

Serves 6

XXXXXXXXXXXXXXXXXXXXXXXXXXXXXXXXXXXXXXXXXXXXXXXXXXXXXXXXXXXXXXXXXXXXXXXXXXXXXXXXXXXXXXXXXXXXXXXX

3 lemons
1 garlic bulb
½ bunch fresh rosemary
1 leg of lamb (about 2.5 kg), boned and rolled
2 tablespoons extra virgin olive oil
salt
1 cup water

Method:

1. Preheat the oven to 180°C. Place a roasting rack in a roasting pan.

2. Slice the lemons into thick rounds and place on the roasting rack in a single layer. Roughly slice the garlic with the skin on and place on the lemon. Then lay the rosemary over the top of the lemon and garlic. This forms the bed upon which the lamb will roast—the juices from these aromatics and the lamb makes a delicious sauce (see Hints and tips).

3. Rub the lamb with the oil and salt, and place on the roasting rack. Add the water to the roasting pan and cover with foil. Put the roast in the oven for about 1 hour. After 1 hour, remove the foil (keep the foil to one side and use to cover the lamb when resting), turn the oven up to 220°C and return the lamb to the oven for 30–40 minutes depending on the size. Use a meat thermometer—45°C for rare, 55°C for medium-rare, 65°C for medium and 75–80°C for well done—or use the old 'time by weight' method of 30 minutes for every 500 g.

4. Once cooked, remove from the oven, cover the roast in foil and let it rest for 20 minutes. While the roast is resting, make the sauce (see Hints and tips) if desired.

HINTS AND TIPS:

* You will need—cutting board, cook's knife, roasting pan, roasting rack (wire cake rack or trivet), spoon and cup measures.

* For a **sauce**—pour the juices from the roasting pan into a saucepan. Add the aromatics under the roast, 200 ml white wine and 500 ml veal or beef stock and over medium-high heat, reduce the sauce by half. Check the seasoning and if need be, thicken with 1 tablespoon cornflour mixed with 1 teaspoon cold water. Strain the sauce before serving with the lamb.

* Even without the bed of aromatics, it's important to place the meat onto a rack so that it doesn't stew in its own juices. If you do not have a rack to place the roast on, then put it directly on the wire rungs of the oven shelf with your roasting pan underneath to catch all the juices.

* If possible, take the meat from the refrigerator about 1 hour before cooking, this allows the meat to come closer to room temperature, which in turn allows the cooking times in the recipe to be true.

* Trim excess fat and any silver sinew if necessary or have your butcher do that for you. Do remember that fat is flavour and it may be better to roast with the fat on and trim after it is roasted to allow the meat to self-baste.

* Resting roasted meat before carving and serving is vital—it enables temperatures to even out and the meat fibres to relax, and evenly redistributes the juices. The relaxed meat becomes more tender and easier to carve with less loss of juices. Any juices collected on the plate the roast was resting on can be used in a sauce. Allow the meat to rest for approximately 5 minutes for every 500 g meat. For example, 15 minutes for a 1.5 kg lamb roast.

* Lamb will shrink during the cooking process so allow for this when purchasing and always allow an extra portion.

* Carve meat across the grain; this enhances tenderness.

* Create insertions, no more than 6, with a sharp knife on all sides of the roast. Make a paste by mixing 3 crushed garlic cloves, ½ tablespoon olive oil, 1 teaspoon dried oregano and ¼ teaspoon salt, divide evenly and place the paste into each cavity to infuse the meat with aroma and flavour while cooking.

* The roast can be basted with the pan juices during cooking.

ROAST PORK AND CRACKLING

Serves 6

XXXXXXXXXXXXXXXXXXXXXXXXXXXXXXXXXXXXXXXXXXXXXXXXXXXXXXXXXXXXXXXXXXXXXXXXXXXXXXXXXXXXXXXXXXXXXXXXX

2 kg joint of pork with skin on (leg, shoulder,
    belly or loin)
salt flakes

Method:

1. Preheat the oven to 220°C.

2. Follow the instructions in **Hints and tips** for
preparing the skin for crackling.

3. Place the pork on a trivet or small cake rack and
place in a roasting pan. Place the pan on a middle
shelf in the oven. Roast for 30 minutes, then reduce
the heat to 170°C for 1¼ hours.

4. Remove from the oven and set aside to rest for
15–20 minutes before carving.

HINTS AND TIPS:

* You will need—cutting board, cook's knife, paper towel, roasting pan and trivet or small wire rack.

* For the **crackling**—there are several theories for perfect crackling and for many cooks their method seems to work and they will stick to it—which is fine. Keep in mind some basic ideas. First, rinse the skin under cold water and thoroughly pat dry with paper towel—moisture is crackling's worst enemy. Make sure the skin is scored in ½–1-cm intervals and through the fat, even if it means re-scoring what the butcher has already done. Rub with salt, cover in plastic wrap and leave on the bench for 30 minutes—the salt will extract excess moisture from the skin. Use paper towel again to remove the excess moisture. DO NOT rub with oil as the pork fat is enough to self-baste the skin. Sprinkle again with salt, this time lightly, and bake as per the instructions given. Some cooks rub the skin with lemon juice and salt, I've tried this method as well, but I also let it stand to extract moisture before baking.

* If, for whatever reason, the pork crackling doesn't work, remove the skin, cover the roast with foil to keep it warm and place the crackling between two pieces of paper towel and microwave on high for 2 minutes. Allow to cool for a couple more minutes before breaking into pieces.

* The salt—it is important to use a good salt for this dish. Table salt or cooking salt are too harsh and bitter in flavour and it is therefore recommended to use a quality flake or sea salt whenever possible. If using a flake salt, it is a good idea to crush the salt in a mortar and pestle to make it fine grained so it really gets into the skin.

* When roasting meats, pork included, bring the meat to room temperature for a more even cooking of the meat. A piece of meat straight from the fridge placed into the oven needs to heat up before it starts to cook— which means the outside is cooking while the inside is still cold, and by the time the inside is cooked, the outer part is dried out and overcooked.

* If you plan on cooking roasts often, then invest in a meat thermometer.

* The quality of the pig is the real test of successful crackling. The water content in the skin ultimately determines the outcome. Excellent pigs raised in a free range or organic lifestyle will always produce perfect crackling. Pork from the supermarket will always frustrate the cook as it will work one week, yet 2 weeks later produce a rubbery result.

SAN CHOY BAO

Serves 6

xxxxxxxxxxxxxxxxxxxxxxxxxxxxxxxxxxxxxxxxxxxxxxxxxxxxxxxxxxxxxxxxxxxxxxxxxxxxxxxxxxxxxxxxxx

150 ml peanut or other vegetable oil
1 tablespoon sesame oil
8 garlic cloves, crushed
100 g ginger, grated
6 shallots (eschalots), finely chopped
1 bunch spring onions, white part thinly sliced
1 kg pork mince
150 ml Chinese cooking wine
200 ml hoisin sauce
200 ml oyster sauce
2 iceberg lettuces, leaves washed and dried
2 tablespoons sesame seeds, to garnish
green part of spring onions, sliced on an angle,
    to garnish

Method:

1. Heat the oil in a wok until smoking. Add the
garlic, ginger, shallots and thinly sliced spring
onion and fry for 1 minute.

2. Stir in the mince and cook until brown. Add the
wine and sauces, work into the mince and stir-fry
until the mince is cooked through.

3. Turn off the heat and set aside.

4. Place the lettuce leaf cups on serving plates, fill
with the cooked mince and sprinkle over the garnishes.

HINTS AND TIPS:

* You will need—wok or large frying pan, wooden spoon or metal spatula, cutting board, cook's knife and liquid, weight and spoon measures.

* It can be a good idea to buy an extra lettuce or two as the leaves can sometimes be awkward to separate; leftover lettuce can always be used in salads or sandwiches.

* To separate the lettuce leaves, cut out the core and run the lettuce under cold water (core side facing the flowing water). The leaves get the water between them and this helps to minimise the risk of tearing, especially in tight lettuce heads.

* A 225 g can chopped water chestnuts can be added for crunch and texture.

* A mixture of 500 g chicken mince and 500 g pork mince can be used.

* A pre-cooked Chinese duck, which can be purchased from Chinese barbecue stores, may also be used instead of the mince for a fancier dish.

* Dry sherry can be substituted for Chinese cooking wine.

* It is a good idea to provide a finger bowl of warm water and lemon slices because eating san choy bao can get quite messy. At the very least, provide napkins or paper towels.

* San choy bao mince can also be made in a saucepan; it will require a longer cooking time because it won't get as hot as a wok. Allow time for the mixture to become relatively dry and manageable, rather than sloppy, bearing in mind that it is essentially eaten with fingers.

* A mix of light soy sauce and teriyaki can be used in the same quantities as the hoisin and oyster sauces and works just as well, but some of the authenticity of the dish will be lost.

* Hot or sweet chilli sauce can be added for extra kick.

SAUSAGES AND MASH WITH PEPPER SAUCE

Serves 4

xxxxxxxxxxxxxxxxxxxxxxxxxxxxxxxxxxxxxxxxxxxxxxxxxxxxxxxxxxxxxxxxxxxxxxxxxxxxxxxxxxxxxx

1 recipe quantity **potato mash**
1 recipe quantity **caramelised onions**
8 sausages of your choice
1 tablespoon olive oil
1 small brown onion, finely diced
250 ml red wine
6 sprigs thyme
250 ml beef stock
1 tablespoon freshly cracked black pepper
2 tablespoons cornflour mixed with 1 tablespoon
    cold water
60 g butter, diced cold
salt

Method:

1. Once the mash and caramelised onions are cooking, cook the sausages in a frying pan or on the barbecue.

2. While the sausages are cooking, make the sauce. Heat the oil in a saucepan and fry the onion over medium heat, stirring, for about 5 minutes or until the onion is softened.

3. Add the wine and thyme and simmer for 10–15 minutes or until the wine is reduced by half.

4. Add the stock and pepper and simmer for 5 minutes.

5. Add the cornflour and cold water paste and whisk as the sauce comes to the boil and thickens—the cornflour will thicken as the sauce begins to boil. Stir in the diced butter and check the seasoning.

6. Remove from the heat and cover with plastic wrap until ready to use.

7. To serve—place a dollop of creamy mash in the centre of 4 plates. Place 2 sausages on each dollop of mash and pour some sauce over the lot. Top with a spoonful of caramelised onion.

HINTS AND TIPS:

---

* You will need—equipment required to make mash and caramelised onions, frying pan or barbecue, saucepan, spoon, weight and liquid measures, whisk, tongs, cutting board and cook's knife.

* This simple combination of ingredients works equally as well with a good steak or grilled chicken breast.

* The sauce can be made in advance and heated before serving.

* If the red wine component appears too much, simply omit the wine and replace with stock or water.

* It is important to mix the cornflour with cold water before stirring into the sauce. This cold 'slurry' is then whisked into the sauce as it boils. Starches like cornflour, arrowroot, rice flour and potato starch reach maximum thickening ability once the liquid has come to the boil, so it is worth noting that only small amounts at a time are added and brought to the boil between each addition.

* A **simple onion gravy** can be made by preparing the **caramelised onions** following the instructions. Add 250 ml beef stock to the onions, bring to the boil and thicken with cornflour and water. Check the seasoning.

STEAK AND KIDNEY PIE

Serves 4

xxxxxxxxxxxxxxxxxxxxxxxxxxxxxxxxxxxxxxxxxxxxxxxxxxxxxxxxxxxxxxxxxxxxxxxxxxxxxxxxxxxxxxxxxx

800 g chuck steak, cut into 3-cm dice
300 ml Guinness
8 lambs' kidneys
½ cup cornflour
1 tablespoon salt
1 tablespoon freshly ground black pepper
3 tablespoons olive oil
2 medium onions, cut into 1-cm dice
100 g button mushrooms, halved
2 carrots, peeled and cut into 1-cm dice
2 celery sticks, chopped
2 garlic cloves, crushed
1 teaspoon fresh thyme leaves
1 litre beef stock or water
1 sheet puff pastry, defrosted
1 egg yolk, for glazing

Method:

1. Place the meat in a glass or plastic bowl and mix
with the Guinness, then set aside to marinate for
several hours or overnight. Drain and discard the
Guinness or keep half the Guinness for the sauce.

2. Trim the lamb kidneys by slicing through the middle
and removing the white fat. Once cleaned, cut each
half into thirds.

3. Mix the cornflour, salt and pepper together, then
toss the beef and kidneys in the mixture.

4. In a heavy-based pot or casserole dish, heat some
of the oil and add a small handful of meat at a time,
browning then transferring to a dish. Repeat until all
the meat is browned. Adding all the meat in one batch
will not work as there is not enough hot surface area
to brown such a large amount.

Method cont.

5. Add another tablespoon of oil to the pot, add the onion, mushrooms, carrot and celery, and cook for 5 minutes or until softened. Add the garlic and thyme, and sauté for 1 minute.

6. Return the meat to the pot with the stock or water and any Guinness (optional). Bring to the boil then reduce the heat and simmer for 2 hours or until the meat is tender.

7. Transfer to a pie dish, adding just enough liquid, if necessary, to cover the meat. Extra liquid can be kept for serving separately with the pie at the table.

8. Cool completely and cover with the puff pastry (the pastry will not rise and crisp as well if the filling is still hot). Make a slit in the top to allow steam to escape. Brush with the egg yolk, refrigerate for 1 minute and brush again with egg yolk.

9. Bake in a preheated 200°C oven for 15 minutes, then reduce the heat to 180°C and bake for another 20–30 minutes to ensure the filling is hot. If the pastry is getting too dark, cover with foil and continue to cook.

HINTS AND TIPS:

* You will need—cutting board, cook's knife, vegetable peeler, weight, liquid, cup and spoon measures, heavy-based pot or casserole dish, 1-litre pie dish and pastry brush.

* The Guinness is used as a marinade in this recipe, although the flavour may be too strong for some. However, if that rich, hoppy flavour is desired, then add the Guinness to the sauce when adding the beef stock and cook as per the instructions.

* Kidneys have a strong flavour and are not to everyone's liking. For a child-friendly pie, simply substitute the kidneys for an extra 200 g beef so the beef totals 1 kg. Substitute the Guinness for water or beef stock and continue as per the instructions to give you a simple yet tasty beef pie.

* The pie filling can easily be made well in advance and refrigerated for 5–7 days or frozen until needed. A cold pie filling is easier to work with when topping with the puff pastry.

THAI BEEF SALAD

Serves 4–6 as an entrée, or 2 as a main

XXXXXXXXXXXXXXXXXXXXXXXXXXXXXXXXXXXXXXXXXXXXXXXXXXXXXXXXXXXXXXXXXXXXXXXXXXXXXXXXXXXXXXXXXXXXX

500 g beef rump or sirloin
8 cherry tomatoes
¼ continental cucumber, thinly sliced on an angle
2 red shallots, peeled and thinly sliced
½ cup fresh coriander leaves, washed and picked
½ cup fresh mint leaves, washed and picked
½ cup Thai basil leaves, washed and picked
2 cups tatsoi leaves, washed and dried well

Dressing
2 garlic cloves
2 tablespoons grated palm sugar
1 bird's eye chilli, cut in half and seeds removed
2 tablespoons lime juice
2 tablespoons fish sauce

Method:

1. Cook the beef in a very hot frying pan, on the
barbecue or even in a wok (as the Thai cooks do). Cook
to your liking (rare to well done), then leave to one
side covered with foil—adding the beef to the salad
still warm is as good as adding it cold.

2. In a large bowl, squash the tomatoes to release
their juice. Add remaining salad ingredients.

3. For the dressing, a mortar and pestle is
recommended to smash the garlic and sugar together,
then pound in the chilli before adding the liquid.
However, chopping and smashing with a knife will yield
a similar result.

4. Slice the beef. Mix the beef into the salad with
the dressing. Serve and eat as soon as the dressing
is added. Dress the salad too soon and all the crisp
greens will wilt, and quickly.

HINTS AND TIPS:

* You will need—cutting board, cook's knife, frying pan or wok or barbecue, large bowl and mortar and pestle, spoon and cup measures.

* Why use rump or sirloin steak in this dish? Flavour. Certainly feel free to use fillet steak to guarantee tenderness, but you will be sacrificing flavour.

* Tatsoi leaf is a small, dark, round, juicy, non-bitter leaf used in Asian salads, stir-fries and soup. It is sold loose or as a head, like a lettuce. Substitute with mizuna leaf or mixed lettuce leaf, or be bold and omit tatsoi or lettuce, adding extra herbs including Vietnamese mint.

* It is important when washing the herbs and lettuce that they are drained thoroughly as residual water will dilute the all-important dressing. I suggest a salad spinner, available in all kitchenware shops.

* Flavour and texture can be enhanced by the addition of 1 teaspoon roughly chopped galangal (do not substitute with ginger).

* Adding 2 very finely shredded kaffir lime leaves to the salad will also create a new dimension. Kaffir lime leaves grow as two leaves joined end to end to make one. Therefore, when asked for 2 leaves, you are really adding 4.

* Toasting 1 tablespoon raw, unsalted peanuts until lightly golden, cooling, then roughly crushing and adding to the salad just before serving will add new crunch to this amazing salad. Blanch the peanuts and cool before toasting to remove some bitterness and give a much cleaner peanut flavour and crunch. It is recommended to toast the nuts in peanut oil to give an even-coloured result.

* Substitute the red shallots for half a small red onion.

* An excellent addition to this salad is 1 tablespoon raw jasmine rice, toasted in a pan until evenly browned, then crushed in a mortar and pestle or in a spice grinder. Do not grind too fine, instead grind to the consistency of very coarse sand. Sprinkle over the salad just before serving.

* Handling hot chilli should be done with great care, the seeds and the white ribs the seeds are attached to is where the heat is concentrated. Caution must therefore be taken not to touch soft areas of skin on your body as the burning effect will last for 30 minutes to 1 hour, no matter how long you wash the burning area in cold water. Food handling gloves are recommended. Try rubbing your hands with the inner part of the discarded lime shell (after squeezing juice from the limes) once the chilli is dealt with.

VEAL SCHNITZEL

Serves 4

XXXXXXXXXXXXXXXXXXXXXXXXXXXXXXXXXXXXXXXXXXXXXXXXXXXXXXXXXXXXXXXXXXXXXXXXXXXXXXXXXXXXXXXXX

4 veal scaloppine (escalopes), about 150 g each
1 cup plain flour
1 teaspoon salt
½ teaspoon pepper
2 eggs, lightly beaten
2 tablespoons milk
2 cups dried bread crumbs
200 ml olive oil
1 lemon, cut into wedges

Method:

1. Place a double thickness of plastic wrap on a
cutting board, place a piece of veal on the plastic
then place another double thickness of plastic wrap
over the veal and lightly flatten with a meat mallet.
The plastic wrap helps to prevent the meat from
tearing and also saves on cleaning the mallet and meat
from the board. Repeat the process until all the meat
is done.

2. Line up 3 bowls on the bench. In the first bowl,
combine the flour, salt and pepper. In the second bowl,
mix the eggs and milk. The last bowl is for the bread
crumbs.

3. Dip each piece of veal first in the flour, then
in the egg mixture and finally in the bread crumbs,
pressing the bread crumbs on to cover and stick
properly. Set on a tray in the refrigerator for
10 minutes.

4. Heat 100 ml of the oil in a nonstick frying pan
over medium heat and cook half the veal for 2 minutes
on one side, turn and cook for another minute. Drain
on paper towels. Heat the remaining olive oil and cook
the remaining veal. If the pan is large enough, all
the veal may be cooked in one batch using less oil.
Serve with lemon wedges.

HINTS AND TIPS:

* You will need—cutting board, cook's knife, plastic wrap, meat mallet, 3 bowls, nonstick frying pan, paper towel, cup, liquid and spoon measures.

* The veal in this recipe can be substituted for chicken breast, sliced in half and gently flattened. Pork loin or fillet can also be used, again, flatten to the same thickness as the veal before crumbing.

* Veal Schnitzel is also known as Wiener schnitzel.

* Veal schnitzel topped with **Napoli (tomato) sauce** and cheese is a pub staple known as **veal parmigiana**. After cooking both sides of the schnitzel, top one side with 2 tablespoons Napoli sauce then sprinkle with 1 tablespoon of your favourite grated cheese—tasty, mozzarella, parmesan or pecorino to name a few. Place on a baking tray and heat under a grill until the cheese melts or place in a hot oven (220°C) for 5 minutes or until the cheese melts. In the UK, it will be topped with a white sauce and cheese and then melted under the grill.

* For **veal Holstein**—top each veal schnitzel with a fried egg and 2 anchovy fillets over the egg.

* Veal schnitzel served with a **mushroom sauce** becomes **Veal Jäger**.

* For **Veal Cordon Bleu** (Blue Ribbon)—you will require 4 slices of good melting cheese like gruyère, Swiss or even tasty cheese, as well as 4 slices of ham. Use a meat mallet to pound the veal until 2 mm thin. Place a piece of cheese and ham at one end, fold the veal over to cover the ham and cheese. Dip in plain flour, then into beaten eggs (2) and finally 1 cup of bread crumbs. Rest in the fridge for 1 hour before pan frying in some butter and oil.

* For great flavour, rub 1 tablespoon crushed garlic into the bread crumbs, then add ½ cup grated parmesan cheese and 2 tablespoons chopped flat-leaf parsley—the results are amazing.

* Try making your own **bread crumbs**. Heat the oven to 110°C, place 12 slices of bread, crust on (white, wholegrain or wholemeal) directly onto the oven racks and leave until completely dry. Roughly break the dry bread into a food processor and blitz until it resembles bread crumbs. Use only what is needed and store the remainder in a freezer bag or plastic container in the freezer until needed. Storing the bread crumbs in the freezer will ensure they do not turn stale and will therefore last at least 6 months in great condition.

----
xxxxxxxxxxxx **7. Vegetables** xxxxxxxxxxxx

BAKED POTATO IN CREAM

Serves 4

XXXXXXXXXXXXXXXXXXXXXXXXXXXXXXXXXXXXXXXXXXXXXXXXXXXXXXXXXXXXXXXXXXXXXXXXXXXXXXXXXXXXXXXXXXXXXXXXXXXX

500 g potato, peeled and very thinly sliced
150 ml thickened cream
60 g parmesan cheese, grated
pinch of freshly grated nutmeg
salt and cayenne pepper
60 g parmesan or gruyère cheese, grated

Method:

1. Preheat the oven to 160°C.

2. To get the potatoes thin enough for this dish, it is best to cut them with a V-slicer or a mandoline. It is important to cut the potatoes as thinly as possible.

3. Mix together the cream, parmesan, nutmeg, salt and cayenne pepper to taste. Add the very finely sliced potato, making sure cream is smothered over all pieces to ensure that the cream to potato ratio is right.

4. Pour into a baking dish that will allow the potato to sit a least 2.5 cm thick. Top with more parmesan or gruyère cheese. Bake in the oven for 40–45 minutes.

5. Although fine to serve immediately from the oven, this dish is especially good made the day before, cut into shapes and reheated in the microwave.

HINTS AND TIPS:

* You will need—cutting board, cook's knife, vegetable peeler, 'V' slicer or mandoline, weight and liquid measures and baking dish.

* The use of a 'V' slicer or a mandoline is paramount to the success of this dish. To cut by hand is something even professionals would not attempt. This is due to the thickness of the potatoes when sliced. If too thick, the potatoes cook unevenly and, even if cooked through, tend to impart a raw potato flavour to the finished dish. The potatoes need to be almost see-through thin.

* This is a rich accompaniment to any special dinner party and is not something that is made on a regular basis.

* If making for the next day, line the base of the dish with baking paper. This will allow you to tip the baked potato out and cut into squares, triangles or circles which can be heated separately if not wanting to reheat the whole dish.

* The cream can be substituted with sour cream.

* Pontiac potatoes are a good varietal to use in this dish.

* Once baked, if the top hasn't browned and formed a crust, then place it under the grill for a few minutes or until crispy brown.

BUBBLE-AND-SQUEAK

Serves 4

xxxxxxxxxxxxxxxxxxxxxxxxxxxxxxxxxxxxxxxxxxxxxxxxxxxxxxxxxxxxxxxxxxxxxxxxxxxxxxxxxxxxxxxxxxxxx

500 g leftover roasted vegetables (potato, pumpkin,
   carrot and parsnip)
250 g cabbage or brussel sprouts
150 g butter
salt and pepper

Method:

1. Chop or crush the cold, leftover vegetables and set
aside.

2. Shred the cabbage or slice the brussel sprouts and
add to the vegetables.

3. Heat a frying pan over medium heat then add the
butter. As the butter melts and begins to foam, add
all the vegetables. With a wooden spoon, mix together.

4. Season with salt and pepper. After about 8 minutes,
the bubble-and-squeak will be hot and the base will
have cooked to form one large patty. Continue to cook,
without stirring, for a couple of minutes so the base
gets brown and crispy. Serve immediately.

HINTS AND TIPS:

* You will need—cutting board, cook's knife, weight measure, bowls, frying pan or sauté pan and wooden spoon.

* This is a classic British leftovers dish. Traditionally served hot with cold meat and pickles, it has become trendy in some restaurants whose chefs roast their favourite vegetables specifically to make a version of this comfort food.

* The cabbage or brussel spouts can be omitted altogether. If you like, you can add 4 spring onions (finely sliced) to the mixture as it cooks.

* To cut back on saturated fats, fry in olive oil (100 ml) instead of the butter, then once cooked, drizzle about 50 ml extra virgin olive oil over the top and sprinkle with some freshly cut flat-leaf parsley.

* To add some saturated fats, when frying bacon, keep the fat in a container in the fridge. Then use 2 tablespoons bacon fat to fry the bubble-and-squeak— nasty but delicious!

* This dish is truly open to interpretation and any combination of cooked vegetables can be reheated in this fashion. However, it is worth remembering that potato and/or pumpkin should be used to act as a binding agent. Basically, as the potato and/ or pumpkin reheat, they break up and mash slightly, holding all the other ingredients together.

* This is a great breakfast dish and once cooked can be moulded into egg rings. Then fry some eggs and place over the top of the bubble-and-squeak.

* Leftover roasted vegetables—as fantastic as they are in bubble-and-squeak—can be used equally as well in a **frittata** and served for breakfast, or for lunch with a light **green salad**.

CORN ON THE COB

Serves 4

XXXXXXXXXXXXXXXXXXXXXXXXXXXXXXXXXXXXXXXXXXXXXXXXXXXXXXXXXXXXXXXXXXXXXXXXXXXXXXXXXXXXXXXXXXXXX

4 ears of sweet corn, husks and silks removed
salt and pepper
1 tablespoon butter (optional)

Method:

1. In a large pot, bring plenty of water to the boil.

2. Add the corn, bring back to the boil, then reduce the heat to low.

3. Simmer the corn for 5 minutes or longer if you like the corn to be softer. Cooking the corn for 5–10 minutes ensures the corn kernels stay crisp and juicy. The longer the corn is simmered, the more juice will be cooked from it, leaving a soft, less sweet and tasty cob of corn.

4. Remove from the simmering water and season with salt and pepper and a knob of butter if desired.

HINTS AND TIPS:

* You will need—saucepan and spoon measure (optional).

* It has been said that adding 'a small amount of sugar to the boiling water' enhances the natural sweetness of the corn, but this is still unfounded chemistry.

* Adding salt to the water in the beginning can affect the cooking time of the corn by toughening the kernels' outer layer, so it is advised not to add salt at this point, but rather season once removed from the water.

* The corn can be seasoned with chilli powder or sumac, which is a sour berry ground to a powder—originally from the Middle East—to suit individual taste.

* Grilling corn on a barbecue hotplate or baking in a hot oven (210°C) requires corn with the husks still intact so as to steam the corn within. Peel the husks back to the stem and remove the silks. Rub with butter or drizzle with olive oil, and season with salt and pepper. Pull husks back over the kernels and tie the ends with cooking twine. Drop in cold water for 2 minutes before placing on the barbecue; this will stop the husks from burning before the corn is cooked. Allow 15 minutes cooking time, turning regularly before serving.

* Leftover cooked corn can be refrigerated for up to 5 days. At any point the kernels can be removed with a knife or grated using a hand grater, then used in **stir-fry**, **fried rice**, **corn fritters**, **bubble-and-squeak**, **chicken and sweet corn soup**, or **chowder**.

* Once the corn has been removed from the boiling water, it can be placed in cold water to halt the cooking process.

* If preparing a large dinner or banquet, the cob can be cut into rounds about 2 cm thick either before or after boiling; these are easier to eat than a large cob and add colour to the plate.

* To clean the cob—grab the husks with as much of the silks as possible and peel down. Once you have pulled away the husks, some of the silk will remain on the cob. To remove, hold one end of the cob and grasp the other end and twist while running your hand along the length of the cob.

* Corn can be microwaved by placing in a bowl with just enough water (about 2 tablespoons) to cover the base of the dish; then cover with plastic wrap and cook on high for 6 minutes; turn the cob after 3 minutes.

PICKLED VEGETABLES

Makes about 3½ kg

xxxxxxxxxxxxxxxxxxxxxxxxxxxxxxxxxxxxxxxxxxxxxxxxxxxxxxxxxxxxxxxxxxxxxxxxxxxxxxxxxxxxxxxxxxxx

500 g green capsicum, seeded and cut into strips
600 g carrots, cleaned and cut into thin strips
1 medium cauliflower, broken into florets
1 cup cooking salt
2 cups distilled white vinegar
2 cups water
½ cup white sugar
4 garlic cloves, sliced
1 bay leaf
2 teaspoons dill seeds
2 teaspoons celery seeds
2 teaspoons yellow mustard seeds
1 teaspoon crushed dried chilli flakes

Method:

1. Combine all the vegetables and the salt in a large
mixing bowl. Cover with ice; let stand for 3 hours.
Drain the vegetables; rinse very well.

2. Combine the vinegar, water, sugar, garlic and
spices in a large saucepan. Cover and bring to the
boil. Remove the lid, add the vegetables, remove
the pan from the heat and allow to cool to room
temperature.

3. Pack into sterilised jars, leaving about 1.2 cm
space at the top of the jar. Remove air bubbles by
gently tapping the jar on the bench. Screw on caps
and store in a cool place until needed. Once opened,
refrigerate.

HINTS AND TIPS:

★ You will need—cutting board, cook's knife, vegetable peeler, cup, spoon and weight measures, large bowl, colander or strainer, large saucepan or pot and jars with lids.

★ Always choose vegetables of the best quality when pickling. This means firm, ripe but not too ripe, and blemish-free vegetables. If there are imperfections, remove them before cooking.

★ The idea of salting the vegetables before they are pickled is to draw out natural water contained in the vegetables. This water would otherwise dilute the pickling solution during storage, which in turn will diminish the preserving quality.

★ Use cooking salt in this recipe as table salt contains a 'free-flowing' chemical which can make the vinegar turn cloudy.

★ Other styles of vinegar can be used—especially recommended are wine vinegar, malt vinegar (contains gluten) and cider vinegar.

★ This recipe can also be used for pickling just cauliflower.

★ The spices in this mixture can stay loose in the solution, even when bottling; be aware, however, that they will continue to impart flavour and may even be too strong if storing the vegetables for a lengthy period. As a suggestion, tie the spices in a piece of muslin cloth and remove once the vegetables have cooled and are ready for bottling.

★ Do not boil the pickling solution for too long. Vinegar is an acetic acid that is volatile and loses strength when boiled for even short periods.

★ When pickling, the liquid solution is best at 50 per cent vinegar and 50 per cent water, and the combined weight of the liquid should equal the total weight of the vegetables.

★ It is a good idea to label the jars with the ingredients and the date they were packed.

★ Store in a cool place away from sunlight as light causes a loss of colour in the vegetables. Mould will also develop if the vegetables are not completely submerged in the pickling solution.

★ Always try and store the pickled vegetables for 4—6 weeks prior to using. This time in storage will help the flavours mellow and combine perfectly.

★ Serve pickled vegetables as part of an antipasto plate with salami, **frittata**, grilled mushrooms and some leafy greens.

POTATO MASH
Serves 6-8

xxxxxxxxxxxxxxxxxxxxxxxxxxxxxxxxxxxxxxxxxxxxxxxxxxxxxxxxxxxxxxxxxxxxxxxxxxxxxxxxxxxxxxxxxxxxxxx

1.5 kg Sebago or Pontiac potatoes, peeled and quartered
salt
50 g butter
150 ml cream
freshly ground white pepper

Method:

1. Boil the potatoes in lightly salted water until tender. Drain.

2. Heat the butter and cream in the microwave or in a saucepan.

3. Use a whisk or potato masher to mash the potatoes, pour in the hot cream and butter, add salt and pepper, and whisk until light in texture. Serve immediately.

HINTS AND TIPS:

* You will need—cutting board, cook's knife, vegetable peeler, large pot, weight and liquid measures, whisk or potato masher and a bowl or small pot to heat cream and butter.

* This style of mash is very smooth and rich and is often the very reason customers in a restaurant are inspired to try and make their mash the same. To be fair, this style of mash is not normal, domestically at least.

* Usually, mash made at home is done with milk and butter, often added cold. If cream seems a bit too much, then use milk—but the real secret is in the heating of the milk and butter. By doing this, there is less chance of the mash being overly lumpy.

* Another good tip to avoid lumpy mash is to invest in what's called a 'potato ricer' or a 'mouli', both of which are tools preferred by the professional cook. An extra—or an extreme—step is to pass the already processed potato through a fine meshed 'drum' sieve. After that, the hot butter and cream are added. Crazy . . . but brilliant at the same time.

* For the health conscious, we have an alternative for you too. Replace the cream and butter with 200 ml extra virgin olive oil. It may seem like a lot but for 1.5 kg potato, it really is just enough. If the flavour of extra virgin olive oil is too strong, then simply use a good olive oil.

* Mashed potato can be stored, covered in the refrigerator for 5 days. To reheat, use the microwave on medium power to avoid burning the potato near the outside of the dish. Alternatively, reheat in a saucepan with an extra dollop of butter or cream.

* Never use a food processor to mash potatoes thinking you will get a smoother texture. All you will get is a pasty batch of potato glue that for some reason still has small lumps in it. The problem with a food processor is that it works the potato starch too vigorously, making a sticky, white mess instead of a fluffy white mash.

* Use white pepper in mash to avoid unsightly specks of black pepper.

* Other good mashing potatoes include—Desiree, Spunta, Delaware, Bison and Toolangi Delight.

* Cold mash is a great base for lentil or chickpea burgers.

RATATOUILLE

Serves 8

XXXXXXXXXXXXXXXXXXXXXXXXXXXXXXXXXXXXXXXXXXXXXXXXXXXXXXXXXXXXXXXXXXXXXXXXXXXXXXXXXXXXXXXXXXXXXX

2 medium eggplants
2 zucchini
1 tablespoon cooking salt
1 large brown onion
3 garlic cloves
3 large ripe tomatoes
1 red capsicum
100 ml olive oil
1 bay leaf
salt and pepper

Method:

1. To prepare the vegetables—cut the eggplant and zucchini into 2-cm dice. Place in a bowl and sprinkle with the salt, cover and set aside for 30 minutes.

2. Peel and finely dice the onion and garlic and set aside.

3. Remove the stem end of the tomato with a paring knife and score the skin at the top with a cross (X). Place the tomatoes in a bowl and cover with boiling water from the kettle. Remove after 20 seconds and peel. Slice in half, remove and discard any seeds. Dice the tomatoes and set aside.

4. Cut the capsicum in half and remove the stem, seeds and any white 'ribs'. Dice the capsicum to the same size as the tomatoes, eggplant and zucchini.

5. Wash and drain the eggplant and zucchini and pat dry.

6. To cook—heat the olive oil in a large pot, add the onion and garlic and cook for 3–5 minutes on low–medium heat without colouring. Add the remaining ingredients, cover with a lid and cook over low heat for 1 hour. Season with salt and pepper and serve.

HINTS AND TIPS:

★ You will need—cutting board, cook's knife, paring knife, liquid measures, bowls, large, heavy-based pot with lid and wooden spoon.

★ Ratatouille is an excellent accompaniment for grilled and roasted meats. It also serves well as a main dish on its own.

★ Leftover ratatouille can be used with pasta or for **vegetarian lasagne**. As a pasta sauce, either keep chunky or blitz in a food processor.

★ Served cold it makes for an excellent salad either on its own or mixed with some cooked and cooled pasta.

★ Salting the eggplant and zucchini is optional. The idea is to draw out excess moisture which would otherwise dilute the sauce as it cooks. Excess moisture in the ratatouille can be cooked out; continue to simmer the dish until it is thick.

★ Fresh tomatoes can be substituted for a can of chopped tomatoes (400 g).

★ Serve cold ratatouille with grilled ciabatta, a squeeze of lemon juice and a drizzle of extra virgin olive oil.

★ Add fresh herbs at the end of cooking. Basil, parsley or oregano can be stirred into the ratatouille with 2 minutes of cooking to go.

★ Covered and refrigerated, this dish will keep for at least 5 days.

ROASTED VEGETABLES

Serves 6

xxxxxxxxxxxxxxxxxxxxxxxxxxxxxxxxxxxxxxxxxxxxxxxxxxxxxxxxxxxxxxxxxxxxxxxxxxxxxxxxxxxxxxxxxxxxx

4 medium potatoes, peeled
300 g pumpkin, peeled and seeds removed
2 carrots, peeled
1 parsnip, peeled
1 sweet potato, peeled
2 medium beetroot, washed
1 brown onion
4 garlic cloves, left whole in their skins
½ cup olive oil
1 teaspoon salt
2 teaspoons dried rosemary

Method:

1. Preheat the oven to 180°C.

2. Cut all the vegetables into even-sized pieces, generally quarters and eighths provide the best roasting size.

3. Place all the ingredients in a baking dish and mix thoroughly with the garlic, olive oil, salt and rosemary.

4. Roast for 45 minutes or until cooked through and crisp, turning once or twice.

HINTS AND TIPS:

* You will need—cutting board, cook's knife, paring knife, vegetable peeler, cup and spoon measures and bowl.

* The vegetables listed are only suggestions, you can mix and match to your particular taste but be mindful that if you are combining root vegetables with soft vegetables, their cooking times differ. So if you are combining both, cut the root vegetables smaller than the soft vegetables to even out the roasting time.

* Other soft vegetables can be roasted separately to the hard root vegetables. A combination of zucchini, eggplant, capsicum, cherry tomatoes, mushrooms, shallots and garlic cloves can be pan-fried in plenty of olive oil to add colour before transferring to a roasting tray to soften for 20 minutes. Serve immediately or cool completely and mix with pesto to serve as a salad.

* All vegetables can be roasted to a softer texture rather than crispy; ½ cup of any stock added to the baking dish before roasting will do this.

* If roasting potatoes on their own, it is highly recommended to peel and quarter the potatoes and simmer them in salted water until tender. Drain and toss in olive oil before roasting for 20 minutes at 200°C.

* Fresh herbs are always best but not necessary for this dish.

* Add 2 tablespoons passata (smooth tomato sauce) for colour and a hint of flavour.

* You can test if the vegetables are ready by inserting a skewer—if it passes easily through, then they are ready.

* Leftover roasted vegetables can be used to make **bubble-and-squeak**. It is a good idea to double the amount so there are leftovers which could also be used in a roasted vegetable salad with a **simple vinaigrette** or **mayonnaise**.

VEGETABLE AND NOODLE STIR-FRY

Serves 2

xxxxxxxxxxxxxxxxxxxxxxxxxxxxxxxxxxxxxxxxxxxxxxxxxxxxxxxxxxxxxxxxxxxxxxxxxxxxxxxxxxxxxxxxxxxxxxxx

400 g mixed vegetables, equal quantities
¼ cup peanut oil
4 garlic cloves, very finely sliced
150 ml chicken or vegetable stock, hot
4 tablespoons oyster sauce
2 tablespoons light soy sauce
1 tablespoon sesame oil
½ teaspoon finely ground black pepper
500 g fresh noodles (hokkien, rice, egg, flat, thin
    or thick), rinsed in hot water and drained

Method:

1. Cut or slice the vegetables into bite-sized pieces.
Mix in a bowl and cover with boiling water. Drain
after 20 seconds.

2. Heat a wok until smoking lightly. Add the peanut
oil, then the garlic. Very quickly add the vegetables
before the garlic burns. Stir the vegetables, do not
toss, as too much heat will be lost.

3. Add the hot stock and cook for 2–3 minutes. Add the
sauces, sesame oil and pepper. Then add the noodles
and mix well. Serve immediately or cook for a further
1–2 minutes if vegetables are still too crisp.

HINTS AND TIPS:

★ You will need—cutting board, cook's knife, bowl or 2 for the vegetables, wok, wok spatula, and cup, liquid, weight and spoon measures.

★ See the tips on stir-fries—wok cooking in Really Useful Information.

★ This recipe serves 2, doubling the recipe is fine but the ingredients will need to be cooked in 2 batches. Too much heat from the wok is lost with the addition of a large amount of food and this tends to stew the ingredients, overcooking the noodles and making the dish gluggy.

★ Always use maximum heat under the wok.

★ Blanching and draining the vegetables ensures rapid cooking times.

★ The best place to buy fresh noodles is at an Asian grocer, not at the supermarket (they contain too many preservatives).

★ Almost any combination of vegetables can be used for stir-fry, depending on what's in season and personal preference. Try baby corn, carrot, purple carrot, broccoli, broccoli stems, broccolini, cauliflower, young kale, baby spinach, rocket, snow pea shoots, tatsoi, fresh mushrooms, dried mushrooms (reconstituted), snow peas, sugar snap peas, bean sprouts, spring onions, onion, chives, capsicum, rhubarb, snake beans, green beans, eggplant, zucchini, celery, Chinese cabbage, bok choy, Chinese broccoli, bamboo shoots, water chestnuts, or sponge gourd.

★ Herbs and spices include—coriander, coriander root, basil, Asian basil varieties, lemon grass, white pepper, Sichuan pepper, ginger, or galangal. Add any fresh herbs to the wok with 10 seconds to go.

★ To make a **chilli stir-fry**—finely chop fresh chilli to taste and add with the garlic in the above recipe.

VEGETARIAN LASAGNE

Serves 8

XXXXXXXXXXXXXXXXXXXXXXXXXXXXXXXXXXXXXXXXXXXXXXXXXXXXXXXXXXXXXXXXXXXXXXXXXXXXXXXXXXXXXXXXXXXX

100 ml olive oil
1 large brown onion, finely diced
4 garlic cloves, crushed
1 large eggplant, diced
200 g button mushrooms, chopped
250 ml white wine
2 x 400 g cans diced tomatoes
2 tablespoons tomato paste
1 carrot, peeled and grated
1 tablespoon dried oregano
1 teaspoon salt
freshly ground black pepper
¼ bunch fresh flat-leaf parsley, chopped
lasagne sheets
500 g firm ricotta cheese
150 g parmesan cheese, grated

Method:

1. In a large pot over medium heat, add the oil, onion and garlic and cook without colouring for 5 minutes. Add the eggplant and mushrooms and continue to cook until softened, about 15 minutes.

2. Add the white wine and reduce by half. Then add the tomatoes, tomato paste, carrot and oregano. Bring to the boil then reduce heat to a simmer and cook, covered, for 30 minutes. Remove the lid and continue to cook until the sauce thickens.

3. Add salt and pepper to taste, remove from the heat and stir in the parsley.

4. Place some of the sauce in the base of a lasagne dish, sprinkle with some ricotta and a small amount of parmesan then top with a layer of pasta sheets. Repeat with 3 more layers. Spread the remaining sauce over the top, and sprinkle with the parmesan.

5. Bake in a preheated 180°C oven for about 45 minutes.

HINTS AND TIPS:

* You will need—cutting board, cook's knife, vegetable peeler, large, heavy-based pot, wooden spoon, lasagne dish, weight, spoon and liquid measures and grater.

* A good alternative to this method is to chargrill vegetables on the barbecue and layer them in the dish. Use roasted capsicum, zucchini, eggplant and potatoes. A quick fix is to visit the local delicatessen and buy the grilled vegetables already done. Then use a pasta sauce to save time.

* Use different cheeses for interesting changes to the base lasagne. Try buffalo mozzarella, goat's cheese, cheddar, fetta or a Dutch smoked cheese.

* Make a traditional **béchamel sauce** or **mornay sauce** to pour over the finished lasagne. You will need about 1 litre for the above recipe. Drizzle some of the hot béchamel sauce in between each layer.

* The combination of vegetables in a vegetarian lasagne can be as basic or as complicated as you want.

* A simple **mushroom lasagne** might consist of 50 g dried porcini mushrooms soaked in hot water for 30 minutes, and 500 g fresh portobello mushrooms, and 500 g button or field mushrooms, both sliced and fried in plenty of butter, olive oil and garlic. Layer with an excellent béchamel sauce and top with freshly grated parmesan cheese.

* Lasagne can be assembled well in advance and cooked when needed. It will also freeze well once assembled. Defrost in the refrigerator overnight before baking in a preheated oven.

* Leftover cooked lasagne reheats well. Simply cover with foil and reheat in a 150°C oven for 30 minutes, or microwave on medium for several minutes or until hot.

ZUCCHINI SLICE

Serves 12

xxxxxxxxxxxxxxxxxxxxxxxxxxxxxxxxxxxxxxxxxxxxxxxxxxxxxxxxxxxxxxxxxxxxxxxxxxxxxxxxxxxxxxxxxxxx

450 g zucchini (approximately 3 medium)
5 eggs, lightly beaten
150 g plain flour
100 ml olive oil
50 g tasty cheese, grated
salt and pepper

Method:

1. Preheat the oven to 170°C. Line a baking dish or slice pan with baking paper.

2. Remove the top and end of the zucchini and grate. Gently squeeze out excess moisture to prevent the slice from being too wet. Place in a bowl and add the remaining ingredients. Mix thoroughly and check the seasoning.

3. Pour the mixture into the prepared baking dish and bake for 35 minutes or until the top is golden and the middle is firm to the touch.

HINTS AND TIPS:

★ You will need—cutting board, cook's knife, grater, bowl, weight and liquid measures, wooden spoon, baking dish (about 28 cm x 18 cm) and baking paper.

★ This is a very basic recipe for zucchini slice, anything else added constitutes it being called a zucchini and (fill in the blank) slice. A popular version is **zucchini and bacon slice**—dice 1 small onion and 2 bacon rashers and fry in 2 tablespoons olive oil until softened and lightly coloured. Cool before mixing into the raw zucchini mixture.

★ When squeezing the excess moisture from the grated zucchini, do not be tempted to wring it dry as it will render the slice too dry. A gentle squeeze over the sink is all it needs.

★ Zucchini are available all year round. Be sure to buy only firm, glossy looking zucchini and wipe thoroughly with a damp cloth before grating.

★ Large zucchini tend to be dry, fluffy and seedy on the inside and are not as flavoursome as the smaller, sweeter ones.

★ Flour is one of the binding agents in this recipe. Gluten-intolerant cooks or coeliacs can replace the flour with 1 cup grated potato, also squeezed of excess moisture before adding to the grated zucchini.

★ The use of self-raising flour, although compatible, will give the slice some rise and therefore have it looking more like a savoury cake than a tasty, thin slice.

★ Zucchini slice is an excellent after-school snack or light lunch served with a **green salad**.

★ Add 2 tablespoons fresh herbs to the mixture—try basil, parsley, dill or thyme.

★ Try toasting ½ cup pine nuts and stir into the mixture before baking.

★ Top the slice with 1 cup grated parmesan cheese before placing in the oven for a cheese crust.

★ Covered and refrigerated, zucchini slice will last for 5 days. It can be frozen but the texture will change slightly so is best consumed fresh.

----
xxxxxxxxxxxxx 8. Salads xxxxxxxxxxxxx

CAESAR SALAD

Serves 4

XXXXXXXXXXXXXXXXXXXXXXXXXXXXXXXXXXXXXXXXXXXXXXXXXXXXXXXXXXXXXXXXXXXXXXXXXXXXXXXXXXXXXXXXXXXXXXXX

4 slices white bread, ciabatta or sourdough
4 bacon rashers
2 tablespoons vegetable or safflower oil
4 cos lettuce or 2 baby cos (see **Hints and tips**)
Caesar dressing
75 g good parmesan cheese, shaved

Method:

1. Dice the bread into 2-cm cubes and cook according
to **croutons** recipe.

2. Cut the bacon into 5-mm strips and fry in the oil
until crispy, drain on paper towel.

3. Remove all the dark outer leaves if using large
cos. Wash and dry the inner leaves, preferably using a
lettuce spinner, and tear into a large salad bowl.

4. Add the croutons and bacon and mix in the Caesar
dressing. Serve with shaved Parmesan over the top.

HINTS AND TIPS:

* You will need—cutting board, cook's knife, bread knife, sauté pan, vegetable peeler, weight and spoon measures, large salad bowl, equipment to make the Caesar dressing and a salad spinner if available.

* Like all great dishes, the quality of the ingredients is paramount to a successful outcome. Good bread made into crispy, dry croutons is very important to help soak up the dressing as well as adding texture. Great quality bacon and parmesan cheese are equally important in balancing the flavours of this decadent salad.

* Regular, large cos lettuces have met some aggressive competition from a new cultivar—the baby cos. Old school cos is at a disadvantage because of the waste factor. All the dark and slightly bitter outer leaves are discarded in search of the light green and sweet inner leaves. A few of the outer leaves can be used in other salads or in sandwiches and rolls, but ultimately they are a forsaken food. Baby cos has about 1 per cent wastage, 1 or 2 outer leaves at worst are sacrificed as the remaining lettuce is put to good use. Baby cos are readily available from supermarkets and green grocers everywhere.

* There are plenty of hints and tips in the recipe for **Caesar dressing**.

* To make a **special Caesar salad**, try adding crispy shards of prosciutto. Purchase thinly sliced prosciutto from a deli—2 slices per person. Place on a baking tray lined with baking paper and bake in the oven at 180°C for 5–10 minutes or until shrivelled slightly and browned; they will go crunchy once cooled.

* Add a **poached egg** to finish off the special Caesar salad.

* If you are a fan of anchovies, drape an extra anchovy over each salad before serving.

* Chargrill the baby cos lettuce briefly. Slice the lettuce in half, keeping the root end intact so the leaves stay attached. Spray with olive oil spray, season with salt and pepper, and place on the chargrill of the barbecue. Cook for 1 minute, place in a serving bowl, drizzle with dressing and top with a poached egg, crispy prosciutto and shaved parmesan.

CHEF'S SALAD

Serves 4–6

xxxxxxxxxxxxxxxxxxxxxxxxxxxxxxxxxxxxxxxxxxxxxxxxxxxxxxxxxxxxxxxxxxxxxxxxxxxxxxxxxxxxxxxxxxxxxx

250 g piece best quality ham
250 g piece cooked turkey breast
200 g vintage cheddar cheese
250 g cherry or grape tomatoes
1 Lebanese cucumber
2 baby cos lettuce
1 cup purchased whole egg mayonnaise
juice of 1 lemon
salt and pepper

Method:

1. Slice or dice the ham, turkey and cheese. Place in a large salad bowl.

2. Add the tomatoes. Slice the cucumber in half lengthways and then slice into 5-mm thick half moons.

3. Wash and dry the lettuce, tear into pieces and add to the salad bowl.

4. For the dressing—in a small, separate bowl, whisk the mayonnaise with the lemon juice and salt and pepper to taste. Check the consistency, which should resemble pouring cream. Add some water to thin the dressing if needed.

5. Pour the dressing over the salad and mix.

HINTS AND TIPS:

* You will need—cutting board, cook's knife, 2 bowls, whisk, mixing spoons, cup and weight measures.

* Chef's salad is said to originate in the US. After that fact, it is very sketchy as to how, where and when it came about. My own guess is that it came into being because many chefs just throw a bunch of handy ingredients together for a quick bite to eat during a 14-hour shift with no breaks. Sometimes the resulting feed is tasty enough to put on the menu— although this is a very rare occurrence.

* Chef's salad is the ideal Boxing Day meal. The ingredients smack of way too many leftover proteins from Christmas Day that can be mixed with lettuce and a dressing.

* You can buy whole pieces of ham from the meat section in the supermarket. They are sold as individual pieces, usually about 300 g in size, vacuum packed and called something groovy like 'double smoked' or 'premium leg ham' or 'spiced gypsy'.

* Cooked turkey breast may be a bit harder to find, but check the freezer section in the supermarket. If no pre-cooked stuff is available, buy raw and cook it yourself. Chicken breast makes a worthy substitute.

* Grape tomatoes are an Australian variety developed by Australian horticultural scientists. This product won a gold medal in France for best new product for fruit and vegetables. Based on the Roma tomato, it is packed with flavour and is my favourite small tomato to use.

* Baby cos lettuce is another exceptional product. See Hints and tips in the **Caesar salad** recipe.

* Lebanese cucumbers are great because of their size. They are like a small continental cucumber. So instead of using and possibly wasting half a continental cucumber, the Lebanese cucumber is ideal. They are available at all supermarkets and greengrocers.

* The creamy dressing is just one option. Substitute with a simple dressing of lemon juice and extra virgin olive oil.

* The theme of a chef's salad is ham, turkey and cheese mixed with lettuce and a dressing. Other salad ingredients can be added to your personal taste.

COLESLAW

Serves 4

XXXXXXXXXXXXXXXXXXXXXXXXXXXXXXXXXXXXXXXXXXXXXXXXXXXXXXXXXXXXXXXXXXXXXXXXXXXXXXXXXXXXXXXXXXXXXXXXX

4 cups shredded cabbage
2 carrots, peeled
½ bunch spring onions, wiped with a damp cloth
1 red or green capsicum, halved, seeds and core removed
1 cup **mayonnaise**
salt and pepper

Method:

1. Place the cabbage in a bowl and set aside.

2. Grate the carrots or for the more skilled cook, julienne (fine strips) the carrot and add to the cabbage.

3. Slice the green tops of the spring onions into rounds about 5 mm thick, and slice the white base a bit thinner, about 1–2 mm. Add to the cabbage and carrot.

4. Dice the capsicum, add to the bowl and mix until combined. Keep refrigerated until ready to serve. Just prior to serving, mix in the mayonnaise and season with salt and pepper if needed.

HINTS AND TIPS:

* You will need—cutting board, cook's knife, grater, vegetable peeler, large salad bowl and equipment for mayonnaise.

* The cabbage for coleslaw can vary. The traditional white cabbage is a sturdy, big-tasting cabbage that holds up well, even when dressed, for days and is ideal for picnics and lunches the following day.

* Red cabbage can be used instead of or in combination with the white cabbage, and is also a sturdy cabbage with lasting crunch. Be aware that the natural purple colouring (anthocyanins) will discolour the salad, turning white into lavender.

* Soft cabbages like Savoy and wombok (Chinese cabbage or napa cabbage) are more delicate in flavour and softer in texture, and give a finer shred to the amateur cook. The only downside is that the leaf won't hold as long once dressed and is not as good the next day. If taking on a picnic, make the salad and keep the dressing separate and mix once at the picnic spot.

* Use a simple **vinaigrette** instead of mayonnaise, adding 1 teaspoon sugar to the dressing to counter the acid of the vinegar.

* This basic recipe for coleslaw can have many other combinations. Different chopped or torn herbs can be added like flat-leaf parsley (1 cup), basil (1 cup) or dill (1 cup), depending on what it is served with.

* For a more Asian feel, use wombok then add 1 cup bean sprouts and 1 cup shredded mixed herbs like mint, Thai basil, coriander and Vietnamese mint. Try adding 2 long red chillies (de-seeded and thinly sliced). Use a simple dressing of 2 tablespoons soy sauce, 1 tablespoon sugar, 1 tablespoon sesame oil, 2 tablespoons lime juice and 4 tablespoons peanut oil.

* Onion, garlic and ginger are considered too strong to use in a coleslaw; however, I'm never one to be a naysayer, so if a big bite is required then use small amounts of any or all of these ingredients.

* Coleslaw is not only good as a stand-alone salad, but is fantastic as a filling in sandwiches and rolls.

* A classic coleslaw dressing has more of a sweet and sour flavour. To 1 cup of mayonnaise add 30 ml white wine vinegar and 15 g castor sugar.

FATTOUSH

Serves 6

XXXXXXXXXXXXXXXXXXXXXXXXXXXXXXXXXXXXXXXXXXXXXXXXXXXXXXXXXXXXXXXXXXXXXXXXXXXXXXXXXXXXXXXXXXXXXXXXXXXXXX

2 continental cucumbers
4 vine-ripened tomatoes, cut in half and de-seeded
1 red onion
½ bunch fresh flat-leaf parsley
¼ bunch fresh coriander
½ bunch fresh mint
2 tablespoons olive oil
3 slices pita bread
3 garlic cloves, finely chopped
150 ml extra virgin olive oil
juice of 2 lemons
freshly ground black pepper and sea salt
1 iceberg lettuce, washed and separated into cups

Method:

1. Slice the cucumber in half lengthways, remove the seeds with a teaspoon, then slice into 5-mm thick half moons.

2. Cut the tomato into dice about the same size as the cucumber. Place both in a large bowl.

3. Finely dice the purple onion and add to the tomato and cucumber.

4. Wash the parsley, coriander and mint, and remove the leaves. Roughly tear the leaves and add to the other ingredients.

5. In a large frying pan, heat the olive oil. Tear the pita bread into small, bite-sized pieces. In 2 batches, fry in the hot oil until crisp and golden. Place the fried pita bread on paper towel to drain and allow to cool.

6. To dress the salad—mix the garlic, extra virgin olive oil and lemon juice with the pepper and salt, pour over the salad and add the fried pita bread.

HINTS AND TIPS:

* You will need—cutting board, cook's knife, large mixing spoon, bowl, liquid and spoon measures, large frying pan and tongs.

* This is a traditional Levantine dish. The Levant area borders the Mediterranean Sea with a landmass mostly in the Arabian Peninsula.

* The seeds in the cucumber and tomato are removed for two reasons: primarily to reduce the water content in the salad and prevent the crisp pita bread from becoming soggy; and secondly, the seeds in both ingredients are slightly bitter.

* Sumac can be sprinkled into the salad to give it a different sour note. Reduce the lemon juice by half. Sumac is a small purple berry that is often soaked in water and it is the water that is used instead of lemon juice as a souring agent when lemons are not in season in some Middle Eastern countries.

* To add more bulk to the salad, use some of the leftover iceberg lettuce, shred and mix with the other ingredients.

* To refine the salad slightly to give it a modern restaurant feel, finely dice the ingredients then place a spoonful of the fattoush into a prepared iceberg lettuce cup and serve on individual plates or a platter similar to the way Chinese **san choy bao** is served.

* This salad is a great way to use up stale pita or flat bread and is fantastic to serve in summer with grilled barbecue meats.

* Try adding ½ cup fetta cheese and ¼ cup black olives to the salad.

GREEK SALAD

Serves 4

XXXXXXXXXXXXXXXXXXXXXXXXXXXXXXXXXXXXXXXXXXXXXXXXXXXXXXXXXXXXXXXXXXXXXXXXXXXXXXXXXXXXXXXXXXXXXXXXX

2 Lebanese cucumbers
2 ripe tomatoes, cut into wedges
1 red onion, thinly sliced
2 teaspoons fresh oregano or marjoram, chopped
½ cup olive oil
1 tablespoon red wine vinegar or lemon juice
¼ teaspoon salt flakes

Method:

1. Peel (optional) and slice the cucumbers in half lengthways and then slice into half moons.

2. Place the cucumber, tomato and onion in a bowl and mix in the oregano or marjoram, olive oil, vinegar and salt. Mix to evenly coat the tomatoes and cucumbers.

HINTS AND TIPS:

* You will need—cutting board, cook's knife, spoon and cup measures, bowl and mixing spoon.

* This is a true Greek salad as compiled by a true Greek friend ... read on.

* It is a common misconception that Greek salad has fetta cheese in it. No self-respecting Greek would add fetta, or olives for that matter, to their salad. Fetta is traditionally served on the side, either on its own or sprinkled with oregano and a slick of olive oil. If you must have fetta in your salad, you can leave it as a slab, rather than diced, and place it on top of the salad. Olives are to be enjoyed on their own.

* If you must use fetta, please do not use the Australian variety for this salad. It is often drier and has a rubbery texture. The European varieties bring much more flavour. If you do this, limit the salt you put in the salad because the fetta is already salty.

* In essence, a Greek salad is a simple, uncomplicated combination of the essentials that are often grown in one's vegetable patch. It forms the base of all other salads but these would not necessarily be a Greek salad.

* Another vegetable that is traditionally used is the banana pepper or white pepper—it looks like a large yellow chilli, after all peppers and chillies are both part of the capsicum family. If you are fortunate enough to source banana peppers, slice one lengthways, remove the seeds and membrane just like a red or green pepper, then finely slice crossways and add to the salad. They are sweeter than other peppers.

* Lettuce of any variety can be added but then it would not be a 'pure' Greek salad. Often a lettuce-style Greek salad is served in Western restaurants or for tourists not familiar with the origins of the salad.

* In Greece, the Greek salad is called 'horiatiki' which translates that each village/region has its own version based on what is available. But it is always kept simple and fresh.

* A squeeze of lemon juice can be added for extra zing. Or add 1 tablespoon white wine vinegar to the salad.

* The oil used in the salad should be the best you can source and afford. Extra virgin olive oil is too strong in flavour which is why regular olive oil is suggested.

* Fresh oregano is best but dried is fine in which case use only 1 teaspoon.

* Always keep an empty jam jar on hand to mix dressings by shaking and pouring easily onto salads.

GREEN SALAD

Serves 4

xxxxxxxxxxxxxxxxxxxxxxxxxxxxxxxxxxxxxxxxxxxxxxxxxxxxxxxxxxxxxxxxxxxxxxxxxxxxxxxxxxxxxxxxx

4 large handfuls mixed lettuce leaves
4 tablespoons **vinaigrette**
sea salt and freshly ground black pepper

Method:

1. Wash and dry lettuce (a salad spinner is best).

2. Just before serving toss, with the dressing and season with salt and pepper.

HINTS AND TIPS:

* You will need—spoon measures and salad spinner.

* One of the most important pieces of kitchen equipment for any serious cook is a salad spinner—available at all good kitchen supply stores. It is an invaluable tool for those who love salads or want to improve the art of making salad. The primary reason for using a salad spinner is to remove as much water as possible from the lettuce without damaging the leaf. This is important because excess water will dilute the flavoursome dressing coating the lettuce leaves. Merely shaking off the water will not have the desired results, the dressing will slip off the water-coated leaves and sink to the bottom of the salad bowl.

* Secondary to the dressing being diluted is the storage of the lettuce which increases by several days as the lettuce is not sitting in its own water, becoming waterlogged and rotting.

* A salad spinner is also ideal for drying washed herbs.

* An important fact to remember is to not overload the spinner, a small handful of leafy matter at a time will guarantee great results.

* This green salad is as simple as it gets and might be seen as a little stingy on ingredients. If you feel the need to bulk out the salad with something chunky, try adding only one or two other ingredients to keep it simple, such as avocado, cucumber, fennel, sunflower sprouts, alfalfa, spring onions, chives, or any soft herbs like parsley, chervil, basil or dill.

* The varieties of lettuce and green leaves can be mixed or singular, choose from—rocket, butter, cos, coral, watercress, frisée, radicchio, lamb's lettuce, tatsoi or mizuna.

* The most important factor when putting together a simple green leafy salad is the timing of the dressing and the lettuce coming together. Added too soon and the salad will resemble compost, therefore it is vital that the salad is dressed just before eating. If it means adding the dressing at the dinner table, then do so. If bringing to a picnic, then pack salad leaves separately to the dressing.

* A basic vinaigrette is used in this recipe, but there are many options available. For the busy cook who cannot find time to squeeze ½ lemon and 4 tablespoons olive oil over the salad, then might I suggest a pre-made dressing from the supermarket.

* Remember the many varieties of vinegars available to add different flavour profiles to a basic salad.

* Try a simple yet tasty dressing of 100 g blue cheese mixed with 150 ml hazelnut or walnut oil, juice of ½ lemon and some freshly ground black pepper.

* Lightly steamed green vegetables are another alternative to a green salad. Broccoli, broccolini, green beans, snow peas or broad beans are perfect with this light salad.

NIÇOISE SALAD

Serves 4

XXXXXXXXXXXXXXXXXXXXXXXXXXXXXXXXXXXXXXXXXXXXXXXXXXXXXXXXXXXXXXXXXXXXXXXXXXXXXXXXXXXXXXXXXXXXXXXX

500 g salad potatoes (chat, kipfler or pink)
2 tablespoons cooking salt
400 g green beans, topped
4 eggs
120 ml extra virgin olive oil
40 ml red wine vinegar
2 teaspoons Dijon mustard
sea salt and freshly ground black pepper
450 g can tuna
2 baby cos lettuces, leaves washed and dried
250 g cherry or grape tomatoes, halved
100 g black olives (kalamata or Ligurian)

Method:

1. Place the potatoes in a large saucepan, cover
with cold water, add the salt and bring to the boil,
then reduce the heat to a simmer and cook until just
tender. Drain and cool completely before slicing into
thick rounds.

2. Place the beans in a bowl or pot and cover with
boiling water from the kettle, let stand for
2 minutes. Drain and refresh (cool) under cold water.

3. Place the eggs in a small saucepan of cold water.
Bring to the boil over high heat. Reduce the heat to
low and simmer, uncovered, for 8 minutes. Drain and
cool under cold running water. Peel and quarter.

4. Combine the oil, vinegar and mustard in a jar with
a lid and shake until combined. Add salt and pepper to
taste.

5. Flake the tuna into large pieces and divide between
4 bowls or place in 1 large bowl. Add the potato,
beans, eggs, lettuce, tomatoes and olives. Drizzle
over the dressing.

HINTS AND TIPS:

* You will need—cutting board, cook's knife, weight, liquid and spoon measures, large salad bowl or 4 serving bowls, 2 saucepans, egg timer, mixing spoon and jar with a lid.

* Niçoise salad is a simple, fresh salad originating from the region of Nice, France. There are many variations to the salad, and, of course, this is one of them.

* Traditionally, Niçoise salad is not served with boiled potato or any cooked vegetables. Original versions of this salad speak of raw vegetables, boiled eggs, anchovies, olive oil and tuna.

* Fresh tuna is an excellent way to enhance this dish to make it less of a basic lunch staple and more of a dinner party hit. Fresh tuna should be ordered as 4 x 150 g tuna steaks from the local fish monger. Lightly seal the tuna in a hot pan. It doesn't need to be cooked all the way through to keep it moist and fresh tasting, but if you prefer it well done, just cook it longer until it resembles the canned tuna.

* Once the potatoes are cooked, they need to cool completely to allow the sticky starches to set and become easy to slice.

* Anchovies are often used in a classic Niçoise salad. I recommend using 2 anchovy fillets per person. Take 8 anchovy fillets and chop them roughly before sprinkling over the salad once assembled.

* Mixed lettuce leaves can be used instead of the cos lettuce suggested.

* It is important to dress the salad just moments before serving. Everything can be prepared and ready, in fact, the salad can be mixed in advance, it is just the dressing that doesn't get added until the last minute. The reason for this—as I recommend for all leafy salads—is that the acid (vinegar or lemon juice) and salt in the dressing burn the delicate lettuce leaves and the salt also draws out moisture, making the leaves wilt and go soggy.

* When boiling eggs for a salad, it is best to use eggs that are 1–2 weeks old. Fresh eggs are best for frying, poaching and for scrambling, but are a nightmare to peel. The older the eggs, the more alkaline they become (losing some of their natural carbon dioxide) and the easier they are to peel.

PANZANELLA

Serves 6

xxxxxxxxxxxxxxxxxxxxxxxxxxxxxxxxxxxxxxxxxxxxxxxxxxxxxxxxxxxxxxxxxxxxxxxxxxxxxxxxxxxxxx

1 large ciabatta, French or sourdough loaf, diced
   (2 cm x 2 cm)
150 ml olive oil
1 tablespoon salt flakes
4 vine-ripened tomatoes
3 garlic cloves, finely chopped
100 ml red wine vinegar
250 ml extra virgin olive oil
½ bunch fresh basil leaves
½ bunch fresh flat-leaf parsley leaves
1 red capsicum, roasted, peeled and sliced
1 yellow capsicum, roasted, peeled and sliced
1 tablespoon capers, rinsed and drained
sea salt and freshly ground black pepper
shaved parmesan cheese (optional)

Method:

1. Preheat the oven to 180°C.

2. Toss the bread in the olive oil and salt flakes
and bake for about 15 minutes or until crispy on the
outside and still a bit soft on the inside.

3. Quarter the tomatoes, remove the seeds and coarsely
chop. Place in a large salad bowl, and mix in the
garlic.

4. Place the bread in with the tomato and garlic,
drizzle with the vinegar and oil, and toss well.

5. Add herbs, capsicums and capers; toss well and
set aside for 30 minutes or until the bread softens
slightly. Season with the salt and pepper to taste.
Serve with freshly shaved parmesan cheese if desired.

HINTS AND TIPS:

* You will need—cutting board, cook's knife, spoon and liquid measures, large salad bowl and mixing spoon.

* Panzanella is a classic Tuscan salad that's perfect for summer months. The bread in the recipe is best used stale and is roasted in the oven to give it a crust on the outside. In some recipes, the bread is not toasted at all, and in others it is soaked in cold water for 10 minutes to soften it up completely, the water is squeezed out and the bread placed in a shallow terracotta dish, drizzled with the vinegar and oil, topped with all the other ingredients and served.

* The best version of this salad simply requires the cook to source the very best ingredients. Serve at room temperature to enhance the ripeness of the tomatoes and basil and to bring out the flavour of the oil. This salad can be made hours in advance and should be taken out of the fridge at least an hour before serving.

* The basic concept of panzanella is to soften stale or toasted bread with a vinegar dressing and add fresh tomato, garlic and basil. From there, any number of combinations can be applied.

* Try adding 400 g canned tuna and 1 finely diced red onion.

* If using onions in this salad, there is a method used to reduce the sharpness of the onions and make them more digestible. Once the onions are cut, soak in cold water and 1 teaspoon salt for 1 hour. Drain thoroughly and add to the salad.

* Take 500 g fresh salmon fillet and cut into 5-cm dice. Lightly sauté in 1 tablespoon olive oil until crisp on the outside and medium-rare inside. Add to the salad.

* For added freshness and crunch, try the addition of half a continental cucumber sliced in half lengthways, seeds removed and sliced into half moons.

* This bread salad can have lettuce added but then it really becomes a lettuce salad with stale croutons and therefore misses the point. Perhaps serve a simple lettuce salad to the side of a more traditional panzanella.

PASTA SALAD

Serves 4

xxxxxxxxxxxxxxxxxxxxxxxxxxxxxxxxxxxxxxxxxxxxxxxxxxxxxxxxxxxxxxxxxxxxxxxxxxxxxxxxxxxxxxxxxxxx

250 g short pasta (shell, bow tie, orecchiette
   or macaroni)
2 tablespoons cooking salt
1.5 litres water
2 tablespoons vegetable oil
2 garlic cloves, crushed
1 teaspoon salt flakes
50 ml balsamic vinegar
200 ml olive oil
½ continental cucumber, seeds removed
1 yellow capsicum, diced
250 g cherry or grape tomatoes
100 g black olives
¼ cup fresh basil leaves
¼ cup fresh flat-leaf parsley leaves
sea salt and freshly ground black pepper

Method:

1. Boil the pasta in the salted water until al dente—
slightly crunchy on the inside (see **Hints and tips**).
Drain the pasta in a colander or sieve (do not rinse),
add the vegetable oil and toss. Spread the pasta
evenly on a baking tray and leave to cool at room
temperature.

2. Place the garlic in a bowl and use a spoon to
squash the salt flakes into the garlic. Stir in the
vinegar and olive oil.

3. Slice the cucumber and place in a salad bowl. Add
the capsicum, tomatoes, olives, herbs and pasta, and
season to taste.

4. Stir in the dressing and serve.

HINTS AND TIPS:

----

* You will need—cutting board, cook's knife, large pot, wooden spoon, weight, liquid, cup and spoon measures, small bowl and large salad bowl.

* Consider cooking extra pasta when making dinner so it can be set aside for a pasta salad the next day.

* The combinations for a pasta salad are limited only by your imagination. Steamed or grilled vegetables, smoked, grilled or roasted meats, ham or salami, herbs and spices can all influence the outcome and style of the salad.

* The method of cooking the pasta is important to understand. Overcooked pasta in a salad is hideous, becoming a pasty mush of carbs and vegetables. The reasoning behind undercooking the pasta is that the pasta will continue to absorb moisture even when cold. So what appears to be undercooked as it comes from the pot becomes just perfect once cooled and mixed with the other ingredients.

* The pasta is tossed in oil while hot to stop it from sticking as it cools. It is never rinsed or cooled under cold water—this rinses flavour from the cooked pasta. Spreading the pasta on a baking tray in a thin layer cools the pasta naturally and keeps the flavour intact.

* If you find garlic too strong in flavour, then omit it from the recipe altogether or simmer the garlic in its skin with the pasta. Once cooked, simply squeeze the garlic from its skin and mash with the salt.

* Grape tomatoes are a tasty variety originating in Australia. Based on the Roma tomato, they are packed with excellent flavour and being similar in size to the cherry tomatoes are brilliant for salads or snacks in school lunch boxes.

POTATO SALAD

Serves 4

XXXXXXXXXXXXXXXXXXXXXXXXXXXXXXXXXXXXXXXXXXXXXXXXXXXXXXXXXXXXXXXXXXXXXXXXXXXXXXXXXXXXXXXXXXXXXX

700 g waxy potatoes (see **Hints and tips**)
2 tablespoons cooking salt
50 ml white wine vinegar
150 ml olive oil
1 teaspoon salt flakes
¼ teaspoon freshly ground black pepper
2 tablespoons chopped fresh flat-leaf parsley

Method:

1. Wash the potatoes thoroughly and place in a pot
with enough cold water to cover. Add the cooking salt,
bring to the boil and simmer until fork tender (about
15–20 minutes, depending on size). When checking for
doneness, a skewer or fork should pierce the potato
with little resistance and slide out easily. Drain the
potatoes and cool on a flat tray—do not rinse under
cold water. Refrigerate the potatoes for several hours
or overnight to allow the starches to set and make
them easier to cut (no sticky residue).

2. The cold potatoes can be peeled easily or used with
their skins left intact. Cut into bite-sized pieces
and place in a bowl.

3. Toss with the vinegar, oil, salt flakes, pepper and
parsley.

HINTS AND TIPS:

* You will need—cutting board, cook's knife, large pot or saucepan, spoon and liquid measures, colander or strainer and large salad bowl.

* Waxy potatoes are a style of potato ideally suited to potato salad because of the stickiness of the starch which holds the potato together once cut and mixed.

* Types of waxy potato for potato salad include—kipfler, pink fir, Ratte, Southern Gold, Bintje, Wilwash, Wilja, Coliban, Pontiac, Nicola and Patrone.

* The dressing in my recipe is a very basic oil and vinegar mixture. Often potato salad is served with a creamy mayonnaise-style dressing—if this is preferred, then use ¾ cup homemade **mayonnaise** or pre-made mayonnaise from the supermarket.

* Alternative dressings include the use of about ¾ cup sour cream, yoghurt or crème fraîche whisked with a few tablespoons of olive oil.

* Try adding 3 hard-boiled eggs (roughly chopped) to the basic recipe.

* Other herbs that can be used include—tarragon, chervil, chives, mint and spring onions.

* Try using different vinegars for the salad like balsamic vinegar, red wine vinegar, sherry vinegar or cider vinegar. Lemon juice is a good substitute for vinegar.

* Mix 1 tablespoon seeded mustard with 4 tablespoons olive oil, 1 tablespoon balsamic vinegar and 2 tablespoons baby capers (chopped). Use this combination as a dressing.

* Chop 4 bacon rashers into 5-mm wide batons and fry in ¼ cup vegetable oil until crisp. Drain on paper towel and mix into the salad immediately before serving to keep the crunch.

* Once mixed, the potato salad can be warmed through slightly (in a microwave-proof bowl) and drizzled with a little truffle oil.

RICE SALAD

Serves 4–6

XXXXXXXXXXXXXXXXXXXXXXXXXXXXXXXXXXXXXXXXXXXXXXXXXXXXXXXXXXXXXXXXXXXXXXXXXXXXXXXXXXXXXXXXXXXX

750 g cooked medium-grain rice (white, brown or
   wild rice)
2 garlic cloves
1 teaspoon sea salt
½ teaspoon freshly ground black pepper
juice of 1 lemon
150 ml olive oil
1 red capsicum
½ continental cucumber, seeds removed
½ bunch spring onions, finely sliced
150 g corn kernels
150 g green peas

Method:

1. Place the cooked rice in a large bowl.

2. For the dressing—finely chop the garlic and place
in a small bowl. Add the salt and pepper and squash
with the back of a spoon to form a paste. Stir in the
lemon juice and oil and set aside.

3. Dice the capsicum and cucumber so they are uniform
in size with the corn kernels and peas and add to the
rice.

4. Add the spring onions.

5. Place the corn kernels and peas in another bowl,
cover with boiling water from the kettle and leave to
stand for 2 minutes (fresh) or 30 seconds (frozen).
Drain and refresh under cold water. Drain thoroughly
and add to the rice.

6. Add the dressing just before serving and stir until
all ingredients are thoroughly combined. Check the
seasoning and serve at room temperature.

7. Leftover salad will last for up to 3 days
refrigerated.

HINTS AND TIPS:

* You will need—pot or rice cooker for the rice, cutting board, cook's knife, small and large bowl, wooden or metal spoon, strainer or colander, kettle and weight, liquid and spoon measures.

* A rice salad is a great way to use up leftover steamed rice. See the tips for **cooking rice** in Really useful information.

* Brown rice is a much healthier alternative and allows the cook to add a variety of nuts and seeds to the recipe—sesame seeds, pine nuts, pepitas and sunflower seeds are just a few ideas.

* Wild rice is another very healthy alternative and although not actually a true rice, it easily transforms an average white rice salad into a dynamic salad for your next party.

* Medium-grain rice is best as the grains stay separated once cooked and remain soft when chilled.

* Long-grain rice can be used for this salad but the cooked grains tend to harden considerably when chilled overnight. This is why cold long-grain rice is ideal for fried rice, but it must be heated slightly or brought to room temperature to soften before use for a rice salad.

* Short-grain rice is too gelatinous and will stick together which will be very frustrating when trying to make a rice salad. It is soft and sticky when cooked and when cold.

* A mixed rice salad is an interesting combination with varying textures, flavours and colours. Use equal parts of each and then add your favourite ingredients.

* Try replacing the dressing provided with 1 cup **mayonnaise** which can be plain or flavoured with 2 tablespoons red curry paste.

TABBOULEH

Makes about 10 cups

XXXXXXXXXXXXXXXXXXXXXXXXXXXXXXXXXXXXXXXXXXXXXXXXXXXXXXXXXXXXXXXXXXXXXXXXXXXXXXXXXXXXXXXXXXXXXX

4 bunches fresh flat-leaf parsley
4 large vine-ripened tomatoes
75 g fine bulgur
juice of 2 lemons
1 small white salad onion, finely diced
½ teaspoon ground allspice
½ teaspoon sumac
2 teaspoons salt flakes
100 ml extra virgin olive oil
1 cos lettuce

Method:

1. Wash and completely dry the parsley. Pick over the parsley removing all the leaves, then with a razor-sharp knife, slice the parsley leaves as finely as possible—a process (known as a 'chiffonade') that takes some time but is worth the effort.

2. Cut the tomatoes into quarters and remove the pulp, place the pulp in a sieve to strain. Reserve the juice (discard the seeds). Chop the tomato flesh into very small dice.

3. Place the bulgur in a sieve and wash under cold running water for 1 minute. Place in a bowl and mix in the lemon juice and the reserved tomato juice and leave to absorb for 30 minutes.

4. Place the parsley, tomato, onion, spices, salt and oil in a large salad bowl and gently fold together with the soaked bulgur.

5. Serve with the washed and separated cos lettuce leaves.

HINTS AND TIPS:

* You will need—cutting board, cook's knife, spoon and liquid measures, juicer, sieve and bowls.

* Tabbouleh can also be spelt tabouleh or tabouli.

* This recipe is like all other traditional recipes that are steeped in history and culture. Every native cook has his or her own twist to the recipe and will not submit to another, declaring theirs to be the best.

* Tabbouleh that is beige in colour is completely wrong. This is due to the fact that some cooks make the bulgur the main ingredient when in fact it should be green and red (parsley and tomato), the colours on the Lebanese national flag.

* Bulgur (or burghul) is wheat that has been soaked, cooked and dried. It can be bought whole or in small broken pieces of varying size, which is used for dishes like pilaf and tabouli. Bulgur should not be confused with cracked wheat which is the whole wheat kernel that has been cracked and takes longer to cook and has less flavour than bulgur.

* For individuals who are wheat- and gluten-intolerant, try replacing the bulgur with quinoa (pronounced—keen-wa) or buckwheat (which is not in fact a type of wheat). Do not be tempted to make it from couscous as it, too, is a wheat-based product.

* Chopping the parsley with a blunt knife will only bruise the leaves and crush the juice and flavour from the parsley, making it more bitter than is necessary. A 'chiffonade' refers to the shredding of any leafy matter—the idea is that the knife only passes through the leaf once, therefore minimising bruising and locking in valuable flavour and moisture.

* Curly parsley can be used and chopped violently to produce a finer result but a stronger parsley flavour.

* Try adding ½ bunch finely shredded mint and 4 finely chopped bird's eye chillies to this recipe.

* Tabbouleh is usually served as an appetiser with cos lettuce used as the vessel to eat it from. It is also ideal at barbecues and in school lunch boxes.

```
------------------------------------------
xxxxxxxx 9. Grains and Pulses xxxxxxxx
------------------------------------------
```

COUSCOUS WITH PRESERVED LEMON AND SAFFRON

Serves 4

xxxxxxxxxxxxxxxxxxxxxxxxxxxxxxxxxxxxxxxxxxxxxxxxxxxxxxxxxxxxxxxxxxxxxxxxxxxxxxxxxxxxxxxxxxxxxxxxxxx

2 cups couscous
1 tablespoon butter
¼ red onion, finely diced
1 garlic clove, crushed
large pinch of saffron threads
2 cups **chicken** or **vegetable stock**
250 g English spinach
1 preserved lemon
salt

Method:

1. Place the couscous in a medium-sized bowl.

2. In a saucepan over medium heat, melt the butter and fry the onion and garlic until transparent.

3. Add the saffron and stock and bring to the boil.

4. Pour over the couscous, cover the bowl with a plate or plastic wrap and leave for 5 minutes. Meanwhile, cover the spinach with boiled water from the kettle, drain immediately, rinse under cold water and drain again.

5. Use a fork to fluff the couscous.

6. Chop the spinach and add to the couscous.

7. Rinse the preserved lemon and remove the flesh. Slice the rind and mix into the couscous then season with salt to taste. It is now ready to serve.

HINTS AND TIPS:

* You will need—cutting board, cook's knife, cup, spoon and weight measures, saucepan, wooden spoon, fork and bowl.

* Couscous, although resembling a grain, is best described as a very small pasta.

* Couscous is a wheat-based product and should be avoided by coeliacs or people with wheat or gluten intolerance.

* For best results every time, a great rule of thumb is to use equal parts couscous to liquid. This general rule only applies to instant couscous, which is more common and readily available in supermarkets.

* Couscous is a perfect accompaniment to stews and casseroles. It is also ideal as a salad, side dish or even as a dessert.

* The real trick to fluffy couscous is in the 'fluffing'. For instant (5-minute) couscous, once the liquid has been added and it has rested (covered) for 5 minutes, it is important to gently scratch at the couscous to loosen the swollen grains. Do not be tempted to rush this stage, as 'digging' at the couscous will only result in lumps which are almost impossible to break down.

* When using pre-made stocks, be aware of the salt content before adding extra salt. Be especially careful when adding preserved lemon, which will also impart its own salty characteristic.

FRIED RICE

Serves 2–4

xxxxxxxxxxxxxxxxxxxxxxxxxxxxxxxxxxxxxxxxxxxxxxxxxxxxxxxxxxxxxxxxxxxxxxxxxxxxxxxxxxxxxxxxxxx

1 teaspoon white sugar

2 tablespoons Chinese cooking wine or dry sherry

1 tablespoon oyster sauce

3 tablespoons soy sauce

½ teaspoon sesame oil

2 tablespoons peanut oil

3 large eggs, beaten

1½ tablespoons finely chopped ginger

4 garlic cloves, diced

2 spring onions, white part only, finely sliced

1 cup roughly chopped Chinese red roast pork

4 cups cooked long-grain white rice

¼ cup frozen green peas

2 spring onions, green part only, finely sliced on the
    diagonal

½ large red chilli, finely sliced on the diagonal

Method:

1. In a small bowl, mix the sugar, wine or sherry,
oyster sauce, soy sauce and sesame oil.

2. Heat 1 tablespoon of the peanut oil in a wok until
it begins to smoke. Pour the beaten eggs into the
wok and cook for about 1 minute, rotating the wok to
spread the mixture around to form a thin 'pancake' and
to ensure even cooking. When almost cooked through,
carefully remove the omelette from the wok with a
spatula or egg flip and cool. When cool, shred with
a knife and set aside.

3. Wipe out the wok with kitchen paper, add the
remaining peanut oil and stir-fry the ginger and
garlic for 1 minute, or until very aromatic. Add the
white of the spring onion and stir-fry for 30 seconds.
Add the pork and stir-fry for a further minute until
heated through. Stir in the sauce mixture and stir-fry
for 30 seconds. Finally, add the rice, omelette and
peas. Stir-fry for 2–3 minutes, or until the rice is
heated through.

Method cont.

4. Divide the rice between individual bowls and garnish with the green of the spring onions and the chilli.

HINTS AND TIPS:

★ You will need—cutting board, cook's knife, bowls to hold each of the ingredients before cooking begins, wok or large frying pan, spatula or egg flip and cup and spoon measures.

★ Probably the single most important thing with making a good fried rice like that found in Chinese restaurants is to use day-old cooked rice. The question most often asked when making fried rice is, 'How do I stop my fried rice from being gluggy?' The answer is cold, cooked rice. Cooling allows the starches in the cooked rice to set which then allows the grains to stay firm and separated when re-cooked as fried rice—the longer cold rice is re-cooked, the more the grains can absorb moisture, soften and turn pasty.

★ Peanut oil is only a suggestion; it can be replaced with any good mild-flavoured cooking oil. If,

however, following a recipe is important, then buy peanut oil from an Asian food store as the aroma is one of freshly roasted peanuts as opposed to supermarket peanut oil which has no aroma at all and could in fact be anything.

★ Red roasted pork can be seen hanging up in the windows of Chinese barbecue shops and restaurants. Often it is cheaper to buy than ham—which is an alternative if there is not a Chinese shop or restaurant nearby.

★ Chinese cooking wine can be purchased from Asian food stores. But, as suggested, a dry sherry will do the job equally well.

★ The vegetables used in this recipe are merely a suggestion. The type of vegetables or the variety going into the fried rice is simply a matter of individual taste. The main thing to remember when adding vegetables to fried rice is to keep them uniform in size

and to add them in stages depending on how hard the vegetable is. For instance, carrot will need to be added early in the cooking process; peas need to be added only 1 minute before serving.

★ Cooked brown rice in fried rice is, without a doubt, the best way to get kids and teenagers eating this wholesome grain.

★ For people with wheat or gluten intolerance, substitute the soy sauce with tamari (a wheat-free soy sauce).

LENTIL BURGERS
Makes 6 burgers

xxxxxxxxxxxxxxxxxxxxxxxxxxxxxxxxxxxxxxxxxxxxxxxxxxxxxxxxxxxxxxxxxxxxxxxxxxxxxxxxxxxxxxxxxxx

1 large potato, peeled and chopped
100 ml olive oil
1 teaspoon ground cumin
1 teaspoon ground coriander
1 large onion, finely chopped
1 carrot, peeled and finely chopped in a food processor
2 celery sticks, finely chopped
400 g can lentils, drained and squeezed (see **Hints and tips**)
1 tablespoon tahini
salt and pepper

Method:

1. Cook the potato in boiling salted water until tender. Mash and set aside to cool to room temperature.

2. Heat 1 tablespoon of the oil in a sauté pan, add the spices and fry for 30 seconds or until fragrant. Add the onion, carrot and celery and cook over low heat until softened. Remove from the heat and cool.

3. Combine the lentils and tahini in a large bowl. Use a potato masher to squash the lentils to a paste, leaving some whole for texture.

4. Add the mashed potato and the onion mixture, mix well and season to taste. Form into 6 burgers and refrigerate for 1 hour.

5. Heat the remaining oil in a large frying pan or on a barbecue hotplate and fry the lentil burgers over medium heat until golden brown and heated through. Serve with a salad or in burger buns.

HINTS AND TIPS:

* You will need—cutting board, cook's knife, saucepan, sauté pan, large frying pan, potato masher, and spoon and liquid measure.

* This recipe calls for canned lentils for ease of use. By all means cook lentils from scratch, but the final outcome really isn't that different. If possible, it is best to use organic lentils; this is because the price difference isn't that big, but the flavour is.

* Canned lentils are usually sold in 400 g cans. But you will need 2 cans to account for the draining, rinsing and then squeezing out as much moisture as possible.

* The final mixture is still very moist and delicate—this is important as the biggest complaint about lentil and chickpea burgers is that they are too dry.

* For **chickpea burgers**, simply substitute the lentils for chickpeas. Pass the chickpeas (drained and rinsed) through a food processor to make a fine crumb before adding to the rest of the mixture.

* For even-sized burgers, use a ½ cup measure—sprinkle a few sesame seeds in the bottom, press the burger mixture into the cup and turn out. Repeat the process, placing the burgers on a tray lined with plastic wrap. Cover and refrigerate for 1 hour before cooking.

* If you want, the patties can be rolled in bran, sesame seeds or even oats before you put them in the fridge.

* This is a gluten-free, vegan-friendly recipe. The use of mashed potato is to avoid the use of bread crumbs, which in conjunction with egg, are often used in burger mixtures to thicken and hold the patties together.

MACARONI CHEESE

Serves 6–8

xxxxxxxxxxxxxxxxxxxxxxxxxxxxxxxxxxxxxxxxxxxxxxxxxxxxxxxxxxxxxxxxxxxxxxxxxxxxxxxxxxxxxxxxxxxx

olive oil spray
500 g elbow macaroni
80 g butter
80 g plain flour
1.25 litres milk
2 teaspoons mustard
pinch of freshly grated nutmeg
salt and pepper
150 g good parmesan cheese, grated
450 g good cheddar cheese, grated
½ cup dried bread crumbs

Method:

1. Preheat the oven to 180°C. Prepare a large ovenproof dish by spraying lightly with olive oil.

2. Cook the pasta according to the instructions on the packet, cool and set aside.

3. In a saucepan, melt the butter and add the flour. Cook over low–medium heat until the flour takes on a sandy colour. Remove from the heat and add all the milk. Return to medium heat and whisk while bringing back to the boil. Simmer for 2 minutes and stir in the mustard, nutmeg, and salt and pepper.

4. Remove from the heat and stir in the parmesan and 200 g of the cheddar cheese.

5. Place the pasta in the prepared dish, pour over the sauce and mix well, top with the bread crumbs and the remaining cheddar cheese. Place in the oven until heated through and golden on top.

HINTS AND TIPS:

* You will need—large pot, colander or strainer, saucepan, whisk, wooden spoon, weight, liquid and spoon measures, plastic spatula, baking dish.

* There are two styles of macaroni cheese: the baked method (provided), and the 'teenage' method where the pasta is cooked and the cheese sauce is mixed through and then eaten—simple.

* The cheese used in macaroni cheese can vary depending on budget and taste. Using all cheddar is the cheaper option. Parmesan, pecorino, asiago, manchego or kefalotyri are all fantastic cheeses available at good delicatessens.

* The recipe I've given uses cheddar cheese but you could also try making a crust before baking by mixing ½ cup dried bread crumbs with 1 cup grated parmesan cheese then sprinkling over the top.

* Other ingredients like bacon, ham, peas or corn could be added, but then it's just a baked pasta with cheese and stuff.

* This dish could be made with any style of short pasta but then it just becomes a cheesy baked pasta—that the kids will still love.

* Adding 2 teaspoons mustard powder is optional although popular among old school cooks who love this classic pasta dish.

* Try adding ¼ teaspoon ground cayenne pepper to the white sauce for a bit of warmth.

* Serve with a fresh simple salad and crusty bread.

* Leftover macaroni cheese will last for 5 days in the fridge. To reheat, place in a microwave-safe dish, add 1 tablespoon milk, cover with plastic wrap and heat until piping hot.

FIRM POLENTA

Serves 6–8

XXXXXXXXXXXXXXXXXXXXXXXXXXXXXXXXXXXXXXXXXXXXXXXXXXXXXXXXXXXXXXXXXXXXXXXXXXXXXXXXXXXXXXXXXXXX

1 litre water or stock
200 g instant polenta
50 g butter
salt

Method:

1. Line a shallow baking tray or slice tray with plastic wrap (spray or lightly brush with oil to help the plastic wrap to stick to the tray).

2. Bring the water or stock to the boil. Slowly add the polenta in a steady stream, whisking constantly until all the polenta is added. Continue to whisk until the polenta comes to the boil, then reduce the heat to a simmer and cook for 3–5 minutes.

3. Add the butter and salt to taste, remove from the heat and stir until the butter is incorporated.

4. Pour into the prepared tray and smooth until evenly spread, then set aside to cool. Refrigerate until needed. Cut into squares, triangles or chip shapes, brush or spray with oil before pan-frying or grilling on the barbecue. When re-cooking, don't turn the polenta too soon, wait until it's fully brown on one side to form a nice crisp crust.

HINTS AND TIPS:

* You will need—shallow baking tray, weight and liquid measures, saucepan and whisk.

* Polenta is dried and ground corn that is slightly finer than corn meal. It can easily be substituted for corn meal.

* Polenta is an ideal food source for those people who have to avoid wheat and gluten in their diet.

* Firm polenta is great to serve as a replacement for potato.

* Top with parmesan cheese and grill before serving or mix ½ cup grated parmesan cheese into the mixture when adding the butter.

* Instant polenta is already cooked and needs only a few minutes to finish. Regular polenta takes about 40 minutes to cook and is a bit of a work-out with a wooden spoon. Be careful as it spits from the pot and is extremely hot. After 20 minutes it may appear cooked, but do not be tempted to finish early as the polenta will still be very grainy and crunchy. Cook until it starts to pull away from the sides of the pot then beat in the butter and parmesan cheese.

SOFT POLENTA

Serves 4–6

xxxxxxxxxxxxxxxxxxxxxxxxxxxxxxxxxxxxxxxxxxxxxxxxxxxxxxxxxxxxxxxxxxxxxxxxxxxxxxxxxx

500 ml milk
60 g instant polenta
100 g taleggio cheese
salt

Method:

1. Heat the milk in a saucepan, sprinkle the polenta into the hot milk and bring back to the boil, stirring all the time with a whisk. Cook gently for 5 minutes until thickened slightly.

2. Remove from the heat, add the cheese and stir until melted. Add salt to taste and serve immediately.

HINTS AND TIPS:

----

* You will need—saucepan, whisk, weight and liquid measures.

* Soft polenta can also be made with chicken stock or vegetable stock.

* Soft polenta is very well suited to slow-cooked dishes served with their own sauce.

* Try **Italian sausages with soft polenta**—4 Italian sausages, 100 ml white wine, 100 g butter, 1 lemon, 1 tablespoon chopped flat-leaf parsley. Grill the sausages on a chargrill until half-cooked. Slice in half lengthways but not all the way through. Place back on the chargrill and continue to cook. In a saucepan, heat the white wine, add the butter and stir. Add the sausages and lemon juice. Finish with salt, pepper and parsley just before serving. Serve with soft polenta.

RISOTTO

Serves 10

xxxxxxxxxxxxxxxxxxxxxxxxxxxxxxxxxxxxxxxxxxxxxxxxxxxxxxxxxxxxxxxxxxxxxxxxxxxxxxxxxxxxxxxxxxxxxxxxxxxxxx

100 ml olive oil
1 small onion, finely diced
1 kg arborio rice
250 ml white wine
1½ litres boiling **chicken stock**
salt and pepper

Method:

1. Heat the olive oil in a pot and sauté the onion until transparent. Add the rice and cook, stirring with a wooden spoon, until the rice is hot, coated in oil and translucent (see **Hints and tips**).

2. Add the white wine, bring to the boil, then reduce the heat to simmering point.

3. Stir in the hot stock, a ladle at a time, with each ladle being absorbed before the next is added. Continue to stir the rice to release the starches, resulting in a creamy risotto. Season with salt and pepper.

4. Spread onto a flat tray to cool quickly. When cooled, place in an airtight container and store in the fridge until needed. Two even cups of cooked rice will serve 1 adult main course.

5. To re-heat allow an extra 1½ litres of stock or water. Sauté any extra ingredients like mushrooms or chicken, add 1 cup white wine, the rice and 2 ladles of hot stock. Continue to add the stock and stir until the rice is al dente and the risotto is creamy and thick.

HINTS AND TIPS:

★ You will need—cutting board, cook's knife, 2 saucepans, ladle, wooden spoon and weight and liquid measures.

★ This risotto base is a method used in most restaurants to speed up the end result. Half-cooking the rice in 1-kg amounts allows you to store the risotto base in the fridge for up to 5 days. This also means different risottos can be made simply by sautéing other ingredients, adding some risotto base and more chicken stock.

★ For **risotto Milanese**— you will need an extra 1½ litres stock (3 litres per 1 kg rice), about 6 strands saffron and 2 cups grated parmesan (grana padano). Following the method, halfway through adding the hot stock, add the saffron strands, continue to cook until the rice is al dente (still a bit crunchy on the inside). Remove the pot from the heat and add the parmesan, whip it in well until the rice is creamy. Serve immediately. Try adding 120 g bone marrow (available from the butcher) when frying the onion.

★ Allow 100 g rice for a main course and 50 g for an entree. Although this doesn't seem like much rice, keep in mind that it absorbs 3 times its volume in liquid plus there are the flavour profiles whether it's a duck and mushroom risotto or seafood risotto.

★ There are some brands of risotto rice that don't require stirring. This is excellent news for the beginner cook but strange to risotto's old school cooks who will tell you that the best risotto is one that has been worked constantly with a wooden spoon, so as to have the rice grains trounce one another, rendering maximum starch which in turn produces the creamy texture.

★ Risotto rice is a medium-grain rice, with a characteristic white dot in the centre of the grain, used specifically for making risotto. There are several varieties, each claiming to produce the best risotto, including carnaroli, violane nano (or simply nano), arborio, baldo, padano and roma. Washing risotto rice is a big no-no. The more starches left with the grain, the creamier the risotto.

★ Risotto is sometimes called 'piedmont rice'.

SPAGHETTI CARBONARA (TRADITIONAL, NO CREAM RECIPE)

Serves 4

XXXXXXXXXXXXXXXXXXXXXXXXXXXXXXXXXXXXXXXXXXXXXXXXXXXXXXXXXXXXXXXXXXXXXXXXXXXXXXXXXXXXXX

3 eggs
1 cup freshly grated
   parmesan
250 g prosciutto, diced
500 g spaghetti
125 g butter, cut
   into dice
freshly ground black
   pepper

Method:

1. Beat the eggs gently with a fork and add ⅓ cup parmesan and the prosciutto.

2. Cook the spaghetti in a pot of rapidly boiling salted water until al dente.

3. Drain the spaghetti, then return to the cooking pan and mix in the butter. Once the butter has melted, quickly stir in the egg and cheese mixture. It is important that this process be performed immediately after draining and replacing the spaghetti in the pan, so that the egg is allowed to cook from the heat retained in the pan. Do not turn the heat back on as it will scramble the eggs.

4. Sprinkle the remaining parmesan over the top, season with the pepper and serve immediately.

HINTS AND TIPS:

* You will need—cutting board, cook's knife, bowl, large pot, colander, fork, grater, wooden spoon.

* Try adding 1 garlic clove (thinly sliced) to the egg mixture as well as ¼ cup shredded flat-leaf parsley.

* This traditional method does not produce a saucy dish but rather the pasta is lightly coated in egg and butter speckled with prosciuttto and black pepper.

* Proscuitto is different to bacon and ham, but all can be interchanged.

SPAGHETTI CARBONARA (WESTERNISED CREAMY VERSION)

Serves 4

xxxxxxxxxxxxxxxxxxxxxxxxxxxxxxxxxxxxxxxxxxxxxxxxxxxxxxxxxxxxxxxxxxxxxxxxxxxxxxx

500 g spaghetti
2 tablespoons olive oil
250 g bacon, diced
1 cup sliced portobello
    or button mushrooms
    (optional)
1 garlic clove, thinly
    sliced
250 ml thickened cream
sea salt and freshly
    ground black pepper
4 eggs, lightly beaten
2 tablespoons chopped
    chives
½ cup grated parmesan

Method:

1. Cook the spaghetti in a large saucepan of rapidly boiling salted water until al dente.

2. Heat the oil in a sauté pan, add the bacon and fry until the bacon is brown and slightly crisp.

3. Add the mushrooms if using and cook until softened. Add the garlic and sauté for another 30 seconds.

4. Add the cream and bring to the boil.

5. Add the pasta and mix thoroughly. Season with salt and pepper.

6. Remove from the heat and stir in the eggs and chives.

7. Serve topped with parmesan cheese.

HINTS AND TIPS:

* You will need—cutting board, cook's knife, 2 bowls, fork or wooden spoon, large saucepan, sauté pan, wooden spoon and spoon, liquid, cup and weight measures.

* In both recipes, it's worth noting that the egg is added away from the heat—this is done so the egg doesn't overcook and scramble. If, on the other hand, the egg doesn't seem to be cooked enough, place the pan over gentle heat, stir until the egg thickens and then serve.

SPRING ROLLS

Makes about 30

XXXXXXXXXXXXXXXXXXXXXXXXXXXXXXXXXXXXXXXXXXXXXXXXXXXXXXXXXXXXXXXXXXXXXXXXXXXXXXXXXXXXXXXXXXX

4 dried shiitake mushrooms
50 g rice vermicelli noodles
300 g white cabbage, finely shredded
2 tablespoons peanut oil
200 g pork or chicken mince
1 carrot, grated
½ bunch spring onions, thinly sliced
100 g fresh bean sprouts
3 tablespoons soy sauce
1½ tablespoons cornflour
1 tablespoon sesame oil
30 spring roll wrappers
2 litres vegetable oil, for frying

Method:

1. Soak the mushrooms in hot water for 15 minutes until soft. Drain, squeeze out the excess water, remove and discard the hard stem, then thinly slice. Soak the noodles in boiling water for 10 minutes. Drain well.

2. Place the cabbage in a bowl, cover with boiling water from the kettle and stand for 2 minutes. Drain, cool and squeeze dry.

3. Heat the peanut oil in a wok or pan over high heat. Add the mince and cook until no longer pink. Add the cabbage, carrot, spring onion, bean sprouts, mushrooms and noodles and toss until heated through.

4. Mix the soy sauce with the cornflour and stir into the mince mixture. Mix well, remove from the heat and stir in the sesame oil. Check the seasoning and add salt if needed. Leave to cool completely before rolling.

5. To roll—place a spring roll wrapper on a flat surface in front of you in a diamond shape. Have a small amount of water in a bowl to use for sticking the pastry together.

Method cont.

6. Place 1 heaped tablespoon of the mince mixture in the centre of the wrap. Fold the wrapper over the mince mixture from the bottom first, fold in the sides and finish rolling the spring roll. Just at the end, dab some water on the tip and roll up to stick together. Continue until all the wrappers are used. Leftover filling can be frozen for another day.

7. Pour the oil into a deep pot and heat to 180°C. Cook the spring rolls turning often to ensure even colouring for 3–4 minutes or until golden brown. Remove from the oil and drain well on paper towel. Serve hot with a dipping sauce.

HINTS AND TIPS:
----

* You will need—cutting board, cook's knife, paring knife, vegetable peeler, 2 bowls, wok or sauté pan, large, deep pot for deep-frying, tongs or slotted metal spoon, and weight, spoon and liquid measures.

* For **vegetarian spring rolls**—replace the mince with extra cabbage, carrot and bean sprouts. Also add bamboo shoots (canned) or water chestnuts (canned) for extra flavour and texture. Chokos can also be grated and added to the mixture as a way to use this vegetable that lacks flavour.

* Fresh chilli can add some bite. Add 2 bird's eye chillies (sliced in half, de-seeded and chopped) to the filling. Alternatively, add 1 teaspoon chilli flakes.

* Spring roll wrappers are readily available in the freezer section at the supermarket as well as all Asian grocers. Spring roll wrappers are made with wheat flour and are not suitable for coeliacs or those with gluten-intolerance.

* For those with nut allergies, simply fry the mince in vegetable or canola oil.

* If you deep-fry at home, you can strain the used oil through paper towel and store in the fridge to re-use later. The oil can be used for day-to-day cooking as well as further deep-frying. Polyunsaturated oils can only be used once, while olive oil and unrefined peanut oil last longer and can be strained and re-used 2 or 3 times.

* Never get into the habit of pouring oil down the sink. Pour cold oil into an empty plastic or metal container with a lid (old milk or cream containers, jam jars and the like) before putting in the rubbish. Some countries have depots where used cooking oil can be dropped off. I suggest giving your local council a call to find out if this service is available to you.

----

xxx **10. Dressings, Sauces and Butters** xxx

SAVOURY SAUCES

AÏOLI
Makes about 1½ cups
xxxxxxxxxxxxxxxxxxxxxxxxxxxxxxxxxxxxxxxxxxxxxxxxxxxxxxxxxxxxxxxxxxxxxxxxxxxxxxxxxxxxxxxxxxxxxxx

3 garlic cloves, crushed
½ teaspoon salt
3 medium egg yolks
300 ml olive oil
1 tablespoon lemon juice

Method:

1. Place the garlic, salt and egg yolks in a bowl.
Gradually whisk in the olive oil in a slow, thin
stream until the sauce thickens and resembles a
mayonnaise.

2. Stir in the lemon juice and if the mixture is still
too thick, add 1 teaspoon water.

3. Keep covered in the refrigerator for up to 2 weeks.

* You will need—cutting board, cook's knife, spoon and liquid measures, bowl, and whisk.

* The amount of garlic used in an aïoli or garlic mayonnaise can vary from a single clove to as many as 6 cloves and is a matter of personal taste.

* One medium-sized garlic clove = approximately ½ teaspoon garlic.

* The one true key to ensuring success with this sauce or any emulsion-style sauce is to go slow. Rush the addition of oil to an egg base and trouble will be guaranteed—by trouble I mean the sauce will separate or split.

* Should your aïoli split while adding the oil, follow the rescue instructions given in **mayonnaise.**

* When making this sauce, keep all equipment at room temperature so that the ingredients will not be exposed to contrasting surface temperatures. This will lessen the chances of the sauce splitting.

* Although traditionally made in a mortar and pestle, the use of a whisk and

bowl (as above), a hand-held blender, hand beaters or even a food processor will also do. If using a food processor, the recipe quantity above will get lost in a large machine and is therefore more suited to a small unit that attaches itself to a hand-held blender.

* Some recipes may call for a teaspoon of Dijon mustard mixed with the egg yolks and although this is not traditional, it is acceptable and can certainly assist in the emulsion of the sauce.

* Aïoli goes well with fish, chicken and vegetables (cooked and raw). It is also great in sandwiches and rolls instead of butter or margarine.

* Use in potato salad or serve alongside roast potatoes.

* Try serving with fresh steamed green beans.

* A cheat's method is to use a store-bought mayonnaise (preferably a good quality 'egg mayonnaise') and replace the oil with the bought mayonnaise and simply stir in the other ingredients without the worry of splitting the sauce.

* Thin the aïoli with even more water and you have a creamy, garlicky salad dressing.

* Add 2 tablespoons grated parmesan cheese and 8 finely chopped anchovy fillets to the aïoli and you have a Caesar dressing.

* Aïoli, the dressing or sauce, shares its namesake with a festive meal. A summer celebration in France known as 'Aioli Monstre de Cotignac' or 'Grand Aioli de Tourtour' is a feast where everyone brings a plate to share of the freshest summer vegetables, boiled eggs, poached fish and baguettes to serve with lashings of aïoli sauce.

* To make a **rouille**, add ¼ teaspoon saffron and ¼ teaspoon cayenne pepper to the dressing when the lemon juice is added at the end. Traditionally served with the French soup 'bouillabaisse', rouille can be served with most cooked seafood or seafood soups.

CAESAR DRESSING

Makes about 700 ml

XXXXXXXXXXXXXXXXXXXXXXXXXXXXXXXXXXXXXXXXXXXXXXXXXXXXXXXXXXXXXXXXXXXXXXXXXXXXXXXXXXXXXXXXXXX

4 egg yolks
6 anchovy fillets
4 garlic cloves, sliced
1 tablespoon Dijon mustard
500 ml light olive oil
2 tablespoons chopped flat-leaf parsley
juice of 1 lemon
salt and pepper

Method:

1. Place the egg yolks, anchovies, garlic and mustard in a food processor and blitz for 1–2 minutes to combine.

2. While the machine is running, very, very slowly begin to drizzle in the oil. When half the oil is added, it is safe to pour it in a bit faster. Once all the oil is added, scrape the dressing into a bowl.

3. Stir in the parsley and lemon juice and check to see if it needs any salt and pepper to taste. If the dressing is too thick, add 1 tablespoon water. Store, covered, in the refrigerator for up to 4 weeks.

HINTS AND TIPS:

* You will need—cutting board, sharp cook's knife, food processor, spoon and liquid measures, bowl and plastic scraper. Have a whisk on hand just in case—read on.

* Caesar dressing, like any egg emulsion sauce (including mayonnaise or hollandaise), requires a deft hand when it comes to adding the oil. If anything goes wrong, this is when it will occur. However, not to scare you, there are some tips to avoid or even remedy the situation should anything go wrong.

* Trust me when I say 'prevention is better than cure'. As a young apprentice, I split many an emulsion sauce, and usually in vast quantities—the remedy is painstakingly mind-bending and worth avoiding, therefore, this next piece of advice is vital for your sanity. When I say 'very, very' slowly in the method, I'm not saying it because I like writing the word often, it's because very, very slowly is the key to success, especially in the early stages of the sauce. When adding the oil slowly, it means a thin steady stream or constant drizzle, the only step less than that is adding

the oil with an eye dropper which is very, very silly. Once the emulsion starts to come together and looks like a dressing (when about half of the oil has been added), then and only then is it safe to begin adding the oil a bit faster. Only trained professionals seem to have the gift of making this sauce in the blink of an eye, but for us mere mortals, slow and steady will still achieve the same result.

* Now, should you suddenly sneeze while drizzling and a huge slick of oil enters the dressing and it begins to split, do not panic. First, try adding 1 tablespoon boiling hot water—this will, in a few instances, bring the dressing back together and you may resume the exciting task of very, very slowly adding the oil. However ...

* Should you almost finish adding all the oil and your past decides to catch up with you and karma makes the dressing separate, then try this debilitating remedy, which works every time—First, you will need a bowl and a whisk as we now go manual. Add to the bowl, 1 egg yolk only, then teaspoon by teaspoon start whisking in the split

dressing, very, very slowly, until all the dressing is added with the remaining oil. Well done!

* In a hurry? Buy a jar of good quality egg mayonnaise from the supermarket and add the anchovies (finely crushed), garlic (finely crushed) and Dijon mustard, then finish with the parsley and lemon juice as mentioned in the recipe.

COCKTAIL SAUCE

Makes about 2 cups

xxxxxxxxxxxxxxxxxxxxxxxxxxxxxxxxxxxxxxxxxxxxxxxxxxxxxxxxxxxxxxxxxxxxxxxxxxxxxxxxxxxx

250 ml mayonnaise
60 ml Worcestershire sauce
60 ml brandy
120 ml tomato ketchup
1 tablespoon horseradish
salt and pepper
60 ml thickened cream,
   semi-whipped

Method:

1. Place the mayonnaise, Worcestershire sauce, brandy, ketchup and horseradish in a bowl and mix well.

2. Check the seasoning, adding salt and pepper if necessary, then fold in the cream.

3. Place in a jar with a lid and store refrigerated for up to 2 weeks.

HINTS AND TIPS:

★ You will need—2 bowls, liquid and spoon measures, whisk and long-handled plastic spatula or wooden spoon for mixing.

★ Homemade **mayonnaise** can be replaced with a quality store-bought variety. Look for a prepared mayonnaise that has ´egg mayonnaise´ on the label as opposed to the very sweet varieties that can be too overpowering in this dressing.

★ Horseradish refers to the jar of prepared horseradish found in all grocery stores. It can be replaced with 1 teaspoon freshly grated horseradish.

★ The semi-whipped cream is added at the end simply to lighten the sauce, it is not entirely necessary and can be omitted. Try replacing the cream with plain yoghurt, sour cream or crème fraîche.

★ In America, cocktail sauce can be just a simple mixture of tomato sauce and prepared horseradish and possibly some Tabasco sauce and lemon juice. A mayonnaise base is favoured in the UK as well as Australia.

★ For an extra kick to the cocktail sauce, try adding 1 tablespoon Tabasco sauce or cayenne pepper.

★ ´Marie Rose sauce´ is another name for cocktail sauce although Marie Rose may differ slightly in some of the ingredients.

★ Another similar sauce is **thousand island dressing**, which is pink in colour but traditionally includes (added to the above recipe) 1 chopped boiled egg, 1 tablespoon minced gherkins, 1 tablespoon Dijon mustard and 1 tablespoon of chopped dill leaves.

★ Cocktail sauce goes with cooked seafood, especially prawns and oysters. It is a classic accompaniment to the popular dinner party dish ´prawn cocktail´.

★ It´s a good idea to hang on to screw-cap jars for when sauces or dressings are made. Make sure that the jar has been thoroughly cleaned with hot soapy water and dried properly before using.

GARLIC BUTTER

Makes about 300 g

XXXXXXXXXXXXXXXXXXXXXXXXXXXXXXXXXXXXXXXXXXXXXXXXXXXXXXXXXXXXXXXXXXXXXXXXXXXXXXXXXXXXX

250 g butter, softened
5–6 garlic cloves, crushed
zest of ½ lemon
2 teaspoons salt
1 teaspoon freshly ground
    black pepper
2 tablespoons chopped
    fresh flat-leaf parsley

Method:

1. Place the butter (see Hints and tips) in a bowl. Add the garlic and mix into the butter with the remaining ingredients.

2. Cover and keep refrigerated until needed. The butter will keep for about 7–10 days. Or wrap in plastic wrap then foil and freeze for up to 3 months.

HINTS AND TIPS:

★ You will need—weight and spoon measures, grater, cutting board, cook's knife, wooden spoon or whisk and bowl.

★ The butter can be simply mixed with the other ingredients or whipped until light and fluffy before adding the other ingredients. The results are only slightly different.

★ For **herb butter**—reduce the garlic content by half or omit altogether. Add 1 cup chopped mixed fresh herbs or ¼ cup dried mixed herbs. Most combinations of mixed herbs work; however, it is the hard herbs that will add the greatest amount of flavour, like rosemary, sage, thyme and oregano. Smaller amounts of soft herbs like curly parsley, basil, dill, tarragon or chives also enhance the flavour.

★ Great ideas for flavoured butters include: 1 tablespoon of garlic butter per person for garlic prawns is a classic. Steamed asparagus topped with a knob of garlic or herb butter is a great way to celebrate spring. Grilled meats benefit from a knob of garlic or herb butter as a simple substitute for making a sauce. Also grilled mushrooms, steamed broccoli, sautéed clams and mussels enjoy the company of garlic butter.

★ If freezing flavoured butters, wrap in plastic wrap, roll into a log shape about 5 cm in diameter, then roll in foil to help protect it from freezer burn. Or refrigerate as a log, then use a hot knife to cut 5-mm discs from the log and store in a clip lock bag in the freezer. Defrost the frozen butter on the bench as the meat or vegetables are cooking.

★ Make garlic bread in advance, wrap in foil and freeze for another day. The classic way of slicing a bread stick almost all the way through and smearing the butter in each opening is easy, but try slicing the bread stick lengthways all the way through. Toast one side, cool and spread the other side with garlic or herb butter then top with some grated parmesan. Place under the grill to melt and brown the cheese. This is my favourite way to have garlic bread.

★ Try adding the zest of 1 lemon or 1 orange to the garlic butter. This is a great accompaniment to **osso buco**.

GINGER SOY

Makes about 900 ml

XXXXXXXXXXXXXXXXXXXXXXXXXXXXXXXXXXXXXXXXXXXXXXXXXXXXXXXXXXXXXXXXXXXXXXXXXXXXXXXXXX

40 ml ginger juice (see
    Hints and tips)
75 ml kecap manis
    (Indonesian sweet soy
    sauce)
125 ml soy sauce
150 ml Chinese cooking
    wine or dry sherry
250 ml oyster sauce
250 ml hoisin sauce

Method:

1. Place all ingredients in a bowl and stir with a whisk or spoon until thoroughly combined. Pour into a container with a lid and refrigerate until required. This sauce will keep refrigerated for at least 2–3 months.

HINTS AND TIPS:

* You will need—juice extractor, bowl, whisk or spoon, and liquid measure.

* This sauce is ideally suited to chicken, fish and vegetable stir-fries.

* To make the ginger juice, place 80 g fresh ginger in a vegetable juice extractor.

* If you can't make the ginger juice, a good substitute is to use 60 g finely grated fresh ginger or 2 tablespoons ground ginger. When grating the ginger, do not peel it, just wash it thoroughly and grate with the skin on, then add to the sauce—be sure to stir the sauce before adding to the stir fry.

* Add 150 g honey to create a **honey ginger soy stir fry sauce.**

* Allow about 100 ml sauce per serve.

* Due to the nature of the individual ingredients, the fridge life of this sauce is quite high. This is mainly because of the high preservative qualities of salt and sugar. Expect a fridge life of up to 3 months. Alternatively, simply make smaller amounts that can be consumed sooner.

* All of the ingredients are readily available at Asian grocers. Supermarkets will stock about 90 per cent of these ingredients.

HOLLANDAISE

Makes about 400 ml

xxxxxxxxxxxxxxxxxxxxxxxxxxxxxxxxxxxxxxxxxxxxxxxxxxxxxxxxxxxxxxxxxxxxxxxxxxxxxxxxxxxxxxxxxxx

4 egg yolks
2 tablespoons white wine
   vinegar
250 ml ghee (clarified
   butter) melted, or
   light olive oil
1 tablespoon lemon juice
sea salt and freshly
   ground pepper

Method:

1. Place a small saucepan with 5 cm hot water in it over medium heat and bring to, and maintain, a low simmer.

2. In a heatproof bowl, whisk the egg yolks and vinegar. Place over the simmering water and whisk until pale, fluffy and double in volume.

3. Remove from the heat and, like mayonnaise, very gradually whisk in the clarified butter or oil.

4. Once all the oil is added, mix in the lemon juice and season with salt and pepper. Use immediately or cover with plastic wrap and keep at room temperature until needed.

HINTS AND TIPS:

* You will need—saucepan, heatproof bowl, whisk, and spoon and liquid measures.

* This is a very quick recipe for hollandaise. Traditionally, what's called a 'reduction' is made first, where (for this recipe) 4 tablespoons white wine vinegar with 6 black peppercorns are set over medium heat and reduced by half, then this is strained over the egg yolks and the whisking begins. This step is good practice but not entirely necessary for the beginner cook or the cook in a bit of a hurry.

* Should any of these sauces look like separating, add 1 tablespoon hot water and whisk. If that doesn't work, then head to the recipe for Caesar dressing for hints and tips on rescuing a separated emulsion sauce.

* Leftover hollandaise does not keep well as the butter in the sauce sets hard in the fridge and then upon reheating splits—which again is why some chefs prefer to use oil as it sets more like a mayonnaise in the fridge and can be used as such the next day.

* There are many derivatives of hollandaise, the most obvious would have to be **béarnaise**—add to the reduction of vinegar 1 tablespoon chopped tarragon stalks. Then add 1 tablespoon chopped tarragon leaves to the sauce. Traditionally, béarnaise is thicker than a hollandaise.

* **Sauce Choron**—peel and de-seed 300 g tomatoes. Chop the tomato flesh and cook in 1 tablespoon butter until dry. Pass through a fine sieve and stir this fresh tomato paste into the béarnaise (see hint above).

* **Sauce Maltaise**—mix the zest and juice of 1 blood orange into the hollandaise.

MAYONNAISE

Makes about 1 cup

xxxxxxxxxxxxxxxxxxxxxxxxxxxxxxxxxxxxxxxxxxxxxxxxxxxxxxxxxxxxxxxxxxxxxxxxxxxxxxxxxxxxxxxx

2 egg yolks
1 tablespoon white wine vinegar
250 ml light olive oil
salt and pepper to taste
1 tablespoon lemon juice

Method:

1. Place the egg yolks and vinegar in a bowl and whisk.

2. Continue whisking and very, very slowly drizzling the oil. Do this by adding only a few drops at a time in the beginning. As the mayonnaise starts to thicken, the oil can be added a little bit faster in a thin steady stream.

3. When all the oil has been added, season with salt and pepper and finish with the lemon juice. Cover and keep refrigerated for up to 4 weeks.

HINTS AND TIPS:

* You will need—bowl, whisk, liquid and spoon measures and container for storage.

* Mayonnaise is notoriously difficult to make due to the ease in which it can separate or split if the oil is added too fast. Refer to the hints and tips in the **Caesar dressing** recipe for more information on what is required to do this task successfully.

* The oil I've suggested to use in this recipe is merely that—a suggestion. Other oils I recommend are safflower, vegetable, grapeseed or peanut. Olive oil, extra virgin olive oil and some nut oils like hazelnut and walnut are too overpowering in flavour for a basic mayonnaise.

* Some recipes call for 1 teaspoon mustard (to the recipe)—this is certainly optional and will help in the emulsion or holding together of the sauce as the oil is being added.

* For people who are accustomed to the taste of the commercial brands that are very white in colour and very sweet in taste, a real mayonnaise may not be to their liking. However, there are some very good commercially made products that contain whole eggs available at the supermarket, and if time is scarce, try one of these as an alternative.

* There are many derivatives of mayonnaise, some I have given recipes for, like **cocktail sauce**, **Caesar dressing**, **aïoli**, **rouille** and **thousand island dressing**. Other derivatives include the following:

* **Ranch dressing**—an American staple made from mayonnaise mixed with sour cream, finely chopped spring onions and other seasonings.

* **Sauce remoulade**—a mayonnaise with mustard, finely chopped gherkins and capers added as well the herbs, parsley, chervil and tarragon. Sometimes minced anchovies are added too.

* **Tartare sauce**—another classic sauce made from the mother mayonnaise. To the mayonnaise add, 1 tablespoon finely chopped gherkins, 2 tablespoons each of finely chopped capers, shallots and curly parsley and mix until evenly combined.

* **Tofu mayonnaise**—150 g silken tofu, 1 tablespoon lemon juice, 1 tablespoon Dijon mustard, 250 ml olive oil. Using a food processor, blitz the tofu, lemon juice and mustard. With the machine running, slowly add the oil, a few drops at a time and then as a slow steady stream until it is emulsified and thick. Store in an airtight container in the fridge for 2 weeks. Add 1 teaspoon cayenne pepper for extra kick.

* Heston Blumenthal, a great chef from the UK, has two pages devoted to the making of mayonnaise in his book *Family Food*. I've gleaned a couple of tips from him—first, the bowl and whisk used are important; the bowl should have a rounded base for even mixing of the dressing and the whisk should have plenty of fine wires (some whisks on the market are thick-wired with large gaps suggesting you may as well make the mayonnaise with a fork). Secondly, and very interestingly, a mayonnaise can be successfully made with just egg white, although he suggests that the flavour will be more neutral. Heston's last point leads me to add that the recipe I've provided could indeed be made using a single whole egg instead of 2 egg yolks.

MEE GORING SAUCE

Makes about 600 ml

xxxxxxxxxxxxxxxxxxxxxxxxxxxxxxxxxxxxxxxxxxxxxxxxxxxxxxxxxxxxxxxxxxxxxxxxxxxxxxxxxxxxxxxxxxx

200 ml tomato ketchup

200 ml soy sauce

100 ml chilli sauce
   (sambal oelek)

100 ml kecap manis
   (Indonesian sweet soy
   sauce)

Method:

1. Place all of the ingredients in a bowl and stir with a whisk or spoon until thoroughly combined. Pour into a container with a lid and refrigerate until required.

HINTS AND TIPS:

★ You will need—liquid measure, bowl, whisk or spoon.

★ This sauce naturally goes with the fried noodle dish 'mee goreng', also known as 'Indian mee goreng'.

★ Although lime juice is not in this recipe, it is important to finish the dish with a squeeze of lime to lift the dish and cut through the salty sweetness of the sauce.

★ Sambal oelek is a basic chilli condiment made by grinding fresh red chillies into a paste. Readily available in supermarkets, sambal oelek is a great way to add fresh chilli to a dish without the messy job of doing it yourself.

★ Kecap manis is a thick, Indonesian sweet soy sauce. It has a syrupy texture similar to molasses, the sweetness is from the addition of palm sugar. If none is at hand make your own substitute by mixing together 3 tablespoons soy sauce (or tamari) with 1 tablespoon dark brown sugar.

★ Allow about 100 ml sauce per serve.

★ Due to the nature of the individual ingredients, the fridge life of this sauce is quite high. This is mainly because of the high preservative qualities of salt and sugar. Expect a fridge life of up to 3 months. Alternatively, simply make smaller amounts that can be consumed sooner.

★ All of the ingredients are readily available at Asian grocers. Supermarkets will stock about 90 per cent of these ingredients.

NAPOLI SAUCE

Serves 6

xxxxxxxxxxxxxxxxxxxxxxxxxxxxxxxxxxxxxxxxxxxxxxxxxxxxxxxxxxxxxxxxxxxxxxxxxxxxxxxxxxxxxxxxxxxx

4 tablespoons olive oil
1 large brown onion, finely
    chopped
2 garlic cloves, crushed
800 g can crushed tomatoes
sea salt and freshly
    ground black pepper

Method:

1. Heat the oil in a pot or saucepan over medium heat, add the onion and fry until just beginning to colour. Add the garlic and fry for 1 minute.

2. Add the tomatoes and salt and pepper, and simmer for 20–25 minutes or until the sauce has reduced slightly and thickens. Check the seasoning.

3. Serve immediately or cool and store in an airtight container in the refrigerator for up to 5 days.

HINTS AND TIPS:

* You will need—cutting board, cook's knife, spoon measure, pot or saucepan and wooden spoon.

* There are many variations of Italian-style tomato sauce, the one provided is quick and easy.

* Fresh tomatoes can be used for this recipe in which case replace the canned tomatoes with 1 kg fresh, very ripe (even over-ripe) tomatoes. Peel the tomatoes, de-seed and roughly chop then cook as per the method. Fresh tomatoes have a higher water content so it may be that the sauce needs to cook for longer, as much as double the time, to achieve a thick sauce.

* Herbs added when the tomatoes go into the pot include any one of—or a mixture of—rosemary, thyme, oregano, marjoram, basil or parsley. One or 2 sprigs is ample to impart a soft perfume from the herbs. Too many fresh herbs can overpower the sauce. Soft herbs like parsley and basil should only be added halfway through the cooking process as their flavour is released quickly. Once the sauce is cooked, remove the stalk and discard. Dried herbs can also be added at the start of the recipe using 1 teaspoon of any of those mentioned above.

* A hot sauce is made by adding 1 tablespoon chilli flakes when the tomatoes are added. If you don't like pieces of chilli in the sauce, add 1 teaspoon cayenne pepper. The amount added entirely depends on how hot you like your tomato sauce.

* For a commercial style **tomato ketchup**—use the same recipe and quantities but omit the oil and add: ½ cup white sugar, ¼ cup red wine vinegar, 1 teaspoon salt, 1 tablespoon Dijon mustard, large pinch ground ginger, ½ teaspoon five-spice powder. Do not fry the onion and garlic, just place all the ingredients in the pot and bring to the boil, reduce heat to a simmer and cook for 45 minutes, uncovered. Remove from the heat, cool slightly and blend either with a hand-held blender or a benchtop blender. Press the mixture through a fine sieve. Place the sauce back in the cleaned pot and bring back to the boil to remove any air bubbles. Pour into a hot sterilised jar (see Basic Preserving), seal and refrigerate.

PAD THAI SAUCE

Makes about 550 ml

XXXXXXXXXXXXXXXXXXXXXXXXXXXXXXXXXXXXXXXXXXXXXXXXXXXXXXXXXXXXXXXXXXXXXXXXXXXXXXXXXXXX

200 ml fish sauce
200 g grated palm sugar or
   white sugar
150 ml tamarind juice

Method:

1. Place all of the ingredients in a saucepan, bring just to the boil, then reduce the heat and cook for 1 minute, stirring until the sugar dissolves. Pour into a container with a lid and refrigerate until required.

HINTS AND TIPS:

★ You will need—liquid and weight measures, saucepan and a wooden spoon.

★ This Pad Thai or Pat Thai sauce matches the noodle dish of the same name.

★ Fish sauce or ´nahm pla´ is a heady condiment used readily in Thai cuisine as a salt. Considering the pungency of fish sauce, it´s surprising that once added to a dish it transforms into a meaty, salty element that marries well with its surrounding flavour profiles. A deft hand needs to be used—as with salt, too much and the dish will be spoilt.

★ Soy sauce is not a suitable replacement for fish sauce.

★ Palm sugar is readily available at Asian grocers and most supermarkets. There are several styles. Some are pale and hard and should be smashed with a mortar and pestle. Others are dark and soft. This recipe calls for the pale version. White sugar will make a good substitute.

★ Allow about 100 ml sauce per serve.

★ Due to the nature of the individual ingredients, the fridge life of this sauce is quite high. This is mainly because of the high preservative qualities of salt and sugar. Expect a fridge life of up to 3 months. Alternatively, simply make smaller amounts that can be consumed sooner.

★ All of the ingredients are readily available at Asian grocers. Supermarkets will stock about 90 per cent of these ingredients.

RED WINE SAUCE

Makes 300 ml

xxxxxxxxxxxxxxxxxxxxxxxxxxxxxxxxxxxxxxxxxxxxxxxxxxxxxxxxxxxxxxxxxxxxxxxxxxxxxxxxxxxxxxxx

500 ml veal or beef stock
300 ml red wine
1 bay leaf
6 black peppercorns
1 sprig thyme
1 tablespoon redcurrant
   jelly
1 tablespoon red wine
   vinegar
sea salt

Method:

1. Place the stock, wine, bay leaf, peppercorns and thyme in a saucepan or in the roasting pan (from which the roast has been removed to rest on a tray, see **roast beef** or **roast lamb** recipe).

2. Place over medium–high heat and reduce the liquid by two-thirds.

3. Add the redcurrant jelly and vinegar and salt to taste. Bring back to the boil, strain through a fine sieve and keep warm, ready to serve.

HINTS AND TIPS:

★ You will need—liquid and spoon measures, saucepan and sieve.

★ This sauce, although sounding a bit lengthy, is quite easy. An easier red wine sauce follows.

★ Veal or beef stock is usually pre-packaged and often already salted, so keep this in mind when seasoning as once the stock reduces, it may be salty enough.

★ Redcurrant jelly adds a sweetness to the sauce to counter the reduced and concentrated tannins in the red wine. If unavailable, then replace with 1 cup port, added with the stock. Or, alternatively, add 1 tablespoon brown sugar.

★ Red wine vinegar can be omitted altogether or replaced with malt vinegar or balsamic vinegar.

★ 2 tablespoons tomato paste can be added to this recipe when the redcurrant jelly and vinegar are added to help thicken and enrich the sauce. Alternatively, add 2 chopped Roma tomatoes and 2 peeled garlic cloves before the stock and wine begin to reduce. When the sauce is being passed through the fine sieve, press the vegetables through to make a paste which will help thicken the sauce.

★ Easy **red wine sauce**—this sauce, also known as ´beurre rouge´, or red wine butter sauce, is a simple recipe to serve with just-cooked steaks. Remove the steaks from the pan and set aside to rest in a warm area. Add

200 ml red wine and 100 ml port to the pan and reduce the alcohol by half over medium heat. Remove from the heat and add 100 g diced butter—do not put the pan back on the heat, simply swirl the pan to melt the butter. Finish this sauce with some sea salt flakes and freshly ground black pepper before serving over the steaks.

★ For an easier sauce— without wine—for steaks, remove and rest the steak, add 1 cup water to the pan and bring to the boil to lift the cooked-on juices on the base of the pan. When the water starts to evaporate, add some salt and pepper, a splash of balsamic or red wine vinegar and a good slug of olive oil while swirling the pan. Remove from the heat and serve.

PLUM SAUCE

Makes about 1½ litres

xxxxxxxxxxxxxxxxxxxxxxxxxxxxxxxxxxxxxxxxxxxxxxxxxxxxxxxxxxxxxxxxxxxxxxxxxxxxxxxxxxxxxxxxxxxx

1 kg plums, halved
1 teaspoon five-spice powder
1 teaspoon ground ginger
1 teaspoon cayenne pepper (optional)
2 cups brown sugar
3 cups white wine vinegar
2 teaspoons sea salt

Method:

1. Remove the stones from the plums, then using a meat mallet, crack half the stones and tie them in a piece of muslin.

2. Place the plums, muslin bag of cracked plum stones, spices, sugar, vinegar and salt in a large stainless steel pot and bring to the boil, stirring until the sugar has dissolved. Cook steadily for 30 minutes or until the plums are very soft. Remove the muslin bag and discard.

3. Cool the sauce slightly and blitz in a food processor or blender then return to the cleaned pan. Bring back to the boil, reduce the heat and simmer for a few minutes or until the sauce is as thick as you would like it. (Remember that the sauce will thicken further when it is cold and it should be of a pouring consistency.) Pour into hot, sterilised bottles or jars, seal, label and date. Leave for at least 1 week before using. This sauce will last up to 12 months in a cool dry pantry. Refrigerate once opened.

HINTS AND TIPS:

* You will need—cutting board, paring knife, meat mallet, muslin, bowl, cup and spoon measures, large stainless steel pot, wooden spoon, food processor or blender, and jars for storage.

* This sauce is really a preserve, for more information on preserves refer to Basic preserving.

* Any fruit sauce or preserve should be made with a premium product. Avoid using fruits that are over-ripe, diseased, damaged or bruised.

* Plum stones are high in pectin, which helps set the sauce slightly. Adding the plums stones can, of course, be left out. But it is a good tip when preserving plums.

* Whole spices can be used in this recipe, in which case they, too, need to be tied into a muslin bag and added at the beginning. Remove the spice bag before making a puree. For the above recipe, try adding 10 black peppercorns, 5 whole cloves and 5 whole allspice.

* Plum sauce with roast pork is a staple in Chinese restaurants, and is also used as a dipping sauce for spring rolls, egg rolls, chicken wings and steamed dumplings. It goes with pork spare ribs (instead of sweet and sour sauce), Peking duck (instead of hoisin sauce), roast turkey, or grilled chicken or pork.

* Like most recipes, feel free to play around with the quantities of vinegar and sugar to adjust the flavour to your liking, whether that be more sweet or sour. The amount of spice can also be adjusted according to individual taste.

* A very easy version of this recipe is to use—1 cup plum jam, 2 tablespoons red wine vinegar, 2 tablespoons hoisin sauce, 1 teaspoon ground ginger, 1 teaspoon dry mustard, ½ teaspoon cayenne pepper. Place all the ingredients in a saucepan, bring to the boil and simmer for 5 minutes. Remove from the heat and store, refrigerated, for up to 2 weeks.

SATAY SAUCE

Makes about 1 litre

xxxxxxxxxxxxxxxxxxxxxxxxxxxxxxxxxxxxxxxxxxxxxxxxxxxxxxxxxxxxxxxxxxxxxxxxxxxxxxxxxxxxxxxxxxxxxx

1 brown onion, chopped

1 lemon grass stalk, bottom quarter only, chopped

1 teaspoon shrimp paste (optional)

1 teaspoon chilli powder

4 garlic cloves, sliced

1 teaspoon ground cumin

1 teaspoon ground coriander

2 cups coconut milk

2 tablespoons peanut oil

300 g peanuts, unsalted and crushed

4 tablespoons sugar

2 tablespoons tamarind paste

4 tablespoons soy sauce

Method:

1. Place the onion in a food processor. Finely chop the lemon grass and add to the onion along with the shrimp paste, chilli powder, garlic and spices. Add enough coconut milk (about 2 tablespoons) to moisten the mixture and blitz to produce a paste.

2. Heat the oil in a wok or heavy-based saucepan over medium heat and gently fry the paste until it turns a pale, pinky brown colour, then reduce the heat to low. If the paste begins to brown too quickly, remove the pan from the heat, reduce the heat and continue cooking.

3. Add the remaining coconut milk and the peanuts and stir to separate the nuts. Simmer until the sauce thickens. Stir in the sugar, tamarind paste and soy sauce.

4. Remove from the heat and serve. Keeps refrigerated for 2 weeks.

HINTS AND TIPS:

* You will need—cutting board, cook's knife, food processor (or a mortar and pestle), wok or heavy-based saucepan, wooden spoon, and weight, cup and spoon measures.

* This is probably one of the more extensive satay sauce recipes based on my time in Thai restaurants. Do not despair if some of these ingredients are not available or if it just seems too much to handle—read on for a very simple alternative.

* A **very simple satay sauce**—1 cup crunchy peanut butter, 2 cups coconut milk and 2 tablespoons hot chilli sauce. Place the peanut butter in a saucepan over medium heat, and stir with a wooden spoon until it begins to melt. Gradually add the coconut milk, and stir until it is thoroughly combined. Cook until sauce consistency then stir in the chilli sauce. Too easy!

* Shrimp paste is written as optional for two reasons. First, it stinks really, really badly and is enough to put people off the idea of cooking this recipe (but it does add a great flavour); and secondly, it is the only meat product in the recipe, so for vegetarians or vegans, simply leave it out.

* A tip on storing shrimp paste—keep it in the packet it came in, place that in a clip lock bag, place the bag in an airtight container, then store until next time— this helps to stop the smell escaping.

* The 1 teaspoon chilli powder can be replaced with 3 teaspoons chilli flakes.

* Satay sauce goes with skewered meats like chicken, beef and fish. It's great for a dipping sauce for **spring rolls** and samosas, and fantastic with **vegetables and noodle stir-fry**.

* Normally for this recipe I use 8 shallots (eschalots). Shallots are milder in flavour but quite fiddly to peel which is why I suggest using 1 onion.

* Tamarind paste is readily available in supermarkets and Asian grocers and is a very sour brown paste often used to balance the hot, sweet, sour and salty flavours in Asian food.

SHALLOT DRESSING

Makes about 1 litre

XXXXXXXXXXXXXXXXXXXXXXXXXXXXXXXXXXXXXXXXXXXXXXXXXXXXXXXXXXXXXXXXXXXXXXXXXXXXXXXXXXXXXXXXXXXXX

100 g peeled shallots
   (eschalots)
100 ml sherry vinegar
750 ml olive oil
1 tablespoon very finely
   chopped curly parsley

Method:

1. Roughly chop the shallots and place in a food processor. (See Hints and tips for method without a food processor.)

2. Add the sherry vinegar and blitz.

3. Very slowly add the oil so the dressing doesn't separate.

4. Once all the oil is added, stir in the parsley and transfer to a bottle or jar and refrigerate until required.

HINTS AND TIPS:

★ You will need—cutting board, cook's knife, liquid and spoon measures, food processor and jar for storage.

★ Salt has deliberately been omitted from this recipe— adding salt will cause the dressing to separate.

★ The addition of ¼ teaspoon freshly ground black pepper is recommended.

★ The recipe yield may seem too much; however, refrigerated this dressing will last for at least 1 month. Or, halve the recipe for a more useable quantity.

★ Shallots are a small, brown-skinned type of onion with a milder flavour and pungency than regular onions (the use of purple shallots is fine). If shallots are unavailable, replace with a small onion of any colour (white, brown or red).

★ Adding the oil very slowly will produce a homogenous dressing, but do not panic if it splits. Simply add the rest of the oil, pour into a large bottle with a lid so that every time you go to use the dressing, you can shake it up to mix the ingredients before pouring over the salad.

★ Sherry vinegar adds a very specific flavour to the dressing; red wine vinegar, white wine vinegar or balsamic vinegar can be used instead. Plain white vinegar is acceptable but will produce a very bland-tasting dressing.

★ For extra dimension to this dressing, try adding 1 tablespoon Dijon mustard to the shallots and vinegar before blitzing—the mustard will also help prevent the dressing from separating.

★ Like all dressings made with vinegar and lemon juice, remember to add the dressing to the salad just before serving to prevent the lettuce from wilting.

★ Try adding a few tablespoons of this dressing to freshly steamed green beans.

SWEET AND SOUR SAUCE

Makes about 500 ml

XXXXXXXXXXXXXXXXXXXXXXXXXXXXXXXXXXXXXXXXXXXXXXXXXXXXXXXXXXXXXXXXXXXXXXXXXXXXXXXXXXXXX

125 ml white vinegar
100 g white sugar
125 ml tomato ketchup
50 ml soy sauce
2 slices canned pineapple,
   diced
pinch of ground ginger
1 tablespoon cornflour

Method:

1. Place the vinegar, sugar, tomato sauce and soy sauce together in a wok or saucepan. Bring to the boil and simmer for 1 minute, stirring constantly. Add the pineapple and ginger. Combine the cornflour and a small amount of water and mix to form a paste. Stir into the sauce and cook until thick—if too thick add a little more water.

HINTS AND TIPS:

★ You will need—cutting board, cook's knife, liquid and spoon measures, wok or saucepan, large spoon.

★ Serve sweet and sour sauce with pork, steamed or grilled fish, chicken or seafood.

★ Leftover sauce can be used as a dipping sauce for fish fingers.

★ Allow about 100 ml sauce per serve.

★ Due to the nature of the individual ingredients, the fridge life of this sauce is quite high. This is mainly because of the high preservative qualities of salt and sugar. Expect a fridge life of up to 3 months. Alternatively, simply make smaller amounts that can be consumed sooner.

★ All of the ingredients are readily available at Asian grocers. Supermarkets will stock about 90 per cent of these ingredients.

TERIYAKI SAUCE

Makes about 350 ml

XXXXXXXXXXXXXXXXXXXXXXXXXXXXXXXXXXXXXXXXXXXXXXXXXXXXXXXXXXXXXXXXXXXXXXXXXXXXXXXXXXXXXXXXX

200 ml dark soy sauce or
   tamari
200 ml sake
300 ml mirin
3 tablespoons white sugar

Method:

1. Place all of the ingredients in a saucepan, bring just to the boil, then reduce heat to medium and cook until the sugar has dissolved and the sauce has reduced by half (about 350 ml). Pour into a container with a lid and refrigerate until required.

HINTS AND TIPS:

----

* You will need—liquid and spoon measures, saucepan, large spoon.

* This sauce is reduced to produce a thick stir-fry sauce for Japanese dishes.

* As a marinade for meats, do not reduce the quantities given, just mix in a bowl and pour over the meat to be marinated.

* Sake is a rice wine, used in cooking (the cheaper styles) and for celebrating (the expensive styles). There are many varieties of sake and it is incorrect to think that they are all the same. I treat sake like wine; if I'm not prepared to drink it, I won't cook with it.

* Mirin is a sweet rice wine and can be substituted with 1 cup of white sugar if it is unavailable.

* Dark soy sauce is readily available, as is tamari which is a gluten-free style of soy sauce.

* Allow about 100 ml sauce per serve.

* Due to the nature of the individual ingredients, the fridge life of this sauce is quite high. This is mainly because of the high preservative qualities of salt and sugar. Expect a fridge life of up to 3 months. Alternatively, simply make smaller amounts that can be consumed sooner.

* All of the ingredients are readily available at Asian grocers. Supermarkets will stock about 90 per cent of these ingredients.

THAI CHILLI SAUCE

Makes about 750 ml

xxxxxxxxxxxxxxxxxxxxxxxxxxxxxxxxxxxxxxxxxxxxxxxxxxxxxxxxxxxxxxxxxxxxxxxxxxxxxxxxxxxx

150 ml yellow bean paste

75 ml fish sauce

125 g caster sugar or
    granulated dark palm
    sugar

150 ml oyster sauce

150 g chilli in soybean
    oil

100 ml tamarind juice

Method:

1. Place all of the ingredients in a bowl and stir with a whisk or spoon until thoroughly combined. Pour into a container with a lid and refrigerate until required.

HINTS AND TIPS:

★ You will need—liquid and weight measures, bowl, whisk or spoon.

★ This sauce suits chicken, vegetable, tofu and tempeh stir-fries.

★ Yellow bean paste is found in Asian grocers. It is usually sold in 600 ml bottles, and is a very thick yellow/brown sauce.

★ Chilli in soy bean oil is rarely seen in supermarkets and can be replaced with chilli paste or sambal oelek.

★ Tamarind juice is a very thick muddy brown pulp. This is readily available in supermarkets and Asian grocers. I prefer to make my own tamarind juice as I find the prepared juice a bit too thick. To make tamarind juice—use a 450 g block tamarind paste (check the ingredients on the back and find a brand with NO added salt), place in a large jug or container with 600 ml hot water. Let stand for 1—2 hours. Squish the paste with your hand or a potato masher to separate the pulp from the seeds and fibres. Pass this mixture through a sieve to leave a smooth juice, then discard the seeds. This mixture yields about 600 ml tamarind juice and keeps for several months, refrigerated.

★ Granulated palm sugar is available at most Asian grocers and is preferred over caster sugar or soft brown sugar.

★ Allow about 100 ml sauce per serve.

★ Due to the nature of the individual ingredients, the fridge life of this sauce is quite high. This is mainly because of the high preservative qualities of salt and sugar. Expect a fridge life of up to 3 months. Alternatively, simply make smaller amounts that can be consumed sooner.

★ All of the ingredients are readily available at Asian grocers.

WHITE SAUCE

Makes approximately 1¼ litres

XXXXXXXXXXXXXXXXXXXXXXXXXXXXXXXXXXXXXXXXXXXXXXXXXXXXXXXXXXXXXXXXXXXXXXXXXXXXXXXXXXXXXXXXXXXX

80 g butter
80 g plain flour
1 litre milk
salt and pepper

Method:

1. Melt the butter in a saucepan over medium-low heat. Add the flour and stir continually with a wooden spoon until the 'roux' reaches a sandy colour and texture; about 3–5 minutes.

2. Remove from the heat, add all the milk and use a whisk to combine the sauce. Return to medium heat and stir with the whisk until the sauce begins to thicken. Gently boil for 2 minutes, being careful not to let it burn.

3. Remove from the heat and season with salt and pepper.

HINTS AND TIPS:

---

* You will need—stainless steel saucepan, weight, cup and liquid measures, wooden spoon, and whisk.

* For a **béchamel sauce**—take a small onion and stud with 10 whole cloves and 1 bay leaf, add to the milk and bring to the boil. Remove from the heat and allow to infuse for 10 minutes before discarding the onion and spice. The milk is now ready to use in the recipe. If using béchamel sauce for lasagne, add an extra 150 ml milk to the recipe to thin it down and remember to keep the sauce hot so it is easy to pour.

* For a **mornay sauce**—add 200 g grated gruyère or tasty cheese once the sauce is removed from the heat. Only season with salt and pepper after the cheese has melted as the cheese may be salty enough. If using mornay sauce for seafood crepes, then try replacing the milk with fish stock for greater flavour.

* For a **white caper sauce**— add 2 tablespoons rinsed and chopped capers and 2 tablespoons chopped parsley.

* Other variations include adding 2 tablespoons curry paste to the cooked 'roux'

before adding the milk. Or add 2 tablespoons of your favourite mustard once the sauce is finished and before it is cool.

* Also try 1 cup chopped and cooked mushrooms or **caramelised onions**, added once the sauce is finished and removed from the heat.

* Adding the milk to the roux bit by bit is a method that is outdated and considered time-consuming by professionals who favour the above method. Using a whisk should only be done when making the sauce in a stainless steel pot because an aluminium pot can tend to make the sauce grey from the reaction of the different metals. Also, a whisk may scratch non-stick coatings.

* A whisk is used to avoid lumps and guarantees a smooth sauce every time.

* For a thicker sauce, add an extra 20 g flour and 20 g butter to the basic recipe and continue as per the method.

* Leftover white sauce can be used to make a toasted French sandwich called 'Croque Monsieur'. Spread 1 slice of bread with some Dijon mustard, place some

ham and 1 tablespoon grated gruyère cheese on top and cover with another bread slice. Place on a baking tray and grill the sandwich under a hot grill on one side. Remove the sandwich from the grill, turn over and spread the un-grilled side with cold white sauce, sprinkle with more grated cheese, return to the grill and cook until golden and bubbling.

* Take the above idea, fry an egg, place on the grilled sandwich and you have what is now called a 'Croque Madame'.

VINAIGRETTE

Makes about 400 ml

XXXXXXXXXXXXXXXXXXXXXXXXXXXXXXXXXXXXXXXXXXXXXXXXXXXXXXXXXXXXXXXXXXXXXXXXXXXXXXXXXXXXXX

60 ml white wine vinegar
30 ml lemon juice
1 teaspoon Dijon mustard
sea salt
300 ml olive oil

Method:

1. Combine the vinegar, lemon juice, mustard and salt in a bowl and whisk until the salt has dissolved.

2. Drizzle in the oil and whisk continuously until the dressing has emulsified.

3. Pour into a jar or bottle with a lid and refrigerate. Shake well before using. Because of the oil and vinegar, this dressing will last for many weeks in the fridge and will probably be used well before it deteriorates.

HINTS AND TIPS:

* You will need—bowl, thin whisk, spoon and liquid measures, and jar with a lid.

* There are many variations of vinaigrette (pronounced vin-aa-gret). Therefore I have provided several options.

* Things to remember—salt will not dissolve in oil, therefore it must be worked into the acid of the vinegar or lemon juice to break it down before adding the oil.

* Dijon mustard is rarely used in a vinaigrette and is added to a dressing to assist in holding it together (emulsify) as well as adding flavour. Do not panic if the dressing splits while it sits in the fridge. Simply shake or whisk well just before adding to the salad.

* A common rule of thumb for this dressing is 1 part vinegar to 3 parts oil. Some recipes may stray from this rule deliberately to offer a milder tasting dressing—to allow the good oil to shine, or depending on its use.

* Olive oil is only one option for a vinaigrette. Strong nut oils like walnut and hazelnut can be used either on their own (very strong) or in equal parts with a mild oil like peanut oil or grapeseed oil.

* In an Asian-inspired dressing, mix a few tablespoons of strongly flavoured sesame oil with a soft oil like peanut.

* Try a combination of vinegars like 50 ml red wine vinegar and 50 ml sherry vinegar to 300 ml olive oil with salt and pepper to taste. No mustard is needed. Place in a sealed jar and store. Shake well before use.

* For a vinaigrette for 1 serving, try 1 tablespoon white wine vinegar, pinch of salt, 3 tablespoons olive oil, whisk together and serve.

YOGHURT DRESSING

Makes about 2½ cups

xxxxxxxxxxxxxxxxxxxxxxxxxxxxxxxxxxxxxxxxxxxxxxxxxxxxxxxxxxxxxxxxxxxxxxxxxxxxxxxxxxx

1 cup natural yoghurt
1 teaspoon crushed garlic
½ teaspoon cayenne pepper
juice of 1 lemon
1 cup light olive oil
sea salt and freshly
    ground black pepper
cold water

Method:

1. Whisk together the yoghurt, garlic, cayenne pepper and lemon juice in a bowl.

2. Slowly add the oil, whisking continuously. Season with salt and pepper to taste and, depending on the thickness of the dressing, add a little cold water to thin slightly.

3. Transfer to a jar with a screw-cap lid or a plastic container with an airtight lid, and refrigerate. This sauce will keep in the fridge for 5–7 days.

HINTS AND TIPS:
----

* You will need—cutting board, cook's knife, bowl, whisk and cup and spoon measures.

* This creamy style of dressing goes well with **potato salad**, green bean salad, **panzanella**, and **green salad**. Or drizzle over steamed broccoli or leftover warmed roast lamb or use as a light marinade for chicken or pork.

* Like most dressings in this book, light olive oil is just one option; alternatives include vegetable oil, peanut oil, grapeseed oil or safflower oil.

* Yoghurt can be replaced with sour cream or crème fraîche.

* Cayenne pepper is also optional, so simply omit if the little bite it offers is still too much.

* Chopped fresh herbs like mint, basil or flat-leaf parsley can be added; if so, use 2 tablespoons of any of these or a combination of all three for the above recipe.

SWEET SAUCES

APPLE SAUCE

Makes about 1½ cups

xxxxxxxxxxxxxxxxxxxxxxxxxxxxxxxxxxxxxxxxxxxxxxxxxxxxxxxxxxxxxxxxxxxxxxxxxxxxxxxxxxxxxxxx

4 Golden Delicious apples, peeled, cored and diced
1 tablespoon lemon juice
1 cinnamon stick
2 strips of lemon zest

Method:

1. Place all of the ingredients in a pot over low heat. Cover and cook gently for 20–30 minutes or until completely broken down and soft, then remove from heat.

2. Remove the cinnamon stick and lemon zest. Mash with a potato masher or puree in a food processor. It may be that the apples have broken down enough that just mixing with a wooden spoon is enough to make a puree. Serve hot or chill for later use.

HINTS AND TIPS:

* You will need—cutting board, sharp knife, vegetable peeler, apple corer (optional), spoon measure, wooden spoon, potato masher or food processor and saucepan.

* Mixing the apple varieties can give an even better result as some apples are very sweet naturally. For this, a mixture of Jonathan, Rome, Gala, Red Delicious, Fuji and Pink Lady can be used, with as many as 4 varieties per sauce batch. However, some just may love the sourness that comes with the classic Granny Smith. Best of all are apples purchased from a country farmers' market.

* The sweetness of this sauce is very individual. The sweet tooth will add sugar while those preferring a more natural flavour will remain faithful to the recipe.

* Some recipes recommend adding a small amount of water to the apples when cooking. Adding water is not necessary as apples are 70 per cent water—the secret is to cook the apples on low heat to slowly draw out the moisture and soften the apples. It is also vital to stir the apples often to

ensure they cook and break down evenly.

* Leaving the skin on is a matter of taste; be aware, however, that as the apple flesh breaks down, the skin will not, therefore leaving chewy pieces throughout the sauce.

* To use a microwave with this sauce, place all the prepared ingredients in a microwave-proof bowl, cover with a lid but have the lid slightly open to allow steam to escape or cover with plastic wrap with a couple of holes in the top. Microwave on high for 10 minutes, being careful when removing the lid or wrap to avoid a steam burn, the nastiest of all burns.

* For a more **exotic apple sauce**, add to the above recipe 1 tablespoon apple brandy (Calvados) or cognac, 1 tablespoon butter, 1 tablespoon honey and ½ teaspoon ground cinnamon.

* Adding a dry spice at the beginning creates a beautiful aroma and flavour. The addition of 1 cinnamon stick or 4 whole cloves to the basic recipe is a good start. Peppercorns (10), bay leaf (1), caraway seeds

(½ teaspoon toasted) or juniper berries (4 crushed) are alternative flavour profiles.

* Often associated with roast pork or pork chops, apple sauce accompanies roast duck and goose equally as well. As a dessert, it can be served with ice-cream or yoghurt.

* Adding butter to the sauce at the beginning can add a rich texture to the finished sauce, but is completely optional, especially if cutting back on unnecessary fats.

* For a simple baby food option, add nothing to the saucepan other than diced apples, cook on low heat, stirring often until completely soft, then cool and store in the refrigerator until needed.

* For toddlers or young children, instead of making an apple puree, simply crush with a fork or potato masher and add some sultanas, currants or dried cranberries.

* Apple sauce freezes very well in airtight containers, for at least 6 months.

BUTTERSCOTCH SAUCE
Makes about 600 ml

XXXXXXXXXXXXXXXXXXXXXXXXXXXXXXXXXXXXXXXXXXXXXXXXXXXXXXXXXXXXXXXXXXXXXXXXXXXXXXXXXXXXXXXXXXXX

150 g unsalted butter
250 g dark brown sugar
300 ml thickened cream

Method:

1. Place the butter and sugar in a saucepan over medium heat and stir until the butter melts and the sugar begins to dissolve.

2. Remove from the heat and whisk in the cream. Place back on the heat and bring to the boil. Strain through a sieve and use immediately, or cool and store in the refrigerator for up to 7 days. To reheat, simply place in a saucepan and bring back to the boil or place in a microwave-proof bowl for 1 minute.

HINTS AND TIPS:

* You will need—saucepan, weight and liquid measures, and wooden spoon.

* Salted butter can be used for this sauce and will, of course, give it a very mild, but not offensive, salty taste.

* Dark brown sugar is a soft brown sugar. The 'dark' refers to the molasses left in the sugar when being refined. The darker the sugar, the richer it is—also the better it is for you. Dark brown sugar is readily available at all supermarkets.

* An alternative to 'dark brown sugar' is 'soft brown sugar' or 'brown sugar', which is less dark due to extra refining at the mill.

* Thickened cream can be replaced with pouring cream or even double cream which would result in a very rich sauce. Thickened cream and pouring cream have fat contents at between 28 per cent and 35 per cent whilst double cream is more like 50–52 per cent.

* After sitting in the fridge for a day or two, the sauce may separate. At the bottom of the dish is a small amount of dark syrup, while the majority of the sauce is a thick, almost solid mass. Do not panic, as it is simply some of the sugars taking a breather from the sauce. Once heated, everything will be as it was.

* Butterscotch sauce goes with date pudding, ice-cream, pancakes, crepes and waffles.

* The fact that butterscotch sauce has the word 'scotch' in it makes you wonder if it really can be made with alcohol. Yes, it can. For an adult version of this sauce, try adding 2 tablespoons Scotch whisky.

* For **simple toffee sauce**— combine 100 g unsalted butter, 200 g soft brown sugar, 1 cup thickened cream, 1 teaspoon vanilla extract in a saucepan, stir over medium–high heat until the sauce comes to the boil, reduce heat and simmer for 5 minutes.

* For a **pecan toffee sauce**—add ½ cup chopped pecan nuts to the sauce once removed from the heat. This is a great accompaniment for sticky date pudding.

CARAMEL SAUCE

Makes about 2 cups

XXXXXXXXXXXXXXXXXXXXXXXXXXXXXXXXXXXXXXXXXXXXXXXXXXXXXXXXXXXXXXXXXXXXXXXXXXXXXXXXXXXXXXXXXXXXXXXXXXXX

100 ml water
150 g granulated sugar
300 ml thickened cream

Method:

1. Bring the water to the boil in a heavy-based saucepan over high heat, add the sugar and reduce the heat to medium. Continue cooking the sugar until the caramel liquid becomes a deep amber colour.

2. Remove the saucepan from the heat immediately and add the cream. Return the saucepan to the heat and bring back to the boil, stirring with a whisk until the caramel is dissolved.

3. Pour into a container and cool. Refrigerate until needed—the sauce can be served cold or reheated.

HINTS AND TIPS:

* You will need—saucepan, whisk, and weight and liquid measures.

* This is a true caramel sauce, often recipes for caramel sauce closely resemble or are identical to **butterscotch sauce**. They are quite different in the method and therefore deserve different names.

* When adding the cream to the caramel, it may bubble and splatter, so take care. To avoid this aggressive reaction, try heating the cream in the microwave and adding it warm or even hot.

* This is a great sauce to go with chocolate desserts, apple pie, hot puddings like sticky date pudding or over ice-cream. The sauce is traditionally always served chilled, but can be warmed through.

* For a smoother more refined caramel sauce, try adding 2 egg yolks. To do this, place 2 egg yolks in a separate bowl, whisk a little of the hot caramel sauce into the yolks and then pour the yolk mixture back into the sauce, mix thoroughly and set aside to cool. Do not put it back on the heat.

* For **caramel ice-cream**—now that egg yolks are in the mixture (see previous tip) and because of the cream content, simply pour this mixture into an ice-cream machine and churn according to the manufacturer's instructions.

* This method of making caramel sauce is known as a 'wet caramel' because water is added to give the cook a more controlled, even result. However, for the more experienced cooks, a 'dry caramel' can be made and takes a fraction of the time. To do this, omit the water completely and place the sugar in the pan over medium heat. The sugar will naturally begin to melt. At this point you need to keep watch, as hot spots can occur and parts of the sugar will begin to caramelise before most of it has melted properly. To avoid this from happening, swirl the sugar in the pan so it is constantly moving and melting evenly. Before you know it, the whole quantity has caramelised and is ready to mix with the cream.

* Caramel sauce will keep in the fridge for 3–5 days, covered; and like butterscotch sauce, after sitting in the fridge for a few days, the sauce may separate: at the bottom of the dish is a small amount of dark syrup, while the majority of the sauce is a thick, almost solid mass. Do not panic, as it is simply some of the heavy sugars separating from the lighter fats of the cream. Reheat or pour into a bowl and whisk.

CHOCOLATE SAUCE

Makes about 3 cups

xxxxxxxxxxxxxxxxxxxxxxxxxxxxxxxxxxxxxxxxxxxxxxxxxxxxxxxxxxxxxxxxxxxxxxxxxxxxxxxxxxxxxxxxxxx

300 g dark cooking chocolate, chopped
250 ml cold water
50 g caster sugar
1 teaspoon vanilla essence
½ cup pouring cream
50 g unsalted butter

Method:

1. Place about 10 cm of hot water in a small saucepan and bring to the boil.

2. Combine the chocolate, water and sugar in a heatproof bowl and place over the boiling water. Reduce the heat to low and simmer gently until the chocolate has melted, stirring the mixture occasionally.

3. When the chocolate mixture is smooth, remove from the heat and stir in the vanilla, cream and butter. Either use immediately or cool and refrigerate, covered, for up to 2 weeks. Once cold, the sauce will have set; to use, spoon out the required amount of sauce and heat gently either in a pan or in the microwave.

* You will need—saucepan, bowl, long-handled plastic scraper, and weight, cup, liquid and spoon measures.

* A chocolate sauce made in this fashion, albeit beautiful, can be time-consuming, so check the method for easy chocolate sauce below.

* **Easy chocolate sauce**—this is the easiest way to make a chocolate sauce. In a saucepan, bring 300 ml cream to the boil, remove from the heat and with a whisk or wooden spoon, stir in 150 g chopped dark cooking chocolate. Stir until all the chocolate is thoroughly combined then transfer to a bowl or jug, cover and refrigerate. This recipe for chocolate sauce is my personal favourite, because it is so easy.

* Chocolate sauce goes with ice-cream, pancakes, crepes, profiteroles, poached pears, in or on soufflé, on toasted brioche and banana cake.

* Adding alcohol to chocolate sauce is very naughty and I therefore thoroughly recommend doing it! Try adding 2 tablespoons of any of the following favourite—Creme de Cacao (chocolate liqueur), Frangelico (hazelnut liqueur), Grand Marnier, Triple Sec or Cointreau (orange liqueurs), Curacao (bitter orange liqueur), Kahlua or Tia Maria (coffee liqueurs), Baileys Irish Cream, or Chambord (raspberry liqueur).

* If all that is in the pantry is cocoa powder and it's too late to buy the ingredients for the above recipe, try this as an alternative—place 125 g caster sugar in a heavy-based saucepan, add 125 ml water and stir over gentle heat until the sugar is dissolved. Bring to the boil and boil for 2 minutes. Remove from the heat, add 50 g sifted cocoa powder and whisk until smooth. Bring back to the boil then remove from the heat. Cool slightly and serve, or store refrigerated. This sauce will lack the finesse of the basic recipe but will do the job until the shops open.

RASPBERRY SAUCE

Makes about 1½ cups

XXXXXXXXXXXXXXXXXXXXXXXXXXXXXXXXXXXXXXXXXXXXXXXXXXXXXXXXXXXXXXXXXXXXXXXXXXXXXXXXXXXXXXXXXXXXX

225 g (1 punnet) fresh raspberries
100 g pure icing sugar
lemon juice, to taste

Method:

1. Place the raspberries in a bowl and coat with the icing sugar, cover with plastic wrap and stand at room temperature for 1 hour to allow the sugar to begin drawing out the juices from the raspberries.

2. Place the mixture in a food processor and puree briefly. Pour into a sieve to remove the seeds. Taste the sauce and add a squeeze of lemon juice to round out the flavour. Place the sauce in a container and refrigerate until required for up to 5 days.

HINTS AND TIPS:

* You will need—bowl, spoon, weight measure, food processor, plastic spatula, and sieve.

* Fresh raspberries are not available all year round and for this particular sauce, frozen raspberries are a perfect substitute. Defrost the raspberries before adding the sugar and follow the method provided.

* Leaving the raspberries and sugar to sit to draw out the juices is not vital, and if you are in a hurry, simply skip this step and proceed to the puree stage.

* Lemon juice is added in some cases as it lends a different sourness to that of the raspberries. For example, if the berries are plump and very sweet, the sauce may lack the characteristic sourness needed to match the dessert it is served with.

* An adult version can be made by adding a liqueur that marries well with raspberries. To the above recipe, add 2 tablespoons of one of the following— Chambord (raspberry liqueur), Hideous (berry and citrus liqueur), Grand Marnier or Cointreau (orange liqueur).

* Caster sugar or even soft brown sugar can be substituted for icing sugar.

* For a mixed berry sauce, use a combination of several different berries to equal the total quantity in the recipe. Blackberries, mulberries, boysenberries, loganberries and youngberries are some varieties that can be used. Blueberries and strawberries could also work with less success.

* Any leftover sauce can be frozen for up to 6 months. After that the ice crystals that form in the sauce will get too large and the sauce will become watery and lack flavour when defrosted.

* Raspberry sauce goes with many, many desserts—for example, over and under ice-cream, used in ice-cream, on pancakes (with ice-cream) and with meringues (and ice-cream).

* If you own an ice-cream machine, pour the sauce into the machine with 1 teaspoon lightly beaten egg white (used as a stabiliser) and follow the manufacturer's instructions to produce a quick raspberry sorbet.

* Leftover raspberry sauce can be used in conjunction with whole fresh raspberries to make **raspberry fool**.

XXXXXXXXXXXX **11. Desserts** XXXXXXXXXXXX

APPLE AND RHUBARB CRUMBLE

Serves 6

xxxxxxxxxxxxxxxxxxxxxxxxxxxxxxxxxxxxxxxxxxxxxxxxxxxxxxxxxxxxxxxxxxxxxxxxxxxxxxxxxxxxxxxxxxx

500 g rhubarb
500 g cooking apples, Granny Smith or
    Golden Delicious
180 g caster sugar
40 g unsalted butter
1 cinnamon stick
juice of ½ lemon

Crumble
125 g unsalted butter
125 g caster sugar
250 g plain flour

Method:

1. Preheat the oven to 180°C.

2. Trim the rhubarb and cut into 2-cm pieces. Peel the apples, remove the core and dice to roughly the same size as the rhubarb.

3. Place the sugar, butter, cinnamon and lemon juice in a stainless steel pan and cook over medium heat until lightly caramelised. Add the rhubarb and cook for 5 minutes, then add the apple and cook for another 5 minutes. Remove from the heat and allow to cool.

4. For the crumble—place all of the ingredients in a bowl and mix well using your hands. Keep mixing and rubbing to form coarse crumbs.

5. To assemble—place the apple and rhubarb mixture in a baking dish or individual ramekins filling to three-quarters full. Top with the crumble mixture and then bake in the oven until the crumble is crisp and pale brown, about 30 minutes. Serve immediately with cream, yoghurt or ice-cream.

HINTS AND TIPS:

* You will need—cutting board, cook's knife, paring knife, vegetable peeler, weight measure, bowl, saucepan, baking dish or 6 ramekins and wooden spoon.

* A friendly reminder: never eat the leaves from rhubarb as they contain the poison oxalic acid. Although only 0.5 per cent of the leaf is oxalic acid, it wouldn't take much to make a person sick.

* The leaves aren't entirely useless, however. Boil 5–6 leaves with 1 litre of water for 30 minutes, strain and mix with ½ teaspoon liquid soap (not detergent), then use in a spray bottle to kill or deter aphids from plants, keeping in mind that it is still a poison and should not be used on edible plants.

* Oxalic acid is also present in the stem but exists in far less and very edible quantities—it's what gives rhubarb that pucker-the-lips effect.

* Remember to wash the rhubarb stalks thoroughly before cooking.

* Try replacing the plain flour with wholemeal flour for a healthier alternative.

* The plain flour can also be halved and replaced with 125 g almond meal.

* For a gluten-free recipe, the plain flour can be replaced with 250 g almond meal. For nut allergies, try replacing the almond meal with 125 g buckwheat flour mixed with 125 g rice flour or 125 g potato flour.

* Another alternative for the crumble topping is to mix 2 cups rolled oats or even raw muesli with the specified quantities of sugar and butter (melt the butter for this version of crumble). If this crumble topping is a bit dry, try adding more melted butter.

* Other cooking apples include the Bramley, Grenadier and Jonathan.

* Some apples, when cooked, turn to mush while others tend to hold their shape quite well. Those that break down include the Bramley, McIntosh and Melba. The firmer holding varieties include Granny Smith, Golden Delicious, Winesap and Baldwin.

* If you are making a large batch and are concerned the apples will discolour after peeling and dicing, then squeeze the juice from a lemon in a bowl and toss in the apple pieces. Often it is recommended to drop the apples in acidulated water, which is a bowl of water with lemon juice squeezed into it. The problem with this method is that the apples absorb too much water by the time they are ready to cook, therefore making the cooked mass too watery.

* Leftover crumble is great the next morning for a breakfast treat served with yoghurt.

APPLE PIE

Serves 10

XXXXXXXXXXXXXXXXXXXXXXXXXXXXXXXXXXXXXXXXXXXXXXXXXXXXXXXXXXXXXXXXXXXXXXXXXXXXXXXXXXXXXXXXXXXXXX

2 x recipe quantities **sweet shortcrust pastry**
200 g unsalted butter
3 kg Golden Delicious apples, peeled, quartered,
    cored and chopped
450 g soft brown sugar
150 ml water
1 teaspoon ground cinnamon
1 tablespoon vanilla extract
1 tablespoon cornflour mixed with 1 tablespoon
    cold water
50 g dried bread crumbs
1 egg yolk

Method:

1. Roll out 1 batch of the pastry about 3–5 mm thick
and drape over a pie dish. Gently press the pastry
into the base and place in the refrigerator to set.

2. Preheat the oven to 180°C.

3. Melt the butter over medium heat in a large pot.
Add the apples and stir. Add the sugar, water,
cinnamon and vanilla and cook, uncovered, for
5 minutes. Stir in the cornflour mixture and cook
until thickened. Pour onto a baking tray and leave
to cool to room temperature.

4. Blind bake the pastry base (see Pastry in Really
Useful Information). Cool slightly, sprinkle with the
bread crumbs and pour the cooled apple filling onto the
pastry. It may appear as if there is too much but it
is meant to be overfull.

5. Roll out the second batch of pastry and drape over
the pie filling. Brush with the egg yolk and bake for
20 minutes or until the top is golden and crispy.

6. Serve hot from the oven or allow to cool and serve
at room temperature.

HINTS AND TIPS:

* You will need—cutting board, cook's knife, vegetable peeler, spoon, liquid and weight measures, 23-cm (9-inch) American-style ceramic or Pyrex pie dish, pastry brush, rolling pin, wooden spoon, baking tray, and large saucepan.

* Add nuts to the pie filling. Roast 250 g walnuts or pecan nuts, chop roughly then mix into the apple mixture.

* The bread crumbs in the base of the apple pie soak up excess moisture so the base stays crispy and light.

* Adding raw apples to the pie filling is fine, but remember to overfill the pie dish as the apples will shrink as they cook.

* This pie can be made in a flan ring with a removable base.

* Serve with ice-cream, whipped cream, crème fraîche, yoghurt or sour cream.

* The trimmings from the pastry can be used to make small leaves to add to the top of the pie.

APPLE STRUDEL

Serves 8

XXXXXXXXXXXXXXXXXXXXXXXXXXXXXXXXXXXXXXXXXXXXXXXXXXXXXXXXXXXXXXXXXXXXXXXXXXXXXXXXXXXXXXXXXXXXXXXXXX

4 large Granny Smith apples, peeled, cored and sliced
zest and juice of 1 lemon
100 g bread crumbs
150 g caster sugar
150 g unsalted butter, melted
1 teaspoon ground cinnamon
50 g sultanas
6 sheets filo pastry
pure icing sugar, for dusting

Method:

1. Toss the apple in the lemon juice.

2. Preheat the oven to 180°C. Line a baking tray with baking paper.

3. Mix the apples, lemon zest, bread crumbs, caster sugar, one-third of the melted butter, cinnamon and sultanas in a large bowl.

4. Lay 1 sheet of filo pastry on the prepared baking tray and brush with a little of the remaining melted butter, lay another sheet on top and again brush with melted butter. Continue until there are 4–5 layers of pastry. Do not brush the last sheet with butter.

5. Pour the apple filling onto the pastry, leaving a 5-cm border all around. Fold in the shorter sides and roll the log over so the seam side is facing down, brush with the remaining butter, and bake for 30 minutes or until golden.

6. Remove from the oven and cool slightly before dusting heavily with icing sugar. Cut serves on an angle and serve with whipped cream.

HINTS AND TIPS:

* You will need—large bowl, small bowl, vegetable peeler, apple corer, weight and spoon measures, pastry brush, and flat baking tray.

* Apple strudel originated in Austria where it is made with a special strudel dough. For a novice or even an intermediate cook, the notion of making the dough is daunting at the very least. The best and easiest alternative is to use paper-thin filo pastry, found in all supermarkets and delis.

* Puff pastry could be used instead of filo; however, because it is thicker, the underside tends to stay wet and therefore doughy and undercooked compared with the top.

* If filo pastry was bought frozen, leave out to thoroughly defrost before using. Slightly frozen, too cold or stale filo pastry is difficult to work with and will often crack and break.

* When working with filo, always remember to work quickly and keep the pastry covered with a damp towel when not using as it dries out and becomes brittle. When storing leftover filo, roll up, place back in the bag it came in, plastic wrap the end tightly and place back in the outer box or bag it came in. Keep refrigerated.

* Individual strudels can be made by using 2 sheets of filo pastry, brushed with melted butter in between, then folded in half. Place 2 heaped tablespoons apple mixture in the centre of the pastry. Gather in the corners, holding them above the apple, then squeeze the pastry together just above the apple mixture to form a closed bag with a sprouting top of pastry. Brush with butter and bake for 15–20 minutes.

* Other dried fruits can be added to this mixture. Instead of sultanas, try currants, raisins, prunes, dates, golden sultanas, dried apricots or pears, or dried cranberries.

* A ¼ cup nuts can also be added, especially suited are walnuts or pecan nuts. Almonds and macadamia nuts also work. Remember to crush or break up the nuts before adding to the apple mixture.

* Using canned apples for this recipe is recommended when time is limited. Always check the label to make sure the can contains 'sliced' apples and not apple puree or diced (pie) apple. Omit the bread crumbs from the recipe if using canned apples. Reduce the cooking time to 15–20 minutes and increase the oven temperature to 210°C—the apples are cooked and so the inside only needs to be heated through and the pastry cooked until golden.

BAKED CHEESECAKE

Serves 10–12 people

xxxxxxxxxxxxxxxxxxxxxxxxxxxxxxxxxxxxxxxxxxxxxxxxxxxxxxxxxxxxxxxxxxxxxxxxxxxxxxxxxxxxxxxxxxxxxx

1 teaspoon butter, for greasing

Base
250 g plain sweet biscuits
125 g unsalted butter, melted

Filling
500 g cream cheese, at room temperature
2 eggs, at room temperature
2 egg yolks, at room temperature
200 ml thickened cream
200 g pure icing sugar
finely grated zest of 1 lemon
juice of 1 lemon

Method:

1. Preheat the oven to 150°C. Grease a 20-cm
springform cake tin with 1 teaspoon butter.

2. For the base—place the biscuits in a food
processor and blitz until finely crushed. Add the
melted butter and process until well combined.
Transfer to the prepared cake tin and use the back of
a spoon to spread evenly over the base and halfway
up the sides of the tin. Place in the fridge until
needed.

3. For the filling—place all of the ingredients in
a bowl and mix with a wooden spoon until thoroughly
combined. Do not beat heavily or use a whisk (see
Hints and tips). Pour onto the base.

4. Bake for 1 hour in the oven or until the centre
of the cheesecake has just set. When given a gentle
shake, the centre should wobble like jelly. At this
point, turn off the oven and leave the door ajar
to slowly cool down (see Hints and tips). When
mostly cool, remove the cheesecake from the oven and
refrigerate. Serve when cold.

HINTS AND TIPS:

* You will need—20-cm springform cake tin, food processor, grater, bowl, wooden spoon, plastic spatula, and weight, liquid and spoon measures.

* This traditional baked cheesecake has many variations. It is the method, however, that seems to cause the greatest problems, especially the outcome—notably that the cheesecake is dry and/or it forms a crack in the middle.

* First—do not be tempted to over-beat or whip the mixture, this will create excessive air bubbles which will make the cheesecake rise and then collapse when cooled, leaving a depression in the surface. The method above suggests mixing all the ingredients together with a wooden spoon to form a smooth paste or custard. Having the cream cheese and eggs at room temperature will help to make this stage easier. Recipes that ask for egg whites to be beaten and folded into the mix are asking for trouble. As do recipes that request the beating of anything until light and fluffy. Light and fluffy are the enemies of a good baked cheesecake.

* Second—do not overcook. A smooth baked cheesecake is basically a custard and only needs to cook until the eggs are just set, cooling slowly and refrigerating finish the setting process. Baking at too high a temperature will overcook the filling, resulting in a cheesecake that is dry and crumbly in texture and has shrunk around the edges.

* Third—the cracked surface of a cheesecake is the result of cooling too quickly. Therefore it is recommended that it begins cooling in the oven with the door ajar before being transferred to the fridge to set.

BAKED QUINCE

Makes about 1½ kg

xxxxxxxxxxxxxxxxxxxxxxxxxxxxxxxxxxxxxxxxxxxxxxxxxxxxxxxxxxxxxxxxxxxxxxxxxxxxxxxxxxxxxxxxxxxxxxxxx

5 quinces
800 g sugar
150 g unsalted butter, diced

Method:

1. Preheat the oven to 160°C. Wash or wipe the quinces, removing any down that may be on the surface.

2. Cut the quinces into quarters and remove the core. Place the quince, unpeeled, in a baking tray cut side up.

3. Sprinkle with the sugar and diced butter.

4. Add a little water to the tray, cover with foil and bake for 1½ hours. Turn quinces and cook for a further 1½ hours.

5. Once cooked, serve immediately or leave to cool and store in the refrigerator for several weeks.

HINTS AND TIPS:

* You will need—cutting board, sharp cook's knife, paring knife, weight measure, and baking tray.

* Quinces, once in season, are delicious. When buying, look for quinces that are free from blemishes and have a pale yellow skin and a fragrance that resembles 'boiled candies'.

* Quinces are a very hard fruit even when ready to cook, so feeling for 'ripeness' will prove futile.

* Cutting quinces must be done with great care, as they are so hard it is easy to slip with the knife. Once cut in half, place the cut surface on the cutting board and cut into quarters to avoid the fruit rolling when trying to cut.

* Quinces are not a fruit for eating out of hand. They need long slow cooking before using in pies, compotes, crumbles, frangipane, cakes or as a paste.

* The theory is that 'the deep red colour of the baked quinces is the guide to doneness'. However, sometimes some of the quinces seem to remain very pale, even when thoroughly cooked and soft. This has to do with the 'ripeness' or 'ready-ness', which can be hard to tell until cooked. If the quinces are not completely yellow, store them at room temperature until they are fully ripened, yellow all over and emit a pleasant aroma, they will be no softer to handle. The cooked fruit still eat well if pale, but lack the depth of flavour of the riper, dark red cooked quince.

* Another method of cooking is to bake at 100°C for 8 hours or even overnight. This long, slow process helps to guarantee the richness in colour that is desired in the fruit.

* Certain spices and peel can be added when baking quinces. Try 2 cinnamon sticks and the zest of 1 lemon, or add 6 whole cloves, 6 black peppercorns, zest of 1 orange and 2 bay leaves.

* Baked quince goes with creamy, natural yoghurt, custard, or whipped cream.

* Cook quince in the same manner but with half the sugar and 1 tablespoon juniper berries. The fruit will be ideal to use as an accompaniment to savoury meat dishes like duck, venison or rabbit.

* For a small quantity, take 1 quince, slice in half and remove the core. Place 1 half on a large piece of foil, cut side up, add ½ cup sugar, 1 teaspoon butter and a piece of lemon zest (optional), and enclose in the foil. Repeat with the other half. Place in an oven preheated to 180°C for 1–2 hours until tender. Serve immediately or cool and refrigerate.

BAKED RICOTTA CHEESECAKE
Serves 8

XXXXXXXXXXXXXXXXXXXXXXXXXXXXXXXXXXXXXXXXXXXXXXXXXXXXXXXXXXXXXXXXXXXXXXXXXXXXXXXXXXXXXXXXXXXXX

500 g ricotta
200 g almond meal
50 g caster sugar
100 g sultanas
4 egg yolks
1 teaspoon vanilla extract
zest of 1 orange
juice of 1 orange
pure icing sugar, for dusting

Method:

1. Preheat the oven to 130°C. Grease and line the base of a baking dish or a springform cake tin with baking paper.

2. Mix all the ingredients in a bowl and pour into the prepared dish.

3. Place in the oven and bake for 1 hour or until the centre is just set. Remove from the oven and cool on a wire rack.

4. When cooled, dust with the icing sugar and serve.

HINTS AND TIPS:

* You will need—large bowl, wooden spoon, plastic spatula, very fine grater, weight, spoon and liquid measures, juicer, 22-cm springform cake tin and baking paper.

* This classic Italian dessert is perfect for the non-sweet tooth. Unlike other baked cheesecakes which are rich and creamy, ricotta cheesecake has a drier consistency and mouth feel, and can do with the company of either a sauce or some pouring cream.

* The ricotta in this recipe refers to the firm ricotta available from all delicatessens. Although the recipe will work with the tubs of soft ricotta, the cake tends to be a bit wet once cooled.

* This cheesecake is often made with plain flour but I have reworked the recipe to make it gluten-free. I also find the almond meal adds to the moistness of the cheesecake. If making it with plain flour, then use 100 g plain flour.

* A good sauce for this dish is a **caramel orange sauce**—place 100 g sugar in a saucepan with 1 tablespoon water and set over medium heat. When the sugar reaches a light caramel colour, add the zest of 1 orange and 100 ml orange juice (carefully), and stir with a whisk until the caramel dissolves in the juice. Mix together 1 tablespoon cornflour and 1 tablespoon cold water in a small bowl and slowly drizzle into the simmering sauce, stirring until thickened slightly. You may not need all of the cornflour. Remove the sauce from the heat, and cool slightly before stirring in 60 ml orange liqueur (Cointreau, Triple Sec or Grand Marnier). This sauce will keep for 4–6 weeks refrigerated.

* Substitute the orange zest and juice in the basic recipe for lemon juice and zest.

* The recipe can be adjusted to accommodate the sweet tooth, simply add an extra 100 g caster sugar.

* Try adding a spice to the mixture—mix in 1 tablespoon ground cinnamon or grate fresh nutmeg over the cheesecake before it goes into the oven.

* Cool the cheesecake thoroughly in the tin. As it cools it will come away from the sides and won't tend to split in the middle.

* Try soaking the sultanas in 100 ml orange liqueur or brandy for 1 hour before adding to the mixture.

BANANA SPLIT

Serves 1

XXXXXXXXXXXXXXXXXXXXXXXXXXXXXXXXXXXXXXXXXXXXXXXXXXXXXXXXXXXXXXXXXXXXXXXXXXXXXXXXXXXXXXXXXXXX

1 ripe banana
100 ml thickened cream
1 teaspoon pure icing sugar
1–3 scoops vanilla ice-cream
100 ml **chocolate sauce**
1 tablespoon crushed peanuts
1 maraschino cherry with stem

Method:

1. Peel the banana and cut in 2 lengthways. Place in an elongated glass dish or a dessert bowl.

2. Whip the cream and sugar until firm peaks form.

3. Place as many as 3 scoops of ice-cream in the centre of the banana halves. Dollop or pipe the whipped cream over the ice-cream. Drizzle with the chocolate sauce, sprinkle with the nuts and top with the cherry.

HINTS AND TIPS:

* You will need—cutting board, cook's knife, banana split dish or dessert bowl, bowl and whisk or electric beaters and spoon and liquid measures.

* Banana split is an American invention and this recipe is about as traditional as it gets. From here on in, it is open slather as to what else goes in.

* Always use 1 ripe banana per serve.

* The ice-cream should be the best quality—and vanilla—is just the beginning. Strawberry, cookies and cream, chocolate and caramel swirl are also highly recommended.

* Making chocolate sauce could be seen as a time-wasting chore on a dessert that should be thrown together in seconds. The homemade sauce is amazing, but a fast alternative is a store-bought chocolate sauce that sets hard when it hits the cold ice-cream.

* While we're discussing cheating, you may as well pick up some 'dairy whip', the whipped cream in a can. Basically half cream and half air with a dose of sugar,

this is what some prescribe as the best cream for banana split.

* The peanuts can also be bought crushed and added straight from the packet.

* Maraschino cherries have a taste that some kiddies just won't like; substitute for a glazed cherry or better still, fresh berries in season.

* **Caramel sauce**, strawberry sauce, **raspberry sauce**, fresh passionfruit pulp or mango puree can all be substituted for chocolate sauce.

* Chop up your favourite chocolate bar and sprinkle over the ice-cream before adding the cream.

* Try toasted almond flakes or crushed macadamia nuts instead of peanuts. Or use smashed peanut brittle or sesame brittle instead of the nuts.

* Grill the banana halves on a barbecue plate or in a sauté pan with 1 teaspoon butter before serving.

* Make a **roasted banana split**—place the banana in its skin in a preheated hot oven (220°C) for 10–12 minutes (or on the

barbecue, turning occasionally). Remove from the oven, carefully slice the skin open, place the banana on a plate (in the skin) exposing the soft cooked flesh, and top with ice-cream, cream, chocolate or caramel sauce, nuts and a cherry. Or use any of the other flavour ideas.

BRANDY SNAPS

Makes about 10–12

xxxxxxxxxxxxxxxxxxxxxxxxxxxxxxxxxxxxxxxxxxxxxxxxxxxxxxxxxxxxxxxxxxxxxxxxxxxxxxxxxxxxxxxxxxxxx

120 g butter
120 g caster sugar
120 g golden syrup
120 g plain flour
1 teaspoon ground ginger
1 teaspoon lemon juice

Method:

1. Preheat the oven to 180°C. Line a baking tray with baking paper.

2. Place the butter, sugar and golden syrup in a saucepan and heat gently until the butter has melted and the sugar dissolved. Remove from the heat and leave to cool slightly.

3. Sift the flour and ginger directly into the mixture, add the lemon juice and stir well. Refrigerate for at least 1 hour before using.

4. Place 1 tablespoon of the mixture on the prepared baking tray and spread out thinly. Repeat until the tray is full. Do not place too closely together as they spread when baking.

5. Bake in the oven for 6–9 minutes. When dark caramel in colour and bubbling, remove from the oven and allow to cool for 30 seconds before handling, then, while still warm, remove from the baking paper with a flat knife or egg flip.

6. Drape over a rolling pin to obtain a nice curved shape or over a cup to form a bowl shape. Allow to cool completely before removing from the mould. The brandy snaps can be used immediately with whipped cream or thick custard and fruit, or stored in an airtight container in the pantry for 1–2 days before they naturally begin to soften.

HINTS AND TIPS:

* You will need—saucepan, spoon and weight measures, sieve, wooden spoon, baking tray, baking paper and rolling pin or cup.

* The brandy snap mixture will last uncooked in the fridge for 2 weeks. Use cold from the fridge before baking for an easy dessert at any time.

* For **maple snaps**—simply replace the golden syrup with the same quantity of pure maple syrup.

* For **raspberry snaps**—replace the golden syrup with **raspberry sauce**, and cook through, trying to retain some of the red colouring from the fruit while allowing it to set properly.

* If, after a couple of days in the pantry, the snaps begin to soften, place them back in a preheated 180°C oven for 1 minute, then repeat the process of forming the desired shape. Cool and store again.

* For a cigar shape, wrap the warm biscuit around a wooden spoon handle, then cool completely before removing.

* Do not be tempted to make too many in one go. Make 2 or 3 at a time—this way you have time to mould and shape the warm biscuit. If you try to make too many, the biscuit may cool too quickly and set flat or break while you're trying to shape it.

* If you try and mould the biscuit straight from the oven, it may be too hot and tear when placed over the rolling pin or inverted cup—be patient.

* If the biscuits are too pale when they come out of the oven, you will find they will not set properly and stay crispy. In this case, place them back in the oven for another 1–2 minutes.

* An uncooked base version of this recipe can work just as well. Cream the butter (softened) and sugar until pale, stir in the golden syrup then sift in the flour and ginger, add the lemon juice, and the mixture is ready to use. To make this even easier, replace the caster sugar with pure icing sugar.

BREAD AND BUTTER PUDDING

Serves 6

XXXXXXXXXXXXXXXXXXXXXXXXXXXXXXXXXXXXXXXXXXXXXXXXXXXXXXXXXXXXXXXXXXXXXXXXXXXXXXXXXXXXX

150 g sultanas

60 ml orange liqueur
(Cointreau or Grand
Marnier)

600 ml full cream milk

300 ml thickened cream

1 teaspoon vanilla extract

6 eggs

150 g caster sugar

16 slices white bread

2 tablespoons unsalted
butter, softened

apricot jam

Method:

1. Soak the sultanas in the orange liqueur for
2–3 hours. Lightly grease a baking dish.

2. Preheat the oven to 150°C.

3. Bring the milk, cream and vanilla to a simmer over
medium heat and remove from the heat.

4. In a large bowl, beat the eggs and sugar until
pale. Slowly add all the milk mixture and stir well.

5. Butter the bread and spread with the jam. Remove
the crusts and cut each jam sandwich on the diagonal.

6. Layer the bread, sultanas and custard in the
prepared baking dish. Let stand for 1 hour.

7. Bake for 1–1½ hours or until the custard has set.

8. The pudding can be served immediately. However, it
is best left to stand for 15 minutes before serving.

HINTS AND TIPS:

★ You will need—cutting
board, cook's knife, 2 bowls,
baking dish, weight, liquid
and spoon measures and wooden
spoon or whisk.

★ Bread and butter pudding
is a classic dish with many
interpretations. It is
important to know that it
is a form of baked custard.
Importantly don't rush the
cooking process. A slow oven
for a longer cooking time
is preferred over a higher
temperature and shorter time
which will curdle the custard
and make it watery.

★ This recipe has many
options, so let's begin by
suggesting the plain white
bread can be replaced with
croissants, ciabatta or
bread sticks. The crust
on these breads can be
left on as they are not as
chewy as commercial white
bread (ciabatta can be
tough though). Fruit bread
or panettone can replace
the bread and the soaked
sultanas.

★ Alcohol can be omitted
all together. Alternatively,
other liqueurs can be used
depending on the flavour and
fruit being matched.

★ Chocolate buttons can
replace the sultanas, with
a dash of Crème de Cacao
(chocolate liqueur) mixed
into the custard.

★ A sprinkle of ground
cinnamon or nutmeg over the
top before baking adds a nice
spice touch.

★ For a dairy-free
alternative, see **bread and
butter pudding with soy**. For
gluten-intolerance, replace
with gluten-free bread; and
if using soy milk, check
there are no wheat products
in the soy milk.

BREAD AND BUTTER PUDDING WITH SOY

Serves 4

XXXXXXXXXXXXXXXXXXXXXXXXXXXXXXXXXXXXXXXXXXXXXXXXXXXXXXXXXXXXXXXXXXXXXXXXXXXXXXXXXXXXXXXX

3 eggs
1½ tablespoons honey
2½ cups vanilla-flavoured
   soy milk
1 tablespoon margarine
2 tablespoons apricot jam
8 slices light rye or
   multigrain bread,
   crusts removed
¾ cup sultanas

Method:

1. Preheat the oven to 160°C. Lightly grease a round ovenproof dish.

2. Place the eggs, honey and soy milk in a bowl. Whisk well.

3. Spread the margarine and jam onto one side of each slice of bread and cut into triangles.

4. Place a layer of bread into the prepared dish and sprinkle with ½ cup sultanas. Gently pour half the custard mixture over the top.

5. Place the remaining bread into dish in a circular pattern, and add the remaining custard. Sprinkle with the remaining sultanas.

6. Place the pudding into a large baking pan filled with enough water to come halfway up the sides of the ovenproof dish. Bake in the oven for 1 hour or until set and browned on top. The pudding can be served immediately. However, it is best left to stand for 15 minutes before serving.

7. For **Hints and tips** please see p. 276.

CHOCOLATE MOUSSE

Serves 4

XXXXXXXXXXXXXXXXXXXXXXXXXXXXXXXXXXXXXXXXXXXXXXXXXXXXXXXXXXXXXXXXXXXXXXXXXXXXXXXXXXXXXXXXXXXXXXXX

150 g good quality dark cooking chocolate
100 ml espresso coffee
4 eggs, separated
pinch of salt
100 g caster sugar
250 ml thickened cream, lightly whipped and
    kept refrigerated

Method:

1. Combine the chocolate and coffee in a heatproof
bowl and place on a pot of just-boiled water that has
been removed from the heat. The residual steam will
gently melt the chocolate.

2. Allow the chocolate mixture to cool slightly before
whisking in the egg yolks.

3. In a separate bowl, beat the egg whites and salt
until beginning to thicken. Slowly add the sugar and
continue to beat until stiff peaks form. Do not overwhip or the whites will be too dry and hard to mix
into the chocolate.

4. Stir the cream into the chocolate mixture until
well combined.

5. Fold one-third of the egg whites into the chocolate
to lighten the mixture. Then gently fold in the
remaining egg whites.

6. Divide the mixture between 4 ramekins, small bowls
or glasses or place in a single bowl and refrigerate,
covered, for at least 3 hours or overnight.

HINTS AND TIPS:

---

* You will need—2 bowls, electric mixer, whisk, saucepan, plastic spatula, liquid and weight measures and ramekins, bowls or glasses for serving.

* Chocolate mousse can be one of the quickest and easiest of all the desserts to make. There are many recipes for mousse which can range from light and fluffy like this recipe, which is served in glasses or moulds, to firm and dense which can be piped or even sliced.

* Traditionally, cream is not used in recipes for chocolate mousse but it does add a smooth, velvety texture.

* Try replacing the coffee with 100 ml Cointreau or brandy, or to be child-friendly, use raspberry cordial or better still, 100 ml pureed fresh raspberries (see **raspberry sauce**).

* Try adding a ¼ cup chopped nuts like macadamias or pecan nuts.

* **Chocolate mousse for piping**—3 egg yolks, 3 eggs, 100 g caster sugar, 800 g dark couverture chocolate, 1 litre semi-whipped cream. Gently melt the chocolate in a heatproof bowl over a saucepan of simmering water and set aside. Turn up the heat and place a heatproof bowl over the pan of boiling water. Make a sabayon by whisking the egg yolks, eggs and sugar until ribbon stage. Remove from the heat. Have someone hold the bowl, whisk in the chocolate and cream, adding a quarter of each at a time, making sure it's well incorporated before adding more, otherwise the mixture will split. Refrigerate once all the ingredients are combined. Spoon or pipe this dense mousse as needed.

* **Free-standing chocolate mousse**—this mousse is based on gelatine and contains no raw egg whites, and can be set in a mould and turned out. It is still light but has the advantage of being served on a plate with different garnishes. You will need—250 g dark chocolate, 2 eggs, 60 ml crème de cacao, 2 gelatine leaves, 600 ml thickened cream (semi-whipped). Melt the chocolate in a heatproof bowl over a saucepan of simmering water and set aside. Soak the gelatine leaves in plenty of cold water until soft. Whisk the eggs and liqueur in a heatproof bowl over a saucepan of simmering water until ribbon stage. Squeeze excess water from the softened gelatine and stir into the egg mixture. Slowly beat the egg mixture into the chocolate until thoroughly combined. Cool to room temperature before stirring in the cream with a plastic spatula. Pour into individual moulds or serving glasses. Cover with plastic wrap and refrigerate. Serves 8–10.

* The best chocolate to use is dark or bittersweet chocolate or couverture, available at good delicatessens, food halls and speciality ingredient shops. If the budget is tight, a good mousse can be achieved using dark cooking chocolate from the supermarket. Other types of chocolate can be adapted to this recipe, including milk and white chocolate; however, as the cocoa butter content in these chocolates is less, the melting of the chocolate needs to be done very, very gently to avoid the chocolate seizing (going grainy).

CHOCOLATE SELF-SAUCING PUDDING

Serves 6–8

xxxxxxxxxxxxxxxxxxxxxxxxxxxxxxxxxxxxxxxxxxxxxxxxxxxxxxxxxxxxxxxxxxxxxxxxxxxxxxxxxxxxxxxxx

150 g soft brown sugar
300 g self-raising flour
4 tablespoons cocoa powder
300 ml milk
3 eggs
100 g butter, melted

Sauce
350 g soft brown sugar
4 tablespoons cocoa powder
500 ml boiling water

Method:

1. Preheat the oven to 180°C. Grease a deep baking dish.

2. Place the brown sugar in a bowl and sift the flour and cocoa powder over the sugar. Mix with a wooden spoon.

3. In a separate bowl, mix together the milk, eggs and butter.

4. Pour the milk mixture over the dry ingredients and stir with the wooden spoon to make a batter. Pour the batter into the prepared baking dish.

5. For the sauce—combine the sugar and cocoa powder in a jug, add the boiling water and stir until the sugar dissolves (see Hints and tips). Then gently pour the sauce over the batter. It is best to pour the sauce over the back of a spoon to avoid disturbing the batter too much.

6. Place in the oven and bake for 45 minutes. When cooked, a skewer or small knife inserted into the pudding part only will come out clean. Serve immediately with cream or ice-cream. If the pudding sits for too long, the sauce will get soaked up by the pudding.

HINTS AND TIPS:

* You will need—baking dish (about 20 cm diameter x 10 cm deep, at least 1-litre capacity), 2 bowls, wooden spoon, whisk, jug for the sauce and liquid, weight and spoon measures.

* This classic recipe for self-saucing pudding is big on flavour. The strong taste of dark cocoa powder may be too strong for some palates. For a very mild-tasting pudding, substitute the cocoa powder (in the pudding and the sauce) for drinking chocolate and reduce the sugar content by half as there is sugar in the drinking chocolate.

* Some recipes for chocolate self-saucing pudding suggest that for the sauce, the sugar and cocoa are mixed together and sprinkled over the pudding batter then hot water is poured over this preparation. The most common problem with this method is sometimes the sugar and cocoa don't mix properly with the boiling water and the result is an uncooked mass of sugar and cocoa in the centre of the pudding. To safely guarantee this won't happen, follow the method I've prescribed.

* For a choc-chip effect in the sauce, add 100 g chopped dark chocolate or small chocolate buttons sprinkled over the batter, then pour the sauce over the pudding.

* Individual puddings can be produced by buttering individual (250-ml capacity) ovenproof moulds. The cooking time will be reduced to 20–25 minutes.

* Dust with icing sugar before serving at the table. This pudding can get quite messy looking, and the icing sugar will cover any ugly bits.

* Self-saucing pudding is notorious for bubbling over the edges of the dish—to avoid heavy cleaning of the oven racks and oven floor, try placing a piece of baking paper on a baking tray, then place the pudding on the lined tray before baking. Serve the pudding and throw out the paper.

CHRISTMAS PUDDING

Makes 4 x 1-litre puddings

XXXXXXXXXXXXXXXXXXXXXXXXXXXXXXXXXXXXXXXXXXXXXXXXXXXXXXXXXXXXXXXXXXXXXXXXXXXXXXXXXXXXXXXXXX

Dry ingredients
100 g dried mixed peel
150 g glacé cherries
150 g blanched almonds, chopped
250 g plain flour
250 g fresh bread crumbs
300 g suet, grated
300 g dark brown sugar
400 g currants
400 g sultanas
500 g raisins
finely grated zest of 1 orange
finely grated zest of 1 lemon
1 carrot, peeled and grated
1 Granny Smith apple, grated
½ teaspoon salt
2 teaspoons mixed spice

Wet ingredients
8 eggs, lightly beaten
350 ml stout or Guinness
150 ml brandy

Method:

1. Mix all the dry ingredients and fruit in a large bowl. In a separate smaller bowl, mix the wet ingredients. Combine the contents of both bowls, cover and store in the fridge for 24–48 hours.

2. Preheat the oven to 150°C. Stir the mixture and divide between 4 pudding bowls. Press the mixture firmly into the bowls, wipe the inner and outer rim with a damp cloth, then cover each pudding with a circle of baking paper. Cover the bowls with a layer of foil and crimp the edges or use large elastic bands to hold the foil in place.

Method cont.

3. Line a large, deep baking tray with a cloth or tea towel, and place the puddings in the tray. Add enough boiling water to the tray to reach halfway up the sides of the bowls (to make a water bath). Place in the oven and bake for 6 hours; check the water level every 1–2 hours and top up with more boiling water to maintain a level halfway up the sides of the bowls. Turn the oven off and allow to cool in the oven. Remove the puddings from the baking tray and leave to cool to room temperature overnight. Store in the fridge until needed.

4. To reheat, place back in a water bath in the oven set at 160°C for 2 hours.

HINTS AND TIPS:

----

* You will need—large mixing bowl, 4 x 1-litre ceramic pudding bowls, large baking tray (8–10 cm deep), wooden spoon, weight, liquid and spoon measures, grater, vegetable peeler, baking paper and foil.

* This pudding can last a year or two if stored correctly (in the fridge) and if you show some self control (I meant well, but mine didn't even see the end of January).

* The long marinating and cooking process is required to ensure richness in flavour and thorough cooking and amalgamation of the ingredients. To cook less results in a raw and somewhat greasy-tasting pudding. Be patient as you tend to only make it once a year.

* Serve with **brandy custard** or **brandy butter sauce** which is made by bringing to the boil 200 g caster sugar, 100 ml water and 50 g glucose. Cook until pale amber in colour, remove from the heat and carefully stir in 200 g unsalted butter and 500 ml thickened cream. Lastly, stir in 100 ml brandy, pass through a fine strainer and serve warm.

* The cooked puddings can be sliced and heated in the microwave briefly before serving—for those who just cannot wait any longer.

CREPES

Makes about 20

XXXXXXXXXXXXXXXXXXXXXXXXXXXXXXXXXXXXXXXXXXXXXXXXXXXXXXXXXXXXXXXXXXXXXXXXXXXXXXXXXXXXXXXXXXXXXXXXX

4 eggs
400 ml milk
170 g plain flour
50 g pure icing sugar
pinch of salt
olive oil spray or butter, for cooking

Method:

1. For the batter—whisk the eggs and milk in a bowl.

2. Sift the flour and salt into a separate bowl. Make a well in the centre, then add the egg mixture. Using a whisk, start drawing in some of the flour, keeping the batter smooth. Set aside for 1 hour to rest (see Hints and tips).

3. To cook the crepes, spray a crepe pan or small nonstick frying pan with oil or add a small knob of butter. Heat over medium–low heat. Add just enough batter to leave a thin coating on the base of the pan, lifting and swirling the pan to ensure the batter is distributed evenly. Cook on one side for 2–3 minutes or until it begins to colour. Use an egg flip to turn and cook the other side for 1 minute, then transfer to a plate or a wire rack. Repeat this process until all the crepe batter is used.

HINTS AND TIPS:

* You will need—2 bowls, whisk, plastic spatula, liquid, weight and spoon measures, egg flip, and crepe pan or nonstick frying pan.

* First, the making of the batter and allowing it to rest are important as the gluten in the flour has been worked and is tight; cooking immediately would make rubbery crepes.

* Use a crepe pan that has been lightly greased. Nonstick crepe pans are available from kitchenware stores and are worthwhile if you plan on making crepes often.

* Crepes eaten immediately after cooking go well topped with freshly squeezed lemon and sugar or spread with good jam.

* The crepe batter will last 3 days refrigerated before it starts to turn grey.

* Crepes can be frozen for later use.

* This recipe is ideal for sweet and savoury crepes.

* Always check the consistency of the batter after the resting period to ensure it is not too thick. If it is, just add more milk.

* If the crepes are to be used for crepes Suzette, try adding 1 teaspoon of orange blossom water, orange liqueur or an orange syrup (made by simmering equal parts sugar and orange juice with the zest of the oranges).

* **Soufflé crepes baked in royale custard**—first, make the crepes and set aside. For the custard—whisk together 250 ml thickened cream, 125 ml cream, 2 eggs, 2 egg yolks, 40 g caster sugar and 10 ml dark rum in a bowl; then set aside. For the filling—whip 30 g unsalted butter (softened), 40 g pure icing sugar and 4 egg yolks; then beat in 400 g cream cheese (softened, at room temperature), 1 teaspoon vanilla extract, and grated zest of 1 lemon; stir in ½ cup sultanas. In a separate bowl, whip 4 egg whites to soft peaks. Gradually beat in 100 g caster sugar. Fold the egg whites into the cheese mixture. To assemble—fold a crepe into quarters to form a pocket, half-fill the pocket with a couple of tablespoons of filling (do not be tempted to overfill). Place the filled crepes in a ceramic baking dish or lasagne dish. Pour the custard on top to come halfway up the sides of the crepes. Place in a preheated

160°C oven and bake until the custard sets, about 30 minutes. Dust with icing sugar and serve with whipped cream. This dish can be made individually using smaller, shallow gratin dishes. Try using mascarpone or quark cheese as an alternative to cream cheese. Sultanas are optional and can be substituted with chocolate buttons.

JUNKET

Serves 6–8

xxxxxxxxxxxxxxxxxxxxxxxxxxxxxxxxxxxxxxxxxxxxxxxxxxxxxxxxxxxxxxxxxxxxxxxxxxxxxxxxxxxxxxxxxxxxxxxxx

1 litre full cream milk
100 g caster sugar
1 teaspoon vanilla extract
4 junket tablets
1 tablespoon cold milk, extra

Method:

1. Place the litre of milk and the sugar in a saucepan and heat gently to body temperature (37°C). Remove from the heat and stir in the vanilla.

2. Crush the junket tablets and mix with the 1 tablespoon cold milk. Add some of the warm milk mixture then pour the junket mixture into the warm milk mixture. Stir and place in a bowl or individual ramekins. Leave at room temperature for 30 minutes or until set, then refrigerate.

3. Top with whipped cream just before serving.

HINTS AND TIPS:

* You will need—saucepan, wooden spoon, weight, liquid and spoon measures, small bowl and 6–8 individual bowls or glasses.

* The availability of junket tablets or powder is said to be diminishing with the decreasing production of junket by some companies. Junket tablets should still be available at supermarkets, independent grocers and health food stores—keep hunting around, you will find them.

* Junket tablets can be bought already flavoured. Buying the plain tablets means adding your own flavour. Use ½ vanilla bean in the milk and allow the flavour to infuse for 10 minutes after heating, then scrape out the seeds from the pod. This gives a beautiful vanilla junket.

* Junket powder is also available and for this recipe use 1 teaspoon mixed into the cold milk, then continue as per the recipe.

* Junket tablets or powder are made from rennet, which is made from an active enzyme known as rennin which comes from the fourth stomach of milk-fed calves. Rennet is used in cheese production as it coagulates the milk proteins to form the curds (the first stage of cheese making). Vegetarians should always check cheese products to see if they contain rennet; vegans don't eat cheese anyway.

* For **orange junket**—add the zest of 1 orange and ¼ teaspoon orange flower water to this recipe (omit the vanilla extract).

* For **chocolate junket**—add 4 tablespoons powdered chocolate milk flavouring while the milk is heating. Stir until dissolved.

* For **coffee junket**—stir 2 tablespoons instant coffee to the milk once heated.

* Full cream milk is specified because skim milk, UHT (long-life milk), soy milk, lactose-free milk and some powdered milks tend not to set.

LEMON DELICIOUS

Serves 6

XXXXXXXXXXXXXXXXXXXXXXXXXXXXXXXXXXXXXXXXXXXXXXXXXXXXXXXXXXXXXXXXXXXXXXXXXXXXXXXXXXXXXXXXXXXXX

Melted butter, for greasing
sugar, for coating baking dish
60 g butter, softened
225 g caster sugar
4 eggs, at room temperature, separated
zest of 2 lemons
150 ml lemon juice (about 3 lemons)
35 g self-raising flour
400 ml milk
pinch of salt

Method:

1. Preheat the oven to 170°C. Prepare a baking dish or individual ramekins by brushing with the melted butter and coating with the sugar.

2. Combine the softened butter and sugar in a bowl and beat until pale. Add the egg yolks one at a time, beating well between each addition.

3. Add the lemon zest and mix in the lemon juice.

4. Stir in the flour and then the milk, a bit at a time, until well combined and the mixture is quite runny.

5. Whisk the egg whites with the salt until soft peaks form, then fold into the lemon mixture. Spoon the pudding mixture into the prepared dish or dishes.

6. Place the pudding dishes in a deep roasting tray lined with a cloth or a tea towel, and add hot water to reach halfway up the sides of the dishes. Bake in the oven for 40 minutes for a large, single pudding, or 20–25 minutes for individual puddings. When risen and browned on top, remove and serve immediately with lashings of cream or ice-cream. Remember when serving to scoop out the lemon sauce that has formed at the bottom of the dish.

HINTS AND TIPS:

* You will need—750-ml capacity pudding dish or 6 x 1-cup capacity soufflé dishes or ramekins, 2 bowls, grater, juicer, liquid, spoon and weight measures, wooden spoon, whisk or electric beaters, plastic spatula and deep roasting tray.

* Lemon delicious—also known as 'lemon delight'—is a classic, tangy self-saucing pudding and like all self-saucing puddings needs to be served immediately or risk the pudding soaking up the sauce if left to sit for too long.

* Brushing the baking dish with softened butter and coating with sugar helps the pudding to rise. Equally effective is to lightly spray the dish with canola or light olive oil before dusting in the sugar.

* Having the ingredients at room temperature helps prevent the mixture from splitting. Usually, a base cake mix splits or separates because the eggs are too cold for the room temperature sugar and butter mixture. However, should this happen, keep making the pudding, as it won't totally ruin the final product.

* The egg whites are beaten to a soft peak and then folded in briefly. If the egg whites are beaten to stiff peaks, they become dry and harder to fold into the batter and because air has been knocked out from the egg whites, the pudding is heavier once baked. It is also recommended when folding in egg whites (especially in the case of soufflés) that you add a quarter of the egg whites and work that faster and harder before gently folding in the remaining three-quarters of the egg whites, which will then be incorporated into the mixture much more easily.

* It is also vital that the pudding is baked in a 'water bath' with a cloth or tea towel underneath the pudding dish (to absorb excess heat from the metal roasting tray); the water bath also allows the sauce to properly form at the base of the pudding.

* Dust the pudding/s with icing sugar before serving.

LEMON MERINGUE PIE

Serves 8

XXXXXXXXXXXXXXXXXXXXXXXXXXXXXXXXXXXXXXXXXXXXXXXXXXXXXXXXXXXXXXXXXXXXXXXXXXXXXXXXXXXXXXXXXXXXXXX

Pastry
200 g plain flour
50 g caster sugar
150 g cold unsalted butter, cut into small dice
1 egg

Filling
180 g caster sugar
180 ml lemon juice (3–4 lemons)
250 ml water
60 g cornflour
75 g unsalted butter, cut into small dice
4 egg yolks
Meringue
4 egg whites
200 g caster sugar

Method:

1. For the pastry—place the flour, sugar and butter in
a food processor, and blitz until sandy in texture.
Add the egg and continue processing to form a paste.
Remove the dough from the processor and work with your
hands to form a smooth, homogenous ball, then wrap in
plastic wrap and refrigerate for 1 hour.

2. On a lightly floured surface, roll out the dough to
5 mm thick, then drape over a shallow pie dish. Do not
trim excess pastry at this stage, place back in the
fridge for 30 minutes (or the pastry will shrink in
the oven).

3. Preheat the oven to 180°C. Line the pastry case
with a round piece of baking paper, half fill with
dried beans, rice or pastry weights and bake for
12 minutes. Remove from the oven, remove the paper
and weights. Place the pastry case back in the oven
for 10–15 minutes or until lightly golden. Remove and
set aside. When cool, trim the overhanging pastry
with a cook's knife by shaving the cooked pastry in a
slightly downward motion away from your body.

Method cont.

4. Reset the oven to 200°C.

5. For the filling—place the sugar, lemon juice, water and cornflour in a saucepan over medium heat and bring to the boil, stirring continuously. Reduce the heat and cook for another minute or until the mixture becomes thick and transparent. Remove from the heat and beat in the butter and egg yolks with a wooden spoon. Pour the warm custard into the pie case.

6. For the meringue—place the egg whites and sugar in the bowl of an electric mixer, whisk until a stiff meringue forms. Dollop and spread on the warm lemon custard.

7. Bake for 8–10 minutes or until the meringue is lightly browned all over. Cool before placing in the refrigerator. Chill completely before slicing.

HINTS AND TIPS:
----

* You will need—weight, spoon and liquid measures, bowls, food processor, electric mixer, rolling pin, 23-cm flan tin or pie dish, saucepan, wooden spoon, plastic spatula, cook's knife and cutting board.

* The warmer the lemon custard is when the meringue is added, the less likely the meringue will slide off the pie when cooled. Therefore, as soon as the custard is made, make the meringue and get the pie into the oven as soon as possible.

* For reasons why the meringue might weep, see **Italian meringue**.

* To save some time, buy a pre-made flan case, available from most supermarkets.

* If you are not used to adding the egg whites and sugar together at the beginning of beating, then stick to the traditional method of whipping the egg whites to soft peaks and then gradually adding the sugar. The meringue will be less dense but will still work. Either method is fine.

* The grated zest of 1 lemon added to the pastry base gives a lovely hint of lemon flavour that ties in nicely with the rest of the pie.

LEMON TART

Serves 10

XXXXXXXXXXXXXXXXXXXXXXXXXXXXXXXXXXXXXXXXXXXXXXXXXXXXXXXXXXXXXXXXXXXXXXXXXXXXXXXXXXXXXXXXXXXXXXXXXX

1 x recipe quantity **shortcrust pastry**
zest of 2 lemons
350 g caster sugar
8 eggs, at room temperature
250 ml lemon juice
250 ml thickened cream

Method:

1. Roll out the pastry and line a 23-cm flan tin. Place in the fridge for 30 minutes to rest. Preheat the oven to 200°C.

2. Place the lemon zest, sugar and eggs in a bowl and whisk to combine.

3. Stir in the lemon juice and fold in the cream.

4. Blind bake (see Pastry in Really Useful Information) the pastry case for 20 minutes. Remove from the oven and while hot, add the lemon filling. Reduce the oven temperature to 150°C and bake the tart for 30 minutes or until the lemon custard is only just set. Remove from the oven and cool completely before serving.

5. Serve at room temperature or chilled with whipped, double or pouring cream.

HINTS AND TIPS:

* You will need—rolling pin, weight, spoon and liquid measures, 2 bowls, grater, juicer, whisk, wooden spoon, baking paper and 23-cm flan tin with a removable base.

* The most important thing to remember when making the filling for this tart is that it is simply a delicate custard. It therefore only needs to just set and will finish setting as it cools. When testing for doneness, give the oven shelf a gentle shake, the centre of the tart should wobble like a jelly.

* Adding the filling to the hot pastry base helps to get the cooking underway and forms a seal on the base to help prevent leakage.

* The cream suggested for this tart is thickened cream or you could use pouring cream with a 35 per cent fat content.

* When making the pastry, try adding the zest of 1 lemon to the pastry. It becomes noticeable when eating the tart and rounds out the overall experience of this delicate sweet.

* To sweeten the pastry, add ¼ cup pure icing sugar to the dough as it is being made. Try also adding ½ cup almond meal to the dough.

* Remember to read the Hints and tips for **shortcrust pastry** as well.

* It is important to rest the pastry once it has been rolled and shaped into the flan tin. The gluten in the flour has been worked from the rolling action and, if baked immediately, will shrink once exposed to the heat of the oven. It is a good idea to leave some overhang when lining the flan tin, which, when cooked can be trimmed off before adding the custard mixture.

* Substitute lemon juice with orange juice, blood orange juice or a mixture of citrus fruit juices.

* You can make a caramelised lemon tart by sprinkling the cooled tart with a thin layer of caster sugar and placing it under the grill set to high for 1 minute or until the sugar caramelises.

* The pastry base can be made and cooked the day before it is needed, as too the lemon filling which will keep for up to 5 days refrigerated. Stir the lemon mixture before pouring into the cooked base.

* Overcooking the tart will cause the filling to curdle on the outer edge, making the lemon custard dry and grainy. An overcooked tart will also tend to split open once cold. It is best to keep the tart in the flan tin as long as possible, even if some slices have been taken from it; this will also help prevent the tart from splitting.

* **Raspberry sauce** is another great accompaniment for this tart.

PANNACOTTA

Serves 6

xxxxxxxxxxxxxxxxxxxxxxxxxxxxxxxxxxxxxxxxxxxxxxxxxxxxxxxxxxxxxxxxxxxxxxxxxxxxxxxxxxxxxxxxxxx

2 gelatine leaves
100 ml cold milk
500 ml pouring cream
100 g caster sugar
1 vanilla bean, split lengthways, or 1½ teaspoons
    vanilla extract
1 piece of lemon zest

Method:

1. Soak the gelatine in the milk for 5 minutes or until the leaves soften.

2. Combine the cream with the sugar, vanilla bean or vanilla extract and lemon zest in a saucepan.

3. Bring just to the boil, remove from the heat and stand for 5 minutes.

4. Pour the hot cream mixture into the gelatine and milk mixture and stir to dissolve the gelatine.

5. Strain the mixture through a fine sieve and pour into 6 dariole moulds. Cover and refrigerate overnight.

HINTS AND TIPS:

* You will need—2 bowls, saucepan, liquid and weight measures, wooden spoon, plastic spatula and ceramic, plastic or metal dariole moulds.

* Pannacotta translates as 'cooked cream'. It is delicious served with fresh berries or **raspberry sauce**. Or serve with **biscotti** or **almond bread**. Or try the pannacotta with fruits in season like peaches (grilled), cherries or mangoes.

* As a general rule of thumb, use 1 gelatine leaf for every 300–350 ml liquid. You would be surprised at how much difference 50 ml of liquid can make. For the beginner, start with 300 ml (as per the recipe above); for the more advanced cook, add 50–75 ml double cream to the cooked mixture to produce a very delicate set cream.

* Pannacotta should have a just-set texture and is therefore delicate when turning out of the mould. To release, dip a small knife in hot water and insert between the very edge of the pannacotta and the dariole mould, remove (this will break the seal and make an air pocket), then invert the pannacotta over a plate and it should gently release itself. If not, then dip the ramekins into hot water for 5 seconds and try again.

* Try adding 2 tablespoons passionfruit pulp to the mixture just before the gelatine is added.

* Halve the sugar and add 2 tablespoons honey to the mixture. Serve with crushed pistachio nuts.

* Although not very traditional, replace half the cream with natural yoghurt or buttermilk, but only heat the cream. Dissolve the gelatine in the cream mixture then pour into the yoghurt or buttermilk.

PAVLOVA

Serves 8

xxxxxxxxxxxxxxxxxxxxxxxxxxxxxxxxxxxxxxxxxxxxxxxxxxxxxxxxxxxxxxxxxxxxxxxxxxxxxxxxxxxxxxxxxxxx

3 egg whites
1½ cups caster sugar
1 teaspoon vanilla extract
1 teaspoon white vinegar
1 teaspoon cornflour
2 tablespoons boiling water

Method:

1. Preheat the oven to 200°C. Line a baking tray with baking paper.

2. Use an electric mixer to whisk the egg whites until soft peaks form. Gradually add the sugar and continue to beat on high until all the sugar is incorporated.

3. Turn the speed to low and add the vanilla, vinegar and cornflour.

4. Slowly add the boiling water and whisk until completely combined.

5. Spoon in 1 large mound on the prepared baking tray. Bake for 1 minute, reduce the heat to 100°C and cook for a further 90 minutes.

6. Turn off the oven and leave the pavlova to stand in the oven until cool or it will split. Store in an airtight container for up to 3 days.

HINTS AND TIPS:

* You will need—cup and spoon measures, electric mixer, plastic spatula, baking tray and baking paper.

* As with any meringue, a clean bowl, free from oil or water, is required to succeed. So make sure no egg yolks drop into the egg whites when separating the eggs, as egg yolks are a type of fat. Should some egg yolk or shell drop into the egg whites, then use an emptied egg shell to scoop out the offenders; this is by far the best method and works without having to fish around for ages trying to get foreign matter out.

* Depending on how you like your 'pav'—thin and crispy or thick and marshmallowy—will determine how you spread it on the tray. Pile it high and rounded to have a marshmallow centre.

* For individual pavlovas, simply dollop small oblong shapes onto the baking paper, but not too close as they will expand.

* The addition of boiling water to the mixture at the end adds steam to the cooking process, making the pavlova lighter and fluffier.

* Pavlova is traditionally served with whipped cream (600 ml for this recipe) and chopped fruit—but not just any fruit. Banana, passionfruit, kiwifruit or strawberries are as varied as it gets. Use a combination of these 4 or theme the pavlova with just one fruit.

* For a **chocolate pavlova**— add 3 tablespoons Dutch cocoa powder (sifted) when adding the cornflour. Once cooked and cooled, serve with whipped cream and fresh raspberries.

* This popular dish is named after the famous ballerina Anna Pavlova, who toured Australia and New Zealand in the 1920s. This brings about the age-old debate—which country can claim the dish as its own? Well, as true blue Aussie as I may be, I have to say that several historians have pointed out quite clearly that there are recipes as far back as 1922 in New Zealand with names ranging from meringue cake to pavlova cake (1933). Australia's first claim to this dish is 1935 when made and named 'pavlova' at the Esplanade Hotel in Western Australia by chef Bert Sachse. But whatever its origins, pavlova will always be an Aussie favourite.

PEACH MELBA

Serves 4

XXXXXXXXXXXXXXXXXXXXXXXXXXXXXXXXXXXXXXXXXXXXXXXXXXXXXXXXXXXXXXXXXXXXXXXXXXXXXXXXXXXXXXXXXXXXX

4 ripe freestone peaches
300 g sugar
500 ml water
1 cinnamon stick
300 ml **raspberry sauce**
4 scoops of best quality vanilla ice-cream

Method:

1. Gently make a light incision with a sharp knife around the outside of each peach.

2. Place the sugar, water and cinnamon in a large saucepan and bring to the boil. Reduce the heat to simmer, immerse the peaches into the simmering liquid and cook for 10 minutes.

3. Carefully remove the peaches. Cool for several minutes, then peel the skin from the flesh with a small knife.

4. To serve—place 1 scoop of ice-cream in the centre of a chilled plate or in a dessert glass. With the back of the ice-cream scoop, press into the centre of the ball of ice-cream to make a small hollow in which to place the peach. Pour a small amount of raspberry sauce over the peach and serve immediately.

HINTS AND TIPS:

---

* You will need—cutting board, paring knife, liquid and weight measures, sieve, 2 bowls and ice-cream scoop.

* This classic dessert was named in honour of the Australian soprano opera singer Dame Nellie Melba. It was invented in London at the Savoy Hotel by Auguste Escoffier, a brilliant contemporary, known as 'the Emperor of chefs', who also named Melba toast after her.

* An alternative to the suggested presentation is to slice the cooked peach in half, remove the stone, place one half on the plate, place the ice-cream ball in the centre of the peach half and sandwich with the other half, then drizzle with the raspberry sauce.

* Substitute the water in the poaching liquid for white wine or champagne, add 2 pieces of lemon zest, and replace the cinnamon stick with a vanilla bean, sliced lengthways. This more expensive and decadent poaching liquor can be cooled and frozen for poaching other fruits like pears, apricots or more peaches.

* Fresh, ripe white peaches are a great substitute for regular yellow peaches.

* Once the peaches have cooked, remove from the syrup, peel and set aside while the syrup cools; then store the peaches in the syrup overnight to absorb extra flavour.

* The peaches requested are free-stone (also known as 'slip stone'), so-called because the stone will pop out easily when sliced in half. Naturally, peaches that have stones that cling to the flesh are known as 'cling stone' peaches. Although these peaches are equally tasty, they are doubly hard to eat in a delicate dessert such as this one.

* Optional is to serve this dessert with a dollop of whipped cream and some toasted slivered almonds, in addition to the ice-cream and raspberry sauce.

* For something different, try slicing the peaches in half, remove the stones, grill on the barbecue, turn and dust with icing sugar. Cook for another minute, transfer to a plate, and add the ice-cream, fresh cream, if desired, and fresh raspberries.

PECAN PIE

Serves 8

XXXXXXXXXXXXXXXXXXXXXXXXXXXXXXXXXXXXXXXXXXXXXXXXXXXXXXXXXXXXXXXXXXXXXXXXXXXXXXXXXXXXXXXXXXX

Pastry

1 x recipe quantity for **lemon meringue pie**

Pecan filling

150 g caster sugar

3 eggs, lightly beaten

250 ml corn syrup or pure maple syrup

75 g butter, melted

1 teaspoon vanilla extract

pinch of salt

200 g shelled, roasted and chopped pecan nuts

Method:

1. For the pastry—follow steps 1–3 in lemon meringue pie.

2. Mix the sugar, eggs, corn syrup, butter, vanilla, salt and half of the pecan nuts with a wooden spoon, until thoroughly combined.

3. Pour into the prepared pie base, and sprinkle with the remaining pecan nuts.

4. Place the flan tin on a baking tray and bake in 180°C oven for 1 hour or until firm and golden brown. Serve warm with whipped or double cream.

HINTS AND TIPS:

★ You will need—weight, liquid and spoon measures, bowls, food processor, rolling pin, 23-cm flan tin or pie dish, baking tray, bowl, wooden spoon, plastic spatula and cooling rack.

★ There are several styles of pecan pie and this is just one of them. They can be thick and pasty with loads of nuts or thin and caramel-like with very few nuts. One thing most aficionados agree—the base should not be soggy or too thick.

★ A different slant on this recipe is to use cream in the filling. Mix 6 egg yolks, 120 ml corn or pure maple syrup, 100 g dark brown sugar, 90 ml bourbon, 200 ml double cream then fold in 250 g pecan nuts. Pour into the base and bake for 45 minutes.

★ Should the pastry start to get too dark, carefully remove the pie from the oven and place a thin layer of foil around the flan to cover the edges, then carefully place back in the oven for the remaining time.

★ To save time, buy a pre-baked flan base from the supermarket.

★ Roasting the pecan nuts at 180°C until lightly golden ensures that they don't go chewy and will enhance the flavour.

★ Keep in mind pecan nuts are seasonal, so check the use-by date and where the nuts are from. Old pecan nuts taste rancid and can completely wreck the pie. Look for locally grown or fresh imports from reputable markets or delicatessens.

★ Try replacing the pecan nuts with chopped macadamia nuts or walnuts.

PUMPKIN PIE

Serves 10–12

xxxxxxxxxxxxxxxxxxxxxxxxxxxxxxxxxxxxxxxxxxxxxxxxxxxxxxxxxxxxxxxxxxxxxxxxxxxxxxxxxxxxxxxxxxxxxxxxx

1 x recipe quantity **Shortcrust Pastry**

Pumpkin filling
3 eggs
450 g fresh pumpkin puree or 425 g can plain pumpkin
    puree
125 ml thickened cream
100 g soft brown sugar
1 teaspoon ground cinnamon
½ teaspoon ground ginger
pinch of ground cloves
pinch of freshly grated nutmeg
½ teaspoon salt

Method:

1. For the pastry—remove the dough from the fridge,
roll out to a thickness of 3–5 mm and drape over a
flan tin or pie dish. Refrigerate for 30 minutes to
allow the gluten to settle and to avoid shrinkage when
baked.

2. Preheat the oven to 180°C. Line a baking tray with
baking paper to catch any spills.

3. For the filling—whisk the eggs lightly (do not
add too much air) in a large bowl. Add the remaining
filling ingredients and gently whisk to combine. Pour
into the pie case and place on the prepared baking
tray.

4. Bake the pie in the oven for 45–55 minutes or until
the filling is set (see **Hints and tips**) and the crust
is brown—the centre will still look wet. Place the
pie on a wire rack to cool.

HINTS AND TIPS:

* You will need—23-cm flan tin or pie dish, rolling pin, baking tray, baking paper, spoon, liquid and weight measures, whisk, wooden spoon, large bowl, plastic spatula and wire rack.

* Hot tip—I highly recommend making a **pecan and ginger biscuit layer** to sprinkle over the uncooked pastry base before adding the pumpkin filling. This tasty layer, from the highly acclaimed pastry cook Rose Levy Beranbaum, absorbs excess moisture, ensuring the pastry base stays dry and crispy after the pie is cooked. Simply combine 25 g pecan nuts (toasted and ground) and 25 g crushed gingernut biscuits.

* Fresh roasted pumpkin is also highly recommended for this dish. You will need approximately 2–3 kg butternut, Japola (Jap) or Kent. Cut the pumpkin in half, remove seeds and fibres, place in a roasting pan and cook at 170°C for 45 minutes to 1½ hours, depending on size, until a knife inserted into the pumpkin has no resistance. Cool the pumpkin, scoop flesh from the skin and puree, then drain in muslin (cheesecloth) or a very fine strainer for several hours to extract as much liquid

as possible (do not force it through). Then weigh the 450 g needed for the above recipe.

* Serve with dolloping cream or plain whipped cream. Or try with **maple cream**— 300 ml thickened cream, 2 tablespoons pure maple syrup. Lightly whip the cream to soft peaks, stir in the maple syrup, then finish whipping to a firm peak. Refrigerate until needed.

* Once again, this is a baked custard-style dessert, therefore there are some basic rules to follow to avoid shrinkage, cracking and drooping of the custard once cooled. Do not overcook, it is best to have the centre slightly wet and undercooked, then turn off the oven and with the door ajar, leave the pie to cool in the oven before removing and placing in the refrigerator to set cold. Also, do not over-mix or whisk the filling too much as the extra added air will first expand and then collapse upon cooling, leaving a depression in the centre.

* This pie is cooked with a raw base compared with some pies that have the base cooked first and then the filling added before being baked. Buying a pre-made flan

or pie base will save time. When adding the pie filling, reduce the oven temperature to 150°C and bake for the same amount of time, even a bit longer. This gentle heat is much better suited to the delicate custard filling. The same rules apply in mixing and cooling to avoid cracking and sinking.

QUEEN OF PUDDINGS
Serves 6

xxxxxxxxxxxxxxxxxxxxxxxxxxxxxxxxxxxxxxxxxxxxxxxxxxxxxxxxxxxxxxxxxxxxxxxxxxxxxxxxxxxxxxxxxxxxxx

300 ml milk
300 ml thickened cream
zest of 1 lemon
50 g unsalted butter
5 egg yolks
75 g caster sugar
50 ml brandy (optional)
100 g fresh white bread with crusts removed,
    torn into small pieces
150 g jam (any flavour is fine)

Meringue
3 egg whites
150 g caster sugar

Method:

1. Preheat the oven to 180°C. Grease a baking dish or 6 individual soufflé moulds.

2. Heat the milk, cream, lemon zest and butter in a saucepan and cook until the butter melts.

3. Whisk the egg yolks, sugar and brandy in a bowl, then whisk in the hot milk mixture. Add the bread and stand for 20 minutes or until the bread swells.

4. Ladle the mixture into the prepared baking dish/es, place in a baking pan and add enough hot water to come halfway up the sides of the dish/es. Carefully place in the oven, making sure water doesn't splash into the pudding.

5. Bake for 35 minutes for a large dish or 20 minutes for individual dishes. The pudding is ready when the centre is set like jelly. Remove from the oven and cool for 5 minutes. Melt the jam in a small saucepan or in the microwave and gently spoon over the pudding, being careful not to break the surface. Reset the oven to 200°C.

Method cont.

6. For the meringue—whisk the egg whites until firm then beat in the sugar in 2 batches. Continue beating until all the sugar is incorporated.

7. Spoon the meringue over the pudding and place back in the oven for 10 minutes to cook and brown the meringue. Serve hot with whipped cream.

HINTS AND TIPS:

★ You will need—1.5-litre baking dish or 6 soufflé moulds, saucepan, deep baking pan, 2 bowls, electric mixer, weight and liquid measures, ladle and plastic spatula.

★ This recipe can be made successfully using all milk instead of the combination of milk and cream.

★ This old school recipe makes use of a classic uncooked meringue. The following option requires a bit more skill, but with amazing results. The only difference is in the meringue finish. Make the pudding base and top with **Italian meringue**. Use a piping bag with a star nozzle and pipe the Italian meringue over the pudding which will NOT need to go into the oven to cook (the meringue is cooked by the boiling sugar syrup). To add colour to the outside, use a cook's blow torch or quickly brown under a hot grill.

★ Once the custard has been made, instead of adding jam, try adding soft fruit compote like rhubarb, peach or pears, then top with the meringue.

★ Make a **Black Forest queen of puddings**—add 60 ml kirsch (cherry liqueur) to the custard before baking, then melt cherry conserve to add over the custard and top with a can of cherries (drained of their liquid). Grate 100 g chocolate over the cherries before adding the meringue. Serve with a **chocolate sauce**.

★ For a special occasion— decorate the cooked meringue with gold leaf which is available at quality food stores or selected delicatessens. Be sure to wear cotton gloves (available at supermarkets in the cleaning supplies area) as the gold leaf will stick to your fingers.

RASPBERRY FOOL

Serves 4

XXXXXXXXXXXXXXXXXXXXXXXXXXXXXXXXXXXXXXXXXXXXXXXXXXXXXXXXXXXXXXXXXXXXXXXXXXXXXXXXXX

300 g fresh raspberries
50 g pure icing sugar
300 ml thickened cream
½ teaspoon vanilla
extract

Method:

1. Place half the raspberries in a bowl with the icing sugar and mash with a fork. Pour into a fine sieve and work with the back of a spoon to press out all the pulp.

2. Whip the cream to soft peaks and gently fold in the raspberry puree; do not mix too much so it has a ripple effect through the cream.

3. Divide the remaining raspberries between 4 small serving glasses—place a few raspberries at the base of each glass, divide the raspberry cream between the 4 glasses and top with the remaining raspberries. Refrigerate for a couple of hours before serving.

HINTS AND TIPS:

----

* You will need—2 bowls, spoon, fork, fine sieve, weight, liquid and spoon measures, whisk or electric mixer, plastic spatula and 4 serving glasses.

* Use leftover **raspberry sauce** to make Raspberry fool.

* Serve with a thin or sponge biscuit like **biscotti**, amaretti biscuits, short bread or savoiardi.

* Try making an adult version by adding 60 ml of sweet liqueur like Chambord (raspberry), Cointreau or Grand Marnier (orange), or Crème de Cacao (chocolate).

* Add 60 ml of quality cordial like elderflower, rose petal or lime. Look out for exotic cordials in the beverage section of the supermarket or health food stores.

* Other flavours include—any style of berry, either on its own or a combination for **berry fool**; fresh mangoes (puree half and dice the remainder) with the same weight ratio makes a refreshing **mango fool**; **rhubarb fool**, using 300 g cooked rhubarb; and **passionfruit and banana fool**, with a single banana diced and added to the glass and the pulp of 6 passionfruit mixed into the semi-whipped cream with 2 tablespoons icing sugar.

STEWED RHUBARB

Makes 1 cup

xxxxxxxxxxxxxxxxxxxxxxxxxxxxxxxxxxxxxxxxxxxxxxxxxxxxxxxxxxxxxxxxxxxxxxxxxxxxxxxxxxxxxxxxx

1 rhubarb stalk
25 ml water
80 g sugar

Method:

1. Chop the rhubarb into 2-cm lengths. Place the rhubarb in a saucepan with the water and sugar, cover with a lid and cook gently until the rhubarb breaks down and most of the water has evaporated (about 10 minutes).

2. Serve warm or cold with cream or custard.

3. Cover and refrigerate for 5–7 days.

HINTS AND TIPS:

* You will need—cutting board, cook's knife, liquid and weight measures and saucepan.

* Peeling rhubarb is not necessary, although sometimes when the stalks are very thick, peeling some strands reduces the stringiness in the dish.

* This small quantity is a guide based on it being enough for 1 serve. To say 'use a bunch', can mean the difference of 2–3 stalks (of average size). Some cooks prefer their rhubarb sweeter or more tart simply by adjusting the sugar content.

* Discard any leaf matter attached to the stalk as it is poisonous. Small amounts are not life-threatening but will make you unwell.

* To what stage the rhubarb is cooked depends on its use. For a compote served on porridge for breakfast, cooking for a few minutes might be enough to begin breaking down the rhubarb while still leaving large pieces for texture (although it won't be crunchy or raw).

* For **poached rhubarb**— here's a technique used by chefs to preserve the shape of the rhubarb for use in elegant desserts or puddings. Make a pink vanilla sugar syrup with 250 g sugar, 250 ml water, 1 vanilla bean (cut lengthways and seeds scraped into the syrup) and any off-cuts and strings from a bunch of rhubarb (to impart flavour and colour). Bring the syrup to the boil and simmer gently for 10 minutes. Cut the rhubarb into 5-cm lengths and place in the simmering syrup for 30–40 seconds only, then remove from the syrup onto a plate and cool. Strain the syrup and cool completely before adding the rhubarb and the vanilla bean back into the syrup and storing in the refrigerator. Covered, poached rhubarb will last for 2 weeks in the syrup. Add the syrup for colour and flavour.

* For **rhubarb pie**—keep the slices chunky, remove from the heat and cool. If a bit watery, drain off some of the liquid before adding to the pie base, or combine cornflour and cold water and mix into the simmering rhubarb to thicken the juices, then cool completely before adding to the base. It may take as many as 2 bunches of rhubarb to fill a 23-cm pie dish. Many recipes for rhubarb pie suggest adding the uncooked rhubarb and the sugar to the uncooked pie base, this works well but be sure to overfill the base because as it cooks, the rhubarb loses its volume as it breaks down.

RICE PUDDING

Serves 4

XXXXXXXXXXXXXXXXXXXXXXXXXXXXXXXXXXXXXXXXXXXXXXXXXXXXXXXXXXXXXXXXXXXXXXXXXXXXXXXXXXXXXXXXXXXXXXXXXXXXX

120 g short-grain rice (not arborio or sushi rice)
1 litre full cream milk
thickly peeled zest of ½ lemon
1 teaspoon vanilla extract
¼ teaspoon salt
100 g caster sugar

Method:

1. Combine the rice, sugar, lemon zest, vanilla and salt in a saucepan, place over medium–high heat and bring to the boil. Stir and reduce the heat to the lowest setting.

2. Continue to stir as the rice can stick to the bottom of the pot.

3. It may appear at first as if there is no way the small amount of rice will thicken this amount of milk. Watch in amazement—after about an hour, it will begin to thicken. The pudding is ready when the milk is absorbed and the mixture is as thick as porridge. Remove from the heat and stir in the sugar. Remove the lemon zest, then cool the pudding and refrigerate. When cold, it is ready to serve. Refrigerated and covered, rice pudding will last 3–4 days.

HINTS AND TIPS:

* You will need—saucepan, wooden spoon, liquid, weight and spoon measures and a vegetable peeler.

* There are so many recipes and styles of rice pudding it was hard to decide which should go in this book. I chose one my kids love to cook that tastes great. For this recipe, we semi-whip 200 ml thickened cream and fold it into the rice once it is fridge cold; it lightens it up and makes it go further.

* Serve with fresh fruit, fruit compote or stewed fruits, add toasted flaked almonds, or simply dust with ground cinnamon or a bit of ground nutmeg.

* This very same recipe can be baked for 3 hours in a 120°C oven. Combine all the ingredients, including the sugar, and pour into a buttered baking dish. Be sure to stir the rice 3–4 times in the first hour as the rice will settle.

* **Portuguese and Spanish rice puddings** are very similar to this recipe, except they start with the rice cooking in water. You need 500 ml water, 225 g short-grain rice, 500 ml hot milk, 225 g sugar, zest of 1 lemon (as above, use a vegetable peeler to make big strips of zest), 1 teaspoon ground cinnamon. Place the water and rice in a medium-sized saucepan, cover and bring to the boil, then reduce the heat and simmer gently for 20 minutes. Add the hot milk, sugar and lemon zest, and cook uncovered until thick like porridge, about 30 minutes, stirring occasionally as it will stick and burn. Remove from the heat, discard the zest, spread the pudding into a shallow pie dish and place in the fridge to set cold. Dust with ground cinnamon before serving. This pudding will set firmer than the main recipe due to the extra rice added to the same liquid quantity.

* A huge range of ingredients can be added to or served with rice pudding. After cooking, try mixing in 100 g currants, sultanas, chopped dried figs or dried chopped apricots.

* If using dried fruits, soak in 30 ml liqueur of choice for a few hours before adding.

* Roasted and chopped nuts, such as almonds, hazelnuts, macadamias, pecans or pistachios can be sprinkled over the top. Instead of vanilla extract, add ½ teaspoon rosewater or orange blossom water.

* For the health conscious— substitute the milk with soy milk and the white rice for a short-grain brown rice (available in health food stores), then use brown sugar at the end. Cook using the same method and times mentioned.

STICKY DATE PUDDING

Serves 4

xxxxxxxxxxxxxxxxxxxxxxxxxxxxxxxxxxxxxxxxxxxxxxxxxxxxxxxxxxxxxxxxxxxxxxxxxxxxxxxxxxxxxxxxxxxxxxxxxxx

200 g pitted dates
1 teaspoon bicarbonate of soda
200 ml boiling water
100 g butter, softened
200 g soft brown sugar
3 eggs, at room temperature
200 g self-raising flour, sifted

Method:

1. Mix the dates, bicarbonate of soda and boiling water in a bowl and stand until completely cool.

2. Preheat the oven to 180°C. Lightly grease a pudding dish or cake tin.

3. Cream the butter and sugar with an electric mixer. Add the eggs, one at a time, beating well after each addition to ensure the mixture stays smooth. If the eggs are cold direct from the fridge, the mixture may split (see Hints and tips).

4. Use a wooden spoon to fold in the flour and date mixture. If the mixture is runny, then everything is fine.

5. Pour the mixture into the prepared dish, place in the oven and bake for 35–45 minutes or until a skewer inserted into the middle comes out clean. Serve with cream or one of the suggested sauces below.

HINTS AND TIPS:

★ You will need—bowl, electric mixer, 1-litre pudding bowl or cake tin, weight, liquid and spoon measures and wooden spoon.

★ Ensure all ingredients are at room temperature to avoid the pudding mixture splitting. Adding cold eggs, even one at a time, to the room temperature butter and sugar will curdle the mixture every time.

★ If, when adding the eggs, the mixture does split, don't panic; continue as per the recipe and surprisingly, once baked, the final product will be fine.

★ Serve cold the next day as a cake or part of school/ office lunches.

★ Serve with **butterscotch sauce, pecan toffee sauce** or **simple toffee sauce**.

★ Try adding 200 g dark or milk chocolate buttons to the batter before it goes into the oven.

★ Make **butterscotch sauce** and pour into the base of a baking dish or cake tin. Pour the pudding batter over the sauce and cook at 180°C for the same time. Test if ready by inserting a skewer into the centre of the pudding. Adjust the cooking time if underdone. When the pudding is cooked, turn out immediately onto a large plate to expose the gooey base.

★ Cooking the pudding in a water bath in the oven is optional and can keep the pudding a bit moister, but add an extra 15–20 minutes to the cooking time. A water bath requires placing the pudding in a deep baking tray and adding boiling water to come halfway up the sides of the pudding bowl.

★ Leftover pudding can be cut into individual serves, wrapped separately and frozen. Defrost and microwave briefly before serving as a quick dessert when a friend drops in or just for you.

SUMMER PUDDING

Serves 8

xxxxxxxxxxxxxxxxxxxxxxxxxxxxxxxxxxxxxxxxxxxxxxxxxxxxxxxxxxxxxxxxxxxxxxxxxxxxxxxxxxxxxxxxxxxx

400 g strawberries, hulled and quartered
550 g raspberries
400 g blueberries
200 g caster sugar
150 ml water
1 loaf fresh, dense white bread, thickly sliced and
    crusts removed

Method:

1. Combine the berries, sugar and water in a medium
saucepan and stir gently over low heat, without
boiling, until the sugar has dissolved. Bring to a
simmer, remove from the heat and allow to stand for
about 5 minutes. Strain the juices from the fruit and
keep to one side.

2. Cut half the bread slices into triangles, leaving
the rest in squares.

3. Firmly pack a layer of the triangular bread slices
into the base of a glass bowl. Line the sides of the
bowl with the squares of bread, overlapping just
slightly.

4. Spoon the strained berries into the centre of the
bowl and pour enough juice over the top to nearly
cover the fruit. Ensure the juices run through the
bread slices lining the bowl. Leave to stand for
2 minutes.

5. Cover the top of the fruit with overlapping
triangular slices of bread. Pour a little more juice
over the top to saturate the bread.

Method cont.

6. Place the bowl in a larger dish to catch any juice that may spill. Cover the pudding with plastic wrap and place a plate or saucer (only slightly smaller than the mouth of the bowl) on top, then weigh down with a couple of cans of tomatoes from the pantry. The weight will cause the juice to bleed through the bread staining it red. Refrigerate overnight to allow the pudding to set. To serve, unmould the pudding onto a serving plate, slice and serve with pouring cream.

HINTS AND TIPS:

* You will need—saucepan, wooden spoon, liquid and weight measures, paring knife, 2-litre capacity pudding bowl (shallow or small casserole dishes will also work), plate to cover and canned food for weights.

* Try different breads like fruit bread, wholegrain, rye or light rye. Very cheap white bread tends to turn a bit slimy, so I like to make this pudding with day-old light rye or at Christmas time with Italian panettone, so the bread remains moist and has some texture even when thoroughly soaked by the berry juices.

* If fresh berries are out of season, substitute with frozen berries in the quantities mentioned. Frozen strawberries are best substituted with frozen blackberries.

* Other berries not mentioned but equally good are blackberries, boysenberries, mulberries and redcurrants. Traditionally, this pudding is made only with raspberries and redcurrants at a ratio of 4 parts raspberries to 1 part redcurrants. With so many fresh ripe berries around, why not make the pudding burst with every variety available.

* Serve with natural yoghurt, crème fraîche, double cream or whipped cream.

* A tip for berry season— when berries sit in the fridge and are not eaten, pop them in clip lock bags and place in the freezer. A collection will soon build— time to make summer pudding.

SYRUP PUDDING

Serves 4

XXXXXXXXXXXXXXXXXXXXXXXXXXXXXXXXXXXXXXXXXXXXXXXXXXXXXXXXXXXXXXXXXXXXXXXXXXXXXXXXXXXXXXXXXXXX

5 tablespoons golden syrup
150 g unsalted butter, softened
150 g caster sugar
2 eggs, at room temperature, lightly beaten
½ teaspoon vanilla extract
140 g self-raising flour, sifted
2 tablespoons milk

Method:

1. Preheat the oven to 160°C. Grease a pudding bowl. Pour the golden syrup into the base of the pudding bowl.

2. Cream the butter and sugar with an electric mixer. Beat in the eggs and vanilla extract. Fold in the flour and stir in enough milk to make the mixture a soft, dropping consistency. Pour into the prepared pudding bowl.

3. Cut a round of baking paper and place on top of the pudding. Cover the top of the bowl with foil and secure with a large elastic band or crimp the edges of the foil to keep it in place.

4. Stand the pudding bowl in a deep baking tray and add boiling water to reach halfway up the sides of the bowl. Place in the oven and bake for at least 2 hours, topping the tray up with water as required during the cooking time.

5. Remove the pudding bowl from the tray and cool a little. Remove the foil and baking paper. To turn out, loosen the pudding with a small knife, place the serving plate over the pudding and invert the two together so the plate is now on the bottom and the bowl is upside down. Remove the bowl to reveal the fabulous pudding. Slice and serve with cream, ice-cream, custard or sauce (see Hints and tips).

HINTS AND TIPS:

* You will need—1-litre pudding bowl, spoon and weight measures, bowl, electric mixer, wooden spoon, sieve and deep baking tray.

* This pudding is known also as 'golden syrup steamed pudding' or 'steamed syrup pudding'.

* For a **steamed ginger pudding**, sprinkle ½ teaspoon ground ginger over the syrup in the base of the bowl and 2 teaspoons ground ginger into the pudding mixture before baking.

* A **sauce** for this pudding can be made as follows— juice and zest of 1 orange, 1 tablespoon dark brown sugar, 3 tablespoons golden syrup and 30 ml orange liqueur (optional). Place the orange juice and zest, sugar and syrup in a saucepan. Bring to the boil then reduce heat to low and simmer for 2 minutes, remove from heat and add liqueur if using. Pour over the hot pudding at the table.

* A simpler sauce would be to just drizzle an extra 3 tablespoons golden syrup over the pudding when it's turned out.

* Cooking the pudding for 2 hours may seem like a long time to wait for a simple dessert. There is an alternative—bake the pudding without the water bath at 160°C for 45 minutes. The resulting pudding is a bit drier than the steamed version but is still very delicious.

* If the pudding is left to sit for several hours or overnight, the syrup is absorbd into the sponge. To serve, simply place a portion in the microwave on high for 30 seconds, drizzle with extra golden syrup and serve with cream or ice-cream.

TIRAMISU

Serves 8

XXXXXXXXXXXXXXXXXXXXXXXXXXXXXXXXXXXXXXXXXXXXXXXXXXXXXXXXXXXXXXXXXXXXXXXXXXXXXXXXXXXXXXXXXXXXXXXXXX

4 eggs
125 g caster sugar
100 ml marsala
500 g mascarpone cheese
450 ml thickened cream, lightly whipped
300 ml espresso coffee
100 ml Kahlua (coffee liqueur)
1 packet sponge biscuits (savoiardi)
drinking cocoa, for dusting

Method:

1. Place the eggs, sugar and marsala in a heatproof bowl over a pot of simmering water and whisk until light, fluffy and at ribbon stage—this is called a zabaglione. For a quick method, whisk the mixture until hot, transfer to an electric mixer and beat on high until the mixture cools.

2. Place the mascarpone cheese in another bowl, add some of the egg mixture and stir until the mascarpone is soft. Add the rest of the egg mixture and mix until well combined. Mix the cream in thoroughly and set aside.

3. In a third bowl, combine the coffee and Kahlua.

4. Dip one biscuit at a time into the coffee mixture very briefly—too long and the biscuit will become soggy and fall apart, as well as make the tiramisu too wet. Place a layer of dipped sponge biscuits in the base of a large bowl, cake tin or rectangular baking dish.

5. Pour half the mascarpone mixture over the biscuits, spreading evenly. Top with a second layer of coffee-dipped biscuits and another layer of the mascarpone mixture.

6. Dust heavily with the cocoa and refrigerate for at least 6 hours, preferably overnight, for the tiramisu to set properly.

HINTS AND TIPS:

* You will need—3 bowls, whisk, electric mixer, sieve, weight and liquid measures, large serving bowl, cake tin or rectangle dish and spatula.

* Every time I write a version of a classic recipe, I fear the backlash from the die-hard lovers of that dish and their banshee-like screams of, 'This is not how you make ...!' Tiramisu is one of those dishes. First, as much as I love tiramisu made with no cream and all mascarpone, it is not always economical as mascarpone is quite expensive, very dense and extremely rich, therefore I have provided a lighter version. The intrinsic flavours of the dish are there—coffee, marsala, coffee liqueur, chocolate and sponge. Please enjoy.

* For a richer tiramisu, leave out the whipped cream altogether. Separate the egg yolks and egg whites, make the zabaglione with the yolks, and in a clean bowl whisk the egg whites to stiff peaks. Mix the mascarpone with the zabaglione then fold in the beaten egg whites. The custard is now ready to layer with the other ingredients.

* For an alcohol-free and child-friendly version, replace the espresso and Kahlua with 400 ml strong hot chocolate cooled to room temperature before use.

* The instruction to 'briefly' dip the sponge biscuits in the coffee mixture is vital. I even press the biscuits between the palms of my hands to squeeze out excess liquid to guarantee that my tiramisu does not develop a pool of diluted coffee at the bottom of the dish after it sets.

* Tiramisu can be successfully frozen for a completely different effect, a cross between ice-cream, granita and cassata.

* A **berry tiramisu** can be made by removing the coffee element. Use sponge cake instead of biscuits, and brush the sponge with Chambord (raspberry liqueur), layer with fresh berries and **raspberry sauce**, and the mascarpone-zabaglione cream.

* Allergic to eggs? An **egg-free tiramisu** uses the same recipe as above, but instead of making a zabaglione with the eggs and sugar, add an extra 100 g mascarpone. Beat the sugar into the whipped cream and mix into the mascarpone. Continue with the same method.

TRIFLE
Serves 12

XXXXXXXXXXXXXXXXXXXXXXXXXXXXXXXXXXXXXXXXXXXXXXXXXXXXXXXXXXXXXXXXXXXXXXXXXXXXXXXXXXXXXXXXXXXXX

Sponge
7 eggs
180 g caster sugar
80 g plain flour
40 g cornflour
extra caster sugar, for sprinkling

Custard
250 ml milk
250 ml cream
1 teaspoon vanilla extract
8 egg yolks
60 g caster sugar
1 tablespoon cornflour

1 packet raspberry jelly or 200 g raspberry jam
300 ml dry masala, Spanish sherry or other liqueur
    like Cointreau
fruit of choice (see **Hints and tips**)

Method:

1. For the sponge—preheat the oven to 200°C. Grease
and flour a lamington tin. Place the eggs and sugar in
a heatproof bowl over a saucepan of simmering water
and whisk until thick and pale, about 10 minutes. Sift
in the flour and cornflour and fold gently to combine.
Pour into the prepared tin and bake for 10–12 minutes
or until cooked and golden on the surface. Cool on a
wire rack, sprinkle with the extra caster sugar and
turn out when cold.

2. For the custard—bring the milk, cream and vanilla
to a simmer in a saucepan. Whisk the egg yolks with
the sugar and cornflour until just combined. Whisk in
the warm milk mixture. Strain the custard back into
the rinsed saucepan, place over a medium heat and
stir constantly with a wooden spoon until the mixture
thickens and coats the back of the spoon. Remove from
the heat and set aside.

Method cont.

3. To assemble—select your best large glass bowl. Make the jelly following the instructions on the packet. Chop the set jelly into chunks. Or if using the jam, place in a microwave-proof bowl and microwave for 1 minute, remove and stir. Continue until the jam is quite soft. Spread the jam over the cooled sponge. Cut the sponge into pieces and divide into 2 batches (the base and middle layer). Put 1 batch of the sponge in the base of the bowl and sprinkle on half the alcohol. Add the fruit then some chopped jelly (if using), and finish this first layer with some custard. Add the second layer of sponge, sprinkle with the remaining alcohol, add more fruit and jelly, then top with the custard.

4. Place the trifle in the fridge overnight before serving with freshly whipped cream and toasted almonds.

HINTS AND TIPS:

----

* You will need—electric mixer, whisk, liquid, weight and spoon measures, wooden spoon, saucepan, lamington tin, sieve, cutting board, paring knife and 2-litre capacity glass bowl.

* The humble trifle is many things to many cooks. Jam or jelly? Sponge or biscuits? Sherry, marsala or brandy? No alcohol at all? Packet custard or homemade English custard? Fruit or no fruit? Nuts or no nuts? This recipe is to be messed with. Adjust it to bring back favourable memories of the trifle you grew up with; or stick with my recipe if the one you recall was too wet and had too much cheap sherry.

* Although best made the day before, a **free-form trifle** is an exciting last-minute dessert where all the components are put together in individual glasses or on a plate. The cook becomes the artist and decides what fruit, custard, sponge cake and alcohol is used—and how they are assembled.

* For a really **quick and easy trifle**, all the ingredients can be bought pre-made: sponge cake, sponge biscuits or jam sponge roll, and pre-made custard in the fridge section of your supermarket. If you are using jelly, that's really the only ingredient you need to make.

* For **alcohol-free trifle**, use cordial; look out for some of the gourmet cordials available at selected supermarkets and delicatessens.

* Use fresh berries and **raspberry sauce**, or poached peaches with peach schnapps.

YOGHURT AND LEMON MOUSSE

Serves 4

xxxxxxxxxxxxxxxxxxxxxxxxxxxxxxxxxxxxxxxxxxxxxxxxxxxxxxxxxxxxxxxxxxxxxxxxxxxxxxxxxxxxxxxxxxxx

250 ml thickened cream
100 g pure icing sugar
300 g firm, drained natural yoghurt (see **Hints and tips**)
juice and zest of ½ lemon
½ teaspoon vanilla extract
2 gelatine leaves
1 tablespoon thickened cream, extra

Method:

1. Place the cream and sugar in a cold mixing bowl and whisk to soft peaks; keep refrigerated.

2. Combine the yoghurt, lemon juice and zest, and vanilla extract in a bowl, and mix well.

3. Place the gelatine leaves in a bowl or pot with plenty of cold water. When the gelatine breaks down and becomes soft, heat the tablespoon of cream in a saucepan or in a microwave. Squeeze the water out of the softened gelatine and stir the gelatine into the hot cream until dissolved.

4. Add a spoonful of yoghurt to the gelatine cream mixture then stir this mixture back into the yoghurt. Fold in the semi-whipped cream then pour into individual glasses or into 1 large dish, and refrigerate until set (at least 4 hours). Serve with fresh berries or **rhubarb compote**. This mousse will keep for 1 week, covered and refrigerated.

HINTS AND TIPS:

* You will need—2 bowls, electric mixer, plastic spatula, spoon, liquid and weight measures, small saucepan or microwave dish and 4 glasses or 1 large dish for serving.

* Drained yoghurt is an overnight job. To make this dish, start the day before and serve the day after the mousse is made. To yield 300 g strained yoghurt, you will need to start out with 500-600 g natural yoghurt. Line a strainer with cheesecloth, muslin cloth or a clean tea towel and place over a bowl or bucket to catch the liquid. Pour the yoghurt into the cloth and cover with plastic wrap, then refrigerate for 24 hours (the longer it drains, the thicker it will get; after 3 days, it becomes a yoghurt cheese called 'labna'). The remaining firm yoghurt may not be exactly the right measure, so make sure there are 300 g. Throw out the residual liquid. Any leftover strained yoghurt can be used to make **tzatziki dip**.

* Gelatine comes from the collagen in animal parts, especially skin, hooves and bones. When boiled, they become sticky and set to a jelly-like texture. Commercial gelatine is available as granules or sheets (known as leaf gelatine). Chefs tend to recommend leaf gelatine (common in European countries) rather than granules, because it translates to a more precise measure. Gelatine granules are sometimes referred to as powdered gelatine (favoured in the US).

* If gelatine granules are easier to use than gelatine leaves, then substitute 2 gelatine leaves with 1 teaspoon gelatine granules.

* Make sure the lemon is washed and dried before any zest is grated. Dirt, wax and insect naughties may be on the surface, so clean before use.

* The pure icing sugar can be substituted for caster sugar.

* To lighten the mousse, beat 2 egg whites with a pinch of salt to soft peaks and fold into the mousse after the cream is added.

* This light and tangy mousse is refreshing on a warm night. Serve with a citrus salad (orange, lime and pink grapefruit with shredded mint) or drizzle with slightly warmed honey.

* Substitute the teaspoon of vanilla extract with ¼ teaspoon rosewater or orange blossom water.

* Scoop into a dessert bowl and serve with a drizzle of **raspberry sauce** and a handful of fresh raspberries.

ZABAGLIONE

Serves 6

xxxxxxxxxxxxxxxxxxxxxxxxxxxxxxxxxxxxxxxxxxxxxxxxxxxxxxxxxxxxxxxxxxxxxxxxxxxxxxxxxxxxxxxxxxxxxx

8 egg yolks
120 g caster sugar
120 ml white wine
30 ml brandy
few drops of vanilla extract

Method:

1. Place the egg yolks and sugar in a large heatproof bowl and whisk until pale and thick. Add the white wine, brandy and vanilla, and mix well.

2. Place the bowl over a saucepan filled to one-third with simmering water. The bowl should sit snugly on the saucepan but the bottom of the bowl should not touch the water. Whisk the zabaglione over medium heat until it thickens and doubles in volume.

3. Remove the bowl from the pan and cool the zabaglione before pouring into serving glasses.

HINTS AND TIPS:

★ You will need—large heatproof bowl, and liquid weight measures, saucepan and whisk.

★ For new cooks who have not had much experience whisking, bring in a friend to share the job. I only say this because it is a long, continuous process and if halted, the sauce could begin to scramble. There is a real chance that the whisking arm will get tired before the sauce is fluffy enough to serve.

★ A fine-wired whisk with many wires is recommended. It is a great investment for any kitchen, and many sauces and dressings in this book make good use of a quality whisk. Hard whisks, that is, a whisk with fewer thick wires, are wasted in a domestic kitchen.

★ Zabaglione is traditionally flavoured with sweet marsala, an Italian fortified wine. If you choose to use marsala, drop the sugar content in this recipe by 20 g. Then use 150 ml marsala instead of the wine and brandy combination.

★ The recipe provided is actually closer to a 'sabayon', the French version of Italy's zabaglione. Simply replace the wine and brandy for 160 ml champagne.

★ Zabaglione is served as a dessert on its own, accompanied by biscotti or savoiardi (sponge biscuits) for dipping.

★ Once the zabaglione has been placed in glasses— whether they be fancy goblets, martini glasses or simple latte glasses—top with a sprinkling of drinking cocoa or grate some excellent quality dark chocolate over the top.

★ Spoon some fresh berries into the base of a shallow bowl and pour the zabaglione over the top. Place under a hot grill to quickly brown the top. This is called 'berries gratin' and is a very easy and impressive dessert to make for your next dinner party.

★ Zabaglione goes well with berries or poached fruit (quince, pears, rhubarb), or baked apples; sprinkled with chocolate, ground cinnamon or nutmeg; or served with almond bread, sable biscuits, langue du chat (small, delicate biscuits resembling a cat's tongue).

★ Add ½ cup semi-whipped cream when the zabaglione has cooled completely and serve instead of custard or cream. This lighter version is great with plain sponge cake, madeira cake, scones or **pavlova**.

----
xxx **12. Cakes, Biscuits and Pastries** xxx

ALMOND BREAD

Makes 30–34 slices

xxxxxxxxxxxxxxxxxxxxxxxxxxxxxxxxxxxxxxxxxxxxxxxxxxxxxxxxxxxxxxxxxxxxxxxxxxxxxxxxxxxxxxxxxxxxxx

5 egg whites
150 g caster sugar
100 g plain flour, sifted
50 g almond meal
150 g almonds

Method:

1. Preheat the oven to 170°C. Grease a loaf tin.

2. Beat the egg whites until soft peaks form. Gradually add the caster sugar, beating well after each addition. Continue to beat until all the sugar is dissolved.

3. Fold in the flour, almond meal and almonds.

4. Spread the mixture into the prepared tin. Bake for 30–35 minutes or until just firm to touch. Turn out of the tin to cool.

5. When cold, wrap in foil and set aside for 2–5 days or place in the refrigerator for several hours to harden. Use a very sharp knife to cut the bread into wafer-thin slices (about 2 mm).

6. Preheat the oven to 120°C. Line 2 baking trays with baking paper.

7. Place the slices on the prepared trays and bake in the oven for 35 minutes or until dry and crisp. Cool and store in an airtight container for up to 2–3 months.

HINTS AND TIPS:

* You will need—electric mixer, wooden spoon, 25-cm x 8-cm loaf tin, sieve, weight measure, cutting board, very sharp cook's knife or serrated knife or electric knife and 2 baking trays.

* The cooked almond bread needs to be firm to slice. Stale or refrigerated almond bread is far easier to handle and cut thinly than a fresh product which will tear easily.

* For a festive feel, replace 50 g almonds with 50 g red and green glacé cherries. Add the cherries when the almonds are added.

* The almonds can have skin on or be blanched.

* For those cooks lucky enough to have a deli slicer (used to cut salami and ham), the bread can be kept in the freezer then sliced very thinly straight from the freezer.

* Try adding the zest of 1 lemon and 25 g dried cranberries.

* Serve almond bread as a dipping biscuit for crème brulee, **zabaglione**, **chocolate mousse** or **rice pudding**. Sandwich a scoop of ice-cream between 2 pieces of almond bread and drizzle with **butterscotch sauce** or **raspberry sauce**.

* Try making a dessert dip using 250 g mascarpone cheese mixed with 60 g pure icing sugar and the juice of ½ a lemon. Place in the centre of the table with a stack of almond bread.

* Almond bread can also be served with a cheese platter.

* A batch of almond bread biscuits tied in a cellophane bag with ribbon makes for a lovely gift at any time of year but especially at Christmas time when made with red and green glacé cherries.

ANZAC BISCUITS

Makes about 36

xxxxxxxxxxxxxxxxxxxxxxxxxxxxxxxxxxxxxxxxxxxxxxxxxxxxxxxxxxxxxxxxxxxxxxxxxxxxxxxxxxxxxxxxxxx

1 cup rolled oats
1 teaspoon salt
½ cup plain flour
½ cup caster sugar
½ cup desiccated coconut
100 g butter
1 tablespoon golden syrup
1 teaspoon baking soda
2 tablespoons boiling water

Method:

1. Preheat the oven to 180°C or 160°C for fan-forced. Line a baking tray with baking paper.

2. Mix the oats, salt, flour, sugar and coconut together in a large bowl, and set aside.

3. Gently melt the butter and golden syrup in a saucepan, and stir until thoroughly combined.

4. Combine the baking soda and water in a small bowl. Pour the foaming baking soda mixture into the warm butter and golden syrup and stir to incorporate—it will foam up again.

5. Gradually add the wet mixture to the dry ingredients, stirring well to incorporate.

6. Place 1 heaped teaspoon of mixture on the prepared tray, and continue until the tray is full, allowing room for the biscuits to spread. You may need to bake in batches. Press down on each biscuit with the back of a fork to flatten. Place on the bottom shelf in the oven and bake for 15 minutes or until golden, taking care not to burn them. Allow to cool on the trays for a few minutes before transferring to a cooling rack. Store in an airtight container.

HINTS AND TIPS:

----

* You will need—cup, spoon and weight measures, wooden spoon, saucepan, baking tray and 2 bowls.

* The original Anzac biscuits—also known as 'soldiers biscuits'—were tough eating. They were originally sent to the troops to provide a high protein, long-lasting and nourishing snack. They were so long-lasting, in fact, that some biscuits from WWI are still on show at the Australian War Memorial museum. Fortunately, today's adapted recipe, although crunchy, is a far cry from the Anzac 'tiles' sent to the frontline.

* If by chance the biscuits burn, and depending on how burnt they are, a solution is to use a grater to file off the burnt spots. Of course, if totally blackened then the bin is a good home for them.

* Should the biscuits become soft from poor storage, all is not lost. Either feed them to starving teenagers or break them up and cook them as if they were porridge— this is not as strange as it sounds. Traditionally, when the biscuits were sent to the troops the soldiers either ate them as they were or crumbled them up, added water and cooked them to make a toasted porridge.

* Try adding ¼ cup chopped nuts like macadamia or blanched almonds to the basic recipe.

* Other additions to this recipe include flaked almonds (¼ cup), sunflower seeds (¼ cup), pumpkin seeds (¼ cup), chopped dried fruit (¼ cup) or chocolate buttons (¼ cup). Any combination of these can be added as long as the amount doesn't exceed a total of ¼ cup.

* Melt some quality cooking chocolate in a bowl over a saucepan of simmering water and drizzle over the cooked and cooled biscuits. Let the chocolate set before storing.

* Try replacing plain flour with rye flour, and the caster sugar with brown sugar for a richer flavour.

* Wholemeal flour is also a good replacement for plain flour.

* Self-raising flour can replace the plain flour/baking soda combination. Keep the flour quantities the same, so use ½ cup self-raising flour in the recipe.

* When a ball of the mixture is flattened slightly with a fork and it falls apart, it's a sign that the biscuit dough is too dry. If this is the case, add another ½–1 tablespoon water to the mixture to soften.

* If using a larger crystal sugar like raw sugar, add to the melted butter and heat to dissolve before adding the golden syrup.

* You might like to use treacle rather than golden syrup.

BAKLAVA

Serves 12

xxxxxxxxxxxxxxxxxxxxxxxxxxxxxxxxxxxxxxxxxxxxxxxxxxxxxxxxxxxxxxxxxxxxxxxxxxxxxxxxxxxxxxxxxxxxxxx

12 sheets filo pastry
400 g crushed walnuts
150 g butter, melted
400 g sugar
400 ml water

Method:

1. Preheat the oven to 180°C. Grease a baking dish.

2. Layer 3 sheets of filo pastry in the baking tray and brush each with the melted butter. Keep the remaining pastry under a damp cloth to prevent it from drying out.

3. Sprinkle with one-third of the walnuts and add another 3 sheets of pastry brushed with butter. Continue until there are 4 layers of pastry and 3 layers of walnuts.

4. Brush the top layer of pastry with butter. Use a sharp knife to cut on the diagonal a diamond shaped pattern on top. Place in the oven and bake for 20–25 minutes or until golden brown.

5. To make the sugar syrup, place the sugar and water in a pot and bring to the boil.

6. Remove the baklava from the oven and pour enough of the hot sugar syrup over the top to almost cover the baklava. Sometimes it will take all of the syrup and sometimes not. Leftover syrup can be used in other dishes (see **sugar syrup**).

7. Allow to cool to room temperature before cutting and serving. Baklava will last at least 2 weeks, covered in the refrigerator.

HINTS AND TIPS:

* You will need—cutting board, cook's knife, pastry brush, saucepan, weight and liquid measures and 5-cm deep 23-cm x 18-cm baking dish.

* Historically, baklava originates from the Ottoman Empire. In those early times, it was made with 7 layers of nuts and 8 layers of pastry; pistachios were considered to be the most prestigious of fillings.

* 400 g walnuts is roughly 3 cups. This recipe has 3 layers of nuts and 4 layers of pastry, therefore allow 1 cup crushed nuts per layer. This formula is handy to know if you decide to make a deeper baklava.

* The method in this recipe prescribes pouring hot sugar syrup over the baklava once removed from the oven. There is an alternative method giving a slightly different end result. Allow the baklava to cool completely to room temperature (at least 4 hours). Pour the hot sugar syrup over the cold baklava, cover with a clean cloth or tea towel and leave overnight to allow the syrup to soak in. The hot syrup over the hot baklava softens the pastry whereas the hot syrup over the cold baklava keeps the pastry crispy. Cover with a cloth or tea towel and not plastic film to prevent the hot syrup from keeping in the steam and softening the pastry.

* Regular walnuts available at the supermarket are best. The 'eating out of hand' walnuts differ to 'baking' walnuts which are darker and fuller tasting; however, baking walnuts are also more bitter and are generally only available at Middle Eastern grocers and nut specialists. The darker baking nut can be too strong to use in this delicate pastry treat.

* Use other nuts like almonds and pistachios mixed in with the walnuts or simply replace the walnuts for another nut.

* Add flavour to the sugar syrup—try the zest of 1 lemon (remember to strain the syrup before pouring over the baklava) or 1 cup honey instead of 225 g (1 cup) sugar, or add 1 tablespoon rosewater or orange blossom water.

* To make eating easier at large gatherings, place slices of baklava in cupcake paper cases.

* To serve, dust with icing mixture.

* Baklava can be frozen, but keeps very well covered and refrigerated or even stored in the pantry. Over a week or two, the baklava tends to get juicier; once it starts to dry out, it is past its use-by date.

* Leftover filo pastry can be wrapped and kept in the freezer for up to 2 months.

BACON AND EGG PIE

Serves 6

XXXXXXXXXXXXXXXXXXXXXXXXXXXXXXXXXXXXXXXXXXXXXXXXXXXXXXXXXXXXXXXXXXXXXXXXXXXXXXXXXXXXXXXXX

1 tablespoon olive oil
8 bacon rashers
½ cup fresh flat-leaf parsley leaves, chopped
1 sheet frozen shortcrust pastry, defrosted
8 eggs
freshly ground black pepper
1 sheet frozen puff pastry, defrosted
1 egg yolk, for glazing

Method:

1. Preheat the oven to 180°C. Use a little of the oil to grease a shallow 22-cm pie or quiche dish with a removable base.

2. In a large sauté pan over medium–high heat, heat the remaining oil and fry the bacon, then remove from the pan and roughly chop.

3. Place the sheet of shortcrust pastry in the base of the dish.

4. Sprinkle the bacon and parsley over the pastry base.

5. Carefully crack the eggs so that the yolks and whites are arranged fairly evenly inside the pastry-lined dish. Grind pepper over the top.

6. Place the sheet of puff pastry over the filling and crimp the edges down with a fork. Trim the excess with a knife.

7. Brush the puff pastry top with the egg yolk, place in the refrigerator for 5 minutes and brush again with egg yolk.

8. Bake in the oven for about 30 minutes or until the pastry is golden brown and flaky. Remove from the oven, and cool slightly in the tin before removing.

HINTS AND TIPS:

* You will need—cutting board, cook's knife, 22-cm pie dish or quiche dish, sauté or frying pan and cup and spoon measures.

* This really is an easy pie to make and one that kids will enjoy being involved in.

* It is fine to eat hot or cold—which means a slice in the school or office lunch box with some salad is a good idea. Or take cold to a picnic.

* Serve warm in summer with a fresh salad and hot in winter with roasted vegetables on the side.

* Simply serve with mashed potato and a salad.

* Although regular bacon is fine to use, try sourcing a thick, smoky bacon for added flavour.

* Try adding a layer of a few slices of fresh tomato and a cup of sliced and sautéed button mushrooms over the bacon and then add the eggs.

* Some cooks love adding peas and corn to the pie, which means it isn't really a bacon and egg pie, just a pie. Add ½ cup frozen peas and ½ cup corn kernels to the bacon and parsley mixture.

* Or you could take 1 leek, slice lengthways and wash out any dirt, then drain and slice crossways. Sauté in 1 tablespoon butter over medium heat until wilted, then mix with the cooked bacon and parsley.

* Sprinkle a cup of your favourite cheese, grated, over the eggs before closing with the pastry lid.

* Buying two types of pastry is preferable; however, if you already have a few sheets of puff pastry in the freezer, then use 1 sheet for the base and 1 sheet for the lid. Shortcrust pastry is not a good substitute for the lid on the pie.

* Brushing the pie with egg yolk twice adds a very rich glaze to the lid, but if you are lacking time and eggs, just brush with milk and bake.

* Use offcuts of puff pastry to make small decorations on the lid of the pie before it goes into the oven.

BANANA BREAD

Makes 1 loaf

XXXXXXXXXXXXXXXXXXXXXXXXXXXXXXXXXXXXXXXXXXXXXXXXXXXXXXXXXXXXXXXXXXXXXXXXXXXXXXXXXXXXXX

3 very ripe bananas
125 ml buttermilk
1 teaspoon vanilla essence
200 g caster sugar
250 g self-raising flour
½ teaspoon salt
2 teaspoons ground cinnamon
60 ml olive oil
1 tablespoon butter

Method:

1. Preheat the oven to 170°C. Grease a loaf tin with oil or butter.

2. Place the bananas in a bowl and mash until smooth. Add the buttermilk and vanilla, and blend until well mixed.

3. Combine the remaining dry ingedients in another bowl and mix until well blended. Add to the banana and milk mixture. Stir in the olive oil and mix thoroughly. Pour into the prepared tin.

4. Bake in the oven for 1 hour or until a small knife or metal skewer inserted in the centre comes out clean. Allow to cool on the bench for 10 minutes before turning out onto a wire rack.

5. Cool completely. Keep refrigerated or frozen until needed. To serve, thickly slice the banana bread, melt the butter in a frying pan over medium heat and when bubbling, add the slices of banana bread. Cook for 1 minute on each side or until golden.

HINTS AND TIPS:

* You will need—21-cm x 11-cm loaf tin, 2 bowls, fork, wooden spoon, weight, liquid and spoon measures and plastic spatula.

* Many recipes for banana bread ask for the butter and sugar to be beaten until pale and fluffy, then the eggs are added one at a time, then the flour and bananas are added. This method and the ingredients are really for a banana cake and although called banana bread, has the consistency of cake. The only difference being that it is baked in a loaf tin and not a cake tin. The idea of banana bread is that it is dry and more like a bread, and it needs to be toasted, usually in a pan with butter, to make it moist.

* For a dairy-free version, replace the buttermilk with soy milk or ½ cup apple puree.

* Try adding ½ cup chopped walnuts or ½ cup sultanas to the recipe. Other nuts and dried fruit could be added in the quantity of ½ cup.

* For a healthier option, replace the plain flour with wholemeal flour and caster sugar with soft brown sugar. Then use mixed spice instead of cinnamon, and yoghurt instead of buttermilk.

* Adding eggs to this recipe is optional. Lightly beat 2 eggs and stir into the batter for a different texture.

* Banana and chocolate are really good friends so try adding ½ cup dark, milk or white chocolate buttons to the batter before baking.

* Fresh or frozen blueberries (½ cup) are delicious in this recipe.

* The banana bread, wrapped in foil, will last for 2 months in the freezer. Place in the fridge overnight to defrost.

* Bananas that are not being eaten and are starting to brown are ideal for baking. Keep overripe bananas in the freezer. To freeze bananas properly, peel and chop into 3-cm pieces, place on a tray lined with plastic wrap and freeze until solid. When frozen, place the banana into small clip lock bags and keep frozen until needed. Or simply peel and freeze as whole bananas.

BANANA CAKE
Serves 8

xxxxxxxxxxxxxxxxxxxxxxxxxxxxxxxxxxxxxxxxxxxxxxxxxxxxxxxxxxxxxxxxxxxxxxxxxxxxxxxxxxxxxxxxxxxxxxxxxxxx

125 g unsalted butter, softened
150 g caster sugar
2 eggs, at room temperature
2 very ripe bananas
2 tablespoons sour cream
1 teaspoon vanilla extract
200 g self-raising flour
1 teaspoon mixed spice or ground cinnamon

Method:

1. Preheat the oven to 180°C. Grease a round or springform cake tin with olive oil spray.

2. Place the butter and sugar in the bowl of an electric mixer and whip until pale and fluffy. Add the eggs, one at a time, making sure the first egg is thoroughly combined before adding the second.

3. Place the bananas in a separate bowl and mash with a fork. Mix in the sour cream and vanilla.

4. Use a wooden spoon to beat the banana mixture into the butter mixture.

5. Sift the flour into the banana batter and stir until thoroughly combined. Pour into the prepared cake tin, place in the oven and bake for 55–60 minutes. Check to make sure the cake is ready by piercing the centre with a metal or wooden skewer. If it comes out clean, remove from the oven to a wire rack; if still a bit sticky in the centre, give the cake an extra 5 minutes in the oven.

6. After 10 minutes cooling, turn out the cake onto the wire rack and cool completely before icing.

HINTS AND TIPS:

* You will need—2 bowls, electric mixer, 24-cm round or springform cake tin, spoon and weight measures, wooden spoon, plastic spatula and wire rack.

* A classic addition to banana cake is walnuts. To the above recipe, add 150 g freshest walnuts, chopped roughly and added to the batter.

* A good **cream cheese frosting** is the best way to finish off this cake.

* Do not waste bananas when they are overripe or excessively brown. These can be frozen and used in banana cake and **banana bread**. To freeze bananas properly, peel, chop into 3-cm pieces, place on a tray lined with plastic wrap and freeze until solid. When frozen, place the banana into small clip lock bags and keep frozen until needed. Or simply peel and freeze as whole bananas.

* For a rich colour in the cake, substitute the caster sugar with dark brown sugar.

* For school lunches, spoon the mixture into muffin moulds and bake for half the time.

* Sour cream can be substituted with natural yogurt or pouring cream with 1 tablespoon lemon juice. If adding the lemon juice, why not grate the zest into the mixture before squeezing the juice.

* Try replacing half the sugar with pure maple syrup, and substitute the mixed spice with ground nutmeg.

* Banana is technically a berry and the tree on which it grows is technically a herb.

* To hasten the ripening of bananas, place in the sun or in a paper bag with a ripe apple (the slow release of ethylene from the apple will trigger ethylene production in the banana). If bananas are ripening too quickly, remove the skin and freeze. A small store of frozen bananas is handy for cakes, muffins or smoothies, or they can simply be blended while still frozen for an instant frozen dairy-free banana treat.

* Bananas can be kept in the fridge; the skin will go brown/black, but the flesh will retain its creamy yellow colour. Long-term storage in the fridge, however, can mean the flesh will begin to break down or decay from the inside out.

BASIC BISCUITS

Makes about 12

XXXXXXXXXXXXXXXXXXXXXXXXXXXXXXXXXXXXXXXXXXXXXXXXXXXXXXXXXXXXXXXXXXXXXXXXXXXXXXXXXXXXXXXXXX

150 g self-raising flour
25 g cornflour
180 g caster sugar
150 g butter or margarine, melted and cooled
½ teaspoon vanilla extract
1 egg, lightly beaten

Method:

1. Preheat the oven to 180°C. Grease a baking tray and line with baking paper.

2. Sift the flours and sugar into a bowl then stir in the butter or margarine, vanilla and egg.

3. Place 1 teaspoonful of mixture on the prepared tray, and continue until the tray is full, allowing room for the biscuits to spread. You may need to bake in batches. With the first tray baked, you will be able to see how much they spread, so the second batch can be put closer together if need be.

4. Cook for 12–15 minutes or until golden. Spread onto a wire rack to cool and store in an airtight container for up to 14 days.

HINTS AND TIPS:

* You will need—2 bowls, weight and spoon measures, wooden spoon, saucepan or microwave bowl to melt butter, sieve, baking tray and baking paper.

* The biscuit dough will last for 3–5 days in the fridge, but if baking the dough straight from the fridge, allow 3–5 minutes extra in the oven.

* Extra dough can be wrapped in plastic wrap, rolled into a log shape and frozen for 3 months. To use, peel back the plastic wrap and cut into 1-cm thick slices, place on a prepared baking tray and leave to defrost on the bench before baking.

* Another technique you could use with the same recipe is to whisk the butter and sugar until light and fluffy, add the egg and vanilla then stir in the sifted flours.

* There are so many combinations of flavours that can be added to this basic biscuit mixture. Try some of the following.

* For **nut biscuits**, add 100 g freshest chopped nuts— macadamias, walnuts, pecans, cashews, almonds or Brazils. Try adding the grated zest of 1 lemon or orange to the dough when adding the nuts.

* Roughly chop 50 g **honeycomb** or 80 g of your favourite chocolate bar and add to the basic mixture.

* Spread the biscuit mixture just a bit with the back of a spoon and dot with Smarties.

* For **chocolate chip biscuits**—stir 100 g dark, milk or white chocolate chips into the biscuit dough. Choc chips can be substituted with excellent quality cooking chocolate, chopped to the size of buttons. Try using soft brown sugar instead of caster sugar for a richer mixture.

* What's the difference between choc chip, double choc chip and triple choc chip? Choc chip has just chocolate chips (see hint above). **Double chocolate chip biscuits** need 1 tablespoon Dutch cocoa mixed into the chocolate chip recipe above. **Triple chocolate chip biscuits** are double choc chip biscuits drizzled with melted chocolate. You will need about 50 g dark, milk or white cooking chocolate, melted in the top of a double boiler and drizzled over the cooled biscuits. Let the chocolate set hard before

storing, if they even make it to storage.

* **Chocolate and nut biscuits**—add 75 g chopped peanuts or macadamias with 100 g chocolate buttons. Or, instead of chopped peanuts, add 2 tablespoons crunchy peanut butter and reduce the butter by 50 g.

* For **strawberry shortcake**— Grease and line 2 x 20-cm cake tins with baking paper. Double the basic biscuit recipe above, divide between the prepared cake tins and bake for 12–15 minutes or until golden. Cool. Prepare 4 cups strawberries (hulled and sliced) and whip 300 ml thickened cream with ½ teaspoon vanilla extract and 2 tablespoons icing sugar. Place one of the shortcakes on a plate, spread a small amount of the whipped cream over the cake, top with half the strawberries then top with the second shortcake; dollop the remaining cream over the top then finish with the remaining strawberries.

BISCOTTI

Makes about 30

XXXXXXXXXXXXXXXXXXXXXXXXXXXXXXXXXXXXXXXXXXXXXXXXXXXXXXXXXXXXXXXXXXXXXXXXXXXXXXXXXXXXXXXXXX

4 eggs, lightly beaten
300 g plain flour
2 teaspoons ground aniseed (optional)
150 g caster sugar
300 g almonds, roughly chopped
grated zest of 2 lemons

Method:

1. Preheat the oven to 160°C. Line a baking tray with baking paper.

2. Place all of the ingredients in a bowl and use a wooden spoon to mix to a smooth dough. Try not to over-work the dough.

3. Turn out onto a lightly floured surface and roll the dough into 2 logs about 30 cm long and three fingers wide. Place on the prepared tray, leaving plenty of space between the logs as they will expand.

4. Place in the oven for 25 minutes. The dough should not take on too much colour.

5. Remove and cool for 5 minutes. Use a sharp serrated knife to carefully slice each log on the diagonal into individual biscotti about 5 mm thick.

6. Place the biscuits, cut side down, on the lined baking tray and bake for another 10 minutes, turning once. Cool completely before storing in an airtight jar.

HINTS AND TIPS:

* You will need—bowl, wooden spoon, weight and spoon measures, baking tray, baking paper, food processor (for the almonds) and grater.

* The ground aniseed adds a beautiful fragrance and sweetness to the biscotti and although similar in smell to star anise, it is in fact a different spice.

* For **chocolate and almond biscotti**—add 2 tablespoons Dutch cocoa, replace the aniseed with ground cinnamon, lessen the flour quantity by 50 g and substitute the lemon zest with that of 1 orange. Try replacing the almonds with roasted hazelnuts. To roast the hazelnuts and remove the skins—preheat the oven to 200°C, roast the hazelnuts on a tray for 10 minutes or until the skins are flaking. Tip the nuts into a tea towel placed over a bowl, fold the edges over and let stand (steam) for 5 minutes, then rub well to remove as much skin as possible. Remove the nuts and chop coarsely.

* For **espresso biscotti**— add 1 tablespoon espresso coffee and 50 g grated dark chocolate to the recipe.

* For a lighter biscuit, substitute plain flour with self-raising flour.

* Be careful in the second stage of cooking because although the biscuits need to dry out, if they bake for too long (15–20 minutes or even longer), prepare to break teeth.

* These biscuits will last for several weeks in an airtight container. After that biscotti will begin to go stale and the nuts will become slightly rancid.

* Serve with coffee, crème brulée or **chocolate mousse**.

* Biscotti, like **almond bread**, make an excellent homemade gift for family and friends at Christmas.

CARROT CAKE

Serves 10

xxxxxxxxxxxxxxxxxxxxxxxxxxxxxxxxxxxxxxxxxxxxxxxxxxxxxxxxxxxxxxxxxxxxxxxxxxxxxxxxxxxxxxxxxxxxx

3 large eggs
1 teaspoon vanilla extract
200 g grated carrot (about 4 carrots)
80 g pecan nuts or walnuts, chopped
250 g soft brown sugar
180 ml vegetable oil
220 g self-raising flour
1 teaspoon ground cinnamon
1 teaspoon mixed spice
1 recipe quantity **cream cheese frosting**
extra 50 g pecan nuts or walnuts, for topping

Method:

1. Preheat the oven to 180°C. Grease a springform cake tin or a loaf tin and line with baking paper.

2. Combine the eggs, vanilla, carrot, chopped nuts, sugar and oil in a large bowl. Sift in the flour, cinnamon and mixed spice. Stir until well combined and pour into the prepared tin.

3. Place in the oven and bake for 55–60 minutes. The cake is ready when a skewer or small knife inserted in the centre comes out clean. If still a bit moist, give the cake an extra 5–10 minutes.

4. Remove from the oven and cover the cake with a clean tea towel, to allow the steam to keep the cake moist. Cool in the tin.

5. Turn the cake out onto a wire rack and spread the top and sides with frosting then sprinkle with the extra nuts. Serve or store the cake in an airtight container in the refrigerator. For maximum flavour, allow the cake to come back to room temperature before serving.

HINTS AND TIPS:

----

* You will need—20-cm springform cake tin or 20-cm x 10-cm loaf tin, baking paper, large bowl, wooden spoon, grater, sieve, weight, liquid and spoon measures, plastic spatula and wire rack.

* Bake at 160°C if using a fan-forced oven. This rule applies to all baking, drop the temperature by 20°C when using a fan-forced oven. The cooking time stays the same.

* For **mini carrot cakes** for school lunch boxes, place the cake batter in muffin moulds and halve the cooking time.

* Try replacing the mixed spice with ground ginger or ground nutmeg.

* Double the recipe for frosting, slice the carrot cake in half horizontally, open up gently and spread the frosting in the centre of the cake, then put the top back on and frost the top and sides.

* Try adding the finely grated zest of 1 orange and 1 lemon to the mixture.

* For an even healthier option, use wholemeal self-raising flour instead of the white self-raising flour.

* Some carrot cakes are presented with little carrot-like garnishes around the top of the cake; here's how to make them. You will need 100 g marzipan (almond paste), and red, yellow and green food colouring. Divide the marzipan in half, and knead in small amounts of food coloring, so they match the colours of the carrots (red and yellow combined for the carrot and green for the carrot tops). Roll the orange-coloured marzipan into a ball the size of a large pea, then roll one side of the ball into the tapered shape of a carrot. With a toothpick, poke a hole in the larger end for the green carrot tops. Make the tops by rolling one small piece of green marzipan into 3 tiny, thin strings. Pinch them together at one end and insert that end into the hole at the top of the carrot. If the stem is a bit loose, then use the toothpick to push the carrot top snugly around the stem. Use a small sharp knife and press small indentations along the length of the carrot, place around the outer edge of the cake with the tip of the carrot facing the middle of the cake.

CHEESE TWISTS

Makes about 10–12 twists

XXXXXXXXXXXXXXXXXXXXXXXXXXXXXXXXXXXXXXXXXXXXXXXXXXXXXXXXXXXXXXXXXXXXXXXXXXXXXXXXXXXXXXXXXXXXX

2 sheets frozen puff pastry, defrosted
¼ cup grated parmesan cheese
¼ cup grated cheddar cheese
2 tablespoons olive oil
1 teaspoon dried oregano
¼ teaspoon salt
½ teaspoon ground cayenne pepper or paprika
1 large egg, lightly beaten
plain flour, for dusting

Method:

1. Preheat the oven to 200°C. Line 3 large baking trays with baking paper.

2. Mix the cheeses, oil, oregano, salt and cayenne pepper or paprika in a bowl. Stir well to combine.

3. Place 1 sheet of puff pastry on a lightly floured surface and brush with the egg. Spread most of the cheese mixture over the pastry sheet.

4. Lay the second pastry sheet over the cheese mixture and sprinkle with a small amount of flour. Use a rolling pin to gently press the layers together without rolling out of shape.

5. Brush the top with more beaten egg and sprinkle with the remaining cheese. Press the cheese into the dough slightly.

6. Use a sharp kitchen knife to cut into 1.5-cm strips.

7. One at a time, grab each strip at either end and twist in opposite directions to form a spiral.

8. Transfer to the prepared baking trays. Place in the oven and bake until golden and puffed, about 10–12 minutes.

9. Remove from the oven and cool before serving or storing in an airtight container.

HINTS AND TIPS:

* You will need—3 baking trays, baking paper, bowl, fork, cutting board, cook's knife, pastry brush, rolling pin and spoon and cup measures.

* Cheese twists are one of the great after-school snacks, if only more people would make them. They are so easy if using pre-made, frozen puff pastry, there really is no excuse for not giving them a go.

* Twisting the filled pastry is just one way to make a tasty snack. An even easier—yet less impressive—way is to simply cut out the shapes and bake as is.

* To make ahead—follow the recipe to the point of twisting the strips (step 7). Place on the prepared baking tray, and brush with the egg mixture and freeze. When frozen, transfer to a clip lock bag and seal. Place back in the freezer for up to 1 month. To bake, preheat the oven to 200°C. Place the frozen strips on a baking tray lined with baking paper. Bake for 15 minutes or until golden.

* Other dried herbs which can be used include basil, mixed herbs or thyme.

* For extra kick—sprinkle with chilli flakes or cayenne pepper, but be sure to let everyone know which ones are likely to bite.

* The cheese suggested in this recipe is only a guide—try using gruyère, gouda, Swiss, tasty, mozzarella or blue cheese. Use as a single flavour or mix two flavours together.

* Finely chopped anchovies, black olives, capers, ham or salami can make their way into the filling to make a pizza-style twist—just make sure the ingredients are finely chopped (maybe use a food processor).

* Serve alongside your favourite dips for a light snack or party food.

* Use a pizza cutter to cut the strips.

* You can make **sweet twists** using a mixture of 1 tablespoon ground cinnamon, ½ cup caster sugar and ½ cup ground almonds; sprinkle between the sheets of pastry and continue as for cheese twists.

* Serve as part of an antipasto platter with prosciutto wrapped around the twists.

CHOCOLATE BROWNIES

Makes about 24

XXXXXXXXXXXXXXXXXXXXXXXXXXXXXXXXXXXXXXXXXXXXXXXXXXXXXXXXXXXXXXXXXXXXXXXXXXXXXXXXXXXXXXXX

250 g dark cooking
   chocolate
250 g unsalted butter
5 eggs
500 g caster sugar
1 tablespoon vanilla
   essence
200 g plain flour
½ teaspoon salt

Method:

1. Preheat the oven to 170°C. Lightly grease and line a large slice tray with baking paper (see Hints and tips).

2. Place the chocolate and butter in a heatproof bowl over a saucepan of simmering water. Reduce the heat to the lowest setting. When melted, set aside to cool slightly.

3. Beat the eggs, sugar and vanilla with an electric mixer for about 10 minutes or until light and fluffy.

4. Beat in the cooled chocolate, sift in the flour and salt and stir until well-combined.

5. Pour into the prepared tin, place in the oven and bake for about 35 minutes. A skewer inserted in the centre should come out with some mixture still on it. Remove from the oven and cool on a wire rack; if it drops in the centre and forms a crust then you have just made the perfect chocolate brownie. Serve or store in an airtight container in the refrigerator for 10 days. Brownies freeze well for 3 months.

HINTS AND TIPS:

★ You will need—large slice tray or 2 smaller trays, baking paper, heatproof bowl, saucepan, electric mixer and bowl, plastic spatula and spoon and weight measures.

★ Brownies are served as a snack on their own with coffee or tea but are equally popular as a dessert with whipped cream or ice-cream— or both. And then there's the blondie.

★ For **blondies**—simply replace the dark chocolate with white chocolate. Melt 200 g white chocolate with the butter; and chop 50 g white chocolate and stir through the mixture with the flour. Cook until browned on top, about 35 minutes. Although called a blondie, they are a very pale caramel colour; blondie refers to the colour of the chocolate before it is cooked.

★ For chocolate nut brownies—add 100 g pecans, walnuts, macadamias, Brazils, pistachios or peanuts when stirring in the flour.

★ Once cooled, cover with a **chocolate frosting** or a **chocolate cream**—heat 150 ml thickened cream, remove from the heat and stir through 200 g chopped dark, milk or white cooking chocolate. Continue to stir (off the heat) until the chocolate has completely melted in the cream and pour over the brownie. Chill before slicing. If heated, the chocolate cream melts and becomes a sauce.

CHOCOLATE CRACKLES

Makes 24

XXXXXXXXXXXXXXXXXXXXXXXXXXXXXXXXXXXXXXXXXXXXXXXXXXXXXXXXXXXXXXXXXXXXXXXXXXXXXXXXX

150 g pure icing sugar
3 tablespoons cocoa powder
4 cups Rice Bubbles
250 g Copha

Method:

1. Spread 24 cupcake paper cases on a tray.

2. Sift together the icing sugar and cocoa. Add the Rice Bubbles and mix well.

3. Melt the copha in a saucepan, pour over the dry ingredients and mix together.

4. Spoon into paper cases and refrigerate. When set, serve or store in an airtight container in the fridge.

HINTS AND TIPS:

★ You will need—tray, cupcake paper cases, bowl, saucepan, sieve, cup, spoon and weight measures and wooden spoon or plastic spatula.

★ Try adding 75 g sultanas to the mixture or 60 g desiccated coconut (or both).

★ Copha is a brand name of solidified coconut oil. It is used also in white Christmas (see below) as well as for thinning chocolate. Classed as a vegetable shortening, it could be used in **Christmas pudding** as a vegetarian or vegan alternative to suet (animal fat). Copha is not available outside Australia so if necessary look for a brand of solid coconut oil or vegetable shortening.

★ Rice Bubbles are known as Rice Crispies in the United States. Brand names aside, any brand of crispy puffed rice will do. The softer, healthier puffed rice will never work as well, becoming quite soggy when the melted copha is added.

★ Chocolate crackles are popular at school fetes and children's birthday parties— it's always interesting to note how many parents sneak one (to appease the inner child).

★ For **white Christmas**—mix 1 cup each of milk powder, desiccated coconut, pure icing sugar and sultanas in a bowl and add 1 teaspoon vanilla extract. Melt 250 g copha and stir into the mixture. When thoroughly combined, press into a baking paper-lined tray and set in the refrigerator. Cut into squares.

CHOCOLATE FUDGE

Here are two recipes for chocolate fudge. The first is a traditional recipe that requires a deft hand to make the sugar syrup; the second recipe is far easier and is the preferred method for beginner cooks and for making decent fudge for school fetes.

CHOCOLATE FUDGE 1

Makes 20 pieces

xxxxxxxxxxxxxxxxxxxxxxxxxxxxxxxxxxxxxxxxxxxxxxxxxxxxxxxxxxxxxxxxxxxxxxxxxxxxxxxxxxxxxxxxxx

80 g Dutch cocoa powder
800 g caster sugar
375 ml milk
60 g butter
1 teaspoon vanilla extract

Method:

1. Lightly grease a 20-cm square cake tin with oil.

2. Sift the cocoa into a large, heavy-based saucepan and add the sugar. Stir in the milk and bring to the boil over medium heat, stirring constantly. Boil, without stirring, until the mixture reaches soft ball stage (see **Hints and tips**)—110°C/230°F on a sugar thermometer. Remove from heat.

3. Add the butter and vanilla, but do not stir. Allow the mixture to cool, at room temperature, until it reaches 45°C/110°F. Beat with a whisk or an electric mixer until the mixture thickens and loses its gloss. Quickly transfer to the prepared tin and spread evenly. Leave to harden at room temperature before cutting into squares.

HINTS AND TIPS:

* You will need—20-cm square cake tin, baking paper, sieve, weight, liquid and spoon measures, sugar thermometer, electric mixer or whisk and saucepan.

* If using a sugar thermometer, the bulb of the thermometer should not rest on the bottom of the pan as the metal of the pan is decidedly hotter than the sugar syrup.

* To test for soft ball stage without a thermometer— fill a cup with cold water. Spoon a small amount of the boiling sugar syrup into the cold water. If the syrup forms a soft ball in the water that flattens when removed, it has reached soft ball stage. Quickly remove the syrup from the heat and add the butter and vanilla.

* If the syrup cooks beyond soft ball stage and into hard ball stage, then the fudge will set very hard and possibly be grainy in texture.

CHOCOLATE FUDGE 2

Makes 16 pieces

XXXXXXXXXXXXXXXXXXXXXXXXXXXXXXXXXXXXXXXXXXXXXXXXXXXXXXXXXXXXXXXXXXXXXXXXXXXXXXXXXXXXXXXXXXXXXXX

400 g quality dark
   chocolate, chopped
395 g can sweetened
   condensed milk
80 g butter

Method:

1. Lightly grease a 20-cm square cake tin. Line the base and sides with baking paper.

2. Combine all of the ingredients in a large heatproof bowl over a saucepan of gently simmering water. Stir for 5 minutes or until smooth.

3. Pour the fudge into the prepared tin and spread evenly. Refrigerate until the fudge is firm.

4. Place a cook's knife in hot water, dry and cut the fudge into small squares. Keep the fudge chilled in an airtight container.

HINTS AND TIPS:

----

* You will need—heatproof bowl, weight measure, saucepan, baking paper, and a 20-cm square cake tin.

* This makes quite a dark fudge. Use 250 g dark chocolate to tone down the big flavour or use a quality milk or 450 g white chocolate as a substitute.

COCONUT ICE

I have included two decisive and very different styles of recipe for the one sweet treat.

COCONUT ICE 1

Makes 20 pieces

XXXXXXXXXXXXXXXXXXXXXXXXXXXXXXXXXXXXXXXXXXXXXXXXXXXXXXXXXXXXXXXXXXXXXXXXXXXXXXXXXXXXXXXXX

3 cups pure icing sugar, sifted
3½ cups desiccated coconut
395 g can condensed milk
1 teaspoon vanilla essence
about 6 drops of pink food colouring

Method:

1. Grease a rectangular slice tray and line with baking paper.

2. Place all of the ingredients in a bowl and mix well.

3. Divide the mixture between 2 bowls and add the pink food colouring to one.

4. Press the white mixture evenly into the base of the prepared tray. Top with the pink mixture, and press firmly and evenly. Refrigerate for at least 1 hour then cut into 3-cm squares or triangles.

COCONUT ICE 2

Makes 20 pieces

XXXXXXXXXXXXXXXXXXXXXXXXXXXXXXXXXXXXXXXXXXXXXXXXXXXXXXXXXXXXXXXXXXXXXXXXXXXXXXXXXXXXXXXXX

125 g copha
(see **Hints and tips**)
400 g pure icing sugar, sifted
250 g desiccated coconut
2 egg whites
1 teaspoon vanilla essence
few drops of pink food colouring

Method:

1. Grease a rectangular slice tray and line with baking paper.

2. Melt the copha in a small saucepan or in the microwave—do not make too hot.

3. Combine the icing sugar and coconut in a bowl. Add the egg whites, vanilla and copha and mix thoroughly. Place half the mixture into a separate bowl and colour with a few drops of pink colouring.

4. Press the white mixture evenly into the base of the tray. Top with the pink mixture, and press firmly and evenly. Refrigerate for at least 1 hour then cut into 3-cm squares or triangles.

HINTS AND TIPS:

* You will need—20-cm x
30-cm rectangular slice
tray, baking paper, small
saucepan, wooden spoon or
plastic spatula, cup, spoon
and weight measures, knife
and 2 bowls.

* The biggest difference
between the recipes is the
use of condensed milk,
copha and egg whites.
The first recipe relies on
condensed milk as its setting
ingredient, while the second
recipe uses copha and egg
whites to set the coconut
ice.

* Both recipes work equally
well but have different
textures when set—it then
comes down to personal
preference and how you
remembered it as a kid.

* The amount of colouring is
also a point of contention.
Some argue that the brighter
the pink, the more it
resembles the commercially
made stuff and the greater
the appeal. True lovers of
coconut ice prefer a softer
shade of pink to represent
that it is homemade.

* The use of raw egg whites
is of concern for the health
conscious and for vegans—
recipe 1 wins out every time.

* It is really important
to check the use-by date
on the desiccated coconut.
Do not be tempted to make
coconut ice with a bag you
discovered in the darkest
corner of the pantry. Coconut
is high in oil, which goes
rancid over time. The fresher
the product, the better the
outcome.

* Dessicated coconut is best
stored in the fridge not the
pantry.

CUPCAKES

Makes 24

XXXXXXXXXXXXXXXXXXXXXXXXXXXXXXXXXXXXXXXXXXXXXXXXXXXXXXXXXXXXXXXXXXXXXXXXXXXXXXXXXXXXXXXXXXXXXXXX

300 g self-raising flour
200 g unsalted butter, softened
200 g caster sugar
3 eggs
1 teaspoon vanilla essence
2 tablespoons milk

Method:

1. Preheat the oven to 180°C. Line 24 muffin moulds with paper cupcake cases. Or simply place the paper cases on a baking tray.

2. Sift the flour into a mixing bowl and add all the other ingredients. Use an electric mixer to slowly incorporate the ingredients. Beat for 5 minutes or until light and fluffy.

3. Spoon the mixture into the paper cases until three-quarters full. Place in the oven and bake for 20 minutes or until golden on top and the cakes spring back when lightly pressed.

4. Remove from the oven and cool on a wire rack. Top with icing (see Hints and tips), **butter frosting** or **butter cream**.

HINTS AND TIPS:

----

* You will need—bowl, sieve, weight and spoon measures, electric mixer, plastic spatula, muffin tray and baking tray.

* If the cupcakes are crumbly in texture, the mixture may not have been beaten for long enough to make it light and fluffy (minimum 3 minutes and no more than 5 minutes), or the oven was too low in temperature, in which case increase by 10°C next time.

* Over-beating the mixture can cause the cupcakes to rise in the middle too much, making icing difficult.

* Store unfrosted or un-iced cupcakes overnight at room temperature, for up to 1 week in the fridge, or once cool freeze immediately for 2 months. Add the frosting just before serving. If needed for the next morning, make the cakes and frosting the night before and keep separate, then ice the cakes in the morning so the icing doesn't become too sticky.

* **Basic icing** for cakes— 250 g pure icing sugar, few drops of vanilla essence, 1 tablespoon hot water. Mix the icing sugar, vanilla and water to form a thick paste. Place over a saucepan of simmering water and stir until the mixture is spreadable. Ice the cakes and set aside. Adding more water to the initial mixture softens the mixture too much and makes it runny.

* Some recipes may call for the butter and cream to be beaten until light and fluffy, the eggs added one at a time, then the flour, vanilla and milk are folded in until well mixed. This method works just as well but takes a bit longer.

* Try the following cupcake flavours.

* **Orange cupcakes**—add the zest of 2 oranges and substitute the milk with orange juice and continue as per the method given.

* **Chocolate cupcakes**—add 2 tablespoons cocoa powder and increase the milk by 1 tablespoon.

* For something quite different, try filling square-based ice-cream cones three-quarters full with the cake batter and bake for the requested time. Then frost and decorate.

* Decorating is limited only by the imagination. As well as the icing or frosting (and any colouring added), there are the sprinkles, silver balls, and the vast array of lollies to make the cakes suit any party.

* For school lunch boxes, it may be a better idea to cut the cakes through the middle and place the icing on one cut side, then sandwich the cake halves together.

* If making mini cupcakes, reduce the cooking time to 10 minutes.

DEVIL'S FOOD CAKE
Serves 12

XXXXXXXXXXXXXXXXXXXXXXXXXXXXXXXXXXXXXXXXXXXXXXXXXXXXXXXXXXXXXXXXXXXXXXXXXXXXXXXXXXXXXXXXXXXXXXXXXXXXXXXX

200 g self-raising flour
50 g Dutch cocoa powder
¼ teaspoon salt
125 g unsalted butter, softened
300 g caster sugar
250 ml milk
2 large eggs, at room temperature, lightly beaten
1 teaspoon vanilla extract
1 recipe quantity **devil's chocolate frosting**

Method:

1. Preheat the oven to 180°C. Lightly grease and flour
2 round cake tins and line the bases with baking
paper.

2. Sift the flour, cocoa and salt once and sift again
into a mixing bowl. Add the butter and mix on low
speed with an electric mixer for 1 minute, or until
the ingredients are combined and the butter is broken
down into very small pieces. Add the sugar and mix
until combined.

3. Add half the milk and beat on low speed for
1 minute. Scrape down the sides of the bowl. Slowly
add the remaining milk, the eggs and vanilla and beat
on low speed. Again scrape down the sides of the bowl
and beat for 1 minute longer or until velvety smooth.

4. Pour the batter into the prepared tins. Place
on the middle shelf in the oven and bake for
25–30 minutes, or until the cake begins to shrink away
from the side of the tin and a skewer inserted in the
centre comes out clean.

Method cont.

5. Remove the cakes from the oven and run a spatula or small knife around the edges to loosen the cakes from the sides of the tins so they don't tear as they shrink during cooling. Finish cooling the cakes to room temperature in their tins. Turn out the cooled cakes and peel off the baking paper just before frosting (making sure to frost only when the cakes are completely cool).

6. Once the cakes have cooled, dollop the frosting onto one cake and roughly and evenly spread it to the edges of the cake. Top with the second cake and spread the remaining frosting on the top and sides. A wispy, somewhat messy top is traditional, but feel free to smooth the frosting with a palette knife dipped in hot water.

HINTS AND TIPS:

* You will need—2 x 20-cm cake tins, electric mixer and bowl, liquid, weight and spoon measures, palette knife and plastic spatula.

* Once iced, devil's food cake should be consumed that day. Keep leftover cake covered at room temperature for another day at most before it turns stale.

* Devil's food cake can have 2 or even 4 layers with the frosting in between and then swirled all over.

* The preference for plain flour for this recipe is common. Substitute the 200 g self-raising flour with 200 g plain flour (known as all-purpose flour in the United States) or better still 150 g plain flour and 50 g cornflour (to resemble what the American cooks call 'cake flour') then add 1 teaspoon baking powder and ¼ teaspoon bicarbonate of soda. Sift twice and follow the recipe.

* Half of the milk can be replaced with strong instant coffee or espresso coffee.

* The batter may appear too thin but continue—all will be fine.

* Try beating the softened butter and sugar until light and fluffy, add the eggs one at a time, then turn the mixer down to low and add the vanilla, flour and cocoa. Lastly add the milk and continue to mix for 1–2 minutes until thoroughly combined. Pour into the cake tins and cook as prescribed.

* Devil's food cake is a stark contrast to angel food cake (or just 'angel cake'). Chocolate and butter reign supreme in the devil's version while the angel is a light egg white and vanilla-based cake that resembles a sponge or chiffon cake.

FLOURLESS CHOCOLATE CAKE

Serves 12

xxxxxxxxxxxxxxxxxxxxxxxxxxxxxxxxxxxxxxxxxxxxxxxxxxxxxxxxxxxxxxxxxxxxxxxxxxxxxxxxxxxxxxxxxxxxx

125 g unsalted butter
200 g quality dark chocolate
4 large eggs, separated
225 g caster sugar
pinch of salt
250 g almond meal

Method:

1. Preheat the oven to 160°C. Line a springform cake tin with baking paper.

2. Place the butter and chocolate in a heatproof bowl over a saucepan of gently simmering water. Remove from the heat and set aside to cool to room temperature.

3. Beat the egg yolks with about three-quarters of the sugar until light and creamy.

4. In a clean, dry bowl, beat the whites, salt and the remaining sugar until soft peaks form.

5. Stir the yolk mixture and the almond meal into the chocolate mixture. Then fold in the egg whites.

6. Pour into the prepared tin and bake for 1 hour or until a skewer inserted in the centre comes out clean.

7. Remove from the oven and cool. Serve with cream and fresh berries. This cake will last for 1 week in an airtight container in the refrigerator.

HINTS AND TIPS:

* You will need—22-cm springform cake tin, 2 bowls, saucepan, set of measuring scales, wooden spoon and wire rack.

* This gluten-free cake that is perfect for coeliacs is enjoyed around the world by lovers of chocolate cake. Its rich, moist texture makes it ideal as a dessert. Try replacing the almond meal with 250 g gluten-free muesli—blitz the muesli in a food processor to resemble the consistency of the almond meal.

* This style of cake tends to collapse in the middle when cooling. This is normal as there is no flour to give the cake body. Body is not important—rich, moist and chocolatey are the order of the day.

* Reduce the sugar to 100 g. This will soften the texture of the crust. The larger proportion of sugar will give the baked cake a crunchy 'brownie' top.

* Although the recipe asks for a springform cake tin, it can be cooked in a regular cake tin. A springform tin simply ensures that the cake doesn't get damaged when turning out. However, as long as the base of a regular cake tin is greased and lined with baking paper, there shouldn't be too much trouble. Remember to let the cake cool completely in the tin to allow it to shrink, making removal easier.

* A different technique with some added ingredients will produce only a slightly different outcome. Try breaking or chopping up the dark chocolate into pieces and placing into the bowl of a food processor. Pulse the chocolate until it begins to break up into smaller bits, then add the sugar and blitz until the chocolate and sugar turn into an even, sandy grain. Slowly add 175 ml hot coffee (instant or espresso) into the chocolate sugar mixture and blitz until the chocolate is melted. Add the butter and 1 tablespoon cocoa powder, and pulse to combine. Add the eggs and vanilla, and process until smooth. The batter will be a smooth liquid. Pour into the prepared tin and bake as per the instructions given.

* Try adding 1 teaspoon ground cinnamon to enhance the chocolate flavour.

* Try adding 1 tablespoon coffee liqueur or instant coffee to the recipe. Coffee has a natural affinity with chocolate and enhances the flavour of the cake.

* As a dessert, drizzle with **chocolate sauce** and serve warm with whipped cream, double cream or a dollop of mascarpone cheese.

* As a cake, top with **devil's chocolate frosting**, or simply dust with drinking cocoa or icing sugar.

FLOURLESS ORANGE CAKE

Serves 10–12

xxxxxxxxxxxxxxxxxxxxxxxxxxxxxxxxxxxxxxxxxxxxxxxxxxxxxxxxxxxxxxxxxxxxxxxxxxxxxxxxxxxxxxxxxxxxxx

2 large oranges (or 3 small–medium size)
250 g caster sugar
300 g almond meal
4 large eggs
1 teaspoon gluten-free baking powder

Method:

1. Preheat the oven to 170°C. Grease a springform cake tin and line with baking paper.

2. Place the oranges in a saucepan and cover with plenty of water. Bring to the boil, reduce the heat to low and simmer for 1 hour. Drain the oranges, place back in the saucepan and cover again with cold water. Bring back to the boil, then simmer for 1 more hour, checking the water level and topping up if need be. Drain and cool. Break the oranges open over a bowl and remove any seeds.

3. Combine the oranges (skin included) and the remaining ingredients in a food processor and process until smooth; scrape down the sides of the bowl and puree for 1 minute more.

4. Pour into the prepared cake tin and bake for 1 hour. Test by inserting a skewer into the centre of the cake—it's ready if it comes out clean. If the cake is still pasty in the centre, cook for 5 minutes longer. Allow to cool in the tin before turning out. Serve or store in an airtight container, refrigerated, for 7 days.

HINTS AND TIPS:

* You will need—22-cm springform cake tin, baking paper, bowl, food processor, saucepan, wooden spoon, plastic spatula, weight and spoon measures and wire rack.

* Another gluten-free—coeliac-friendly—cake. See also **flourless chocolate cake**.

* The oranges tend to float in the water instead of being covered, so top with a round piece of baking paper and weigh down slightly with a small plate or saucer when the water is turned down to a simmer.

* A faster way to cook the oranges is to place them in a microwave-safe bowl, and cover with water and plastic wrap. Microwave for 20 minutes on high, pierce with a skewer which should have little resistance when inserted (cook an extra 1–2 minutes if still too firm) then strain and cool.

* Removing the seeds is not entirely necessary but it makes the cake less bitter.

* Make an **orange syrup cake**—combine 200 ml orange juice and 200 g caster sugar in a small saucepan and bring to the boil, stirring constantly, until the sugar dissolves. Pour over the cake and stand for 4 hours before serving. Orange syrup cake is a popular Middle Eastern treat.

* For a **flourless orange and poppy seed cake**, add ½ cup poppy seeds to the cake mixture. To make a regular **orange and poppy seed cake**, place the following ingredients in a mixing bowl—150 g softened unsalted butter, 200 g caster sugar, zest and juice of 2 oranges, 3 eggs, 200 g self-raising flour, and 100 ml milk. Beat until light in colour, stir in ½ cup poppy seeds and pour into a prepared cake tin. Bake for 35–40 minutes or until the centre springs back when gently pressed. Cool and top with **orange frosting**.

* If almond meal (ground almonds) is unavailable, then use blanched almonds and a little sugar and process in a food processor until very fine. The sugar stops the almonds from getting too oily and becoming a paste.

* Serve with natural yoghurt, whipped cream or ice-cream.

* Or try mixing 250 g mascarpone with 125 g icing sugar, 2 tablespoons orange marmalade and a few drops of orange flower water, then spread over the cooled cake.

* Top with **orange frosting**.

* If strictly gluten-free, check the ingredients list on the baking powder, it is often made with wheat starch. Gluten-free baking powder is available at the supermarket and is labelled clearly.

FRIANDS

Makes 10–12

XXXXXXXXXXXXXXXXXXXXXXXXXXXXXXXXXXXXXXXXXXXXXXXXXXXXXXXXXXXXXXXXXXXXXXXXXXXXXXXXXXXXXXXXXXXXXXXXX

180 g butter
150 g almond meal
200 g pure icing sugar, sifted
55 g plain flour or gluten-free rice flour
5 egg whites
1 teaspoon finely grated lemon zest,
100 g blueberries

Method:

1. Preheat the oven to 220°C. Lightly grease 10–12 friand or muffin moulds.

2. Melt the butter in a saucepan over medium heat and cook until it starts to turn pale golden brown. Set aside to cool slightly.

3. Place the almond meal, icing sugar and flour in a mixing bowl, then add the unbeaten egg whites and lemon zest and mix well. Add the browned butter and mix thoroughly.

4. Fill the prepared moulds no more than three-quarters full. Top each with a few blueberries. Place onto a baking tray and bake in the oven for 5 minutes; then reduce the oven to 180°C and bake for a further 10–15 minutes.

5. Remove from the oven and leave the friands for about 5 minutes before turning out. Serve with a dusting of sifted icing sugar over the top. These friands keep well for 3–5 days in an airtight container. Freeze for 2 months.

HINTS AND TIPS:

* You will need—friand moulds or muffin tray, bowl, sieve, saucepan, wooden spoon or plastic spatula, weight and spoon measures and wire rack.

* The browning of the butter is important as it creates a beautiful nutty flavour in the friands.

* Friands, also known as 'financiers', are a typical French pastry cake or light tea cake. Financiers are usually baked in small rectangular-based moulds while friands are baked in small oval-based moulds.

* The oven is set to very hot to get the characteristic 'explosion' in the middle of the friand, then the heat is turned down to cook through the little cakes properly.

* The recipe provided is made with blueberries, probably the most common way to have them. Other flavours that work well include: **pecan nut and maple syrup**— 100 g pecan nuts (chopped), 200 ml maple syrup (to replace the 200 g icing sugar recipe); **orange and poppy seed**—zest of 2 oranges and 2 tablespoons poppy seeds); **raspberry**—100 g; and **chocolate chip**—150 g grated chocolate or buttons.

* Frozen blueberries or raspberries are ideal for this recipe and should be added to the mixture straight from the freezer. If a 'ripple' effect is wanted, then defrost the berries and stir into the mixture before baking.

* A few drops of almond essence can be added to the mixture as well as sprinkling some almond flakes on the top before baking—leave out the fruit and zest—to make **double almond friands**.

* Friands could be topped with **basic frosting** and a fresh berry.

* Friand moulds are available at quality kitchenware shops and are sold as individual moulds or as trays in groups of 6 or 12.

FRUIT CAKE

Serves 12

XXXXXXXXXXXXXXXXXXXXXXXXXXXXXXXXXXXXXXXXXXXXXXXXXXXXXXXXXXXXXXXXXXXXXXXXXXXXXXXXXXXXXXXXXXXXXXXXX

400 g sultanas
250 g currants
250 g raisins
150 g pitted prunes, chopped
100 g dried figs, chopped
150 g glacé cherries
100 g mixed candied peel
250 ml dark sherry (Pedro Ximenez) or brandy
250 g unsalted butter, at room temperature
275 g dark brown sugar
5 eggs, at room temperature
400 g plain flour
2 teaspoons mixed spice
200 g macadamia nuts, chopped
grated zest of 1 orange
grated zest of 1 lemon

Method:

1. Place all the dried fruits, cherries and candied
peel in a bowl. Mix in the sherry or brandy, cover and
refrigerate overnight or for 2 days.

2. Next day, preheat the oven to 150°C. Lightly grease
a cake tin and line the base and sides with a double
layer of baking paper (grease in-between the layers of
paper to help them stick together), making sure the
paper protrudes 5 cm above the rim of the tin. Wrap a
sheet of folded newspaper or brown paper around the
outside of the tin to match the height of the baking
paper and secure with cooking string. Place 5 layers
of newspaper on a baking tray.

3. Cream the butter and sugar on high speed until
light and fluffy. Add the eggs, one at a time, beating
well between each addition.

4. Sift the flour and mixed spice directly into the
butter mixture. Mix with a wooden spoon and stir in
the marinated fruit, nuts and zest.

Method cont.

5. Add the mixture to the prepared tin, levelling and smoothing the top with the back of a spoon. Place on the prepared baking tray and transfer to the middle shelf of the oven. Bake for about 3 hours.

6. Check the cake after 2½ hours—insert a skewer into the centre of the cake: if it comes out clean, then the cake is done; if not cook for the full time. If the cake starts to get too dark on top, cover with a piece of foil.

7. Remove from the oven, and leave the cake to cool in the tin on a wire rack. When cold, turn the cake out of the tin and remove the first layer of baking paper, leaving one layer on the cake. Wrap in foil and store in a cool, dark place for up to 3 months.

HINTS AND TIPS:

★ You will need—large bowl, spoon, liquid and weight measures, sieve, wooden spoon, 23-cm cake tin, cooking string, baking paper, baking tray, plastic spatula, electric mixer, foil and wire rack.

★ This is not just a fruit cake but also a **Christmas cake**—decorate with whole almonds, place on top of the cake batter once poured into the prepared cake tin.

★ To keep extra moist and naughty, sprinkle 1 tablespoon brandy or sherry over the cake every 2 weeks while in storage.

★ Pedro Ximenez is a very rich, sweet, sticky, Spanish sherry and is optional. A sweet sherry, quality brandy or amaretto happily replace the Spanish sherry.

★ It's important to have the eggs at room temperature so the mixture doesn't curdle.

★ For an **iced Christmas cake**—use a good quality marzipan (about 500 g) and roll out, then lift carefully onto the cake, easing it around the sides. Trim off the excess with a small knife. Allow to dry overnight before decorating. Use pre-made 'ready-to-roll' icing for a quicker, easier cake covering. Roll out on icing sugar. Brush the marzipan-coated cake with sherry, and cover with the rolled-out icing. Smooth the top and sides of the cake with a metal spatula.

★ Use silver balls and extra ready-to-roll icing cut into star shapes and dried until hard to decorate the cake. And then there is the holly ...

FRUIT MINCE PIES

Makes 12

XXXXXXXXXXXXXXXXXXXXXXXXXXXXXXXXXXXXXXXXXXXXXXXXXXXXXXXXXXXXXXXXXXXXXXXXXXXXXXXXXXXXXXXXXXXXXXXXXX

Fruit Mince

3 Granny Smith apples, peeled and grated
250 g raisins, chopped
250 g sultanas
250 g currants
125 g candied mixed peel
125 g dried apricots, finely chopped
125 g dried figs, finely chopped
100 g slivered almonds, chopped
200 g soft brown sugar
2 tablespoons honey
2 teaspoons mixed spice
2 teaspoons ground cinnamon
zest and juice of 3 oranges
100 g suet or solidified vegetable oil, grated
100 ml orange liqueur or brandy

1 recipe quantity shortcrust pastry
sifted icing sugar, for dusting

Method:

1. Combine all of the fruit mince ingredients in a large bowl and mix well. Place in the fridge for 1 week, stir occasionally.

2. For the mince pies— preheat oven to 180°C. Lightly grease a patty pan tray.

3. Rest the pastry in the fridge for 1 hour, roll out on a lightly floured surface until 3 mm thick. Cut out 12 rounds and place into the patty pan moulds.

4. Place tablespoons of fruit mince into each pastry case. Roll out the scraps of pastry on a lightly floured surface, and cut into desired shapes (e.g. stars). Brush each pastry shape with egg and place shape, egg side down, on the fruit mince.

Method cont.

5. Bake in the oven for 20 minutes, or until lightly browned. Cool and lightly dust with icing sugar before serving. Store the cooked fruit mince pies for 1 week in an airtight container.

HINTS AND TIPS:

★ You will need—equipment to make the shortcrust pastry, cutting board, cook's knife or food processor (to chop the dried fruit), weight, spoon and liquid measures, large bowl, wooden spoon, 12-hole shallow patty pan tray and pastry brush.

★ The recipe for fruit mince makes about 2 kg. Leftover mince can be stored in sterilised jars for several months. Leftover fruit mince can be used in **fruit cake**.

★ Fruit mince can be bought pre-made in the supermarket, so too can the shortcrust pastry (frozen in sheets). So if strapped for time, use one or the other and follow the baking method above.

★ Suet or solidified vegetable oil is available in supermarkets near the butter and margarine section. I find melting the suet and pouring it into the mixture at room temperature is far less messy than grating (same for **Christmas pudding**).

★ There are so many different dried fruits available today that it is just a matter of taste as to which fruit is in and which can stay on the supermarket shelf. For a more tropical taste, look into using dried papaya and pineapple instead of apricots and figs.

★ Try drying your own fruit using a dehydrator, then chop the fruit and add to the mixture.

★ Add chopped walnuts, pecan nuts or macadamia nuts to the mixture.

GINGERBREAD PEOPLE

Makes about 10

xxxxxxxxxxxxxxxxxxxxxxxxxxxxxxxxxxxxxxxxxxxxxxxxxxxxxxxxxxxxxxxxxxxxxxxxxxxxxxxxxxxxxxxxxxxxxx

450 g self-raising flour
¼ teaspoon salt
2 teaspoons ground ginger
1 teaspoon ground cinnamon
¼ teaspoon ground nutmeg
½ teaspoon ground allspice
125 g unsalted butter, at room temperature
125 g soft brown sugar
1 large egg
160 ml molasses

Method:

1. Sift the flour, salt and spices into a large bowl.
Set aside.

2. Cream the butter and sugar until light and fluffy.
Add the egg and molasses and beat until well combined.

3. Use a wooden spoon to stir in the flour mixture,
working until thoroughly mixed.

4. Wrap the dough in plastic wrap and refrigerate for
at least 2–3 hours.

5. Preheat the oven to 180°C. Line 2 baking trays with
baking paper.

6. Lightly flour the work surface, cut the dough in
half and roll out the dough to 6–7 mm thick. Use a
person-shaped cutter to cut through the dough. With
a flat spatula or egg flip, lift the dough onto the
prepared baking trays and place about 5 cm apart. Bake
for 12 minutes depending on the size and thickness.
They are ready when firm to touch and the edges are
just starting to colour.

7. Remove from the oven and cool on the baking trays
for about 2 minutes. Then transfer to a wire rack to
cool completely before decorating.

HINTS AND TIPS:

* You will need—bowl, electric mixer, wooden spoon, weight, liquid and spoon measures, baking tray, baking paper, person-shaped biscuit cutter, flat spatula or egg flip and wire rack.

* It may appear that I'm being politically correct in using the term 'people' when we all grew up with them being called 'gingerbread men'. This is not a political statement because 1. They never did look very manly, and 2. There is nothing attached to the biscuit to suggest that it is either masculine OR feminine—so people is fine.

* To avoid the molasses sticking to the measuring jug or cup, lightly grease with oil before measuring and the molasses will easily pour out with little, if any, residue.

* These biscuits are great for hanging or as a gift. Make a hole at the top of each biscuit with a straw before they go into the oven. Then when cold, hang with ribbon or attach gift cards to the holes.

* Try pressing currants, silver or coloured balls (also known as 'cachous') or lollies into the biscuits for eyes and buttons as soon as they come from the oven and are still very warm. If the biscuits have gone cold and you wish to decorate them, use some icing mixture as a glue to attach the eyes and buttons.

* The unbaked biscuit dough will last for 2 days wrapped in the refrigerator before it starts to discolour. Or freeze for up to 3 months— defrost overnight in the fridge before rolling out.

* The nutmeg in this recipe can be replaced with ground cloves—the spice often associated with this recipe.

* The colouring of the biscuit is determined by the sugar (white or brown) and the molasses content. Some recipes replace half the molasses with water and use white sugar instead of soft brown sugar, resulting in a biscuit that is quite a pale beige colour.

* Molasses can be substituted with treacle or golden syrup; however, the flavour and colour are not as strong.

HEDGEHOG

Makes about 20 pieces

xxxxxxxxxxxxxxxxxxxxxxxxxxxxxxxxxxxxxxxxxxxxxxxxxxxxxxxxxxxxxxxxxxxxxxxxxxxxxxxxxxxxxxxx

250 g unsalted butter
250 g caster sugar
60 g desiccated coconut
60 g cocoa powder
450 g plain sweet biscuits
3 eggs, lightly beaten
1 recipe quantity
   chocolate icing

Method:

1. Lightly grease or line a slice tray with baking paper.

2. Place the butter, sugar, coconut and cocoa in a saucepan, bring to the boil and cook for 2 minutes. Remove from the heat and cool.

3. Place the biscuits in a bowl and crush, leaving some pieces chunky.

4. Beat the eggs into the cocoa mixture with a wooden spoon and pour over the crushed biscuits. Pour the mixture onto the prepared tray and set for 2 hours in the refrigerator.

5. Cover with chocolate icing and serve.

HINTS AND TIPS:

* You will need—saucepan, 2 bowls, wooden spoon, 20-cm x 30-cm slice tray and baking paper.

* When breaking up the biscuits, break half into large chunks and the other half into finer crumbs.

* Lining the tray with baking paper makes it easier to remove the slice when set and topped with icing. Just make sure there is some overhang to grab onto for lifting out.

* Try adding 100 g chopped nuts to the recipe—walnuts, pecans and macadamias are the most popular for this recipe.

* Add ½ cup chopped glacé cherries to the mixture.

* Keep refrigerated for 3 days, the biscuits then begin to lose their crunch.

* Plain sweet biscuits can be substituted with gingernut biscuits, sweet digestive biscuits or even chocolate, but changing the biscuit will change the flavour of the slice.

* You could also try icing the slice with ½ the recipe quantity of **devil's chocolate frosting**.

* Instead of icing the hedgehog, simply sprinkle with extra coconut and press into the slice to make it stick.

HONEYCOMB

Makes about 20 pieces

XXXXXXXXXXXXXXXXXXXXXXXXXXXXXXXXXXXXXXXXXXXXXXXXXXXXXXXXXXXXXXXXXXXXXXXXXXXXXXXX

1 cup sugar
4 tablespoons corn syrup
2 teaspoons bicarbonate of soda
1 dessertspoon water

Method:

1. Line a lamington tin with baking paper. Cut the paper 5 cm larger than the tray on all sides then make a diagonal cut 5 cm long from each corner so it fits snugly in the tin, overlapping at the corners. Lightly spray or brush with oil.

2. Melt the sugar and corn syrup in a large heavy-based saucepan for about 5 minutes, stirring gently. Increase the heat and bring to boiling point. Cook without stirring for about 10 minutes. Sift the bicarbonate of soda into the water and stir until dissolved.

3. As soon as the surface turns a pale straw colour, sprinkle the bicarbonate of soda mixture over as wide an area as possible and stir through as quickly but as gently as you can—be sure to take only a few seconds or you'll lose the volume. The mixture will froth up—the trick is to combine the bicarbonate without bursting too many bubbles. Don't worry if tiny specks of bicarbonate of soda remain.

4. Pour into the prepared tin, and leave to harden at room temperature.

5. Once cold and hard, break into shards or rough squares and keep in airtight containers or pack into bags or cellophane for gifts.

HINTS AND TIPS:

★ You will need—25-cm x 30-cm lamington tin, baking paper, pastry brush, large saucepan, wooden spoon and cup and spoon measures.

★ Corn syrup is available from health food shops and some supermarkets.

★ For **honeycomb butter**— 250 g unsalted butter, 125 g honeycomb. Soften the butter without melting it. Break the honeycomb into smaller pieces and mix through the butter. Roll into logs, place in plastic wrap and freeze until needed. When ready to use, cut discs of butter, remove any plastic wrap and serve on pancakes, French toast, ricotta hotcakes or muffins.

HOT CROSS BUNS

Makes 12

xxxxxxxxxxxxxxxxxxxxxxxxxxxxxxxxxxxxxxxxxxxxxxxxxxxxxxxxxxxxxxxxxxxxxxxxxxxxxxxxxxxxxxxxxxxxxx

750 g plain flour
2 teaspoons dried instant yeast
½ teaspoon salt
2½ tablespoons mixed spice
150 g currants
300 ml full cream milk
125 g unsalted butter
100 g soft brown sugar
3 eggs, beaten
4 tablespoons plain flour
2 tablespoons cold water
1 egg, beaten, for glazing
sifted pure icing sugar, for dusting

Method:

1. Place the flour, yeast, salt, mixed spice and currants in a bowl and make a well in the centre.

2. Heat the milk, butter and sugar to approximately 37°C. Pour the milk mixture into the well and add the beaten eggs. Mix until a soft dough is formed.

3. Turn out onto a lightly floured bench and knead until the dough is elastic and homogenous (about 15 minutes).

4. Place the dough in a lightly oiled bowl, cover with plastic wrap or a damp tea towel and leave to rise in a warm place until doubled in volume (about 1½ hours).

5. Meanwhile, make the mixture for the crosses. Combine the flour and cold water in a small bowl and mix to make a thick, sticky paste. Take small balls of the paste and, on a floured work surface, roll into 24 thin strips. Set aside.

Method cont.

6. Turn out the dough onto the lightly floured work surface and knead for a few minutes. Divide the mixture into 12 and roll each into a bun shape. Transfer to a greased baking tray and place a cross on each bun with the strips of paste, then leave in a warm area for 15 minutes or until doubled in size.

7. Preheat the oven to 200°C. Brush the top of the buns with the beaten egg and bake for 15–20 minutes.

8. Remove the buns from the oven and dust immediately with icing sugar then cool on a wire rack.

HINTS AND TIPS:

* You will need—large bowl, weight, liquid and spoon measures, pastry brush, saucepan, baking tray and wire rack.

* What makes a great hot cross bun is simply determined by a matter of individual taste. For some, a light, soft bun with a little spice and a crusty top is perfect; for others, a bun dense with fruit and spice with a marzipan cross is the only way to go. The blasphemy that is the chocolate hot cross bun is something a new generation cannot live without. Like all recipes, adjust according to taste.

* Starting with the spice, for ease of use I have suggested the simple and ready-to-use mixed spice. However, for a more individual taste, substitute with the following combination—½ teaspoon each of ground cinnamon, ground ginger and ground allspice, plus ¼ teaspoon each of ground coriander, ground nutmeg and ground cloves.

* Try soaking the currants in 2 tablespoons brandy or cognac for several hours before adding.

* Try adding 2 tablespoons dried mixed peel and 1 tablespoon chopped, dried apricots.

* If adding nuts, try 4 tablespoons chopped walnuts, pecans or macadamias.

* Making a sweet cross from marzipan requires 200 g, rolled and shaped as for the flour paste.

* Instant dried yeast can be added to the flour mixture immediately and is the simplest and most effective way to begin using and understanding yeast. More advanced cooks swear by the virtuous flavour of fresh yeast.

HUMMINGBIRD CAKE

Serves 12

xxxxxxxxxxxxxxxxxxxxxxxxxxxxxxxxxxxxxxxxxxxxxxxxxxxxxxxxxxxxxxxxxxxxxxxxxxxxxxxxxxxxxx

375 g plain flour, sifted

1 teaspoon bicarbonate of soda

450 g soft brown sugar

1 teaspoon ground cinnamon

250 ml canola or safflower oil

3 large eggs, at room temperature, lightly beaten

1 teaspoon vanilla extract

230 g canned crushed pineapple

4 large ripe bananas, mashed or chopped

2 recipe quantities **passionfruit frosting**

Method:

1. Preheat the oven to 170°C. Grease 2 round cake tins, dust with flour and line the bases with baking paper.

2. Combine the flour, bicarbonate of soda, sugar and cinnamon in a large bowl.

3. Add the oil, eggs and vanilla and mix with a wooden spoon until well combined. Do not beat.

4. Stir in the pineapple and banana and pour into the prepared tins.

5. Bake for 45–50 minutes or until a skewer inserted into the centre comes out clean.

6. Cool in the cake tins for 10 minutes before turning out onto a wire rack. When cold, ice one cake with frosting, top with the second cake and ice the top with the remaining frosting. Decorate, if desired, with extra crushed pineapple or simply dust with ground cinnamon.

HINTS AND TIPS:

----

* You will need—2 x 23-cm round cake tins, baking paper, weight, liquid and spoon measures, large mixing bowl, wooden spoon and wire rack.

* This is a delicious, super-moist dessert cake originating from South America. Hummingbird cake should be dense and moist, not light and fluffy.

* A constant reminder with all cakes that mention the whipping of sugar and butter and then the addition of eggs, one at a time—the eggs must be at room temperature. Cold eggs added to the butter mixture will cause it to split. A second reminder—should the mixture separate, continue making the recipe as mentioned, it will still be fine.

* The method recommends to mix the ingredients together but 'do not beat'. Beating the mixture will work the gluten in the flour and toughen the cake.

* Try adding 1 cup chopped pecan nuts or walnuts to the mixture when adding the pineapple.

* Try halving the cinnamon and using ½ teaspoon ground ginger instead.

* Top the cake with 1 mango (diced).

LUMBERJACK CAKE

Serves 10

XXXXXXXXXXXXXXXXXXXXXXXXXXXXXXXXXXXXXXXXXXXXXXXXXXXXXXXXXXXXXXXXXXXXXXXXXXXXXXXXXXXXXXXXXX

2 Granny Smith apples,
   peeled and grated
180 g pitted dates,
   chopped
1 teaspoon bicarbonate of
   soda
1 cup boiling water
125 g unsalted butter
225 g sugar
2 eggs, at room
   temperature
1 teaspoon vanilla extract
200 g plain flour
½ teaspoon salt

Topping

60 g butter
120 g soft brown sugar
100 ml milk
80 g shredded coconut

Method:

1. Place the apples in a bowl. Add the dates, bicarbonate of soda and boiling water and mix well. Allow to cool to room temperature.

2. Preheat the oven to 180°C. Grease a cake tin and line the base with baking paper.

3. Cream the butter and sugar. Add the eggs and vanilla and beat well.

4. Sift the flour and salt into the butter mixture. Stir in the date and apple mixture.

5. Pour into the prepared tin and bake for about 50 minutes (see Hints and tips).

6. For the topping—combine the butter, sugar, milk and coconut in a small saucepan. Stir over low heat until the butter has melted and the sugar dissolved.

7. When the cake is cooked, spread the coconut topping over the top and bake for a further 20 minutes or until the topping is golden.

8. Remove from the oven and cool on a wire rack. Store in an airtight container for 3–5 days.

HINTS AND TIPS:

★ You will need—cutting board, cook's knife, paring knife, vegetable peeler, grater, 20-cm round or square cake tin, baking paper, cup, liquid, weight and spoon measures, whisk, wooden spoon, 2 bowls, sieve, plastic spatula, small saucepan and wire rack.

★ The size of the cake tin affects the initial cooking time of the cake. A cake in a larger, shallow tin may only require 40 minutes in the oven and then 20 more with the topping. A smaller, high-sided 18 cm tin may take 1 hour to cook, then another 20 minutes for the topping.

★ There really is no variation to this recipe—it is one of the few cakes that stay the same as far as quantities go. Which means if you are looking for a better recipe for lumberjack cake— you really won't find one.

★ The addition of alcohol is optional and not mentioned in any lumberjack recipe; however, try adding 60 ml dark rum or brandy to the date mixture.

MACAROONS

Makes about 50

XXXXXXXXXXXXXXXXXXXXXXXXXXXXXXXXXXXXXXXXXXXXXXXXXXXXXXXXXXXXXXXXXXXXXXXXXXXXXXXXXXXXXXXXXXXXX

200 g pure icing sugar
150 g almond meal
4 egg whites
pinch of cream of tartar

Method:

1. Line 2 baking trays with baking paper and spray lightly with canola oil.

2. Sift the icing sugar into a bowl and mix in the almond meal.

3. Use an electric mixer to whip the egg whites and cream of tartar to firm peaks.

4. Fold in the sugar and almond mixture until well combined.

5. Use a piping bag with a 5-mm nozzle, fill the bag with the macaroon mixture and pipe 2-cm rounds approximately 2 cm apart onto the prepared baking trays. Alternatively, use 2 teaspoons to dollop small amounts onto the trays. Leave to sit on the bench uncovered for at least 1 hour to dry out slightly and form a skin.

6. Preheat the oven to 150°C. Bake for 15–20 minutes or until firm to the touch. Rotate the trays (e.g. from top shelf to bottom shelf) halfway through cooking.

7. Remove from the oven and cool before removing from the trays. Serve or store in an airtight container for 2–3 days.

* You will need—2 baking trays, sieve, electric mixer, 2 bowls, weight measure, plastic spatula, piping bag with 5-mm nozzle or 2 teaspoons and airtight container.

* Macaroons are very easy to make; however, to get them as perfect as some of the French pastry shops, time, practice and a reliable oven are needed.

* Macaroons should be crunchy on the outside and chewy on the inside.

* A few drops of food colouring can be added to the mixture. Divide the mixture in half and to one half add some red food colouring to make pink macaroons. To the other half, add a few drops of yellow food colouring. Bake as per the recipe.

* Once piped onto the baking trays, the small peaks created can be smoothed by dipping your finger in a bowl of cold water and gently patting down before baking.

* Macaroons are usually stuck together. This can be as simple as using strawberry jam to sandwich 2 macaroons together or use **butter cream**.

* This recipe is for a classic French almond macaroon; another popular style of macaroon is made with coconut. For **coconut macaroons**—replace the almond meal with 1 ½ cups desiccated coconut that has been lightly toasted (180°C on a flat tray, tossing after 3 minutes), and add 1 teaspoon vanilla extract.

* Try adding 40 g Dutch cocoa to either the almond or coconut mixture. Sift the cocoa together with the icing sugar before folding into the beaten egg whites.

MARSHMALLOWS

Makes about 15–20

XXXXXXXXXXXXXXXXXXXXXXXXXXXXXXXXXXXXXXXXXXXXXXXXXXXXXXXXXXXXXXXXXXXXXXXXXXXXXXXXXXXXXXXXXXXXXXXX

½ cup icing mixture (see **Hints and tips**)
2½ tablespoons powdered gelatine
125 ml cold water
350 g caster sugar
125 ml light corn syrup
125 ml water, extra
1 tablespoon vanilla extract

Method:

1. Very lightly oil a slice tray and dust with one-third of the icing mixture.

2. Combine the gelatine and cold water in the bowl of an electric mixer and set aside.

3. Mix the sugar, corn syrup and extra water in a saucepan over low heat and stir until the sugar is dissolved.

4. Place a sugar thermometer in the saucepan, increase the heat to high and, without stirring, boil the mixture until it reaches 120°C, also known as the 'firm ball' stage.

5. Remove the pan from the heat and slowly pour the sugar mixture into the gelatine mixture while beating on low speed. When all the syrup has been added, turn the mixer to high speed and beat for 10–15 minutes or until thick and white and almost tripled in volume. Add the vanilla extract and beat for 2 minutes.

6. Pour the marshmallow mixture into the prepared tray and dust with another one-third of the icing mixture. Allow to stand, uncovered, for at least 4 hours or overnight to dry out.

7. When ready, turn the marshmallow out of the tray and onto a cutting board and cut into squares with a hot, dry knife. Dust all over with the remaining icing mixture.

HINTS AND TIPS:

★ You will need—23-cm x 25-cm deep slice tray, electric mixer, cup, liquid, weight and spoon measures, saucepan, sugar thermometer, plastic spatula, cutting board and cook's knife.

★ Marshmallows were once made from the juices extracted from the root of the marshmallow plant, a practice which has been replaced by using a mixture of corn syrup and gelatine or gum arabic.

★ Icing mixture contains cornflour whereas icing sugar, also known as pure icing sugar or confectioners' sugar, doesn't. Cornflour is added to pure icing sugar to keep the sugar from forming lumps and going hard. Icing mixture is ideal for dusting over cakes and desserts, but is not suitable for baking with, as it is not a pure form of sugar.

★ Often recipes for marshmallow contain egg white which is not necessary but can make a more **fluffy marshmallow**. You will need to beat 2 egg whites to stiff peaks and add to the beaten sugar/gelatine mixture. Although fluffier, uncooked egg whites lead to issues of salmonella and food poisoning, therefore the safe option is to follow the basic recipe.

★ Try boiling 6 cardamom pods or the zest of 1 lemon in a small amount of water, then straining the water and using the flavoured water in the recipe.

★ Add 1 tablespoon rosewater, orange flower water or vanilla extract to the basic recipe.

★ Instead of dusting with icing mixture, lightly toast 1 cup desiccated coconut and use to coat the marshmallow.

★ An alternative and very simple recipe for marshmallows—without the use of a sugar thermometer—and worth a try is to: boil 1 kg granulated sugar with 550 ml water until the sugar dissolves. Add 4 tablespoons gelatine powder, remove from the heat and stir until the gelatine has dissolved, then add 1 tablespoon vanilla extract and a good pinch of cream of tartar. Whip with an electric mixer until stiff peaks form. Pour into the prepared tray and leave to set before cutting with a hot knife and dipping in icing mixture or desiccated coconut.

MELTING MOMENTS

Makes 24

XXXXXXXXXXXXXXXXXXXXXXXXXXXXXXXXXXXXXXXXXXXXXXXXXXXXXXXXXXXXXXXXXXXXXXXXXXXXXXXXXXXXXXXXXXXXX

125 g unsalted butter, softened
2 tablespoons pure icing sugar
¼ teaspoon vanilla extract
150 g plain flour
60 g cornflour

Filling
60 g unsalted butter, softened
150 g pure icing sugar
4 drops of vanilla extract

Method:

1. Preheat the oven to 160°C. Line a baking tray with baking paper and lightly grease with oil or butter.

2. Use an electric mixer to whip the butter and sugar until light and fluffy. Add the vanilla.

3. Add the flour and cornflour, and stir to combine.

4. Dip your hands in some flour and roll teaspoonfuls of mixture into balls. Place the balls onto the prepared baking tray and press with a fork, also dipped in flour.

5. Bake in the oven for 15 minutes or until slightly golden in colour.

6. Cool on the tray for 5 minutes before transferring to a wire rack.

7. For the filling—combine the butter, sugar and vanilla in a bowl and beat until pale and creamy.

8. To assemble—spoon some of the filling onto the base of a biscuit and top with a second biscuit. Repeat with the remaining biscuits and filling. Store in an airtight container.

HINTS AND TIPS:

* You will need—weight and spoon measures, electric mixer, baking tray, wire rack, bowl and teaspoon measure.

* Also known as 'yoyos'—2 biscuits are held together by a white paste, resembling a yoyo.

* For a children's party, try gluing the biscuits together with a dollop of ice-cream.

* Melting moments keep in an airtight container stored at room temperature for up to 4 days.

* The biscuits by themselves keep well for 1 week before needing to be filled (if indeed they last that long).

* Often when purchasing melting moments from a good deli or cake shop, the biscuit has a yellow colour to it; this can be achieved by replacing the cornflour with custard powder, measure for measure. Custard powder is flavoured with vanilla so it is not necessary to add the vanilla extract.

* Try adding 2 tablespoons passionfruit pulp to the filling. Passionfruit pulp can be purchased in small tins from the supermarket when not in season.

* Instead of the suggested filling provided, you can use your favourite jam.

* The biscuits can be enjoyed on their own simply dusted with icing sugar.

* A mascarpone filling is a great alternative. For **orange and mascarpone melting moments** try this filling—110 g mascarpone cheese, 75 g cream cheese, 75 g icing sugar, and the zest and juice of 1 orange. Whisk together until smooth and creamy, refrigerate for 1 hour before using then fill the biscuits and eat on the day they are made.

MERINGUES

Serves 6

XXXXXXXXXXXXXXXXXXXXXXXXXXXXXXXXXXXXXXXXXXXXXXXXXXXXXXXXXXXXXXXXXXXXXXXXXXXXXXXXXXXXXXXXXXXXX

100 g egg whites
100 g caster sugar
100 g pure icing sugar,
   sifted

Method:

1. Preheat the oven to 120°C. Line a baking tray with baking paper.

2. Place the egg whites in a very clean bowl and beat with an electric mixer until soft peaks form.

3. Gradually add the caster sugar in small amounts and beat for 10 minutes or until smooth and glossy.

4. Fold in the icing sugar, taking great care not to overwork the mixture.

5. Place small spoonfuls of the meringue on the prepared tray and transfer to the oven. Immediately reduce the temperature to 100°C and bake for 1¾ hours or until the top and base are dry to touch. Keep for 2 weeks in an airtight container.

HINTS AND TIPS:

* You will need—1 baking tray, baking paper, electric mixer and bowl, spatula, cup and weight measures, spoon or piping bag and nozzle for shaping.

* Success with meringues and pavlova relies on persistence and correct oven temperatures.

* Meringues made on a rainy or humid day will struggle to dry properly.

* If beads form on the surface of the meringue or liquid seeps from the base, the oven temperature is too low—try increasing by 10°C.

* Allow meringues to finish cooling in the oven after the oven has been turned off.

* Cracks form when the meringue has cooled too quickly, because it has been removed from the oven while still warm.

* Overcooked meringues? Once they have cooled, they can be crushed and used in, on or around cakes, or mixed into or sprinkled over ice-cream. (And, let's face it, overdone or underdone, to a child, any meringue is good.)

* **Snow eggs**—are a classic, soft poached or baked meringue. Made with egg whites and caster sugar then served on crème anglaise, these meringues are made by beating egg whites to a soft peak, adding the sugar then poaching spoonfuls (quenelles) in slightly sweetened milk for 6 minutes, turning once. They can also be piped into small tins or ramekins and baked at 140°C for 10 minutes.

* 'Vacherins' are French meringues piped into cup or vol au vent shapes. Once cooked they are filled with fruit, ice-cream, cream or custard.

MUFFINS

Makes 6

XXXXXXXXXXXXXXXXXXXXXXXXXXXXXXXXXXXXXXXXXXXXXXXXXXXXXXXXXXXXXXXXXXXXXXXXXXXXXXXXXXXXXXXXX

100 g unsalted butter,
   melted
150 g caster sugar
3 eggs, lightly beaten
1 teaspoon vanilla extract
250 g self-raising flour

Method:

1. Preheat the oven to 180°C. Lightly spray a 6-mould muffin tray with canola or light olive oil.

2. Whisk the butter and sugar in a bowl.

3. Add the eggs and vanilla and stir until combined.

4. Sift the flour into another bowl and make a well in the centre. Mix in the butter mixture with a wooden spoon until just combined. Do not work the mixture too much or the muffins will be tight and rubbery.

5. Dollop into the prepared muffin tray and bake in the oven for 20–25 minutes or until just firm to the touch. Remove and cool in the tray before turning out.

HINTS AND TIPS:

* You will need—2 bowls, weight and spoon measures, wooden spoon, whisk and muffin tray.

* Treat muffins as you would a scone mixture, mixing in the flour just enough to incorporate but to not overmix and work the gluten. Ideally, a muffin mixture is lumpy and looks like a mistake. Then it's ready to cook.

* When adding flavours, do so before the flour is mixed in.

* A good muffin should 'mushroom' out of the tray, ensuring a crispy top and a soft, moist base. Muffin moulds need to be filled to no more than 5 mm from the top. Any less and the muffins will only rise to just above the tray, looking more like a cupcake. Add too much and it will spill over and become one large mass.

* For **simple chocolate muffins**—sift 3 tablespoons cocoa powder with the flour before adding to the wet mixture. For **double chocolate chip muffins**—add 2 tablespoons chocolate buttons or chocolate pieces to the wet mixture before adding the flour and cocoa mixture as for chocolate muffins.

* For **blueberry muffins**— add 1 cup fresh or frozen blueberries to the wet mixture before adding the flour.

* For **savoury muffins**—wet mixture with the flour added carefully at the end. Replace the sugar with grated parmesan cheese. Be sure to omit the vanilla extract as well. With this as the base, any number of savoury flavours can be added. Try 3 tablespoons **pesto**, or 250 g spinach leaves sautéed in butter, cooled and chopped then mixed with 2 tablespoons fetta cheese, or 1 cup each grated zucchini and cooked bacon.

NANAIMO BARS

Makes about 12

XXXXXXXXXXXXXXXXXXXXXXXXXXXXXXXXXXXXXXXXXXXXXXXXXXXXXXXXXXXXXXXXXXXXXXXXXXXXXXXXXXXXXXXXXXXXXXX

Base

125 g unsalted butter
125 g caster sugar
50 g cocoa powder
1 egg, lightly beaten
175 g sweet plain biscuits, crushed
60 g desiccated coconut
60 g walnuts, finely chopped

Middle layer

125 g unsalted butter
3 tablespoons milk
2 tablespoons custard powder
250 g pure icing sugar

Top layer

125 g dark chocolate, chopped
50 g unsalted butter

Method:

1. For the base—combine the unsalted butter, sugar and cocoa in a heatproof bowl and place over a saucepan of simmering water. Heat until the butter has melted and stir until thoroughly mixed.

2. Stir in the egg and continue to heat until the mixture thickens. Remove from the heat (keep the water simmering for the topping) and stir in the biscuits, coconut and walnuts.

3. Line the base of a slice tray with baking paper, press the mixture into the base firmly and set aside.

4. For the middle layer—place the butter, milk, custard powder and icing sugar in the bowl of an electric mixer. Use the whisk to slowly incorporate the ingredients. Turn the machine to high and whip until light and fluffy. Spread this layer over the base.

Method cont.

5. For the top layer—combine the chocolate and butter in a heatproof bowl and place over the pan of simmering water. Remove the pot from the heat to allow the residual heat to slowly melt the chocolate and butter. Once melted and thoroughly combined, cool completely before pouring over the middle layer.

6. Refrigerate for 2 hours or until set firm. Cut with a hot knife.

HINTS AND TIPS:
----

* You will need—23-cm rectangular or square slice tray about 5-cm deep, 2 heatproof bowls, electric mixer, saucepan, weight and spoon measures, food processor (for the biscuits and walnuts), wooden spoon, and plastic spatula.

* Nanaimo bars are to Canada as caramel slice is to Australia. They are simple to make and delicious as a sweet snack. The major difference between the two slices is the middle layer—both have a sweet, compact biscuit base and a chocolate topping, but caramel slice has a distinct firm caramel filling as opposed to the thick, buttery sweet custard centre of the Nanaimo.

* Any plain sweet biscuit can be used in this recipe. Graham crackers (sweet digestive biscuits) are the preferred biscuit in the Nanaimo bar's native Canada. Equally successful is the use of 1 cup rolled oats mixed with 75 g soft brown sugar.

* The use of custard powder (for flavour) in the middle layer is preferred. For alternative flavours, keep the custard powder the same and add vanilla extract (1 teaspoon) or peppermint essence (1 teaspoon plus 1–2 drops green food colouring) or coffee (2 teaspoons instant coffee powder).

* Nanaimo bars are very rich, cut into 5 cm x 5 cm squares before serving.

PEANUT BRITTLE

Makes about 800 g

xxxxxxxxxxxxxxxxxxxxxxxxxxxxxxxxxxxxxxxxxxxxxxxxxxxxxxxxxxxxxxxxxxxxxxxxxxxxxxxxxxxxxxxxxxx

300 g sugar

200 ml light corn syrup

200 ml water

30 g butter

¼ teaspoon salt

½ teaspoon vanilla extract

1 teaspoon bicarbonate of soda

300 g unsalted, roasted peanuts

Method:

1. Line 2 slice trays with foil and lightly spray with canola or light olive oil.

2. Combine the sugar, corn syrup and water in a heavy-based saucepan over medium heat and stir until the sugar dissolves.

3. Place a sugar thermometer in the syrup and continue to cook without stirring until the syrup reaches the 'crack' stage—144°C. Add the butter and stir with a wooden spoon, then allow the mixture to come back to the 'soft ball' stage—112°C. Remove from the heat.

4. Quickly stir in the vanilla and bicarbonate of soda and as it froths, stir in the nuts until well combined. Pour immediately into the prepared trays and set aside to cool completely. Break up when cold. Peanut brittle can be stored for several weeks in an airtight container.

HINTS AND TIPS:

★ You will need—2 x 23-cm x 18-cm slice trays, for one, halve the recipe), foil, heavy-based saucepan, sugar thermometer, wooden spoon and liquid, weight and spoon measures.

★ This type of cooking really is a science and needs some precision to get it the same every time. A sugar thermometer is not a waste of money as it can be used to make **marshmallows**, **Italian meringue**, **jams** and **marmalade**.

★ As the peanut brittle cools, mark it with a knife to form the shapes it will be broken into. It can just be broken randomly into large and small shards.

★ Try replacing the peanuts with roasted macadamia nuts, roasted whole blanched almonds or fresh roasted pecan nuts.

★ The light corn syrup is added to prevent the sugar syrup from forming crystals, the same reason it is used when making honeycomb.

★ Strangely enough, peanut brittle gets better with age, so store in an airtight container in single layers separated with foil or baking paper.

★ Bicarbonate of soda is used in this recipe for two reasons—first, it lightens the texture of the mixture; and second, it neutralises the slight bitterness produced from the caramel.

PECAN BISCUITS

Makes about 30

XXXXXXXXXXXXXXXXXXXXXXXXXXXXXXXXXXXXXXXXXXXXXXXXXXXXXXXXXXXXXXXXXXXXXXXXXXXXXXXXXXXXXXXXXXXX

125 g unsalted butter,
   softened
2 tablespoons caster sugar
1 teaspoon vanilla extract
125 g chopped pecan nuts
100 g plain flour
100 g pure icing sugar

Method:

1. Preheat the oven to 180°C. Line a baking tray with baking paper.

2. Use an electric mixer to cream the butter and sugar until light and fluffy.

3. With a wooden spoon, stir in the vanilla and the pecans.

4. Stir in the flour until thoroughly mixed then roll into balls about 2 cm in diameter.

5. Place on the prepared baking tray and bake for 12–15 minutes.

6. Cool on a wire rack and coat heavily in icing sugar. Store in an airtight container, if they make it that far.

HINTS AND TIPS:

* You will need—baking tray, baking paper, bowl, weight and spoon measures, electric mixer, wooden spoon and wire rack.

* This is another very simple-to-make biscuit recipe that is rich because of the butter content.

* Substitute pecan nuts for macadamias, almonds, pistachios or walnuts.

* These biscuits can be made in advance, frozen flat on a tray and then transferred to a freezer bag. Take out only what is needed and defrost in the refrigerator overnight before baking.

* Try incorporating other flavours into the basic recipe, like chocolate chips (125 g) or add 2 tablespoons cocoa powder to the flour before sifting.

* This style of biscuit is a good, simple recipe for children to get into. Like the **muffins** recipe, it gives children a basic understanding of baking and the science of cooking without too much to think about.

PIKELETS

Makes about 16

XXXXXXXXXXXXXXXXXXXXXXXXXXXXXXXXXXXXXXXXXXXXXXXXXXXXXXXXXXXXXXXXXXXXXXXXXXXXXXXXXXXXXXXX

180 g self-raising flour
50 g caster sugar
1 egg
180 ml milk
1 tablespoon white vinegar
20 g butter, melted
extra butter, for cooking

Method:

1. Sift the flour into a bowl and add the sugar. Make a well in the centre.

2. Combine the egg, milk, vinegar and melted butter in a second bowl and whisk. Add nearly all of the wet ingredients—it is best to reserve some just in case the batter becomes too runny—to the dry ingredients. Mix together until the batter is smooth and runny without being too liquid.

3. Heat a frying pan over low heat, add some of the extra butter and then add spoonfuls of the batter to form discs 8–10 cm in diameter.

4. When the top of each pikelet forms bubbles, turn over with an egg flip or spatula. Cook the other side for 1 minute before removing to a plate. Serve with your favourite topping.

HINTS AND TIPS:

* You will need—2 bowls, whisk or wooden spoon, spoon, liquid and weight measures, frying pan and spatula or egg flip.

* 180 g flour is about 1 heaped cup.

* For a savoury snack, omit the sugar from the recipe. Cook the pikelets and top with smoked salmon and crème fraîche mixed with chopped dill, or shaved leg ham and mustard pickles.

* Some cooks use the same recipe for pancakes and pikelets. Essentially one is just a small version of the other. Then why do I offer recipes for pancakes and pikelets in this book? It's because I grew up believing that there was an intrinsic difference between the two, and I have a strong belief in the virtues of batter, so I have made a point of offering two quite different recipes to distinguish a pancake from a pikelet. My **pancake** recipe can be found in the Breakfast chapter.

* Pikelets are a tidy little snack that most children have devoured at some point or other on finishing the day's toil of schooling ... and there never seemed to be enough. Topped with strawberry jam and sweet whipped cream (naughtily hiding its few drops of vanilla and spoonfuls of icing sugar), this was THE after-school snack to rival all others.

* A clever cook makes umpteen times the recipe so there are plenty of pikelets after school, plenty for lunch boxes the next day, and still plenty for the 24th hour after first ingestion. In other words, make a big batch to last a day and a half (including breakfast).

PRALINE

Makes about 500 g

XXXXXXXXXXXXXXXXXXXXXXXXXXXXXXXXXXXXXXXXXXXXXXXXXXXXXXXXXXXXXXXXXXXXXXXXXXXXXXXXXXXXXXXXXXX

250 g sugar
50 ml water
250 g almonds, toasted

Method:

1. Line a baking tray with foil and lightly spray with canola oil or grease with butter.

2. Place the sugar and water in a heavy-based saucepan, bring to the boil and cook without stirring until it reaches a light caramel colour (about 170°C on a sugar thermometer).

3. Remove from the heat, add the nuts and mix well using a wooden spoon. Pour the mixture onto the prepared tray and allow to become cold before crushing with a rolling pin or in a food processor to a granular texture. Store in an airtight container in a dry, cool area or in the freezer.

HINTS AND TIPS:

* You will need—baking tray, foil, saucepan, weight measure, wooden spoon and food processor or rolling pin.

* This classic praline is crushed and used on any number of sweet and sometimes savoury dishes (see **Thai beef salad**). Try sprinkling over ice-cream, mix into semifreddo, or serve on and around iced cakes and desserts.

* The rule of thumb for a basic praline is the sugar and nuts are measured in equal parts, with a small amount of water added to help control the caramel.

* Any type of nut or combination of nuts can be used as long as they are unsalted and roasted to maximise flavour. Therefore, keep in mind the following— hazelnuts (roasted and skins removed), macadamias, cashews, peanuts, walnuts, pecans and Brazil nuts.

* This style of praline is French, but there is another style of praline which is more of a nut brittle than true praline and is known as a **New Orleans praline**—mix 125 g soft brown sugar, 125 g sugar, 50 ml evaporated milk, 20 g butter and 250 g pecan nuts (or nuts of your choice). Place ingredients in a saucepan and, use a sugar thermometer to bring the mixture to soft ball stage

112°C. Remove from the heat and stand for 5 minutes before stirring in ½ teaspoon vanilla extract. Beat with a wooden spoon until thickened. On a tray lined with greased foil, place 2 teaspoons of mixture for individual pralines (makes about 20).

* Without a sugar thermometer, gauging when a hot sugar syrup is at the 'soft ball' stage requires the use of a bowl of iced water. Spoon a few drops of the syrup into the water and if the syrup forms a fudge-like 'soft ball' when rolled between the thumb and forefinger, it is ready.

QUICHE LORRAINE

Serves 8

XXXXXXXXXXXXXXXXXXXXXXXXXXXXXXXXXXXXXXXXXXXXXXXXXXXXXXXXXXXXXXXXXXXXXXXXXXXXXXXXXXXXXXXXXXX

250 g butter, cut into 1-cm dice
250 g plain flour
½ teaspoon salt
⅓ cup cold water
2 tablespoons olive oil
4 streaky bacon rashers, chopped
1 large leek, sliced and washed
4 eggs, at room temperature
2 cups pouring cream
salt and pepper

Method:

1. For the pastry—place the butter and flour in a food processor and blend until the mixture resembles rolled oats. Add the salt and water and continue to blend until a dough ball forms.

2. Remove from the machine, wrap the dough in plastic wrap, flatten slightly and refrigerate for 30 minutes to 1 hour. It is vital the dough remains cold.

3. Lightly flour a work surface and roll out the dough to a thickness of 3–5 mm.

4. Use a rolling pin to pick up the pastry and lay over a flan tin. Do not despair if at this point it breaks. Pick up any broken pieces and push into any areas where gaps appear. Allow the pastry to hang over the edge of the tin.

5. Place the pastry case back in the fridge for another 30 minutes—this step is also vital.

6. Meanwhile, for the filling—heat the oil in a pan over medium heat. Add the bacon and leek and fry until the leek has softened and the bacon is fragrant, about 8 minutes. Do not colour. Set aside.

7. Combine the eggs, cream and salt and pepper in a bowl and mix well.

Method cont.

8. Stir in the bacon and leek mixture and set aside.

9. Preheat the oven to 200°C.

10. Remove the pastry case from the fridge, cover with foil and add 2 cups dried beans or pie weights (to prevent the base from collecting steam and becoming concave). Bake in the oven for 15 minutes, remove from the oven and carefully remove the foil and weights (the weights are hot and the foil could still cut into the soft pastry). Return the base to the oven and cook for a further 7–10 minutes. Remove the pastry from the oven and reduce the oven temperature to 150°C.

11. While the pastry case is still hot, pour the filling into the case and return to the oven. Bake for 1 hour or until the quiche has set with the middle having a slight wobble when moved.

12. Remove from the oven and cool before serving. It is best the next day when cutting a slice will be much easier and can be warmed in the microwave.

HINTS AND TIPS:
----

* You will need—food processor or electric mixer with dough hook and bowl, cup, weight and spoon measures, rolling pin, cutting board, cook's knife, frying pan, bowl, whisk, deep 23-cm flan tin, foil and pie weights.

* Pre-made shortcrust pastry from the freezer section of the supermarket is a good alternative to homemade.

Bases made with filo pastry or puff pastry also work well.

* The main thing to remember with a quiche is that the filling is a delicate savoury custard that need only just set. Cooking at a high temperature or for too long will make the egg proteins separate or coagulate, leaving the custard watery and sponge-like. Take your time for a smooth result.

RASPBERRY CHEESECAKE

Serves 12

xxxxxxxxxxxxxxxxxxxxxxxxxxxxxxxxxxxxxxxxxxxxxxxxxxxxxxxxxxxxxxxxxxxxxxxxxxxxxxxxxxxxxxxxxxxx

Base

250 g plain sweet or chocolate biscuits

125 g unsalted butter, melted

Filling

375 g fresh raspberries (3 punnets)

150 g pure icing sugar

600 g cream cheese

400 g can condensed milk

300 ml thickened cream

8 gelatine leaves

Method:

1. For the base—place the biscuits in a food processor and blitz to form fine crumbs. Add the butter and pulse until combined. Scrape into a springform cake tin and, with the back of a spoon, press into the base of the tin and halfway up the sides. Place in the fridge.

2. For the filling—place the raspberries in a bowl and sprinkle with the sugar, then set aside for 5 minutes. Place in the food processor and blitz for 30 seconds. Use a plastic spatula to scrape the raspberry puree into a sieve and press out all of the pulp. Do not wash the food processor bowl, add the cream cheese, condensed milk and cream and blitz until smooth. Pour into a bowl then add all but ½ cup of the raspberry sauce and mix through.

3. Place the gelatine in plenty of cold water to soften, about 5 minutes. Squeeze out the excess water. Heat the remaining ½ cup raspberry sauce in a small saucepan. Bring to a simmer, add the gelatine, remove from the heat and stir with a spatula until the gelatine has dissolved. Add 1 cup cream cheese mixture to the gelatine mixture, combine thoroughly then pour into the remaining cream cheese mixture and stir until evenly combined.

Method cont.

4. Pour the filling onto the chilled base. Set for 6 hours in the fridge or overnight.

5. Dip a small knife in hot water and run the knife around the inside of the cake tin, then release the springform. Cut into serves with a larger knife also dipped in hot water. Serve on its own or with **raspberry sauce** and whipped cream.

HINTS AND TIPS:
----

* You will need—bowl, food processor, plastic spatula, sieve, 20-cm springform cake tin, liquid and weight measures, paring knife and cook's knife.

* Cheesecakes set with gelatine are rarely done these days because baked cheesecakes take less time and are less challenging. The results, however, are very different and so this recipe is worth a try.

* For those cooks who are used to using powdered gelatine, use 5 tablespoons sprinkled over ½ cup hot raspberry sauce; when dissolved, continue as per the method.

* For a lighter texture, semi-whip the cream to soft peaks and add last, folding into the cheesecake mixture once the gelatine/raspberry mixture is thoroughly combined.

* Decorate with fresh raspberries.

* If raspberries are out of season or are too expensive, use the same quantity of frozen raspberries.

* For a simple flavour, make a **lemon cheesecake**—omit the raspberry puree altogether and use 100 ml lemon juice, 1 tablespoon vanilla extract and the zest of 2 lemons. Dissolve the gelatine in the heated lemon juice. Place the lemon zest in a sieve and pour boiling water over the zest to remove the bitterness. Add some of the cheesecake mixture to the lemon juice/gelatine then pour back into the main mixture.

* For **simple cheesecake** with no gelatine—beat 200 g softened cream cheese with an electric mixer until light and fluffy. Slowly add 1 can condensed milk (to avoid lumps) and 120 ml lemon juice. Pour this mixture into the prepared base and set overnight. This filling is much softer and reminds me of how my grandmother makes a cold set cheesecake. Serve with whipped cream.

SAUSAGE ROLLS

Makes about 36

xxxxxxxxxxxxxxxxxxxxxxxxxxxxxxxxxxxxxxxxxxxxxxxxxxxxxxxxxxxxxxxxxxxxxxxxxxxxxxxxxxxxxxxxxx

300 g sausage mince
300 g beef mince
1 medium carrot, grated
1 medium brown onion, grated
1 tablespoon chopped fresh flat-leaf parsley
salt and pepper
3 sheets puff pastry, defrosted
2 eggs, lightly beaten

Method:

1. Preheat the oven to 200°C. Grease a large baking tray.

2. Mix the sausage meat, beef mince, carrot, onion, parsley and salt and pepper until well combined.

3. Take 1 sheet of the pastry and cut in half. Place a thick 'sausage' of the mince mixture along one long side of the pastry about 1 cm from the edge. Brush the egg along the long sides of the pastry and fold the pastry over the mince to form a log. Trim off any excess pastry. Cut into 6 pieces. Repeat with the remaining pastry, and mince mixture.

4. Brush the top with the egg, arrange on the baking tray and bake for 20 minutes or until golden brown.

HINTS AND TIPS:

* You will need—cutting board, paring knife, vegetable peeler, bowl, weight and spoon measures, mixing spoon and large baking tray.

* Serve with tomato sauce or with **tomato chutney**.

* When piping the mixture it is important to only half fill the piping bag. This will make handling the mixture and piping much easier.

* For a simple mixture try using 600 g sausage mince, 1 packet French onion soup, 1 tablespoon tomato paste, 1 egg and ½ cup bread crumbs and salt and pepper to taste.

* Any leftovers can be left in the fridge for 5 days and reheated as a snack.

* These rolls can be frozen easily and baked when necessary, just allow 15 minutes for them to thaw slightly before placing in a pre-heated oven. When freezing the uncooked sausage rolls, place on a tray lined with baking paper to prevent them from sticking to the tray. Once frozen solid, transfer to an airtight container or clip lock bag until needed.

* You can add 1 tablespoon dried chilli to the mixture, but do not be too liberal because it is not to everybody's taste.

* For a better quality meat mixture, buy your favourite sausages, run a knife down the length to break the casing membrane and use this meat instead of the sausage mince.

* Sausage mince already prepared for sausage rolls often contains gluten meal as a means of thickening the mixture and for moisture retention. Using regular minced meat, even with bread crumbs added, can tend to wet the pastry, making the base of the sausage roll soggy.

* Sausage rolls are great as finger food but can be left larger for a meal served with a green salad.

* You can cook off the onion, carrot and parsley in 1 tablespoon butter to add depth of flavour.

* The parsley can be substituted with other herbs—coriander always gives an interesting twist. Serve with a sweet chilli sauce.

* Sesame seeds or poppy seeds can be sprinkled on top of the rolls before baking.

* To make sausage pinwheels, spread 1 thawed puff pastry sheet with the mixture to within 1 cm from the edges. Brush the edges with lightly beaten egg and roll up like a Swiss roll. Cut roll into 3-cm wheels, and bake on a baking tray.

SCONES

Makes about 12

xxxxxxxxxxxxxxxxxxxxxxxxxxxxxxxxxxxxxxxxxxxxxxxxxxxxxxxxxxxxxxxxxxxxxxxxxxxxxxxxxxxxxxxxxxxxxxxxxxx

450 g self-raising flour
50 g cold butter, diced
300 ml cold milk
extra milk, for brushing

Method:

1. Preheat the oven to 220°C. Lightly flour a baking
tray.

2. Sift the flour into a bowl, add the butter and work
into the flour using your fingertips. Once combined, the
mixture will resemble coarse sand.

3. Make a well in the centre and add the milk. Use a
bread and butter knife to mix the dough to ensure it
doesn't become overworked or mix using your fingertips.
When the dough just comes together, turn out onto a
lightly floured surface.

4. Flatten the dough with your hands so it is
approximately 2.5 cm thick. Use a sharp scone cutter
to cut out the scones. Do not twist the cutter as
this will make the scones rise unevenly. Transfer the
scones to the prepared baking tray and place so they
are almost touching (1–2 mm apart). Brush the tops
lightly with the extra milk.

5. Bake in the oven for 12 minutes or until golden and
firm to touch.

6. Serve immediately with jam and whipped cream.

HINTS AND TIPS:

* You will need—weight and liquid measures, bowl, bread and butter knife, scone cutter and baking tray.

* The most important factor for great scones is not to over-mix the dough, hence a blunt knife is used to only just bring the mixture together without beating or kneading the dough. Working the dough too much will make the scones tight, hard and doughy instead of light and flaky.

* Try using half milk and half water in the recipe to lighten the mixture even more.

* The butter should be cold from the fridge and mixed only with your fingertips to avoid melting it; the milk should also be added cold. This ensures the scones stay flaky with a light crumb.

* When placing the scones on the tray, they can be touching so they support each other and make soft-sided scones with only a few having the odd crispy side.

* Wrap the cooked scones in a clean tea towel to keep the outer crust soft. For a crunchy crust, cool the scones uncovered.

* Make **mini savoury scones** to use as a base for canapés for a cocktail party. Make the dough only 1.5 cm high, bake, cut in half and top with crème fraîche and smoked salmon. You could also mix ½ cup of your favourite grated cheese into the flour before mixing in the milk or water.

* A favourite recipe of mine is **lemonade scones**. These are easier to make than the classic scone. To 450 g self-raising flour, add 250 ml lemonade and 250 ml thickened cream, mix with a knife and bake until golden. Ensure the lemonade and cream are chilled and this recipe will be perfect every time.

* Try using a scone dough, rolled to 1 cm thick, as a topping for apple pie or instead of a crumble mixture.

SPANAKOPITA

Serves 6

xxxxxxxxxxxxxxxxxxxxxxxxxxxxxxxxxxxxxxxxxxxxxxxxxxxxxxxxxxxxxxxxxxxxxxxxxxxxxxxxxxxxxxxxxxxxx

1 bunch spinach
500 g Australian fetta, crumbled
500 g fresh firm ricotta
3 eggs, lightly beaten
1 tablespoon chopped flat-leaf parsley
1 tablespoon mint or dill (optional)
1 teaspoon salt
8 filo pastry sheets
3 tablespoons olive oil

Method:

1. Preheat the oven to 180°C. Prepare a baking dish by lightly greasing with oil.

2. Wash the spinach thoroughly and place in a pot of boiling water. Cook for 20 seconds or until wilted. Drain and run under cold water to refresh and stop the cooking. When cool, squeeze the excess water from the spinach. You will have approximately 2 cups cooked spinach.

3. Place the spinach in a bowl, add the fetta, ricotta, eggs, parsley, mint or dill (if using) and salt, and mix thoroughly.

4. Place four sheets of filo in the prepared baking dish and brush each layer with oil. This forms the bottom layer.

5. Spread the spinach mixture evenly over the filo. Repeat the filo layers for the top, brushing each sheet with oil.

6. Bake in the oven for 25 minutes or until golden and crispy on top.

HINTS AND TIPS:

---

* You will need—cutting board, cook's knife, weight and spoon measures, pastry brush, baking dish (28 cm x 18 cm x 8 cm deep), large bowl and large pot.

* More spinach can be used in this recipe or alternatively reduce the cheese content. Many Westernised recipes use less than half the cheese I have suggested. My Greek cooking guru Vasiliki and her extended family would not hear of reducing this quantity and I am convinced and somewhat scared and so it is written.

* Pine nuts can be added; toast 2 tablespoons pine nuts, crush in a mortar and pestle, and add with the cheese.

* Use fetta of choice but Australian fetta is less salty than European fetta, therefore allowing the cook to control the saltiness of the dish. Fetta should be rinsed under running water to reduce saltiness if coming straight from the brine.

* Fetta cheese should be purchased in its own brine as it keeps the cheese moist. If the brine is too salty, the fetta can be stored in a milk bath to keep it moist and reduce saltiness.

* Ricotta is a low fat, low salt, mild-flavoured cheese produced from whey, a by-product of cheese manufacture, therefore ricotta is not actually a cheese at all. Ricotta means 'cooked again' and refers to its production method: the whey is reheated and an acid, such as vinegar, is added to coagulate and set the ricotta.

* When preparing filo pastry, always cover the remaining sheets of filo with a damp tea towel as you brush the sheets you are working with. It dries out very quickly, making it difficult to work with.

* To make **Tiropita**—use 500 g ricotta, 500 g fetta, replace parsley for mint, and omit the spinach.

* To make **Hortopita**— use 1 bunch spinach, 2 tablespoons chopped parsley, 1 tablespoon chopped mint, ½ cup chopped spring onions, 1 teaspoon salt, ½ teaspoon pepper, 2 tablespoons raw short-grain rice, combine in a bowl and follow the basic method.

* Spanakopita can be made in advance and frozen before cooking.

* Puff pastry can be used instead of filo. Place 1 sheet on the bottom of the dish and 1 on top.

* Spanakopita is ideal for finger food, make into mini triangles and roll with a sheet of filo pastry.

* If serving as finger food, sweet chilli sauce or tomato relish can be used as a dipping sauce.

* This can also be made without pre-cooking the spinach if in a hurry: add 1 tablespoon raw short-grain rice with the cheeses to soak up the water the spinach releases.

* Reheat spanakopita in the oven, covered with foil, to keep its crispness; if reheated in the microwave, it will go soggy.

SPONGE CAKE

Serves 10

XXXXXXXXXXXXXXXXXXXXXXXXXXXXXXXXXXXXXXXXXXXXXXXXXXXXXXXXXXXXXXXXXXXXXXXXXXXXXXXXXXXXXXXXXXXXXXXXXXX

5 eggs, at room temperature, separated
pinch of cream of tartar
¾ cup caster sugar
2 tablespoons custard powder
¾ cup cornflour
1 teaspoon baking powder
½ teaspoon bicarbonate of soda

Method:

1. Preheat the oven to 175°C. Grease 2 round cake tins
with canola or olive oil, line the bases with a round
of baking paper and dust with cornflour. Lightly tap
out the excess flour.

2. Whisk the egg whites with the cream of tartar to
soft peaks and gradually beat in the sugar. Add the
egg yolks and whisk until combined.

3. Sift the custard powder, cornflour, baking powder
and bicarbonate of soda 3 or 4 times.

4. Gently fold the dry ingredients into the egg
mixture.

5. Pour into the prepared cake tins and bake for
20–25 minutes.

6. Allow the cakes to cool thoroughly in the tins,
then invert onto a wire rack. Top with icing or
whipped cream and strawberries (see Hints and tips).

HINTS AND TIPS:

★ You will need—2 x 20-cm round cake tins, plastic spatula, electric mixer, sieve, cup and spoon measures and wire rack.

★ Sponge cake or foam cake is the lightest and most delicate of all the cakes and is often deemed the blue ribbon baking item in metropolitan shows, Royal shows and small country town shows.

★ A sponge cake differs to a génoise or chiffon cake, as the latter, although quite light, has a denser crumb because it uses plain or cake flour (instead of cornflour) and adds butter.

★ This recipe for sponge cake is very similar to 'angel food cake'—both methods separate the eggs and make a meringue. This recipe has the egg yolks added back to the mixture whereas an angel food cake is pure meringue with no added fat. In a regular sponge cake the whole eggs are beaten to a foam with the sugar before the flour is folded in.

★ For a light crust on the sponge cake, try sprinkling the batter with caster sugar before it goes into the oven.

★ For best results, a sponge cake should be made and used on the same day. It can be successfully frozen, which should be done as soon as it is cooled, and kept frozen for 2–3 months.

★ Any number of fillings and toppings can go with a basic sponge cake. **Frosting** can top the sponge beautifully. Or sandwich the cakes with 300 ml whipped cream mixed with 2 tablespoons pure icing sugar. Or gently mix the whipped cream with 150 g grated chocolate or 250 g chopped berries, such as strawberries.

★ There are many opportunities for a basic sponge to turn into a disaster. The thermostat in most domestic ovens is inaccurate, therefore it is recommended that you use an oven thermometer to get an exact reading from your oven.

★ Lopsided? If your cakes are constantly lopsided, you have a problem with hot spots in the oven. Rotate the cake 180 degrees in the oven halfway through cooking to even things up. If it is too far gone, cool the cake then slice off the top to even it up, turn it over and ice or frost the base (which is now the top).

★ If a cake is undercooked and removed from the oven too soon, it will collapse. Check for doneness by touching the centre gently—it should spring back. The sides of the cake should have shrunk slightly too.

★ If the cake is not for show purposes, use a ring-shaped cake tin (also known as a tube tin) to allow the cake to cook from the inside out.

★ Dull coloured tins are best as shiny surfaced cake tins reflect heat, taking longer to cook; while black tins absorb heat, causing the cake to brown on the outside before the inside is done.

SWISS ROLL

Serves 10

XXXXXXXXXXXXXXXXXXXXXXXXXXXXXXXXXXXXXXXXXXXXXXXXXXXXXXXXXXXXXXXXXXXXXXXXXXXXXXXXXXXXXXXXXXXXXXXXXXXXX

6 egg yolks
120 g caster sugar
2 teaspoons vanilla extract
60 g plain flour
6 egg whites
pinch of cream of tartar
2 tablespoons caster sugar extra, for sprinkling
½ cup strawberry jam, melted
300 ml whipped cream
sifted icing sugar, for dusting

Method:

1. Preheat the oven to 180°C. Line a shallow baking tray with baking paper and dust with flour.

2. Combine the egg yolks, caster sugar and vanilla in a bowl, and whisk until pale. Stir in the flour.

3. Use an electric mixer to whisk the egg whites and cream of tartar until stiff peaks form.

4. Add a large dollop of the egg whites to the egg yolk mixture and thoroughly mix; this step loosens the mixture. Gently fold in the remaining egg whites. Pour the batter into the prepared baking tray and bake for 15–20 minutes or until the sponge springs back when touched.

5. Lay a large piece of baking paper on the bench and sprinkle with the extra caster sugar.

6. Turn out the sponge onto the sugared paper straight from the oven and gently peel off the baking paper. Allow to cool for only 2–3 minutes. While the sponge is still very warm, use the sugared baking paper to lift one end of the sponge and roll up. Cover with a clean tea towel and leave, rolled up, to cool completely—this can take more than an hour.

Method cont.

7. Once cool, gently unroll the sponge. Brush with the melted jam, spread with the whipped cream and roll up. Dust with icing sugar and serve. Keep refrigerated and covered for 1–2 days.

HINTS AND TIPS:

* You will need—rectangular 23-cm x 18-cm baking tray, 2 bowls, electric mixer, cup, liquid, spoon and weight measures, plastic spatula and pastry brush.

* The single biggest issue for cooks making a Swiss roll is the cracking or splitting of the cake when it is rolled up. The reason this happens is that all too often the sponge is left to cool as a flat slab, and is then filled and rolled, causing the stiff sponge to break. To avoid this, the sponge must be rolled while it is still very warm and then allowed to cool in this position until it sets cold. When gently unrolled then filled, it will roll up easily. If the delicate sponge is rolled hot from the oven, it tends to squash from the steam in the sponge; by allowing it to sit for a few minutes, the sponge can begin to set and hold its shape before being rolled.

* Should the sponge not work out as you hoped, it could still be used in a trifle or cut into squares and used for lamingtons.

* For a **lemon Swiss roll**— add the zest and juice of 1 lemon to the sponge mixture. Then fill with **lemon curd** or if in a hurry, pre-bought lemon butter.

* For a **chocolate Swiss roll**—add 3 tablespoons cocoa powder to the egg yolk mixture before folding in the whites. Fill with a **rich chocolate ganache**: heat to boiling point 150 ml thickened cream, remove from the heat, add 250 g chopped dark chocolate, and stir until the chocolate has melted. Cool completely before spreading onto the roll.

* For another decadent filling try **mascarpone and muscat cream**—combine 100 g mascarpone cheese, 100 ml thickened cream, 2 tablespoons icing sugar and 40 ml muscat and spread onto the roll.

TEA CAKE

Serves 8

xxxxxxxxxxxxxxxxxxxxxxxxxxxxxxxxxxxxxxxxxxxxxxxxxxxxxxxxxxxxxxxxxxxxxxxxxxxxxxxxxxxxxxxxxxxxxxxxx

125 g unsalted butter,
    softened
180 g caster sugar
1 teaspoon vanilla extract
3 eggs, at room
    temperature
250 g self-raising flour,
    sifted
125 ml milk

Topping
1 tablespoon unsalted
    butter
1 teaspoon ground cinnamon
1 tablespoon caster sugar

Method:

1. Preheat the oven to 180°C. Line a cake tin with baking paper.

2. Place the butter, sugar and vanilla in a mixing bowl and beat with an electric mixer until light and fluffy. Scrape the sides to make sure all ingredients are combined. Add the eggs, one at a time, making sure each is fully incorporated before adding the next.

3. Fold in the flour and milk in 2 batches. Pour into the prepared tin and bake for about 30 minutes or until the cake is cooked when tested with a wooden skewer.

4. Remove from the oven and rest in the tin for 5 minutes before turning out onto a wire rack. Add topping while the cake is still hot.

5. For the topping—melt the butter and brush over the top of the cake. Mix the cinnamon and sugar and dust evenly over the top. Serve warm.

HINTS AND TIPS:

★ You will need—mixing bowl, electric mixer, weight, spoon and liquid measures, sieve, 20-cm or 22-cm cake tin, pastry brush and wire rack.

★ Another method that works quite well is to place all the cake ingredients into a bowl and beat for 4–5 minutes until pale, then pour into the cake tin and bake.

★ For a **lemon tea cake**—add the zest of 1 lemon to the batter and replace the cinnamon with lemon juice.

★ For a simple **apple tea cake**—peel and core 1 large Granny Smith apple, quarter and thinly slice, then arrange the apple slices, overlapping slightly, over the cake batter before baking. Brush with butter and sprinkle with cinnamon sugar.

★ For the apple tea cake, make a simple crumble mixture to go over the top of the sliced apples before the cake goes in the oven. Rub 50 g cold butter into 50 g plain flour, then mix in 50 g caster sugar.

★ For a **pear tea cake**— peel, core and quarter 2 pears and thinly slice, overlap slightly on the cake batter, then sprinkle with 2 tablespoons soft brown sugar before baking.

★ Tea cake is served hot soon after coming from the oven, although it can freeze well when cooled; defrost and microwave briefly before serving.

TOFFEE

Makes 12 to 15

XXXXXXXXXXXXXXXXXXXXXXXXXXXXXXXXXXXXXXXXXXXXXXXXXXXXXXXXXXXXXXXXXXXXXXXXXXXXXXXXX

450 g white sugar
200 ml cold water
1 tablespoon brown vinegar
sprinkles (optional)

Method:

1. Lightly spray paper cupcake cases with oil.

2. Place the sugar, water and vinegar in a saucepan. Stir over medium heat until the sugar dissolves. Bring to the boil but do not stir. Cook until the syrup is golden brown.

3. Remove from the heat and allow the bubbles to settle. Pour into the prepared paper cases. If desired, decorate with sprinkles.

HINTS AND TIPS:

* You will need—12–15 paper cupcake cases, saucepan and wooden spoon.

* For **toffee apples**, prepare 12 small red delicious, or another sweet eating apple, by washing, drying and pushing an icy-pole stick into the base of each apple. Mix 900 g white sugar with 250 ml water in a saucepan and bring to the boil. When the sugar has dissolved, stir in ½ teaspoon cream of tartar and 2 teaspoons red food colouring. Reduce the heat and simmer the syrup until it reaches hard crack stage—about 20 minutes. Remove from the heat and when the syrup stops bubbling, dip in 1 apple at a time, tipping the saucepan on an angle to thoroughly coat the apple. Place on a tray lined with baking paper. Repeat with remaining apples. Allow to cool to room temperature before storing.

* There is a large range of decorative toppings available in the supermarket. Traditionally topped with hundreds and thousands, have fun with the many variations of sprinkles, decorative sugar flowers, cachous or alphabet letters made from sugar.

* Toffees can be made up to a week in advance and stored in an airtight container.

* For coloured toffees add 1–2 teaspoons of liquid food colouring at the end of the cooking, just as the mixture is removed from the heat.

* The caramel will take about 15 minutes, so it is important to stay at the stove top to ensure it doesn't burn. If you own a sugar thermometer, then cook to the 'crack' stage, which is 160°C.

* It is important to decorate toffees while they are still hot and runny so the decorations stick and set with the toffees. Allow at least 15 minutes for them to set before moving.

* Toffees are another favourite for school fetes and kid's parties.

* Spraying the paper cases with oil stops the toffees from sticking as much when the kids eat them.

VANILLA SLICE

Makes 6–8 slices

XXXXXXXXXXXXXXXXXXXXXXXXXXXXXXXXXXXXXXXXXXXXXXXXXXXXXXXXXXXXXXXXXXXXXXXXXXXXXXXXXXXXXXXXXXXXXXXXXX

2 sheets frozen puff pastry, defrosted
250 g white sugar
60 g custard powder
75 g cornflour
1 litre milk
60 g unsalted butter
2 egg yolks
1 teaspoon vanilla extract
sifted pure icing sugar

Method:

1. Preheat the oven to 200°C. Line a baking tray with baking paper. Line a square baking dish with foil, allowing the foil to drape over the edges of the dish.

2. Place the pastry sheets on the prepared baking tray and bake for 15 minutes until browned and puffed. Remove and cool.

3. Trim the cooked pastry sheet to fit the baking dish then place 1 pastry sheet in the base of the lined dish.

4. For the custard—combine the sugar, custard powder and cornflour in a large saucepan.

5. Mix in just enough milk to form a paste, then gradually mix in the rest of the milk—this will prevent lumps from forming.

6. Bring to a simmer, stirring constantly (use a whisk to keep the custard smooth), and simmer for a further 3 minutes. Remove from the heat and stir in the butter, egg yolks and vanilla.

7. Pour the custard onto the puff pastry base. Top with the second piece of pastry.

8. Dust with the icing sugar or spread with a layer of **basic icing for cakes**. Refrigerate for at least 3 hours or until cold, then cut into 6 or 8 pieces. The slice will last for 3–5 days covered and refrigerated.

HINTS AND TIPS:

* You will need—22-cm square baking dish, aluminium foil, baking paper, flat baking tray, cutting board, cook's knife, large saucepan, wooden spoon, whisk, plastic spatula and liquid, spoon and weight measures.

* Puff pastry can be substituted with 'Sao' biscuits (no cooking required).

* For a **rich custard filling** that is super light and fluffy, try the following recipe—500 g **pastry cream** (freshly made and hot), 5 gelatine leaves, 600 ml thickened cream, 100 g icing sugar, 1 teaspoon vanilla extract. Once the pastry cream is made, set aside and keep hot. Soak the gelatine in cold water until softened. Place the softened gelatine in a small saucepan and melt over medium heat, add a large spoonful of the pastry cream and whisk. Remove from the heat and whisk in the remaining pastry cream until smooth. In a bowl, whisk the cream, icing sugar and vanilla until soft peaks form. When the custard has cooled to room temperature, beat the cream into the custard and pour onto the prepared puff pastry base. Top with the puff pastry

lid and cover with icing. Refrigerate overnight.

* Try adding 2 tablespoons cocoa powder to the mixture before cooking. **Chocolate slice**, although tasty, is not traditional and would never win a prize at the national vanilla slice competition held in Ouyen, in Victoria's northwest. Traditional will always win out.

* The thickness is determined by the dish the slice is set in. A larger dish (30-cm) will mean a shallow vanilla slice. A 20-cm or less dish will mean a very thick slice that is too big for the mouth to get around.

XXXXXXXXXXXX **13. Toppings** XXXXXXXXXXXX

BASIC ICING

Makes about 1½ cups

xxxxxxxxxxxxxxxxxxxxxxxxxxxxxxxxxxxxxxxxxxxxxxxxxxxxxxxxxxxxxxxxxxxxxxxxxxxxxxxxxxxxxxxxx

250 g pure icing sugar
1 tablespoon unsalted
  butter, softened
1 teaspoon vanilla essence
1 tablespoon boiling water

Method:

1. Sift the icing sugar into a bowl. Add the butter and vanilla, then pour in the boiling water and beat well.

2. Spread immediately over the cake and leave to set.

HINTS AND TIPS:

★ You will need—bowl, spoon and weight measures and wooden spoon.

★ For **basic chocolate icing**—add 1½–2 tablespoons cocoa powder with the icing sugar.

★ Pure icing sugar is different to icing sugar mixture. Icing sugar has a starch (cornflour) added to keep it from hardening with age. Icing mixture can be used in icings but is not recommended for baking as it is not a pure form of sugar and can have an effect on the recipe. If you're gluten-intolerant, use pure icing sugar rather than icing sugar mixture.

CREAM CHEESE FROSTING

Makes about 2 cups

xxxxxxxxxxxxxxxxxxxxxxxxxxxxxxxxxxxxxxxxxxxxxxxxxxxxxxxxxxxxxxxxxxxxxxxxxxxxxxxxxxxxxxx

60 g unsalted butter,
   softened
125 g cream cheese,
   softened
250 g pure icing sugar
1 teaspoon vanilla essence

Method:

1. Use a wooden spoon to beat the butter and cream cheese until soft and thoroughly combined. Alternatively use the (K) paddle on an electric mixer.

2. Stir in the icing sugar and vanilla (or use the slowest setting on the electric mixer) until a smooth paste is formed. Whip or beat on high for 2–3 minutes until light and fluffy. Spread over the cake.

HINTS AND TIPS:

★ You will need—weight and spoon measures, wooden spoon or electric mixer, bowl and plastic spatula.

★ For **orange frosting**—add the zest of 1 orange. Be sure to wash the orange before grating the zest to remove any dust and wax. Substitute the orange with the zest of 1 lemon, 2 limes or 2 mandarins. Use specifically on orange cake, banana cake, hummingbird cake and carrot cake with the butter and cream cheese.

★ Replace the vanilla essence with 1 tablespoon fresh passionfruit pulp.

DEVIL'S CHOCOLATE FROSTING

Makes about 4 cups

XXXXXXXXXXXXXXXXXXXXXXXXXXXXXXXXXXXXXXXXXXXXXXXXXXXXXXXXXXXXXXXXXXXXXXXXXXXXXXXXXXXXXX

180 g dark cooking
   chocolate
500 g pure icing sugar
125 g unsalted butter,
   softened
1 teaspoon vanilla essence
100 ml thickened cream

Method:

1. Gently melt the chocolate in a heatproof bowl over a saucepan of simmering water or in the microwave set on low. Cool to room temperature.

2. Mix the sugar and butter with a wooden spoon, then mix in the melted chocolate and vanilla.

3. Heat the cream to luke warm, stir into the chocolate mixture and beat with an electric mixer for 2–3 minutes or until thickened.

HINTS AND TIPS:

----

* You will need—weight, spoon and liquid measures, heatproof bowl, saucepan or a microwave-proof bowl, wooden spoon and electric mixer.

* As the name suggests, devil's chocolate frosting is for **devil's food cake**. This frosting is equally good on **vanilla** or **chocolate cake**, as well as **cupcakes**.

* Thickened cream is an Australian style of cream that has a thickening agent added. For more on **Cream** see **Really Useful Information**. This recipe will work just as well with any cream with a minimum fat content of 35 per cent.

* I recommend using pure icing sugar, but you could try icing sugar mixture, which has a small amount of cornflour added.

CUSTARD

Makes about 3 cups

XXXXXXXXXXXXXXXXXXXXXXXXXXXXXXXXXXXXXXXXXXXXXXXXXXXXXXXXXXXXXXXXXXXXXXXXXXXXXXXXXXXXXXXXXXX

500 ml milk
½ vanilla bean, split
   lengthways, or
   1 teaspoon vanilla
   extract
5 egg yolks
150 g caster sugar

Method:

1. In a medium saucepan, bring the milk and vanilla to a simmer and remove from the heat.

2. Use a whisk to beat the egg yolks and sugar in a bowl until light and fluffy.

3. Pour the hot milk onto the egg mixture, whisking quickly as the milk is added.

4. Return the custard to the saucepan and over medium heat, stir constantly (in a figure 8 shape) with a wooden spoon until the mixture coats the back of the spoon.

5. Strain the custard into a bowl or jug and serve, or refrigerate. Serve hot or cold.

HINTS AND TIPS:

* You will need—saucepan, bowl, whisk, wooden spoon, sieve, and spoon, liquid and weight measures.

* This is a real custard, also known as a 'crème Anglaise' or 'English custard'.

* Because there is no flour in this recipe, there is a real chance the custard could curdle or separate if it is cooked for too long or too fast over high heat. Should this happen, one way to try and fix it is to use a hand-held blender; this will help disperse the curdled egg in the mixture though it results in a different consistency.

Cool as quickly as possible by placing in an ice bath, which means having a larger bowl than the one the custard is in and half-filling it with cold water and ice cubes.

* An option to avoid this in the first place—other than watching carefully how the custard is thickening—is to add 1 tablespoon cornflour (starch) to the egg yolk and sugar mixture before adding the hot milk. The cornflour will help hold the egg yolks even if overcooked; it will also mean a thicker custard, similar to the pre-made stuff.

* If using a vanilla bean in this recipe, it is advised to slice the vanilla bean in half lengthways before adding

to the milk to allow the tiny black seeds to escape. Once the milk is brought to simmering point, remove from the stove and stand for 10 minutes for the vanilla to infuse before adding to the egg mixture. Then remove the bean and with the back of a small knife, scrape out as many of the black seeds and add to the mixture. The remaining vanilla pod can be rinsed under cold water, dried with paper towel and stored in the sugar jar to perfume the sugar, as well as being used again in a custard but without as much intensity.

ITALIAN MERINGUE

Makes about 2 litres

XXXXXXXXXXXXXXXXXXXXXXXXXXXXXXXXXXXXXXXXXXXXXXXXXXXXXXXXXXXXXXXXXXXXXXXXXXXXXXXXXXXXXXXXXX

60 ml water
300 g caster sugar
1 tablespoon glucose (optional)
5 egg whites

Method:

1. Place the water, sugar and glucose in a saucepan and bring to the boil. Place a sugar thermometer in the syrup once it comes to the boil.

2. When the sugar reaches 110°C on the thermometer, whisk the egg whites with an electric mixer until firm peaks form. Constantly watch the sugar thermometer, remove the syrup from the heat once it reaches 120°C (soft ball stage).

3. Turn the electric mixer to the slowest speed and slowly pour the hot sugar syrup into the egg whites in a thin steady stream. Continue to beat on slow until all the syrup has been added, then increase the speed to medium and continue beating until the mixture is cool, about 15 minutes. The meringue is now ready to use on or in any number of popular desserts or icings.

HINTS AND TIPS:

★ You will need—saucepan, liquid, weight and spoon measures, sugar thermometer, electric mixer with whisk attachment and plastic spatula.

★ To make this successfully, you will need a sugar thermometer.

★ Italian meringue can be kept for 2 days in an airtight container in the refrigerator.

★ Glucose is not necessary in the recipe and the meringue will work well without it. Glucose will, however, prevent sugar crystals from forming around the edge of the bowl or in the egg whites.

★ Scoop the mixture into a piping bag and pipe the meringue onto cooked puddings or Bombe Alaska. The meringue is cooked from the sugar syrup, so it does not need to go into the oven. To brown, simply use a blow-torch, being extremely careful as it will burn very, very easily.

★ Another form of cooked meringue is **Swiss meringue**—combine 3 egg whites and 300 g pure icing sugar in a heatproof bowl. Place the bowl over a saucepan of boiling water and beat the mixture until thick and glossy. Remove from the heat, transfer to an electric mixer and whisk until completely cold. This dense, firm meringue can then be piped into decorative shapes or simple meringue nests and placed on a lined baking tray and cooked in a preheated 120°C oven until crispy, about 1½ hours.

★ To make **shogi sticks** that are used to decorate the outside of cakes—add to the cold beaten Swiss meringue, 40 g sifted cocoa powder and 200 g roasted hazelnut meal. Then pipe into sticks the size of a little finger and bake for 10–15 minutes in a preheated 180°C oven. Leave to cool before removing from the tray. Store in an airtight container for 7 days.

★ Italian meringue is used in **butter cream**—make the recipe quantity of Italian meringue, although increase the sugar by 100 g to total 400 g. Follow the method to the end, but keep the mixer whisking at medium speed and begin adding, in small amounts, 500 g softened, unsalted butter. Do not be inclined to add it too fast or the mixture might split. Beat for a further few minutes. The butter cream is now ready for use on or in cakes and biscuits. Store in an airtight container for up to 2 weeks in the refrigerator or frozen in smaller batches for up to 3 months. Leave at room temperature for a least 1 hour before using. Butter cream made from Italian meringue is beautiful as it is not sickly sweet or overly rich the way butter cream made with just butter and sugar can be.

LEMON CURD

Makes approximately 900 ml

xxxxxxxxxxxxxxxxxxxxxxxxxxxxxxxxxxxxxxxxxxxxxxxxxxxxxxxxxxxxxxxxxxxxxxxxxxxxxxxxxxxxxxxxxxx

5 egg yolks
500 g caster sugar
zest of 4 lemons
200 ml lemon juice
   (approximately
    4 lemons)
150 g butter, diced

Method:

1. Place about 10 cm of water in a saucepan and bring to a simmer.

2. Place in a heatproof bowl over the saucepan but do not let it touch the water. Mix the egg yolks and sugar until combined and stir in the zest and juice. Add the butter and place over the simmering water. Use a whisk or plastic spatula to stir the mixture constantly until it heats through and begins to thicken. Remove from the heat, strain into a clean bowl and stir until slightly cooled.

3. Transfer to sterilised jars, cover and refrigerate until needed. The lemon curd will last for up to 1 month refrigerated.

HINTS AND TIPS:

* You will need—cutting board, cook's knife, saucepan, juicer, grater, whisk, plastic spatula, weight and liquid measures, 2 bowls, and jars for storage.

* Lemon curd is also known as 'lemon butter' and 'lemon cheese'.

* It is important to use the double boiler method to control the heat and prevent the eggs from scrambling. It also produces a smoother texture by cooking the curd slowly over simmering water.

* Lime juice produces a good albeit tarter alternative.

* For **passionfruit curd**—use 200 ml strained passionfruit pulp then add 1 tablespoon of the seeds back into the juice.

* Lemon curd can be used as a spread on warm toast or scones. It can also be used as a filling for tartlets and cakes—either as a frosting or sandwiched in a **sponge cake** or **Swiss roll**.

* To make juicing lemons easier, roll the lemon on the benchtop, applying pressure with the palm of your hand; this 'bruising' tenderises the membranes within. Alternatively, try microwaving the lemon for 20–30 seconds before juicing.

PASTRY CREAM

Makes 700 ml

XXXXXXXXXXXXXXXXXXXXXXXXXXXXXXXXXXXXXXXXXXXXXXXXXXXXXXXXXXXXXXXXXXXXXXXXXXXXXXXXXXXXXXXXXX

500 ml milk
1 vanilla bean, split
   lengthways
5 egg yolks
150 g caster sugar
50 g plain flour, sifted

Method:

1. Place the milk and vanilla bean in a saucepan, and bring just to the boil. Remove from the heat and stand for 10 minutes to allow the vanilla to infuse.

2. Whisk the egg yolks and sugar until pale. Add the flour and stir until combined.

3. Remove the vanilla bean from the milk and, with the back of a small knife, scrape the tiny black seeds from the bean and add to the egg and sugar mixture.

4. Pour a quarter of the milk into the egg mixture and stir to loosen the mixture, then add the remaining milk and mix well.

5. Pour the mixture back into the saucepan, stir continuously over medium heat and bring to the boil. Boil for 2 minutes and remove from the heat.

6. Pour the pastry cream into a bowl and place a piece of plastic wrap directly on the custard to prevent it from forming a skin. Cool completely before using. Keep covered and refrigerated for up to 5 days.

HINTS AND TIPS:

* You will need—weight and liquid measures, bowl, small paring knife, whisk and saucepan.

* Pastry cream is a staple of all pastry cooks. It is used in a vast array of sweet treats from fruit flans, éclairs and profiteroles to soufflé bases, crème chiboust and mousselines.

* Use a stainless steel bowl, saucepan and whisk when making this recipe. Using aluminium will make the pastry cream turn grey and taste metallic.

* Once the vanilla bean has been used, wash and pat dry. Leave to air dry for a few hours then store in the sugar container to scent the sugar. It can be used again (with less pungency) to make another pastry cream.

* Replace the plain flour with gluten-free cornflour for a coeliac-friendly recipe.

* To make a **chocolate pastry cream**, replace 1 tablespoon flour with 1 tablespoon cocoa powder and add 1 tablespoon more of sugar.

MARMALADE

Makes about 5 litres

xxxxxxxxxxxxxxxxxxxxxxxxxxxxxxxxxxxxxxxxxxxxxxxxxxxxxxxxxxxxxxxxxxxxxxxxxxxxxxxxxxxxxxxxxxx

1 kg Seville oranges
juice of 1 lemon
½ teaspoon cooking salt
3 litres cold water
3–4 kg white sugar

Method:

1. Wash the oranges thoroughly to remove any dust, dirt and wax. Slice the top and bottom from the oranges and discard.

2. Slice the oranges thinly, remove and keep any seeds. Wrap the seeds from the oranges and any from the freshly squeezed lemon in muslin or cheesecloth and tie with cooking string.

3. Place the sliced oranges, salt and muslin bag of seeds in a large ceramic bowl or stainless steel pot and add the cold water. Cover and refrigerate overnight.

4. The following day, measure the volume of water and fruit before placing the fruit, muslin bag and water into a heavy-based saucepan. Bring to the boil, reduce the heat and simmer for 30–40 minutes or until the orange rinds are tender.

5. Measure the sugar to equal the volume of the orange and water (about 3.6 kg). Add the sugar and lemon juice to the hot orange mixture and bring to the boil, remove any froth or scum that forms on the surface.

6. Cook until it becomes a jelly consistency, about 20 minutes. This can be tested by spooning a small amount onto a plate and refrigerating for 5 minutes; when pushed with your finger, it will have a wrinkly skin. If it is not ready, keep boiling and testing every 5–10 minutes until it is at setting point.

Method cont.

7. Discard the bag of seeds and remove the marmalade from the heat. Set aside for 15 minutes to allow the marmalade to cool slightly and the pieces of fruit to settle throughout the mixture; the fruit will float to the top if poured into jars immediately.

8. Pour into sterilised jars and store for up to 6 months. Refrigerate after opening.

HINTS AND TIPS:

* You will need—large 5-litre pot or bowl for soaking the fruit, cutting board, cook's knife, spoon and weight measures, wooden spoon, muslin or cheesecloth, cooking string, juicer, ladle and jars with lids for storage.

* Seville oranges are very sour and have a high pectin level, which significantly helps in the gelling of the marmalade. Marmalade made with sweet oranges struggles to set properly without added setting agents; they also lack the bitterness—the determining factor in a good marmalade—producing something that resembles an orange jam rather than a marmalade.

* Like any preserve, always use the best and freshest fruit available, void of any blemishes or rot.

* Soaking the fruit for 24 hours helps to soften the rind and remove some bitterness. It also reduces the cooking time and keeps the fruit in the marmalade tasting fresh.

* Using the seeds from the freshly squeezed lemon as well as from the oranges helps to gel the marmalade.

* Other citrus fruits ideal for marmalade include cumquats, lemons, limes and grapefruits.

* Citrus fruits are often coated with a wax which is hard to remove. It is best to buy fruits that are sold as 'unwaxed' to avoid damage when scrubbing them yourself.

* If you own a sugar thermometer, the setting point for the marmalade is 105°C. Remove from the heat and rest for 20 minutes before bottling in hot sterilised jars.

* For tips on how to sterilise jars, see Basic Preserving.

STRAWBERRY JAM

Makes about 3 cups

XXXXXXXXXXXXXXXXXXXXXXXXXXXXXXXXXXXXXXXXXXXXXXXXXXXXXXXXXXXXXXXXXXXXXXXXXXXXXXXXXXXXXXXXXXXXX

400 g white sugar
500 g strawberries, hulled
50 ml lemon juice plus any seeds

Method:

1. To sterilise the jars to be used, see Basic Preserving. Place 2 saucers in the freezer (to check the jam's consistency later). Preheat the oven to 140°C.

2. Place the sugar in a cake tin and place in the oven.

3. Place the strawberries, in a heavy-based saucepan, add the lemon juice and seeds and slowly bring to the boil over medium heat.

4. After 10 minutes, slowly stir in the warmed sugar, increase the heat to high and boil until the sugar dissolves and the jam thickens, about 15 minutes. Stir occasionally to prevent the jam from sticking to the bottom of the pot. Remove any scum that may have formed on the surface.

5. Test the jam by placing a teaspoonful onto a chilled saucer, place back in the freezer for 30 seconds, then remove and run the handle of the spoon through the jam; it should wrinkle around the edges when done. If not, continue to boil for another 5 minutes and test again on the second cold saucer.

6. When the jam is ready, remove from the heat and leave to stand for 15 minutes for the fruits to settle evenly. (Hot jam poured immediately into the jars can cause the fruit to rise and sit at the top of the jam.) Remove any seeds that were added and discard. While still warm, pour the jam into the sterilised jars. Seal the jam jars, label with a name and a date. Store in a cool, airy, dry, dark place for up to 1 year. Refrigerate once opened.

HINTS AND TIPS:

----

* You will need—cutting board, paring knife, juicer, heavy-based saucepan, wooden spoon, weight and liquid measures, cake tin and jars for storage.

* The yield from this recipe varies depending on the ripeness of the fruit and the time taken to reach setting point.

* The amount of sugar used in a jam recipe depends on the ripeness or tartness of the raw fruit. With this in mind, a very general rule of thumb is that the fruit and sugar quantities are close to equal.

* It is always recommended to make any jam in small batches to maintain the flavour and integrity of the fruit. Never exceed more than 1 kg fruit at a time. Cooking a large batch of fruit for too long to get it to reach setting point can break down the fruit to the point of losing valuable flavour.

* The faster the jam is cooked, the more it will retain its colour and flavour.

* It is important to remove any scum that develops as the fruit and sugar mixture comes to the boil and before packing as it tends to

solidify, is unsightly and may cause fermentation of the jam.

* Always use a premium fruit when making jam.

* Try adding 2 pieces of lemon or orange zest to the jam for added flavour. Be sure to wash the zest and remove any pith (white flesh) before adding at the beginning of cooking; then remove when removing the seeds.

* Warming the sugar before adding to the fruit is said to aid in maintaining clarity in the jam as the warm sugar dissolves faster, allowing the jam to reach setting point sooner. The sugar added to a cake tin or tray should be no deeper than 3 cm nor should it be spread too thinly, which allows the sugar to start to melt. This heating process should take about 10 minutes, about the same amount of time it takes to slowly bring the strawberries and lemon juice to the boil.

* Other berries adapt very well to this recipe—try blackberries, raspberries or mulberries. Try making a mixed berry jam using the best quality fruit in season.

* This jam is ideal with homemade **scones** and **whipped cream**.

----
xxxxxxxxxxxxx 14. Drinks xxxxxxxxxxxxx

BANANA SMOOTHIE

Serves 1

xxxxxxxxxxxxxxxxxxxxxxxxxxxxxxxxxxxxxxxxxxxxxxxxxxxxxxxxxxxxxxxxxxxxxxxxxxxxxxxxxxxx

6 ice cubes
1 ripe banana, chopped
250 ml full cream or skim
   milk or soy milk
1 tablespoon honey
ground cinnamon or nutmeg
   (optional)

Method:

1. Place the ice in a blender and blitz to break up.

2. Add the banana, milk and honey and blend until smooth and thick.

3. Serve immediately. Sprinkle with a bit of ground cinnamon or nutmeg, if desired, before serving.

HINTS AND TIPS:

----

* You will need—cutting board, cook's knife, liquid and spoon measures and blender.

* Bananas need to be very ripe for a great smoothie. Look for bananas that have brown spots—called 'sugar spots'—all over the skin as this is a classic sign that the starch in the bananas has turned to sugar.

* Freezing leftover bananas is a great idea. Bananas should be frozen when it is apparent that they will turn black and mushy before they are consumed. Peel and chop the bananas into 4 pieces and place in a plastic bag or airtight container before freezing. Peel bananas before freezing so the skin doesn't freeze to the flesh. Cutting into 4 pieces means the banana is ready to go straight into the blender. As well, knowing that 4 pieces = 1 banana is handy if using frozen bananas in other recipes, such as **banana cake** which may call for 3 bananas (12 pieces).

* Smoothies are a great, high protein way to start the day.

* For a **super-thick smoothie**—replace the ice cubes with a scoop of ice-cream, and replace the milk with 1 cup natural or vanilla yoghurt.

* For a **berry smoothie**—replace the banana with 1 cup of mixed berries or very ripe strawberries.

* For a **healthy breakfast smoothie**—try 1 cup fresh or toasted muesli blitzed with the ice, ½ banana, ½ cup strawberries, 1 cup natural yoghurt (or milk) and 1 tablespoon honey.

* Try adding 2 tablespoons peanut butter and 2 tablespoons wheatgerm to the mixture. Or nut meals can be added (2 tablespoons) to the above recipe to add protein.

* To 'power-up' your smoothie—replace the honey with molasses and add 1 teaspoon brewer's yeast. Both molasses and brewer's yeast are available at health food shops.

* To 'iron-boost' your smoothie—add 1 teaspoon magnesium supplement powder, available at health food shops.

EGGNOG

Makes about 8 cups

XXXXXXXXXXXXXXXXXXXXXXXXXXXXXXXXXXXXXXXXXXXXXXXXXXXXXXXXXXXXXXXXXXXXXXXXXXXXXXXXXXXXXXX

6 eggs, separated
180 g caster sugar
125 ml white rum
375 ml brandy or cognac
500 ml milk
500 ml thickened cream
freshly grated nutmeg

Method:

1. Place the egg yolks and half the sugar in a bowl and whisk until light and fluffy.

2. Stir in the rum and brandy or cognac and add the milk. Place in the refrigerator.

3. Whip the cream until soft peaks form (semi-whipped). Fold the cream into the egg mixture and place back in the fridge.

4. Whisk the egg whites and half the remaining sugar with an electric mixer until stiff peaks form. Fold into the eggnog and refrigerate until serving. Sprinkle with the nutmeg.

HINTS AND TIPS:

* You will need—3 bowls, liquid and weight measures, and electric mixer.

* Eggnog has a long history and many tales about how it became known as 'eggnog' and what should and shouldn't go into it. This book is not the vehicle to thrash out a debate over such matters but rather its aim is to provide one of the many versions of this festive heart warmer/stopper.

* The first controversy is the raw egg element in the recipe. Research shows that it is approximately 1 in 20 000 eggs that is said to carry potentially harmful bacteria. But for those concerned with statistics, then there is an alternative. Try cooking the eggs. This would mean NOT separating the yolks from the whites. Combine the sugar and eggs in a heatproof bowl, then add the rum. Place the bowl over a saucepan of simmering water (a double boiler) and whisk furiously and continuously until the egg mixture triples in volume, is thick and velvety—and any bacteria are dead. Add the brandy or cognac and milk and refrigerate until chilled. Whip the cream as directed and fold into the cooked 'nog'.

* For kiddies who want to be a part of the festivities, try the following. Use the cooked egg method in the previous tip and beat the eggs, sugar, 250 ml grape juice and 1 tablespoon vanilla extract over the double boiler until light and fluffy. Add the milk and chill. Fold in the whipped cream and serve. Apple juice or orange juice also work well.

HOT CHOCOLATE

Serves 2

XXXXXXXXXXXXXXXXXXXXXXXXXXXXXXXXXXXXXXXXXXXXXXXXXXXXXXXXXXXXXXXXXXXXXXXXXXXXXXXXX

600 ml milk
150 g quality dark
   chocolate, chopped
2 tablespoons caster sugar

Method:

1. Bring the milk to the boil. Remove from the heat, add the chocolate and sugar and stir until the chocolate has completely dissolved.

2. Serve immediately (see Hints and Tips for serving suggestions).

HINTS AND TIPS:

----

* You will need—saucepan, liquid, weight and spoon measures and small wooden spoon or whisk.

* A great hot chocolate is made using chocolate not cocoa powder.

* The chocolate is added to the milk away from the heat because the residual heat of the milk is more than enough to melt the chocolate and dissolve the sugar. It also cools the milk to avoid scalding your tongue.

* The obvious choice to finish off a hot chocolate is to add a couple of marshmallows to the mug. Or try simply dusting the top with powdered drinking chocolate (cocoa powder with added sugar).

* Try frothing the hot chocolate. For this you will need a hand-held blender or a benchtop blender. Pour half the hot chocolate into the mugs then blend the remaining half to create a fine froth, pour and spoon the froth into the mugs and serve immediately.

* For a naughty night cap, add 1 nip (30 ml) of your favourite bedtime drink. Cognac, brandy or whisky are very conservative, for a bit more fun try Bailey's Irish Cream, Kahlua or Crème de Cacao.

* A decadent twist for the kids could mean replacing the caster sugar with dark brown sugar and adding 1 teaspoon vanilla extract— an extra marshmallow wouldn't go astray either.

* If all that is in the pantry is cocoa powder, then try this—combine 1 cup water with 75 g cocoa powder in a saucepan, bring to the boil then add 500 ml milk and 2 tablespoons soft brown sugar. Bring back to the boil, remove from the heat and cool slightly. Serves 2.

* For a truly rich encounter, replace half the milk with pouring cream.

* For an easy dinner party idea, make the hot chocolate in advance. When ready to serve, reheat the hot chocolate, place a scoop of chocolate ice-cream into a coffee glass and top with hot chocolate.

LEMON AND GINGER TEA

Serves 2

xxxxxxxxxxxxxxxxxxxxxxxxxxxxxxxxxxxxxxxxxxxxxxxxxxxxxxxxxxxxxxxxxxxxxxxxxxxxxxxxxxxxxxx

500 ml cold filtered water
½ lemon
5-cm knob of ginger,
    washed and sliced

Method:

1. Bring the cold water to the boil.

2. Squeeze the lemon into a teapot, chop the squeezed lemon into pieces and add to the pot with the ginger.

3. Pour in the boiled water then let rest for 5 minutes before serving.

HINTS AND TIPS:

* You will need—cutting board, cook's knife, liquid measure and teapot.

* If making a large pot of tea, invest in a teapot that has an infuser or use a coffee plunger. The ginger will not need to be removed but the flavour will intensify if left to rest for a long period of time.

* Honey can be added for sweetness.

* Only use fresh ginger for this; powdered or bottled ginger will not work at all.

* Try this tea when you have a cold and you need to soothe a sore throat.

* To make a stronger concoction for a sore throat use: 1 nip scotch, 1 teaspoon honey and 1 whole clove, allowing the ginger and clove to infuse for an extra 2 minutes.

* Try adding 1 native lemon myrtle leaf per person.

* Ginger aids digestion, stimulates the circulatory system, and can prevent nausea and travel sickness.

* Lemon is an antiseptic, aids digestion and stimulates the immune system which is why this tea is great when suffering from a cold.

LEMONADE

Serves 6

xxxxxxxxxxxxxxxxxxxxxxxxxxxxxxxxxxxxxxxxxxxxxxxxxxxxxxxxxxxxxxxxxxxxxxxxxxxxxxxxxxxxxxxxxxxxxx

225 g white sugar

250 ml water

250 ml lemon juice (about
   4–5 lemons)

1 litre still or sparkling
   mineral water

2 cups ice

1 lemon, sliced

Method:

1. Place the sugar and water in a saucepan and bring to the boil. Reduce the heat and simmer for 5 minutes or until the sugar dissolves.

2. Remove from the heat and cool slightly, then add the lemon juice.

3. Set the base lemon syrup aside to cool, add the mineral water, ice and slices of lemon and serve in a jug.

HINTS AND TIPS:

★ You will need—weight and liquid measures, saucepan, wooden spoon, cutting board, cook's knife, juicer and 2-litre jug.

★ It is not necessary to strain the lemon juice before adding. Any pulp that goes into the lemonade adds a certain homemade feel to the drink. Just be careful not to let the seeds go in.

★ The lemon syrup can be made and stored separately. This lemon concentrate is ideal not just for lemonade but for adult drinks as well. Over ice, add a nip (30 ml) of vodka, tequila or gin, and 2 nips of lemon syrup then top up with sparkling mineral water or tonic water.

★ Oranges can replace the lemons to produce a much sweeter drink. Add to the orange syrup, 1 tablespoon orange blossom water, found in Middle Eastern grocers and health food shops.

★ When limes are abundant, make the syrup with lime juice. You may need to increase the sugar content by as much as 100 g to counter their extra astringency.

★ Once the lemonade is made, try adding 3 sprigs of mint. Bruise the mint with your fingertips before plunging into the jug of iced lemonade.

★ Not all lemons are the same. The three main varietals are the Eureka, Lisbon and Meyer. The Meyer is the most prized with its thin skin and sweeter flavour.

★ Make double the recipe and freeze some of the lemonade as ice cubes, then add these lemonade cubes to the drink to prevent the lemonade from diluting.

PUNCH

Serves 10

xxxxxxxxxxxxxxxxxxxxxxxxxxxxxxxxxxxxxxxxxxxxxxxxxxxxxxxxxxxxxxxxxxxxxxxxxxxxxxxxxxxxxx

1 kg ice
500 ml orange juice
500 ml pineapple juice
250 ml peach or apricot
   nectar
100 ml lemon juice (about
   2 lemons)
500 ml dry ginger ale
500 ml sparkling mineral
   water
400 g can crushed
   pineapple
1 small can passionfruit
   pulp
½ bunch mint, leaves
   washed and chopped

Method:

1. Place the ice in a large punch bowl (at least 5-litre capacity).

2. Pour all the ingredients over the ice and stir with a ladle until well mixed.

HINTS AND TIPS:

* You will need—cutting board, cook's knife, liquid measure, ladle and punch bowl.

* Punch, as in fruit punch, can be any combination of drinks, usually non-alcoholic, mixed with fruit juices and poured over ice.

* Fruit pieces add to the texture of the drink and mint adds fresh flavour and perfume.

* For an adult version, try adding 750 ml vodka or dark rum. Gin, Cointreau, Frangelico, white rum, Limoncello or Schnapps are also popular.

* Strangely, fruit punch appears to be out of fashion or is it that punch bowls are too daggy? Whatever the reason, punch is a brilliant kids' party drink that must surely beat a boring bottle of fizzy drink sitting on a table.

* The ultra healthy version of punch consists of homemade fruit juices and your own mixture of crushed or finely chopped fresh tropical fruits.

----
xxxxxxxxxx **15. Basic Recipes** xxxxxxxxxx

APPLE, PRUNE AND SPICE STUFFING

Makes about 4 cups

xxxxxxxxxxxxxxxxxxxxxxxxxxxxxxxxxxxxxxxxxxxxxxxxxxxxxxxxxxxxxxxxxxxxxxxxxxxxxxxxxxxxxxxx

50 g butter
1 small onion, finely diced
2 bacon rashers, chopped
100 g dried apple rings, chopped
100 ml Calvados (apple brandy)
250 g fresh bread crumbs
150 g pork mince
2 eggs
1 Granny Smith apple, grated with skin on
1 cup pitted torn prunes
1½ teaspoons mixed spice
100 g pine nuts
salt and pepper

Method:

1. Melt the butter in a pan, add the onion and bacon and cook until softened with little colour. Set aside to cool.

2. Soak the dried apple in the Calvados for 20 minutes.

3. Mix the bread crumbs, mince, eggs, chopped dried apple, grated apple, prunes, mixed spice, nuts and seasoning in a bowl. Add the cooled onion and bacon and mix until thoroughly combined.

HINTS AND TIPS:

* You will need—cutting board, cook's kife, sauté pan, wooden spoon and cup, spoon, weight and liquid measures.

* Use this stuffing inside a whole turkey, or press between the skin and breast meat on a turkey buffet. This requires the cook to use the fingers, to separate the skin without tearing from the meat. Do not force all the stuffing in as it will expand as it cooks.

* The pork mince in this recipe adds body and moisture to the stuffing but can be replaced with 150 g fresh bread crumbs if preferred. The eggs can also be replaced with 100 g melted butter or extra virgin olive oil.

* **Chestnut and wild mushroom stuffing**—this is a combination of fresh or tinned chopped chestnuts mixed with dried and reconstituted wild mushrooms imported from Europe and available at specialist delis and European-style produce stores. Use the basic recipe but replace the apples, prunes, pine nuts and spice with 200 g chestnuts and 100 g wild mushrooms (known as 'forestiere' mixture), soaked in hot water for 20 minutes. It is important to remember when straining the mushrooms after soaking, that sand will have collected at the bottom of the dish, so be careful not to strain that back into the mushrooms.

* **Onion and sage stuffing**— use the basic recipe, but replace the apples, prunes and spice with another small onion (finely chopped) and ¼ cup finely shredded fresh sage leaves.

* The stuffing could also be rolled into balls and cooked alongside the turkey roast, just add when there is 45 minutes of roasting time to go.

BEER BATTER

Makes about 2½ cups

XXXXXXXXXXXXXXXXXXXXXXXXXXXXXXXXXXXXXXXXXXXXXXXXXXXXXXXXXXXXXXXXXXXXXXXXXXXXXXXXXXXXXXXXXX

150 g rice flour
20 g cornflour
375 ml cold beer
½ teaspoon ground black pepper
¼ teaspoon paprika

Method:

Place all of the ingredients in a bowl and mix with a
wooden spoon. Stir until just combined. The mixture
will resemble lumpy, runny cream. Do not strain,
amazingly the lumps disappear when the batter is
fried. Use this batter immediately; the longer it
sits, the more the air bubbles from the beer break
down so the batter won't be as light and crispy.

HINTS AND TIPS:

* You will need—bowl, wooden spoon and weight, liquid and spoon measures.

* There are many variations to this batter, but whichever recipe you use, it is still important to not beat or whisk the mixture as this works the flour (especially if using plain flour) too much, making a smooth but tighter and tougher batter. The less it is mixed, the lumpier and rougher looking it is, but it's also lighter and crispier.

* Plain flour can be substituted for rice flour in this batter. However, wheat flours (plain or self-raising) contain gluten which when fried tend to absorb fat and moisture far more than non-gluten flours like rice or cornmeal.

* For non-beer drinkers, replace beer with soda water or sparkling mineral water—as long as it is ice cold. A very cold liquid means a very cold batter which helps keep it thick without adding extra flour. Adding extra flour causes the cooked batter to be to bread-like and chewy.

* If the batter is too thick (too much flour), the batter after frying will be crisp on the outside and wet and doughy on the inside.

* If the batter is too thin, there is the risk of it breaking apart when it hits the oil.

* If the oil is not hot enough, the batter will soak up the oil making greasy beer-battered food.

* If the oil is too hot, the batter will crisp and cook before the food on the inside. The oil temperature for frying batter should be between 170°C and 180°C—certainly no higher than 180°C.

* The addition of ¼ teaspoon bicarbonate of soda is optional but can produce extra bubbles in the batter to make it lighter.

* One egg white, whisked to soft peaks and folded into the batter, is another way to lighten the batter.

* For hits of flavour, try adding 1 teaspoon dill seeds or fennel seeds to the batter before frying. Cumin seeds or caraway seeds also provide an interesting character to the batter.

* It is necessary to coat the food in flour before dipping in the batter. The flour provides a rough-textured surface for the wet batter to stick to; without it, the batter will mostly break away from the food being fried.

* For a **fruit-friendly beer batter**, try substituting regular bitter ale for a dessert beer or fruit beer, then whip 4 egg whites until soft peaks form and fold into the batter. Thread a strawberry or cut pieces of fruit onto a wooden skewer, dip into the batter and place into a pot of hot oil on the stovetop. Because the batter is so light, the fruit 'fritters' tend to be quite buoyant and you will need to roll the fritter around using the skewer sticking out of the pot. When golden, remove to a plate and dust with icing sugar. Serve with a fruit sauce, like **raspberry**, or **chocolate sauce**.

BLINI

Makes about 20 small or 8 large

xxxxxxxxxxxxxxxxxxxxxxxxxxxxxxxxxxxxxxxxxxxxxxxxxxxxxxxxxxxxxxxxxxxxxxxxxxxxxxxxxxxxxxxxx

375 ml milk
125 g unsalted butter
7 g sachet or 2½ teaspoons dry yeast
100 g buckwheat flour
50 g plain flour
2 tablespoons white sugar
¾ teaspoon salt
2 large eggs, separated
125 g butter, for frying

Method:

1. Combine the milk and butter in a microwave-safe
bowl; microwave on high in 1-minute increments until
the butter is melted, stirring between each minute.
Cool slightly so the temperature is about 37°C.
Sprinkle the yeast over the top and stand for about
5 minutes to dissolve the yeast.

2. Combine the flours, sugar and salt in a separate
mixing bowl. Pour the milk mixture over the dry
ingredients, add the egg yolks and mix until just
combined. Cover the bowl tightly with plastic wrap and
sit in a warm place for 1 hour or until the mixture is
bubbly and has expanded by one-third. (At this point,
the batter can be refrigerated overnight and the
recipe completed the following day. Allow the batter
to come back to room temperature before continuing.)

3. Whisk the egg whites until soft peaks form and fold
into the batter.

4. Heat a nonstick sauté or frying pan over medium-
high heat. Melt 1 tablespoon of the remaining butter
in the pan; drop small spoonfuls of batter into the
pan to form small pancakes. Cook until the edges look
a bit dry and small bubbles form on the surface. Flip
to cook the other side. Remove from the pan when the
second side is browned. Move the cooked blini to a
wire rack to cool. Repeat with the remaining batter.

Method cont.

5. Once cool, either use immediately or store in an airtight container in the fridge until needed. Blini freeze very well and will last for up to 3 months sealed in a bag or plastic container. Simply defrost overnight in the fridge before using.

HINTS AND TIPS:

----

* You will need—liquid, weight and spoon measures, 1 small and 1 larger bowl, whisk, wooden spoon, frying or sauté pan and cooling rack.

* Blini are traditional Russian pancakes that are usually served with sour cream and caviar. Blini is plural for the word 'blin' referring to a small pancake.

* Heating the milk and melting the butter can be done just as successfully in a saucepan on the stovetop. As long as the yeast is added at about body temperature, which is vital to activate the yeast.

* Although traditionally made with just buckwheat flour, the addition of a small amount of plain flour, which is common in Western cooking, lightens the mixture.

* Making blini without yeast could be seen as a travesty; however, for cooks who are unsure of the workings of yeast or are simply in a hurry and can't wait for the yeast reaction, simply skip this part of the method and continue with the recipe.

* Try adding ½ cup creamed corn and ¼ cup crab meat to the batter before folding in the egg whites, then top these blini with **guacamole.**

* The size of the blini depends entirely on their use. If serving as cocktail food, then 3–5 cm diameter is ideal. For an entrée, the traditional size of 10 cm diameter is needed—blini are never any bigger than this.

* Cooking blini in a nonstick pan with spray oil is perfect if cutting back on fats.

* Another traditional topping for blini is the very common, smoked salmon with crème fraîche and dill. Try topping with a small amount of your favourite dip and some fresh herbs. Other suggestions are cottage cheese and smoked trout or whipped Persian fetta with sundried tomatoes or taramasalata and fresh cucumber.

CHICKEN STOCK

Makes 2–3 litres

xxxxxxxxxxxxxxxxxxxxxxxxxxxxxxxxxxxxxxxxxxxxxxxxxxxxxxxxxxxxxxxxxxxxxxxxxxxxxxxxxxxxxxxxxxxxxxxxx

2 kg chicken necks or bones, rinsed in cold water
2 onions, skin on and quartered
2 carrots, washed and roughly chopped
2 celery sticks, roughly chopped
1 **bouquet garni**
water

Method:

1. Combine all the ingredients in a large pot and add enough cold water to cover the chicken bones by 5 cm.

2. Bring slowly to the boil, then immediately reduce the heat to bring the stock to a rolling simmer. Simmer for 2 hours, topping up with cold water if it reduces to the level of the bones. Have a ladle handy to remove any scum that floats to the surface—this is important (see Hints and Tips).

3. After 2 hours, remove stock from the heat and stand for 30 minutes before straining through a fine sieve or colander lined with muslin cloth. Allow to cool on the bench before placing in the fridge or freezing.

HINTS AND TIPS:

* You will need— cutting board, cook's knife, large stock or soup pot and fine sieve or colander and muslin cloth or cheesecloth.

* It is important to rinse the bones before cooking to remove excess blood and fat, the impurities that would otherwise turn the stock cloudy. A good stock, if done properly and not rushed, will always be clear.

* One option is to place the bones only in the pot, add water to cover, bring to the boil, drain and rinse under cold water. This 'blanching' of the bones ensures that most of the impurities are removed. It is argued that this initial cooking extracts flavour, but this is not the case—the reason stock is cooked for as long as instructed is because it takes that long to permeate the bones for maximum flavour.

* It will always be insisted upon to begin any stock with cold water. This is because cold water, even ice cold water will set the otherwise soluble and loose proteins in and around the bones. If hot water is used to begin the stock, the proteins begin to dissolve into smaller particles and as such, a cloudy, grey liquid will then turn into a dull and murky finished stock. The flavour would also be impeded, tasting a bit like soapy dishwater.

* The skin on the onions is not to be removed. The pigmentation of the skin can lend a very slight straw colouring to the stock.

* If a brown chicken stock is asked for, then place the raw bones on a roasting tray—lined with baking paper to save on washing the tray—then place in a very hot oven to brown. This, in effect, is like blanching the bones before making a stock, in that it cooks most of the proteins through, leaving very little to cloud the stock. The resulting stock should take on a good caramel colour.

* Vegetables in a meat stock play a very small role, so much so, that they can be entirely unnecessary if all that is needed is a pure meat flavour. Vegetables and spices lend only a slightly sweet flavour and aroma to a stock. The Chinese, for example, do not like adding vegetables to their 'master' stocks as they believe that vegetables absorb valuable meat flavours, especially when you consider that a meat stock can simmer for as long as 12 hours compared to a **vegetable stock** which takes only 45 minutes to cook.

* A meat stock will last 4–5 days in the fridge. If unsure how long the stock was in the fridge, say 6–7 days, it may still be okay. Stock should always be boiled before use and a tell-tale sign of a stock that is way passed due date is when it has a life of its own and begins to bubble in the fridge. A stock that may have only just gone off will have a very slight sour taste to it.

* It is recommended that any leftover stock be frozen for another day. Frozen stock will last 3–4 months but is best used within a month as the water crystals begin to 'take over' the 'flavour' crystals. Freezing in 1-cup volumes is recommended as is freezing in ice cube trays and then transferring to plastic bags.

CLARIFIED BUTTER

Makes approximately 375 g

XXXXXXXXXXXXXXXXXXXXXXXXXXXXXXXXXXXXXXXXXXXXXXXXXXXXXXXXXXXXXXXXXXXXXXXXXXXXXXXXXXXXXXXXXXXXXXX

500 g unsalted butter

Method:

1. Chop the butter into cubes and place in a saucepan. Bring gently to the boil and reduce the heat to low.

2. As the butter cooks, three layers will form. A white scum collects on the surface; this is the whey and needs to cook until the water evaporates from it, leaving a skin that can be easily removed with a spoon. (Often cooks will stand constantly over the pot removing the white foam wondering if it will ever stop forming, it is best just to let it evaporate.) The bottom layer is the casein and the middle layer is the butterfat, a clear, golden liquid used in cooking.

3. Once the skin has been removed, stand for 5 minutes to cool slightly, then pour the fat away from the casein into a clean container. The clarified butter can be stored, sealed, at room temperature, but is best kept refrigerated.

HINTS AND TIPS:

* You will need—cutting board, cook's knife, saucepan, spoon and container for storage.

* Clarified butter has had water, milk solids and any salts (if using salted butter) removed.

* Clarified butter is popular in cooking because it is a pure fat that cooks at higher temperatures compared to butter, which browns quickly because of the milk solids.

* Take into account that approximately 25 per cent of the original weight will be lost to skimming and straining. So for every 500 g of butter clarified, about 125 g is wastage, leaving roughly 375 g clear butter fat.

* Another name for clarified butter is 'drawn' butter, more common in North American cookbooks.

* One of the best known uses for clarified butter is for **hollandaise sauce**. It is also favoured in genoise cakes and madeleines where butter is melted not creamed.

* Clarified butter stores better than regular butter, up to 6 months, refrigerated. This is because the milk solids are a protein, and like all proteins, their shelf life is limited, so when the proteins begin to break down, the butter fat is affected and turns rancid.

* Ghee, the purest form of clarified butter (all water has been removed), is used heavily in Indian cooking. It is found in all supermarkets, and Indian and Middle Eastern food stores. Ghee has a nuttier flavour than the French style of clarified butter as it is cooked for slightly longer. This process cooks the casein residue that sinks to the base of the pot, browning the casein and in turn providing the distinct flavour. This is, of course, the easy answer to having clarified butter for cooking. Note, however, it is more expensive than butter because of the extra process and packaging it must go through.

* For people who are lactose-intolerant, ghee (more so than homemade clarified butter) is digestible as the protein has been cooked out, leaving a lactose-free cooking fat similar to a vegetable or nut oil. Still, it is best to see your physician before ingesting this product.

* Clarified butter and ghee can be used wherever oils are called for. In pastries, this style of butter is still semi-soft and creamy at room temperature, and aids in a flaky pastry.

CLUB SANDWICH

Makes 4

XXXXXXXXXXXXXXXXXXXXXXXXXXXXXXXXXXXXXXXXXXXXXXXXXXXXXXXXXXXXXXXXXXXXXXXXXXXXXXXXXXXXXXXXXXXXX

12 slices of bread
¾ cup mayonnaise
1 cos lettuce, leaves washed and dried
4 tomatoes, each cut into 4 thick slices
salt and pepper
500 g cooked turkey breast, sliced
16 streaky bacon rashers, crispy fried

Method:

1. For the first layer, toast 4 slices of the bread and place on the bench.

2. Begin toasting the next 4 slices of the bread.

3. Spread the first 4 slices with a quarter of the mayonnaise and top each with lettuce leaves and 4 thick slices of tomato. Season with salt and pepper. This first layer is always meat free.

4. Spread another quarter of the mayonnaise on the second batch of toast. Toast the last 4 slices of bread. Place the second batch of toast on the first layer, mayonnaise side facing the tomato. Spread another quarter of the mayonnaise on the exposed toast and top with a layer of lettuce, sliced turkey and bacon. Spread the remaining mayonnaise on the final batch of toast and place, mayonnaise side down on top of each sandwich. Pin the sandwiches together using the toothpicks, arranging in such a way that allows each sandwich to be cut into 4 diamond shapes. Without the toothpicks, the sandwiches may fall apart when served.

HINTS AND TIPS:

* You will need—cutting board, cook's knife, frying pan, tongs, cup measure, toaster and 16 toothpicks.

* Also know as a 'clubhouse sandwich', it is thought to have originated at the Saratoga Clubhouse, Saratoga, New York, in 1894.

* This is the perfect way to use up leftover ham and turkey from Christmas, using sliced ham instead of the bacon, making for a very easy Boxing Day lunch idea.

* As this is such a large sandwich, one whole sandwich per person may be too much. Serve on a platter as a shared meal idea, allowing half a sandwich per person.

* Chicken breast or roast beef can easily replace the turkey breast as is often the case when served in restaurants.

* Marinated chicken thigh meat, grilled on the barbecue, is a great alternative and a cheaper option than breast meat. (Marinating is optional.)

* Iceberg lettuce, rocket or mixed lettuce leaves can replace the cos lettuce.

* It is not recommended to make these sandwiches too far in advance, as the ingredients soften the toast and the desired effect is lost.

* Vary the flavour of the mayonnaise by adding ½ teaspoon sliced bird's eye chilli or 2 tablespoons **pesto** or 1 teaspoon wholegrain mustard.

* The type of bread used is simply a matter of taste. Traditionally made with basic squares of white bread, the use of grain breads, sourdough and crusty Vienna is fine.

* Adding other ingredients like avocado, cheese and cucumber, although fine, tends to add too many layers and extra thickness, and makes it even more difficult to wrap your mouth around the sandwich. It then isn't a club sandwich but just a very BIG and ominous double-decker sandwich.

CRÈME FRAÎCHE

Makes 2 cups

XXXXXXXXXXXXXXXXXXXXXXXXXXXXXXXXXXXXXXXXXXXXXXXXXXXXXXXXXXXXXXXXXXXXXXXXXXXXXXXXXXXX

300 ml thickened cream
   (minimum 35 per cent
   fat)
3 tablespoons buttermilk

Method:

1. Pour the cream into a saucepan and gently heat to body temperature (37°C) or slightly warmer—do not boil.

2. Remove from the heat and stir in the buttermilk, then transfer to a clean bowl and cover with plastic wrap.

3. Leave on the bench for 12–24 hours. Stir once, cover again and refrigerate for 8 hours before using. Crème fraîche will last in the fridge for 7–10 days and can be frozen in small amounts for up to 3 months.

HINTS AND TIPS:

* You will need—saucepan, bowl, spoon, and liquid and spoon measures.

* Crème fraîche is pronounced krem fresh.

* The number-one concern for cooks when deciding to make their own crème fraîche is hygiene. How can a cream product survive at room temperature (preferably a very warm area that can maintain approximately 40°C) for so long without spoiling? This is due to the benign bacteria in the buttermilk which grow and protect the cream from any harmful bacteria forming.

* Crème fraîche is used in recipes because it adds a distinct flavour and it

doesn't split when cooked. This is because it is high in fat and low in protein.

* Crème fraîche thickens after it is chilled, so do not panic if it appears slightly runny before it enters the fridge.

* Do not substitute crème fraîche with sour cream if the dish is to be cooked over high heat as sour cream has a much lower fat content and will curdle in the heating process.

* For cold or gently heated sauces, crème fraîche can be substituted in equal measure with sour cream or yoghurt or with equal parts thickened cream and sour cream.

* To make a **herbed crème fraîche**—mix into the basic recipe 1 tablespoon chopped fresh herbs; either a mixture of parsley, chervil, chives and basil, or a single herb flavour including any of the aforementioned or try oregano, sage, tarragon or mint.

CROUTONS

Makes 2 cups

xxxxxxxxxxxxxxxxxxxxxxxxxxxxxxxxxxxxxxxxxxxxxxxxxxxxxxxxxxxxxxxxxxxxxxxxxxxxxxxxxxxxxxx

2 cups stale crustless
   bread cut into 1-cm
   dice
½ cup melted butter,
   clarified butter, ghee
   or olive oil

Method:

1. Preheat the oven to 180°C. Line a baking tray with baking paper.

2. Place the bread in a bowl and pour the butter or oil around the edge of the bowl, then using a spoon or your hands, quickly toss the croutons so as to evenly distribute the butter or oil.

3. Spread evenly and in a single layer on the prepared baking tray, and bake for 20 minutes or until golden and crunchy.

4. Remove from the oven and cool. Store the croutons in an airtight container in the fridge for up to 1 month or even longer if made with olive oil.

HINTS AND TIPS:

* You will need—cutting board, cook's knife, saucepan, bowl, spoon, cup measure, baking tray, baking paper and airtight storage container.

* The main role of a crouton is to soak up the liquid to which the crouton has been added, whether that be salad dressing, soup, meat juices or even sauces.

* The most basic crouton recipe of all is to simply oven-dry bread cut in any fashion, with no butters or oil and no seasoning or flavours added. Once this

style of crouton is made, it is ideal to blitz in a food processor to make bread crumbs.

* For great flavour—add 1 tablespoon chopped fresh herbs or ½ tablespoon dried mixed herbs to the butter or oil before tossing with the croutons.

* Two chopped garlic cloves can be added to the butter as it melts to infuse the flavour and produce a tasty garlic crouton. Garlic and herbs can be mixed together too.

* Cutting croutons into dice is only one method. Another popular method is to use a French stick, slice

into rounds or on an angle approximately ½ cm thick, then brush with melted butter or oil and dry in the oven.

* See **French onion soup** for another recipe for cheese croutons which can be used in a salad or simply as a snack for hungry kids after school.

* For large croutons served in a salad, use a sourdough loaf or French stick sliced into rounds 1-cm thick and brushed with garlic oil (see **roasted garlic**) then dried in the oven for 30 minutes at 100°C.

CURRY POWDER

Makes about 2½ cups

XXXXXXXXXXXXXXXXXXXXXXXXXXXXXXXXXXXXXXXXXXXXXXXXXXXXXXXXXXXXXXXXXXXXXXXXXXXXXXXXXXXXXXXXXXXXXX

1 cup coriander seeds
½ cup cumin seeds
1 tablespoon fennel seeds
1 tablespoon fenugreek seeds
1 cinnamon stick, broken into small pieces
1 teaspoon whole cloves
1 teaspoon cardamom seeds
2 tablespoons ground turmeric
2 teaspoons chilli powder
2 tablespoons rice flour

Method:

1. It is important to toast the whole seeds to enhance their flavour and to make grinding them much easier. To dry fry the coriander seeds, place them in a frying pan and cook over medium heat, shaking the pan often to evenly toast, until the seeds begin to smoke. Remove from the heat and place on a tray to cool. Repeat this process by separately frying the cumin seeds, fennel, cinnamon, cloves and cardamom, placing each onto the tray to cool. It is fine to mix all the toasted seeds together when cooling.

2. Once cool, begin the process of grinding the spices to a powder. Sift the spice mixture through a coarse strainer to remove any husks and larger pieces of spice (you may prefer to skip this step to keep the spice mixture rustic).

3. Place the toasted and ground spices in a bowl and mix in the turmeric, chilli powder and rice flour. Transfer to an airtight container and store in a dry, dark place, away from sunlight. This curry powder, like all dry spice mixes, will begin to lose pungency and flavour from the moment it is stored and so it is recommended to use within 3 months for best results.

HINTS AND TIPS:

* You will need—sauté or frying pan, baking tray, bowl, spoon, cup and spoon measures, mortar and pestle and container for storing.

* It is important to remember that there is no such thing as a curry powder in India. Curry powders, as we know them, were invented in the West. The closest thing India has to a curry powder is what's called a 'masala', which can be a varied mixture of spices, herbs and seasonings and in any combination. So really this is a recipe for a masala rather than a curry powder. Curry pastes form the base for many of the curries produced in India, as well as other Asian countries like Thailand and Malaysia.

* It is important to toast the different seeds separately as they are all different shapes, sizes and weights and therefore cook differently, some toasting faster and more evenly than others. To rush this process could mean burning some of the spices, making the powder slightly acrid (bitter taste and smell).

* Making curry powder from scratch—although laborious—produces a much more pungent and lively tasting curry compared to the pre-made, store-bought versions.

* If serious about making spice mixes, then investing in a spice grinder or coffee grinder is money well spent. Working from a mortar and pestle, albeit romantic, is also very hard work when making volumes of spice mixes.

* The degree of heat in a curry powder is simply determined by the amount of chilli powder in the recipe. This is a medium-hot mix to the average palate, and so adding another teaspoon of chilli powder will take it up a notch, whereas removing the chilli powder altogether will make it mild and child-friendly.

* Variations to this spice mix are many and it is encouraged that the cook omit 1 or 2 spices in favour of others. Only through experimenting will a suitable 'masala' be achieved.

DASHI STOCK

Makes 1 litre

xxxxxxxxxxxxxxxxxxxxxxxxxxxxxxxxxxxxxxxxxxxxxxxxxxxxxxxxxxxxxxxxxxxxxxxxxxxxxxxxxxxxxxxxxxxxxxxxxx

1 small piece (about 30 g)
  kombu (dried kelp)
1 litre water
2 tablespoons dried bonito
  flakes

Method:

1. Wipe the kombu with a damp cloth (do not wash), add to the cold water in a saucepan and bring just to the boil. Remove the kombu and discard.

2. Sprinkle the bonito flakes over the stock and remove from the heat. As soon as the bonito flakes sink to the bottom of the pot, strain the stock and discard the flakes. Cool and refrigerate. This stock keeps for 3–5 days in the fridge.

HINTS AND TIPS:

* You will need—saucepan, sieve, liquid and spoon measures.

* Dashi stock is the base for soups and simmered dishes in Japanese cuisine—most famous of all are **miso soup** and udon soup.

* There are several types of dashi made from kelp (seaweed), bonito flakes (skipjack tuna), dried sardines or dried shiitake mushrooms. They can be made using an individual flavour or a combination of 2 ingredients.

* For vegans and vegetarians, it is best to make either kombu dashi or hoshi-shiitake dashi. For **kombu dashi**—use the basic recipe and simply omit the bonito flakes. For **hoshi-shiitake dashi**—use the basic recipe but replace the kelp and bonito flakes with 4 large or 6 medium dried shiitake mushrooms and allow to soak for 15 minutes once removed from the heat.

* For **niboshi dashi** (sardine stock)—place 15 g small dried sardines (remove the heads) in 4 cups water and soak for 1 hour. Bring to the boil and simmer for 2 minutes. Remove from the heat and strain.

* Dashi is definitely the easiest stock to make; however, if pressed for time, instant dashi stock— a powder that simply needs water added—is available at Japanese grocers and some supermarkets.

* Fish-flavoured dashi stock (bonito or sardines) can be used as a quick fish stock if called for in other recipes.

FISH STOCK

Makes about 1 litre

XXXXXXXXXXXXXXXXXXXXXXXXXXXXXXXXXXXXXXXXXXXXXXXXXXXXXXXXXXXXXXXXXXXXXXXXXXXXXXXXXXXXXXXXXXXX

1 kg fish trimmings, bones
   and head (eyes removed)
2 tablespoons olive oil
½ onion, chopped
1 celery stick, chopped
5 parsley stalks
   (optional)
10 white peppercorns
250 ml white wine
cold water

Method:

1. Rinse the fish trimmings in cold water to remove any impurities and blood.

2. In a pot, heat the oil and fry the onion, celery and parsley stalks (if using) without colouring, about 5–7 minutes.

3. Add the fish trimmings, peppercorns and white wine and enough water to cover the fish. Bring to the boil and reduce heat to a simmer. Skim any grey impurities that may float to the surface. Simmer for 20 minutes.

4. Remove from the heat and pass through a fine sieve or muslin cloth-lined colander. Keep refrigerated for up to 5 days or place in the freezer for 3 months.

HINTS AND TIPS:

★ You will need—cutting board, knife, large pot, spoon, liquid and spoon measures, sieve, colander or muslin cloth. See p. 454.

★ When buying fish trimmings and bones or heads, purchase only white, lean fish like whiting, snapper or blue eye. Do not use oily fish like salmon, trout, marlin or swordfish as the flavour is too strong and they will make the stock cloudy in appearance.

★ Remove the eyes from the head as they can make the stock cloudy in appearance.

★ Fish stock should never boil during its making as fish gelatine breaks down at temperatures below boiling point.

★ Refer to **chicken stock** as to why any stock is started with cold water, not hot.

★ Fish stock is only cooked for 20–30 minutes because the bones are much finer than those of chicken (2–4 hours cooking time) or beef and veal (6–12 hours cooking time). Cooking for longer is said to make the stock turn bitter, which is rarely true and has more to do with the overcooked bones breaking down and causing the stock to turn cloudy and somewhat chalky. Maximum flavour and gelatine extraction occurs within a very short time frame and this is therefore a very easy stock to prepare.

★ Do not panic if any of the ingredients listed in the recipe are not available— except, of course, the fish bones and the water—because a successful fish stock can still be made without one or all of the aromatics (vegetables, pepper, or even wine).

★ Other flavours that can be added to the stock are: lemon zest (2 strips), thyme or lemon thyme (4 sprigs), fennel bulb (1 slice), or garlic (1 clove, sliced).

FONDUE

Serves 4

xxxxxxxxxxxxxxxxxxxxxxxxxxxxxxxxxxxxxxxxxxxxxxxxxxxxxxxxxxxxxxxxxxxxxxxxxxxxxxxxxxxxxxxxxxx

350 g emmental cheese
350 g gruyère cheese
1 tablespoon cornflour
3 tablespoons kirsch
350 ml white wine
juice of ½ lemon
pinch of nutmeg
pinch of ground white pepper

Method:

1. Remove any rind on the cheeses and roughly chop into ½-cm dice.

2. Mix the cornflour and kirsch together to form a paste.

3. Heat three-quarters of the wine in a saucepan until warm but not boiling, then add the lemon juice and the cheese, ½ cup at a time.

4. Stir constantly over medium heat and simmer until the ingredients are melted and smooth. Add the rest of the wine.

5. Stir the cornflour/kirsch paste into the fondue and simmer for a further 2 minutes. Transfer the saucepan carefully onto a fondue burner to keep warm and serve immediately.

6. Serve with bread chunks. Dip the bread into the fondue using a figure 8 motion with your skewer so as to swirl the mixture and keep it smooth. Reduce the intensity of the flame as the fondue is consumed.

HINTS AND TIPS:

* You will need—cutting board, knife, weight, liquid and spoon measures, saucepan and fondue set.

* Fondue originated in Switzerland and has become famous around the world as a novel shared table dinner party dish.

* The idea of fondue is to use 2 or more cheeses heated with white wine and kirsch (a clear cherry brandy), then dip and swirl crusty, slightly stale bread into it.

* It is important to keep your eye on the heat as the fondue risks curdling if boiled even though alcohol is added to try and prevent this from happening.

* For a child-friendly, non-alcoholic version, use apple juice instead of white wine. **Chicken stock** could also replace wine in this recipe with a pleasing result.

* Other cheeses to consider for fondue are raclette, comtè, beaufort, tilsit, appenzeller or even a cheddar. For an Italian twist, use a mixture of 350 g provolone, 200 g mozzarella and 150 g parmesan.

* The fondue is best cooked in a saucepan on the stovetop and then transferred to the pot from the fondue set. Using a ceramic pot to cook and serve the fondue is another good option.

* Adding lemon juice to the fondue is important as the acid helps to break down the protein in the cheese.

* Foods for dipping in fondue vary greatly. Try bagels or foccacia, salami, pepperoni, chorizo or ham, capsicum, artichoke hearts, steamed broccoli or cauliflower, or grilled zucchini or eggplant.

* If doubling the recipe for a larger crowd, the wine should not be doubled, add instead 500 ml to the recipe.

* If the fondue becomes too thick, return to the stovetop over medium heat and add some more wine. If it is too thin, mix another 1 tablespoon wine (or water) with another 1 tablespoon cornflour and mix through.

* Leftover fondue will set in the fridge overnight; it can then be used in omelettes and frittatas or re-melted and used as a cheese sauce on steamed vegetables.

FRITTATA

Serves 4 to 6

xxxxxxxxxxxxxxxxxxxxxxxxxxxxxxxxxxxxxxxxxxxxxxxxxxxxxxxxxxxxxxxxxxxxxxxxxxxxxxxxxxxxxxxxxx

8 large eggs
100 ml water
4 tablespoons grated parmesan cheese
1 tablespoon chopped fresh flat-leaf parsley
salt and pepper
75 g butter

Method:

1. Break the eggs into a bowl and add the water, parmesan, parsley and seasoning.

2. Beat the eggs lightly, just so the ingredients are mixed. If adding leftover vegetables or any meat, stir them into the mixture at this stage (see Hints and Tips).

3. Melt the butter in a deep nonstick frying pan over medium heat.

4. When the butter is bubbling, pour in the egg mixture and reduce the heat to the lowest setting. Cover the pan with a lid and cook until the frittata has set, about 15–20 minutes. Check every 5 minutes and give the pan a shake to ensure it isn't stuck to the bottom or burning.

5. When cooked, remove from the heat, place a large plate over the pan and turn the pan over, holding the plate with the other hand. The frittata should just fall out onto the plate. Leave on the bench to cool before serving. If the frittata has stuck to the bottom of the pan, let it sit for a further 5 minutes and try again. If all else fails, use an egg flip or spatula to remove it from the pan.

HINTS AND TIPS:

* You will need—bowl, cutting board, cook's knife, fork, weight and spoon measures, deep nonstick frying pan and large plate.

* Frittata, an Italian omelette, is a great way to use up leftover meat and vegetables for lunch the next day.

* A good formula for frittata is—for every egg, add a ¼ cup of ingredients, so no matter how big or small the frittata, the egg-to-filling ratio will be consistent.

* Any ingredients added to a frittata must be pre-cooked and cooled completely to avoid making the frittata soggy. Any seafood needs to be seared, chicken must be cooked through and vegetables steamed, boiled or roasted. Any of these ingredients must be cut or torn into small pieces before being stirred into the egg mixture, especially if the frittata is to be cut into small wedges and served as finger food.

* Frittata can also be baked in the oven which can cut the cooking time in half. To do this, preheat the oven to 180°C, make the frittata, but only cook for 1 minute on the stovetop before placing the pan in the oven (make sure the pan handle is ovenproof) for 10–15 minutes.

* Frittata can be served as finger food with drinks or with a leaf salad for lunch, or as part of an antipasto platter with **pickled vegetables**, bean salad, marinated artichoke hearts, stuffed mushrooms and cured meats.

* Leftover frittata can be sliced and used as a sandwich filling—especially good in a French stick with lettuce and mayonnaise.

* This frittata recipe is for a base mixture and should have other ingredients added. Combinations include the following:

* **Pancetta, scallop and sage**—50 g fried pancetta, 6–8 seared scallops, 8 torn sage leaves.

* **Ham and pea**—200 g diced ham and 100 g defrosted frozen peas.

* **Sundried tomato, mushroom and spinach**—100 g sun-dried tomatoes, 150 g sliced and fried mushrooms, 100 g spinach leaves (cooked in 1 teaspoon olive oil then drained and chopped).

* **Potato and rosemary**—300 g potato (roasted or steamed and cut into small pieces), 1 teaspoon finely chopped rosemary.

* **Chorizo, prawn and chilli**—100 g sliced and fried chorizo sausage, 200 g prawns (peeled, cooked and chopped), 1 bird's eye chilli (de-seeded and chopped).

* **Olive, fetta and zucchini**—½ cup pitted black olives, ½ cup fetta cheese, 2 small or 1 large zucchini (cut into cubes and fried in 1 tablespoon olive).

GARLIC BREAD

Serves 8

XXXXXXXXXXXXXXXXXXXXXXXXXXXXXXXXXXXXXXXXXXXXXXXXXXXXXXXXXXXXXXXXXXXXXXXXXXXXXXXXXXXXXXXX

150 g butter, softened
2 tablespoons olive oil
   (optional)
4 garlic cloves, crushed
2 tablespoons chopped
   fresh flat-leaf parsley
   or chives
¼ teaspoon freshly ground
   pepper
2 French bread sticks

Method:

1. Preheat the oven to 180°C.

2. For the garlic butter—combine the butter, olive oil, if using, garlic, parsley and pepper in a bowl and mix with a wooden spoon until well combined.

3. Slice the bread at 2.5-cm intervals, leaving the slices attached to the loaf at the base.

4. Spread the garlic butter on either side of each slice.

5. Wrap the bread sticks in a double layer of foil and heat for 15 minutes in the oven.

6. Remove from the oven, carefully peel back the foil and serve.

HINTS AND TIPS:

* You will need—bowl, wooden spoon, weight and spoon measures, cutting board, cook's knife, bread knife, baking tray, foil and butter knife. A garlic press is optional.

* Use regular salted butter. The olive oil is optional and is added to keep the butter soft.

* The parsley can be replaced with any number of fresh herbs; however, many herbs are strongly flavoured so add only 1 tablespoon oregano, thyme, rosemary, sage or basil. Dried herbs can also be used, again only add 1 tablespoon.

* Try adding 2 tablespoons grated parmesan cheese to the basic recipe for extra flavour.

* Sourdough can be sliced, toasted, cooled and then buttered. Sprinkle with grated parmesan and toast under the grill or heat in a preheated oven at 220°C until the cheese melts.

* Try pita bread—brush the tops with garlic butter, sprinkle with parmesan cheese, heat for 5 minutes in a preheated oven at 220°C and cut into quarters.

* The foil-wrapped bread can be cooked on the barbecue, turning the bread often, and will be ready in about 10 minutes.

* Once the bread has been buttered and wrapped in foil, it can be frozen for up to 6 months. To cook from frozen, allow 30 minutes at 170°C in the oven.

* The garlic butter can also be made, wrapped in plastic wrap and frozen until needed. Allow to defrost overnight in the fridge before using.

GARLIC CONFIT

Serves 16

xxxxxxxxxxxxxxxxxxxxxxxxxxxxxxxxxxxxxxxxxxxxxxxxxxxxxxxxxxxxxxxxxxxxxxxxxxxxxxxxxxxxxxxxxx

8 garlic bulbs
approximately 1 litre
   olive oil

Method:

1. Preheat the oven to 130°C (110°C fan-forced).

2. Slice the top off the garlic—just enough to expose the garlic. Place the garlic bulbs, cut side down, in a baking dish. Add enough olive oil to reach three-quarters up the side of the garlic.

3. Place in the oven for 1 hour, after which the garlic should be turned over and cooked for a further 30 minutes. Remove from the oven and cool. The garlic confit can be stored in the refrigerator for several weeks, in an airtight container, so the smell doesn't permeate other foods in the fridge.

HINTS AND TIPS:

----

* You will need—deep baking dish big enough to hold the garlic, cook's knife and cutting board.

* When buying garlic, look for firm, blemish-free bulbs without visible signs of sprouting. If possible, buy only what is needed for the coming week.

* Garlic that has sprouted can still be used; simply remove and discard the green sprouting germ from the centre and slice or mince the remaining clove for stir-fry or pasta sauce. Sprouting garlic should not be used for confit or roasting whole.

* The oil from the garlic confit is excellent when used for cooking—especially great on roast meats.

* **Roasted garlic** is easy to do and is very similar to confit. Prepare the garlic as per the method above. Place the garlic in the roasting tray and lightly drizzle a bit of oil over the top, cover with foil and bake at 180°C for 50 minutes until very soft in the middle—then cool and refrigerate. Roasted garlic can be used in much the same way as garlic confit, but should be used within a week.

* Serve bulbs of garlic confit at dinner parties and as a starter served with

goat's cheese or **tzatziki** and toasted flat bread or grilled slices of sourdough bread drizzled with extra virgin olive oil.

* Use a few cloves of the garlic confit when mashing potato.

* Mix into a **red wine sauce** for use on roasted or grilled red meats.

LAVOSH

Makes about 450 g

xxxxxxxxxxxxxxxxxxxxxxxxxxxxxxxxxxxxxxxxxxxxxxxxxxxxxxxxxxxxxxxxxxxxxxxxxxxxxxxxxxxxxxxxxxxx

250 g plain flour
1 egg, lightly beaten
150 ml water
2 tablespoons poppy seeds
20 ml vegetable or olive oil
¼ teaspoon sea salt

Method:

1. With a wooden spoon or your hand, start mixing the flour and egg in a bowl, gradually add the water. Add the poppy seeds, oil and salt and continue to work the dough. You may or may not need all the water.

2. Knead the dough until smooth and homogenous. Allow to rest, covered with a tea towel or plastic wrap, for 20 minutes before rolling.

3. Preheat the oven to 200°C. Line a baking tray with baking paper.

4. Roll by hand with a rolling pin, or through a pasta machine, depending on how rustic it needs to look. Either way, the dough needs to be rolled thin, 1–2 mm.

5. Cut to the desired shape, place on the prepared baking tray and bake until light golden in colour, about 12 minutes.

6. Cool on a wire rack before storing in an airtight container for up to 10 days.

HINTS AND TIPS:

* You will need—bowl, spoon, liquid and weight measures, wooden spoon, rolling pin or pasta machine, baking tray, baking paper and wire rack.

* Lavosh is a versatile unleavened, yeast-free crisp bread that is easy to make at home. A pasta machine will give a quick result with minimum fuss.

* Lavosh is perfect to serve with cheese, dips and antipasto at a light lunch or dinner party.

* Try adding 1 tablespoon lemon zest to the recipe for a lovely flavour and aroma.

* Try replacing the poppy seeds with 1 tablespoon chilli flakes.

* Lavosh dough can be kept refrigerated for 3–5 days, after which it will begin to grey and lose its fresh flavour. The dough freezes well for 1–2 months. Defrost in the fridge before using.

* Cut the rolled out dough into different shapes. Use a round scone cutter to make a biscuit similar to a water cracker. Off-cuts can be reformed and rolled through the pasta machine again.

* Dried herbs (1 tablespoon per recipe) are brilliant in this recipe—my favourites are rosemary or thyme.

* Once rolled and placed on the baking tray, try sprinkling with sea salt flakes or freshly ground black pepper, pressing the seasonings gently into the surface of the uncooked lavosh before baking.

* Broken pieces of lavosh can be kept and used in **fattoush** or **panzanella**.

* For church-goers looking for an unleavened bread for communion, make the lavosh plain, without any seeds, nuts, herbs or seasonings.

NACHOS

Serves 4

xxxxxxxxxxxxxxxxxxxxxxxxxxxxxxxxxxxxxxxxxxxxxxxxxxxxxxxxxxxxxxxxxxxxxxxxxxxxxxxxxxxxxxxxxx

1 large onion, chopped
2 garlic cloves, crushed
2 tablespoons olive oil
500 g beef mince
425 g can chopped tomatoes
2 teaspoons chilli powder
2 teaspoons ground cumin
½ teaspoon salt
100 g black olives, pitted and chopped (optional)
400 g can refried beans
200 g bag corn chips
150 g cheddar or mozzarella cheese, grated
sour cream, for serving (optional)
guacamole, for serving (optional)

Method:

1. Fry the onion and garlic in the oil over medium heat until softened. Stir in the beef mince and cook until brown.

2. Add the tomatoes, stir well, reduce heat to low and simmer for 30 minutes or until mixed thoroughly and thickened.

3. Mix in the chilli powder, cumin and salt. Remove from the heat and stir in the olives, if using. Set aside until needed.

4. Spread a thin layer of refried beans over the base of a baking dish.

5. Spread a layer of corn chips over the beans, top with a layer of cheese, then add the beef mince. Repeat until all the ingredients are used. Or, since this recipe usually makes about 4 layers, you can divide all the toppings into 4 portions for even layering.

6. Microwave on high until heated through, about 6–8 minutes, or bake at 180°C for 20–30 minutes. Serve warm with sour cream and guacamole dip, if desired.

HINTS AND TIPS:

* You will need—cutting board, cook's knife, spoon and weight measures, wooden spoon, sauté pan and baking dish.

* How many young cooks do you think have 'invented' a version of this dish with great pride on the night and little recollection of it the next day? That is the sort of dish nachos is: even the most rank amateur cook can have a go and succeed.

* What can possibly go wrong? Too much cheese and the whole thing becomes a large weapon. Too much sauce and the corn chips go soggy. Too much heat and the corn chips and cheese burn. Too little heat and the cheese in the centre won't melt. In other words there are basic things that can spoil a relatively easy dish.

* What makes for a good nachos? This question asked of any dish, anywhere, will get the same answer and that is—it depends on who's eating it. Some love loads of cheese and little sauce, others prefer to skimp on the cheese and so on and so forth. Adhere to the basic rules applied in my method and by all means personalise your nachos based on the love of some ingredients over others. Cooking is interpretational, a cookbook is a only guide and the cook has the right to enhance a recipe based on personal preference, market forces or even budget. No questions asked.

* Nachos loves being served with ice cold beer and tequila—refer to the second tip. Enjoy!

* Naturally there are easier ways to construct nachos than the one I recommend. It usually involves buying everything pre-made.

PASTA DOUGH

Makes approximately 500 g

xxxxxxxxxxxxxxxxxxxxxxxxxxxxxxxxxxxxxxxxxxxxxxxxxxxxxxxxxxxxxxxxxxxxxxxxxxxxxxxxxxxxxxxxxx

500 g pasta flour or plain flour (see Hints and Tips)
1 teaspoon salt
4 eggs

Method:

1. Using a food processor, blitz the flour and salt quickly before adding the eggs. Process until the dough begins to come together.

2. Remove the dough from the machine and knead on a lightly floured benchtop. Work the dough for 5 minutes with your hands until it is smooth. Cover and rest for 30 minutes before rolling out.

3. To roll out, cut the dough into 4 manageable pieces, roll out with a rolling pin, and pass each piece through the widest setting on a pasta machine. There is no need to dust the dough with flour as it rolls through, as this will only add more flour and make it heavy and stodgy when cooked.

4. Continue to roll the pasta until it reaches the second last setting or even the last, depending on how thin you need it. After it is rolled, lightly sprinkle it with flour to stop it from sticking together. If cutting the pasta into shapes, allow it to sit and dry for 10 minutes before cutting.

5. To cook fresh pasta, bring at least 3 litres of water to the boil, add all the pasta at once, stir and cook for 2 minutes only, then drain and serve.

* You will need—bowl, pasta machine, rolling pin and food processor.

* Fresh pasta doesn't need to be hung over a broom handle to dry out unless you plan on storing it in an airtight container for a month or two. Otherwise dust it in plenty of fine semolina and keep refrigerated for 2–3 days, after which it begins to turn grey.

* Pasta flour or 00 flour—available at good delicatessens—is different to plain flour in that it has a higher gluten content, which means it can tolerate the constant stretching through a pasta machine without tearing; plain flour, being softer, needs to be handled gently when rolling.

* A gluten-free pasta can be made using—250 g potato flour, 250 g rice flour, ½ teaspoon salt, 1–½ teaspoons xanthan gum, ½ teaspoon guar gum, 4 eggs, 1 tablespoon olive oil. Mix the flours, salt and gums together, make a well in the centre and add the eggs. Work the flour into the eggs and when a dough begins to form, knead the dough for 5 minutes. Allow to rest for 30 minutes before rolling out. Xanthan gum and guar gum are available from health food shops.

* Continental flour is a fine semolina also used for making pasta and is available at good delicatessens.

* Flours also have a moisture content making it difficult to be precise with the number of eggs (which vary in size), so the dough could become sticky or too dry. Therefore be ready to compensate by adding more flour if too sticky or some water should it be too dry and not coming together.

* See cooking pasta in the Really Useful Section for more tips on cooking pasta properly.

* Once the pasta is rolled, it is important to keep it from sticking together. This requires the cook to have a bowl of flour or semolina to one side so that the dough can be constantly dusted as it is rolled through the pasta machine. Once the pasta is cut to the desired shape, it will require more flour to be dusted over the cut pasta to account for the exposed edges which can become sticky. Shake off excess flour before dropping into the boiling water.

* An important note for owners of a pasta machine—DO NOT WASH IT! Use a pastry brush to brush away excess or built-up flour on the machine. Washing will cause the components to rust, and any built-up flour to become pasty and set hard, as well as the rollers losing their very smooth surface.

PASTRY

SWEET PASTRY

Makes about 500 g

XXXXXXXXXXXXXXXXXXXXXXXXXXXXXXXXXXXXXXXXXXXXXXXXXXXXXXXXXXXXXXXXXXXXXXXXXXXXXXXXXXXXXXXXXXXX

250 g plain flour, sifted
125 g cold unsalted
   butter, diced
100 g caster sugar
pinch of salt
2 eggs

Method:

1. Place the flour and butter in a food processor and blitz until the mixture resembles coarse sand.

2. Add the sugar, salt and eggs and continue processing until the dough comes together to form a ball.

3. Remove the dough to a lightly floured benchtop and work briefly until well combined.

4. Wrap in plastic wrap and refrigerate until required.

HINTS AND TIPS:

★ You will need—food processor, weight measures and plastic scraper.

★ This recipe is enough for 1 flan tin or 23 cm deep pie dish or tart tin.

★ Sweet pastry is one of the three main French pastries mentioned here. It is also known as 'pâte sucrée'.

★ As the butter is only half the quantity to flour, this pastry is easy to work with once rested and gives a good result in any tart or flan—it is only bettered by the more delicate sweet shortcrust pastry.

★ This pastry is simple to do by hand if a food processor is not available. Place the sifted flour and salt in a bowl, and rub in the butter with your fingertips until it reaches a granular texture. Make a well in the centre, add the sugar and eggs, and mix until it forms a smooth dough. Wrap and refrigerate.

SWEET SHORTCRUST PASTRY

Makes about 375 g

xxxxxxxxxxxxxxxxxxxxxxxxxxxxxxxxxxxxxxxxxxxxxxxxxxxxxxxxxxxxxxxxxxxxxxxxxxxxxxxxxxxxxxxx

50 g plain flour, sifted
200 g cold unsalted
    butter, diced
100 g caster sugar
2 egg yolks

Method:

1. Place the sifted flour and butter in a food processor and blitz until the mixture resembles coarse sand.

2. Add the sugar and egg yolks and continue processing until the dough just comes together to form a ball.

3. Place the dough on a lightly floured benchtop and work briefly until well combined.

4. Wrap in plastic wrap and refrigerate until required.

HINTS AND TIPS:

* You will need—food processor, weight measures and plastic scraper.

* This recipe makes enough for one tart.

* Also known as 'pâte sablée sucrée', this pastry is very short, because it has so much butter in it. The butter content means the gluten is unable to form, making it a very delicate, rich and soft pastry both raw and cooked.

* Unless you are a trained professional, rolling out and lining a pie dish or flan tin with sweet shortcrust pastry is nigh impossible because the pastry rips and tears very easily. For novice, intermediate and most domestic cooks, it is always suggested that the dough is broken into small pieces and scattered into the tin or dish and pressed into place. Rest in the fridge for at least 30 minutes before baking.

* This is a great pastry to simply roll into logs, dust in caster sugar and set cold in the fridge. Slice 5-mm discs from the cold logs and bake for 15 minutes at 180°C to produce a tasty little shortbread biscuit. Once cold, try dipping the biscuits in melted chocolate for a treat at your next dinner party.

SHORTCRUST PASTRY

Makes about 325 g

XXXXXXXXXXXXXXXXXXXXXXXXXXXXXXXXXXXXXXXXXXXXXXXXXXXXXXXXXXXXXXXXXXXXXXXXXXXXXXXXXXXXXXXXXX

250 g plain flour
150 g butter, diced and
    softened
1 egg, at room temperature
pinch of sugar
1 tablespoon milk

Method:

1. Place the flour in a bowl, make a well in the centre and add the butter, egg and sugar. Begin to mix with one hand and when almost completely combined, add the milk. Continue to mix until a smooth dough forms. Wrap in plastic wrap and chill for 2–3 hours.

2. Alternatively, place all of the ingredients in a food processor and blitz until a dough is formed. Remove and work the dough for a minute to ensure it is smooth. Wrap in plastic wrap and refrigerate.

HINTS AND TIPS:

* You will need—bowl, food processor, weight measures and plastic scraper.

* Also known as ´pâte brisée´, shortcrust pastry is often used as a base for pies and quiche.

* This is quite a rich, short savoury pastry. Other savoury pastries tend to be made using water and lard instead of eggs, butter and milk.

* Using fresh lard in place of the butter will produce a more **flaky pastry**, try making this alternative called ´pâte à foncer´—250 g plain flour, 2 pinches salt, 125 g lard, 100 ml cold water. Use the

same method as for shortcrust pastry.

* Yet another interesting alternative is called ´pâte à pâte´ or **hot water pastry**—125 ml water, 100 g lard, 250 g flour, 2 pinches of salt. Heat the water and lard to boiling point, remove from the heat and stir in the flour and salt. Cool and refrigerate until required.

QUICK PUFF PASTRY

Makes about 600 g

xxxxxxxxxxxxxxxxxxxxxxxxxxxxxxxxxxxxxxxxxxxxxxxxxxxxxxxxxxxxxxxxxxxxxxxxxxxxxxxxxxxxxxxxxxxxx

250 g plain flour
250 g butter, cut into
   5-mm dice
½ teaspoon salt
125 ml iced water

Method:

1. Place the flour on the work surface and make a well in the centre. Add the butter and salt and begin to work the butter into the flour with your fingertips.

2. Once the butter is smaller in size but not fully incorporated, make another well in the flour and butter mixture and add the water. Gradually draw in the flour to make a dough which is homogenous yet still flecked with butter.

3. Lightly dust the work surface with flour and roll out the pastry to 40 cm x 20 cm.

4. Fold the 2 ends into the centre to make three layers, give the pastry a quarter turn and roll out again to 40 cm x 20 cm. Fold into 3 once more, wrap and refrigerate for 20 minutes.

5. Repeat this process 2 more times, then rest once more for at least 20 minutes in the fridge before using.

6. Wrap in plastic wrap and keep refrigerated for up to 3 days.

HINTS AND TIPS:

----

* You will need—weight, spoon and liquid measures and rolling pin.

* This is meant to be a quick puff pastry—also known as 'flaky pastry' or 'demi-feulleté'—although it still takes about 2 hours to make. The conventional method requires a large piece of butter to be incorporated into the dough and takes an extra 2–3 turns and resting periods. The quick method saves 1½ hours overall.

* Once the pastry has been rolled out and cut into shapes, it can be wrapped and frozen ready for another day.

* It is important to note when using any puff pastry (homemade or commercially made) that when the cut pastry is ready to bake and it is being brushed with egg for glazing, the egg should not go over the edge of the pastry or it will act like a glue and prevent that spot from rising, producing a lopsided puff pastry shape.

* It is also vital that the dough is kept cold so the butter doesn't melt and affect how flaky the pastry is.

CHOUX PASTRY

Makes about 450 g

xxxxxxxxxxxxxxxxxxxxxxxxxxxxxxxxxxxxxxxxxxxxxxxxxxxxxxxxxxxxxxxxxxxxxxxxxxxxxxxxxxxxxxxxxxx

200 ml water
100 g butter
½ teaspoon salt
½ teaspoon sugar
100 g bread flour
3 egg whites
1 egg
1 egg, lightly beaten, for glazing

Method:

1. Preheat the oven to 150°C. Line a baking tray with baking paper.

2. Place the water, butter, salt and sugar in a saucepan and bring to the boil. As soon as the water comes to the boil, add the flour all at once while still on the heat. Beat the dough with a wooden spoon until it forms a ball and begins to come away from the sides of the pan. Remove from the heat and leave to cool on the bench.

3. It is important to cool the dough before adding the eggs to avoid any heat in the dough cooking the eggs.

4. When the dough is cool enough to touch, beat in 1 egg white at a time, beating well after each addition. Beat in the egg.

5. Fill a piping bag and pipe 3-cm balls (for **profiteroles**) or 2.5-cm wide x 8-cm long fingers (for **éclairs**) at least 2 cm apart onto the prepared baking tray.

6. Brush the top with the beaten egg and place on the bottom shelf of the oven. Turn up the oven to 220°C and bake for 10–15 minutes or until golden brown and puffed. Reduce the oven temperature to 150°C to dry the puffs out and bake for a further 15 minutes. Turn the oven off, use a small knife to poke a hole in the bottom of each puff and leave to cool in the oven.

Method cont.

7. Transfer to an airtight container and keep for 2–3 days or freeze for up to 2 months.

HINTS AND TIPS:
----

* You will need—saucepan, wooden spoon, baking tray, baking paper, weight, liquid and spoon measures and piping bag.

* Choux pastry—also known as 'pâte à choux'—is used for many dishes, sweet and savoury, from **profiteroles** and éclairs to cheese puffs and potato Dauphine (mashed potato mixed with choux paste and deep-fried).

* It is important to use bread (strong) flour in choux pastry as the higher proteins in the flour produce greater gluten elasticity making lighter puffs. Use plain flour if only making choux pastry on rare occasions.

* Adding the flour to the boiling water is also very important to ensure the starches in the flour swell and absorb the water instantly.

* Often recipes for choux pastry use whole eggs. Using mostly egg whites will guarantee a lighter, crispier and drier puff. For a lighter puff again, try reducing the water content in the recipe by 50 ml and adding another egg white at the end—be aware that the resultant puff, although light in texture, will have a stronger egg flavour.

PIZZA DOUGH

Makes about 4 bases

xxxxxxxxxxxxxxxxxxxxxxxxxxxxxxxxxxxxxxxxxxxxxxxxxxxxxxxxxxxxxxxxxxxxxxxxxxxxxxxxxxxxxxxxx

350 g plain flour
1 tablespoon dry yeast
1 teaspoon salt
1 teaspoon sugar
3 tablespoons olive oil
250 ml warm water

Method:

1. Mix the flour, yeast, salt, sugar, olive oil and
water in a bowl.

2. Tip onto the benchtop and with extra flour at hand,
knead the dough until it is smooth and elastic.

3. Rub the bowl with a small amount of oil and add the
ball of dough.

4. Cover with a tea towel or plastic wrap and keep in
a warm place until doubled in size, an hour or more
depending on how warm it is.

5. Once doubled in size, remove the cover and punch
the dough back to its original size.

6. Roll and stretch the dough to fit a large round
pizza tray or baking tray.

7. Spread with toppings and bake in a preheated 220°C
oven for 20 minutes.

HINTS AND TIPS:

* You will need—large bowl, spoon, weight and liquid measures, plastic wrap or tea towel, rolling pin and pizza tray or rectangular baking tray.

* Like most bread products, the best flour for the job is 'strong' flour—also known as 'bread' flour. However, for most beginner cooks, plain flour is easily recognised and readily available and does a good job.

* If it is not to your liking the first time, do not despair—dough making is an art and over time can be refined until you get a feel for it. It can vary greatly depending on the consistency and age of the flour, the yeast and the temperature. Once you start, the quest for the perfect crust is on.

* If it is cold and you need to find a warm spot, an old trick passed on to me by my wise Greek friend is to place the dough in bed with the electric blanket on. It sounds strange but it works!

* Not all pizzas are round; you can make long rectangular ones or mini pizzas.

* If you will be making pizza often, it is worth investing in pizza trays or a pizza stone. Try and find pizza trays that are 'matt' grey or black as these absorb heat and make for a crispier base, whereas a shiny silver pizza tray reflects heat and the base of the pizza may not brown as well.

* Use the dough to make **calzone**; this is like an Italian pasty. Make a filling, spread a large mound of it along half of the rolled out round of pizza dough. Brush lightly whisked egg along the edges, fold over the other half and press the edges down firmly. Brush with more egg and bake in a 220°C oven until golden.

* Use the dough to make **cheese twists**.

* Substitute the dry yeast for live yeast which can be purchased from delis or bakeries.

* You may need to add a dusting of flour from time to time as you knead the dough to reduce stickiness.

* You will know when the dough is ready when it no longer sticks to your hands.

* The dough can be frozen for several months, but be mindful that it will continue rising for a little while before its temperature drops, so wrap it tightly or place in a clip lock bag. When using the dough, remove from the freezer and defrost in the fridge overnight. Then bring it back to room temperature before rolling out, otherwise the dough will tear.

PRESERVED LEMONS
Makes 12

XXXXXXXXXXXXXXXXXXXXXXXXXXXXXXXXXXXXXXXXXXXXXXXXXXXXXXXXXXXXXXXXXXXXXXXXXXXXXXXXXXXXXXXXXXXXXXXXXX

12 lemons
1 cup coarse salt

Method:

1. Wash and dry the lemons before salting, remembering that it is the skin only that is eaten.

2. Use a sharp knife to make 2 vertical cuts in each lemon in a cross about two-thirds of the way through the lemon, but all the way along (do not panic if it cuts through, it is still good to use).

3. Stuff the cuts in each lemon with plenty of salt.

4. Place a lemon carefully at the bottom of a sterilised wide-mouthed glass jar. Proceed in this manner with the remaining lemons, compressing them into the far edges of the jar until no space is left and the lemon juice rises to the top.

5. Seal with the lid and leave on the kitchen bench.

6. More lemons may be added in the following 2–3 days as the lemon rinds begin to soften.

7. Make sure the lemons are covered with juice at all times, adding fresh lemon juice if necessary.

8. The lemons are ready to use when the rinds are very tender, 4–6 weeks.

9. Rinse the lemons thoroughly and discard any flesh and seeds before using. Refrigerate after opening. Preserved lemons will keep for up to 6 months in the refrigerator after opening.

HINTS AND TIPS:

★ You will need—cutting board, cook's knife, cup measure and large jar with screw-cap lid.

★ A sealant may be used once the lemons have been placed in the jar. This can be a slick of vegetable oil, enough to cover the surface. Alternatively, use waxed paper and cellophane discs. Make your own from a waxed paper roll purchased from the supermarket. Ensure the rim of the jar is clean and place on top, wax side down, then dampen the cellophane disc, place on top of the rim, moist side up, allow some overhang, and secure with an elastic band. When dry, the cellophane will shrink and create a tight seal.

★ When ready, the lemon pulp is discarded and only the peel is used.

★ Limes can also be preserved this way.

★ Extra flavourings may be added, for example: 1 dried bay leaf, 1 cinnamon stick, 2 whole cloves, 2 dried red chillies, 1 teaspoon black peppercorns, 1 teaspoon coriander seeds, or ½ teaspoon cumin seed. Don't add all these together.

★ Preserved lemons can be added to stews, fish dishes, stuffings for chicken, tagines and salads.

★ Traditionally, thinner skinned lemons are utilised because they tend to be juicier. Thick-skinned varieties can be preserved but require extra juice to cover them.

★ If a white mould forms, it is harmless and can be rinsed off before the lemon is used.

★ Six medium-sized lemons fit nicely into a 1-litre jar. Don't be afraid to tightly pack the jar because the lemons shrink.

★ Unopened, preserved lemons can last 24 months; kept in a dark, dry, cool place.

SUGAR SYRUP

Makes approximately 350 ml

XXXXXXXXXXXXXXXXXXXXXXXXXXXXXXXXXXXXXXXXXXXXXXXXXXXXXXXXXXXXXXXXXXXXXXXXXXXXXXXXXXXXXXXXXXX

1 cup water
1 cup white sugar

Method:

1. Pour the water into saucepan and add the sugar.

2. Allow the sugar to dissolve over medium heat, stirring occasionally.

3. Once it comes to the boil, reduce to low heat and allow to simmer for 5 minutes, without stirring, to thicken slightly.

4. Pour into a sterilised bottle, cover and store in the refrigerator.

HINTS AND TIPS:

★ You will need—cup measures, saucepan and wooden spoon.

★ The syrup, properly covered to prevent it from taking on odours, can be stored in the refrigerator for up to 12 months. Left at room temperature, sugar syrup can form mould so it is always recommended to store refrigerated.

★ Sugar syrup is a 50/50 combination of water and sugar. It can differ in density depending on the sugar to water ratio.

★ It is good to have on hand because it lasts well and can be used in many recipes, for example **baklava**, syrup cakes or sorbet.

★ Add an extra ½ cup water to make a poaching syrup for fruit. If the fruit is quite tart, then leave the ratio at equal parts sugar to water. Flavour the poaching syrup by adding 30 ml (1 nip) liqueur or ½ cinnamon stick or ½ vanilla bean. Other spices can also be used including black pepper, star anise or cardamom pods.

★ Try adding a piece of lemon or orange zest to the sugar mixture before it boils. Keep the zest in the stored syrup to continue flavouring it. Use this lemon-flavoured syrup as a base for **lemonade**.

★ Sugar syrup is frequently used in cocktails because it combines well with alcohol. One example is a French 75. Combine 15 ml each of gin, fresh lemon juice and sugar syrup in a champagne flute and top up with chilled sparking wine or French champagne.

★ Sugar syrup is often referred to as a 'simple syrup' in cocktails, in the professional kitchen it is often known as a 'stock syrup'.

★ If you don't have a sugar thermometer, you can test the stages of cooked sugar syrups using the iced water method, note the following:

★ **Soft ball**—drops of syrup in chilled water will form a fudge-like 'soft ball' when rolled between the thumb and forefinger.

★ **Firm ball**—drops of the syrup cooled in the iced water will produce a 'firm ball' ideal for making caramel.

VANILLA SUGAR

Makes 2 cups

XXXXXXXXXXXXXXXXXXXXXXXXXXXXXXXXXXXXXXXXXXXXXXXXXXXXXXXXXXXXXXXXXXXXXXXXXXXXXXXXXX

500 g caster or pure icing
    sugar
1 vanilla bean

Method 1:

1. The easiest way to do this is to pour the sugar into a jar or other sealed container, cut the vanilla bean into 3 pieces and store in the sugar. Over the coming days and weeks, the aroma permeates the whole container of sugar.

2. Once the sugar is used, the vanilla pieces can be added to another batch of sugar.

Method 2:

1. This method requires the use of a food processor. Place 2 tablespoons sugar in the food processor with the vanilla bean that has been chopped into smaller pieces. Process until the vanilla bean is little more than small black grains.

2. Add the remaining sugar and process to incorporate all the vanilla and sugar.

3. Store in an airtight container.

HINTS AND TIPS:

----

* You will need—cutting board, paring knife, weight measure, and food processor (optional).

* Vanilla sugar is available at good delicatessens and selected supermarkets.

* Use vanilla sugar wherever you use regular sugar.

* Making vanilla sugar is a great way to utilise vanilla beans that have already been used in desserts and sauces. Wash the used vanilla bean and leave to dry at room temperature. Follow the instructions given in either method above.

VEGETABLE STOCK

Makes about 2 litres

xxxxxxxxxxxxxxxxxxxxxxxxxxxxxxxxxxxxxxxxxxxxxxxxxxxxxxxxxxxxxxxxxxxxxxxxxxxxxxxxxxxxxxxxxxxx

¼ cup light olive oil or vegetable oil
500 g onions, peeled and chopped
400 g carrots, peeled and chopped
500 g leeks, white part only, chopped, washed
   and drained
1 small fennel bulb, chopped (optional)
2 bay leaves
2 sprigs thyme
50 g parsley stalks

Method:

1. Heat the oil in a large soup or stock pot.

2. Add all the ingredients and cook on medium heat for 5 minutes.

3. Add enough cold water to cover the vegetables by 5 cm.

4. Increase the heat to bring just to the boil then reduce the heat so the stock is simmering.

5. Cook for 45 minutes only. Remove from the heat, stand for 10 minutes then strain.

6. Cool before storing in the fridge. Vegetable stock loses flavour very quickly and by day 3, although not off, is hardly worth using. Best used on the day or on day 2, or freeze.

HINTS AND TIPS:

★ You will need—cutting board, cook's knife, vegetable peeler, cup and weight measures, large pot and wooden spoon.

★ Vegetable stock can be anything from a carefully boiled-up array of root vegetables to the liquid leftover after boiling mixed vegetables for dinner (which can be saved for making soups, making bread or vegan risotto.)

★ Sauté the vegetables before adding the water to bring out their flavour.

★ For a more intensified, sweeter tasting stock, roast the vegetables for 45 minutes before cooking in the above method (for 45 minutes).

★ The stock will take about 20 minutes to cook if the vegetables are cut small, or up to 1 hour if they're kept whole. After an hour, the vegetables are well and truly spent and any herbs left to steep may turn bitter, so strain everything out. (All the flavour and nutrients are now in the liquid, so eating these soggy leftovers would be the equivalent to tucking into boiled cardboard.) To intensify the flavour, you can then reduce the stock by half.

★ This is an easy stock to prepare and have on hand for soups, risotto and sauces; especially for vegetarians and vegans.

★ Like all stocks in this book, it freezes well and will last for 2 months in the freezer. Keeping stock in the freezer for too long will change the make up of the stock. The ice crystals become larger, affecting the flavour when defrosted.

★ For a light amber colour to the stock, leave the skin on the onions.

★ For a dark vegetable stock, brown the vegetables in the pan before adding the water, being careful not to burn the vegetables which would impart a burnt flavour. A simple way to colour the stock is to add some soy sauce or mushroom soy sauce, just enough to change the colour but not to overpower.

★ Adding other vegetables will certainly add a richness and depth of flavour, but do remember these vegetables are a throwaway item used for flavour only.

★ Adding leafy green matter like spinach or soft herbs is not a great idea as these ingredients tend to become slimy, bitter or grassy tasting which could affect the final delicate flavour of the stock.

★ Homemade vegetable stock should be made from quality ingredients, not the old, wilted leftovers fermenting in the bottom of the crisper. As tempting as it may seem to use up the 'compost' at the bottom of the fridge, ask yourself, Would I eat these normally? If the answer is, no then discard and use fresher vegetables.

```
-------------------------------------------------------
xxxxxxxxx The Really Useful Information xxxxxxxxx
-------------------------------------------------------
```

AVOCADOS

There are close to 30 varieties of cultivated avocado, from the Anaheim to the Zutano, and each has specific qualities, tastes and oil content (from 12-25 per cent). Haas (the best quality), with its dark, pebbly-green skin, and Fuerte, with a smooth green skin, are the most common. The many others from around the world tend to have short seasons, but are worth sourcing when available. Avocado leaves can be slightly toasted in a pan, cooled then ground with a mortar and pestle to release their subtle fragrance of anise and hazelnuts. Use the crushed leaves in stews, chicken or fish dishes, and salads made with avocado.

TIPS

* To check ripeness, gently press at the narrow, stalk end of the fruit, not at the bulbous, seed-filled end. This is where the fruit is most dense; if it is ripe, it should give when pressed at this end.
* To hasten ripening, place an avocado in a paper bag with a ripe apple (the slow release of ethylene from the apple initiates ethylene production in the avocado).
* Store ripe avocados in the fridge for 4-10 days—how long they last depends on the variety. As a general rule, the smooth, green-skinned varieties bruise more easily and do not store for as long as the rougher, dark-skinned avocados.
* To remove the seed, cut the avocado in half, give the seed a firm (not aggressive) hit with the knife blade, twist and pull. Either peel or use a large spoon to scoop out the flesh in one go.
* The flesh of an avocado inevitably browns after you've cut into it. To help prevent browning, brush with lemon or lime juice, mash and mix with more lemon or lime juice, or leave the seed in the half not being used, cover and refrigerate.
* Avocado flesh can be stored in the freezer for up to 2 months.

BEANS

FRESH BEANS

So many beans, so little space. Beans are usually divided into 2 groups: those with edible pods and those where only the seeds are eaten (see also **Dried Beans**). Beans grow either on a bush or trained on a pole. Bush beans grow close to the ground and need no support, while pole beans are climbing, vine-like plants. Fresh beans are also known as 'shelling beans' in the US.

Types of fresh bean
Broad beans are best in the spring; out of season they tend to be mealy and dry, good only for soups and purees. Shell the beans and remove their outer skins. This skin toughens as the bean matures (sometimes becoming grey or even pink-tinged); so the older and larger the bean, the more likely you will want to remove it before eating. Cook first (approximately 3 minutes) then pop the beans out of the remaining skins. Young, tender, fresh beans can also be eaten raw. Mature beans (also known as 'foules') are often best pureed or dried. Also known as 'fava beans' in the US (although in many other countries fava refers exclusively to the dried bean), Windsor beans or horse beans.
  Edible soy beans, known in Japan as 'edamame', are harvested as young green-shelled beans, before they mature into soy beans. In Japan, edamame are eaten as snacks and

appetisers; the pods are boiled for 10 minutes before the bean is shelled. In China and other countries, the shelled soy beans are cooked with meat and vegetables in various dishes. The pods can be frozen (cooked or uncooked) for later use.

Green beans are many and varied, the most common being the string or French bean and the flat green bean. String beans are now bred with little or no sign of the chewy string of old, while flat green beans are tougher, larger and less palatable. The yellow bean, also known as 'wax bean' or 'butter bean' (not to be confused with the lima bean), is a varietal of the green bean with a delicate, tasty flavour, although it deteriorates faster than green beans. Also available is the purple bean which cooks green. Baby green beans are now sold in punnets. They are sweet and can be eaten raw.

Snake beans, also known as 'Chinese long beans', 'asparagus beans', 'bodi beans' and 'yard-long beans', can be cut into lengths and cooked like normal green beans.

Wing beans are used in stir-fries and in soups and can be found at Asian grocers. They have four wings running the length of the bean. Always buy them fully green and crisp; older ones bend too easily and the wings turn brown and decay.

DRIED BEANS

Dried beans (also known as 'shell-outs') are pulses (see **Legumes** for a definition). They should be soaked for some hours, usually overnight, before cooking. The beans are soaked for 2 reasons: first, to speed up the cooking time; and secondly, because the flatulence often associated with eating beans can be attributed to the sugars in the bean that are water-soluble, so by soaking the beans and diluting the sugars, potent gases are reduced.

HOW TO SOAK DRIED BEANS

For long soaking, cover the dried beans with 3 times their volume of water and stand in the refrigerator for 12 hours or overnight. Drain.

For quick soaking, place the beans in a saucepan, cover with 3 times their volume of water and bring to the boil. Boil for 2 minutes. Remove from the heat, cover and stand for 1 hour. Drain.

Most dried beans take 1–1½ hours to cook once they are soaked, or 15–30 minutes in a pressure cooker. Most beans can be cooked in the water they have soaked in, except soy, kidney beans and chickpeas which should be drained and cooked in fresh water as the soaking water retains bitterness from the beans. When cooking dried beans, it is recommended to add a dash of oil to reduce the amount of foaming.

If a recipe calls for cooked or canned beans when you have dried, or vice versa, here is a rule of thumb for replacing one with the other.

1 cup dried beans = about 3 cups cooked beans
500 g dried beans = 2½ cups dried beans = about 7½ cups cooked beans
400 g (14 oz) can beans = about 1½ cups drained beans
540 g (19 oz) can beans = about 2 cups drained beans = approximately ¾ cup dried beans

Types of dried bean

Azuki/adzuki beans are primarily grown for bean seeds, which in turn are used for soups, desserts and cake pastes and are the main ingredients in red bean paste and sweet bean paste. The young fresh bean pods can be eaten like snow peas.

Black beans, also known as 'turtle beans', are a small black-skinned bean used in stews, soups and salads; not to be confused with fermented black beans which are a type of soy bean. Black-eye beans are also known as 'black-eyed peas', 'cornfield', 'turtle beans', 'Mexican beans' and 'valentines'. These earthy tasting beans cook in 1 hour and are a popular addition to dishes from the Caribbean, Mexico and the southern states of the US.

Borlotti beans have a distinct marking of pink or red streaks. They are available fresh but are more often used dried. With their hammy, nutty flavour, the dried beans are a great salad and soup bean, while the fresh beans are wonderful in pasta. Sometimes called 'cranberry beans' or 'Roman' or 'Romano beans'.

Lima beans or *butter beans* are the favourites of Rabbit in *Winnie-the-Pooh* and a must-have ingredient for the side dish succotash. This flat, kidney-shaped bean has a buttery texture and flavour.

Marrow beans are said to taste of bacon (I can neither confirm nor deny this claim). They swell considerably after cooking so make a great salad bean; also good as a puree or in soups.

Red kidney beans are so named for their shape. They have a full flavour and mealy texture and are often used in salads.

Runner beans are available fresh or dried. They are quite large (although may take less than 1 hour to cook) so can be served braised or stewed as a dish on their own, where a slow-cooking method suits.

Soy beans have a higher protein content (35 per cent) than other beans. Dried soy beans contain an enzyme inhibitor that can make them indigestible so they should be soaked for 24 hours (change the water every 8 hours) then cooked in fresh water for 3–4 hours. Once cooked, they have a silky-smooth texture but little flavour, although they can be enhanced by adding flavours such as onion, tomato, rosemary, soy sauce, garlic or thyme in the last hour of cooking. I personally prefer eating soy beans in their many other forms (fresh, sprouts, bean curds, sauces) to avoid this long drawn-out process of cooking the dried bean.

Fermented black beans (also known as 'salted black beans', 'Chinese black beans' or 'ginger black beans') are black soy beans that have been cooked, innoculated with a mould and fermented in their cooking brine for about 6 months then partially dried. The better quality brands are then flavoured with Chinese five-spice powder, orange zest and ginger. The beans now have a salty soy taste and a firm, pliable texture, and will last indefinitely in the cupboard. Once opened, they can be stored for months in an airtight container in the refrigerator. Although some recipes recommend soaking and/or rinsing the beans to reduce their saltiness, this is frowned on by Chinese chefs.

White beans is a general term that describes cannellini, great northern beans, haricot beans (also known as 'navy beans' or 'Boston beans') and the white bean itself. Any of these can be interchanged in recipes.

Bean flakes are similar to instant rolled oats in that they cook very quickly into a paste. They are ideal in soups or as a side dish or puree.

CHEESE

TIPS FOR BUYING AND STORING CHEESE:

* Don't be afraid to ask for a sample of cheese before buying (although a supermarket is the last place this service would be offered). If you are unable to sample the cheese, look carefully before buying: avoid any wrapped cheeses that show weeping or shrinkage and any unwrapped cheeses that show signs of drying around the edges or cracking in harder cheese.

* Stored in its original wrapper, unopened, in the coldest part of the refrigerator, cheese (especially hard cheese) can live a grand life, often beyond its 'use by' date. However, cheese is a living food and needs to breathe to develop. The best way to store it is wrapped in a calico cloth or waxed paper. (Don't use plastic wrap or foil.) Ideally, keep cheese in a cool, moist cave, with good ventilation and a stable air temperature from 8–12°C. As most houses lack a good cave, the refrigerator will have to suffice.

* Mould spores from blue cheese can spread to other cheese and food in the same storage area, so make sure blue cheese in particular is thoroughly wrapped.

* Freezing cheese is not recommended, although leftover grated cheese and some semi-hard cheeses keep well in the freezer. Soft cheeses like brie and camembert do not appreciate this treatment.

* Remove cheese from the fridge and stand at room temperature for 1–2 hours before serving. This allows the flavour and aroma to develop.

TIPS FOR A CHEESE BOARD:

* Don't feel the need to always serve a vast array of different cheeses at a dinner party. Choose 2 or 3, ranging in texture from hard to semi-hard to semi-soft, allowing 80–100 g of cheese per person, less if cheese is to be served before or after a dessert.

* Make sure your guests enjoy a particular cheese before spending your money—blue cheese is not for everyone.

* Serving cut fruit on the same plate as the cheese is an insult; cheese should be served simply on its own. Any fruit to be enjoyed with the cheese, whether fresh, dried or as a paste, can be served on a separate plate. Offer bread as well as biscuits with cheese; fruit breads, nut breads and wine breads are all suitable.

CHILLIES

CHILLI HEAT RATINGS

Chilli heat is measured in Scoville heat units. The capsaicin is chemically extracted from the chilli and subjected to high performance liquid chromatography. Basically, these units represent the number of times the extracted capsaicin dissolved in alcohol can be diluted with a quantity of sugar water before the capsaicin can no longer be tasted.

1–10	Scoville units	Chilli name
0	0	capsicum
1	100–500	cherry, pepperoncini, NuMex, R-Nak, Mexibel, aji flor
2	500–1000	Santa Fe Grande, anaheim, sandia, Big Jim
3	1000–1500	Española, poblano, mulato, ancho, Española improved, pasilla, chilaca, hot cherry, NuMex 64
4	1500–2500	rocotillo, cascabel
5	2500–5000	TAM jalapeño, mirasol, cayenne (large thick), guajillo, cascabella, Hungarian wax, Peter pepper, Turkish
6	5000–15 000	aji amarillo, romesco, jalapeño, serrano, yellow wax, wax
7	15 000–30 000	de arbol, catarina, japones
8	30 000–50 000	aji, cayenne, cayenne (long thin), prik khee nu, dundicut, tabasco, costeno, rocoto, piquin
9	50 000–100 000	yatsafusa, chipotle, santaka, Thai, chiltepin, aji limon, aji or cusqueno, datil
10	100 000–300 000	habanero, Bahamian, Jamaican hot, bird, bird's eye, Scotch bonnet
10+	300 000–577 000	Red Caribbean, savina
	15 000 000+	pure capsaicin

CHOCOLATE

Chocolate has a long history as a glamour food, the food of the gods. The very best chocolate fetches top dollar for its smooth texture and pure flavour, which unfortunately means that much of the chocolate we consume is often churned into cheap confectionery and crude compound cooking blocks—sad, milk-laden versions of the good stuff. The good stuff displays its cocoa butter content proudly (from 33 per cent), and is a real treat to use and eat.

Store chocolate at room temperature (ideally at 20°C) in a cool, dry place, in its original wrapper or in foil. Dark chocolate has a shelf life of several years, while milk chocolate should be used within 12 months. Don't store chocolate in the fridge or freezer, as it will have a greater tendency to bloom once thawed. (Bloom is the name given to the grey/white spots that appear on the surface of chocolate when the cocoa butter separates from the solids.) Why would you freeze it anyway? Eat it!

Chocolate is made from the cacao bean. The rarest cacao tree, whose bean is the most expensive and sought after by the world's best chocolate makers, is the 'criollo' (which means 'native'), although 90 per cent of the world's production of cacao beans comes from the 'forastero' (translated as 'foreigner'); 'trinitario' ('third') is a hybrid of the two.

The cacao bean is fermented then dried before being roasted and ground to form cocoa liquor or chocolate liquor. Chocolate liquor is bitter and can be put aside to set to be sold as bitter chocolate. It is about 50/50 cocoa solids and cocoa butter; the solids provide the chocolatey taste in the final product and the butter provides smoothness and 'mouth feel'. Next, the chocolate liquor goes through a hydraulic press that separates the cocoa butter and solids, and this is the stage when the chocolate maker applies recipes and techniques that ultimately define their brand. Commonly added are sugar, milk solids and flavours such as vanilla. The next step in the process is conching, when the chocolate liquid mass is stirred and mixed at 55–75°C to give it a smooth texture. This process causes friction between the added sugars and the cocoa, leaving a polished cocoa particle. Invented by chocolate manufacturer Rudolf Lindt, conching gets its name from the shell-like shape of the machine's rollers. Lower-quality chocolates may not have been through this conching stage, resulting in a grainy, average-tasting chocolate. Others are conched for hours, even days, for a more luxurious texture. Valrhona, one of the best chocolate makers in the world, conches its chocolate for 5 days. The final stage in making chocolate is tempering: the chocolate is slowly heated then slowly cooled. Tempering allows the chocolate to harden properly and prevents the cocoa butter from separating. Adding flavours, conching and tempering are fine arts with idiosyncratic results. The two things to look for when you're choosing chocolate are the percentage of cocoa liquor compared to other additives, and the percentage of cocoa butter to cocoa solids (the latter is often hard to determine from the label).

TIPS FOR MELTING CHOCOLATE

Put the uninitiated cook around chocolate and they quickly become the painter's apprentice, slopping it around and coating everything, including the inside of the cutlery drawer. There are two methods for melting chocolate effectively:

* In the microwave: melt at 50 per cent power for 20–30 second intervals, stirring each time. Don't omit the step of stirring, as warmed chocolate keeps its shape, and may look like it needs more time when in fact it has begun to melt.
* In the double boiler: bring the water to the boil in the lower saucepan, then turn off the heat. Place the chocolate in the upper saucepan or in a heatproof bowl over the boiled water and let the residual heat from the water slowly melt the chocolate. Rush this process and you run the risk of scorching the chocolate, making it stiff, lumpy and grainy.
* To add liquid to melted chocolate: heat the liquid first. If you add cold liquid, the chocolate will solidify or seize. Even the moisture from a wet spoon is enough to tamper with melting chocolate. Alternatively, you can add liquid before you start melting the chocolate and heat them both together.

PROBLEM SOLVING

* Seized? Once chocolate has seized, it is unlikely to remelt (although you can try adding a spoonful of vegetable oil which can soften the chocolate enough to continue). The best use for it then is to make chocolate sauce or ganache.
* Bloomed? Blooming often occurs when chocolate is chilled and then returned to room temperature. Chocolate that blooms is still edible with only the slightest difference in flavour and texture. You can melt it to regain its original texture.

TYPES OF CHOCOLATE

Bittersweet chocolate is the chef's choice for desserts because of its stronger flavour. It contains more cocoa liquor (at least 35 per cent) than semi-sweet and sweet chocolate (semi-sweet contains 15–35 per cent and unsweetened chocolate is pure cocoa liquor) and less added sugar.

Cacao is the fruit from which the cacao bean is extracted. Although the words 'cacao' and 'cocoa' are often used interchangeably to describe products derived from the cacao tree, 'cacao' ought only to refer to the tree and the bean it produces, while 'cocoa' refers to the products derived from them—butter, powder, liquor, etc. The cacao bean is made up of 54 per cent cacao butter, 11.5 per cent protein, 9 per cent starch, 5 per cent water, and hundreds of other elements like theobromine, caffeine and aromatic oils. Cacao beans are processed in a similar way to coffee beans.

Cocoa butter is created during the chocolate-making process. It determines the viscosity of chocolate (the best chocolates have a higher percentage, 33–40 per cent, of cocoa butter). It can be bought separately and used to thin chocolate. Cocoa butter is also an important ingredient in pharmaceuticals and cosmetics.

Cocoa powder is a product derived from the cacao bean during the chocolate-making process. Cocoa liquor and cocoa butter are extracted from the cacao bean, and the dry cake that remains after pressing is ground into cocoa powder. Cocoa powder is mildly acidic and can be bought as low-fat and medium-fat. Drinking cocoa or drinking chocolate contains cocoa powder, sugar, malt extracts, milk powder, lecithin and vanilla. It is used in sweetened chocolate drink mixes. *Dutch cocoa* was invented by Coenraad Johannes van Houten in the Netherlands. It is cocoa powder that has been alkalised to leave a darker, smoother, less bitter and more soluble powder. If a recipe calls for Dutch cocoa and all you have is ordinary cocoa powder, add a very small amount of baking powder when sifting the cocoa. This will help alkalise the mix.

Compound chocolate, manufactured as a cheap alternative to chocolate, is made with vegetable oil and cocoa powder instead of cocoa liquor. It melts at a higher temperature, making it manageable for the novice cook. It is sometimes called 'compound chocolate coating', 'decorators' chocolate' or 'confectioners' chocolate'.

Couverture means 'covering', which is its intent. It is a chocolate made to coat truffles, cakes and sweets, but is used by anyone who knows their chocolate for all manner of cooking. Its high cocoa butter content gives couverture its characteristic viscosity (the cocoa butter thins the chocolate to a smooth, glossy and quite runny texture compared with poorly made or cheaper styles of chocolate which when melted stay quite firm). It can be replaced with dark chocolate or compound chocolate, but neither will guarantee the excellent results gained from couverture.

Dark chocolate is sweetened but has no added milk solids. (This is the chocolate you might have stolen from your dad's private stash as a child, only to decide that, if it isn't milk chocolate, it isn't chocolate at all.) Dark chocolates range from bittersweet and semi-sweet to sweet.

German chocolate has nothing to do with Germany. It was formulated in 1852 by Samuel German, to make life easier for bakers by adding more sugar to the chocolate, and is seen as the predecessor to bittersweet chocolate.

Mexican chocolate has added cinnamon, sugar and sometimes nuts and is used for hot drinks and mole sauce. For homemade Mexican chocolate—combine, 1 tablespoon cocoa powder, ½ teaspoon caster sugar and ¼ teaspoon ground cinnamon. Makes the equivalent of 30 g Mexican chocolate.

Milk chocolate or sweet chocolate is rarely used in cooking, as the added milk solids can interfere with baked goods. However, it can be used successfully in a mousse.

Semi-sweet chocolate is similar to bittersweet chocolate, but contains less cocoa liquor (15–35 per cent). An excellent cooking chocolate for good domestic cooks in the know. (Sweet chocolate has more sugar.)

Unsweetened chocolate or *bitter chocolate* is made with 100 per cent cocoa liquor and is bitter and not to be eaten straight from the pantry. It is favoured by professional bakers, as they have more control over the quantities of sugar, etc. in the final product. If necessary, unsweetened chocolate can be replaced with cocoa powder (not drinking chocolate). For homemade unsweetened chocolate—mix together 1 tablespoon vegetable oil and 3 tablespoons cocoa powder. Makes the equivalent of 30 g unsweetened chocolate.

White chocolate is made from what's leftover after the cocoa liquor has been removed, so contains only cocoa butter, sugar, milk solids and vanilla. Different brands contain varying amounts of cocoa butter, and some contain none at all. As a rule of thumb, those made with cocoa butter are ivory-coloured, while those with little or none are a brighter white. All white chocolate must be melted at very low temperatures to keep it from scorching and turning lumpy.

ALTERNATIVES TO CHOCOLATE

Interchange different styles of chocolate with caution, as the properties of each type will react differently.

Carob, the most commonly used alternative, is the fruit of the carob tree (technically a legume) which humans have been harvesting for some 5000 years. It is very high in sucrose (40 per cent) and other sugars (up to 70 per cent). Carob is ground into a cocoa-like powder, roasted or left raw, and is used for drinks and in baking. Carob bars and chips are used for cooking, and the pod can be boiled in water to produce a thick, syrup-like molasses. Carob is used as an alternative to chocolate as it contains a third of the calories, is almost fat-free (chocolate is half fat), is high in pectin, and it doesn't interfere with the absorption of calcium (as chocolate does). It is also caffeine-free so the seeds can be roasted and made into a coffee substitute. Carob can be substituted measure for measure with chocolate, but it has a milder flavour so play with the recipe, perhaps adding more carob to compensate.

CORN

Corn, as in sweet corn, whole-kernel corn, corn on the cob or maize, is best cooked and eaten immediately after harvesting. As corn ages, the sugars rapidly break down into starches and flavour is lost. Only buy corn with a full husk; corn that is presented with the tops cut off or packaged with no husk at all will be old and starchy. If you intend to grill corn, first soak the ears, husk and all, in water for a couple of hours. Cook in the husk on the grill, turning regularly, then remove the husk (shuck) when it's done. Corn can be boiled with its husk on or off, then either eaten immediately or cooled and stripped of the juicy kernels for salads, fritters or succotash.

The sweet corn plant (part of the maize family) is a type of grass, the cobs are the seed heads, the largest of any grass type, edible or inedible. An edible fungus that grows on corn stalks (a strange, purplish growth) is considered a delicacy by some. Baby corn is not young sweet corn but a different variety.

CREAM

The different types of cream sold in different countries and used in recipe books around the world can be one of the more frustrating things to deal with as a cook (or a tourist). Essentially, it is the fat content in cream that affects the final outcome of a dish. As the European, American, South African, Australian and New Zealand dairy fraternities continue to churn creams with differing fat contents and use different marketing names, it can be decidedly challenging to guarantee a perfect result. The list I've provided attempts to explain the main types of cream. My advice is to understand the recipe that the cream is to be used in and work out whether it needs a low, medium or high fat content, and whether it's required for whipping, pouring or for use as is.

TYPES OF CREAM

Clotted cream is made from rich, unpasteurised milk that is heated to 85°C for about 1 hour. In this time, yellow clots of coagulated cream form on top of the milk. This rich cream with a fat content of 55 per cent is also known as 'Devonshire cream'. It can be used as a substitute for qaimaaq.

Crème fraîche is a naturally soured cream (also known as 'racreme', and 'clabber'/'clabbered cream'). It doesn't curdle when heated, which is why it is used for cream-based sauces. It is easy to make at home. For homemade crème fraîche—mix 1 cup whipping cream with ½ cup sour cream or 2 tablespoons buttermilk and pour into a glass bowl. Cover with plastic wrap and leave on the kitchen bench for 8–14 hours (until set). Stir and refrigerate. It will last for 7–10 days in the fridge.

Double cream, generally speaking, has a fat content of 45–48 per cent. (Note that UK cookbooks ask for double cream when they want a pure cream of 30-35 per cent fat content: you'll just have to see whether the recipe works and if not, try a different cream next time.)

Double cream with a high fat content can be whipped but be mindful that it is easy to overwhip, becoming grainy in texture and looking somewhat separated. To help prevent this try adding 15 ml milk to every 300 ml double cream before whipping.

Extra thick single cream is an English product made from single cream (18 per cent fat) which has been homogenised, pasteurised and then cooled. This cream which cannot be whipped is a thick spooning cream similar to Australian double cream.

Half and half is half milk and half cream. It is an American product that is not readily available elsewhere, but you can make your own by using equal parts milk and pouring cream. It cannot be whipped as it contains only 12 per cent fat.

Pouring cream is an Australian product, the equivalent of single cream (with a minimum of 18 per cent fat) in the UK and light cream (18–30 per cent fat) in the US. It can also be called 'pure cream', 'coffee cream' and 'table cream'.

Qaimaaq is a type of cream that is also known as 'breakfast cream'. If necessary, substitute with clotted cream.

Sour cream is cream that has been soured with lactic acid bacteria. The degree of sourness varies between countries-if you're from Ireland, you may like it very sour; if from the US, quite mild. It can be made at home, using buttermilk or yoghurt as the starter. The recipe can be varied, but try the following. For homemade sour cream—mix 250 ml cream (18–36 per cent fat, no additives) with approximately

2 tablespoons or 50 ml yoghurt or buttermilk and leave in a bowl overnight or for 24 hours in a warm area while the mixture sets. Depending on how thick you like it, use immediately or strain through muslin cloth or cheesecloth for several hours until the desired thickness.

Sterilised cream (23–28 per cent fat), also known as 'manufacturer's cream' or 'ultra sterilised cream', is heat-treated which results in a caramelised flavour. This European product, sold in tins or Tetra Paks, cannot be whipped but is spoonable enough to accompany desserts. If unavailable, use pouring cream instead.

Thickened cream is an Australian product, about 35 per cent fat, which contains a thickener such as halal gelatine or vegetable gum. These thickeners are added to stabilise the cream when whipped. Sometimes mineral salts are also added. Use when your British cookbooks call for whipping cream (35–38 per cent fat) and American cookbooks call for heavy cream or heavy whipping cream (35–42 per cent fat).

TIPS FOR WHIPPING CREAM:

★ Chill the bowl you plan to use in the refrigerator. This ensures the cream stays chilled and reduces the chance of it separating.

★ Expect cream to increase in volume by 2–2½ times when whipped. To gain maximum volume, begin the whipping process at a slower speed, and increase the speed as the cream begins to thicken.

★ If the cream begins to turn yellow, it has begun to overwhip and separate. Try mixing in more cream with a spatula until combined. If the cream is too far gone, however, your only hope is to turn it into butter and buttermilk—continue whipping until the milk solids have separated from the milk fat.

★ Add sugar to whipped cream when tracks begin to form. This helps to maximise its volume.

★ To make cream lighter, add a dash of milk to the final stages of whipping. This mixture will not stand for as long.

EGGS

TIPS:

* When I speak of eggs, I mean the freshest possible eggs you can get your hands on: their flavour is incomparable. If, like me, you're an egg snob, the best place to buy eggs is at a local market direct from the farmer. Alternatively, the next best eggs are free range or organic.
* To set the record straight, a rooster is not needed for egg production in itself but for producing fertile eggs—that is, eggs that will hatch a chick after incubation. A rooster is good for waking people up at an ungodly hour, attacking the hand that feeds it, and mating with an entire yardful of hens. (Fertilised eggs can be eaten if they are collected as soon as they are laid—it takes 21 days of a hen sitting on an egg continuously to develop it into a chick.) Fertile and infertile eggs are equally nutritious.
* Brown eggs and white eggs are exactly the same in flavour, quality and nutrition—the pigmentation is genetic, not to do with a hen's diet or condition. Eggs only vary in flavour according to the conditions the hens are kept in.
* A blood spot on a yolk is not a sign that an egg has been fertilised; it simply shows that a blood vessel on the yolk's surface burst while the egg was forming.
* Store eggs in the fridge in their cardboard box. (Eggs are porous and absorb odours from the fridge, which taints their natural flavour; the box will help protect them.)
* Buy eggs with a plan in mind. If baking a cake which may only use one or two eggs, plan on making an omelette or other egg-based dishes within a day or two of purchase.
* For cake and pastry recipes, room temperature eggs are a must, so remove from the fridge and rest on the bench for at least half an hour before starting the recipe. A cold egg mixed with room temperature batter will seize or cool the mixture and won't mix in smoothly. Without a smooth, airy emulsion at this stage, a cake or pastry may become dry and grainy in texture or flat in appearance, cook unevenly or even sink slightly.
* Cream of tartar can also be used to stabilise egg whites: use ⅛ teaspoon cream of tartar for 1 egg white.
* When whipping egg whites, remember that there are four definitive stages that the whites go through. Stage 1 is the just beaten 'foamy' stage: the bubbles are big and the whites are still quite runny. Stage 2 is 'soft peak' where beating takes the whites to a foam which is white, shiny and forms a soft peak that folds over as the beater is lifted from the whites. Stage 3 is 'firm peak' where the whites have been beaten to their maximum size. It will form a stable peak of fine white foam when the beater is removed. The last stage (4) is known as 'dry foam'. The foam is much drier, with no sheen and forms clumps. When the beaters are lifted, the 'dry foam' tends to break easily. This last stage is to be avoided.
* Beating egg whites in a copper bowl is proven to enhance the stability of the egg whites by imparting tiny copper particles. The slightly golden colour is a natural and safe result of the copper bowl. The only drawback is the expense and upkeep involved in owning copperware. A pinch of cream of tartar can also stabilise beaten egg whites so that they are less likely to fall apart.

EGG SIZES

	weight	size
jumbo, very large or extra large	more than 73 g	0–1
large	63–73 g	1–3
medium	53–63 g	3–5
small or pee wee	less than 53 g	5–7

HOW TO COOK EGGS

Omelette is probably the only egg dish that should be cooked at a high heat. All other egg dishes should be cooked at moderate temperatures so as not to make the white turn rubbery. (Omelettes cook so quickly that the whites don't have time to react in this manner.)

For the perfect *hard-boiled egg*, without the nasty grey rim around the yolk, try this method. Place room temperature eggs in a pot of cold water and bring to the boil. Set the timer for 8 minutes from the moment the water begins to simmer. The water should never actually boil, just simmer. (Note that egg protein is delicate and should be cooked gently; boiling eggs makes the yolks hard and the whites rubbery.) When cooked, pour off the water, and place in plenty of cold water to halt the cooking process. For easy peeling, tap the eggs all over to crack the shell and place back in the cold water. Fresh eggs are always much harder to peel than older eggs, and chunks of the white will often come away. See boiled egg for more hard-boiled egg ideas.

For *coddled or soft-boiled eggs* for dipping toast soldiers, try this—bring plenty of water to simmering point. You can add salt and vinegar to help prevent the eggs from cracking. Use room temperature eggs, not eggs straight from the fridge (again to prevent cracking). Cook for 3, 4 or 5 minutes depending on how soft an egg you desire. See boiled egg for more soft-boiled egg ideas.

Scrambled eggs should be cooked over gentle heat with a bit of patience, otherwise you'll end up with a hard, rubbery mass of weeping egg. Mix the eggs with water, milk, cream or (if you're feeling decadent) mascarpone. Use a ratio of 1 egg to 1 tablespoon liquid. Add herbs towards the end of cooking. See scrambled egg for more scrambled egg ideas.

For *poached eggs*, there's one true secret to producing the golf ball/comet-looking eggs found in the best breakfast joints around the world: freshness. The fresher the egg, the better the egg white will cling to the yolk. You can help this along by creating a whirlpool effect in the pot of simmering water and releasing the egg into the centre of the vortex. Adding salt or vinegar to the water may also help the whites to become firm. But at the end of the day, these tricks are irrelevant if the egg is not as fresh as possible. If you place an egg into the water and you find the white floats and disperses on the top while the yolk sinks to the bottom with merely a tail of white intact, chances are this egg is reasonably old and hardly worth eating.

For *fried eggs*, heat butter over medium heat until it begins to bubble, then turn the heat down, break in the eggs and cover the pan. The lid will enclose the steam which slowly cooks the whites on the surface. (I despise a crispy underside to my fried eggs. Heston Blumenthal, 'the alchemist of British cooking', separates the yolk from the white, gently fries the white, then adds the yolk towards the end of cooking—a great method that works well but isn't always practical.)

PROBLEM SOLVING

* Leftover egg yolks? Try hard not to break the yolks and place them in a glass or bowl. Cover with a bit of cold water and refrigerate for up to 3 days. I suggest making a mayonnaise or fresh custard. Leftover egg yolks can be frozen but will be gummy and unusable unless you add a pinch of salt or sugar before freezing. Label your yolks 'savoury' or 'sweet', depending on which you added, then defrost in the refrigerator before using as you would a fresh yolk.

* Leftover egg whites? Store in the freezer. Wash and thoroughly dry an empty plastic container with a screw-top lid. Add leftover egg whites and freeze. Continue to add whites until 2 cm from the top. Don't forget to date the container, as whites will be at their best in the freezer for up to 3 months. Use egg whites for meringues and pavlovas. The problem then becomes one of volume, not numbers. Where a recipe asks for 3 egg whites, you now have a cupful at your disposal. As a guide, the white of one 55–65 g egg weighs 25–35 g. In other words, a little under half the weight of the entire egg is the white.

* Dirty eggs? Wipe with a dry cloth. If you wash an egg, it will become even more vulnerable to absorbing fridge odours.

* Stuck to the carton? Wet the carton and the egg will come out with ease.

* How do I tell if it's fresh? A fresh egg will sink when placed in water (unless it has been damaged). An egg that floats has lost moisture, which has been replaced by air in the blunt, fat end of the egg. The white of a fresh egg clings to the yolk when the egg is cracked onto a plate and the chalazae—(pronounced Kuh-Lay-zee) the two strands of connective tissue attached to the yolk which extend to either end of the shell's membrane and anchor the yolk in the centre of the egg—is prominent. Also, egg white becomes more transparent as the egg ages (caused by the slow escape of carbon dioxide); fresh eggs have a cloudier white.

* Separating eggs and there's eggshell shrapnel or egg yolk in the whites? Remove with an empty half eggshell. If a lot of yolk has managed to infiltrate the white, keep it for scrambled egg and start again.

* Separating eggs and there's egg white in the yolk? Don't worry. It is highly unlikely that the white will affect the further use of the yolk.

* Undercooked boiled eggs? If they're still quite raw in the centre, peel all eggs, mash them together and quickly sauté in a bit of butter in a pan on the stove, just until the yolks have set. Cool immediately and use in sandwiches or eat while hot as a form of scrambled egg.

* Curdled fresh egg custard? Take to it with an electric mixer. The sauce will now be fluffier and a little thinner than intended, but still usable.

* Collapsed soufflé? A collapsing soufflé is known as the 'double deflation method'—as you helplessly watch the soufflé plunge below the rim of its receptacle, you witness too the deflation of your culinary ego. Turn the soufflé out of the mould and onto a baking tray. Place the turned out soufflé back in the hot oven for another minute or 2 and called it 'twice-baked soufflé'. Although it will not rise the second time around, this dense, eggy pudding will have a more concentrated flavour. Serve it on a plate garnished with sauce or ice-cream or both.

* Egg stuck to the dishes? Always use cold water to wash dishes with egg stuck to them. Hot water will only cook the egg onto the plate.

OTHER TYPES OF EGG

Eggs for cooking are most commonly those from hens. Eggs from other birds tend to be recipe specific and are rarely interchangeable.

Duck eggs (available from Asian grocers) can be used in many recipes that specify hens' eggs, but the flavour is stronger, oilier and richer, and not to everybody's taste. The flavour, naturally, is a cross between duck meat and egg. Duck eggs are also larger, so do not substitute 1 duck egg for 1 hen's egg. Duck egg whites cannot be whisked successfully as they lack globulin, a protein that, when whisked, holds air bubbles. In Vietnam, fertile duck eggs are incubated until the foetal stage then boiled for 15 minutes and eaten with ginger, Vietnamese mint and soy sauce.

Quail eggs are readily available from poultry shops as well as some supermarkets. These delicately flavoured little eggs can be brutal on your patience if you have to boil and peel them, as the shell is delicate and somewhat elastic. If poaching or frying, always cut the top off them rather than cracking them in the middle like a hen's egg, and pour onto a shallow dish or saucer before placing in the pan. Quail eggs take about 2 minutes to poach. When boiling quail eggs, swirl the water for half the cooking time to centre the egg yolk. They will take 3–4 minutes to hard boil.

Thousand-year eggs are not a thousand years old, because that would be just silly. There are three varieties: hulidan, dsaudan and pidan. For pidan eggs, duck's or hen's eggs are coated in a clay-like plaster of red earth, garden lime, salt, wood ash and tea. Once coated in this alkaline mud, they are buried in soil for 100 days to cure. The eggs can be eaten raw—usually with soy and ginger—or cooked after the coating is removed (scrape off and wash under running water). The flavour resembles lime and pungent ammonia. As for the colour, the whites turn amber to black and have a gelatinous texture and the yolk is dark-green with a creamy texture. Hulidan eggs are covered with a mix of salt and clay or ash and left in a cool, dark space for 1 month. When opened, the eggs have a partly solidified white and yolk with a salty flavour. Dsaudan eggs are packed in a mixture of salt and cooked rice and then stored for a minimum of 6 months, in which time the shell will soften and the insides will coagulate, producing an egg that is mildly salty and winey tasting. Also known as century eggs, hundred-year eggs, fermented eggs, ancient eggs or Ming dynasty eggs.

ALTERNATIVES TO EGGS

Eggs act as a binding agent in recipes which makes it hard to find an exact replacement with equal properties.

'Egg replacer' is a powdered leavening agent made from toasted soy flour, wheat starch, lecithin, dextrose and guar gum. It is made to use measure for measure instead of whole eggs in baking: 10 g powder mixed with 40 g water = 1 egg.

For savoury dishes, the tofu-based products mock egg salad, imitation scrambled eggs and egg-free mayonnaise might be appropriate.

Not enough eggs for baking? Replace every third egg with 1 tablespoon cornflour. For recipes with 3 or more eggs, egg replacer is the best option. For recipes using 1 egg, use egg replacer or one of the following: 1 tablespoon soy flour mixed with 1 tablespoon water; ¼ cup ripe mashed banana or apple or prune puree; 3 tablespoons mashed tofu; or 1 teaspoon ground flaxseed mixed with 3 tablespoons water.

'Egg cream' contains neither eggs nor cream, but rather milk, chocolate and seltzer or soda water. It is a drink asked for in New York. When made with love, the froth on top resembles beaten egg whites.

FATS

Essential fatty acids (EFA) are essential to human health but our bodies can't make them so they must be supplied through food or supplements. The two vital EFAs are omega-6 and omega-3 (see polyunsaturated and superunsaturated fats). EFAs are highly perishable, deteriorating rapidly when exposed to light, air, heat and metals, so they cannot be dried, powdered or stored for long periods. To get the most out of EFAs, choose fresh products.

Monounsaturated fats are good for us and should be included in our diet. Foods rich in monounsaturated fatty acids are generally liquid at room temperature and semi-solid when refrigerated (for example, olive oil). Other foods high in monounsaturated fatty acids include peanuts, pecans, cashews, macadamias, avocados and canola oil.

Polyunsaturated fats, also known as omega-6 EFAs, are the good guys and are found in grapeseed, corn, cottonseed, pumpkin, sesame, soy and walnut oils, and in safflower, sunflower and hemp (which have the highest EFA reading). However, polyunsaturated fats can be harmful when commercially processed.

Saturated fats are bad because they clog your arteries. Found especially in butter, eggs, beef, lamb, chicken and pork, saturated fats become especially harmful when prepared with high heat, that is, barbecued, fried, grilled or cooked at a temperature over 105°C. Cooked at low temperatures, saturated fats are less harmful. All oils and fats contain some saturated fatty acids-some other foods with high levels are palm kernels (88 per cent), coconut, cocoa butter and shea nut butter. Of course, these fats also provide flavour which is why it's a good idea to cook the chicken with the skin on, or the steak with the fat left on, to keep the food moist and flavoursome, then remove the skin and fat before serving (before it goes on the plate, to avoid temptation).

Superunsaturated fats are often referred to as omega-3 EFAs and they're another of the good guys. They are harder to come by than omega-6, but the richest source is flaxseed. They are also found in tuna, salmon and trout and in blackcurrant seed oil. In land animals, the brain, eyeballs, adrenal glands and testes are rich in superunsaturated fatty acids.

Trans fatty acids are the really evil ones. They are the result of a chemical alteration, or transformation, that converts 'natural' unsaturated fats into 'unnatural' unsaturated fats that act like saturated fats. However, trans fatty acids are worse for you than saturated fats because they interfere with the work that the natural essential fatty acids must do. Margarines, shortenings, shortening oils, and hydrogenated and partially hydrogenated vegetable oils contain a large amount of trans fat. Salad oils, butter, milk and meats generally have small amounts of trans fatty acids.

Vegetable fat is sold in a block form like butter and is generally used to replace butter in baking (although some are produced as solid oils for frying). Its use varies depending on the brand. Trex (UK) is used to replace butter in vegan cooking, especially baking. (When replacing butter with Trex, use 20 per cent less than the specified amount of butter, as Trex contains no water.)

FISH

Fish and other seafood have such a staggering variety of species that they would have to be at the top of the list when it comes to the confusion surrounding names. On an international level, it becomes far more confusing, as each country and their respective cookbook authors call on seafood native to that region. To supply a universal dictionary of the names of all fish caught globally would be a mammoth task: even fishing bodies struggle to standardise a market name for each of their own country's species, let alone collaborate to solve international naming frustrations. So although I have listed many of the more common alternative names for crustaceans and fish in this book, this general advice is probably the most useful: when using foreign cookbooks or travelling overseas, the key is to establish what kind of texture and flavour the recipe requires. Is it firm-fleshed or flaky, lean or oily, flat or round? (See below for a discussion of these categories.) Then ask for a fish with these specific qualities at the local market or fish shop rather than struggling with unfamiliar names.

The two main categories of fresh fish are flatfish and round fish. Flatfish are bottom-dwellers which swim parallel to the ocean floor. The side that faces down is pale, while the upper side is dark and contains both eyes. Species include flounder, sole, brill, turbot (halibut) and plaice. You usually lose about 50 per cent of a whole flatfish in cleaning, preparation and removal of inedible parts; while the waste ratio of round fish is higher (60 per cent) due to the larger head. Flatfish are lean, and the best of them is probably the halibut (the largest flat fish in the world).

Round fish are, as the name suggests, rounder in shape, and have eyes on either side of the head. They are then divided into a further three categories of lean, moderate and high fat content. The higher the fat content, the darker, firmer and more distinctively flavoured the flesh becomes. 'High' fat means on average 12–14 per cent, although in eel it can be as high as 30 per cent. Fish in this category include butterfish, mackerel, tuna, salmon and sardines (pilchards). Fish species with lean fat content tend to carry their oil in the liver rather than the flesh. At about 2.5 per cent fat, lean fish are mild in flavour and lightly coloured. Fish in this category include red fish, snapper, bream, garfish and perch.

Fish with moderate fat content (6 per cent or less) include swordfish, whiting, ocean trout and barramundi.

TIPS FOR BUYING FISH:

* Use your eyes—and nose. First, look at the fish: you want to see bright, clear and often protruding eyes and a shiny, bright-coloured skin. The gills should be red to bright pink (as a fish ages, its gills turn to a light pink, then grey and finally to a greenish or dull brown). The outer skin should be firm to press and, if it hasn't been scaled, it will have a natural film or slime. Your fish (and fish shop) should smell of the ocean, without any strong smell of overt fishiness or of ammonia.
* Ask the fishmonger to gut (draw) and scale (dress) the fish for you. This can save not only time but an unbelievable mess. A fully dressed fish usually means gutted and scaled, with gills, head, fins and tail removed.
* When buying fish fillets or cutlets, look for cleanly cut, firm, elastic, shiny, translucent flesh. Any fillets that appear dull and watery may well be old or defrosted. Fillets with drying or browned edges are not acceptable.
* Frozen fish should be bought tightly wrapped. If you notice freezer burns after unwrapping, take it back.

* Frozen seafood can, in some cases, be superior in quality to fresh. After being caught, fish to be sold fresh is held on fishing trawlers in ice slurries or in chilled sea water at 0°C. It could be days before it reaches the shop, while fish which is sold as frozen is 'snap' or 'fast' frozen on the ship so it doesn't run the same risk of being overhandled, bruised or deteriorating in quality.

HOW TO COOK FISH

Fish is a delicate protein that I associate with egg white. In their raw state, both fish and egg white are translucent protein. Apply heat and both react in the same way: they change colour (from translucent to opaque) and texture (becoming firm). However, there the similarities end, as egg white can be cooked for a lengthy period and will still be quite edible, while fish needs to be monitored closely so it doesn't become dry and tough. The proteins in fish need to only just set: the juices change from clear to white and the flesh becomes opaque but remains moist. If you continue to cook beyond this point, the fish will begin to 'bleed': the juices are forced from the flesh, leaving blobs of white protein on the surface of the cooked fish. The more juices forced from the flesh, the drier the meat you are left with.

Cooking fish in the microwave is asking for trouble, as the risk of overcooking is high. There are better ways.

For the best results with defrosted fish, cook while it is still icy (before it starts to drip). Follow the recipe as if the fish were fresh but give it a longer cooking time—as much as 25 per cent more—and allow for it having a little extra moisture.

STORAGE AND PREPARATION

Fresh fish is said to have a shelf life of 12 days from the moment it is caught, provided it is stored at 0°C, which should mean you have about 7 days with it. However, as most refrigerators sit on 4°C this cuts shelf life back to about 3–4 days after purchase.

Be aware that the entrails of freshly caught or whole uncleaned fish decay faster than the flesh, which means you run the risk of spoiling your catch if you don't clean it before storing.

Use a sharp pair of poultry scissors to trim the dorsal and tail fins from the body of the fish. This prevents them from burning if the fish is cooked near or over a naked flame.

When filleting flatfish at home, remove the fillets from the pale or white side first. This will make taking the fillets from the darker side easier.

Frozen raw fish lasts about 6 months in the freezer. Defrost the fish, covered, in a refrigerator. This takes about 24 hours. Once defrosted, it does not have the tight, firm flesh characteristic of fresh fish and in some cases may be waterlogged or seem like a dish sponge, so take account of this when you are deciding what to cook with it.

Never re-freeze fish: it will cause the flesh to break down, go watery and lose flavour, and it poses a greater risk of food poisoning when the fish is defrosted the second time.

FLOUR

Flour is classified by its extraction rate, which is the percentage of wheat grain present in the flour. At the top end, coming in at 100 per cent, is wholemeal flour, with brown flour around 80–85 per cent, followed by plain flour at 75–80 per cent. The protein content determines how the flour performs during baking, as it is the protein that forms gluten. Generally speaking, bread and pasta is made with flour with a high protein content or hard flour (11–14 per cent) (in the case of pasta, this is because pasta dough must be rolled very thin which is easier with the elasticity of high-gluten flour); while cake-making or soft flour has a low protein content (7–10 per cent). Cakes or biscuits made with high-gluten flour will be chewier, especially if the dough or batter is mixed excessively. Vigorous mixing of any flour-based recipe (whether hard or soft) will work the gluten, which is why some recipes for scones, sponges, short pastry, etc. suggest mixing as lightly as possible. The protein content of flour is marked on the packet.

TIPS:

★ Sift flour two or three times before mixing with other ingredients. This aerates the mixture, as well as removing any lumps or foreign matter. Aerating ensures that the final product is given every chance of being light and fluffy.

★ Add the sifted flour to the wet mixture, not the other way around. Use a metal spoon or a rubber or plastic spatula to fold the flour into the mixture. This cutting and folding also ensures the final mixture retains as much of the air as possible.

★ If you find small brown insects (psocids or booklice, often mistaken for weevils) in your flour, dispose of it immediately. To avoid these little pests, buy smaller quantities of flour and store in an airtight container in a dry, cool place. Humidity can wreak havoc on dry goods in the tropics, so try storing flour products in the fridge, but remember that keeping them airtight is the key.

★ Plain flours have a shelf life of 6–9 months if stored correctly. Wholemeal or brown flour's shelf life is considerably less due to its fat content, so 2–3 months is recommended.

Types of flour

In the following list of flours, w-f indicates wheat-free and g-f indicates gluten-free.

Amaranth flour (w-f, g-f) is made from the tiny seeds of amaranth, a plant that is related to spinach and beetroot (beets). (The leaves of the plant are also edible.) Amaranth flour is not designed for making leavened breads, as the result is too dense, but is great for flat breads, pasta, biscuits (cookies), pancakes and muffins.

   Arrowroot flour (w-f, g-f)—also called 'arrowroot starch' or simply 'arrowroot'—is made from the arrowroot, *Maranta arundinacea* (although some varieties are made from plants such as banana, potato or tropical roots). It is higher in fibre than all other starches, by as much as 25 per cent, yet is still smooth, and has 1½ times the thickening power of plain flour. It's great in baking and as a thickener, where it mixes clear, not cloudy (which is handy to know if thickening a clear liquid) and is often better than cornflour because it doesn't impart a chalky taste if undercooked. Like all starches, mix arrowroot with a little cold water first to make a wet paste before adding it to the hot liquid.

   Barley flour (w-f) is made from barley and although barley contains gluten, the gluten is quite weak, so mix it with wheat flour when baking. For bread, a good ratio is to make the barley flour 25 per cent of the mixture. For other baking, mix 50/50 with other flours.

Bean flour (w-f, g-f) can be used to make pasta, crepes and flat breads, and some traditional Middle Eastern dishes.

Besan flour (w-f, g-f)—also known as 'garbanzo flour', 'gram flour' and 'chickpea flour'—is made from finely milled chickpeas or pigeon peas (chana dhal or bengal gram). Used extensively in Indian cuisine as a batter, it also makes an excellent binding and thickening agent as well as panisses (chickpea fritters), breads, dips and desserts.

Bleached flour is whiter and contains less vitamin E than unbleached. Use it exactly as you do unbleached flour.

Buckwheat flour (w-f, g-f) is also known as 'Indian wheat'. Pancakes and soba noodles are two well-known products made from buckwheat flour. Although the word 'wheat' appears in its name, buckwheat is totally wheat- and gluten-free.

Cake flour is a US product not readily available on European and Australasian supermarket shelves. Cake flour is made from soft wheat with as little as 9 per cent protein compared to the 10–12 per cent in plain flour and 12–14 per cent in strong flour. It is bleached with chlorine gas, which, besides whitening the flour, also makes it slightly acidic. This acidity makes cakes set faster and gives them a finer texture. If a recipe calls for the use of cake flour or soft wheat flour, use plain flour but substitute 10 per cent of the quantity with cornflour or potato flour. This will help soften the mixture.

Cassava flour (w-f, g-f) is made from the tuberous root of the cassava and is used to create tapioca products. For tapioca, a starch, the fibre element of cassava (approximately 12 per cent) has been removed. Pearl tapioca and tapioca flour are used as thickeners in soups and sauces or used in desserts. Tapioca flour can be used to make gluten-free bread, where it imparts a chewy texture.

Chestnut flour (w-f, g-f) is a sweet flour used in desserts and batters. It should be fresh if it smells of chestnuts. Do not substitute with water chestnut flour, found in Asian grocers, which is used as a thickening and binding agent or to make water chestnut crackers.

Cornflour (w-f, although many brands are made with wheat so check the labels before buying, g-f) has a very fine texture and is used as a thickener or in baking to lighten the texture of a product. It is known as 'cornstarch' in the US, and should not be confused with cornmeal.

Durum wheat flour is a hard wheat flour used to make pasta and noodles. ('Hard' in this case doesn't refer to the level of gluten or protein but to the physical properties of the wheat which splinters when ground.) It is also referred to as 'durum wheat semolina', 'fine ground semolina' or 'continental flour'. See also *Semolina flour*.

Gluten, while not a type of flour, is a substance found in wheat flour which affects the elasticity and texture of a dough. Some people require a gluten-free diet, most often those who are diagnosed with coeliac disease, also known as gluten-sensitive enteropathy. They must avoid wheat, oats, rye and barley, among other products.

Gluten flour, made by the removal of the starch and the bran, can be added to plain flour to boost its gluten level so it resembles strong flour (see below).

Gluten-free flour is sold commercially. This flour is usually made from wheat with the gluten removed, so is often not suitable for people with wheat allergies. See also Gluten.

Graham flour is a US product similar to wholemeal flour (which can be used as substitute).

Jerusalem artichoke flour (w-f, g-f) is a useful alternative for people with hypoglycaemia and diabetes. It doesn't thicken as other flours do, so is suited to pasta, pie crusts and biscuits.

Kamut flour is an ancient grain, twice the size of wheat and with 30 per cent more protein. It is used for baking (bread and biscuits) and pasta.

Kuzu/kudzu (w-f, g-f) is a starch (found in Asian grocers) made from the roots of the kudzu plant. It is used for thickening soups and sauces, and for coating food to be deep-fried.

Legume flour (w-f, g-f) can be made from any legume: yellow or green peas, red or green lentils, or white, broad or lima beans. These flours can be mixed with other flours to add extra protein to gluten-free baking.

Lotus flour (w-f, g-f) has a moderate, pleasant taste that hints of sour, salt, bitter and—of all things—mild cheese. A truly unique taste (which can be neutralised with the addition of a little salt to the recipe). It is used for baking (breads and biscuits) and pasta.

Malanga flour (w-f, g-f), from the taro family, is considered to be the most easily digested complex carbohydrate because the grains in the starch are so fine. Also said to be the most hypoallergenic of all the flours, it is used in baking and as an excellent thickener.

Matzo is a Jewish unleavened bread made from flour and water and cooked very quickly so it doesn't ferment or rise (hence it is said it must be mixed and cooked within 18 minutes). The resulting thin crisp cracker is then eaten as is or cooled and processed further as matzo flour (finely ground, for cakes and biscuits), matzo meal (coarsely ground, as a replacement for bread crumbs and for matzo balls or dumplings) or matzo farfel (little cubes used as a noodle or bread cube substitute).

Millet flour (w-f, g-f) is made from millet seed. Millet and millet by-products are considered animal fodder to many Westerners but they are a staple in African, Indian and Asian countries. The flour can be mixed with plain flour in baking, in a proportion of up to 30 per cent millet flour. Try mixing in some whole millet seeds for texture.

Nut flour (w-f, g-f) is derived from the ground 'cake' formed when oil is pressed from nuts such as almonds, macadamias, walnuts, chestnuts and pecans to name a few. Store in the fridge or freezer and use soon after purchase. See also Nut meal.

Nut meal (w-f, g-f) is ground from whole nuts, with the oil retained, to leave a coarse, oily mix which can turn rancid within weeks. Store in the fridge or freezer and use soon after purchase. See also Nut flour.

Oat flour (w-f) is used for thickening stews and soups. It is great in biscuits, muffins, breads and desserts.

00 flour (double O flour) is an Italian wheat flour with a low protein content. If none is available, use plain flour. Most commonly used for making pasta.

Pastry flour is a US product used for making pastries (as its name suggests), and sits somewhere between cake flour and plain flour in the protein content. It's great for pie dough if ever you find it.

Plain flour, or all-purpose flour in the US, is the most common of the white flours. Use within 9 months or, for a long duration, keep in the fridge or freezer and bring to room temperature before cooking.

Poi flour or poi starch (w-f, g-f) is made from dehydrated, fermented paste from taro stems. It is used extensively in Polynesian cuisine.

Potato flour (w-f, g-f) is used primarily as a thickener and in gluten-free baking. However, it makes a great addition to cake recipes because of its ability to absorb moisture. Experiment with replacing some plain flour with potato flour in baking for a moister or drier final product. Try replacing 10 per cent of the flour or you can replace 1 cup of wheat flour with ⅝ cup potato flour.

Quinoa flour (w-f, g-f), made from the quinoa (pronounced keen-wah) fruit, is sometimes found in pre-made pasta.

Rice flour (w-f, g-f), both white and brown, has a very light and airy texture and a slightly sweet flavour. It is used in desserts, cakes and biscuits, and as a gluten-free thickener.

Rye flour (w-f) is usually mixed with wheat flour to make bread; the lighter the bread, the more wheat flour in the mixture. Pumpernickel bread is high in rye, strong in flavour and deep in colour. Rye flour is low in gluten.

Sago flour (w-f, g-f), made from the stem of the sago palm, is used to make pearl sago for desserts, and to thicken soups, sauces and stir-fries.

Self-raising flour (self-rising flour in the US) is plain flour that has baking powder added. I suggest making your own when needed, as the baking powder in packaged self-raising flour absorbs atmospheric moisture over time and loses its leavening ability, even if stored in an airtight container. It is sometimes called 'phosphated flour' or 'pancake flour'. For homemade self-raising flour-mix together: 1 cup plain flour, 1½ teaspoons baking powder and ½ teaspoon salt.

Semolina flour is used for making couscous and pasta. Semolina is made from the coarsely ground endosperm of durum wheat. It is sold as extra fine, fine, medium and coarse, each of which are suited to specific cooking methods. Extra fine is used in fresh pasta and specialty breads. Known as 'creamed wheat' or 'cream of wheat' in the US and sometimes 'farina', fine semolina is used as a porridge or in cakes and biscuits. Medium and coarse are often used in dessert or pudding recipes.

Sorghum flour (w-f, g-f) is nutritionally packed and adds a great flavour to gluten-free baking when combined with other flour products.

Soy flour (w-f, g-f) should be stored in the fridge or freezer, and must be mixed with another flour; by itself it is unappetising. It is rich in protein, so is used as a bread improver, and can help goods keep moist and last longer. Try replacing 2 tablespoons in every 1 cup flour with soy flour. Remember that baked products will brown more quickly if they contain soy flour, so use a temperature about 10°C lower than the recipe suggests. Soy flour can also be toasted before use to intensify its nutty flavour—do so in a dry pan over medium heat until the colour just begins to change.

Spelt flour (w-f) is very low in gluten, and makes an excellent substitute for wheat, with its delicious nutty flavour. If making bread with spelt flour, use only three-quarters of the water specified in the wheat flour recipe.

Stone ground flours are wholemeal, either plain or self-raising. The best are organic and milled in small batches by water-powered stone mills—this crushes and grinds the whole grains slowly so flavour and nutritional oils are distributed throughout. (In contrast, most flour milling is done by high-speed steel cylinders or hammer mills, which heats and oxidies the grain, killing healthy enzymes and allowing oils to become rancid.) They have a slightly fresher flavour, a courser texture and a slightly better nutrient value than regular wholemeal flour.

Strong flour is also known as 'bread flour', 'high gluten flour' or 'hard wheat flour'. The high gluten content of this flour makes it the ideal product for making bread, giving the final loaf a better structure.

Teff flour (w-f, g-f), made from the world's smallest grain, is packed with nutrients (proteins and calcium) and has been enjoyed for centuries by highland Ethiopians. It is used to make the spongy, sour flat bread 'injera' which is used to scoop up meat and vegetable stews and to line the trays on which stews are served, soaking up juices as the meal progresses—when this edible tablecloth is eaten, the meal is officially over.

Wholemeal flour, or whole wheat flour in the US, is a more nutritious flour than plain, as it contains all the bran and wheatgerm.

HERBS

I will always encourage people to try growing fresh herbs at home, in the garden or in pots on the windowsill or balcony. If you opt for potted herbs, I recommend the following four as a starting combination: flat-leaf parsley, rosemary, basil and thyme.

TIPS:

* Wash herbs only just before using them, as excess water can be absorbed through the leaves, causing black, slimy spots.
* Store fresh herbs from the market in a plastic bag with the stem end wrapped in wet paper towel.
* If the herbs have been purchased with the root still intact, stand them in a small amount of cold water in the fridge, covered with a plastic bag.
* As a general rule, add woodier herbs (rosemary, thyme) early in cooking and soft herbs (basil, mint) at the very end of cooking.
* Dried herbs certainly have their place in the kitchen, but when they've lost their punch, toss them out and start again: replace any not used within a year of purchase.
* When substituting dried herbs for fresh, use about half the amount the recipe calls for, as dried herbs contain concentrated oils: 1 teaspoon fresh herbs = ½ teaspoon dried. If you have dried your own recently, it may be wise to use only one-third of the dried herb compared to fresh, as the dried herb will still have quite a kick.

PROBLEM SOLVING

Leftover herbs? The best option is to avoid leftovers by planning a second recipe to use up the remainder of the bunch. However, there are many uses for leftovers:
* Dry your own—not all herbs enjoy being dried. The best are those that contain volatile oils: rosemary, marjoram, savory, bay and thyme. Either hang them over the stove area or place on a tray in a warm, dry area of the house. Once dry, store in airtight jars.
* Store in vinegar—softer herbs, like parsley, tarragon, basil, dill and mint, lose more in the drying process so a good option is to steep in vinegar, then splash a little on the dish instead of the fresh herb.
* Store herbs in oil—chop finely or crush in a mortar and pestle then mix with a little oil. Store in the fridge for several weeks with the layer of oil sitting on top. Ideal for basil, coriander and dill.
* Freeze—most herbs can be frozen, left intact on the branch. The less you handle them before freezing, the better chance they have in the freezer. Wash, pat dry carefully (so as not to bruise them and release their oils), then pack in plastic bags, removing as much air as possible before freezing. Remember not to overcrowd the bag and to keep it flat. When you need the herb, just snap off the amount required and cut while still frozen. Defrosting the herb will make it too wet to work with. Another way to freeze herbs is to puree with water then store in ice trays. The ice cubes of herbs can be stored in plastic bags and then used for soups, stews or sauces.
* Make herb butter—chop and mix with softened butter, roll in foil and freeze for later use. Try on herb bread or take a slice to have with a steak.

TYPES OF HERBS

Basil This fragrant herb doesn't like to be heated for long periods so add at the end of cooking. Use in salads, or blend with cream cheese and use as a spread in sandwiches. Basil (and other leafy herbs) should be torn rather than cut to avoid bruising and loss of flavour. There are some amazing varieties of basil that are worth trying: look for holy basil, excellent with fish and seafood dishes of Asian inspiration: cinnamon basil, for use in biscuits and desserts; lemon basil, for curries, seafood, poultry, veal and salads; purple basil for flair; and Thai basil or horapa basil, with its strong aniseed aroma, for stir-fries, soups, curries and salads.

Bergamot is both a citrus fruit and a herb of the mint family that has edible flowers and leaves. The herb is similar to eau de cologne mint, which is also known as orange mint. Dried bergamot is popular in the US for tea infusions (similar to lemon balm). Its aroma is not dissimilar to the bergamot orange, but the herb and fruit are not related.

Chervil is a herb with a delicate anise flavour, usually used to finish a dish or in a salad. Chervil is a component in the classic herb blend 'fines herbes'.

Chinese parsley see Coriander.

Cilantro see Coriander.

Coriander leaves and seeds taste very different so cannot be substituted for one another. Coriander leaf, also known as 'cilantro' in the US or 'Chinese parsley', is my favourite herb, with its enticing aroma and bold, refreshing and incomparable flavour. It is definitely one that should only be used fresh—when cooked or dried, the flavour diminishes greatly. The root is used extensively in Thai cuisine where it is pounded into pastes and dressings. Unfortunately, coriander root can be hard to come across, especially in supermarkets. If a recipe calls for root when none is available, try doubling the quantity of finely chopped stem, but bear in mind that this will produce a slightly different texture (slimier) and will not match the depth of flavour the root can provide. Coriander sold with its root intact can be stored in a small amount of water (1–2 cm only) and covered with a plastic bag—it will last for 1–2 weeks and longer if you change the water.

Curry leaf, a delicate herb with a pungency that resembles curry, can be found fresh in Asian grocers (sold in bags of small stems of soft, dark green leaves) although dried leaves are more readily available. The fresh leaves are vibrant, while the pre-packed dried leaves have little flavour. Fresh leaves can be toasted or oven-dried just before use to release the essential oils, then added to soups, sauces and curries. They are also delicious finely shredded in a spring roll or samosa mixture. Packets of leaves can be frozen (as you would kaffir lime leaves) then added to the dish straight from the freezer. And if you really like the flavour, it might even be worth planting one of these decorative leafy trees in the garden.

Epazote is a pungent herb used especially in bean dishes in Central American countries, Mexico and New Mexico. It is said to make the beans more digestible. It is also available as a powder.

Fines herbes is a mixture of chopped herbs, usually chervil, chives, parsley and tarragon.

Marjoram and *oregano* are very similar herbs of the same genus, *Origanum*. Oregano is said to be a hardier plant, liking arid soils, and is stronger in flavour and more pungent; it is suited to Mediterranean-style cooking, with strong flavours. Marjoram is more delicate, appreciates a lighter cooking style (added to sauces or soups towards the end of cooking, or eaten raw in a salad) and is ideal as a pot herb. (Oregano has a root system that does not take to potting.) However, the difference isn't substantial, and their flavour can be just as strongly determined by where the herb is grown: in plenty of sunlight, essential oils within the plant are more prominent and heighten the flavour. Both herbs like to be dried. Use fresh in salads, especially where tomatoes and onions feature.

Mint is an easy-to-grow herb. The three main types are spearmint, peppermint and pennyroyal. Spearmint (garden mint) is the one most often used in the kitchen.

Orange mint see Bergamot.

Oregano see Marjoram.

Parsley is one of the most popular culinary herbs. The two main varieties of this herb are prepared quite differently. Curly parsley can be chopped ferociously, this way and that, and still present well. (The old method of wrapping the finely chopped parsley in a towel, washing it and then squeezing out whatever flavour and chlorophyll was left in it, ready to sprinkle over every dish on the menu, must surely be vanquished.) Flat-leaf parsley (also called 'Italian parsley' or 'continental parsley') should be torn by hand or run through with the blade of a knife once or twice only—a chiffonade of leaf, if you will. Any ferocious chopping attacks on this type of parsley bruise and damage the leaf. Flat-leaf parsley has more flavour and less bitterness than curly parsley. A third common variety is celery-leaf parsley: this is often tagged Italian parsley but is in fact a different breed altogether, and has a much tougher texture and stronger flavour. Parsley root, also known as 'turnip-rooted parsley' and 'Hamburg parsley' (although the Germans call it 'Dutch parsley'—seems nobody wants to own up to its origin), is a subspecies grown for its beige root, which tastes like a parsley–celeriac cross. It's used in parts of Europe in soups, stews and simply as a vegetable. Choose firm roots with feathery, bright-green leaves. All fresh parsley can be stored refrigerated in a plastic bag for up to a week.

Rosemary is a tough herb that can be added at the beginning of cooking. Remove the leaves and grind in a mortar and pestle with sea salt to make a rub for lamb, chicken, beef or veal cuts. Rosemary keeps well in the fridge, but not in water: keep it dry in an airtight bag. You can also tie a string around the end of the bunch and hang it in the kitchen to dry. Rosemary flowers are also edible, if slightly bitter.

Sage has a powerful flavour so tends to be used 1 or 2 leaves at a time. Drying the remainder is an excellent option, as dried sage holds well in cooking for long periods. One way to use a bunch of fresh sage quickly is to make a chicken or veal ragoût, a long slow-cooking process well matched to this herb. Sage butter and sage oil are delicious (see **Herbs—Problem Solving**) and, need I say it, sage stuffing. Store sage in the same way as rosemary, dry and airtight in the fridge.

Shiso is a very popular herb in Japan, where the green leaves are used in salads, to wrap food, and in tempura, sushi and sashimi as a garnish. Also known as 'perilla', 'Chinese basil' and 'wild sesame'. Red shiso is named 'beefsteak leaf' because of its colour. It is used extensively as a colouring and mild flavouring agent in pickled plums.

Thyme comes in many varieties, all of which can be interchanged successfully, despite obvious differences in pungency. Common thyme and lemon thyme suit most foods. I find myself drying the bunch as soon as it gets home—using it and hanging it up at the same time.

Za'atar, the Arabic word for 'wild thyme', is both a herb and a spice mix used in Middle Eastern cooking. It is sprinkled on bread before baking, and on soups, seafood, barbecued mutton and grilled meats. It is a blend of sumac, sesame seeds and the herb za'atar, and can be bought ready-made in Middle Eastern and Lebanese produce shops.

LEMONS

TIPS:

* Lemons are a rich source of vitamin C and their ascorbic acid content prevents oxidisation. Use lemon juice to stop some fruit and vegetables from browning, like bananas, apples and artichokes.
* Always wash and dry lemons before using the zest in cooking. This removes dust, mould and dirt which could affect the dish being cooked; and in the case of non-organic lemons, removes the insecticides, colour dye or wax they can be sprayed with (these can all be removed with soapy water).
* When grating the zest, place a piece of baking or silicon paper over the outside of the grater where it will stick to the rough edges. Grate to your heart's content, peel off the paper and all the zest will come off with it.
* To get more juice from a lemon, roll it on the benchtop, applying pressure with the palm of your hand. This 'bruising' tenderises the membranes within the lemon. Or place the lemon in the microwave for 20–30 seconds before juicing.
* Leftover lemon juice can be frozen in ice-cube trays and when frozen kept in a clip-lock bag. Lemon zest also freezes well.
* For a dinner party, lemon halves wrapped and tied in muslin make an attractive addition to the table. A half lemon should last each person the entire meal, and the muslin prevents the seeds from popping everywhere.

MEAT

One way of thinking about different types of meat—rather than the usual divide between white and red—is whether the animal is ruminant or non-ruminant. Ruminant refers to any cud-chewing or cloven-hoofed animal with four legs. Keep in mind that recipes for one animal could lend themselves to another. Horsemeat, although not eaten in many countries, is popular in many European countries, especially Belgium, France and Sweden, where it outsells lamb and mutton combined.

The best mince meat is the type you make yourself. If you don't have a mincing machine, try cutting larger pieces of meat (usually scraps, off-cuts or cheaper cuts like skirt or flank) into 1–2 cm pieces before putting in the food processor on pulse so you can control how finely it is chopped. Hand-cutting meat for a good meat sauce is better left to a chef.

CUTS OF MEAT AND COMMON TERMS

* Chuck steak is known as 'round steak' in the US, and is also called 'stewing beef' or 'casserole beef'.
* Corned beef is known as 'cured beef' or 'corned silverside' in the UK and can be called 'salt beef'. Canned corned beef is known as 'bully beef' in the UK.
* A cutlet is the lean loin with the bone on.
* A chop is a cut, bone in, from the shoulder and neck, and also the middle loin.
* An eye fillet steak or fillet steak is known as 'tenderloin steak' in the US and is also called 'filet mignon'.
* Mince is referred to as 'ground meat' in the US.
* Offal is known as 'variety meats' or 'organ meat' in the US.

* Rump steak is called 'sirloin steak' in the US, while sirloin in Australia or the UK refers to what Americans call 'porterhouse'.
* Skirt steak is called 'flank steak' in the US and can be called stewing steak.
* A joint of meat is a large cut of meat with the bone.

HOW TO COOK MEAT

Bring meat to room temperature before cooking. Meat to be roasted, pan-grilled or barbecued should be left out of the fridge for a period of time (30 minutes to 1½ hours) to reach room temperature. This reduces the core temperature and the overall cooking time of the meat.

Rest grilled or roasted meat after cooking. When raw meat hits the pan or oven, it begins to contract, and as it cooks and contracts, the juices (blood) are forced to the centre of the meat. If you cut into it immediately it is cooked, the juices will still be concentrated in the centre. Allowing the meat to rest and cool a little, relaxes the meat fibres and lets the juices redistribute evenly throughout the meat. The more juices, the more flavour and tenderness. The larger the cut of meat, the longer the resting time required. Rest the average steak in a warm place for 5–10 minutes, and a large roast for up to 1 hour covered in foil. (Braised or stewed meats do not need to be rested.)

Frying or grilling
Remember 'hot' when exposing meat to a pan or grill top; a continual sizzling sound should always be present. Brown the meat on both sides in a hot pan then adjust the heat to finish, but be careful not to drop the heat so much that the meat starts to stew. It is sometimes recommended that thick-cut steaks be finished in a hot oven. This practice helps those who are in the habit of turning their meat 50 times to stop it from burning before it is cooked, but is really only suitable for those who enjoy cremating their food.

Sealing meat to lock in the juices
New research shows that it is in fact a fallacy that moisture is retained by sealing meat (see also *Braising*). However, browning the meat before finishing the cooking enhances its flavour and texture: it adds a delicious crust that contrasts satisfyingly with a rare centre.

To salt or not to salt?
When anything with a water content, whether meat, fruit or vegetables, comes into contact with salt, the salt will begin to draw out the water. The amount of salt and the time the food is exposed to it will determine the extraction rate of moisture. So a steak that is salted and left to sit while the pan heats up will lose valuable juices, while a steak that is salted after it is cooked misses the point, as the meat has already been sealed. The best option is to season the meat with salt just before it hits the pan, ready to be sealed. This way the salt cooks onto the meat, enhancing the flavour of the cut, without drawing out valuable juices. Watch as crystal salt flakes caramelise on the surface of the meat when exposed to a hot pan.

Roasting
Having the meat boned then netted or trussed by the butcher is recommended to hold plain or filled roast cuts in an even shape while roasting, portioning and carving. Season the joint with salt and pepper, spice rubs or pastes or chopped herbs.

Seal or brown very lean cuts of meat (beef, veal or lamb) before roasting. Pre-sealing a roast in a hot pan improves colour and flavour, particularly when using small, very lean beef or lamb cuts that need only a short amount of cooking.

Sealing a joint before moving it to the oven forms a crust and cooks on the seasonings, and allows the oven to be kept on a lower temperature (160°C).

A digital meat thermometer (probe) is a wise investment if you roast a lot of red meat. Insert the thermometer into the thickest part of the meat, away from any fat or bones (which have a higher temperature reading while cooking), as it goes into the oven and leave it there the entire time the meat is roasted. Depending on how you like your meat cooked, the core temperature will let you know when to remove the roast. This is as close to foolproof as you can get. Core temperatures for doneness are: 45°C = rare; 55°C = medium-rare; 65°C = medium; 75–80°C = well to very well done. Also take into account that while the meat is resting, it is in fact still cooking and the core temperature can rise by another 2°C for a small roast to 8°C for a large joint of meat.

If a thermometer is not available then the old 'time by weight' method will do just fine. Allow 30 minutes for every 500 g. For example, 1½ hours for a leg of lamb that weighs 1.5 kg.

Crumbing or breading

Never add salt to meat before crumbing. It will draw out the moisture and make the crumbs turn soggy. Instead, season the egg mixture and the flour with salt and pepper.

To add flavour to the meat, you can stuff it or marinate it (remember to pat dry with paper towel before crumbing). To add flavour to bread crumbs, rub in freshly crushed garlic (2 teaspoons crushed garlic for every 500 g bread crumbs will get you started) or add freshly ground black pepper and torn or roughly shredded flat-leaf parsley. Your homemade parmigiana will never taste the same again.

Braising

For most braised dishes, the cut of meat is first dredged in flour then pan-fried. The flour acts as a thickening agent as well as adding colour to the sauce. The purpose of this is not to lock in the juices, as braising meat may take several hours in which time any juices that were 'locked in' have well and truly escaped into the braising liquor. Never assume that the longer meat braises the better off it will be. Meat can overbraise to the point where it falls off the bone or turns into mush. Depending on the type, size and cut of meat, stick to the requested time limit, check for done-ness, then give or take time after checking.

Pot roasting

Resist adding too much liquid or the pot roast will become a stew.

Problem solving

★ Steak curls as it cooks? Some cuts have a tough membrane attached to the meat that when exposed to heat causes the cut of meat to curl or twist, making the opposite side near impossible to brown evenly. Simply place small incisions at intervals in the membrane, making sure the cut goes through to the meat.

★ Is the steak done? When pressed with a finger, a cooked steak will feel different (softer, firmer, springier) depending on how well it is done. The professional cook learns by experience to tell a rare from a medium-rare steak, but for domestic cooks who don't cook hundreds of steaks a year, telling the difference can be difficult. A good way to learn is to make a small incision in one side of the steak and look to see how done it is. (Remember to serve with the cut side down.) Of course, the sealed surface area has now been cut, allowing valuable juices to escape. So once the incision has been made, also press the meat with a finger and remember what that pressure feels like. Soon you will be able to tell what a rare steak feels like without having to cut into it.

* Undercooked one person's steak? Slice it in two (lengthways) and place back in the pan for another minute or so; now you have two steaks.
* Undercooked roast? As you usually don't discover it's undercooked until you've started carving, placing it back in the oven is not an option. The best thing to do is slice the meat a bit thicker and finish cooking each piece as a steak.
* Burnt a casserole, stew or soup? Don't stir it! Plonk the pot immediately into a sink of cold water to stop the cooking. This is an important step. Then lift out the ingredients without disturbing the bottom of the pot, and place in a fresh pot or dish. Taste the food to assess whether the burnt flavour has permeated the liquid and if so, by how much. If it's really bad, the bin is the only option. If it tastes only slightly burnt, try masking the flavour with a sauce such as Worcestershire sauce, barbecue sauce or tomato paste, or with other strong flavours such as garlic, chilli or onion (sautéed first in a separate pan) or spices (dry-roasted first).

BEEF

Aged beef is beef that is hung in the butcher's cool room for as little as 5 days or as long as 21 days (any longer and the meat is thought to deteriorate). Hanging the beef (which can be done by several methods) allows enzymes within the meat to start breaking down muscle fibres, rendering it tender and tasty. Some muscle groups age at different rates, depending on the hanging method, and generally only the best cuts are reserved for hanging. There is little advantage in hanging stewing beef or beef ready for mincing.

Tips:

* I recommend the personal experience of buying beef from a butcher, who, if you're loyal, will source, cut, hang (age) or put aside meat just for you. It beats peering for colour and marbling through the plastic wrap in the supermarket, and has the advantage that they can help choose the best cut for the dish you are planning.
* Remove any 'silver skin' from beef (and other meats) with a sharp knife to prevent the meat from contorting when cooked. Better still, ask your butcher to remove it for you to save time and wastage of precious meat.
* Grass-fed versus grain-fed—the majority of the world's population wouldn't know the difference, nor would the majority of the world's professional cooks. Keep in mind that many things determine the outcome of the final product, from stress and drought experienced by the animal while still alive, through to ageing and cooking technique. Most of the beef in Australia is grass-fed, and is generally favoured for its flavour.
* Bone-in versus bone-out—cooking meat on the bone does contribute to flavour, and the bone can also act as a mild heat conductor to help in the cooking process. However, if you are in a hurry and lack carving skills, buy your meat boned and rolled; the loss in flavour is not significant.

LAMB AND MUTTON

Mutton was often considered tough and stringy, but due to modern breeding and farming methods, the meat produced now is both tender and flavourful. Mutton has a more robust flavour than lamb, an off-white fat that springs back to the touch (lamb has a firm, creamy-white fat), and it turns cherry-red when cut, then darkens with age (lamb stays a pinkish-red colour). Darker mutton may still be good, strong in aroma, and should be cooked and eaten immediately. As mutton is a tougher piece of meat, marinating or tenderising with a meat mallet will soften the connective tissues. Mutton is not easily available, but can be purchased at butchers.

PORK

Pork is often associated in Western countries with a roast and the crackling that accompanies it. Yet there is so much more on offer, from the lean fillets to the very tasty neck. Pork is the most important meat in Chinese cuisine, and in fact is the most consumed meat in the world (it makes up 44 per cent of the world's consumption compared to 28 per cent beef and 24 per cent chicken).

Roast pork is ready when the juices run clear after the meat is speared with a skewer. Overcooked pork meat is, in general, dry and tough and needs a bucket of moist apple sauce to compensate. People tend to overcook it for fear of the disease trichinosis which is caused by a parasite. However, trichinosis is, in fact, associated with raw pork products and wild game, and has never been reported in Australia. It's important to follow correct food handling and storage methods, but there's no need to cook pork until it becomes a leather substitute.

Crackling or *pork rind*—there never seems to be enough of the stuff. I admit to once standing over a spit roast with a large joint of pork rotating in front of me, and with one other's help, successfully eating the entire provision of crisp, bubbled rind in a very short period of time. Funny thing, karma—I broke a tooth, such were my gluttonous ways. I suggest you ask for an extra slab of pork rind, fat intact, when you buy your roasting joint. (The fat that runs along the back of the pig, just under the skin, is also called 'fatback' or 'speck' and, when rendered, becomes lard.) You can remove the skin from the joint to maximise the yield of crackling, remembering that roasting the crackling (rind/skin) off the meat can mean major shrinkage because the skin will no longer protect the tender white meat from drying out too much.

RABBIT

There is no greater deceit than lying about what you're feeding people, and discovering as a kid that the chicken I thought I was eating was in fact rabbit was just not cool. Although I licked the plate clean, I admit I would not have touched it had I first been told what it was. Some 20 years later, I marvel at the comeback and chic appeal of rabbit and hare on restaurant menus. European cooks never lost touch with rabbit and hare, and have developed countless ways of preparing them. Marinades are often used, with hare in particular, to improve the flavour, and braising and casserole cooking have long been favoured to retain juiciness. However, a saddle of young hare or rabbit, quickly roasted until well browned but still quite pink in the centre, can be one of the juiciest and most tender cuts of meat.

Rabbit and hare are readily available at butcher's and specialty game and poultry shops. Rabbit is low in cholesterol, and it's still an economical meat. Rabbits usually weigh 800 g–1 kg. Farmed white rabbits, known as New Zealand white rabbits, are less widely available, as there are very few licensed farms. Farmed rabbits weigh about 1.5–2 kg and the meat is whiter, more tender and slightly fattier. Due to disease and the release of a killer virus in 1997, wild rabbits are no longer available on the retail market in New Zealand. Incidentally, possum meat is similar in size and taste to rabbit and therefore rabbit recipes can be easily adapted.

MUSHROOMS

* Although we think of mushrooms as a vegetable, they are in fact the fruiting bodies of higher fungi. The fruiting body is the sexual stage in the life cycle of the fungus.

TIPS:

* When buying mushrooms, look for smooth, firm caps, free from major blemishes. The mushroom's surface should be dry but not dried-out looking.
* Store mushrooms in paper bags or, if packaged, remove the plastic wrap and cover loosely with paper towel. Place in the refrigerator for 5 days or longer. Avoid airtight plastic bags—this causes moisture condensation which speeds degradation.
* Most mushrooms can be frozen successfully—the texture will change, but the flavour won't. (Add to the dish while still frozen.) Delicate mushrooms such as oyster or enoki should not be frozen.
* Brush any dirt or foreign matter from mushrooms with a damp cloth or paper towel. Mushrooms shouldn't be washed as they absorb water. Use a pastry brush to remove other debris clinging to the underneath or stem.
* The white flesh of mushrooms will brown after being sliced. This does not affect the taste but you can avoid it by brushing with lemon juice.
* Not all mushrooms should be prepared in the same manner; some shine with most cooking methods, in soups, stews, ragoûts, sauces and stir-fries, while others love just oil and butter. European mushrooms do well sautéed or used in cream sauces, while Asian varieties excel in soups and stir-fries.

OIL

TIPS:

* Always check the use-by date on oil before buying. Oils should also carry a 'packaged on' date and the closer to the packaged date you can buy an oil, the fresher it is. Be wary of oils that are reduced in price, as they could well be old.
* Keeping oil in the fridge is not necessary but is an option. Oils higher in fat content, such as olive oil, tend to solidify and turn opaque in the fridge. Simply bring to room temperature before use. If preparing freshly chopped garlic or chillies to store in the fridge, it is best to use a vegetable oil to avoid having it solidify in cold storage.
* Buy oil in smaller quantities if you keep it near the stove.
* Keep oil out of direct sunlight. Store in a place that is cool, dry and dark, such as a pantry or cupboard. Buying oil in a tin is advantageous, as light cannot penetrate the container.
* All fats and oils eventually break down and become rancid with prolonged exposure to air, light and heat. The only way to tell if an oil is old or rancid is to open it and smell.

Rancid oils have a stale, soapy smell and lose the strong characteristics of that particular oil as well as forming free radicals (which change cell membranes, suppress the immune system and promote the development of cancer and arteriosclerosis). If an oil is rancid, take it back to the shop if it is newly purchased or throw it out, there is nothing that can be done. Once you are used to detecting the rancid odour, you may well be surprised at how often you encounter the smell in other fat- or oil-based products.

* Oils made from nuts are the most unstable of all oils (although macadamia is the best of them), so buy in smaller quantities and try to use well before the use-by date.

* If you deep-fry often, speak to your local council as they may have a collection depot nearby where you can drop off used cooking oil to be sold to companies that make truck fuel or soap—true.

* Recycled oil can be used for day-to-day cooking as well as further deep-frying. Polyunsaturated oils can only be used once, while olive oil and unrefined peanut oil last longer and can be strained and reused two or three times.

* Oil that has had seafood cooked in it should not be reused to cook sweet foods, but can be reused to cook more seafood. However, oil that has been used to cook say, donuts, can be reused to cook seafood.

* Never get in the habit of pouring oil down the sink. Pour cold oil into an empty plastic or metal container with a lid (old milk or cream containers, jam jars and the like) before putting in the rubbish. Some countries have depots where used cooking oil can be dropped off. If you feel you go through enough oil to justify a trip to the depot, then I suggest giving your local council a call to find out if this service is available to you.

THE BEST OIL FOR THE JOB

For salads and other cold dishes where the oil will be tasted clearly, try the stronger oils like walnut, hazelnut, macadamia and extra virgin olive oil. Flavoured oils like citrus, chilli, coffee, herb, garlic and others are intended to give flavour and lift to an otherwise drab dish or salad. Sesame oil is misunderstood and often abused: use it in small quantities as a seasoning, as you would salt and pepper, in stir-fries or Asian-style dressings.

For cooking, use unrefined oils. A quality roasted peanut oil is good for cooking as well as salads but unrefined peanut oil is better for frying. There is a school of thought that believes any oil becomes toxic once heated and so oil should never be used for cooking—here is not the place to analyse that theory. Certainly, the hotter the oil gets, the faster it will oxidise and break down. Shortly before smoking point, oils begin to decompose, thus forming free radicals and acrolein, a toxic smoke. Oil at smoking point is generally considered not fit for human consumption, as it cannot be properly digested by the liver.

The following fats and oils are low in essential fatty acids (see Fat), therefore produce the lowest amount of toxic molecules when heated. So although most of them are saturated fats, they are considered the better option for cooking: butter, lard, tropical fats (coconut and palm oil), high oleic sunflower (not ordinary sunflower) oil, high oleic safflower (not ordinary safflower) oil, peanut oil, sesame oil, canola oil and olive oil—in that order of preference.

Choose **unrefined oils** where possible. **Refined oils** are unbalanced oils. They have had vital elements removed to extend shelf life and profitability. Often removed are lethicin (which makes digesting oil easier), anti-oxidants (like vitamin E and carotene), phytosterols (which provide protection for the immune and cardiovascular system), and chlorophyll (an essential source of magnesium, which is required for muscle, heart and nerve functions). In addition, these elements are removed with corrosive bases, window-washing acids and bleaching clays. The oils are then heated to frying temperatures before being packed into bottles or tins. Sunflower, safflower, canola, soy bean, corn and vegetable oils are just some of those on the supermarket shelf that are worth thinking twice about.

Palm oil can be white or red. Red palm oil is extracted from the fibrous flesh around the nut of the fruit of the oil palm, while the white oil comes from the palm kernel itself. It is used liberally in soups and sauces, yet without making them greasy or oily. Both palm oils are high in saturated fats, although the red (50 per cent) has far less than the white (80 per cent). Palm oil is also known as 'manja' or 'zomi'.

ONIONS

PROBLEM SOLVING

How to prevent tears while working with onion? There's no perfect answer, short of engineering a genetically modified onion void of all sulphur compounds, but the following can help: keep onions in the fridge, as the cold subdues the substance known as allicin, produced when an onion is cut; peel onions under water, although this washes away the natural 'bite' onions produce; and leave the root end intact when peeling, as this contains the largest amount of sulphuric compounds. Onions grown in soil that contains a higher level of sulphur compounds are stronger and more tear-inducing.

TYPES OF ONION

Brown onions (yellow onions in the US) are the most common cooking onion. They're usually too strong to be eaten raw.

Eschalots are indeed favoured by chefs over onions because of the sweeter flavour. Peeled and kept whole, eschalots are ideal for roasting, braising or for pickling.

Green onions are a general term used to describe both the salad onion and the spring onion (see below) and any harvested bulb with green shoots intact.

Pickling onions are small and good for cooking as well as pickling. Pearl onions, boiling onions (small brown onions) and cippolini onions are all pickling onions.

Red onions are sweeter than brown and are often eaten raw but cook just as well. There. are several varieties of red onion, some a little more elongated with a bit of a green sprout at the top (Burmuda onions). Red onions are sometimes mistakenly called 'Spanish onions'.

Salad onions are a slightly more developed spring onion, harvested from 4 months on, giving them a more rounded bulb. Salad onions have the advantage that they are sold separately, not in a bunch, so if ever a recipe calls for a small amount of spring onions, you can buy a salad onion or two instead, and use the inner green leaves only. The bulbous part can be used in salads or in cooking. They are known as 'spring onions' in the US and 'green onions' in the UK.

Shallots grow as a small group or cluster of onion bulbs. Popular in French and Asian cuisines, shallots have a brown/golden skin or a pink/purple skin. Shallots are favoured in sauces for their mild flavour. 'Shallot' is a name used for the spring onion in New South Wales where the word 'eschalot' refers to the true shallot.

Spanish onions are similar to brown onions only larger and sweeter and they are seasonal (spring to summer).

Spring onions are green onions, harvested from 8 weeks after seed to prevent a bulbous end forming (so they are an even width from top to bottom). Buying a whole bunch can mean wastage so, to lengthen storage time, divide into 3 smaller bunches, wrap each in plastic wrap and keep in the fridge. In many parts of the world, the misnomer 'scallions' or 'shallots' is used to describe spring onions.

White onions are sharper and spicier than brown onions but lack their big, rounded flavour. Their tang makes them a popular choice in Hispanic cooking.

PASTA

Pasta is often made with durum wheat (semolina) flour (see Flour) because of its high protein content (15 per cent, too high for successful bread-making). The protein forms strong gluten strands which help the dough retain elasticity when it is extruded through the pasta machine. Pasta made with soft wheat flour is usually mixed with eggs to reinforce the dough, which is not necessary with the strong durum flour. However, eggs can be added to any flour for a richer pasta (pasta all'uovo). Experiment with hen's or duck eggs, starting with 1 egg for every 200 g flour.

Some brands of dried pasta (pasta asciutta) can be just as good if not better than fresh pasta (pasta fresca). Dried pasta has a shelf life of up to 2 years. Fresh pasta is best used immediately or stored in an airtight container in the fridge for up to 5 days. It may also be stored in a cupboard for up to a month but obviously will dry out in that time.

TIPS FOR COOKING PASTA:

* 500 g (1 lb) dried pasta will give the same cooked volume as 750 g (11/2 lb) fresh.
* The size of a single serve varies, of course, but a good starting point is 100 g dried or 150 g fresh per person.
* Al dente translates as 'to the tooth'. When a recipe asks for something to be cooked al dente, that doesn't mean the food should be as hard as a tooth, but rather that it is cooked through while still firm to the bite. Al dente usually refers to cooking pasta or rice, but can sometimes be used to describe other cooked foods.
* The most important thing is to use plenty of boiling, salted water: 1 litre plus a very generous pinch of salt for every serve (100 g) of pasta. Salt is important, as it brings out the flavour of the pasta. (Obviously, you'll make your own judgement if you are trying to reduce your salt intake.)
* Fresh pasta should be ready in 2–3 minutes, gnocchi are ready when they rise to the top, and dried pasta is ready in 5–12 minutes, depending on the type (follow the instructions on the packet). I like to undercook the pasta and then finish cooking it in the sauce.
* Adding oil to pasta water is absolutely not necessary. With the exception of fresh lasagne sheets, pasta does not benefit from the addition of oil. The real secret to stopping it sticking together is to stir the pasta for the first 2 minutes after adding it to the pot. Move the pasta around the pot with a wooden spoon, this allows the water to cook the outer part of the pasta, making it slippery, not a starchy glue.
* Once it is cooked, drain the pasta, setting some of the cooking water aside as this can be used to thin pasta sauces if stock is not available.
* Never rinse pasta in water after draining as this washes away the natural sticky starches that help the sauce stick.
* If you are keeping the pasta for later use, toss it in olive or vegetable oil after draining, then spread thinly on trays, allowing the pasta to cool quickly. To reheat, either drop it in boiling water for 10-15 seconds or microwave, covered, for 30 seconds.

PROBLEM SOLVING

Pasta stuck together? Cooked pasta that is really stuck together is best kept for a baked pasta dish. Cool the pasta, then mix with sauce, vegetables or tinned tuna and cheese, and place in a hot oven for 30 minutes.

PASTRY

Bought pastry, although handy, will never match the quality of rich, fresh homemade pastry: mass-produced commerical pastry is made in bulk using a rolling machine and inferior fats, and pastry made at home with butter and in small batches will always be tastier. See Pastry recipes.

TIPS:

* Always chill raw pastry for 30 minutes before rolling it out, then for another 20–30 minutes before putting it in the oven. This allows the gluten in the flour to relax, preventing unnecessary shrinkage while baking.
* Pastry rolled out on marble is significantly better than other surfaces due to the marble's capacity to absorb heat. This keeps the butter or fats within the pastry cool and workable.
* Transferring pastry from the workbench to the tart tin or pie dish can be the cause of much frustration. Work quickly and confidently. The longer you work it, the warmer it gets, becoming soft and unmanageable. This is especially true of shortcrust or sweet pastries. Here are two methods:

1 Quickly roll out the dough between layers of plastic wrap. Ensure the plastic wrap is wide enough that the pastry won't spill out the sides. Then remove the top layer of plastic, pick up the bottom piece with the pastry stuck to it and transfer to the pie dish.
2 Roll out the dough on a work bench, dust lightly with flour, fold into quarters, transfer to the dish with the point of the fold in the centre of the dish, then simply unfold.

* Brush a little water around the top edge of the pie base before covering with the pastry lid. This helps strengthen the seal when the two are crimped together.
* Once the dough or pastry has been moulded into the tin or dish, allow it to rest in the fridge for at least 20 minutes before baking.
* For a glossy pie crust, brush with egg white before baking. Puff pastry, whether bought or homemade, should be glazed carefully before baking for the best presentation.
* Splashing milk or egg wash over the outer cut edges of the pastry will act as a glue and retard the rising of the pastry when baked.
* Get into the habit of placing a tray or large baking dish in the oven under the pie to catch spillage.

COOKING PASTRY

Blind baking pastry is the technique of partially cooking the pastry case before the filling is put in it. This ensures that the pastry is cooked through and that it is crisp, so it doesn't get soggy when the filling is added. (It is particularly useful for wet fillings.)
To prevent steam building up under the pastry, causing it to bubble, the uncooked pastry is weighed down in the dish or pricked all over before baking. To blind bake, cover the pastry case with a sheet of baking paper, then scatter rice, dried beans or pie weights on top.

Cook for 10–12 minutes. Alternatively, you could freeze the prepared pastry case for 15–20 minutes before baking. If any bubbles appear while the pastry is baking, pop them with the tip of a knife.

Docking pastry means placing small holes around the dough with a pastry docker or a fork. This helps prevent the dough from bulging while it is baking. The downside is that it leaves small holes in the cooked pastry.

A *pie funnel* is a hollow funnel, usually about 7.5 cm tall, that is placed in the centre of the pie before cooking. It aids heat distribution, supports the top pastry crust and allows liquids to reduce, thus enhancing flavour and helping avoid soggy pastry. It is also known as a 'pie bird', as many are made to resemble blackbirds (I shall stop short of reciting the rhyme), and other shapes like elephants, chefs and songbirds are common. I've also seen 'tweety bird' and 'naked women' pie funnels—don't ask.

PROBLEM SOLVING

* Parts of the pastry colouring too quickly? Remove from the oven and cover the 'burning' pastry with a strip of foil.
* To avoid soggy pastry in a tart case, remove it from the oven after blind baking, take out the paper lining filled with beans, rice or weights, then, while still hot, brush with a beaten egg and return to the oven for the prescribed time, usually another 10 minutes. The egg will cook, forming a glaze or impervious layer, ready for the filling. Alternatively, you could brush a thin layer of melted chocolate inside the case when it is cold: allow the chocolate to set before filling.
* Soggy lid? Use a pie funnel. If you don't have one, try putting a piece of dried pasta such as rigatoni or large macaroni into the centre of the pie. This will act as a chimney, allowing excess heat and steam to escape.
* Shrunk pastry? Pastry shrinks during baking because of high water content in the dough. As the water evaporates, the dough loses volume. So try using less water next time. If the dough was made without water yet still shrinks, chances are the pastry was stretched and forced into the dish, or that you didn't rest it in the fridge before baking.

POTATOES

New and old, waxy or floury, so many styles and varieties—cooking with potatoes can be a laboratory full of experiments. Selecting the best potatoes for boiling, frying, mashing, roasting, salads, gratins, baking, steaming, sautés or even for gnocchi can be a trial-and-error journey. In general, waxy are good for salads, steaming and boiling and do not take well to mashing, roasting and baking. Floury potatoes are better suited to dry baking, roasting, mash and chips. They can be used like waxy if they are not overcooked, as they will dry and crumble.

For fluffy mashed potato, heat the milk or cream before adding it with a touch of butter to the mashed potatoes. Potatoes can also be mashed with a good extra virgin olive oil or a non-dairy dip instead of milk, cream or butter.

BEST USE FOR DIFFERENT VARIETIES OF POTATO

Baking (dry)—King Edward (the best), Bintje, Pontiac, Crystal, Sebago, Delaware, Kennebec, Wilwash.

Frying—Idaho (Russet Burbank, the best), Kennebec, Maris Piper, Crystal, Sputna, Delaware.

Gnocchi—Desiree (the best), Toolangi Delight, Purple Congo (although the colour may be too much for some).

Mashing—Sebago (the best), Pontiac, Toolangi Delight, Desiree, Spunta, Bison, Kennebec.

Roasting—Desiree (the best), Spunta, Crystal, Delaware, Idaho (Russet Burbank), Kennebec, Pontiac, Bison.

Salad—choose the waxy variety, whose starches settle and hold firm after cooking (take care not to overcook them and allow to cool thoroughly before use)—Kipfler (the best), Ratte, Pink Fir, Pink Eye (Southern Gold), Bintje, Wilwash, Wilja, Coliban, Pontiac, Nicola, Patrone.

Sweet potato

Sweet potato comes in differing shapes, colours and sizes. Due to the texture of all sweet potatoes, they are best roasted or baked whole in their skins or wrapped in foil with butter/oil and seasonings, or sliced and grilled. They shouldn't be boiled as, like pumpkin, they lose too much texture, volume and, more importantly, flavour. Sweet potato can be white- or orange-fleshed with orange, white, brown or purple skins. The orange-fleshed, brown-skinned sweet potato is known as a 'yam' in the US, where sweet potato refers only to the white-fleshed variety. (The true yam is called a 'tropical yam' in the US.) Boniato is a type of sweet potato favoured for its fluffier texture once cooked, but lacking the sweetness and flavour of regular sweet potato. Kumara is a cultivar of sweet potato popular in New Zealand and the Pacific region.

POULTRY

Poultry refers to domesticated or game birds, but most often chicken. If there is one thing that passionate cooks despise, it is the declining quality of most chicken meat available to the general public. Meat from poorly reared birds lacks flavour and texture and can be more susceptible to harmful bacteria. Of course, mass-produced chicken is cheaper so it's up to the individual to balance the pros and cons of cost, differences in flavour and texture, and the risk of bacteria, such as *E. coli*, *Salmonella* and *Campylobacter*.

All poultry is highly susceptible to the growth of harmful (and not so harmful) bacteria, from the moment it is killed to the time you ingest it. There is not much you can do about the first phases of meat production, but once at home you can reduce contamination through proper storage and cooking. All poultry should be kept refrigerated at 0–4°C and used within 2 days. If frozen, whole or in pieces, the meat must be kept cold while defrosting. When freezing pieces of chicken, separate each piece with plastic wrap or baking paper. This way if only one piece is needed, it can be removed easily without having to defrost a whole lump of chicken. Also, freeze as flat as possible (not pushed into a ball at the back of the freezer), before piling into one bag. This will ensure that the meat freezes quickly, halting bacteria growth, but also that it defrosts evenly. Never defrost poultry by leaving it out at room temperature. Leave it in the fridge for a day or two until it is completely thawed before cooking.

HOW TO COOK POULTRY

Poultry meat can be broken into three categories: red meat, white meat and giblets, each of which is treated differently when cooked.

The 'red' meat is the working muscles of the bird, the legs and wings, which produce a tough, fibrous, dark meat better suited to long, slow cooking (although nothing like the cooking times required for tough red meat from beef or lamb). Having said that, leg meat with sinew and gristle removed is tender enough to stir-fry, sauté, barbecue or bake to shred for sandwiches. The red meat is considered to have more flavour than the white meat—the source of many arguments over the drumstick of a roasted bird.

The 'white' meat is the breast of the bird. In chicken and turkey, it is white and delicate; it must be cooked through, but overcooking will render it dry and tough. The 'white' meat of game birds isn't really considered white meat at all and can be treated like a beef steak, in that it is best served rare to medium rare. (Asking for the breast of game to be cooked well done in a restaurant is frowned upon as much as a well-done steak.)

Giblets are the heart, liver and gizzards of poultry. Often sautéed, grilled, fried or used to make gravy, they can also be steamed or simmered and then ground into a stuffing.

When chicken and turkey—whether whole or as pieces—are cooked perfectly, the juices will run clear rather than cloudy-white or pink.

As chicken and turkey are soft proteins, they prefer gentle rather than fierce cooking methods. This allows the proteins to set rather than having them contract too fast and force out valuable juices.

Skin off versus skin on? The skin tends to be the fattiest part of poultry so does little for the waistline, which is why it is often recommended to buy skinless chicken breasts. On the other hand, the skin is poultry's built-in basting mechanism. So, although it takes a little more self-control, I recommend that you buy chicken breast and cook it with the skin on, letting the fat from the skin render, basting the lean white meat beneath, then remove the skin before eating the succulent meat. (This method doesn't work with poaching and steaming.)

COOKING A WHOLE BIRD

Preparation—remove any bits and fat left inside the carcass. Rinse in cold running water and then pat dry, inside and out, with a lint-free towel (paper towel, especially cheap ones, can leave paper fibres on the meat). If stuffing the cavity, remember not to pack it in too tight because the mixture expands as it cooks.

Cooking times—when roasting whole birds, the breast will cook faster than the legs. (If you want to avoid this, try packing a stuffing between the breast skin and breast or cutting 2–3 lines into the leg muscles to allow heat to penetrate.) And a stuffed bird will take a little longer than one without stuffing because it takes longer for the heat to penetrate to the centre. Allow 2 minutes resting time per kilogram before you carve the beast, and remove the wishbone for easy carving. (Hang the wishbone out to dry for the kids to fight over—the smart child will have figured out that whoever keeps their little finger above their opponent's will always win.)

Types of poultry

Battery hen is a term for a practice that will one day end. This barbaric method of supplying eggs to meet high demand is appalling, and you need only witness the conditions under which these eggs have been produced to change the way you eat. Once these chickens are deemed useless as productive layers (their lifespan is no more than 18 months), they are transported, bruised and broken-boned, to a slaughterhouse, where their calcium-deficient, toxin-infused, pathetic excuse for a carcass is transformed into food such as pies, loaves, soups, pet food and other chicken by-products that conceal the true state of the battery chickens' flesh and miserable lives. That's why you should buy only certified free-range or organic eggs—and here endeth the lesson.

Boiler hen (or stewing hen in the US) is a tough-fleshed hen reserved for stocks, pies, broth and—if desperate—picked over for chicken salad or sandwiches. Not for roasting, the hen needs to be cooked or boiled for several hours. The flavour of boiler chicken is strong and the flesh firm, making for an ideal stock.

Broiler hen is a US term for a meat-producing hen (as opposed to an egg-producing one); also marketed as 'fryers'. A broiler's genetic make-up means it is inappropriate as an egg layer. The broiler is slaughtered at about 6–7 weeks.

Capon is a surgically neutered rooster, slaughtered at 10–12 weeks. It has a heavier carcass than ordinary chicken, yielding lighter, generous amounts of white flesh and is sold particularly for roasting.

Cockscomb is the often red, fleshy excrescence found on the head of roosters and other poultry. It is traditionally served in France as a garnish or a small entrée. Not likely to make a comeback because of their scarcity apart from anything else—you'll have more fun with a bag of parson's nose.

Corn-fed chicken is a label that is occasionally abused. In many cases, it has been shown that no more than 50 per cent of the hens' feed has included corn or maize during the fattening stage. The best corn-fed chickens are also free-range, fed on a diet of corn and corn gluten meal (70 per cent) and soy bean meal (15–20 per cent) with the remainder made up of salts, vitamins and minerals. The resulting chicken is plump, meaty and has a yellow tinge, not just on the skin, but also to the flesh. This yellow pigmentation is derived from the natural yellow colouring in corn called 'xanthophyll'.

Duck in most Western countries is still the meat we go out for. Due to a high fat-to-meat ratio and the expense compared to chicken, duck has struggled to adorn domestic kitchen tables. Duck is processed from 6–15 weeks of age, depending on the breed. Most duck available to the public is the Pekin or Peking duck (this is the name of the breed as well as the famous dish). For a stronger game flavour, try to source the big-scented Muscovy duck. Duck's web (the membrane between its webbed toes) is up there with chicken feet and cockscomb when it comes to challenging ingredients.

Free-range chicken is a marketing term that should be broken into two groups for the consumer. For a chicken to be free-range, at least half its life must be spent outside. 'Traditional free-range' requires greater access to outside living, fewer chickens in the space and a higher minimum age at slaughter. Then there is 'free-range total freedom': similar to traditional but with no restrictions to daytime open-air living. Be rightfully suspicious of labels such as 'farm fresh' and 'country fresh'; these do not guarantee free-range conditions.

Game bird is generally what you enjoy on your travels through Europe, and is not quite the same elsewhere. These are wild birds such as grouse, woodcock, partridge, guinea fowl, snipe and pheasant. Some species, especially quail and pheasant, are now being farmed. When buying quality game birds, look for these points: the beak should break easily, the breast plumage ought to be soft and the breast plump, and the quill feathers (those close to the body) should be pointed, not rounded. Most game birds are hung before cooking to mature and tenderise the meat and develop flavour. Hanging is a matter of taste, however, as some people find that hung or 'high' meat has an overly strong gamey smell and flavour. Game meat sold in supermarkets usually has a milder flavour. Quail are too small and gain nothing from hanging, so consume immediately. When cooking game birds, follow a good recipe. Keep 'medium-rare' in mind and you're off to a good start: The lean meat from game birds (including flightless birds such as emus and ostrich) can be dry and nasty if overcooked.

Goose usually only appears, if ever, at the Christmas table alongside many other meats. Geese are processed at about 20 weeks old and usually only two or three times a year (young geese or gosling are favoured over mature birds as their meat is more tender). The flavour is similar to duck, although wild geese are gamier. Roasting goose is similar to cooking duck, as geese also store plenty of fat under the skin. Season the goose inside and out with sea salt and pepper. Roast at 210°C for 20 minutes, reduce the heat to 180°C and cook for a further 30 minutes per kilogram or 45 minutes per kilo if stuffed. Drain the fat every 20 minutes. When cooled, you can store the fat in the fridge for future use in roasts or casseroles.

Grain-fed chicken is fed on a blend of wheat, corn and sometimes barley, which makes up about 70 per cent of its feed. The other 30 per cent is made up of mainly protein, such as soy bean or occasionally canola or fish meal, as well as vitamins and minerals.

Male chicken refers to one of the thousands of millions of those cute, fluffy new chickens that were unfortunate enough to be hatched at a commercial egg farm. No sentiment is wasted on these 'useless' animals which are either ground up while still alive for fertiliser, gassed or suffocated in bags or containers. This information may have little to do with your cooking, but it will give you something to mull over next time you order sunny-side-up.

Poussin is a chicken that is slaughtered at 21–28 days old. These young chickens are usually reserved for grilling or roasting and can be served as an individual portion. Spatchcock is another word for poussin that can also describe a method in which it is cooked—butterflied and grilled—which is both quick and easy.

Pullet is a female chicken under 12 months old. (After that she becomes known as a hen.)

Turkey, like Santa Claus, is recognised only once a year in many countries, with the exception of the US. Turkey is processed from 4 weeks–10 months old. If cooked properly, turkey yields succulent, tasty white meat, just as good hot as it is cold. The problem lies in the fact that unlike, say, roast lamb, that gets a workout several times a year, turkey is rarely cooked, and the inexperienced cook is scared into overcooking it, thereby rendering the meat drier than a salted pretzel. Turkey, like chicken, prefers gentle cooking and its juices will run clear when cooked. Here's a very rough guide to times for the first-time turkey roaster: try 30–35 minutes per kg (no stuffing) or 40–45 minutes per kg (with stuffing) at 170°C. See **How to Cook Poultry** and **Cooking a Whole Bird**.

Young roaster is a US term for a broiler-style chicken, generally older and heavier than a broiler, slaughtered at around 10 weeks.

QUINCES

TIPS:

* Quinces, although related to the apple family, aren't eaten like apples. Quinces benefit from long slow cooking methods which develop the deep red colour that they are known for.
* Quinces sold in fruit shops will not ripen once home. If the fruit is blemished or soft in spots, it indicates it is beginning to rot and should be discarded.
* Look for bright yellow fruit with small patches of soft brown 'down' over the skin—this down washes off easily. Slightly under-ripe fruit is great to use in quince paste.
* Perfectly ripe fruit has a delicious aroma akin to those little jars of boiled mixed lollies. This is when they are at their peak for roasting, baking or stewing.
* Quinces are often cooked and mixed with apples or pears in pie recipes or as an accompaniment for roast pork.

RICE

Rice is a member of the grass family and lives a short life of 3–7 months. The three main categories of rice are: indica, javanica and japonica. Different varieties have different levels of the two starches found in rice and this affects how they cook: the starch 'amylose' makes the rice grains separate and fluffy, while 'amylopectin' gives the grains a sticky consistency.

Indica or *long-grain rice* is a slender rice that is 4–5 times longer than its width. It is grown in countries with a warm climate such as India, Thailand, Vietnam, Pakistan, Australia, Brazil and southern USA. Once cooked, long-grain rice stays separated and fluffy, making it the perfect accompaniment to curries or sauce-based dishes.

Javanica is a plump but not round grain of rice 2–3 times longer than its width. It has glutinous properties like short-grain rice and is only grown in Indonesia. When cooked, medium-grain rice is more moist and tender than long-grain.

Japonica or *short-grain rice* has a rounded grain that tends to remain sticky once cooked. It is grown in cold-climate countries such as Japan, Korea and northern China.

All rice should be stored in a dry place, below 18°C. Red, brown and black rice (see below) should be consumed within 6 months of purchase. White rice has a longer storage time.

HOW TO COOK RICE

The various types of rice behave differently when cooked, mainly because of variations in their ratio of the starches amylose and amylopectin. There are many methods to cooking rice and, depending on the type, the times can vary by up to 10 minutes. Very generally speaking, rice takes about 20 minutes to cook.

Some recommend that white rice be washed in a small amount of cold water, then rinsed and swirled (but not stirred with a hand or implement as this can break the grains) until the water runs clear. This removes excess rice starch, ensuring the rice is not overly starchy or sticky. Others say that washing is unnecessary.

Opinion is similarly divided about soaking rice: some people swear by it, others abhor the practice. In general, glutinous (short- and medium-grain) rice does benefit from soaking; long-grain rice does not (it will reduce the cooking time slightly but gives it the potential to become soggy).

There is no exact measure of what proportion of water to rice is best, as rice will absorb water at different rates depending on its type and age (young rice still has a moisture content so needs less water). One method is the 'index finger' gauge, where you add water to cover the rice to the height of the first knuckle of your index finger with the fingertip touching the rice. My advice is to cook rice often until you find a method and a measure that is foolproof for you.

TIPS FOR COOKING RICE:

* Adding a small amount of ghee to the rice before cooking can help keep the grains separate: a method used by some Indian cooks that also adds a bit of flavour.
* Whether you salt rice or not is optional. Some say it is best left unseasoned so the focus is cast onto the food it is served with.
* All rice should be left to stand for 10–20 minutes after cooking. It should be stirred occasionally while standing.
* Rice cookers are a brilliant way to cook rice, but need to be cared for. Never use metal implements when removing the rice, and always make sure the base of the bowl is dry before placing it on the element.
* Cooking rice in the microwave takes about 12 minutes (give or take 1–2 minutes depending on the type of rice.)
* For the stovetop method, rinse the rice in water to remove excess starch. For every cup of rice, add 1½ cups water. Bring the rice to the boil, uncovered, on a high–medium heat. Once it is boiling, turn the heat down to low. Place the lid on the pot, keeping the lid tilted to let steam escape. Simmer gently for another 15 minutes. Let stand for 10 minutes. Fluff up rice before serving.
* Steamed rice is a method employed by few outside the Thai community. It takes time and patience, which Western cooks are often short of. The rice should be soaked for 3 hours (long-grain jasmine) or overnight (short-grain) then rinsed and drained. For long-grain rice, add boiling water to only just cover the rice. Place in a steamer basket, cover, and cook over medium heat for 30–60 minutes depending on quantity. For short-grain sticky rice, place directly in a mound in the steamer (only a few grains will drop through so there's no need to use a plate) then cover and cook for approximately 25 minutes. Check the centre of this mound to ensure the rice is cooked through, then cover with a cloth to prevent it drying out.

PROBLEM SOLVING

* Burnt rice? Burning can leave a scorched smell through the cooked rice. Take a crust of bread and place it on top of the rice. Depending on the extent of the burning, this can absorb most, if not all, of the aroma.

TYPES OF RICE

Arborio rice is a commonly available medium-grain rice used for making risotto. This grain has a higher than normal amount of soluble starch and it needs to be cooked slowly and stirred continuously to expose the starch that gives risotto its tell-tale creaminess. Its cooking time is about 18–20 minutes. See also Risotto rice, below.

    Baldo rice is Italian-grown and used in risotto, desserts, stuffings, soups and salads. Considered to be the 'daughter' of arborio rice, baldo rice is also popular in other Mediterranean dishes. If unavailable, replace with arborio.

    Basmati rice, a quality rice with an excellent flavour, is grown in India. It has long grains which stay separate, fluffy and somewhat dry once cooked. When cooked, it swells and lengthens to 2–3 times its raw size. White basmati rice takes less water and less time to cook than ordinary long-grain rice: try using equal quantities of rice to water. Unhulled or brown basmati has even more flavour and takes longer to cook.

Bhutanese red rice hails from the small Himalayan kingdom of Bhutan. This is a short-grain red rice that cooks in 20 minutes and finishes with a nutty, earthy flavour and a red russet colour. If unavailable from delis or Asian grocers, substitute with Christmas rice (or as a last resort, another short-grain rice).

Black glutinous rice is also known as 'black sticky rice' or 'black forbidden rice'. It has a much richer flavour than white sticky rice and can be either medium- or long-grain. Once cooked, black rice is a deep, dark purple with a nutty flavour and a wholegrain texture. Because of its striking appearance, it is often used for festive desserts, steamed in banana leaves or in salads. Before cooking (particularly if you plan to steam the rice), soak in water overnight; this allows the rice to absorb water, swell and then cook in less time.

Black japonica rice is a hybrid of a red medium-grain and a black short-grain japonica type of rice. It is often sold unhulled and therefore cooks like a brown rice (about 45 minutes).

Broken rice is the damaged white rice which is separated from the intact grain at the production stage, and is used in other areas such as animal feed, beer brewing or flour processing.

Brown rice has a chewier texture and nuttier flavour, is a natural source of bran, and is high in fibre and vitamin B. The difference between brown and white rice is that brown has had only the hull or husk removed, leaving the bran intact. This long-grain rice takes longer to cook than white rice (about 40–45 minutes).

Calrose rice is also known as sushi rice. It is quite round and short and belongs to the japonica group.

Carolina rice is a long-grain rice originally grown in that part of America at the end of the 17th century. It is now grown throughout the US.

Christmas rice is a short-grain red rice. When cooked, it has a sticky, dense character and a musky aroma.

Converted rice is also known as 'parboiled rice'. In fact, it hasn't been parboiled but rather soaked, steamed and dried before being husked or hulled. It retains more nutrients than white rice and, due to reduced surface starch, stays well separated after being cooked. It cooks perfectly in approximately 20 minutes.

Dirty rice is a recipe rather than a type of rice. It is white rice cooked with minced chicken livers, gizzards, onions and seasonings, giving it its 'dirty' appearance. This Cajun specialty is far more tasty than it sounds.

Fermented rice is used in Asian desserts and in savoury dishes where its sweetness can counterbalance a salty or sour dish. This sweet rice has a small alcohol content and is available in most Asian grocers.

Flattened rice (or rice flakes) is used in desserts or batters. It sometimes has a slight green colouring, produced by the introduction of pandanus.

Glutinous rice, despite its name, contains no gluten. Rather, the name describes the sticky nature of the rice once cooked. This short-grain rice is used in sushi and Asian desserts. It may also be referred to as 'sticky rice', 'sweet rice' or 'Chinese sweet rice' (again, this is about the way it is used rather than its content; there is no sugar in the grain), as well as 'botan rice', 'Japanese rice', 'mochi rice', 'pearl rice', 'sushi rice' and 'waxy rice'.

Himalayan red rice is a long-grain rice which can be substituted for brown rice-the only difference is the colour of the husk.

Instant rice, or 'precooked rice' as it is sometimes called, is not always readily available, is more expensive and, with its mushy texture and insipid flavour, is less appealing than ordinary rice. It has been precooked and dehydrated and is available white or brown, taking 5 and 10 minutes respectively to cook. Instant rice might help if you're in a hurry but considering normal rice takes only 15–20 minutes to cook, why bother with an inferior product? If a recipe calls for precooked rice, be clear whether this means instant rice or rice that has been boiled or steamed by you earlier.

Jasmine rice has a perfume more like pandanus than jasmine flowers; the name in fact refers to the pearl-like sheen of the grain. This long-grain aromatic rice is favoured in Thailand and has become popular worldwide. Jasmine takes less water and less time to cook than normal long-grain rice: Try using equal quantities of rice to water. Leftover cold jasmine rice makes excellent fried rice. It is also known as 'hom mali rice' or simply 'fragrant rice'.

Kalijira rice (also known as 'baby basmati rice') is a fast-cooking, short-grain rice favoured in desserts. Kalijira rice is produced in Bangladesh.

Patna rice is a long-grain rice originally from the region Bihar (the capital of which is Patna) in India. The name now describes a generic, long-grain white rice that is grown the world over.

Pearl rice is another name for short-grain rice (and is different from 'pearled rice' which simply refers to white rice in general).

Pecan rice or **wild pecan rice** is a new hybrid similar to popcorn rice and basmati. It has a long grain with a chewy texture and nutty flavour and aroma.

Popcorn rice is a new hybrid similar to, but cheaper than, basmati. When cooked, it has the aroma of—what else?—popcorn. Available in white and brown, it is also known as 'American basmati', 'della rice' and 'gourmet rice'.

Popped rice is also known as 'poona rice', available in Indian produce stores and is used in festive desserts and sweetmeats.

Risotto rice is, as the name suggests, used specifically for making risotto. It is a medium-grain rice with a characteristic white dot in the centre of the grain. There are several varieties, each claiming to produce the best risotto, including carnaroli, vialone nano (or simply nano), arborio, baldo, Padano and Roma. Washing risotto rice is a big no-no. The more starches left with the grain, the creamier the risotto. Some brands claim that no stirring is required, thus freeing you from the stove for 15–20 minutes, but old-school risotto lovers will tell you that the best risotto is one that has been worked constantly with a wooden spoon, so as to have the rice grains trounce one another, rendering maximum starch which in turn produces the creamy texture. Risotto rice is sometimes called 'Piedmont rice'.

Rough rice or paddy rice is the unhulled kernel, which is inedible until it is processed for cooking or packaging.

Spanish rice can be medium- or long-grain. Valencia produces a medium- to short-grain style that is favoured for paella (long-grain rice is never used for paella), and another paella rice is granza rice. Andalucia produces a long-grain rice perfect for pilaff. For rice dishes of Spain, the rice is never washed; the starch too valuable to run down the sink.

White rice is also known as 'polished rice', 'pearled rice' (pearled as in polished) or 'fully milled rice', due to it being stripped of its husk and bran layers.

Wild rice is also known as 'Indian rice'. You've heard it before, now hear it again—wild rice is not a rice at all but a grass seed (a trifle confusing, as essentially rice is a grass seed too). It takes longer to cook than white rice, has more nutrients and a nutty flavour and chewy texture that suits poultry, game meats and vegetable dishes. Rinse then cook for 40–50 minutes, after which time most of the grains will have split open or 'blossomed' but still retain a bite.

SALT

Love it or hate it, salt is essential to our diets. As our bodies cannot produce salts for themselves, they rely on us to find it. Then it becomes an issue of what type and how much we should feed our bodies. Some home cooks, made paranoid by the propaganda of 'too much salt causes high blood pressure and heart attacks' and believing that our salt requirements can be met with Vegemite on toast for breakfast, omit salt from all cooking, presenting the family with bland meals. Meals in restaurants often taste significantly better than those cooked at home. Other than the fact that food cooked by anyone other than yourself seems to taste better anyway, the reason for this could be as simple as the professional cook's respect for salt's place in food. Basically, good quality salt enhances the natural flavour of food. You should add salt not once but several times in small amounts, tasting and testing in between each addition.

As well as standard table and cooking salts, many fancy salts are now on the market. These can be better for you but unfortunately often carry heavy price tags, so rarely grace the home kitchen. I recommend the more affordable and still excellent quality salt flakes for the home cook.

TIPS FOR USING SALT:

* Add small amounts of salt several times, stirring and tasting between each addition.
* Before reaching for the salt shaker on the table, whether at home or in a restaurant, taste the food! Chances are, the cook has added just the right amount. High on the list of what chefs hate is the customer who dowses the meal in salt and pepper before trying even one mouthful. (Equally annoying to the customer is the waiter with the baseball-bat-sized pepper grinder offering you pepper before you've tasted your meal—next time ask them to leave the grinder with you until you've tried your food.)

PROBLEM SOLVING

* Added too much salt? Act immediately! Remove everything you dropped in, even if it means scooping out some of the other ingredients (they can always be replaced). Stir the mixture well. Or add a peeled potato or two and cook gently until the potatoes have absorbed most of the salt. Gently remove and discard the potato.
* Still too salty and you can't bring yourself to throw it out? Cool down completely then freeze in smaller portions. Use one of these frozen salt blocks the next time you prepare the same dish by adding it (defrosted overnight) to the new batch.
* Need to eat less salt? First, note that salt (especially iodised salt) is important to our natural diet and it's not recommended to omit it completely. If you need to reduce your salt intake for medical reasons:
    —use a salt that is low in sodium
    —replace salt with seaweed granules

—use salt-reduced products

—check product labels for key words—sodium, salt, soy sauce, brine, corned, pickled, cured and smoked—as these can indicate excess salt

—make your own stocks instead of using packaged cubes or Tetra packs.

TYPES OF SALT

Black salt is a true misnomer if ever there was one, as this is a grey/pink salt, mined from the Ganges plains in central India. Ask for black salt in Indian food stores. Its characteristic smoky flavour and pungent smell means you cannot make a true Indian chaat (a type of salad) without it.

Celtic sea salt is a hand-farmed salt from the marshlands of Brittany. (Like any farmed product, a good crop depends on the weather.) Natural Celtic sea salt is sold as fine white crystals or larger grey crystals. The unwashed, almost dirty, appearance of this salt ensures that it retains all its natural goodness.

Cooking salt is slightly coarser than table salt, and is often made up of several salts. It is used in bulk in commercial kitchens. This is the best salt to season the water for cooking pasta, rather than wasting your good sea salt or salt flakes.

Fleur de sel translates as 'flower of salt'. It is hand-harvested like Celtic sea salt, and used as a finishing salt, in small quantities. Fleur de sel is produced from the salt crust on top of the salt pond, so it is the least salty and purest part of the saline. It is taken from a single day's harvest. See also Sel gris.

Hawaiian black lava salt is a sea salt that is evaporated with purified black lava rock, then mixed with activated charcoal for its colour and apparent detoxifying effects. Although hard to find, it can be ordered over the internet.

Hawaiian red clay salt or *red alae salt* is a sea salt harvested in ponds, with baked Hawaiian clay added after it is dried. It can be ordered over the internet.

Iodised salt has a small amount of potassium iodide added to help prevent goitre, a thyroid condition. As little as 40 mg of potassium iodide is added per kilogram of near pure sodium chloride.

Korean bamboo salt or *red bamboo salt* (biosalt) is made from sun-dried salt stuffed into bamboo hollows and sealed with yellow clay. It is then baked 9 times, for 8 hours each time. After each baking period, the bamboo stub is replaced. The resultant salt is red in colour, sweet-flavoured, and very salty, and its odour may not be appealing. High in minerals, bamboo salt is favoured in medicine, cosmetics and cleaning, and as a finishing salt in cooking.

Kosher salt, because it is. Kosher salt can be an overly refined salt with little nutrient value, sourced, like table salt from land deposits, or Kosher sea salt, a crystal salt with no additives, ideal for pickling meats because of its larger crystal that absorbs moisture. Kosher sea salt is best in a salt grinder if it is to be used as a table salt.

Malian red clay salt or *Saharan salt* is valued in Africa (and by a few New York chefs, hell-bent on unearthing another trendy salt to adorn their menu). It is sourced from salt mines just south of the Sahara in Mali, Africa.

Murray River salt harvested from the underground brines of the Murray–Darling Basin in Victoria acts not only as a top-end flake salt for restaurants and the domestic market, but more importantly is one answer to controlling the ever-increasing salinity problem of that area. The earthy, light pink salt is favoured by chefs and gourmet cooks Australia-wide.

Pink Peruvian lake salt is a form of sea salt harvested from wells lined with rose quartz. The pink colouring comes from the tiny pieces of rose quartz present in the salts.

The Incas and Mayans have used this salt for its powerful spiritual and healing properties. You can eat it at a top New York restaurant, then contemplate the spiritual healing the salt has brought you as you pay for the meal. If money isn't an issue, buy a quarter of a pound of the stuff and bathe in it.

Rock salt is procured from halite, a mineral that was once a sea salt but is now buried underground, sometimes in very large deposits. The rock salt is mined and ground into coarse chunks. Further refining to different-sized grains produces cooking salt or table salt. The coarse rock crystals can be used in a salt mill or dropped straight into water for cooking pasta. They are also used when curing meats like salmon (gravlax) or preserving lemons and in baking where large cuts of meat or whole fish are coated in a thick slurry of salt mixed with a little water or egg white.

Saltpetre or *potassium nitrate* is classed as a salt and preserving agent. A pinch of saltpetre added to a duck liver parfait mixture before it is cooked keeps it pink on the inside long after it has cooled.

Salt spray is a pure form of seawater used as a seasoning and sold in pump spray bottles. On the rare occasion I've used salt spray, I have found its simplicity appealing, although it is similar to fish sauce, in that it requires delicate handling to avoid oversalting. Use a ratio of 2 sprays = 1 pinch of regular salt.

Sea salt and *rock salt* are the preferred salts for everyday cooking. Sea salt has a high mineral content and a clean salty flavour, and is sold as coarse crystals, flakes or granules. In a bygone era, it was referred to as 'bay salt'. Maldon sea salt is a globally recognised salt-flake brand, which has spawned the trend for other countries to cash in on this abundant mineral.

Sel gris is from the same farmers who bring you Celtic sea salt and fleur de sel. However, sel gris is harvested throughout an entire season (for every 150 kg sel gris produced, only about 10 kg fleur de sel is harvested).

Smoked salt can lend a little of its smoky character to a casserole or steak. Styles available include hickory-smoked sea salt, Mediterranean oak-smoked sea salt, and the elusive and extremely expensive smoked Danish salt.

Table salt is the most refined product of rock salt. It contains anti-caking agents such as calcium silicate added (at less than 0.5 per cent) to ensure that it flows freely in any weather condition, especially in the tropics where humidity plays havoc with dry food. Table salt is a very fine-grained, harsh-tasting salt.

SAUCES

Ah, sauces! Those magical liquids that can cover a cook's feeble mistakes or, at best, lift the main ingredient to new heights. For some, meat without sauce is like the moon without darkness; while for others, making a sauce is an arduous task. For these people, I say widen your view of what a sauce is—think of bolognaise or any stew or casserole.

Butter sauces vary from the rich beurre blanc to a simple herb or flavoured butter which becomes a sauce as it melts over the meat or dish. Add butter to pan juices with wine or stock to help thicken the sauce. The trick is to remove the pan from the heat then add small cubes of butter, whisking or stirring until it has melted. Do not boil once the butter has been incorporated as it will split. Flavoured butters can be rolled first in plastic wrap, then in foil to hold their shape, then refrigerated until solid. When hard, cut into rounds and freeze in a plastic bag for later use.

The most common *egg-based sauces* are emulsion sauces, made up of eggs (or more often just egg yolks) combined slowly with a fat, either oil or butter; mayonnaise and hollandaise with its ten or so derivatives are probably the best known. Sabayon can be either sweet or savoury and consists of eggs or egg yolks combined with a liquid (stock, juice or alcohol), then whisked until light or ribbon stage. It is cooked in the top of a double boiler, and great care must be taken not to overcook or scramble the egg. Sabayon can be the beginning of a hollandaise sauce or can be used as a sauce on its own, as in zabaglione, a sweetened sabayon served with sponge biscuits. Another common egg-based sauce is crème anglaise or English custard, a sweetened egg yolk mixture cooked with cream then gently heated to thicken (again with great care as boiling the sauce can lead to separation or curdling). Cold, hard egg sauces such as sauce Gribiche, sauce Vincent, Cambridge sauce and sauce Sardalaise are often served with fish, shellfish, tongue or, if you're in the mood and who isn't, calf's head.

Purees, whether from fruit, nuts or vegetables, make a good alternative to other more time-consuming sauces. Cook the ingredients then thicken with a béchamel (white) sauce, cream, butter, flour (or other starch) or by reducing to enhance the quality of this style of sauce.

See recipes in **Dressings, Sauces and Butters**.

HOW TO THICKEN A SAUCE

Deglaze the pan but don't let the liquid evaporate entirely. Now thicken the sauce by reducing it (continue to cook the sauce over high heat until much of it evaporates and the remaining liquid is intensified in flavour) or by adding another ingredient, such as butter, cream, blue cheese, cornflour, arrowroot or potato or rice flour (mixed first with a little cold water) and cooking gently to combine. A beurre manié (2 parts soft butter mixed with 1 part flour) is another thickening option but I don't favour it as the flour particles need time to cook out and the method doesn't provide this extra time. (The method is to add a beurre manié to the boiling liquid, bring it back to the boil, then turn off the heat source. This leaves the sauce with a grainy texture.)

PROBLEM SOLVING

* Burnt sauce? Try to disguise it by adding a strong flavour profile, such as Vegemite, peanut butter, fruit juice, vinegar, Worcestershire sauce or chilli sauce. Or throw the sauce away and serve the meal with a wedge of lemon instead.
* Lumpy sauce or gravy? Strain the sauce through a sieve. To avoid lumpy sauce in future, use a sauce whisk (metal or plastic) as you begin to bring the sauce together, then use a wooden spoon while the sauce simmers.
* Added too much salt? The only answer is to sacrifice the few to save the many—ladle out the drop zone, including sauce, then bulk out the remaining sauce with stock, cream or wine. Or, if you've mixed in the salt already, pour off two-thirds of it (freeze this in an ice tray and use later as instant salt cubes to add flavour to future sauces), then bulk out the remaining sauce with stock, cream or wine.
* Curdled or split/separated dressing or sauce? Remember Rule No. 1: follow the recipe. If a method states 'add slowly', then snail's pace is fast enough. There is no rushing the first stage of making a mayonnaise or hollandaise (or any derivative of these emulsion-type sauces). Get it right the first time and spare yourself the agony of repairing it. If an emulsion sauce is looking a bit thin, start adding small amounts of very hot water—this will aid in 'cooking' the egg within the sauce, helping to bring it back. Then slowly add the oil again. If the sauce has separated, start again, using 1 fresh egg yolk at room temperature. This time add the separated sauce to the egg instead of oil.

SEAFOOD

Abalone is available fresh, tinned, frozen and dried, each requiring different treatment. To shuck fresh abalone from the shell, cut the connector muscle then pry out the flesh. Trim and discard the viscera (soft organs), remove the dark skin from the foot and scrub the meat to remove the black coating. The cleaned abalone can now be cut into thick steaks against the grain of the meat, then tenderised. (Note that pounding fresh abalone flesh to within an inch of disintegration is frowned upon by Asian cooks, who take immense pride in serving this expensive product; one does not need to treat abalone like octopus to guarantee tenderness.) Fresh abalone need only be sliced very thinly and cooked very quickly, whether poached (steamboat style) or stir-fried. In a restaurant, fresh abalone should be presented to you in the shell, with the wriggling flesh exposed, before being taken away and cooked. Frozen abalone is not a substitute for the fresh product. It is better suited to soups or stewed in rich sauces and is the least exciting of the abalone styles available. Dried abalone resembles a rock, both in appearance and in texture, but the drying process, considered an art form in Japan, actually enhances the flavour. Experienced Chinese chefs cook dried abalone whole, in a sauce that is considered just as important as the abalone itself. The recipe is a well-kept secret, but involves a rich stock of chicken, pork and ham, and up to 13 hours of slow cooking. Abalone is also known as 'paua' in New Zealand.

Bacalao is dried salted cod, popular in Italy, Spain and France. The best bacalao is said to come from Norway as it is less salty and softer. To prepare bacalao for cooking, soak for 2–3 days in cold water, changing the water 2–3 times a day. It can now be served with rice, and cooked in casseroles, stews and risottos, among many other dishes—the Portuguese claim more than 300 uses for this salty fish. Baccalà is one of the many alternative spellings.

Crab should be bought either alive or precooked. When buying live, look for a creature that has a bit of kick in it. Crabs are usually tied with twine to prevent them from latching onto stray fingers. When buying precooked crustaceans, the outer shell should be bright orange to red in colour, free from any disagreeable odours, with white, firm flesh on the inside. Soft, pasty flesh indicates an animal that was stressed before being cooked. As a general guide: 450 g crab in the shell will yield 1 cup flaked crab meat.

HOW TO COOK LIVE CRAB

The RSPCA recommends crabs be placed in the freezer for 4–5 hours before cooking. Alternatively, they can be drowned in a tub of water (although this takes 6–8 hours). If cooked alive, crabs will shed their limbs. Bring sea water or salted water (1 litre water to ½ cup rock salt) to a vigorous boil, then add the crab and cook for about 8 minutes for every 500 g. The shell will turn a bright orange when the crab is cooked. Lift out of the water and place in a tub of chilled water or under cold running water, then refrigerate. This fully cooked crab is now ready to be picked over. If you plan to sauté the crab, it should merely be blanched in boiling water first: use the method above but remove from the water and cool after 5 minutes.

Crab stick is also known as 'sea legs' or 'surimi'. There's not even a whiff of crab in a crab stick. It is made from white fish, usually Alaskan pollock (also used to make other fake seafood products such as imitation scallops or prawns or fish patties). Real Californian rolls should be made with the leg meat of crab, kept whole, not thin strips of this faux crab.

Crayfish are a freshwater crustacean (although usage of the word varies—see Rock lobster). Crayfish species are abundant in North America and Australasia (100 or so species in Australia and 250 in North America) but less common in most other parts of the world. Crayfish are generally much smaller than rock lobsters, with many species considered too small to eat. The Tasmanian crayfish (endangered) is the largest in the world, followed by the Murray River crayfish (hard to find). Yabbies, redclaw and marron are three well-known crayfish in Australia. Marron is the third largest freshwater crayfish in the world, and is indigenous to Western Australia. Its meat is considered to be the finest of all crayfish. About 31 per cent of its total body weight is meat (compared to 15–20 per cent for yabbies). Redclaw, a native of Queensland, is best eaten in that region, as it does not travel well. The American crawfish is a smaller version of the Australian yabby.

All of the species of crayfish have many edible parts: the tail, the claws, the 'mustard' and the 'coral', and the shell can also be used to flavour soups and sauces. The tail and claws represent about 40 per cent of total body weight. The 'mustard' is the orange-brown liver found in the carapace (main shell) which connoisseurs enjoy spread over the tail meat. The 'coral' is the developing egg sac found in the carapace of the female, which can be eaten on its own or whisked into a sauce.

Crayfish and lobster should be bought either alive or precooked, not dead and raw. When buying them live, look for a lively creature: The tail should tuck underneath and not hang down when the crustacean is picked up. When buying precooked crustaceans, all of the outer shell should be bright orange to red in colour, free from any disagreeable odours, with firm white flesh on the inside. Soft, pasty flesh indicates an animal that was stressed before being cooked.

HOW TO COOK LIVE CRAYFISH

Place in the freezer for 2–3 hours to avoid stressing the animals by cooking them while still alive. Drop into boiling salted water until they have turned a bright orange/red. Remove and refresh in iced water.

Jellyfish is often sold dried and salted. It is favoured for its crunchy texture rather than flavour. Soak for 24 hours, changing the water several times, then drop into boiling water for 15–20 seconds. I suggest shredding finely and using in a salad.

Marinara mix or seafood extender might be convenient but resembles cat food in its quality. This pre-mixed array of poor quality seafood will never be touched by anyone who values the succulence of fresh seafood. Instead, try making your own as a special occasion treat: simply combine a selection of fresh seafood and fish pieces.

Mussels, like all shellfish, are at their best when still alive and in their shell. Before buying, check whether they're alive by tapping the shell, which will then tightly close. Any with gaping shells are dead, and should not be purchased. The 'beard' of a mussel is actually the byssal threads, produced by glands near the foot area, which allow the mussel to cling to rocks or hard surfaces in the water.

HOW TO DE-BEARD A MUSSEL

To remove the beard, yank it firmly towards the hinge of the mussel rather than the opening end. (Pulling towards the opening will kill the mussel and can rip out some of the inner flesh.)

Octopus—the best tip for cooking octopus is to tenderise the flesh before cooking. Ideally this is done by beating over a rock in the Greek Islands. Alternatively, precook by blanching in water, tenderise with a meat mallet, or rub with daikon for its tenderising properties. Some people are allergic to the handling of sea creatures and so food-handling gloves are recommended. Buy tentacles or a whole baby octopus, and if you don't fancy cleaning the guts out at home, buy them pre-cleaned. They should be firm to touch and sweet to smell, with no slimy residue or wafts of ammonia.

Oysters—all shellfish should be bought when still alive and in their shell, but this is particularly important nectar: if you buy oysters that have already been shucked, they should be plump, with a natural creamy colour and a clear liquid.

Prawns are usually known as shrimp in the US (although sometimes the word 'prawns' can be used to denote large, extra-large and jumbo prawns), but elsewhere 'shrimp' refers to very small, peeled prawns, as in the classic retro dish, shrimp cocktail—usually frozen or in brine or those labelled for the US export market. They are also sometimes called 'jumbo shrimp' or 'shrimp scampi' in the US. The many species of prawns available worldwide ensure varied flavours, but wherever you are, the methods for buying and handling prawns are the same.

Uncooked prawns are green-grey and can be purchased with the shell on or as cutlets (shell off). I advise you to buy whole green prawns, but if you do buy pre-cooked, they should be plump and bright orange, with no signs of having been defrosted. (Frozen cooked prawns can be watery, rubbery or flavourless when defrosted.) As a general rule: 325 g cooked prawns in the shell will yield 1 cup of prawn meat.

PREPARING AND DE-VEINING PRAWNS

Most recipes suggest de-veining prawns (removing their digestive sac, also known as the sand vein) either before or after cooking, as it is too unsightly or gritty for many people. However, it is edible, and some don't mind it. Occasionally, a batch of prawns can have a very clean vein, and usually the veins of small prawns or shrimp are too small to be removed and contain little if any digestive matter. Sometimes a mass of green, beige or orange goop covers the digestive sac from head to tail, mostly at the head end. This is the prawn ovary, the different colours representing the different stages of the ovary, which turns orange or cream once cooked. (But now you know what it is, will you ever eat it again?) While prawns can be peeled and de-veined either before or after cooking, before cooking is probably better if they are to be served whole, after cooking if they are to be presented in a salad.

HOW TO COOK WHOLE RAW PRAWNS

Bring seawater or salted water (1 litre water to ½ cup rock salt) to a vigorous boil, then add the prawns and cook until they curl and turn a bright orange. (Another sign they are cooked is when they float on the surface.) Lift out the prawns and drop into iced water. Do not reheat or re-cook pre-cooked prawns.

HOW TO DE-VEIN WHOLE GREEN PRAWNS

Use a skewer or a toothpick to pierce the meat at the top of the head end, just below where the vein runs. Gently lift and jiggle the skewer, and as you lift the vein should begin to release itself from the body of meat.

OR

Run a small knife blade along the back of the prawn, enough to pierce the flesh and scrape out the vein. This method is great if the prawns are to be butterflied for quick cooking and presentation.

Ray and skate are similar fish in appearance, although ray have long wire-like tails, while skate are larger and have a shorter, stumpier tail. None of this stops the names being used interchangeably. The wings of both are the only edible part. They are sold with or without skin (as it can be hard to remove, I suggest you buy skinless). Beware of ray and skate wings being passed off as scallops in cheap restaurants after being cut into disks of the same shape—the taste isn't dissimilar but the texture can be stringy.

Rock lobster and *crayfish* are names that are continually interchanged, and shouldn't be. Australian rock lobsters (in Europe called 'spiny lobster', 'lobster' or 'European lobster') do not have front claws; while the American lobster is prized for its large front claws; and the Norwegian lobster, while smaller, is also adorned with front claws. Flat lobsters are also known as 'shovel-nosed lobsters', 'butterfly crays' and 'slipper lobsters'. Two common Australian species are the Balmain bug and the Moreton Bay bug.

Scallops are rarely sold live, as they must be gutted as well as shucked, leaving only the white abductor muscle and the roe (the orange, pink or light tan-coloured flesh attached to the meat). Shucked scallops should be plump, with no sign of damage to the roe. Interestingly, scallops are hermaphrodites—that is, a single scallop has both male and female organs, and the roe or gonad takes on an orange, pink or purple colour (female ovary) or white to pale tan colour (male testis) at different times.

Scallops should be served medium-rare—in other words, barely cooked on the inside, for the best flavour and to retain succulence. Cook them quickly on a high heat: 30 seconds to 1 minute is all it takes in most cases. Frozen scallops, although of a good standard, do retain water. After defrosting, cook them separately from the sauce so they don't water it down, then add to the sauce just before serving. Some recipes ask for the roe (the pinky-orange bit) to be removed from the eye or abductor muscle (the round, white bit). This is because some people don't like the stronger flavour of the roe (or the fact that it is the reproductive gland)—so it's really a matter of personal preference. In the US, the eye of the scallop is preferred and is sold without the roe; in Europe, the roe is often kept on.

The best scallops are, of course, bought fresh, in the shell, to be shucked yourself.

Dried scallops are used sparingly (they're expensive) to sweeten or add flavour to soups, stews and stocks, especially high quality stock. They should be soaked in water for 30 minutes before use.

Scampi are also known as 'Dublin Bay prawns', 'Norway lobsters', 'deep sea lobsters', 'lobsterettes' (US) or 'langoustines' (France). Scampi resemble giant prawns (hence the confusion) although the species is classified as a lobster. True scampi, like those caught in deep-sea fishing off New Zealand or Australia, are a narrow pincer-clawed species with slender bodies and a more delicate flavour than rock lobster. Be wary of restaurants in the US that serve 'shrimp scampi', believing diners will think of it as a special Italian dish because it's cooked with garlic and olive oil or butter—what next, 'veal vitello'?

Shark—a dozen or so edible species of shark are caught for their meat, although as many as half of the 350 species are deemed useless to the fishing industry (only 7 per cent are classed as highly important). Shark is similar in appearance to dogfish, and the several species of dogfish as well as the elephant fish can be referred to as shark. All shark is marketed as 'flake' in its filleted form. Flake is popular in fish and chip shops for its price and the fact that it is boneless.

Squid, calamari and *cuttlefish* are all in the same family. Sometimes 'calamari' and 'squid' are used interchangeably, and although separately they could be mistaken for one another, line them up and the differences are apparent. The word 'calamari' is often mistakenly used to describe cleaned squid and, just to confuse matters, is a term used by Italians and

Greeks to describe more than one squid. Cuttlefish is a stumpier type of squid, favoured by professional cooks for its stronger flavour, tenderness and its ink.

Cuttlefish, squid and calamari should be bought whole. Pre-cut calamari or squid rings tend to be cut from a larger specimen, and the larger the creature, the tougher it will be.

Dried squid is enjoyed as a late-night drinking snack. It can also be used as a seasoning, soaked and then shredded before adding to soups, sauces, stir-fries and salads.

SPICES

Spices, like dried herbs, should be used as close to their date of manufacture as possible. Many people believe a jar of supermarket spice will outlive their grandchildren, when in fact it is probably already past its pungent best. Best of all is to buy whole spices and grind them as you need them. And as the spice snob knows all too well, the best place to buy a particular spice is from a shop based on the cuisine it is used in which ensures a high turnover of that spice.

The list below will help you identify which spices are associated with which cuisines so you can source them from a grocer dealing in that produce. It concentrates on indigenous spices with some common spices in daily use:

Africa—allspice, chilli, clove, coriander seed, cumin seed, ginger, pepper;

Australia—lemon myrtle, Tasmanian pepper;

Central and northern Europe—aniseed, black pepper, blue fenugreek, caraway seed, celery seed, cinnamon, clove, dill seed, fennel seed, juniper berry, nutmeg, paprika, poppy seed, saffron;

South Asia—ajowan, black cardamom, black cumin, cardamom, chilli, cinnamon, ginger, turmeric;

South-east and east Asia—cassia, chilli, clove, cubeb pepper, Indonesian and Vietnamese cinnamon, galangal, garlic, ginger, nutmeg, Sichuan pepper, star anise, turmeric;

Mediterranean region—allspice, aniseed, black pepper, cardamom, cinnamon, clove, coriander seed, cumin, fennel, fenugreek, mace, nutmeg, onion seed, saffron, sumac, thyme;

West and central Asia—asafoetida, black mustard seed, cardamom, chilli, cumin seed, dill seed, fenugreek, garlic, ginger, poppy seed;

West India and the Americas—allspice, cayenne, celery seed, chilli, clove, filé, paprika, vanilla.

SPICE MIXES AND PASTES

Making your own spice mix is a rewarding culinary challenge that is, unfortunately, rarely undertaken due to the many commercial products available. Recipes for spice mixes can be found in specific cookbooks and on the internet—choose reputable recipes that encourage the use of the freshest possible ingredients. If you're not prepared to make your own, then I recommend pastes available at Indian or Asian food stores or from the family flogging their wares at the local Sunday market.

The aromatics of spices are activated and heightened when exposed to heat. This is why pastes are sautéed before being added to other ingredients, and whole spices are dry-roasted before grinding and mixing into a spice mix. To dry-roast means to cook in a dry pan over medium heat, remembering to shake the pan or stir. Spices should be dry-roasted one at a time as different spices take different lengths of time and you will be in danger of burning some if you cook them all together. Remove from the heat when the spice begins to smoke and transfer to another dish immediately to stop the cooking. Crush whole spices in a mortar and pestle, a food processor, a pepper grinder or a coffee grinder. (After putting spices through a coffee grinder, clean it by grinding a handful of plain rice.) See also Bengali five spice; Garam masala; Kebsa; Mixed spice; Quatre épices; Ras el hanout; Togarashi.

Types of spice

Ajowan is a member of a large family of spices that includes cumin, dill and caraway. The dried seed is reasonably hot with a strong thyme-like flavour. It is used mostly in Indian cuisine.

Allspice is the dried, unripe berry from a tree of the myrtle family. Although the name suggests a mix of different spices, in fact it derives from the aroma's likeness to a mix of cloves, cinnamon, pepper and nutmeg. If necessary, you can replace allspice with equal parts of those four spices. Not to be confused with mixed spice, allspice is also known as 'English spice' and 'Jamaica pepper' (and in some places 'pimento'). For really fresh allspice, buy the whole berry and pound or grind your own powder.

Anise is similar in appearance to dill seed. Although often used in cakes and biscuits, it is mainly harvested for use in alcohol (Pernod, ouzo and raki). Anise should not be confused with star anise.

Anise pepper see Sichuan pepper.

Annatto is a small, triangular, brick-red spice with only the slightest sweet and peppery flavour. It is used more often as a colouring, in cheese, butter and confectionery, and in Filipino, Latin American and Caribbean cuisine (described in *Food* by Waverley Root as a spice 'with which red Americans colored their bodies and white Americans color their butter'). There is no real substitute for annatto, as few other foods can provide this natural food colouring without also imparting their stronger individual flavour, thus the similarly coloured saffron, turmeric or paprika will alter the nature of the dish. A small quantity of cochineal will impart a deep-red hue similar to annatto (but then vegans would miss out, as cochineal is made from crushed and dried beetles). Also known as 'achiote', annatto can be bought in Asian and Indian grocers.

Asafoetida is sometimes called 'giant fennel', although it smells nothing like fennel and comes from the sap of the stem or roots of the asafoetida plant (a member of the parsley family). What it does smell like is more in tune with its colloquial names, 'stinking gum' or 'devil's dung'. The name comes from the Persian word 'aza' meaning 'resin' and the Latin word 'fetida' meaning 'stinking'. The unpleasant smell mellows when cooked, however, leaving an aroma more like onion. Important in any authentic Indian or Middle Eastern cooking, it is used in place of garlic and as a flavour enhancer and a digestive aid.

Bengali five spice or panch phora is used in curries and for fried vegetable and seafood dishes. It contains cumin seed, fennel seed, fenugreek seed, mustard seeds and nigella seeds.

Black onion seeds see Nigella.

Caraway is from the same family as parsley. Its fresh leaves and roots can also be eaten but most often the caraway seed is eaten (technically the fruit of the plant). Caraway seeds taste of a combination of dill and anise with a tangy, almost nutty flavour and are popular in the cuisines of Austria, southern Germany and North Africa. When a recipe calls for you to grind your own caraway seeds, you will find it hard going unless you dry-roast them first. The roasted seeds are much easier to crush.

Cardamom is sold as powder, seeds or pods. The pods can be green or off-white. The more common green cardamom is the Indian variety; white cardamom, the size of a pea, is less common and less pungent than the green. Black or brown cardamom is a different spice which has a camphorous taste, and cannot be interchanged with green cardamom. If the recipe calls for seeds or powder, it is best to buy cardamom in pods and remove or grind the seeds yourself. (Roast the pods whole before removing the seeds.) Often the pod is simply bruised (crushed with the flat of a knife) and added whole to the dish.

Chinese five-spice powder is used as a seasoning in sauces, marinades and cooked red meat dishes. It contains equal parts cinnamon, cloves, fennel seeds, star anise and Sichuan pepper.

Chinese pepper see Sichuan pepper.

Cinnamon can be bought as sticks (quills) or ground. The best quality cinnamon is Ceylon cinnamon, Indonesian cinnamon is a medium quality option, and Vietnamese cinnamon is of poor quality, resembling cassia in appearance and flavour.

Cloves tend to lose volatile oils through evaporation, so shouldn't be stored for long periods. To check freshness, drop some in water: if they sink or float upright, all is well, but if they lie on their side, they are stale. I have seen fresh cloves on the stem in markets, looking evocative with their pink and light-green buds, but have found no references to using them in cooking. These unopened buds from the clove tree can be picked from the stem, laid on a mat and dried in the sun (about 4 days, weather permitting), leaving you with the dark brown, tack-like spice we all know. This freshly dried clove will be pungent, high in volatile oils and ready to use.

Coriander seeds are technically the fruit of the plant. As with most whole spices, the powder is best made by lightly roasting and then grinding whole seeds in a mortar and pestle. This freshly ground coriander is far superior to the ground coriander found on supermarket shelves.

Cubeb, a hollow black spice from the pepper family, is hard to source in the West. Used in Indonesian curries, cubeb can be replaced with black pepper mixed with a little allspice.

Dukkah, a North African (Egyptian) condiment, is delicious with bread dipped in extra virgin olive oil or as a coating for meat and fish. It is made up principally of coriander seeds, cumin seeds, nuts (usually hazelnuts), brown sesame seeds, salt and pepper, all roasted and then coarsely ground together.

Fennel seed (technically the fruit of the plant) has a pale-green tinge when dried; the greener the seed, the better the quality. It has a sweet anise aroma and flavour, excellent in pickled vegetable mixes, in bread and with seafood.

Fenugreek is used as a spice although it is in fact a legume (and used as one in Ethiopian cuisine). As many as 50 varieties exist, differing in colour from red-brown to yellowish-green. Dried fenugreek has no discernible smell, but once ground and cooked, its true character is revealed: it has a strong, acrid curry smell with a slightly bitter taste that strangely resembles maple syrup. It is an indispensable addition to curries and chutneys in India and Pakistan. Fresh fenugreek leaves are sold in bunches (the stalks are discarded, as they are too bitter to eat).

Garam masala is a ground spice mix made from a base of cumin and coriander along with cardamom, cinnamon, black peppercorns and Indian bay leaves. There are many variations, some containing up to 12 spices (such as nutmeg, mace, dried chilli, ground ginger and fenugreek). Garam masala is usually added towards the end of cooking a dish.

Jamaica pepper see Allspice.

Kebsa is a spice mix from Saudi Arabia and the Gulf. A mix of cardamom, cinnamon, cumin, cloves, nutmeg, coriander seed, loomi, red chilli and black pepper, it is used in soups, as a dipping spice for bread and olive oil, and as a rub for meats. A very quick kebsa spice blend can be as simple as cinnamon, cumin and allspice. There is also a meal known as kebsa, a Saudi tradition of hospitality, a feast of goat, lamb, chicken, salads and fruit.

Mace the spice has nothing to do with chemical mace, the spray used to disable an attacker in a dark alley. It is similar to nutmeg but recommended for use in savoury dishes.

Mixed spice is used in biscuits, cakes and puddings in Western cuisine. It is a mix of allspice, cinnamon, cloves, ginger, nutmeg and a small amount of black pepper. Making your own mixed spice can be an exercise in individuality; play with the quantities or add other sweet spices such as ground coriander, cardamom or anise.

Nigella, also known as 'kalonji' or 'charnushka' (US), are the teardrop-shaped, black and pungent seeds from a bush found throughout India. This aromatic, slightly bitter spice is used to give a nutty edge to curries and breads, and in Middle Eastern and Turkish cuisine. Nigella should not be confused with black sesame seeds (nigella have a more angular shape to the seeds), black onion seeds (which is a misnomer), or black cumin (although, to confuse matters, 'black cumin' is the literal translation of the Hindi word for kalonji).

Nutmeg can be bought whole or powdered. The whole kernels can be grated directly onto or into food, but be careful not to add too much. In its natural state, the nutmeg kernel has a lacy, scarlet covering, known as 'mace', which, when removed and dried, turns an orange/yellow colour and has the flavour of nutmeg. The general rule is, nutmeg for sweet dishes, mace for savoury.

Panch phora see Bengali five spice.

Pepper, no matter what its colour, begins life as the unripe, green peppercorn. Black pepper is the most aromatic pepper, produced by picking the clusters of berries when not quite ripe, then leaving them in piles to ferment. After a few days, the individual berries are spread out and left to dry in the sun for 2 or 3 more days or until they are shrivelled and nearly black. Black pepper from India is regarded as the best, especially the Malabar and Tellicherry varieties. One of the hottest black peppers is from Lampong province in Sumatra and it, too, is highly regarded. White pepper is the most pungent of the peppers, but the least aromatic. It is produced from the fully ripened berries that are just about to turn red. After harvest, the clusters are packed in bags and soaked in water for more than a week. This softens the outer coating, or pericarp, so that it may be removed to reveal the grey centres. The peppercorns are then spread out to dry in the sun where they naturally bleach to white. Green peppercorns are harvested while still immature and cured in brine. They can be used in curry pastes (soak in cold water for 30 minutes then pound into the paste), or added whole (first rinse in cold water) to cream sauces or stews, and to pâtés, terrines and dressings, for a musky, peppery bite with far less pungency than black or white. Tasmanian pepper, also known as 'mountain pepper' and 'native pepper', is native to Australia and hard to source from outside the country. It resembles black pepper in size and appearance, but there is no substitute for this flavour. Tasmanian pepper has gained popularity through the 'bush food' movement in Australia.

Pink peppercorns are not actually peppercorns but berries. They are sweet and aromatic and make a good (although less fragrant) alternative to juniper berries. Sold either dried or in brine, they are used in sauces, with fish or poultry, or ground to use as a final dusting for garnish. Freeze-dried pink peppercorns are often sold mixed with black and white peppercorns for people to use in clear grinders—the purpose is more for display than flavour. They should be used in moderation, as large quantities have been said to cause respiratory ailments or irritation of mucous membranes.

Quatre épices (literally 'four spices') is a favourite spice in France, North Africa and the Middle East, made up of white pepper, ground nutmeg, ground ginger and ground cloves. It is used in French charcuterie, and Middle Eastern meat dishes.

Ras el hanout is a superbly fragrant and complex Moroccan spice blend. It roughly translates as 'top of the shelf' or 'head of the shop', which for a spice merchant represents the best blend of spices on offer. Although consisting of up to 15 different ingredients, it is subtle, and the addition of rose petals and lavender can impart a fantastic aroma, colour and underlying flavour. Like many of the spice blends, ras el hanout can be made with varied spice combinations and quantities, although often the spices are mixed in equal portions. A basic blend might include black pepper (Tellicherry), cardamom, ginger, cinnamon, mace, turmeric, allspice, nutmeg, saffron, galangal, cayenne, coriander, cassia, cloves and nigella. Ras el hanout can be added to couscous and rice as they cook, and is also used in meat and potato tagines (casseroles), meatballs and lamb dishes. It is best to roast the ground spice mix before using.

Sansho pepper see Sichuan pepper.

Seven-flavour spice see Togarashi.

Sichuan pepper is also known as 'anise pepper', 'Chinese pepper' and 'spice pepper'. It has an aromatic, woody/lemony flavour with a slight anaesthetic feel on the tongue. The aroma comes from the pod and not the seeds. The seeds will have already been removed from store-bought pepper, as they have an unnecessary bitterness about them. You should also remove any fragments of stem that you find as they are tough and pointy, which could be harmful on swallowing. Sichuan pepper can be used as a condiment: first mix with salt, dry-toast in a wok until it begins to smoke, then cool and grind coarsely. Chinese sichuan pepper is the most common but you can also buy Indonesian sichuan, North Indian sichuan and Nepalese sichuan. The Japanese version is called 'sansho' and is used in togarashi.

Spice pepper see Sichuan pepper.

Star anise is a star-shaped spice (each star has 8 points) with the distinct flavour and aroma of aniseed or licorice. It is collected from a small evergreen shrub in Japan yet used significantly in Chinese cuisine. Moderation is the key when using this pungent spice. It is usually added whole to a dish, but each point in the star contains a seed which can be removed and roasted separately then ground. Star anise should not be confused with anise.

Sumac is a tree, whose seed or berry is dried, ground and mixed with salt to produce the spice sumac. This tart, dark red spice is sprinkled over cooked rice, bread doughs, fish or lamb (before being cooked) and salads. Sumac is found in Middle Eastern grocers, and the dried seeds can also be purchased whole: crush and soak the seeds in warm water for about 20 minutes, then strain to produce a juice that is sour enough to be used instead of lemon juice. Note that some wild versions of sumac can be very poisonous.

Togarashi or seven-flavour spice, is a popular Japanese spice mix used as a condiment to sprinkle over hotpots and noodle dishes, or for sukiyaki, or as a seasoning. The seven flavours are ground chilli, poppy seeds, sansho pepper, black sesame seeds, white sesame seeds, rape seeds and ground tangerine peel. The amount of chilli can be varied according to taste.

Za'atar, the Arabic word for wild thyme, is both a herb and a spice mix used in Middle Eastern cooking. It is sprinkled on bread before baking, soups, seafood, barbecued mutton and grilled meats. It is a blend of sumac, sesame seeds and the herb za'atar, and can be bought ready-made in Middle Eastern and Lebanese produce shops.

SUGAR

Sugar comes in many forms—dried, powdered, dark sticky liquids—in different grades, and is mostly produced from sugar cane or the white root of sugar beets. (The by-product of sugar cane and sugar beet refining is molasses.) Screened sugars have been through a sifting method to divide the sugar into various sizes for different uses. The result is granulated sugar, such as plain or caster sugar. Different screened sugars are used for commercial products, depending on the granule size required: coarse sugar, Crystal 750, sugar, nonpareil, fine sugar and extra fine sugar. Milled sugar refers to powdered sugars such as icing sugar. Most of these contain free-flowing agents, such as starch, tri-calcium phosphate or maltodextrin.

Need I go on about the over-consumption of refined sugars in our diets? Suffice to say that with diabetes an ever-increasing diagnosis in Western society, and obesity on the rise in young children, moderation is essential.

PROBLEM SOLVING

Lumpy sugar? Pour through a sieve, gently squash in a mortar and pestle or keep to one side and use in hot caramel, toffee, hot beverages or any other dish where free-flowing sugar is not required.

TYPES OF SUGAR

Blended sugar is cane or beet sugar with dextrose (derived from corn) added, which makes for a cheaper product. It is not as sweet as granulated sugar. Because dextrose is hygroscopic (attracts water from the air), using blended sugar in a recipe could alter the end result.

Brown sugar can be light or dark, both quite moist. The flavour varies slightly according to the richness of the molasses content. Brown sugar can replace most other brown (especially muscovado) and even white granulated sugar, as well as coconut sugar and palm sugar.

Caster/castor sugar is the finest of the screened sugars. Most often used in domestic baking and dessert/sweets, because its small granule dissolves quickly, it can be replaced with white granulated sugar that has been blended until the grains are as fine as possible.

Cinnamon sugar is, as the name suggests, sugar with cinnamon added. To make your own, use 7 parts caster sugar to 1 part ground cinnamon.

Coconut sugar is made from the sap of the coconut tree. (Gathering the sap eventually renders the tree useless for quality coconut production.) The sugar is very dark brown, with less flavour than pure palm sugar—it is similar in taste to dark brown sugar which can be used to replace it if necessary. It is sold in a moist block.

Demerara sugar is a light brown crystal sugar. When made properly, it is only partially refined, which leaves the natural molasses intact, but unfortunately most demerara sugar available is made from refined white sugar with molasses added. (To find the genuine stuff, look on the packet: there should be no list of ingredients as demerara sugar is just that, not sugar and molasses.) It can be replaced with light brown sugar or raw sugar.

Date sugar is made from the sap of the date palm. It adds a delicate flavour to baked goods, beverages and other foods.

Dry fondant sugar, used to make fondant, contains 10 per cent spray-dried glucose.

Evaporated cane sugar juice is one for the vegans. It hasn't gone through the final stages of clarification over charcoaled animal bones that some other sugars are subjected to.

Fondant sugar is slightly different to dry fondant sugar, which is used in royal icing for cake decorating and fondant making. It is a very fine, pure form of icing sugar (without glucose).

Icing sugar or *pure icing sugar*, known in the US as 'confectioners' sugar', is a milled sugar. Unlike many of the milled sugars, pure icing sugar contains no additives. It can be replaced with a homemade icing sugar mixture: blend 1 cup granulated sugar with 1 tablespoon cornflour until powdery. It can also be called 'powdered sugar' and '10 x sugar'.

Muscovado sugar, also known as 'Barbados sugar', is a rich, moist, brown sugar which is less refined than most other brown sugars. Replace with dark brown sugar if necessary.

Palm sugar is also know as 'jaggery', 'java sugar' or 'gula melaka'. (The latter name also refers to a Malaysian dessert made from tapioca or sago, coconut milk and a palm sugar syrup.) This hard block sugar is found in Asian grocers and some supermarkets. Read the ingredients as several brands are made from cane sugar and molasses, not from the sap of the sugar palm. It is available light coloured and very hard or as a dark, almost black and moister block (which may in fact be coconut sugar—check the label). Palm sugar has a flavour unto itself which other sugars will not bring to the dish.

Pearl sugar is used in the baking industry for decorative purposes. Also known as 'decorative sugar' or 'sanding sugar', these are simply lumps of refined sugar particles.

Preserving sugar is designed for jams and preserves. It has large white crystals which dissolve slowly and so do not settle in the bottom of the pan, reducing the need for stirring and the risk of burning. In addition, less froth results in a clearer preserve.

Raw sugar is a semi-refined product similar to turbinado. It has a light caramel/molasses flavour, and is also called 'plantation sugar' or 'sugar in the raw'. In Canada, however, 'raw sugar' refers to the product imported simply for refining into other sugars and is therefore not sold to the consumer, as it still contains impurities.

Rock sugar, also known as 'Chinese rock sugar' or 'rock candy', is made from very pure white sugar and comes as large white crystals, either clear or yellow. Not as sweet as granulated sugar, it is used for red roasting and (the yellow variety) as a decorative sugar, as well as in cooking.

Rolled fondant, also known as 'sugar paste', 'pastillage' and 'roll out icing', is a mix of icing sugar, cornflour and gum arabic. It is used in cake decorating as it's easy to mould, shape and colour. Once applied, it needs to dry before decorating.

Silk sugar is a new product which, as the name suggests, is as smooth as silk when commercially made into fondant; however, it is not readily available to the public.

Snow sugar or *MR sugar* is a commercially available product favoured by bakers and chefs who have their sweet goods on display. This moisture-resistant product tastes of sugar and looks like icing sugar, but it won't dissolve when dusted over berries or cakes. It cannot be used in the cooking process, so is strictly aesthetic.

Soft icing mixture is a milled sugar that is better used for frosting on a cake than in baking, as it contains a starch as a free-flowing agent. See also Icing sugar.

Sugar syrup, known as 'simple syrup' in the US, is a syrup of water and sugar, which has been boiled until the sugar dissolves. Used for sweetening bar drinks (cocktails) and as a base for fruit sauces it is usually made with equal parts sugar and water, but can vary depending on the sweetness required (a sweeter mix may be 2 parts sugar to 1 part water).

Turbinado sugar is a light brown crystal sugar similar to demerara. Use light brown sugar or raw sugar as a substitute.

SUGAR TEMPERATURES

	°C	°F	Use
small thread	100	212	
large thread	104	219	
small pearl	106	220	
large pearl	109	228	
soft ball	112	234	fudge, fondant
medium ball	114	237	marshmallows
firm ball	118	244	caramels
hard ball	120	248	toffee (taffies, US)
very hard ball	124	255	
light crack	135	275	
crack	144	291	
hard crack	152	306	butterscotch, brittles, spun sugar
caramelised sugar	155–70	310–38	

ALTERNATIVES TO SUGAR

In baking, sugar provides a chemical reaction as well as acting as a sweetener. Be aware of this when substituting with another sweetener in cooking, because the alternatives may not provide the bulk and colouring sugar can provide. There are numerous synthetic sweeteners on the market, as well as some good natural sweeteners, which in some cases are many hundreds of times sweeter than sugar. Do your research to establish the benefits and problems of alternatives, depending on your reason for cutting back on sugar. As a note, vegans may choose not to consume white sugars because they can be refined with the use of charcoal made from animal bones.

Agave nectar is a sweetener extracted from the agave, a large succulent plant with thick fleshy leaves. It is a very thick liquid that goes a long way.

Corn syrup is available light or dark. The light syrup has been clarified, removing colour and cloudy particles. Dark syrup has had refiners added to produce a stronger-tasting, dark-coloured syrup. Corn syrup is high in fructose, which absorbs and retains moisture well, so using it in baked goods can result in a moist product that stays fresher for longer. Corn syrup can be replaced with other syrups but is not as sweet as, say, honey or maple.

Fructose is a term for sugar found in honey, corn and certain fruits. The sweetest of the simple sugars, it is almost twice as sweet as sucrose and turns into glucose once ingested. Fructose can be bought in granulated form.

Fruit juice makes for a good sweetener, but for many diabetics, a concentrated fruit juice is still off limits. Fruit crystals, although hard to find, are available.

Glucose powder is made from grapes or fruit, and is closer to a pure glucose. Both are sold at chemists as dietary supplements, as syrup, powder or tablets. Glucose is much less sweet than sugar, and is valued as an energy booster because it heads straight for the blood stream.

Glucose syrup is more dextrin than glucose and is made from maize syrup.

Honey is as much as 60 per cent sweeter than sugar, with a higher caloric count. Honey should never be served to babies, as contaminated honey is the only food product that can cause infant botulism. For true vegans, honey is a no-no, as it is considered that commerical honey production exploits bees. (Bees naturally produce extra honey for the winter; beekeepers take all the honey, feeding bees a cheap, low-grade corn syrup instead, which shortens their life span 2–3 years compared to 6 years for wild bees. Some exclusive keepers rotate honey supplies, ensuring the bees have enough for their winter period, but although honey from these keepers 'tastes great, it has a far smaller yield, is hard to source, expensive and not commercially viable.)

Maple crystals are a wonderful product with a high price tag. Much sweeter than sugar, they have the umami factor: tiny crystals with an excellent maple explosion in the mouth. Finding the product outside Canada can be a little frustrating.

Maple syrup is sweeter and better for you than sugar. Buy organic maple syrup wherever possible, as it doesn't contain the mould inhibitors or formaldehyde that may taint other pure maple syrups. Maple-flavoured syrup is a very cheap imitation of the good stuff. It is a blend of corn syrup (pure sugar) with artificial flavours.

Rice syrup is only half as sweet as cane sugar, with a similar viscosity to honey. It is not recommended as a sugar alternative in cakes and baked goods.

Stevia is a sweetener made from the South American plant *Stevia rebaudiana* 'Bertoni'. It is a green powder 30 times sweeter than sugar, with no calories and a sweet herby taste. It is not recognised by world health authorities, but it may be that stevia is controversial only because it poses a threat to synthetic brands and the sugar industry. You're most likely to find it as a dietary supplement in health food shops, and stevia cookbooks are available.

Stevioside is a white powder derived from stevia, but further refined and without the slight herb flavour. It is 300 times sweeter than sugar so should be used sparingly.

Sucanat is a whole cane sugar which contains the juice of pressed cane sugar with molasses added. Still a sugar as far as diabetics are concerned, it contains a small amount of vitamins, minerals and trace elements which help to reduce the negative effects of long-term white sugar use. Sucanat can be substituted for brown sugar, measure for measure.

Sucrose is the sugar extracted primarily from sugar cane and sugar beet.

Synthetic (toxic) *sweeteners* include many brands that are now household names. Use these products at your own discretion, and research them before believing they are good at what they do. Types of synthetic sweeteners include: neotame; aspartame (NutraSweet, Equal); sucralose, which is 600 times sweeter than sucrose (Splenda); and acesulfame-k, which is 200 times sweeter than sucrose (Sunette, Sweet n Safe, SweetOne).

TOMATOES

Tomatoes arrive in all their glorious shapes, sizes and colours. And like most fruit and vegetables, the tomato can indeed be a wondrous fruit when home grown—tasting sweet and delicious—or it can be a sad, pale, tasteless ball of water that has been mass-produced. By supporting farmers' markets you will be joining the chorus; This is how tomatoes used to taste.

TIPS:

* Fragrance is a better indicator of a good tomato than colour; use your nose to smell the stem end. The stem should retain the garden aroma of the plant itself. If it doesn't, your tomato will lack flavour.
* Keep tomatoes on the windowsill to ripen, then store at room temperature. If tomatoes are fully ripe or starting to soften, use them immediately or move them to the fridge.
* The best knife for cutting tomatoes has a serrated edge, is about 15 cm long, and has finer teeth than a bread knife.
* Add to a leafy salad at the last minute to prevent the acid and weight of the tomatoes from breaking down the lettuce.
* To avoid soggy sandwiches, place each slice of tomato on a piece of paper towel to absorb excess water before it goes on the bread.
* The acid in fresh or canned tomatoes will strip an iron pan of its natural nonstick coating leaving it susceptible to rusting-choose something like stainless steel for cooking.
* Tomato 'water', the clearish liquid that escapes from a sliced tomato, can be used as a low-acidity stand-in for lemon juice. Try it for marinating raw fish.
* To peel a tomato, score the skin very lightly with the point of a sharp knife. Then blanch for 10–15 seconds, no more—the longer the tomato cooks, the more flesh will be ripped off when you peel the tomato. Don't drop the tomatoes in iced water after blanching, as this will dilute the flavour.
* Unripe, green tomatoes can be sliced, dipped in polenta and fried.
* Rehydrate dried tomatoes (those not sold in oil) in hot water for 15 minutes. Drain and then marinate in olive oil, chopped herbs, and balsamic or white wine vinegar (1 part vinegar to 5 parts oil). Store in an airtight container in the refrigerator.

TYPES OF TOMATO

Beefsteak tomatoes are bright red and flat ribbed with solid, juicy flesh. Good for slicing.

Cherry tomatoes, teardrop tomatoes and *grape tomatoes* are, respectively, small and round, teardrop or oblong in shape. They are red or yellow, ideal for salads or mixed into pasta at the very last minute.

Purple tomatoes from South America are very tasty raw, but can be cooked as well.

Roma tomatoes are also known as 'plum tomatoes', 'sauce tomatoes' and 'egg tomatoes'. These medium-sized, oblong tomatoes are ideal for soups, pasta sauces, drying, roasting and salads, as it has few seeds.

Tiger tomatoes are novel and very tasty raw.

Yellow tomatoes can be pear-shaped, round or oblong and suit all dishes, pickling, roasting and eating fresh.

FOOD ALLERGIES, INTOLERANCES AND FOOD ADDITIVES

A food allergy should not be mistaken for a food intolerance. A food allergy is often caused by the immune system responding to proteins within the food and overloading on chemicals such as histamine, which in turn brings about an allergic reaction, such as swelling, wheezing, hives, etc. On the other hand, an intolerance or a sensitivity to a food or an ingredient within food is often linked to other health problems. It has more to do with digestion and has less defined symptoms. Food allergies in adults are rarely curable, while food sensitivities may often improve or disappear over a period of time. Allergy symptoms range from localised hives and swelling to the life-threatening anaphylaxis, which causes difficulty in breathing and/or a drop in blood pressure (shock). Vomiting, diarrhoea, blocked or runny nose, an intense sense of fear, dizziness, swelling of the face and throat (extreme swelling and immediate facial disfigurement are not uncommon), difficulty in thinking and tightness in the chest are also signs to beware of.

Allergies from food occur in around 1 in 20 children and 1 in 100 adults. In up to 80 per cent of cases, children grow out of these; but allergies to nuts, seeds and seafood often continue into adult life and must be monitored. The most severe allergies, which can cause anaphylaxis, are to peanuts, tree nuts (such as pistachios, walnuts, almonds, pecans, brazil nuts and macadamias) and shellfish. Other common allergies are to cow's milk, soy, eggs, fish and gluten.

Seek immediate advice from a medical practitioner if you have an adverse reaction to any food or drink.

ALTERNATIVES TO ALLERGY-CAUSING FOODS

Allergy-causing foods can often be successfully replaced with alternative ingredients, but some alternatives will change the flavour. Milk, eggs, wheat and gluten have alternatives, for example, but it's hard to replace nuts and seafood without changing the nature of the dish. Beware of cross-contamination when preparing food for a guest with an allergy. Even the smallest amount can trigger a nasty reaction. Food should be prepared on completely different cutting boards and benches and cooked in different pans.

ALTERNATIVE FLOURS

Gluten is a substance found in grains such as wheat, oats, rye and barley. Some people require a gluten-free diet, most often those who are diagnosed with coeliac disease (gluten-sensitive enteropathy). See the section on flour which gives an extensive list of wheat- and gluten-free flours.

ALTERNATIVES TO PRODUCTS CONTAINING GLUTEN

Xanthan gum (derived from the fermentation of corn sugar with a bacterium) or *guar gum* (derived from the seeds of a plant originating in India, Cyamoposis tetragonolobus) help gluten-free baked products to bind and hold their shape. For best results, use a combination of the two gums in the proportions of 2 parts xanthan to 1 part guar. Add a small quantity of water to the recipe to encourage the gums to become sticky. Add ½–1 teaspoon of the combined gums and water to a single recipe of biscuits, cakes or bread. For larger quantities, you will have to experiment with the quantites of gum and different proportions of flours.

For **homemade gluten-free baking powder**-mix together: ¼ cup bicarbonate of soda and ½ cup cream of tartar.

For **homemade gluten-free flour**-in recipes, replace 1 cup plain flour with one of the following gluten- and wheat-free alternatives: 1½ cups rolled oats (try putting the rolled oats in the food processor to change the texture); ½ cup soy flour and ½ cup rice flour; ½ cup soy flour, ¼ cup rice flour and ¼ cup potato flour; ½ cup soy flour and ½ cup cornflour; or ¼ cup soy flour, ¼ cup tapioca flour and ½ cup brown rice flour.

ALTERNATIVES TO EGGS

See the Eggs section, **Alternatives to Eggs**, for suggestions.

ALTERNATIVES TO MILK

Almond milk can be easily made at home. It tastes great, has no cholesterol and can be substituted for cow's milk measure for measure when baking. For **homemade almond milk**—blend 1 cup shelled raw almonds to a fine powder. Add 2 cups water and blend for 2 minutes. Keep the blender running while slowly adding another 2 cups water. Strain slowly through muslin or cheesecloth. Almond milk will keep in the fridge for 4–5 days. There will be close to 1 cup almond fibre leftover. You can keep this in the fridge and use it as a body moisturiser in the shower.

Fruit milks are usually made from very ripe bananas, rockmelon or honeydew melon. For banana milk, simply blend 1 very ripe banana with 1 cup of water. For the rockmelon and honeydew, scoop the flesh straight into the blender and puree to form a creamy, milky texture.

Horchata and *Mexican horchata* are both used as milk substitutes.

Goat's milk contains lactose (as does the milk of all mammals) but some people find it more digestible than cow's milk, so it is sometimes recommended as an alternative.

Lactose-reduced milk is exactly that. Lactose has been reduced by 40–100 per cent. People with lactose intolerance can look into these alternatives, but for those allergic to milk proteins, move on.

Non-dairy creamers and whiteners are common in the US but rare elsewhere. These dairy alternatives, usually reserved for beverages, contain corn syrup solids and palm oil, and are free of lactose, cholesterol, allergens and milk protein. Some contain coconut oil, canola oil or other such ingredients.

Oat milk is a good replacement for drinking and in cooking, with excellent health benefits, although it's not suitable for people who are gluten-intolerant.

Rice milk can be used on cereal, for drinking, in baking and as a thickening agent.

Soy milk is an alternative although some people are allergic to Soy.

ALTERNATIVES TO SEAFOOD

For those allergic to seafood, there is no substitute. Allergic reactions to seafood (which includes fish and shellfish, the most common being prawns or shrimp) are the third most common food allergy after eggs and milk. The allergy is usually life-long, and if anything, the reactions can become more aggressive after each exposure to seafood. In severe cases, even the vapours from cooked seafood can trigger a reaction.

ALTERNATIVES TO MEAT

Ardent meat lovers would argue that there are no substitutes, but that does not help vegetarians, vegans or anyone changing the way they eat. Many techniques and accompaniments that work with meat can successfully be applied to non-meat products.

Mushrooms have long been considered meat for vegetarians. Cut into large chunks or kept whole, mushrooms bulk out a curry, stir-fry or casserole perfectly, adding a meaty texture that other vegetables fail to deliver.

Pureed nuts and seeds are a good source of protein in place of meat.

Seitan is made from gluten, is high in protein and has a meat-like texture when cooked. Seitan absorbs flavours well and can be sliced and diced, then used in stir-fries, casseroles or cooked in a sauce.

Tempeh is a fermented soy bean product that is an excellent high-protein meat substitute. Tempeh is one of the most versatile alternatives to meat and it takes to marinating, stir-frying, grilling, braising, sautéing and baking.

Tofu, another soy product, can be purchased ready-made (burgers, steaks, hot dogs) as well as in blocks.

TVP (Textured Vegetable Protein) is dried, minced soy protein used as a substitute for minced meat. TVP has no discernible flavour of its own so relies on added ingredients for a boost. Any recipe made from minced beef can be recreated using TVP.

Food additives

This list of additives is designed as a quick reference to the main food additives ever present in packaged foods. If you still have concerns, you can have a checklist sent to you from your country's governing food authority that deals with additives, genetically modified foods, labelling, irradiation, food standards and safety.

Some additives are not labelled, and this is legal when an ingredient within a processed food itself contains additives. Confusing? Yes, but the simple answer is to contact the manufacturer for this ingredient information. Otherwise send for a complete 'code breaker' from your national food authority.

Food additives are an important component in the preservation of our food, ensuring longevity and ease of use. Additives are also used to improve the taste and appearance of the food. However, with the good comes the bad, and some additives do have an adverse effect on some people. Most intolerances are blamed on the additive, when in fact the intolerance may be attributable to a naturally occuring food component such as amines, glutamates and salicylates. In either case, people with allergies want to know what it is they are consuming, others simply don't like the amount of added extras thrown into a tasty snack.

The varied functions of food additives are: colouring agents, flavouring, colour retention agents, preservatives, flavour enhancers, mineral salts, food acids, humectants, emulsifiers, food acids, anti-caking agents, stabilisers, thickeners, vegetable gums, propellants, glazing agents, and flour treatment agents.

There are so many food additives out there, with equally confusing names, that code numbers have been added to simplify their identification. This list (sourced from the Australian and New Zealand Food Authority) is an international list, and the codes are universal, but keep in mind it is not the most extensive list, and each country may allow and use additives that are not used and accepted in other countries. A letter in front of the numbers simply denotes a country; for example 'E100' is still turmeric, but found on packages in the UK.

The following list shows code number, prescribed name and use. Additive numbers are in **bold-face** type, followed by the name in Roman, then the use in brackets.

100 curcumin [colouring]
100 turmeric [colouring]
101 riboflavin [colouring]
101 riboflavin 5´ phosphate
sodium [colouring]
102 tartrazine [colouring]
103 alkanet [colouring]
104 quinoline yellow Cl
47005 [colouring]
110 sunset yellow FCF
[colouring]
120 carmines [colouring]
120 cochineal Cl 75470
[colouring]
122 azorubine [colouring]
123 amaranth [colouring]
124 ponceau 4R [colouring]
127 erythrosine [colouring]
129 allure red AC Cl 16035
[colouring]
132 indigotine [colouring]
133 brilliant blue FCF
[colouring]
140 chlorophyll [colouring]
141 chlorophyll-copper
complex [colouring]
142 food green S [colouring]
150 caramel [colouring]
151 brilliant black BN
[colouring]
153 activated vegetable
carbon [colouring]
153 carbon blacks [colouring]
155 brown HT [colouring]
160 carotene, others
[colouring]
160a beta-carotene
[colouring]
160b annatto extracts
[colouring]
160e beta-apo-8´ carotenal
[colouring]
160f E-apo-8´ carotenoic
acid methyl or ethyl
ester [colouring]
161 xanthophylls [colouring]
162 beet red [colouring]
163 anthocyanins [colouring]

170 calcium carbonate mineral
salt [colouring]
171 titanium dioxide
[colouring]
172 iron oxide, red, black,
yellow [colouring]
174 silver [colouring]
181 tannic acid [colouring]
200 sorbic acid
[preservative]
201 sodium sorbate
[preservative]
202 potassium sorbate
[preservative]
203 calcium sorbate
[preservative]
210 benzoic acid
[preservative]
211 sodium benzoate
[preservative]
212 potassium benzoate
[preservative]
213 calcium benzoate
[preservative]
216 propylparaben
[preservative]
218 methylparaben
[preservative]
220 sulphur dioxide
[preservative]
221 sodium sulphite
[preservative]
222 sodium bisulphite
[preservative]
223 sodium metabisulphite
[preservative]
224 potassium metabisulphite
[preservative]
225 potassium sulphite
[preservative]
228 potassium bisulphite
[preservative]
234 nisin [preservative]
235 natamycin [preservative]
242 dimethyl dicarbonate
[preservative]
249 potassium nitrite
[preservative, colour

fixative]
250 sodium nitrite
[preservative, colour
fixative]
251 sodium nitrate
[preservative, colour
fixative]
252 potassium nitrate
[preservative, colour
fixative]
260 acetic acid, glacial
[food acid]
261 potassium acetate [food
acid]
262 sodium acetate [food
acid]
262 sodium diacetate [food
acid]
263 sodium acetate [food
acid]
264 ammonium acetate [food
acid]
270 lactic acid [food acid]
280 propionic acid
[preservative]
281 sodium propionate
[preservative]
282 calcium propionate
[preservative]
283 potassium propionate
[preservative]
290 carbon dioxide
[propellant]
296 malic acid [food acid]
297 fumaric acid [food acid]
300 ascorbic acid
[antioxidant]
301 sodium ascorbate
[antioxidant]
302 calcium ascorbate
[antioxidant]
303 potassium ascorbate
[antioxidant]
304 ascorbyl palmitate
[antioxidant]
306 tocopherols concentrate
[mixed antioxidant]
307 dl-a-tocopherol

[antioxidant]
308 g-tocopherol
[antioxidant]
309 d-tocopherol
[antioxidant]
310 propyl gallate
[antioxidant]
311 octyl gallate
[antioxidant]
312 sodecyl gallate
[antioxidant]
315 erythorbic acid
[antioxidant]
316 sodium erythorbate
[antioxidant]
319 tert-butylhydroquinone
[antioxidant]
320 butylated hydroxyanisole
[antioxidant]
321 butylated hydroxytoluene
[antioxidant]
322 lecithin antioxidant
[emulsifier]
325 sodium lactate [food
acid]
326 potassium lactate [food
acid]
327 calcium lactate [food
acid]
328 ammonium lactate [food
acid]
329 magnesium lactate [food
acid]
330 citric acid [food acid]
331 sodium acid citrate
[food acid]
331 sodium citrate [food
acid]
331 sodium dihydrogen citrate
[food acid]
332 potassium citrates [food
acid]
333 calcium citrate [food
acid]
334 tartaric acid [food
acid]
335 sodium tartrate [food
acid]

336 potassium acid tartrate
[food acid]
336 potassium tartrate [food
acid]
337 potassium sodium tartrate
[food acid]
338 phosphoric acid [food
acid]
339 sodium phosphates
[mineral salt]
340 potassium phosphates
[mineral salt]
341 calcium phosphates
[mineral salt]
342 ammonium phosphates
[mineral salt]
343 magnesium phosphates
[mineral salt]
349 ammonium malate [food
acid]
350 dl-sodium malates [food
acid]
351 potassium malate [food
acid]
352 dl-calcium malate [food
acid]
353 metatartaric acid [food
acid]
354 calcium tartrate [food
acid]
355 adipic acid [food acid]
357 potassium adipate [food
acid]
365 sodium fumarate [food
acid]
366 potassium fumarate [food
acid]
367 potassium fumarate [food
acid]
368 ammonium fumarate [food
acid]
375 niacin [colour retention
agent]
380 ammonium citrate [food
acid]
380 triammonium citrate
[food acid]
381 ferric ammonium citrate

[food acid]
385 calcium disodium
hylenediaminetetraacetate
[preservative]
400 alginic acid [thickener,
vegetable gum]
401 sodium alginate
[thickener, vegetable
gum]
402 potassium alginate
[thickener, vegetable
gum]
403 ammonium alginate
[thickener, vegetable
gum]
404 calcium alginate
[thickener, vegetable
gum]
405 propylene glycol alginate
[thickener, vegetable
gum]
406 agar [thickener,
vegetable gum]
407 carrageenan [thickener,
vegetable gum]
407a processed eucheuma
seaweed [thickener,
vegetable gum]
409 arabinogalactan
[thickener, vegetable
gum]
410 locust bean gum
[thickener, vegetable
gum]
412 guar gum [thickener,
vegetable gum]
413 tragacanth [thickener,
vegetable gum]
414 acacia [thickener,
vegetable gum]
415 xanthan gum [thickener,
vegetable gum]
416 karaya gum [thickener,
vegetable gum]
418 gellan gum [thickener,
vegetable gum]
420 sorbitol [humectant]
421 mannitol [humectant]

422 glycerin [humectant]

433 polysorbate 80 [emulsifier]

435 polysorbate 60 [emulsifier]

436 polysorbate 65 [emulsifier]

440 pectin [vegetable gum]

442 ammonium salts of phosphatidic acid [emulsifier]

444 sucrose acetate isobutyrate [emulsifier, stabiliser]

450 potassium pyrophosphate [mineral salts]

450 sodium acid pyrophosphate [mineral salts]

450 sodium pyrophosphate [mineral salts]

451 sodium tripolyphosphate [mineral salts]

452 potassium tripolyphosphate [mineral salts]

452 sodium metaphosphate, insoluble [mineral salts]

452 sodium polyphosphates, glassy [mineral salts]

452 potassium polymetaphosphate [mineral salts]

460 cellulose, microcrystalline and powdered [anti-caking agent]

461 methylcellulose [thickener, vegetable gum]

464 hydroxypropyl methylcellulose [thickener, vegetable gum]

465 methyl ethyl cellulose [thickener, vegetable gum]

466 sodium carboxymethylcellulose [thickener, vegetable gum]

470 magnesium stearate [emulsifier, stabiliser]

471 mono- and di-glycerides of fatty acids [emulsifier]

472a acetic and fatty acid esters of glycerol [emulsifier]

472b lactic and fatty acid esters of glycerol [emulsifier]

472c citric and fatty acid esters of glycerol [emulsifier]

472d tartaric and fatty acid esters of glycerol [emulsifier]

472e diacetyltartaric and fatty acid esters of glycerol [emulsifier]

473 sucrose esters of fatty acids [emulsifier]

475 polyglycerol esters of fatty acids [emulsifier]

476 polyglycerol esters of interesterified ricinoleic acid [emulsifier]

477 propylene glycol mono- and di-esters [emulsifier]

480 dioctyl sodium sulphosuccinate [emulsifier]

481 sodium oleyl lactylate [emulsifier]

481 sodium stearoyl lactylate [emulsifier]

482 calcium oleyl lactylate [emulsifier]

482 calcium stearoyl lactylate [emulsifier]

491 sorbitan monostearate [emulsifier]

492 sorbitan tristearate [emulsifier]

500 sodium bicarbonate [mineral salt]

500 sodium carbonate [mineral salt]

501 potassium carbonates [mineral salt]

503 ammonium bicarbonate [mineral salt]

503 ammonium carbonate [mineral salt]

504 magnesium carbonate [anti-caking agent, mineral salt]

507 hydrochloric acid [acidity regulator]

508 potassium chloride [mineral salt]

509 calcium chloride [mineral salt]

510 ammonium chloride [mineral salt]

511 magnesium chloride [mineral salt]

512 stannous chloride [colour retention agent]

514 sodium sulphate [mineral salt]

515 potassium sulphate [mineral salt]

516 calcium sulphate [flour treatment agent, mineral salt]

518 magnesium sulphate [mineral salt]

519 cupric sulphate [mineral salt]

526 calcium hydroxide [mineral salt]

529 calcium oxide [mineral salt]

535 sodium ferrocyanide [anti-caking agent]

536 potassium ferrocyanide [anti-caking agent]

541 sodium aluminium phosphate, [acidic acidity regulator, emulsifier]

542 bone phosphate [anti-caking agent]

551 silicon dioxide [anti-caking agent]
552 calcium silicate [anti-caking agent]
553 talc [anti-caking agent]
554 sodium aluminosilicate [anti-caking agent]
556 calcium aluminium silicate [anti-caking agent]
558 bentonite [anti-caking agent]
559 kaolin [anti-caking agent]
570 stearic acid [anti-caking agent]
575 gluconod-lactone [acidity regulator]
577 potassium gluconate [stabiliser]
578 calcium gluconate [acidity regulator]
579 ferrous gluconate [colour retention agent]
620 1-glutamic acid [flavour enhancer]
621 monosodium 1-glutamate [flavour enhancer]
622 monopotassium I-glutamate [flavour enhancer]
623 calcium di-1-glutamate [flavour enhancer]
624 monoammonium 1-glutamate [flavour enhancer]
625 magnesium di-1-glutamate [flavour enhancer]
627 disodium guanylate [flavour enhancer]
631 disodium inosinate [flavour enhancer]
635 disodium 51-ribonucleotides [flavour enhancer]
636 maltol [flavour enhancer]
637 ethyl maltol [flavour enhancer]
640 glycine [flavour enhancer]
641 1-leucine [flavour enhancer]
900 dimethylpolysiloxane [emulsifier, anti-foaming agent, anti-caking agent]
901 beeswax, white and yellow [glazing agent]
903 carnauba wax [glazing agent]
904 shellac, bleached [glazing agent]
905b petrolatum [glazing agent]
905a mineral oil, white [glazing agent]
914 oxidised polyethylene [humectant]
920 1-cysteine monohydrochloride [flour treatment agent]
925 chlorine [flour treatment agent]
926 chlorine dioxide [flour treatment agent]
928 benzoyl peroxide [flour treatment agent]
941 nitrogen [propellant]
942 nitrous oxide [propellant]
950 acesulphame potassium [artificial sweetening substance]
951 aspartame [artificial sweetening substance]
952 sodium cyclamate [artificial sweetening substance]
952 cyclamic acid [artificial sweetening substance]
952 calcium cyclamate [artificial sweetening substance]
953 isomalt [humectant]
954 sodium saccharin [artificial sweetening substance]
954 saccharin [artificial sweetening substance]
954 calcium saccharin [artificial sweetening substance]
955 sucralose [artificial sweetening substance]
956 alitame [artificial sweetening substance]
957 thaumatin [flavour enhancer, artificial sweetening substance]
965 maltitol and maltitol syrup [humectant, stabiliser]
966 actitol [humectant]
967 xylitol [humectant, stabiliser]
1001 choline salts and esters [emulsifier]
1100 amylases [flour treatment agent]
1101 proteases papain, bromelain, ficin [flour treatment agent, stabiliser, flavour enhancer]
1102 glucose oxidase [antioxidant]
1104 lipases [flavour enchancer]
1105 lysozyme [preservative]
1200 polydextrose [humectant]
1201 polyvinylpyrrolidone [stabiliser, clarifying agent, dispersing agent]
1202 polyvinylpolypyrrolidone [colour stabiliser]
1400 dextrin roasted starch [thickener, vegetable gum]
1401 acid treated starch [thickener, vegetable gum]
1402 alkaline treated starch [thickener, vegetable gum]
1403 bleached starch [thickener, vegetable gum]
1404 oxidised starch

[thickener, vegetable gum]

1405 enzyme-treated starches [thickener, vegetable gum]

1410 monostarch phosphate [thickener, vegetable gum]

1412 distarch phosphate [thickener, vegetable gum]

1413 phosphated distarch phosphate [thickener, vegetable gum]

1414 acetylated distarch phosphate [thickener,

vegetable gum]

1420 starch acetate esterified with acetic anhydride [thickener, vegetable gum]

1421 starch acetate esterified with vinyl acetate [thickener, vegetable gum]

1422 acetylated distarch adipate [thickener, vegetable gum]

1440 hydroxypropyl starch [thickener, vegetable gum]

1442 hydroxypropyl distarch

phosphate [thickener, vegetable gum]

1450 starch sodium octenylsuccinate [thickener, vegetable gum]

1505 triethyl citrate [thickener, vegetable gum]

1518 triacetin [humectant]

1520 propylene glycol [humectant]

1521 polyethylene glycol 8000 [antifoaming agent]

BASIC PANTRY ESSENTIALS

A well-stocked kitchen pantry is fundamental to good cooking; however, even the most basic of pantry ingredients can deliver a meal when it appears all is lost. This basic list is one that should be maintained regularly—because of the influences of a multicultural society, it may appear to some cooks as if I have left out some great staples. It is certainly up to the individual cook to add to this list based on their own experiences and influences—it may be that one cook's anchovies are another cook's fish sauce, but to include both these ingredients is to then provide a pantry list that moves from basic to gourmet. Remember to use this as a guide and then add a few of your own favourite pantry items that you could not live without.

I have deliberately omitted from the list any pre-packaged foods relating to the school lunch box. This, in part, is due to the fact that pre-packaged foods are rapidly growing in number, as is the concern for the health benefits they may or may not offer. From a parent's point of view, it is too subjective to decide what basic lunch box items should be included.

Basic packet food	Basic canned/bottled food	Value adding
Plain flour	Crushed tomatoes	Cornflour
Self-raising flour	Tomato paste	Drinking chocolate
Custard powder	White beans	Cooking chocolate
Cocoa powder	Chickpeas	Packet cake mix (for
Caster sugar	Pasta sauce	emergencies)
Bread crumbs	Soup	Oyster sauce
Pasta	Baked beans	Chilli sauce
Rice	Condensed milk	Sesame oil
Couscous	Vegetable oil	Coconut cream
Stock cubes	Extra virgin olive oil	Rice noodles
Onion soup mix	Vanilla extract or essence	Anchovies
Cereals	Mayonnaise	Capers
Biscuits	Tomato sauce	Gherkins
Cooking salt	Soy or tamari sauce	Black olives
Dried herbs (oregano and	Worcestershire sauce	Muesli bars
basil)	White vinegar	Dried fruits
Peppercorns	Balsamic vinegar	Soft brown sugar
Spices (cinnamon, nutmeg,	Jam	Maple syrup
chilli)	Peanut butter	Mexican salsa
UHT milk	Honey	Corn chips
	Mustard	Cajun spice
	Curry paste	Canned fruits
		Canola or olive oil
		spray

ESSENTIAL KITCHEN EQUIPMENT

KNIVES

Knives are among the most essential pieces of kitchen equipment, and a basic selection is vital to setting up your kitchen. The three styles mentioned below are a great starting point, but the more experienced you become, the more styles you may feel you need. For example, the cook's knife is fine for slicing roasts, filleting fish and portioning steaks, although knives specific to each of these jobs are available. What you spend on these knives is personal, depending on budget, but remember, the most expensive knives may not necessarily be the best for your hand size and wrist strength or be the most pleasing aesthetically.

Cook's knife—is a large blade used for daily cutting and slicing of most ingredients. Available in 8-in. (20-cm), 10-in. (25-cm) and 12-in. (30-cm) blades. Only one is needed, not one of each size.

Serrated knife—is a must for cutting bread, cakes, tomatoes and passionfruit.

Paring knife—is a small utility knife, and a must for all the small, fiddly jobs where the size of a cook's knife is excessive. Used for cutting fruit and vegetables, scoring tomato skin or removing stems and seeds, etc.

MEASURING EQUIPMENT

A selection of measuring cups, spoons, jugs and weight scales is important, especially if you love baking and dessert making. I suggest one set of graduated measuring cups (metal or plastic), one set of graduated measuring spoons and at least one measuring jug of 1- to 2-litre capacity. Electric or not, measuring scales are a very handy addition to the kitchen.

STOVETOP

Saucepans—are a stovetop's best friend. There are many different shapes and sizes, and buying in sets is not necessarily the best option. Keeping your budget in mind, and remembering that if you buy quality the first time, you'll never have to buy them again, look for a heavy-based style of saucepan of 1–4-litre capacity with a tight-fitting lid and an ovenproof handle. Then decide how many you think you may need. Two might get you started, and then add more over time. Note: keep in mind that induction cooktops are the way of the future and if you are looking to upgrade your kitchen soon, then it could be wise to invest in induction cookware (which works equally as well on a gas hob).

Sauté pans—also known as 'skillets', these can have a nonstick coating and be made from cast iron, stainless steel or aluminium. Professionals lean towards cast iron, especially for grilling steaks and small roasts, as well as for doing a perfect 'tarte Tatin'. However, such is the technology of nonstick pans that even professional cooks consider these for their kitchens. Ranging in size from 6 in. (15 cm) to massive diameters, if a large sauté pan is asked for, they will be talking of a 12-in. (30-cm) pan. Always look for pans with an ovenproof handle; especially good if meat has been seared and needs a few minutes in the oven. Two to three pans of varying sizes are a good start.

Wok—it is said that up to 70 per cent of kitchens in Australia now have a wok. Stir-frying is extremely popular because of the time it takes to cook a meal. Flat bottomed woks are ideal if you have an electric or induction cooktop; round-bottomed woks are better suited to a gas cooktop. Like sauté pans, woks now come in all types of metal and coating; the cheap carbon steel wok from Asian supermarkets is still the most popular.

Stock pot—it may seem odd to list this as a basic piece of equipment for the kitchen, and to some point that's true; this is an optional addition. However, consider this—if you have people over for dinner and you plan on serving soup, stew, bolognaise sauce or the like, a big pot would be needed. The fact that it's called a stock pot and you don't plan on making stock is irrelevant. Also, this is a brilliant pot for cooking pasta in, as well as using as a deep-fryer.

OVENS AND OVENWARE

Ovens—accurate oven temperatures are important, especially for baking. Unfortunately, the thermostat is often the first thing that breaks in an oven. Ten degrees out and that delicate baked custard could resemble omelette when the timer goes off. The best solution is to get to know your oven, or invest in an oven thermometer. The more expensive solution is to call in a specialist, to check and/or replace your thermostat.

Ovens—conventional ovens have a gas burner or electric element(s) heating from the bottom. As the heat rises, it creates different temperature areas or zones within the oven. The hottest area is at the top, the centre is moderate, while the coolest part is at the bottom of the oven. This can limit the amount of food that can be cooked at the one time or cause problems with baked goods if the oven is overloaded.

Gas ovens can cook at a lower temperature than electric, while electric ovens can produce a higher heat.

Self-cleaning ovens are certainly recommended for those cooks who bake often. These ovens cost more but merely need wiping out after the cleaning phase. Basically the oven is set to clean, the temperature rises to about 500°C, vaporising any built-up matter and turning it into dust. The oven then cools and simply needs to be wiped out to leave a sparkling clean oven ready to use—brilliant.

The following types of oven, less common in the domestic market, are sometimes referred to as 'zoned ovens'.

Fan-assisted ovens (available in gas and electric) operate like conventional ovens but with the addition of a fan at the rear. As the heat rises from the bottom, it's circulated by the fan to create a more even temperature. The fan can be turned on or off so, for example, a pie can be baked using the fan-assisted function, and then its top browned using the oven conventionally.

Fan-forced or *convection ovens* have an in-built fan that circulates heated air around the oven. This results in an even temperature throughout the entire oven, allowing all shelves to be used simultaneously. Fan-forced ovens heat more quickly, can cook food at lower temperatures, and use up to 35 per cent less energy than conventional ovens. They are available in electric only.

Combination cookers combine convection and microwave cooking in the same oven. The advantage of these ovens is that food can be browned or crisped on the outside using convection cooking, while the microwave energy reduces the actual cooking time.

See also Oven temperatures conversion chart.

Roasting pan—you need at least one large roasting pan for, well, roasts.

Casserole/lasagne dish—a deep rectangular or square ovenproof dish (glass, ceramic or cast iron).

Gratin dish—can be a ceramic multi-functional dish for dishes like potato gratin, nachos, quiche or pasta bake. The right gratin dish could double up as a pie dish as well.

Pizza tray—at least one, even two, of these is handy, as more and more, people tend to find making their own pizza enjoyable. Dark, matte-finished pizza trays are best for the domestic oven, as they absorb the heat better and give a better base colour. Remember, domestic ovens don't produce the base heat of a wood-fired oven.

Cake tins—at least one to begin with, maybe a round one, possibly springform. The more cakes you plan to make, the more you'll need to add to your collection—choose from round, square, rectangular, solid and springform as well as those made from silicon. A loaf tin is not an essential start-up piece of bake ware, but could be considered the next thing you buy.

Baking trays—are very handy for every thing from reheating bread to baking pavlova (baking trays are known as 'baking sheets' in the USA). I recommend black, nonstick ones with a very small (5-mm) lip around the edge. I will also mention slice trays here as well; one of those rectangular 23-cm x 18-cm x 2.5-cm one-sided trays is fantastic for baking a variety of sweet and savoury dishes.

UTENSILS

When buying utensils, try not to hoard, only buy what you think you will need, then add, only if you think you will use the item. Too many gadgets crowd your drawers only to end up at a garage sale 5 years later.

THE FINAL LIST

Knives—20-cm cook's knife x 1, serrated knife x 1, paring knife x 1

Saucepans—with ovenproof handles and tight-fitting lids x 2 or 3

Saute pans—with ovenproof handles x 1 or 2

Wok x 1 (depends on style of cooktop-see Wok)

Stock pot—5-10-litre (optional but handy if cooking loads of soup and pasta) x 1

Measuring-set of measuring cups x 1, set of measuring spoons x 1, 1–2-litre measuring jug x 1

Scales x 1 (weight measures up to 5 kg in 10–20-g increments)

Roasting tray x 1

Casserole/lasagne dish x 1

Gratin dish x 1 (ceramic)

Pizza tray x 1 (large)

Muffin tray x 1 (6- or 12-muffin capacity)

Cake tin x 1 (23-cm springform

Cake rack x 1

Wooden spoons x 2

Metal spoon x 1 (for serving)

Metal slotted spoon x 1

Ladle x 1

Vegetable peeler x 1

Can opener x 1

Sieve x 1

Colander x 1

Lettuce spinner x 1

Mixing bowls x 3 (stainless steel)

Whisk x 1

Grater x 1

Pastry brush x 1

Tongs x 2 (1 with long handles)

Electric mixer x 1

COOKING TECHNIQUES

Bain marie, also known as a 'water bath', is a method for cooking food such as custards and other delicate egg or meat dishes. The food is placed in a dish that is in turn placed in a container of water (usually filled to halfway up the side of the dish), then cooked in an oven or in some cases on the stovetop at a low temperature. The idea is that the water prevents dry heat from scorching the outer parts of the food and produces steam to gently cook the food evenly through to the centre. A cloth, paper towel or newspaper is often placed at the base of the container before the water is added—as insulation to help maintain an even temperature. Bain marie can also refer to the device used to keep food hot at (hopefully) safe temperatures for long periods of time—seen anywhere from cheap snack bars and chicken shops to dubious all-you-can-eat smorgasbords and the more controlled hotel buffets.

Bake is to cook food in the dry heat of an oven. Note that the degree of dryness in the oven is determined by the food that is being baked. This means that if a batch of biscuits is in the oven, and then a roast is thrown in as well, the moisture or steam produced from the roast can and most probably will affect the outcome of the biscuits, both in texture and flavour.

TIPS FOR BARBEQUING:

* Barbecue tools are essential and should be maintained with the great care you would give a good knife. After use, wash the tools in hot soapy water, rinse and dry well. Store in the kitchen drawer or allocated area under your barbecue.

* A wire brush and a long-handled scraper (a paint scraper for windows will do) are excellent for cleaning the grill and scraping the hotplate, especially when there is a large build-up on the flat plate. A quality wire brush is essential—spare no expense as the cheaper ones tend to lose their wire bristles which may get left on the grill plate and ultimately end up in the food, undetected and dangerous in small windpipes.

* Paper towel should always be at the ready to wipe down hot or cold barbecues and the surrounding area.

* The best time to clean a barbecue is while it is still quite hot. The built-up oil and grease is easier to remove when hot. It may not mean doing it immediately after cooking, but for a good clean, turn the barbecue on, get it hot, turn it off and start cleaning.

* As tempting as it is to not scrape down after cooking, residual food and fat become a serious attraction to rodents, cockroaches and birds.

* Utilise the wok burner on the side of many barbecues to boil small potatoes and then toss in butter and parsley. Or have a pot of hot water on to cook beans or broccoli.

* When cooking red meats (beef, veal and lamb), leave the meat, covered, on the kitchen bench and bring to room temperature. This will reduce the cooking time as well as ensuring a more evenly cooked piece of meat.

* White meats (chicken, pork and seafood) should remain refrigerated until cooking as the protein is more delicate than in red meats.

* Only add salt to meat just before it is to go on the grill. Seasoning with salt after it is cooked is okay, but the meat should rest and seasoning afterwards can draw out moisture. Adding salt too far in advance will draw out the meat's natural juices and dry it out when it is cooked.

* There is a big difference between well done and cooked beyond recognition. It is entirely possible to have a juicy well-done steak—juicy as in moist not blood juicy.

★ Buy a meat thermometer/probe to help you produce the best cooked steaks and roasts. It takes the guesswork out of how long to cook meat by taking a reading of the internal temperatures—rare = 35°C, medium rare = 45°C, medium = 55°C, medium well done = 65°C, and well done = 75°C.

★ Marinating meat before cooking adds flavour and tenderises. Green papaya and kiwifruit both contain an enzyme that tenderises tougher cuts of meat and octopus. Add to the marinade or rub the meat with the fruit no more than 2 hours before it is to be cooked. Any longer than this and the enzymes will break the meat fibres down too much and make it mush. Marinate red meats overnight or for at least 4 hours; pork and chicken benefit from a 4-hour marinate; while fish needs only to marinate for about 20–30 minutes.

★ Salads for a barbecue are many and varied. The best tips for any salad are to keep it refrigerated until ready to serve and then add the dressing just before it hits the table. Do not add the salad dressing too soon or the acid (vinegar or lemon juice) will begin to wilt the vegetables or lettuce. A few exceptions to this rule are potato, pasta or rice salad.

★ When making lettuce-based salads, it is not only important to wash and drain the lettuce, but to dry it properly. Any water left on the lettuce leaves only serves to dilute the dressing, which will end up at the bottom of the salad bowl not evenly coating the ingredients. Other than quality barbecue tools and a sharp knife, most professional cooks would agree that a lettuce spinner is vital in all kitchens—available at all kitchenware supply stores.

★ Professional cooks have a catchphrase they all work by—Mis en place—which roughly translates as pre-preparation. In other words, have everything you need on hand before you start to barbecue—even if you don't think it will get used. This step saves extra trips to the kitchen—during which time your food may burn. Make good use of the side table attached to the barbecue, fill it with condiments, utensils and paper towel.

★ Some foods, like fish with white soft flesh, tomatoes and cevapcici (skinless sausages) can fall apart, burn or stick on the grill. To avoid this, brush a piece of foil with oil, add the meat or vegetable, seal into a package, fold at the corners, and cook until done.

★ Pay attention to the temperature of your barbecue. Try and keep the temperature even and adjust it for varying outdoor weather conditions.

★ Include a good basting brush in your barbecue tool kit. The best one for the job has silicon bristles which don't melt with the high heat, unlike the straw-like bristles of a pastry brush.

★ To lessen the amount of oil you cook in, use an oil spray—either vegetable or olive oil—and lightly spray the food, then season and grill; there will be less residual oil on the barbecue potentially causing a flare up.

★ Do not be tempted to constantly turn and play with the food. Cook on one side for 2–4 minutes, turn and cook for half the time on the second side. However, if the meat is rounded and marinated, then turning constantly will give it a 'spit roast' effect and it will constantly baste itself; this will also stop the marinade from burning.

★ Keep annoying bugs away while barbequing by burning citronella candles or garden torches. They also look beautiful and provide the perfect ambience for backyard dinner parties.

Bard is a technique similar to larding, designed to add fat to an otherwise lean cut of meat. Fat (bacon rashers or pork fat) is draped, wrapped or tied around a piece of meat. Poultry and terrines are often barded as a means of self-basting; a terrine mould is lined with bacon, filled and then cooked in a bain marie in the oven. Game birds like pheasant and quail do well covered with fat in this way; to brown the skin, the fat should be removed a few minutes before the bird is taken from the oven. A simple meat loaf can also benefit from being wrapped in bacon, keeping the contents moist and tasty.

Blanch is to plunge food into boiling or simmering water for a very short period of time, so it is only partly cooked. The food is then drained and refreshed in iced water. Blanching enhances the natural properties of the food and is sometimes done in preparation for further cooking. The time it takes to blanch food depends on the size and type of food.

Blind baking refers to the technique of baking unfilled flans or pie cases. Tarts or flans that are to be filled require the raw pastry to be lined with baking paper and weighed down with dried beans, rice or specific ceramic pie weights before being baked. This process ensures the pastry doesn't become curved (convex) due to a build-up of steam between the pastry and the base of the tin. Once cooked, the weights are removed and the pastry returned to the oven briefly to dry out.

Boil is to cook food in boiling liquid (at a temperature no less than 100°C). For a rolling boil, the surface of the liquid must continuously rise and break.

Braise is a method of cooking meat in liquid. The term braising is usually reserved for larger cuts of meat, while stewing is used for smaller cuts of meat. As a general rule, add enough liquid to reach halfway up the item being braised. Although a recipe may specify the cooking time, my advice is to start checking the meat with an hour to go and possibly every 15 minutes after that, so as not to overcook it. Braised vegetables take 45 minutes, never longer. See also Meat, How to cook, Braising.

Broast is not a cooking technique but a trademarked application from the US-based Broaster Company, available only to the food service industry (hence the description 'broasted' will only ever be seen on a restaurant menu). It is a system that pressure-cooks chicken while frying it and includes a marinating process. This method locks in the juices while locking out the oil.

Broil is a US term meaning to expose food to a high heat, either on a hotplate or under an oven broiler or grill. An oven broiler is the toaster section in an oven with the heat source directly above but not touching the food. In the restaurant industry these overhead broilers are called 'salamanders'.

Candy is a US term that refers to cooking foods in sugar for preservation and flavour. It can also simply mean to coat in sugar.

Caramelise is to cook sugar or the natural sugars within food to a light brown or caramel colour. White sugar caramelises at 160°C.

Casserole can mean an ovenproof dish or container with a lid. More importantly it refers to a meal cooked inside this container. Commonly, cuts of meat with tough connective tissue are cooked slowly with vegetables and liquid until the connective tissue breaks down and becomes soft and gelatinous.

Chargrill is short for 'charcoal grill' and means to cook over the high heat produced by burning coals; also known as 'char-broil' in the US. The smoky characteristics that define chargrilling are as prominent as the grill lines left on the food being cooked. A ribbed grill plate leaves the same markings as a chargrill but does not add the flavour. Both methods are considered a healthy way to cook—as the fats drain away, basting the meat as they drain to leave it succulent.

Coddle is to cook eggs gently in water at just below boiling point or by covering them with boiling water long enough for the whites to barely set. The term can also apply to cooking fruit.

Confit is to cook food in its own fat or juices, then preserve it in the very same fat or liquid. (Although you can make confit of garlic, lemon or other fruits by cooking the food slowly in oils, fruit juices and/or with salt.) Confit of duck, goose and pork is a specialty of the region of Gascony in France where the meat is first rubbed with salt—to extract juices and almost cure the meat—before it is slowly cooked then sealed and preserved in its own fat.

Cure is a method of preserving food. The most common method is salt-curing where salt is added to meat which is then left to stand for a period of time to draw off the water content. What remains is a semi-dried salty tasting piece of meat. Salted beef and corned beef are examples of cured meat. Meat is dry-cured when the salt mix is applied to the meat, which is refrigerated, then washed before being cooked. Hams and bacon are examples of dry-cured meat. Sugar-curing is when sugar is added to the salt mix to sweeten the food.

Deep-fry is to cook in large quantities of fat, usually oil. The principle behind deep-frying is that the high temperature of the oil immediately seals the food so it cooks crisp on the outside without getting oily inside. Fortunately, the days when deep-frying meant slapping food into a hot smoking vat of scalding animal fat are long gone. Successful deep-frying requires careful monitoring of temperatures, choice of oil, straining or disposal of oils, and cleaning of equipment. The temperature at which to deep-fry food depends on size and quantity. As a general rule, 180°–195°C will do. Keep in mind that the oil temperature drops, in some cases significantly, when food is added. Don't overcrowd the pan as the temperature will drop too quickly and the food won't be sealed, becoming soggy and oily instead of crisp. There is no single 'best' oil for deep-frying, but oils such as cottonseed, vegetable, soy, corn, safflower, peanut and canola are often recommended because they have a higher smoking point. Oil smokes at the point when it begins to decompose and create the nasty-smelling compound acreolein. Lard or animal fat is no longer considered appropriate for deep-frying because of the high fat content and low smoking point.

Deglaze means not getting out another pan to make the sauce. Remove the food (usually meat) from the pan and set to one side to rest, covered with foil. Place the pan back on the heat and add wine, flavoured vinegar, stock, cream or even water, then stir to lift any cooked-on juices that have browned in the base of the pan.

Double boil is a cooking method that avoids the direct fierceness of naked heat. This is a controlled way to melt or thicken food like chocolate, lemon curd, sabayon and hollandaise, to name a few. Bring water to the boil in a saucepan then place a heatproof bowl containing the ingredients over the pan of water. Usually the heat source is turned to very low or removed altogether after the water has boiled, allowing the residual heat to do the job. Patience is the key to success when double boiling.

Double boilers can be purchased as just that—a saucepan with a curved insert (with a handle). But a regular saucepan and a heatproof bowl larger than the saucepan will work equally as well.

Glaze refers to any stock that has been reduced to a gelatinous consistency. This sticky reduction can only be made from fresh stock; if you try to make it from commercial stock, you'd be left with a small blob of dark salt. Glaze is used to strengthen the flavour of or thicken sauces, as a coating for meats or terrines, and as the base for a sauce which then has cream or butter added. Commercial veal glaze may be found in specialty food shops, delis or food halls (be prepared to pay premium prices). Glaze may also refer to brushing products to be baked with milk, egg whites or egg wash (milk and eggs) to give them a glossy surface.

Grill is to cook with the heat source either beneath or above the food. If the heat source is beneath, food is cooked on a grill plate or griddle, either flat or ribbed. If the heat source is above the food, the method refers to using an oven grill or broiler. Here, the element does not make contact with the food. Grilling is often referred to as broiling in the US. See also Chargrill.

Indirect grilling is a term used mainly to refer to the preparation of ribs. Like parbaking, it sets the ribs up for their final grill session. The heat comes from the outside or one side of the charcoal grill while the middle section or larger portion of the grill remains off. The meat is placed in the centre of the grill or to the off side, with a bowl of water underneath to catch the drips and to produce steam to help the meat slowly tenderise. The hot coals can be sprinkled with wood chips for a smoky flavour. The meat is covered and cooked until tender. It is then ready for saucing and grilling.

Jug is an old English cooking technique. Jugged hare involves the hare being placed in a tall jug, that is set in a pan of water, and cooked slowly over a long period. The blood is drained before cooking and reserved and (with its natural clotting abilities) used to the thicken the sauce. Jugged kippers is a favoured method to avoid the house smelling of fish. The kippers' heads and tails are removed, they are placed in a jug, head-end first, and boiling water is poured on top. They are then covered with a lid or plate and left to stand for 4–5 minutes.

Liaison is a mixture of cream and egg yolks used to thicken white sauces and soups. It must be heated very gently. (As the word derives from the French, meaning 'to bind', it can also be used to refer to other thickening processes.)

Microwave can refer to the implement or the cooking technique. The first microwave oven was built in 1947. It was nearly 6 feet tall, weighed more than 750 pounds and cost US$5000 to buy. Now these compact metal boxes are standard-issue equipment in most households in developed countries. Microwaves are a form of electromagnetic radiation that is very similar to sunlight and radio waves. Microwave energy occurs when an electric current flows through a conductor. Thanks to Dr Percy Lebaron Spencer, whose chocolate bar melted in his pocket while he was toying with a new experiment which had nothing to do with food, we now have the microwave oven. There are many and varied books on cooking in a microwave, but many avid cooks like me see it simply as the best tool for reheating or melting food rather than a way to cook dishes from scratch. No doubt microwave cooks beg to differ.

MICROWAVE COOKING

Metal and foil

Metal objects should not be used in a microwave as the metal reflects the microwave energy. Any plates or dishes that have silver or gold trim will cause an electrical discharge in the microwave, potentially harming the oven. Some butters are wrapped in a silver packet lined with paper, and these will also spark and ignite. Always place food in appropriate microwave-safe dishes.

Be wary of plastic ties on bags when reheating as the tie may have a wire strip running through the centre which can ignite.

Aluminium foil can be used in the microwave if you follow some simple rules. Use only in small amounts to prevent excess heat from penetrating some of the more delicate areas of chicken wings, ends of fish and cakes. It is also important to ensure the foil doesn't touch the sides of the oven.

Plastic, ceramic and china dishes, and plastic wrap
Not all dishes are microwave-safe—if unsure, test the dish by sitting a microwave-safe glass filled with water next to the dish to be tested and microwave on high for 1 minute. If the testing dish is warm and the water in the glass is still cool, then the dish is not microwave-proof. The dish being tested should remain cold for suitable microwave cooking.

Plastic wrap is microwave safe. However, extended periods of time can distort the shape of the wrap and form a dangerous airtight seal over the food. Carefully lift the wrap away from you to avoid a steam burn. The use of a pair of tongs is recommended or prick the plastic wrap with a fork to release the pressure, allowing the steam to escape before unwrapping.

Cleaning and odours
A microwave should be cleaned immediately after use, especially when there is spillage or food has exploded. If there are some lingering stains and odours from cooking, then try placing 500 ml water and the juice of 1 lemon or 1 tablespoon vanilla essence in a 1-litre microwave-safe bowl or jug and heat for 7–8 minutes on high. Wipe out the condensation and any stains with it. The microwave should smell fresh and clean.

Reheating
Impatience is the biggest reason for food not being reheated properly (hot on the outside and cold in the middle). It seems that society has become so time-poor that even the speed of a microwave is not fast enough. For a more even reheating of food, lower the power on the microwave oven to medium, cover with plastic wrap, poke 1 or 2 holes in the plastic and heat for longer than normal. Once reheated, let the food stand for 30 seconds before removing the plastic wrap to avoid a steam burn.

Tips
* To soften butter, place in a microwave-safe container and heat for 30 seconds on medium-low (30 per cent). Cream cheese is softened also at medium-low (30 per cent) for 1 minute (remember to remove its foil casing).
* Piercing some foods that have a skin is vital to prevent a steam build-up and an ultimate explosion in the oven. Potatoes, tomatoes, sausages, chicken skin and eggs (if being poached) are the main ingredients that need a few prods from a skewer.
* Melting chocolate is done at medium (50 per cent) power. Chocolate is deceptive when melted as it holds its shape. To look at it, you may think it needs more time when in fact it may have already melted. As a guide, for every 100 g chocolate, heat for 2 minutes.
* Heat plates for a dinner party by stacking 4 plates with a damp piece of paper towel between each plate and heating on high for 2–3 minutes.
* Damp facial cloths like those offered in Chinese restaurants are great for your next dinner party, especially if food that requires the guests to use their fingers is offered. To do this, wet the cloths, fold in half and roll up, place on a plate and heat for 5 minutes on high. Remember to warn the guests that the cloths will be hot and it is best to offer them the cloth by unravelling it with a pair of tongs and handing it to them so it loses some heat.

Pan-broil is to cook in a nonstick or ribbed pan on the stovetop with little or preferably no oil and no lid. Any fats that may build up during cooking are drained as the food cooks. The idea is for the meat or vegetable to cook quickly over high heat, so food to be pan-broiled is cut thinner or smaller than usual to help it cook quickly.

Pan-fry is also known as 'saute' and means to cook in oil or fat in a pan on the stovetop with no lid.

Pan-sear refers to searing or browning meat (often steak, chicken or fish) in a pan before finishing in the oven.

Par-bake refers to breads and occasionally biscuits that have been proven, then partly baked (to hold the shape) and frozen so the home cook can finish the baking. Different levels of par-baked bread are available. Some are frozen immediately after the proving stage, allowing the home or commercial cook to do all the baking. Others are 90 per cent baked and sold at room temperature so that they only require 5 minutes of final baking time at home. Par-baking is also used in reference to spare ribs that are partly cooked before being finished on the grill.

Parboil see Blanch.

Pasteurise is a heat treatment used in some countries to kill harmful bacteria in dairy products and some alcoholic drinks (beer, wine, cider). It extends the life of milk, purportedly without affecting its taste and nutrient value. Purists and admirers of raw milk cheese argue that, although this process may kill bad bacteria, it also kills good bacteria and changes the molecular make-up and therefore the taste of the milk and what is made from it. (I should know, I lived on a farm, and on winter mornings would squirt warm cow's milk directly into my mouth. As for bacteria, it's hard to say if any of us became sick after I defrosted my hands in the bucket of very warm milk before I brought the pail back to the house.)

Poach is the delicate process of cooking food in a liquid set below simmering point (approximately 75–80°C). The liquid (water, stock, sugar syrup, alcohol) should never come to the boil. The idea is to preserve the natural shape of the food and retain a delicate flavour. The foods most commonly poached are eggs, fish, meat, poultry and fruit.

Poêlé is a method of slow-cooking meat or vegetables in butter in a covered pan in the oven at a temperature hot enough to braise the food, yet not so hot as to colour the butter solids. Sometimes wrongly referred to as 'butter roasting', 'pot roasting' or 'white braising'.

Pot roasting is a similar method to braising, only it is used for larger joints or cuts of meat. The meat (e.g. beef topside, oyster blade or fresh silverside in a 1.5–2-kg piece) is cooked in a deep, covered pot with very little or no liquid. The meat is first seared or browned in a little butter or oil, then placed on a bed of browned root vegetables, or bones and vegetables. The pot is tightly covered and the meat cooked gently. A pot roast may be cooked in a pot, a pressure cooker or in the oven. The small amount of liquid and the vegetables together produce sufficient steam to make this moist heat method ideal for the medium-tender roasting cuts. Resist adding too much liquid or it will become a stew.

Red cooking is associated with Chinese cooking, a method where meat (often pork, but also beef and chicken) is braised in a soy sauce-based liquid to tenderise and colour it a dark reddish-brown. Other ingredients include ginger, onion, sweet rice wine, Chinese five-spice and powder sugar. A cheap form of red cooking might simply mean rubbing the meat with sugar, salt and red food colouring, then slow roasting to produce a piece of meat that looks very red on the outside but normal on the inside.

Reduce is to cook a liquid down to a fraction of its original volume in order to enhance and concentrate its flavour or to thicken it. Don't add salt before reducing as the salty flavour will be concentrated too. Creams are thickened by reduction; a stock can be reduced by many times its volume to produce a glaze.

Refresh, although not technically a cooking method, is often done after blanching or parboiling. Food is removed from the water, then placed in iced water to halt the cooking process and lock in the colour. It is also known as 'shock'.

Render is to reduce the fat content of meat. This can be done in a pan, in the oven, in water or on the grill, as long as heat is used to remove the fat. Rendering is best achieved at a lower temperature.

Roast is to cook meat or vegetables in the dry heat of the oven; see also Bake.

Sauté see Pan-fry.

Scald is to heat a liquid (often milk) to a point just before boiling. If you boil milk, you will burn the proteins and the result will be scorched milk. Milk used to be scalded to kill bacteria, but we now have pasteurisation to do that job. These days, a recipe may suggest scalding milk to make working with other ingredients easier (for instance, to help added ingredients to dissolve or melt) or simply out of habit.

Sear is to seal the surface of meat or fish with a high heat in a pan or on a grill, with or without oil, either as a style of cooking (for example, for fresh tuna) or as a first step before further cooking. The idea is that it locks in the juices, although the validity of this theory is now being tested and questioned.

Shallow-fry is similar to pan-frying, only using a little more fat. The excess fat is then poured from the pan after the cooking.

Simmer is to cook in a liquid just below boiling point, at a temperature of 85°C, when small rolling bubbles start to break the surface. The great recipe tautology is the instruction to 'gently simmer' because 'simmering hard' would mean to boil.

Smoking means flavouring of meat and vegetables via a hot- or cold-smoking method. Smoking is also what many professional cooks do as a coping mechanism when faced with the pressure of service: the smoke is an aromatic blend of nicotine and tobacco, but sometimes other herbs and spices are thrown into the mix.

Smother is to add a small amount of liquid to a food that has been sautéed. The pan is then covered with a lid, the temperature reduced and the food cooked over a low heat until done.

Steaming is considered the healthiest way to cook vegetables, as there is no agitation in boiling water and the steam doesn't dilute or remove in great amounts the nutrients within the food. Meat, fish, rice and fruit can also be steamed. A liquid, usually water, at boiling point (105°C) or higher produces steam which is caught in a lidded receptacle (make sure the food stays out of the water or it will be boiled rather than steamed). Steam burns can be nasty, so be careful when lifting the lid on the steamer, open it away from the face or arms to allow the severest heat to escape before removing the lid entirely.

Stewing is a slow wet-cooking method where food and liquid are cooked in a pot or pan and allowed to simmer for long enough to be completely tender. Although very similar in technique to braising, meat to be stewed is cut smaller, usually diced. Fruits and vegetables can also be stewed but pay close attention to the time required for cooking, as fruit will only take a fraction of the time it takes to stew meat.

Stir-fry commonly refers to wok-cooking, although frying in a very hot pan for a very short time can also be referred to as stir-frying. The key to stir-frying is the 'stir'-the food is kept moving at all times in a very hot pan.

TIPS FOR STIR-FRYING:

* Never overload the wok with food. You'll lose the intense heat and ultimately ending up with a 'stir-braise'. A wok is designed for small amounts of food at a time, especially on domestic hotplates which don't usually produce enough heat for ideal stir-frying.
* A good peanut oil is recommended for stir-frying.
* Wok implements are vital tools for wok cooking. I prefer the 'hok': the ladle-shaped, long-handled implement, so I can scoop and turn the food. It is also very handy when it comes to serving, whether soup, noodles or vegetables. The flat, shovel-like lifter is good for moving the food around the wok, ensuring it is cooked quickly.
* Always heat the wok to very hot before adding the oil, then quickly add the remaining ingredients. If you heat the oil as the wok heats, you'll burn the oil.
* Some books tell you to heat the wok until it is 'smoking', then add the oil—right they are.
* If you have a traditional thin metal Chinese wok, do the following every now and again to help keep the wok sealed and prevent food from sticking. Heat the wok until it's almost white-hot (watch as the bottom of the wok begins to turn white), remove from the heat, cool slightly and carefully wipe with a cloth, then return the wok to the heat and again ensure an intense heat is produced before adding oil and the ingredients.
* If you have an electric wok, a nonstick wok or you're using a pan or skillet, the smoking point is irrelevant. Instead add a few droplets of water and watch as they form small, tight balls that roll around. This is when it is hot enough. Just remember to remove or evaporate the water before adding the oil.

Sweating means cooking vegetables in a little oil or butter over a medium heat, in a covered pot or pan, to release moisture and intensify the flavour. Sweating is also a method of cooking chefs, usually in the middle of summer, and usually in a small kitchen with no air flow. For best results, wrap them in long-sleeved jackets, long pants, thick socks and steel-capped boots, and reduce valuable heat loss by covering their heads with a silly looking hat. Pressure cook for 12–14 hours until sweating profusely. Best served with a beer!

   White braising is a method seldom used today because of the time it takes. It is designed for meat, such as veal, lamb, kid and other young animals. The meat is cooked on the stovetop in a brown stock which is reduced to a glaze and topped up 3 times. It is then packed snugly into a baking tray and more brown stock is added (to cover about half the meat). The tray is covered and the meat cooked in the oven until tender.

BASIC PRESERVING

Preserving can mean many things to many cooks on many levels. The beginner cook may not realise that by simply chopping leftover fresh herbs, placing them in an airtight container and freezing them is a method of preserving, and a great one at that. A Greek friend of mine who is a great cook employs this method and has an abundance of fresh, frozen herbs ready to be part of in the many traditional dishes she cooks.

From the simple preserving method of freezing to the more complex array of jams, jellies, chutneys, pickles, mustards, fruit candies, sauces, bottled fruits, smoked, cured and dehydrated, preserved foods is a ritual that in a few short generations went from a necessity born from recessions and depressions to a seldom practised art form reserved for passionate stall holders at farmers' markets.

In this book there are some classic recipes for relish, marmalade, jam and chutney, so I've included a guide to basic preserving.

BASIC EQUIPMENT

* Heavy-based stainless steel saucepan or pot
* Set of plastic funnels
* Sugar thermometer
* Cutting board
* 20-cm cook's knife and paring knife
* Strong, heatproof jug
* Labels for dating and naming
* Measuring equipment—cup, liquid, weight and spoon measures
* Several wooden spoons
* Strainer
* Storing jars and bottles with lids

STERILISING

Use glass jars with matching lids. Jars need to be washed in soapy water, rinsed well and drained (do not use a towel to dry). Then place, right way up, in a cold oven and turn the oven temperature to 150°C for 15 minutes. Remove from the oven and fill with the hot preserves to be bottled. Metal screw-top lids to the jars need to be sterilised in the same manner.

Boiling the jars in water for 10 minutes then drying in a cool oven (110°C) is another method for sterilising. Rubber seals, corks and lids should also be immersed in boiling water for a few seconds.

PACKING

* Jams, marmalades, relishes, chutneys and sauces need to be packed while the mixture is still warm and the sterilised jars are hot from the oven. Leave to cool covered with a clean cloth. Once cool, cover the preserves with a circle of waxed paper or jam covers available from supermarkets.
* Jam, marmalade, relish and chutney jars should be filled right to the top.
* Sauces should be filled to within 2 cm of the rim.
* Pickles can be added cold to a jar as the high concentration of vinegar will inhibit mould.

★ Once packed, wipe the jars or bottles and dry them thoroughly before attaching labels marked with the name of the preserve as well as the 'packed on' date.

STORING

★ Light has an adverse effect on bottled preserves and it is therefore recommended to store them in a cool, dark and dry place.
★ Should you live in a wet, humid climate, then it is best to keep the preserves in the refrigerator.
★ Once any preserve has been opened then it is necessary to keep the opened jar in the fridge.

ESSENTIAL PRESERVING INGREDIENTS

Sugars—used for preserving jams, marmalades, candying fruits and in curing meats.
Salts—used for brines, pickling and curing meats.
Acids—used in jams to prevent discoloration (lemon juice, citric acid and tamarind).
Vinegars—used for pickles, chutneys and relishes.
Fats and oils—used as a sealant.

PECTIN

★ Pectin has its own entry due to the important role it has in setting jams and marmalades. Fruits have varying pectin levels so it is important to check the cooked fruit to determine if pectin needs to be added. To test for pectin content—combine 1 tablespoon of the cooked, unsweetened fruit juice with 1 tablespoon of methylated spirits. Stir for 2–3 minutes or until the fruit juice starts to clot. A large clot or lump indicates a high pectin content, while many small, broken clots mean a low pectin content.
★ Lemon juice is added to fruit with a low pectin content to compensate by drawing out the pectin in the fruit. It also prevents the jam from crystallising.
★ Fruit high in pectin include—apples, redcurrants, quinces, black currants, citrus fruit and gooseberries.
★ Raspberries, passionfruits, plums and apricots have a medium pectin content.
★ Strawberries, peaches, mangoes, figs, pineapples, rhubarb and cherries have a low pectin content, and therefore need added pectin when making into jams.
★ Commercial jam setting agents can be purchased from supermarkets.

SUGAR THERMOMETERS

Do not even think about making jam without a sugar thermometer. When a jam is heated to 105°C, the high sugar content reacts with the pectin and forms a gel. If you do not have a sugar thermometer, then test by spooning some jam onto a plate and check its consistency when cold.

SUGAR IN JAMS

★ It's important to note that sugar is not just added in large amounts to sweeten a jam. Its main purpose is to prevent the fruit from fermenting or forming mould. Add too much sugar and you run the risk of the jam becoming syrupy and not setting properly. Add too little sugar and the jam may not set and will deteriorate faster.

* A good rule of thumb is to allow 800 g to 1 kg sugar for every 1 kg of prepared fruit (fruit that is peeled, cored and chopped, ready to cook).

THE 10 RULES OF JAM MAKING

1. Always use premium fruit. Avoid fruit that is overripe, damaged or covered with blemishes. Under-ripe fruit takes too long to cook and sabotages the setting temperature.
2. When cooking fruit with the skin on, do not add the sugar until the skins have softened completely. Once the sugar is added, the skins will not break down further.
3. Use a large pot to make jams. Jam boils, bubbles and splatters, and may give a nasty burn if cooked in a small saucepan.
4. Do not be tempted to make large quantities in one go. Colour and flavour retention is best achieved in smaller batches (less than 2 kg of fruit and sugar combined).
5. Avoid using too much sugar thinking the jam will set better. Quite the opposite is true—too much sugar counters the pectin and leaves the jam syrupy.
6. Not enough sugar in the jam causes rapid deterioration as well as poor setting.
7. Avoid burning the jam—it is important to stir the jam in the initial stages to lift fruit from the base of the pan.
8. Do not be tempted to cook the jam for longer than is required. Going past the recommended 105°C can cause the jam to harden or become slightly chewy once it is cold.
9. Be very aware of the fruit used for jam making and recognise the fruit's pectin levels. Jam making really is an exact science.
10. Patience, understanding and persistence are the 3 key elements of successful jam making.

Good luck!

CONVERSION CHARTS

COMMONLY USED ABBREVIATIONS

°C	degrees Celsius (centigrade)
°F	degrees Fahrenheit
cc cl	centilitre
cm	centimetre
dl	decilitre
dr	dram (drachm)
fl oz	fluid ounce
g	gram (gramme)
gal	gallon
in.	inch
kg	kilogram
L	litre
l.	litre
lb	pound
min	minim
ml	millilitre
mm	millimetre
oz	ounce
pt	pint
qt	quart
T	tablespoon
tbsp	tablespoon
tsp	teaspoon

OVEN TEMPERATURES

A common frustration for many cooks is trying to decipher what a 'moderate' or 'slow' oven is. Conversions between gas marks, Celsius and Fahrenheit can also be confusing. To prove conclusively that cooking really does have an element of guesswork to it, we have four columns of oven settings, all of which are only close to an exact reading. It is highly recommended that an 'ovenproof' thermometer be used. Often domestic and even professional ovens have a malfunctioning thermostat which can really have an effect on baked goods.

Celsius	Fahrenheit	Gas mark	Definition
100	200		very cool
110	225		very cool
120	240		cool/slow
130	250	1	cool/slow
140	275	2	cool/slow
150	300	3	cool/slow
170	325	4	moderate
180	350	5	moderate
190	375	6	moderate
200	400	7	hot
220	425	8	hot
230	450	9	very hot
240	475	10	very hot
250	500	10	very hot

CELSIUS/FAHRENHEIT CONVERSION

This conversion chart is a handy guide to all manner of cooked or chilled foods in cookbooks that use one or both temperature readings. When comparing these exact conversions to, say, that of an oven, then naturally it is assumed that the cook will round up or down as it is nigh impossible to set an oven to exactly 401°F or 113°F, but much easier to set it to its metric equivalent.

°C	°F	°C	°F
-18	0	130	266
0	32	135	275
5	41	140	284
10	50	145	293
15	59	150	302
20	68	155	311
25	77	160	320
30	86	165	329
35	95	170	338
40	104	175	347
45	113	180	356
50	122	185	365
55	141	190	374
60	140	195	383
65	149	200	392
70	158	205	401
75	167	210	410
80	176	215	419
85	185	220	428
90	194	225	437
95	203	230	446
100	212	235	455
105	221	240	464
110	230	245	473
115	239	250	482
120	248	255	491
125	257	260	500

LIQUID CONVERSION

Metric volume	Exact imperial equivalent	Imperial approximation	Also known as
1 ml	0.0338 fl oz		1 cc, 16 min, 20 drops
3.7 ml	0.1251 fl oz		1 fl dr, 60 min
5 ml	0.1691 fl oz		1 tsp, 60 drops thin liquid
10 ml	0.3381 fl oz		1 dessertspoon, 1 cl
15 ml	0.5072 fl oz		1 tbsp (US, UK)
20 ml	0.6762 fl oz		1 tbsp (Australia)
25 ml	0.8453 fl oz		¼ dl, 8 fl dr
30 ml	1.0143 fl oz	1 fl oz	2 tbsp (US, UK)
50 ml	1.76 fl oz	2 fl oz	½ dl, 1 jigger
75 ml	1.66 fl oz	2½ fl oz	¾ dl
100 ml	3.52 fl oz	3½ fl oz	1 dl
120 ml	4.06 fl oz	4 fl oz	1 gill (US), 32 dr
125 ml	4.40 fl oz	4½ oz	¼ pt, ½ cup (Australia)
150 ml	5.28 fl oz	5 fl oz	1 gill (UK) (137.7 ml)
200 ml	7.04 fl oz	7 fl oz	
250 ml	8.81 fl oz	9 fl oz	0.25 L, 1 cup (Australia), 16 tbsp
275 ml	9.68 fl oz	9½ fl oz	½ pt
300 ml	10.56 fl oz	10 fl oz	1 cup (UK)
500 ml	17.63 fl oz	18 fl oz	5 dl, 2 cups (Australia), 0.5 L, 1 pt (US), 2¼ cups (US)
575 ml	20.27 fl oz	20 fl oz	1 pt, 4 gill
1 L	35.26 fl oz	35 fl oz	1¾ pt (UK), 2 pt (US), 1 qt, 4 cups (Australia, UK), 1000 ml
1.1 L	37.18 fl oz	37 fl oz	1 dry qt
3.8 L	128.44 fl oz	128 fl oz	1 gal (US), 4 qt, 16 cups (Australia, UK), 8 pt (US)
4.5 L	158.67 fl oz	160 fl oz	1 gal (UK)
34 L	1149.2 fl oz	1150 fl oz	1 firken

WEIGHT CONVERSION

Imperial weight	Exact metric equivalent	Metric approximation	Also known as
¼ oz	7 g	5 g	
½	14.1 g	15 g	
1 oz	28.3 g	30 g	16 dr
2 oz	56.6 g	55 g	
3 oz	84.9 g	85 g	
4 oz	113.2 g	110–115 g	¼ lb
5 oz	141.5 g	140–150 g	
6 oz	169.8 g	170 g	
7 oz	198.1 g	200 g	
8 oz	227 g	225 g	½ lb
9 oz	255.3 g	250 g	¼ kg
10 oz	283 g	280 g	
11 oz	311.3 g	300–310 g	
12 oz	340 g	340–350 g	
13 oz	368.3 g	370 g	
14 oz	396.6 g	400 g	
15 oz	424 g	425 g	
16 oz	454 g	450 g	1 lb
17 oz	482.3 g	500 g	1 lb, 0.5 kg
2 lb	898.0 g	900 g	
2.2 lb	1 kg		2 lb + 3.27 oz
4.41 lb	2 kg		4 lb +6.55 oz

LESS COMMON MEASURES

A10 can	a large commercial can of food (weight can vary from approx. 1.8 to 3 kg)
baker's dozen	13
bush (US imperial dry measure)	8 gal (4 pecks, 35 L dry)
bushel (US imperial dry measure)	8 gal (4 pecks, 35 L dry)
3 bushels	1 sack
deck	10 bunches
dram (fluid)	3.7 ml
gill (UK)	137.7 ml
gill (US)	118.3 ml
gallon (UK)	4.546 L
gallon (US)	3.785 L
head	1 only (used for vegetables such as cauliflower and cabbage)
No. 1 can (US)	310 g, 11 oz
No. 2 can (US)	560 g/600 ml, 20 oz
No. 2 1/2 can (US)	850 g/840 ml, 28 oz
No. 303 can (US)	450 g/ 480 ml, 16 oz
peck (pk) (US imperial dry measure)	8 qt (8.8 L dry)
pint (UK)	568.3 ml
pint (US)	473.2 ml
5 quarters	1 load (ld)
12 sacks	1 chaldron

COMMON DIMENSIONS OF COOKING EQUIPMENT

These conversions are based on what recipe books commonly call for when specifying items such as cake tins, frying pans and cutters. They are not exact conversions. For example, 30 cm is not exactly 12 in., but a cookbook will usually ask for a 30-cm/12-in. diameter tin or pan.

1 cm	½ in.
2.5 cm	1 in.
4 cm	1½ in.
5 cm	2 in.
8 cm	3 in.
10 cm	4 in.
12 cm	5 in.
23 cm	9 in.
28 cm	11 in.
30 cm	12 in.
33 cm	13 in.

EQUIVALENT QUANTITIES FOR SOME COMMON FOODS

Weights are equivalent to 1 cup (250 ml) of the product
+ means just over the weight specified
- means just under the weight specified

almonds, shelled, whole	150 g	+5 oz
almonds, choppped or flaked	+75 g	+3 oz
almonds, ground	150 g	+5 oz
apples, sliced	175 g	6 oz
apples, chopped	100 g	4 oz
apricots, fresh/raw, sliced	225 g	8 oz
apricots, fresh/raw, chopped	150 g	+5 oz
apricots, cooked, chopped	75 g	3 oz
apricots, dried	150 g	+5 oz
asparagus, fresh/raw, chopped	125 g	-5 oz
asparagus, tinned/cooked, chopped	175 g	6 oz
bacon, raw, chopped	225 g	8 oz
baking powder	180 g	+6 oz
bananas, fresh/raw, sliced	225 g	8 oz
bananas, fresh/raw, chopped	200 g	7 oz
bananas, fresh/raw, mashed	300 g	11 oz
beans, dried (all varieties)	200 g	7 oz
beans, black or kidney, cooked	60 g	2½ oz
beans, lima or navy, cooked	75 g	3 oz
beans, green, fresh/raw, chopped	150 g	+5 oz
beans, green, cooked, chopped	180 g	+6 oz
beef, cooked, chopped/diced	150 g	+5 oz
beetroot, raw, sliced/diced/grated	150 g	+5 oz
beetroot, cooked, sliced/diced	200 g	7 oz
biscuit crumbs	100 g	4 oz
blueberries, fresh/raw	100 g	4 oz
breakfast cereals, All Bran	50 g	2 oz
breakfast cereals, bran flakes	37 g	1½ oz
breakfast cereals, Cornflakes	25 g	1 oz
breakfast cereals, crushed flakes	75 g	3 oz
breakfast cereals, Rice Bubbles/Crispies	25 g	1 oz
breakfast cereals, puffed rice	-25 g	-1 oz
bread, fresh/stale, broken into pieces	50 g	2 oz
bread crumbs, fresh	50 g	2 oz
bread crumbs, dry	90 g	3.5 g
broccoli florets, fresh/raw	175 g	6 oz
Brussels sprouts, fresh/raw	100 g	4 oz
bulgur wheat, raw	225 g	8 oz

bulgur wheat, cooked	250 g	9 oz
butter	225 g	8 oz
cabbage, cooked, chopped	225 g	8 oz
candied fruit	225 g	8 oz
candied peel	75 g	3 oz
capsicum, choppped	175 g	6 oz
carrots, cooked/raw, chopped	50 g	2 oz
cashew nuts, whole/chopped	150 g	+5 oz
cauliflower florets, fresh/cooked	325 g	-12 oz
celeriac, cooked, chopped/mashed	200 g	7 oz
celery, raw, chopped	100 g	4 oz
celery, cooked, chopped	225 g	8 oz
cheese, hard, grated	100 g	4 oz
cheese, hard, cubed	125 g	-5 oz
cheese, cottage or cream	225 g	8 oz
cheese, soft, grated	100 g	4 oz
cherries, fresh, pitted	225 g	8 oz
chicken, cooked, shredded (meat only)	125 g	-5 oz
chocolate, grated	125 g	-5 oz
chocolate chips	175 g	6 oz
citrus fruit, segment/large pieces (flesh only)	225 g	8 oz
cocoa powder	100 g	4 oz
coconut, flaked/grated	75 g	3 oz
cod, flaked (flesh only), cooked	200 g	7 oz
coriander, fresh, chopped	50 g	2 oz
corn kernels, fresh	175 g	6 oz
corn, canned	250 g	9 oz
cornflour	125 g	-5 oz
cornmeal	150 g	+5 oz
corn syrup	300 g	11 oz
crackers, broken	175 g	6 oz
cranberries, fresh/raw	100 g	4 oz
cucumber, raw, chopped	150 g	+5 oz
currants (e.g. black or red), fresh	100 g	4 oz
dried currants,	150 g	+5 oz
dates, whole	225 g	8 oz
dates, pitted, chopped	175 g	6 oz
eggplant, raw, chopped	250 g	9 oz
eggs, hard-boiled, chopped	225 g	8 oz
figs, chopped	150 g	+5 oz
flour, white, rye or barley	150 g	+4 oz
flour, wholewheat	150 g	-5 oz
flour, chickpea	75 g	3 oz

flour, cornflour	100 g	3½ oz
flour, potato	125 g	5 oz
flour, rice	125 g	+5 oz
flour, tapioca	100 g	−5 oz
frozen vegetables, chopped	150 g	+5 oz
garlic flakes	140 g	−5 oz
ginger, fresh, chopped	100 g	4 oz
grapefruit, segments/large pieces (flesh only)	225 g	8 oz
grapes, whole	+100 g	+4 oz
grapes, halved, pitted	175 g	6 oz
greens, raw, chopped	100 g	4 oz
greens, cooked, chopped	225 g	8 oz
haddock, flaked (flesh only cooked)	200 g	7 oz
ham, cooked, chopped	150 g	+5 oz
hazelnuts, whole	150 g	+5 oz
hazelnuts, chopped	175 g	6 oz
jam	325 g	−12 oz
lard	225 g	8 oz
lentils, uncooked	200 g	7 oz
lentils, cooked	75 g	3 oz
lettuce, chopped	75 g	3 oz
margarine	225 g	8 oz
meat (red), minced	225 g	8 oz
meat (red), cooked, chopped	150 g	+5 oz
milk powder	125 g	−5 oz
mint, fresh, chopped	+25 g	+1 oz
molasses	325 g	−12 oz
mushrooms, fresh, whole	125 g	−5 oz
mushrooms, fresh, chopped	100 g	4 oz
mushrooms, fresh, sliced	+75 g	+3 oz
nectarines, fresh, peeled and sliced	225 g	8 oz
noodles, uncooked	75 g	3 oz
noodles, cooked	150 g	+5 oz
nuts see individual nuts		
oatmeal	−100 g	−4 oz
okra, raw	100 g	4 oz
onion, raw, sliced	100 g	4 oz
onion, raw, chopped	150 g	+5 oz
orange, segments/large pieces (flesh only)	225 g	8 oz
oysters, without shell	225 g	8 oz
parsley, fresh, coarsely chopped	25 g	1 oz
pasta, short cut, uncooked	100 g	4 oz
pasta, short cut, cooked	200 g	7 oz

peaches, fresh, sliced	225 g	8 oz
peanut butter	250 g	9 oz
peanuts, shelled	150 g	+5 oz
peanuts, chopped	125 g	-5 oz
pearl barley	200 g	7 oz
pears, fresh, peeled and sliced	225 g	8 oz
pears, canned, drained and chopped	+175 g	+6 oz
peas (green), shelled, fresh or frozen	150 g	+5 oz
peas, split, uncooked	225 g	8 oz
peas, split, cooked	100 g	4 oz
pecan nuts, shelled, halved	100 g	4 oz
pecan nuts, shelled, chopped	125 g	-5 oz
pineapple, fresh, skinned, chopped	200 g	7 oz
pineapple, crushed	225 g	8 oz
pistachio nuts, whole	150 g	+5 oz
pistachio nuts, chopped	100 g	4 oz
plums, fresh, stoned	175 g	6 oz
poppy seeds	125 g	-5 oz
potatoes, raw, chopped	175 g	6 oz
potatoes, cooked, chopped or mashed	225 g	8 oz
prunes	175 g	6 oz
prunes, cooked, stoned	125 g	-5 oz
pumpkin, cooked, chopped	150 g	+5 oz
pumpkin, cooked, mashed	225 g	8 oz
quince, fresh, cored	175 g	6 oz
raisins	150 g	+5 oz
raisins, cooked	200 g	7 oz
raspberries, fresh/raw	125 g	-5 oz
rhubarb, fresh/raw, chopped	100 g	4 oz
rhubarb, cooked, fresh or canned and drained	200 g	7 oz
rice, raw	225 g	8 oz
rice, cooked	250 g	9 oz
rolled oats, uncooked	100 g	4 oz
salmon, canned, drained, flaked	225 g	8 oz
sauerkraut	150 g	+5 oz
semolina, dry	200 g	7 oz
shallots, raw, sliced	100 g	4 oz
shallots, raw, chopped	150 g	+5 oz
shortening	225 g	8 oz
soy beans, cooked	75 g	3 oz
spaghetti, uncooked	100 g	4 oz
spaghetti, cooked	50 g	2 oz
spinach, cooked (450 g raw weight)	225 g	8 oz

spinach, raw	75 g	2½ oz
squash (summer), cooked, chopped	125 g	-5 oz
squash (winter), cooked, mashed	450 g	16 oz
strawberries, fresh/raw, halved/sliced	200 g	7 oz
suet, shredded	125 g	-5 oz
sugar, granulated, caster or superfine	225 g	8 oz
sugar, brown	200 g	7 oz
sugar, icing	125 g	-5 oz
sultanas	150 g	+5 oz
swede, raw, chopped	150 g	+5 oz
swede, cooked, chopped or mashed	200 g	7 oz
sweet potatotes, raw, chopped	150 g	+5 oz
sweet potatoes, cooked, mashed	200 g	7 oz
tapioca, dry	150 g	+5 oz
tomatoes, fresh/raw, chopped	200 g	7 oz
tomatoes, canned	225 g	8 oz
tomato paste or sauce	225 g	8 oz
tuna, flaked (flesh only)	225 g	8 oz
turkey, cooked, shredded (flesh only)	125 g	-5 oz
turnips, raw, chopped	150 g	+5 oz
turnips, cooked, chopped or mashed	200 g	7 oz
walnuts, shelled, halved	100 g	4 oz
walnuts, shelled, chopped	125 g	-5 oz
yam, raw, chopped	150 g	+5 oz
yam, cooked, chopped	200 g	7 oz
yoghurt	250 g	9 oz
zucchini, sliced	150 g	+5 oz
zucchini, chopped	175 g	6 oz

CUP MEASUREMENTS

What a luxury it would be if metric were to become the universal measurement, which seems rational in these modern times. See Weight and Liquid conversion tables for equivalents for US customary, British imperial and metric measurements.

Tips for measurements:

* Cookbooks assume you will use proper cup and spoon measuring utensils. Household cups and spoons are not useful. Keep this in mind when working from these books, especially when baking delicate goods.
* Australian cookbooks tend to use a mix of metric and British imperial.
* US cookbook measurements refer to volume rather than weight for dry ingredients.
* Take particular care with cup measurements, as all three are different:
    1 US cup = 237 ml
    1 British cup = 284 ml
    1 Australian cup = 250 ml
* When measuring with a cup or spoon, always use level quantity (scant) unless the recipe states 'heaped'.
* Scant, as in scant ½ cup, or scant pinch of salt, is also known as a 'struck measure'. It means just the measurement specified.

----

xxxxxxxxxxxxx **The Indexes** xxxxxxxxxxxxx

Recipe index

xxxxxxxxxxxxxxxxxxxxxxxxxxxxxxxxxxxxxxxxxxxxxxxxxxxxxxxxxxxxxxxxxxxxxxxxxxxxxxxxxx

aïoli 222
ajo blanco 55
almond bread 326
anzac biscuits 328
apple and rhubarb crumble 260
apple pie 262
apple prune and spice stuffing 430
apple sauce 248
apple strudel 264
apricot chicken 90

baba ghanouj 20
bacon and egg pie 332
bacon, spinach and goat's cheese omelette 11
baked potato in cream 156
baklava 330
banana bread 334
banana cake 336
banana smoothie 422
banana split 272
banana, strawberry and passionfruit salad 6
béarnaise sauce 229
béchamel sauce 245
beef brisket, braised 118
beef casserole 112
beef, roast 138
beef stroganoff 114
beer batter 432
berries gratin 323
berry tiramisu 317
bircher muesli 2
biscotti 340
biscuits, basic 338
Black Forest queen of puddings 305
blini 434
blueberry muffins 381
boiled eggs 4
bolognaise sauce 116
brandy butter sauce 283
brandy snaps 274

bread and butter pudding 276
bubble and squeak 158
butter cream 413
butterscotch sauce 250

Caesar dressing 224
Caesar salad 178
caramel ice-cream 253
caramel orange sauce 271
caramel sauce 252
caramelised onions 21
carrot cake 342
cauliflower soup 46
cheese croutons 52
cheese twists 344
cheesecake, baked 266
cheesecake, baked ricotta 270
cheesecake, lemon 391
cheesecake, raspberry 390
cheesecake, simple 391
chef's salad 180
chicken and sweet corn soup 48
chicken Kiev 92
chicken liver parfait 94
chicken, roast 100
chicken soup with matzoh balls 48
chicken stock 436
chilli con carne 122
chilli jam 22
chocolate and nut biscuits 339
chocolate blondies 346
chocolate brownies 346
chocolate cake, flourless 356
chocolate chip biscuits 339
chocolate chip friands 361
chocolate crackles 347
chocolate cupcakes 353
chocolate fudge 348, 349
chocolate ganache 401
chocolate icing 408
chocolate mousse 278
chocolate muffins 381
chocolate pastry cream 415

chocolate pavlova 297
chocolate sauce 254
chocolate self-saucing pudding 280
chocolate slice 405
chocolate Swiss roll 401
chorizo, prawn and chilli frittata 451
choux pastry 464
Christmas cake 363
Christmas pudding 282
chutney, tomato 38
citrus fruit salad 7
clarified butter 438
club sandwich 440
cocktail sauce 226
coconut ice 350
coconut macaroons 375
coleslaw 182
corn on the cob 160
corned beef 124
couscous with preserved lemon and saffron 204
crab cakes 74
crab chowder 51
cream cheese frosting 409
crème fraîche 442
crepes 284
crispy skin chicken breast 96
Croque Madame 245
Croque Monsieur 245
croutons 443
cupcakes 352
curry powder 444

dashi stock 446
devil's chocolate frosting 410
devil's food cake 354
double almond friands 361
duck in orange sauce 103
duck with cherry sauce, roast 102

eggnog 423
eggs, boiled 4
eggs, scrambled 12

fattoush 184
fish, cooking whole 72
fish fillets, pan-fried 76
fish pie 77
fish stock 447
flourless chocolate cake 356
flourless orange cake 358
fondue 448
French onion soup 52
French toast 5
friands 360
fried rice 206
frittata 450
fruit cake 362
fruit mince pies 364
fruit salad 6

garlic bread 452
garlic butter 227
garlic confit 453
garlic prawns 78
garlic, roasted 453
gazpacho 54
ginger pudding, steamed 315
ginger soy dressing 228
gingerbread people 366
Greek salad 186
green salad 188
guacamole 24

ham and pea frittata 451
ham, baked 108
hash brown potato 8
hedgehog 368
herb butter 227
hollandaise sauce 229
honeycomb 369
honeycomb butter 369
hortopita 397
hot chocolate 424
hot cross buns 370
hummingbird cake 372
hummus 25

icing, basic 408
Italian meringue 412
Italian sausages with soft
    polenta 213

junket 286
lamb, roast 140
lamb shanks, braised 120
lasagne 128
lasagne, vegetarian 172
lavosh 454
lemon and ginger tea 425
lemon cheesecake 391
lemon curd 414
lemon delicious 288
lemon meringue pie 290
lemon Swiss roll 401
lemon tart 292
lemonade 426
lemonade scones 394
lentil burgers 208
lumberjack cake 373

macaroni cheese 210
maple snaps 275
marmalade 416
marshmallows 376
matzoh balls, chicken soup
    with 48
meat loaf 130
mee goring sauce 232
melon fruit salad 6
melting moments 378
meringue, Italian 412
meringue, Swiss 413
meringues 380
minestrone 56
mint jelly 26
miso soup 58
moussaka 132
muffins 381
mushroom lasagne 173
mushroom soup 59
mushroom, tomato and spinach
    omelette 11

nachos 456
Nanaimo bars 382

napoli sauce 233
Niçoise salad 190
nut biscuits 339

olive, fetta and zucchini
    frittata 451
omelette 10
onion, caramelised 21
onion jam 28
orange and marscarpone
    melting moments 379
orange and poppy seed cake 359
orange and poppy seed friands
    361
orange cake, flourless 358
orange cupcakes 353
orange syrup cake 359
osso buco 134

pad thai sauce 234
pancakes, super fluffy 16
pancetta, scallop and sage
    frittata 451
pannacotta 294
panzanella 192
passionfruit curd 414
pasta dough 460
pasta salad 194
pastry 460–64
pastry cream 415
pavlova 296
pea and ham soup 60
peach Melba 298
peanut brittle 384
pecan and maple syrup friands
    361
pecan biscuits 385
pecan pie 300
pecan toffee sauce 251
Peking duck 98
pesto 30
pickled vegetables 162
pikelets 386
pineapple, papaya and mint
    salad 7
pistou 32
pizza dough 466
plum sauce 236

polenta, firm 212
polenta, soft 213
pork, roast 142
potato and leek soup 61
potato and rosemary frittata 451
potato, baked in cream 156
potato mash 164
potato salad 196
praline 387
prawn cocktail 80
prawns, garlic 78
preserved lemons 468
puff pastry 463
pumpkin pie 302
pumpkin soup 62
punch 427

queen of puddings 304
quiche Lorraine 388
quince, baked 268
quince paste 33

ranch dressing 231
raspberry cheesecake 390
raspberry fool 306
raspberry sauce 256
raspberry snaps 275
ratatouille 166
red wine sauce 235
rhubarb pie 307
rhubarb, poached 307
rhubarb, stewed 307
rice pudding 308
rice salad 198
ricotta cheesecake, baked 270
risotto 214
rissoles 136
roast beef 138
roast chicken 100
roast duck with cherry sauce 102
roast lamb 140
roast pork and crackling 140
roasted vegetables 168

salmon patties 81
salsa verde 34
salt and pepper squid 82
san choy bao 144
satay sauce 238
sauce Choron 229
sauce Maltaise 229
sauce remoulade 231
sausage pinwheels 393
sausage rolls 392
sausages and mash with pepper sauce 146
scones 394
scrambled eggs 12
seafood chowder 64
seafood crepes 84
seafood gumbo 64
shallot dressing 240
shogi sticks 413
shortcrust pastry 462
snow eggs 380
soufflé crepes baked in royale custard 285
spaghetti carbonara 216, 217
spanakopita 396
spare ribs, barbecue-style 110
sponge cake 398
spring rolls 218
squid, salt and pepper 82
steak and kidney pie 148
steamed ginger pudding 315
sticky date pudding 310
strawberry, grape and mango salad 7
strawberry jam 418
strawberry shortcake 339
sugar syrup 470
summer pudding 312
sundried tomato, mushroom and spinach frittata 451
sweet and sour sauce 241
sweet pastry 460
sweet shortcrust pastry 460
Swiss roll 400
syrup pudding 314

tabbouleh 200
tartare sauce 231
tea cake 402
teriyaki sauce 242
Thai beef salad 150
Thai chilli sauce 243
thousand island dressing 226
tiramisu 316
tiropita 397
toffee 403
toffee sauce 251
tofu mayonnaise 231
tomato chutney 38
tomato jam 42
tomato relish 40
tomato soup 66
tomatoes, slow-roasted 14
trifle 319
tropical salad 7
tzatziki 43

vanilla slice 404
vanilla sugar 471
veal Cordon Bleu 153
veal Holstein 153
veal Jäger 153
veal schnitzel 152
vegetable and barley soup 68
vegetable and noodle stir-fry 170
vegetables, roasted 168
vegetarian lasagne 172
vegetarian spring rolls 219
vichyssoise 61
vinaigrette 246
white caper sauce 245
white Christmas 347
white sauce 244

yoghurt and lemon mousse 320
yoghurt dressing 247
Yorkshire pudding 139

zabaglione 322
zucchini slice 174

General index

abalone 523
African spices 527
agave nectar 534
aïoli 222
ajo blanco 55
ajowan 528
allicin 21
allspice 528
almond
  bread 326
  chocolate and almond
    biscotti 341
  double almond friands 361
  macaroons 374
  milk 538
  praline 387
amaranth flour 493
American spices 527
anchovies
  Niçoise salad 191
  salsa verde 34
  tapenade 36
anise 528
anise (Sichuan) pepper 530
annatto 528
Anzac biscuits 328
apple
  crumble, apple and rhubarb
    260
  lumberjack cake 373
  pie 262
  sauce 248
  strudel 264
  stuffing, apple, prune and
    spice 430
  toffee apples 403
apricot chicken 90
arborio rice 515
  risotto 214
arrowroot flour 493
asafoetida 528
Asian spices 527
Australian spices 527

avocados 476
  guacamole 24
azuki/adzuki beans 477

baba ghanouj 20
bacalao 523
bacon see ham and bacon
bain marie 549
bake 549
baklava 330
  sugar syrup for 470
baldo rice 516
banana
  bread 334
  cake 336
  hummingbird cake 372
  roasted banana split 273
  smoothie 422
  split 272
  strawberry, banana and
    passionfruit salad 6
banana pepper 187
barbequing 549–50
bard 551
barley and vegetable soup 68
barley flour 493
basil 498
  pesto 30
  pistou 32
  slow-roasted tomatoes with
    15
basmati rice 516
bean flakes 478
bean flour 494
beans 476–8
béarnaise sauce 229
béchamel sauce 245
beef 503
  braised brisket 118
  braising 502
  casserole 112
  chilli con carne 122
  cooking 501
  corned 124

cottage pie 126
  cuts 500
  girello 125
  gravy 139
  lasagne 128
  red wine sauce for steaks
    235
  roast 138
  roasting generally 501–2
  steak and kidney pie 148
  stroganoff 114
  Thai beef salad 150
beer batter 432
Bengali five spice 528
bergamot 498
berries gratin 323
berry tiramisu 317
besan flour 494
beurre manié 522
beurre rouge 235
Bhutanese red rice 517
bircher muesli 2
biscotti 340
  chocolate and almond 341
  espresso 341
biscuits
  Anzac 328
  basic 338
  biscotti 340
  chocolate and nut 339
  chocolate chip 339
  gingerbread people 366
  hedgehog 368
  honeycomb 339
  macaroons 374
  melting moments 378
  nut 339
  pecan 385
  strawberry shortcake 339
black beans 478
  fermented 478
black cumin 530
Black Forest queen of
  puddings 305

black glutinous rice 517
black japonica rice 517
black salt 520
black sesame seeds 530
black sticky rice 517
blanch 551
bleached flour 494
blended sugar 532
blind baking 509, 551
blini 434
blueberry
   berries gratin 323
   friands 360
   muffins 381
   pancake topping 17
   summer pudding 312
bocconcini 129
boil 551
boiled eggs 4, 487
bolognaise sauce 116
   lasagne 128
borlotti beans 478
braised beef brisket 118
braised lamb shanks 120
braising 502, 551
brandy butter sauce 283
brandy snaps 274
bread and butter pudding 276
   soy 277
breadcrumbs 153
breakfast burrito 13
broad beans 476
broast 551
broil 551
broken rice 517
brown rice 199, 207, 517
brown sugar 532
bubble and squeak 158
   roasted vegetables 169
buckwheat flour 494
bulgur (burghul) 201
   tabbouleh 200
butter cream 413
butter sauces 521
butterscotch sauce 250
   sticky date pudding with
      311

cabbage
   bubble and squeak 158
   coleslaw 182
   Savoy 183
   wombok 183
cacao 482
cacao bean 480
Caesar dressing 224
Caesar salad 178
cake flour 494
cakes
   baked cheesecake 266
   baked ricotta cheesecake
      270
   banana 336
   carrot 342
   chocolate cupcakes 353
   Christmas 363
   cupcakes 352
   devil's food 354
   flourless chocolate 356
   flourless orange 358
   fruit 363
   hummingbird 372
   icing see icing
   lumberjack 373
   orange and poppy seed 359
   orange cupcakes 353
   orange syrup 359
   sponge 398
   Swiss roll 400
   tea 402
calrose rice 517
candy 551
capers
   pickled 35
   salsa verde 34
   salted 34
   tapenade 36
   white caper sauce 245
capon 513
capsicum
   chilli jam 22
   gazpacho 54
   panzanella 192
   pickled vegetables 162
   roasted vegetables 169
caramel ice-cream 253

caramel orange sauce 271
caramel sauce 252
caramelise 551
caramelised lemon tart 293
caramelised onions 21
   sausages and mash with 21,
      147
   white sauce with 245
caraway 528
cardamom 528
carob 483
Carolina rice 517
carrot cake 342
cassava flour 494
casserole 551
   beef 112
   burnt 503
caster/castor sugar 532
cauliflower soup 46
celtic sea salt 520
chargrill 551
cheese 479
   buying and storing 479
   chef's salad 180
   croutons 52
   fondue 448
   twists 344
cheese board 479
cheesecake
   baked 266
   baked ricotta 270
   lemon 391
   raspberry 390
   simple 391
chef's salad 180
cherry sauce, roast duck with
   102
chervil 498
chestnut and wild mushroom
   stuffing 431
chestnut flour 494
chicken 511–14
   apricot chicken 90
   bacteria, risk of 511
   battery hen 512
   boiler hen 512
   broiler hen 512
   club sandwich 441

cooking 512
corn-fed 513
crispy skin chicken breast 96
free-range 513
grain-fed 514
herb butter with 97
Kiev 92
liver parfait 94
mushroom sauce for 97
pesto and camembert, with 31
poussin 514
pullet 514
rinsing 101
roast 100
rosemary skewers 97
soup, chicken and sweet corn 48
soup with matzoh balls 50
spatchcock 514
stock 436
stuffing 101
tapenade and ricotta, with 37
trussing 101
types 512–14
chickpeas
    braised lamb shanks with 121
    burgers 209
    canned 25
    hummus 25
chiffonade 201, 499
chilli 480
    con carne 122
    heat ratings 480
    jam 22
    stir-fry 171
Chinese cooking wine 207
Chinese five-spice powder 529
Chinese parsley (coriander) 498
Chinese (Sichuan) pepper 530
chocolate 480–83
    alternatives 483
    biscotti, chocolate and almond 341

biscuits, chocolate and nut 339
biscuits, chocolate chip 339
bitter 483
bittersweet 482
Black Forest queen of puddings 305
blondies 346
blooming 480, 481
brownies 346
cacao 482
cocoa butter 482
cocoa powder 482
compound 482
conching 481
couverture 482
crackles 347
cupcakes 353
dark 482
devil's chocolate frosting 410
devil's food cake 354
flourless chocolate cake 356
free-standing mousse 279
friands, chocolate chip 361
fudge 348, 349
ganache 401
German 482
hot chocolate 425
icing 408
junket 287
melting 481
Mexican 482
milk 483
mousse 278
mousse for piping 279
muffins 381
pastry cream 415
pavlova 297
problem solving 481
sauce 254
self-saucing pudding 280
semi-sweet 483
slice 405
sweet 483
Swiss roll 401
types of 482

unsweetened 483
white 483
chorizo, prawn and chilli frittata 451
Christmas cake 363
Christmas pudding 282
    brandy butter sauce for 283
Christmas rice 517
cilantro (coriander) 498
cinnamon 529
cinnamon sugar 532
citrus fruit salad 7
clam chowder 51
clarified butter 438
cloves 529
club sandwich 440
cockscomb 513
cocktail sauce 226
cocoa butter 482
cocoa powder 482
coconut ice 350
coconut macaroons 375
coconut sugar 532
coddled eggs 487, 552
coeliac disease 537
    food alternatives see gluten/wheat intolerance
coffee junket 287
coleslaw 182
confit 552
conversion charts 561–71
cooking salt 520
cooking techniques 549–57
coriander 498
    leaf 498
    root 498
    seeds 498, 529
corn 484
    chicken and sweet corn soup 48
    on the cob 160
corn syrup 534
corned beef 124
corned beef hash 125
cornflour 494
cottage pie 126

couscous 205
  preserved lemon and
      saffron, with 204
crab 523
  see also seafood
  blini 435
  buying 523
  cakes 74
  chowder 51
  cooking 523
  meat 85
  stick 523
crayfish 523–4
  see also seafood
cream 484–5
  butter 413
  clotted 484
  crème fraîche 442, 484
  double 484
  maple 303
  pastry 415
  potato baked in 156
  pouring 485
  qaimaaq 485
  sour 485
  sterilised 485
  thickened 485
  whipping 485
cream cheese frosting 409
crème anglaise 522
crème fraîche 442, 484
crepes 284
  seafood 84
  soufflé crepes baked in
      royale custard 285
  Suzette 285
Croque Madame 245
Croque Monsieur 245
croutons 443
  cheese 52
cubeb 529
cucumber
  chef's salad 180
  fattoush 184
  Greek salad 186
  Lebanese 181
  tzatziki 43
cupcakes 352

cure 552
curry leaf 498
curry powder 444
custard 411

dairy intolerance 537
  alternatives to milk 538
  bircher muesli 3
  ghee 439
  mushroom soup 59
  omelette 13
  soy bread and butter
      pudding 277
dashi 58
  hoshi-shiitake dashi 446
  kombu dashi 446
  miso soup 58
  niboshi dashi 446
  stock 446
date sugar 532
deep-fry 552
deglaze 552
demerara sugar 532
devil's chocolate frosting
      410
devil's food cake 354
dirty rice 517
double boil 552
double boilers 552
dry fondant sugar 532
Dsaudan eggs 489
duck
  eggs 489
  orange sauce, in 103
  Peking duck 98
  roast duck with cherry
      sauce 102
  san choy bao 145
dukkah 529
durum wheat flour 494

egg cream 489
eggnog 423
eggplant
  baba ghanouj 20
  moussaka 132
  ratatouille 166
  roasted vegetables 169

salting 167
  vegetarian lasagne 172
eggs 486–9
  alternatives 489
  bacon and egg pie 332
  bacon, spinach and goat's
      cheese omelette 11
  beating egg whites 486
  boiled 4, 487
  chorizo, prawn and chilli
      frittata 451
  coddled 487, 552
  dirty 488
  Dsaudan 489
  duck 489
  egg replacer 489
  eggnog 423
  French toast 5
  fried 487
  frittata 450
  ham and pea frittata 451
  hard-boiled 487
  hollandaise sauce 229
  hulidan 489
  leftover yolks/whites 488
  meringue *see* meringue/s
  mushroom, tomato and
      spinach omelette 11
  olive, fetta and zucchini
      frittata 451
  omelette 10, 487
  pancetta, scallop and sage
      frittata 451
  pidan 489
  poached 487
  problem solving 488
  quail 489
  quiche Lorraine 388
  salads, boiling for 191
  scrambled 12, 487
  separating 488
  sizes 487
  soft-boiled 487
  storing 486
  sundried tomato, mushroom
      and spinach frittata
      451

thousand-year 489
whipping egg whites 486
English spice (allspice) 528
epazote 498
eschalots 507
essential fatty acids 490
evaporated cane sugar 532

fats 490
fattoush 184
fennel seed 529
fenugreek 529
fermented rice 517
fetta 187, 397
  Greek salad 187
  olive, fetta and zucchini
    frittata 451
  Persian 29
  spanakopita 396
fines herbes 498
fish 491–2
  see also seafood
  buying 491
  cooking 492
  flatfish 491
  pan-fried fish fillets 76
  pie 77
  preparation 492
  round fish 491
  salmon patties 81
  stock 447
  storing 492
  tuna see tuna
  whole fish, cooking 72
flattened rice 517
fleur de sel 520
flour 493–4
fondant sugar 532
fondue 448
food additives 539–44
food allergies and
    intolerances 537–8
  alternatives to allergy-
    causing foods 537–9
  dairy see dairy intolerance
  gluten or wheat see gluten/
    wheat intolerance
French onion soup 52

French toast 5
friands 360
fried rice 206
frittata 450
  chorizo, prawn and chilli
    451
  ham and pea 451
  olive, fetta and zucchini
    451
  pancetta, scallop and sage
    451
  sundried tomato, mushroom
    and spinach 451
fructose 534
fruit cake 362
fruit juice
  punch 427
  sweetener 534
fruit milks 538
fruit mince pies 364
fruit salad 6
fudge, chocolate 348, 349

game birds 513
garam masala 529
garlic
  aïoli 222
  bread 452
  butter 227
  confit 453
  pistou 32
  prawns 78
  roasted 453
gazpacho 54
gelatine 321
ghee 439
ginger pudding, steamed 315
ginger soy dressing 228
gingerbread people 366
glaze 552
glucose powder 534
glucose syrup 534
gluten 494
gluten flour 494
gluten-free baking powder 537
gluten-free flour 494, 538
gluten/wheat intolerance 537
  alternatives foods 537

apple and rhubarb crumble
  260
apricot chicken 91
bircher muesli 3
bread and butter pudding
  276
couscous, avoiding 205
flour suitable for 493–4,
  537
flourless chocolate cake 356
flourless orange cake 358
gluten-free baking powder
  537
gluten-free flour 494, 538
hash brown pizza base 9
lasagne 129
lentil burgers 208
pasta dough 459
quinoa 201
spring rolls not suitable
  218
tabbouleh 201
tamari 207, 242
glutinous rice 517
goat's milk 538
goose 514
Graham flour 494
grape tomatoes 195, 536
gravy
  beef 139
  onion 147
Greek salad 186
green beans 477
green onions 507
green salad 188
gremolata 135
grill 553
guacamole 24
  blini with 435
guar gum 537

ham and bacon
  bacon and egg pie 332
  bacon, spinach and goat's
    cheese omelette 11
  baked ham 108
  chef's salad 180
  club sandwich 440

ham and bacon (*continued*)
  freezing ham 109
  ham and pea frittata 451
  pancetta, scallop and sage
    frittata 451
  pasta bake 87
  pea and ham soup 60
  potato salad with bacon 197
  spaghetti carbonara 216,
    217
  zucchini and bacon slice
    175
hash brown potato 8
Hawaiian black lava salt 520
Hawaiian red clay salt 520
hedgehog 368
herb butter 227
herbs 497–9
  problem solving 497
  types 498–9
Himalayan red rice 518
hoisin sauce 99
hollandaise sauce 229
  clarified butter 439
honey 535
honeycomb 369
  biscuits 339
  butter 369
horchata 538
horiatiki 187
hortopita 397
hot chocolate 425
hot cross buns 370
hulidan eggs 489
hummingbird cake 372
hummus 25

icing
  basic 408
  chocolate 408
  cream cheese frosting 409
  devil's chocolate frosting
    410
  orange frosting 409
icing sugar 533
Indian spices 527
indirect grilling 553
instant rice 518

iodised salt 519, 520
Italian meringue 412
Italian sausages with soft
  polenta 213

jaggery (palm sugar) 533
jam-making 558–60
Jamaica pepper (allspice) 528
japonica rice 515, 517
jasmine rice 518
java (palm) sugar 533
javanica rice 515
Jerusalem artichoke flour 494
jug 553
junket 286

kalijira rice 518
kalonji (nigella) 530
kamut flour 494
kebsa 529
kecap manis 232
kefalograviera 133
kitchen equipment 546–8
knives 546
Korean bamboo salt 520
Kosher salt 520
kumara 511
kuzu/kudzu 495

lamb 504
  braised lamb shanks 120
  cooking 501
  crumbing 502
  cuts 500
  Frenched lamb shanks 121
  moussaka 132
  osso buco variant 135
  rissoles 136
  roast 140
  roasting generally 501–2
  shepherd's pie 127
  tzatziki with 43
  white braising 557
lasagne 128
  mushroom 173
  vegetarian 172
lavosh 454
leek and potato soup 61

legume flour 495
lemon 500
  caramelised lemon tart 293
  cheesecake 391
  couscous with preserved
    lemon and saffron 204
  curd 414
  delicious 288
  dressing 247
  freezing juice 500
  grating zest 500
  lemonade 426
  marmalade 417
  meringue pie 290
  preserved 469
  Swiss roll 401
  tart 292
  tea, lemon and ginger 425
  varieties 426
  yoghurt and lemon mousse
    320
lemonade 426
lemonade scones 395
lentil burgers 208
lettuce
  drying 189, 550
  green salad 188
  san choy bao 144
  varieties 189
liaison 553
lima beans 478
lobster 526
lotus flour 495
lumberjack cake 373

macaroni cheese 210
macaroons 374
mace 530
malanga flour 495
Malian red clay salt 520
manja (palm oil) 507
maple cream 303
maple crystals 535
maple snaps 275
maple syrup 535
marjoram 498
marmalade 416
marron 524

marrow beans 478
marshmallows 376
matzo 495
matzoh balls, chicken soup
    with 50
mayonnaise 230
  cocktail sauce 226
  derivatives 231
  leftover egg yolks 49
measuring equipment 546
meat 500–5
  see also beef; lamb; pork;
      veal
  alternatives 538–9
  barbequing 549–50
  braising 502, 551
  cooking 501–2
  crumbing 502
  cuts 500
  marinating 550
  pot roasting 502, 555
  problem solving 502
  roasting 501–2
  salting 501
meat loaf 130
Mediterranean spices 527
mee goring sauce 232
melon fruit salad 6
melting moments 378
meringue/s 380
  butter cream 413
  Italian 412
  pavlova 296
  shogi sticks 413
  snow eggs 380
  Swiss 413
  vacherins 380
Mexican chocolate 482
Mexican horchata 538
microwave cooking 553–4
milk alternatives 538
millet flour 495
mince pies 364
minestrone 56
  pesto in 31
  salsa verde in 34
mint 499
mint jelly 26

mirin 242
miso soup 58
  dashi stock 446
mixed berry and mango salad 7
mixed spice 530
monounsaturated fats 490
mornay sauce 245
mouli 165
moussaka 132
muffins 381
Murray River salt 520
muscovado sugar 533
mushrooms 505
  beef stroganoff with 115
  chestnut and wild mushroom
      stuffing 431
  hoshi-shiitake dashi 446
  lasagne 173
  meat alternative 539
  mushroom, tomato and
      spinach omelette 11
  roasted vegetables 169
  soup 59
  spaghetti carbonara 217
  sundried tomato, mushroom
      and spinach frittata
      451
  veal Jäger 153
mussels 524
  see also seafood
mutton 504
nachos 456
  tomato relish with 38
Nanaimo bars 382
Napoli sauce 233
New Orleans praline 387
Niçoise salad 190
nigella seeds 530
nut allergies 537
nut biscuits 339
nut flour 495
nut meal 495
nutmeg 530
nuts, pureed 539

oat flour 495
oil 505–7

olives
  Greek salad 186
  olive, fetta and zucchini
      frittata 451
  pitting 37
  tapenade 36
omega-3 fatty acids 490
omega-6 fatty acids 490
omelette 10, 487
onions 507
  caramelised 21
  French onion soup 52
  gravy 147
  jam 28
  onion and sage stuffing 431
  problem solving 507
  types 507
00 flour 495
orange
  cake, flourless 358
  cake, orange and poppy seed
      359
  cupcakes 353
  friands, orange and poppy
      seed 361
  frosting 409
  junket 287
  marmalade 416
  melting moments, orange and
      marscarpone 378
  syrup cake 359
oregano 498
osso buco 134
  gremolata with 135
ovens and ovenware 547–8
oysters 525
  see also seafood

pad thai sauce 234
palm oil 507
palm sugar 243, 533
pancakes, super fluffy 16
pancetta, scallop and sage
      frittata 451
panch phora 528
pan-fry 555
pan-sear 555
pannacotta 294

pantry essentials 545
panzanella 192
par-bake 555
parsley 499
  chiffonade 201, 499
  chopping 201, 499
  curly 201, 499
  flat-leaf 201, 499
  root 499
  tabbouleh 200
passata 15, 169
passionfruit
  banana, strawberry and
    passionfruit salad 6
  bircher muesli with 3
  curd 414
  frosting 409
pasta 508
  bake 87
  bolognaise sauce 116
  cooking 508
  dough 458
  gluten-free 459
  lasagne 128
  macaroni cheese 210
  Napoli sauce 233
  problem solving 509
  salad 194
  spaghetti carbonara 216,
    217
  tapenade pasta sauce 37
  tuna bake 86
  vegetarian lasagne 172
pasteurise 555
pastry 460–65, 509–10
  blind baking 509
  cheese twists 344
  choux 464
  cream 415
  docking 510
  filo 265
  pie funnel 510
  problem solving 510
  quick puff 463
  rolling 509
  shortcrust 462
  spanakopita 396
  sweet 460

  sweet shortcrust 461
  sweet twists 344
  tapenade, potato and
    rosemary 37
pastry flour 495
patna rice 518
pavlova 296
pea and ham soup 60
peach melba 298
peaches 299
peanut brittle 384
peanut oil 207, 506
pearl rice 518
pearl sugar 533
pecan
  biscuits 385
  friands, pecan and maple
    syrup 361
  pie 300
  rice 518
  toffee sauce 251
pectin 559
Peking duck 98
pepper 530
pesto 30
  pizza base 31
  tomato soup, in 67
pheasant 513
pickled vegetables 162
pickling onions 507
pidan eggs 489
pie
  apple 262
  bacon and egg 332
  fish 77
  fruit mince 364
  lemon meringue 290
  pecan 300
  pumpkin 302
  rhubarb 307
  steak and kidney 148
pikelets 386
pineapple
  hummingbird cake 372
  pancake topping 17
  pineapple, papaya and mint
    salad 7
  sweet and sour sauce 241

pink peppercorns 530
pink Peruvian lake salt 520
pistou 32
pizza base
  hash brown 9
  pesto 31
  tapenade 37
  tomato relish 38
pizza dough 466
plain flour 495
plum sauce 236
poach 555
poached eggs 487
poached rhubarb 307
poêlé 555
poi flour 495
polenta
  firm 212
  Italian sausages with 213
  soft 213
polyunsaturated fats 490
popcorn rice 518
popped rice 518
pork 504
  apple sauce for 248
  barbecue-style spare ribs
    110
  Chinese red roast pork 206,
    207
  quince paste with 33
  roast pork and crackling
    142
  san choy bao 144
  trichinosis 504
Portuguese rice pudding 309
pot roasting 502, 555
potato flour 495
potato ricer 165
potatoes 510–11
  baked in cream 156
  best use for different
    varieties 511
  corned beef hash 125
  cottage pie 126
  frittata, potato and
    rosemary 451
  hash brown 8
  mash 164, 510

mouli 165
Niçoise salad 190
Pontiac 157
roasted vegetables 168
salad 196
sausages and mash with
    pepper sauce 146
shepherd's pie 127
soup, potato and leek 61
tapenade, potato and
    rosemary pastries 37
waxy varieties 197, 511
poultry 511–14
    see also chicken; duck;
    turkey
    bacteria, risk of 511
    cooking 512
    game birds 513
    types 513–14
poussin 514
praline 387
prawns 525
    see also seafood
    chorizo, prawn and chilli
        frittata 451
    cocktail sauce for 226
    cooking 525
    de-veining 525
    garlic prawns 78
    prawn cocktail 80
preserved lemons 469
    couscous with saffron and
        204
preserving 558–60
preserving sugar 533
pullet 514
pumpkin 63
    pie 302
    roasted vegetables 168
    soup 62
    types 63
punch 427

qaimaaq 485
quail 513
quail eggs 489
quatre épices 530
queen of puddings 304

quiche Lorraine 388
quince 269, 515
    baked 268
    buying 269, 515
    paste 33
quinoa 201, 495
quinoa flour 495

rabbit and hare 504
ranch dressing 231
ras el hanout 531
raspberry
    berries gratin 323
    berry tiramisu 317
    cheesecake 390
    fool 306
    friands 361
    jam 419
    sauce 256
    snaps 275
    summer pudding 312
ratatouille 166
raw sugar 533
red cooking 555
red kidney beans 478
red onions 507
red wine sauce 235
reduce 555
refresh 556
render 556
rhubarb 261, 307
    apple and rhubarb crumble
        260
    oxalic acid 261
    pancake topping 17
    pie 307

poached 307
poisonous leaves 261, 307
stewed 307
rice 515–18
    brown 199, 207, 517
    converted 517
    cooking 515–16
    dirty 517
    flakes 517
    fried 206
    indica 515

instant 518
japonica 515, 517
javanica 515
long-grain 199, 515
medium-grain 199, 215
piedmont 215
problem solving 516
pudding 308
risotto 214
salad 198
short-grain 199, 515
soaking 515
types 516–18
wild 199, 519
rice flour 496
rice syrup 496
ricotta cheesecake, baked 270
risotto 214
    Milanese 215
    rice 215, 518
rissoles 136
    tomato relish with 41
roast beef 138
roast chicken 100
roast lamb 140
roast pork and crackling 142
roasted vegetables 168
    bubble and squeak 169
    salsa verde with 34
roasting 556
    meat 501–2
rock salt 521
rock sugar 533
rolled fondant 533
rosemary 499
    potato and rosemary
        frittata 451
    skewers, for chicken 97
    tapenade, potato and
        rosemary pastries 37
rough rice 518
rouille 223
runner beans 478
rye flour 496

sabayon 323, 522
sage 499
    onion and sage stuffing 431

sage (*continued*)
  pancetta, scallop and sage
    frittata 451
sago flour 496
sake 242
salad onions 507
salad spinner 189
salads
  boiling eggs for 191
  Caesar 178
  chef's 180
  coleslaw 182
  fattoush 184
  fruit 6
  Greek 186
  green 188
  Niçoise 190
  panzanella 192
  pasta 194
  potato 196
  rice 198
  tabbouleh 200
  Thai beef 150
salmon croquettes 81
salmon patties 81
salsa verde 34
  pumpkin soup, in 63
salsa verde agrodolce 35
salt 519–20
  problem solving 519
  types 520–21
salt and pepper squid 82
salt spray 521
saltpetre 521
sambal oelek 232
san choy bao 144
satay sauce 238
saturated fats 490
saucepans 546
sauces 521–22
  apple 248
  béarnaise 229
  béchamel 245
  bolognaise 116
  brandy butter 283
  butter 521
  butterscotch 250
  Cambridge 522

caramel 252
caramel orange 271
chocolate 254
Choron 229
cocktail 226
egg-based 521
Gribiche 522
hollandaise 229
Maltaise 229
mee goring 232
mornay 245
mushroom 97
Napoli 233
pad thai 234
plum 236
problem solving 522
purees 522
raspberry 256
red wine 235
remoulade 231
sabayon 323, 522
Sardalaise 522
satay 238
sweet and sour 241
tartare 231
teriyaki 242
Thai chilli 243
thickening 522
toffee 251
tomato 15
Vincent 522
white caper 245
sausage pinwheels 393
sausage rolls 392
  tomato relish with 41
sausages
  caramelised onions with 21,
    147
  chorizo, prawn and chilli
    frittata 451
  Italian, with soft polenta
    213
  mash and pepper sauce, with
    146
  onion gravy 147
savoury muffins 381
savoury scones 395
scald 556

scallops 526
  see also seafood
  cooking 526
  dried 526
  pancetta, scallop and sage
    frittata 451
scampi 526
scones 394
scrambled eggs 12, 487
sea salt 521
seafood 523–5
  see also crab; fish; prawns
  abalone 523
  allergies 537
  alternatives 538
  bacalao 523
  calamari 83, 526
  chowder 51
  cocktail sauce for 226
  crayfish 523–24
  crepes 77, 84
  cuttlefish 526
  gumbo 64
  jellyfish 524
  marinara mix 524
  marron 524
  mussels 524
  oysters 525
  pie 85
  rock lobster 526
  salt and pepper squid 82
  scallops 526
  scampi 526
  shark 526
  squid 83, 526
  yabbies 524
sear 556
seitan 539
sel gris 521
self-raising flour 496
semolina flour 496
sesame oil 506
seven-flavour spice 531
shallot dressing 240
shallots 507
shallow-fry 556
shepherd's pie 127
shiso 499

shogi sticks 413
shrimp paste 239
Sichuan pepper 531
silk sugar 533
smoked salt 521
smoking 556
smother 556
snake beans 477
snow eggs 380
snow sugar 533
soft icing mixture 533
sorghum flour 496
soufflé crepes baked in royale
    custard 285
soup
    ajo blanco 55
    cauliflower 46
    chicken and sweet corn soup
        48
    chicken soup with matzoh
        balls 50
    crab chowder 51
    croutons for 52, 443
    French onion 52
    gazpacho 54
    minestrone 56
    miso 58
    mushroom 59
    pea and ham 60
    potato and leek 61
    pumpkin 62
    seafood chowder 51
    seafood gumbo 64
    tomato 66
    vegetable 69
    vegetable and barley 68
    vichyssoise 61
South Asian spices 527
South-east Asian spices 527
soy beans 476, 478
soy flour 496
soy sauce
    dark 242
    tamari as substitute 207,
        242
spaghetti carbonara
    creamy style 217
    traditional 216

spanakopita 396
Spanish rice 518
Spanish rice pudding 309
spare ribs, barbecue-style
    110
spatchcock 514
spelt flour 496
spice (Sichuan) pepper 531
spices 527–1
spinach
    bacon, spinach and goat's
        cheese omelette 11
    hortopita 397
    mushroom, tomato and
        spinach omelette 11
    spanakopita 396
    sundried tomato, mushroom
        and spinach frittata
        451
sponge cake 398
spring onions 507
spring rolls 218
    satay dipping sauce 238
    vegetarian 219
squid 83, 526
    see also seafood
    calamari distinguished 83,
        526
    dried 527
    salt and pepper squid 82
star anise 531
steak and kidney pie 148
steamed ginger pudding 315
steaming 556
stevia 535
stevioside 535
stewing 556
sticky date pudding 310
stir-fry 556–7
    chilli 171
    vegetable and noodle 170
stock
    chicken 436
    dashi 446
    fish 447
    vegetable 472
stone ground flours 496

strawberry
    berries gratin 323
    jam 418
    shortcake 339
    strawberry, grape and mango
        salad 7
    summer pudding 312
stroganoff, beef 114
strong flour 496
stuffing
    apple, prune and spice 430
    chestnut and wild mushroom
        431
    onion and sage 431
    roast chicken, for 101
sucanat 535
sucrose 535
sugar 532–3
    alternatives 534–5
    jams, in 559
    problem solving 532
    temperatures 534
    thermometers 559
    types, 532–3
sugar syrup 470, 533
sumac 185, 531
summer pudding 312
superunsaturated fats 490
sushi rice 517
sweating 557
sweet and sour sauce 241
sweet potato 511
    roasted vegetables 168
    soup 63
    varieties 511
sweeteners 534–5
Swiss roll 400
synthetic sweeteners 535
syrup pudding 314

tabbouleh 200
table salt 521
tamari 207, 242
tamarind juice 243
tamarind paste 239
tapenade 36
tartare sauce 231
    crab cakes with 75

tatsoi leaf 151
  Thai beef salad 150
tea cake 402
tea, lemon and ginger 425
teff flour 496
tempeh 539
teriyaki sauce 242
Thai beef salad 150
Thai chilli sauce 243
thousand island dressing 226
thousand-year eggs 489
thyme 499
tiramisu 316
tiropita 397
toffee 403
toffee apples 403
toffee sauce 251
tofu 539
  egg alternative 489
  mayonnaise 231
  meat alternative 539
  miso soup 58
togarashi 531
tomatoes 536
  bolognaise sauce 116
  chilli jam 22
  chutney 38
  gazpacho 54
  Greek salad 186
  green tomato chutney 39
  green tomato jam 42
  green tomato relish 41
  Napoli sauce 233
  panzanella 192
  passata 15, 169
  pasta salad 194
  relish 40
  roasted vegetables 169
  sauce 15
  slow-roasted 14
  soup 66
  sundried tomato, mushroom
    and spinach frittata
    451
  types 536
trans fatty acids 490

trifle 318
tropical salad 7
tuna
  bake 86
  Niçoise salad 190
  omega-3 fatty acids 490
  panzanella 193
  tapenade and tuna pasta
    sauce 37
  tapenade made with 37
turbinado sugar 533
turkey 514
  apple, prune and spice
    stuffing 430
  chef's salad 180
  chestnut and wild rice
    stuffing 431
  club sandwich 440
  cooking 105
  onion and sage stuffing 431
  quince paste with 33
  roast turkey buffet 104
TVP (textured vegetable
  protein) 539
tzatziki 43

utensils 548

vacherins 380
vanilla slice 404
vanilla sugar 471
veal
  Cordon Bleu 153
  crumbing 502
  Holstein 153
  Jäger 153
  osso buco 134
  schnitzel 152
  white braising 557
vegetable and barley soup 68
vegetable and noodle stir-fry
  170
  satay sauce 238
vegetable fat 490
vegetable soup 68
vegetable stock 472

vegetables, pickled 162
vegetables, roasted 168
vegetarian lasagne 172
  leftover ratatouille 167
vegetarian spring rolls 219
vichyssoise 61
vinaigrette dressing 246

walnuts 331
  baklava 330
whisking 323
white beans 478
white braising 557
white caper sauce 245
white Christmas 347
white onions 508
white rice 518
white sauce 244
wholemeal flour 496
wild rice 199, 519
  chestnut and wild rice
    stuffing 431
wok 546
wok-cooking 556–7

xantham gum 537

yabbies 524
yellow bean paste 243
yoghurt
  dressing 247
  tzatziki 43, 321
  yoghurt and lemon mousse
    320
Yorkshire pudding 139

za'atar 499, 531
zabaglione 322, 522
zomi (palm oil) 507
zucchini
  olive, fetta and zucchini
    frittata 451
  ratatouille 166
  roasted vegetables 169
  salting 167
  slice 175